春秋繁露

LUXURIANT GEMS OF THE *Spring and Autumn*

TRANSLATIONS FROM THE ASIAN CLASSICS

春秋繁露

LUXURIANT GEMS OF THE *Spring and Autumn*

Attributed to Dong Zhongshu

EDITED AND TRANSLATED BY

Sarah A. Queen

& John S. Major

Columbia University Press *New York*

Columbia University Press
Publishers Since 1893
New York Chichester, West Sussex
cup.columbia.edu

Columbia University Press wishes to express its appreciation for assistance given by the Chiang Ching-kuo Foundation for International Scholarly Exchange in the preparation of the translation and in the publication of this series.

Library of Congress Cataloging-in-Publication Data
Names: Dong, Zhongshu, active 2nd century B.C. |
Queen, Sarah A. (Sarah Ann) editor. | Major, John S., editor.
Title: Luxuriant gems of the spring and autumn ; attributed to Dong Zhongshu ;
edited and translated by Sarah A. Queen and John S. Major.
Other titles: Chun qiu fan lu. English
Description: New York : Columbia University Press, [2016] |
Series: Translations from the Asian classics | Includes bibliographical references and index.
Identifiers: LCCN 2015008489| ISBN 9780231169325 (cloth : acid-free paper) |
ISBN 9780231539616 (e-book)
Classification: LCC PL2470.Z7 D6613 2016 | DDC 931/.03—dc23
LC record available at http://lccn.loc.gov/2015008489

Columbia University Press books are printed on permanent and durable acid-free paper.
This book is printed on paper with recycled content.
Printed in the United States of America

COVER IMAGE: Bronze base for a bell rack in the form of a dragon, from the tomb of Liu Fei, king of Jiangdu, whom Dong Zhongshu served as administrator in the 130s B.C.E. (Photo courtesy of the Archaeological Research Institute, Nanjing Museum)
COVER & BOOK DESIGN: Lisa Hamm

For Thomas and Benjamin, and for Steve

Contents

Group 7: Ritual Principles 491

Group 8: Heavenly Principles 555

Acknowledgments

WE ARE grateful to the many friends and colleagues who gave us encouragement and good advice during the years it took us to complete this book. Joachim Gentz and Newell Ann van Auken very generously shared perspectives on the *Spring and Autumn* and its commentaries. Michael Loewe kindly shared information from his book-length study of Dong Zhongshu in advance of its publication in 2011. We are grateful to David Pankenier for generously sharing with us his notes from a reading of the *Chunqiu fanlu* with the legendary scholar and teacher Aisin-gioro Yu-yun. The anonymous peer reviewers for Columbia University Press made many helpful suggestions for improving the manuscript. Nathan Sivin did us a huge favor by reading a complete but still rough draft of the entire manuscript, providing us with a detailed critique of the work as a whole and suggesting hundreds of specific corrections. We are grateful to Nancy Lewandowski for her management of successive digital and physical copies of the manuscript.

Jennifer Crewe, Jonathan Fiedler, Irene Pavitt, Lisa Hamm, and their colleagues at Columbia University Press worked with consummate professionalism on the editing, design, and production of the book. Anne Holmes worked her customary magic on the book's index. Our thanks to all of them.

We owe a tremendous debt of gratitude to Graham Majorhart for his tenacity and excellent negotiating skills in tracking down and obtaining for us the beautiful image that graces the cover of this book. Thanks also are due to Mr. Chen Xingcan, deputy director of the Institute of Archaeology, Chinese Academy of Social Sciences, who facilitated Graham's initial contact with the relevant authorities, and especially to Mr. Lin Liugen, director of the Archaeological

Research Institute at the Nanjing Museum, who provided the actual image and permission to use it. We are delighted that, through their efforts and goodwill, we are able to use on the cover of this book the image of a cast-bronze dragon that was found in the recently excavated tomb of Liu Fei, king of Jiangdu (r. 153–128 B.C.E.). Dong Zhongshu, the putative author of the *Chunqiu fanlu* (and the actual author of some of it), served as administrator of Jiangdu during the 130s B.C.E., and it is a remarkable privilege to be able to adorn this book's cover with an object—the base of a bell-rack—that Dong may well have seen in use in Liu Fei's court.

As always, we owe deepest thanks to our respective families for their encouragement, support, and forbearance.

春秋繁露

LUXURIANT GEMS OF THE *Spring and Autumn*

Introduction

THIS BOOK is the first complete English translation of the *Chunqiu fanlu*, a compendium that has been associated with the Han-dynasty Confucian scholar Dong Zhongshu (ca. 195–104 B.C.E.) since the sixth century C.E., when the title of this work first began to appear in bibliographical treatises.[1] As the title suggests, the book ostensibly draws on the *Spring and Autumn* (*Chunqiu*, a chronicle kept by the dukes of the state of Lu from 722 to 481 B.C.E.) as a source of "luxuriant gems" (*fanlu*) of wisdom, especially about the organization and conduct of government.[2] By the beginning of the Han dynasty (206 B.C.E.–220 C.E.), many intellectuals had come to believe that the *Spring and Autumn* had been written or edited by Confucius himself, using an esoteric language of praise and blame to indicate approval or disapproval of the recorded historical events. The chronicle therefore was viewed as a canonical source of guidance for rulers and their ministers. In fact, though, the *Chunqiu fanlu* is a collection of very disparate materials, composed by several people over a period spanning several generations. Some of its content does indeed rely on, or

1. The earliest reference to a book titled *Chunqiu fanlu* is found in *Qi Lu* (*Seven Records*) attributed to Yuan Xiaoxu (479–536). Han sources attribute three works to Dong Zhongshu: *Dong Zhongshu* (*Dong Zhongshu*) in 123 *pian* 篇 ("bundles" [chapters]); *Gongyang Dong Zhongshu zhiyu* (*Legal Judgments of Gongyang* [*Scholar*] *Dong Zhongshu*) in 16 *pian*; and *Zai yi zhi ji* (*Records of Disasters and Anomalies*). For the biographical details of Dong Zhongshu and a detailed discussion of the textual history of Dong's oeuvre, see Sarah A. Queen, *From Chronicle to Canon: The Hermeneutics of the "Spring and Autumn" According to Tung Chung-shu* (Cambridge: Cambridge University Press, 1996), chaps. 2 and 3.
2. However, as we will explain, *fanlu* was originally the name of the book's first chapter and only later was applied to the entire work.

at least refer to, the *Spring and Autumn* as a fountainhead of prescriptive wisdom, but in some chapters this connection is tangential or absent.

Fate has not been kind to this text. Many of its chapters are fragmentary and garbled, and over the centuries, scholars have questioned the authenticity of the text, or parts of it.[3] The factors conspiring against scholarly acceptance of the *Chunqiu fanlu* have been numerous and compelling. The text's late appearance on the literary scene, its inclusion of materials that clearly postdate Dong's life, and the poor quality of the collection—with respect to both its literary style and the condition of the various editions that have survived—have led some readers to treat it dismissively and have challenged those scholars who have attempted to understand, interpret, and defend it. In turn, the questionable authenticity of the text has cast a long shadow over the figure of Dong Zhongshu himself.

A Brief Biography of Dong Zhongshu

What little we know about Dong Zhongshu comes from two accounts of his life preserved in the Han official histories: the chapter "The Biographies of Confucian Scholars" in the *Shiji* and the "Biography of Dong Zhongshu" in the *Han shu*. The latter biography draws on its *Shiji* predecessor but expands on it by including a number of Dong's official communications and other writings. Appendices A and B at the end of this volume contain full translations of these two biographies. By way of background, we briefly summarize here some of the most important events in Dong's life.[4]

The early years of Dong Zhongshu's life occasioned little comment from his chief biographers, Sima Qian and Ban Gu. Although Dong's birth date is not recorded, he most likely was born sometime around 195 B.C.E., just after the reign of the first Han emperor, Gaozu, drew to a close. Both historians note only that Dong Zhongshu was a native of the kingdom called Guanquan (part of present-day Hebei Province)[5] and that at an early age he mastered the *Spring*

3. See, for example, Saiki Tetsurō 齋木哲郎, "*Shunjū hanro* no gishosetsu ni tsuite" 春秋繁露の偽書說について (On Theories That the *Chunqiu fanlu* Is a Forgery), *Kyūko* 汲古 17 (1990): 17–22.

4. For longer and more detailed biographical studies, see Queen, *From Chronicle to Canon*, chap. 2; Michael Loewe, *Dong Zhongshu, a "Confucian" Heritage, and the "Chunqiu fanlu,"* Brill China Studies, no. 20 (Leiden: Brill, 2011), 43–80; Marianne Bujard, "La vie de Dong Zhongshu: Enigmes et hypothèses," *Journal Asiatique* 280 (1992): 145–217; and Gary Arbuckle, "Restoring Dong Zhongshu (BCE 195–115): An Experiment in Historical and Philosophical Reconstruction" (Ph.D. diss., University of British Columbia, 1991), 1–83.

5. *HS* 27/1317; *HS* 56/2527.

and Autumn. The circumstances under which he was able to do this and who served as his teacher are not described. In short, the details of Dong's early life remain beyond the historian's reach.

During the reign of Emperor Jing (r. 157–141 B.C.E.), an avid patron of the Daoist arts of Laozi and the Yellow Emperor[6] and less so of the classical arts associated with Confucius,[7] Dong Zhongshu traveled to the Han capital, Chang'an. There he took up his first official post as an Erudite (a court-appointed scholar) of the *Gongyang Commentary* to the *Spring and Autumn* and first transmitted his teachings.[8] He is said to have embraced his teaching responsibilities with a single-minded determination[9] that spawned a number of hagiographical vignettes over the centuries, beginning with that of Sima Qian, who claimed: "His concentration was such that verily for three years he did not glance at his garden."[10] Dong's teaching also was marked by a degree of formality that must have been atypical for his time, as it was noted in his biography that "[from behind] a lowered curtain, he lectured to and recited for his disciples, who in turn transmitted [his teachings] from those with greatest seniority to those with least seniority, so that some of his disciples never even saw his face."[11] His reputation as an honest, forthright scholar and a man of propriety was said to have spread quickly, and before long, "scholars regarded him as a teacher to be respected."[12]

At the court of Emperor Jing, Dong Zhongshu's colleagues included a wide array of scholars and practitioners representing various positions on the rich and varied spectrum that constituted Han intellectual life. Dong served alongside devotees of the Daoist arts, such as Wang Guokai, Ji An, Zheng Dangshi, and Sima Tan's teacher, Master Huang,[13] and others appointed as Erudites of the Confucian classics, such as Yuan Gu, an expert on the *Odes*, and Master Huwu (also known as Huwu Zidu), a fellow scholar of the *Spring and Autumn*. Master Huwu was said to have followed the regional interpretations from the

6. Emperor Jing's patronage of the Daoist arts was apparently the outcome of familial pressures. His mother was a devoted adherent of various techniques associated with the Yellow Emperor and Laozi and compelled her son to "revere their techniques" (*SJ* 49/1975; *HS* 97/3945).
7. "Emperor Jing did not employ Confucians. Consequently, numerous Erudites occupied official posts and awaited imperial inquiries but did not advance [to high political office]" (*SJ* 121/3117–18).
8. *SJ* 121/3127; *HS* 56/2495; *HS* 27A/1317.
9. *HS* 56/2495.
10. See also *HS* 56, and *Lunheng* 44, where this familiar line about not looking at his garden is repeated. Dong is mentioned twenty-six times in the *Lunheng*.
11. *SJ* 121/3127.
12. *HS* 56/2495.
13. For their respective biographies, see *HS* 50/2312; *SJ* 120/3105 and *HS* 50/2316; *SJ* 120/2323 and *HS* 120/3112; and *SJ* 130/3286–3287 and *HS* 62/2709.

kingdoms of Lu and Qi, while Dong followed those associated with Zhao.[14] Despite differences due to the regional flavor of their teachings, it appears that Dong Zhongshu came under the influence of Master Huwu before the latter returned home to Qi to teach: Ban Gu notes that Dong Zhongshu composed works praising Master Huwu's virtues.[15]

Shortly after Emperor Jing's successor, the teenage Emperor Wu, ascended the throne in 141 B.C.E., Dong Zhongshu finally had an opportunity to participate in an imperial inquiry and gain the emperor's support.[16] The moment was laden with possibilities: Would Dong Zhongshu gain the emperor's confidence and secure a promotion to high political office? Or would his ideas prove disagreeable to the young emperor and result in his being relegated to a less influential post? As the emperor struggled to gain a foothold in a court dominated by his regent, Empress Dowager Dou, it was anyone's guess which political faction and attendant view of empire would eventually win dominance at court. For his part, Dong Zhongshu addressed the emperor's inquiries with a series of frank and forthright responses. Although his remarks were couched in the self-abasing rhetoric that was conventional when addressing the throne, Dong's responses bravely challenged the emperor to recognize his own shortcomings and criticized the state of affairs under his reign at every turn.[17]

How did the emperor respond? Around 134 B.C.E., Emperor Wu appointed Dong Zhongshu to the post of administrator[18] to the kingdom of Jiangdu (in present-day Jiangsu Province). Could that appointment have been an implicit signal that Dong's responses were simply too forthright and critical for the young emperor to tolerate? Perhaps such an outspoken scholar could be effectively neutralized with an assignment far from the central court. Sending Dong to Jiangdu not only removed him from the central court but also made him an effective muzzle for Liu Fei, Emperor Wu's elder brother, who reigned as King Yi of Jiangdu.

King Yi was well known for his martial inclinations, having established a reputation for military acumen during the Revolt of the Seven Kingdoms

14. *SJ* 121/3118.
15. *HS* 88/3615.
16. *HS* 56/2495.
17. For a detailed analysis of Dong's memorials to Emperor Wu, see Sarah A. Queen, "The Rhetoric of Dong Zhongshu's Imperial Communications," in *Facing the Monarch: Modes of Advice in the Early Chinese Court*, ed. Garret Olberding, Harvard East Asian Monographs (Cambridge, Mass.: Harvard University Press, 2013), 166–202.
18. Michael Loewe translates this title as "Chancellor" in *A Biographical Dictionary of the Qin, Former Han, and Xin Periods (221 BC–AD 24)* (Leiden: Brill, 2000), 70–73, and *Dong Zhongshu*, 46–48.

in 154 B.C.E., when he quelled the rebellion in Wu on behalf of the imperial court.[19] Sima Qian and Ban Gu also emphasize that the king was arrogant and extravagant.[20] A ruler with such character traits was hardly likely to put up with the uncompromising and frank Dong Zhongshu. The two men could not have had more different personalities and agendas. Yet Ban Gu reports that Dong was able to influence the king and, as a teacher does his disciple, ultimately "rectify and correct" him.

During the same period, Dong became known for his interpretations of disasters and anomalies recorded in the *Spring and Autumn*, particularly those that informed the ritual practices he implemented when seeking rain in times of drought and stopping rain in times of flood. Sima Qian remarks:

> By consulting ominous changes such as natural disasters and strange events recorded in the *Spring and Autumn,* he deduced the causes of disorderly interactions between yin and yang. Therefore when inducing rain, he repressed yang and released yin; when stopping rain, he inverted these techniques. When he implemented these techniques in this single state, he never failed to obtain the desired results.[21]

Despite the suspicions that such a hyperbolic conclusion might prompt, it is clear from Sima Qian's remarks that Dong's stint as administrator in Jiangdu afforded him the opportunity to link his exegetical approaches, cosmological principles, and ritual practices into a potent mixture that was to have major implications for the later stages of his official career. Nonetheless, despite these successes, he was abruptly dismissed from his post as administrator in Jiangdu

---

19. Under the system of government established by the Han founding emperor, Liu Bang (Emperor Gao), the western half of the empire was under direct imperial control, and the eastern half was divided into semiautonomous kingdoms ruled by imperial kinsman and allies. Han records uniformly describe these kings as rebellious and unruly, and they may well have been so; but it also is likely that some of the royal "rebellions" were provoked or even fabricated by an imperial regime seeking to restrain or eliminate the neofeudal kings and incorporate their territory into the imperial domain. See John S. Major, Sarah A. Queen, Andrew Seth Meyer, and Harold D. Roth, trans. and eds., *The "Huainanzi": A Guide to the Theory and Practice of Government in Early Han China* (New York: Columbia University Press, 2010), 2–6. As we shall see, Dong Zhongshu advocated a hard-line imperial policy against the neofeudal kings.

20. *SJ* 59/2096; Burton Watson, trans., *Records of the Grand Historian*, rev. ed. (New York: Columbia University Press, 1993), 1:391. Liu Fei died in 128 B.C.E. His tomb was found accidentally in 2009 by quarry workers in Xuyi County, Jiangsu Province, and excavated in 2009 to 2011. The tomb contained a wealth of artifacts, including bronze vessels, musical instruments, chariots, and thousands of coins. For a brief report, see Sarah Griffiths, "Chinese King's Mausoleum Unearthed," *Daily Mail*, August 5, 2014, http://www.dailymail.co.uk/sciencetech/article-2716538/2100-year-old-kings-mausoleum-discovered-China-Tombs-contain-treasures-including-chariots-afterlife.html (accessed January 28, 2015).

21. *SJ* 121/3128.

and sent back to Chang'an, where he was appointed to the lesser post of grand master to the palace.[22] This may have happened because Dong would not be silenced or domesticated. Despite being forced from the center of power to a peripheral kingdom, he continued to express his uncompromising views when addressing King Yi and refused to bow to the king's hawkish pressures. This fact is well documented in the official written record of an exchange between Dong Zhongshu and the king that is preserved in both the *Han shu* and the *Chunqiu fanlu*.[23] Moreover, it is clear that this exchange was prompted by the king's desire to gain imperial approval for a military expedition against the Xiongnu, a coalition of northern peoples who threatened the empire's frontier. Dong argued strongly against military action. When King Yi failed to win the emperor's approval, he may very well have held Dong Zhongshu personally responsible.

Back in Chang'an, as grand master to the palace, Dong Zhongshu once again offered instruction in the ways of the *Spring and Autumn*. He is said to have received orders from the emperor himself to instruct one of his favorite courtiers, Wuqiu Shouwang.[24] Beyond this single reference, little is known about the students whom Dong instructed or the methods of instruction he employed in this second leg of his journey as a teacher.

At that time, Dong became involved in a political intrigue initiated by his opponents at court that nearly cost him his life. The intrigue began when after paying Dong a visit, the official Zhufu Yan absconded with a potentially volatile memorial that Dong had drafted, in which he analyzed the significance of a fire that had occurred in the mortuary temple of Emperor Gao. Zhufu Yan sent the memorial to the emperor, who summoned a number of scholars, including Dong's disciple Lü Bushu, to examine and appraise the draft memorial. The memorial was roundly denounced, even by Dong's disciple, who apparently did not know that the author was his very own teacher! Dong Zhongshu was then turned over to the legal officials, who tried him for "privately composing a book on disasters and anomalies" and charged him with "the crime of immorality."[25]

To understand why Zhufu Yan may have felt threatened enough by the memorial to use it against Dong Zhongshu, it is necessary to consider its content and the political agenda it addressed. The memorial concerned two fires that occurred in 135 B.C.E, destroying both the imperial mortuary temple in

22. Loewe, *Biographical Dictionary*, 70.
23. *HS* 56/2523–24; *CQFL* 32. For more details about this exchange, see Queen, "Rhetoric."
24. *HS* 64A/2794.
25. *HS* 36/1930. This incident also is described by Wang Chong (*Lunheng* 84/362/17–20).

Liaodong and the side halls in the funerary park to Emperor Gao in Chang'an. It was widely believed that fires that destroyed imperial palaces, ancestral halls, temples, or other buildings associated with the ruling clan were particularly inauspicious for the reigning dynasty. Dong argued that this double catastrophe at sites commemorating the founding emperor of the Han at both the periphery and the center of the empire was an unequivocal warning from Heaven that the emperor must deal decisively and harshly with the corresponding sources of trouble in these locales—that is, the unruly royal relatives in the distant kingdoms and the corrupt officials in the metropolitan area.[26]

Zhufu Yan likely found the memorial personally threatening on at least two accounts. Infamous for taking bribes and other kinds of payoffs, he no doubt feared that he was one of the very officials whom Dong had in mind when he argued that Heaven was sending the following message to the emperor: "Spy out your trusted couriers in the capital area who have engaged in dishonest practices and those who are honored but not upright and execute them without mercy, just as I have burned down the side halls in the funerary park to Emperor Gao."[27] Moreover, Zhufu Yan and Dong Zhongshu were pitted against each other in one of the crucial debates of the period: how to resolve the pressing political challenges posed by the regional kings, relatives of the emperor who ruled the various kingdoms of the Han Empire. Dong advocated taking a hard line on the status of the potentially rebellious regional kings; Zhufu Yan was more conciliatory.[28]

No doubt these factors weighed on Zhufu Yan's mind when the emperor ordered him, together with other officials, to judge this case. The verdict was as harsh as it could be: Dong Zhongshu was sentenced to death. His only hope was an imperial pardon, and that is precisely what happened, though the emperor's motives for pardoning Dong were not recorded. Dong's unambiguous show of loyalty to the central court on the question of the regional kings may have earned the emperor's favor. Judging from the policies that the emperor subsequently adopted on this issue, his own views were not far from Dong's, and therefore he may have had some sympathy for him. Or perhaps the emperor understood Zhufu Yan's real motivations for embroiling Dong in a trumped-up court case. In any event, Dong escaped execution.

26. *HS* 27A/1332.
27. *HS* 27A/1332.
28. For details of this debate, see Queen, *From Chronicle to Canon*, 26–30; and *HS* 112/2961.

Having scarcely recovered from the episode with Zhufu Yan, Dong once again found his life threatened by yet another political opponent at court, this time Gongsun Hong, who had had a meteoric rise from pig herder to powerful minister. Gongsun Hong was instrumental in persuading Emperor Wu to appoint Dong to a position certain to put his life in danger: he was named administrator to the court of the imperial kinsman Liu Duan, who reigned as King Yu of Jiaoxi (in present-day Shandong Province). The king was notoriously unstable and infamous for the brutal treatment he meted out to officials sent by the central government to rein him in. Dong took up residence in Jiaoxi and quickly was able to foil Gongsun Hong's plot. Before becoming embroiled in the king's machinations and being accused of some imaginary crime, Dong managed to resign on grounds of illness and retreat from Jiaoxi unscathed.[29] No doubt this personal experience of serving in the kingdoms of Jiangdu and Jiaoxi contributed to shaping the policies he promoted with regard to the regional kings, policies that informed in significant ways his reading of the *Spring and Autumn* and its *Gongyang Commentary*.

After Dong returned to the capital, his fate improved. Judging from various events, his interpretations of the *Spring and Autumn* appear to have finally won the emperor's respect and support. Dong Zhongshu's rise to prominence was marked by three key events. Some time around 122 B.C.E., the emperor directed him to debate the scholar Duke Jiang of Xiaqiu, who was known for his expertise on the *Guliang Commentary* and the *Classic of Odes*.[30] Presumably this was an opportunity for both sides to debate current policy issues, drawing on canonical authority to support their respective positions. "Well versed in the Five Classics, a capable and exceptional speaker, who excelled at linking various literary passages," in contrast to his opponent, who stammered his way through the debate, Dong won by a clear and decisive margin.[31] The debate must have been a significant event at the court because it is recorded that Dong's nemesis Gongsun Hong, who was then serving as counselor-in-chief, presided over the debate, compiled the debaters' respective opinions, and followed Dong's policy recommendations. Although the specific recommendations were not recorded,

29. *SJ* 121/3218; *HS* 56/2525.

30. This debate took place just at the time of the death of Liu An, king of Huainan, patron and editor of the *Huainanzi*, who committed suicide in 122 B.C.E. when he was summoned to the imperial capital to face charges of harboring imperial ambitions. Dong Zhongshu was about fifteen years older than Liu An, and they both were politically active during the first two decades of Emperor Wu's reign. Their views differed on many points of philosophy and policy. If they were personally acquainted or interacted with each other in any way, history preserves no record of it.

31. *HS* 88/3617.

they clearly marked the rise to prominence of Dong's particular interpretations of Gongyang Learning.[32] Not only did Dong's performance convince the counselor-in-chief that his policy recommendations were worth pursing, but it impressed the emperor. Emperor Wu then directed Dong to instruct the heir apparent, the future Emperor Zhao, in his interpretations of the *Gongyang Commentary* to the *Spring and Autumn*.[33] Moreover, during this time the emperor himself appears to have solicited Dong's opinions: "When there were important deliberations at court, the emperor often sent messengers to Dong's home, including even the chamberlain for law enforcement, Zhang Tang, to question him."[34] The memorials written by Dong at this time attest to his influence at court, as Emperor Wu often enacted his policy recommendations.[35]

This eminent scholar, teacher, and official left behind sons, grandsons, and hundreds of disciples who achieved high office.[36] Dong Zhongshu also was highly praised by the most prominent scholars of his age. Reflecting on his teachings, Sima Qian wrote: "From the rise of the Han down to the reign of the fifth generation of rulers, only Dong Zhongshu established a reputation for elucidating the *Spring and Autumn*."[37] Pondering his influence and integrity, Ban Gu composed the following effusive encomium:

抑抑仲舒	Elegant and refined Zhongshu,
再相諸侯	twice minister to the Lords of the Land,
身修國治	by cultivating his person he stabilized [their] kingdoms.
致任懸車	Serving diligently until retiring his carriage,
下帷章思	with lowered curtain pronouncing his thoughts,
論道屬書	discoursing on the Way in his writings,
讜言訪對	with bold words and searching responses,
為世純儒.	he was the unsullied Confucian of his era.[38]

The famous bibliographer and editor Liu Xiang compared Dong with cultural paragons of antiquity: "Dong Zhongshu possessed the ability to assist a true king. Even Yi [Yin] and Lü [Wang] lacked the means to augment [his talents],

32. *SJ* 121/3129; *HS* 88/3617.
33. *HS* 88/3617.
34. *HS* 56/2525.
35. Queen, *From Chronicle to Canon*, 32–35.
36. *SJ* 121/3129; *HS* 56/2525. For the biographies of Dong's disciples, see Queen, *From Chronicle to Canon*, app. 2.
37. *SJ* 121/3128.
38. *HS* 100B/4255.

while the likes of Guan [Zhong] and Yan [Ying] certainly did not compare with him."[39] Even though he suffered political setbacks for his views, making powerful enemies time and again, Dong ultimately secured a reputation that far outweighed the fleeting achievements of his competitors and far outlasted the acclaim they enjoyed in their time.

The *Gongyang Commentary* and Gongyang Learning

The *Gongyang Commentary* (*Gongyang zhuan*) is one of three extant ancient commentaries on the *Spring and Autumn*, the others being the *Guliang Commentary* (*Guliang zhuan*) and the *Zuo Commentary* (*Zuo zhuan*).[40] The *Gongyang Commentary*, as we explain at greater length in the introduction to group 1, "Exegetical Principles," was traditionally regarded as having been written or edited by Confucius's disciple Zixia and then transmitted within the Gongyang family until it was written down during the reign of the Han emperor Jing (r. 157–141 B.C.E.). Contrary to this traditional account, it seems likely that the *Gongyang Commentary* already existed at least partly in written form by the end of the Warring States period, although it seems to have become prominent in the intellectual world of the Han only during and after Emperor Jing's reign. The *Guliang Commentary* is thought to have been written down somewhat later than the *Gongyang Commentary*. The *Zuo Commentary* was traditionally ascribed to Zuo Qiuming, who is said to have been a contemporary of Confucius, but most scholars now consider the *Zuo Commentary* to be a composite work of the fourth to third centuries B.C.E.

The content of the *Gongyang* and *Guliang* commentaries is similar. Both agree that Confucius composed the *Spring and Autumn*.[41] Both are written in

39. *HS* 56/2526. All the individuals mentioned were famous ministers of antiquity.

40. For a cogent description of the *Spring and Autumn* and its ancient commentaries, see Anne Cheng, "Ch'un ch'iu 春秋, Kung yang 公羊, Ku liang 穀梁, and Tso chuan 左傳," in *Early Chinese Texts: A Bibliographical Guide*, ed. Michael Loewe, Early China Special Monograph Series no. 2 (Berkeley: Society for the Study of Early China and the Institute of East Asian Studies, University of California, 1993), 67–76.

41. The earliest extant reference that attributes the authorship of the *Spring and Autumn* to Confucius is found in the *Mencius* 3B.9: "Confucius was apprehensive and composed the *Spring and Autumn*. He said: 'Those who understand me will do so on account of the *Spring and Autumn*; those who condemn me will do so on account of the *Spring and Autumn*.'" The claim that Confucius was the author of the *Spring and Autumn* appears only once (Duke Zhao 10.12.1) in the *Gongyang* itself. Interestingly, there too the question of liability or blame arises, as Confucius is quoted as saying, "As for the wording, I, Qiu, take the blame for that."

question-and-answer style, and both embrace the "praise-and-blame" theory, according to which Confucius used "subtle language" to express his approval or condemnation of events recorded in the *Spring and Autumn*. Erudites—scholars given official posts on the basis of their learning—specializing in the *Gongyang Commentary* were active during the middle decades of the Western Han period, under Emperors Jing and Wu. The *Guliang Commentary* gained official recognition in the mid-first century B.C.E. The *Zuo Commentary* (which differs from the other two by emphasizing historical anecdotes and paying less attention to the language of praise and blame) rose to prominence as an object of study several decades later, at the very end of the Western Han period.

All three commentaries offer a wealth of historical detail to supplement the bare-bones chronicle of the *Spring and Autumn*. But where this detail comes from remains an open question. There are several possibilities, not mutually exclusive: (1) oral transmission through officials of the pre-Qin states and/or through masters and disciples of various lineages of learning; (2) transmission in writing in documents (such as hypothetical chronicles of pre-Qin states in addition to Lu) that are no longer extant; and (3) imaginative reconstruction, effectively historical fiction, by later writers, including the authors of the chronicles themselves. Most modern scholars agree that the commentaries cannot be relied on as sources of historical information in the absence of corroboration (as is sometimes found, for example, in bronze inscriptions).

Nevertheless, it is clear that Dong Zhongshu and his fellow *Gongyang* Erudites, along with their students and followers—to whom we refer collectively as the Gongyang Learning—accepted the accounts in the commentary as being historically true and that those events, properly explained, revealed Confucius's views on ethics, ritual, government, and other matters. They believed, and advocated, that a correct understanding of Confucius's "subtle language" in the *Spring and Autumn* could provide a template for good government in their own time. One modern scholar has observed that the *Spring and Autumn* follows clear rules in the use of names and titles and in the inclusion or omission of individual names,[42] showing that the idea of praise and blame through the use of coded language, though perhaps a Han misreading of the *Spring and Autumn*, is not, after all, completely far-fetched. (This does not, of course, in any way support the traditional claim that Confucius wrote or edited the *Spring and Autumn* itself.)

42. Newell Ann Van Auken, "Who Is a *rén* 人? The Use of *rén* in *Spring and Autumn Records* and Its Interpretation in the Zuǒ, Gōngyáng, and Gǔliáng Commentaries," *Journal of the American Oriental Society* 131, no. 4 (2011): 555–90.

The Question of Han Confucianism

The status of the commentaries to the *Spring and Autumn* in the Former Han period is relevant to the discussion in contemporary Sinology about Han Confucianism—whether it existed and, if so, how it might be characterized. A number of scholars, notably Robert Eno, Michael Nylan, and Michael Loewe, have argued that there was no such thing as Han Confucianism (in the sense of a coherent body of doctrine), that the notion of a "Han Confucian synthesis" is at best an oversimplification, and that the idea that Dong Zhongshu presided over a "triumph of Confucianism" during the reign of Emperor Wu is simply illusory.[43] We agree with much of this critique. In particular, we agree that the old idea of Dong Zhongshu as the architect of a "Han Confucian synthesis" cannot be correct because it rests on a reading of the *Chunqiu fanlu* as a comprehensive expression of Dong's views, integrating the Five-Phase chapters, for example, into a framework founded on the *Spring and Autumn* and the *Gongyang Commentary*. As we show in *Luxuriant Gems of the "Spring and Autumn,"* such a unitary view of the *Chunqiu fanlu* is insupportable.

Eno, Nylan, Loewe, and others who have followed their lead thus make a point of avoiding the use of the word "Confucianism" in connection with the Han period, or of using "Confucian" as a translation of the Chinese word *ru* 儒. That term, whose original meaning is obscure (its possible connotations of "softness," "bending," or "yielding" offer little clarification), came to be applied in the Warring States and Han periods to certain scholars or groups of scholars. The recent trend has been either not to translate the term *ru* or to try to find another term, such as "classicist" or "literati," that might be suitable. In our view, not translating *ru* merely perpetuates an obscurity, and "classicist" casts too broad a net. Many scholarly lineages in the Warring States and Han periods had texts that they regarded as "classics" (such as the *Laozi*) that were foreign to the *ru* tradition. Likewise, "literati" includes many individuals who were not *ru*. Accordingly, we translate *ru* as "Confucian," and we refer to Dong Zhongshu and his fellow practitioners as Confucians. We feel that some scholars' current aversion to the term "Confucianism" with reference to the Han period is unnecessarily

43. This case is made very forcefully by Loewe in *Dong Zhongshu*. See also Michael Nylan, *The Five "Confucian" Classics* (New Haven, Conn.: Yale University Press, 2001); and Robert Eno, *The Confucian Creation of Heaven: Philosophy and the Defense of Ritual Mastery* (Albany: State University of New York Press, 1990).

stringent and hampers, rather than promotes, understanding. We regard "Confucianism" as a capacious, somewhat baggy term, rather like "Christianity" or "Marxism." In our view, to call Dong Zhongshu and some of his contemporaries Confucians is not in any way to suggest that their views were the same as the Neo-Confucianism of a thousand years later, or those of seventeenth-century Han Learning, but to acknowledge that they regarded Confucius as the preeminent sage of human history and the author of the *Spring and Autumn* and accepted that text (seen through the lens of the *Gongyang Commentary*) as the authoritative and canonical guide to creating a good society and a just and effective government in their own time. If that does not merit the designation "Confucian," it is hard to see what might. In the same way, both Thomas Aquinas and John Calvin can be termed Christians with little risk of anyone's assuming that their doctrines and teachings were identical. To insist on too much "rectification of names" is, we think, a mistake.

An Example from the *Gongyang Commentary*

The *Gongyang Commentary* is keyed to the information contained in the *Spring and Autumn*, expanding on the frequently brief and laconic entries under the rubrics of the dukes of Lu and the years of their reign, supplying large amounts of supplementary circumstantial information, and indicating in its characteristic question-and-answer format how the basic text praises or blames the persons concerned. In most cases, largely because of considerations of space, we do not quote at length from the *Gongyang Commentary*, although we often summarize, paraphrase, or quote briefly from a *Gongyang* passage. Where the *Chunqiu fanlu* links directly to a passage in the *Spring and Autumn*, we identify the source passage by duke, year, and paragraph. Interested readers then can find both the *Spring and Autumn* passage and the *Gongyang* explication.[44] The following is an example:

---

44. Passages from the *Chunqiu fanlu*, citing chapter/page/line, are from D. C. Lau, *Chunqiu fanlu zhuzi suoyin* 春秋繁露逐字索引 (*A Concordance to the "Chunqiu fanlu"*), Ancient Chinese Text Concordance Series, Chinese University of Hong Kong, Institute of Chinese Studies (Hong Kong: Commercial Press, 1992). Passages from the *Spring and Autumn* and the *Gongyang Commentary*, cited in the form of duke plus year, will lead readers to Gören Malmqvist's translation of passages from the *Gongyang Commentary* (though not all passages appear in the translation): "Studies on the Gongyang and Guliang Commentaries, Parts 1–3," *Bulletin of the Museum of Far Eastern Antiquities* 43 (1971): 67–222; 47 (1975): 19–69; 49 (1977): 33–215.

Chunqiu fanlu 7: Zhao Dun of Jin was a lone knight, without a foot or an inch of land or a single person in his entourage; yet Duke Ling, who possessed the honor and power bequeathed to him by his hegemonic ancestors, [feared him and] desired to kill him.

Though [Duke Ling] used every kind of artifice and utmost deceit,
With deceit overflowing and his strength fully employed,

[nevertheless] the calamity that [eventually] fell on his own person was great. Zhao Dun's heart [was such that] had he been the ruler of [even] a small state, who would have been capable of destroying him? [*CQFL* 7/19/9–11]

Spring and Autumn, Duke Xuan 7.6.1: Spring. Zhao Dun of Jin and Sun Mian of Wey invaded Chen.

Gongyang Commentary: Zhao Dun assassinated his ruler. Why does he reappear here?
Zhao Quan was the one who with his own hands assassinated the ruler. Since this was so, why does the text lay the blame for this deed on Zhao Dun? [He] did not punish the assassin. Why does it say that he did not punish the assassin? The historian of Jin recorded the crime as follows: Zhao Dun of Jin assassinated his ruler Yi Gao. Zhao Dun said: "Oh Heaven! I am innocent! I did not assassinate the ruler. Who says that I am the one who assassinated the ruler?" The historian said: "You are the most benevolent and righteous [of men]. Someone assassinated your ruler, and you returned to the capital but did not punish the assassin. If this was not to assassinate the ruler, then what is?"

Under what circumstances did Zhao Dun return to the capital? Duke Ling behaved in a reckless manner. He ordered the great officers to attend the court and then he took up a position in a tower and shot pellets at them. They ran hurriedly to avoid the pellets. Only in such games did the duke take pleasure.

Zhao Dun had already come out from his audience [with the duke] and was standing in the court with the other great officers when somebody came out of the inner apartments carrying a bamboo basket. Zhao Dun asked: "What is that? Why should that basket appear from the inner apartments?" He called the man, but he did not come. [Someone] said: "You are a great officer. If you want to have a look at it, then go closer and do so!" When Zhao Dun went closer and had a look at it, he found to his horror that it was the body of a dead man. Zhao Dun asked: "Who is that?" The man replied: "It is the cook. The dish of bear paws that he was cooking was not ready. The duke got angry, hit him with the ladle,

> and killed him. [The duke] had [him] dismembered and wishes me to dispose of the body." Zhao Dun said: "Oh!" and hurriedly entered the palace. Duke Ling, who from a distance saw Zhao Dun approaching, was frightened and saluted twice. Zhao Dun, while still facing the duke, withdrew a few steps, saluted twice and kowtowed, and then left hurriedly.
>
> Duke Ling was ashamed in his heart. He wished to kill him and thus ordered a certain brave soldier to go and kill Zhao Dun. When this brave soldier entered [Zhao Dun's] main gate, nobody was there to guard it. When he entered his inner apartment, nobody was there to guard it, and when he went up to the hall, no one was there either. He bent down, peeked under the door, [and saw that] Zhao Dun was just eating a [simple] meal of fish. The brave soldier said: "Ah, you, sir, are indeed a good man! When I entered your main gate, no one was there. When I entered your inner apartment, nobody was there. When I came up to your hall, no one was there. This shows how relaxed you are. You are an important minister in the state of Jin and yet you sup on fish. That shows your frugality. The ruler wants to kill you, but I cannot bear to do so. But at the same time, I also cannot face my ruler again." And so he cut his throat and died. When Duke Ling heard about this, he became furious and wished all the more to kill Zhao Dun. None of the people could be made to go forward and kill him.

The Gongyang Learning's exegetical tradition forms an essential part of the background for understanding the *Chunqiu fanlu*. But because the *Chunqiu fanlu* is a complicated text, woven from many strands, in our view it requires a new approach to understanding it.

A New Reading of the *Chunqiu fanlu*

With this translation, we hope to guide specialists and generalists alike through a new reading of the *Chunqiu fanlu,* based on and developed from insights first presented in Sarah A. Queen's *From Chronicle to Canon*, published in 1996. Guided by the organization of the text itself, we divided the work into eight groups of chapters according to their common themes. In the introductions to those groups, we discuss in detail the discoveries and interpretations derived from our close work with the *Chunqiu fanlu*. In this general introduction, we offer an overview of the text and discuss our approaches to it.

The new reading of the *Chunqiu fanlu* that we propose is based on the following four principles:

1. Reading the *Chunqiu fanlu* as the record of a living and thriving tradition of exegesis, based on the *Gongyang Commentary* to the *Spring and Autumn*, that addresses some of the most pressing concerns of the Han era, is a far more fruitful approach than one confined to assessing the authenticity or inauthenticity of the text based on the attribution of all, some, or none of its contents to Dong Zhongshu.

2. This frame of interpretation will enable historians to fill a long-standing lacuna in Confucian history by showing how the tradition of Gongyang Learning may have evolved in the critical years after the *Gongyang Commentary* was committed to writing during the reign of Emperor Jing (r. 157–141 B.C.E.) but before the seminal work of He Xiu (129–182 C.E.) formulated what became the orthodox interpretation of that tradition.[45]

3. With this new frame of reference, the multiple voices of the *Chunqiu fanlu* are not dismissed as problematic because not all of them derive from authentic works of Dong Zhongshu. They all are invaluable evidence for understanding how masters of Gongyang Learning transmitted their teachings and how their disciples during the Western and Eastern Han received and developed those teachings. We know the names of some Gongyang masters and those of some of their disciples; there were many others whose names have been forgotten. In this reading of the *Chunqiu fanlu,* all are potential participants in the discussions preserved in the text.

4. Finally, if we regard the *Chunqiu fanlu* correctly as a composite work, compiled by an unknown editor from diverse sources long after Dong Zhongshu's death, and value it as a record of the development and intellectual influence of Gongyang Learning, then issues of authenticity become unimportant. There is no rational basis for an equation that says "by the actual hand of Dong Zhongshu, good; not by the actual hand of Dong Zhongshu, bad (or, at least, less good)." The undoubted fact that the date and authorship of many chapters of the *Chunqiu fanlu* cannot be established with certainty is no grounds for relegating parts of the text to the dustbin of history. It is valuable for understanding an exegetical tradition whose contributions were of great importance to Chinese political and intellectual life. That exegetical tradition sustained a

45. He Xiu, *Chunqiu Gongyang jiegu* (*Explanatory Notes to the "Gongyang Commentary" on the "Spring and Autumn"*), a subcommentary to the *Spring and Autumn*.

constellation of Confucian values and ideals that generations of scholar-officials drew on again and again through the centuries to fulfill their roles as guardians and custodians of the Way. We do indeed propose a stratification of the text, but we downplay the long-standing issue of "authenticity" in favor of regarding the *Chunqiu fanlu* as representing a tradition that developed and changed over time.

The Content and Organization of the *Chunqiu fanlu*

The Content of the Text

Our reading of the *Chunqiu fanlu* rests on a particular understanding of its content and organization. We believe that it is the work of an anonymous compiler living between the fourth and the sixth century C.E. who brought together a number of writings associated with Dong Zhongshu and other masters and disciples of Gongyang Learning. The editor's interest in preserving for posterity the teachings associated with this preeminent Han master and others who transmitted their interpretations of the *Spring and Autumn* through the lens of the *Gongyang Commentary* is readily apparent from the content and organization of the text. As the reader will discover, the majority of essays preserved in the *Chunqiu fanlu* take up and develop various themes derived from the *Gongyang Commentary*, but in different ways and with different foci. In other words, groups of chapters in the *Chunqiu fanlu* address different principles gleaned from the *Gongyang Commentary*. Because these thematically linked principles generally cluster in chapters in close proximity, we grouped these chapters accordingly and provided titles for these thematic groups that speak to their central concerns. In doing so, we hope to make transparent to the reader both the method of compilation that no doubt guided the hands of our anonymous compiler and his motives for undertaking the task. As the reader will see, each group of chapters elucidates a particular aspect of the "great principles" to be derived from the *Spring and Autumn* by revealing the coded messages—as the Gongyang exegetes believed they were—embedded in its text. Taken together, the chapters reveal a utopian vision of flourishing humanity rooted in the unified rule of King Wen of Zhou, a vision designed to serve as a blueprint for implementing the plan for perfected government that the Gongyang Learning masters saw as the precious legacy of the great sage Confucius.

The Organization of the Text

Traditionally, the content of the *Chunqiu fanlu* was arranged according to two overlapping systems. In the first, the content is divided into seventeen "books" (*juan* 卷 [scrolls]), each with a variable number of "parts" (*pian* 編), totaling eighty-two *pian*. In the second system of arrangement, the eighty-two *pian* are numbered consecutively as chapters. In our translation, although we preface each chapter with its appropriate book and part number as well as its consecutive chapter number, our references and cross-references to text material are always to the consecutively numbered chapters. The following list shows the relationship among books, parts, and chapters:

Book 1	2 parts	Chapters 1–2
Book 2	1 part	Chapter 3
Book 3	2 parts	Chapters 4–5
Book 4	1 part	Chapter 6
Book 5	7 parts	Chapters 7–13
Book 6	7 parts	Chapters 14–20
Book 7	6 parts	Chapters 21–26
Book 8	4 parts	Chapters 27–30
Book 9	4 parts	Chapters 31–34
Book 10	6 parts	Chapters 35–40
Book 11	7 parts	Chapters 41–47
Book 12	7 parts	Chapters 48–54
Book 13	7 parts	Chapters 55–61
Book 14	4 parts	Chapters 62–65
Book 15	6 parts	Chapters 66–71
Book 16	6 parts	Chapters 72–77
Book 17	5 parts	Chapters 78–82

Our own division of the text's material into eight groups of chapters obviously differs considerably from the traditional arrangement of the text as "books" and "parts." In our view, the diverse materials preserved in the *Chunqiu fanlu* should be organized according to the principles that apparently guided its anonymous compiler. He grouped together materials that address common themes associated with the *Spring and Autumn* in the text of the *Chunqiu fanlu*, as well as materials intended to fill out specific areas of inquiry not addressed in the *Spring and Autumn*. The groups of chapters move in a somewhat orderly and progressive manner from the beginning to the end of the text. For example, the *Chunqiu fanlu* begins with copious and detailed discussions of the "subtle language" of the *Spring and Autumn*, thereby laying the groundwork for appreciating the claims of later chapters. Reading the text from beginning to end, one can construct a comprehensive overview of Gongyang Learning. Following the contours of these different theoretical and practical realms of concern, the *Chunqiu fanlu* divides into eight groups, to which we have given the following titles:

1. Exegetical Principles (chapters 1–17)
2. Monarchical Principles (chapters 18–22)
3. Regulatory Principles (chapters 23–28)
4. Ethical Principles (chapters 29–42)
5. Yin-Yang Principles (chapters 43–57)
6. Five-Phase Principles (chapters 58–64)
7. Ritual Principles (chapters 65–76)
8. Heavenly Principles (chapters 77–82)

We preface each of these eight groups with a critical introduction, giving readers an overview of each group by identifying its main theme or themes and providing brief descriptions of its constituent chapters. Each group introduction also addresses issues of dating and attribution as well as the general historical context and the issues defining that context.

The Condition of the Text

Having claimed that the *Chunqiu fanlu* exhibits a coherent organization in which the principles of compilation guiding its anonymous compiler become apparent through the proper grouping, dating, and attribution of its chapters, we also recognize the importance of acknowledging the generally poor condition of the text as a whole. Thus despite its structural bones, which give the *Chunqiu fanlu* a strong and coherent form, some of the chapters and sections within chapters contain features that betray the fragmentary and poorly preserved materials of which they are composed. For example, some chapters contain multiple essay fragments from separate sources that have been stitched together to give a semblance of a coherent whole. Still others include essays that diligent scholars have restored from fragments that had migrated to different parts of the text. Accordingly, one of the several principles of sectioning we used in our translation is to alert readers to this fragmentary quality of the text. We explain these principles in greater detail later, in the section "Methods of Translation."

The Title of the Work

Our claims about the compilation and general character of the text find further support in the title by which the collection has come to be known: the *Chunqiu fanlu*. This title is typically rendered into English as either *Luxuriant Dewdrops of the "Spring and Autumn"* or *Luxuriant Gems of the "Spring and Autumn*." The two are quite close, diverging only in their understanding of the title's fourth character. The first version captures the literal meaning of the word *lu*, with its connotations of the "sweet dew" (*gan lu*) that was believed to descend on and moisten and fructify such lands as were ruled by a monarch sagely enough to attract it. The second takes the word metaphorically to refer to strings of gems that hang from the ruler's ritual headgear, shielding his visage from the gaze of lesser men while also reminding the monarch that his view of the world is necessarily partly obscured.[46] Whether literal or metaphorical, the dewdrops or gems of the *Spring and Autumn* are the various principles—from the exegetical and political (Monarchical and Regulatory) to the ethical and cosmological (Ethical, Yin-Yang, Five-Phase, and Heavenly)—addressed in the different groups of chapters of the text. Thus although the title *Chunqiu fanlu* does not appear in the Han sources, it is invaluable for understanding the intent of its anonymous compiler as well as the work's actual content. As we will see, it adds up to a genealogy of Gongyang Learning in the Han.

Individual Chapter Titles

In reconstituting the traces of Han Gongyang Learning, our anonymous compiler no doubt searched far and wide for the materials that constitute the *Chunqiu fanlu*. As our discussions in the successive group introductions demonstrate, both the content and the form of the materials preserved in the text suggest that this is so. Moreover, the notion that the anonymous compiler drew from

46. For a discussion of the various interpretations of this title, see Su Yu, *Chunqiu fanlu yizheng* (hereafter cited as *CQFLYZ*), 1.

multiple source-texts is further supported by the *Chunqiu fanlu*'s chapter titles, which differ in length, and the principles of naming chapters appear to change as one moves through the text. Significantly, the different types of chapter titles correspond to the eight different groups of material we have identified, further supporting our notion that the compiler worked purposefully and methodically, organizing his materials according to certain principles of compilation and borrowing from more than one source-text. Recognizing and analyzing which chapter titles exhibit what general trends and which depart from them is another way to try to resolve the mystery of how this text came together, from what kinds of sources, and what the original order of its chapters may have been.

The chapter titles of group 1, "Exegetical Principles," are mostly, but not invariably, two characters long, but there is an important distinction between the first five titles and the last twelve: the first five chapter titles (assuming "Fanlu" to be the original title of chapter 1, as proposed by Su Yu) are purely decorative, whereas the last twelve titles concretely describe the central themes of their respective chapters (or, in the case of chapter 17, identifies it as a postface to the entire group). As we explain in the introductions to these chapters, this difference is one of several factors suggesting that two different source-texts were combined to constitute this first group.

GROUP 1: EXEGETICAL PRINCIPLES, CHAPTERS 1–17

1. 繁露 *Fanlu* Luxuriant Gems (楚莊王 *Chu Zhuang Wang*, King Zhuang of Chu)
2. 玉杯 *Yu bei* Jade Cup
3. 竹林 *Zhu lin* Bamboo Grove
4. 玉英 *Yu ying* Jade Brilliance
5. 精華 *Jing hua* The Quintessential and the Ornamental
6. 王道 *Wang dao* The Kingly Way
7. 滅國 (上) *Mie guo (shang)* Annihilated States, Part A
8. 滅國 (下) *Mie guo (xia)* Annihilated States, Part B
9. 遂本消息 *Sui ben xiao xi* Waxing and Waning in Accord with the Root
10. 盟會要 *Meng hui yao* The Essentials of Covenants and Meetings
11. 正貫 *Zheng guan* The Rectifying Thread
12. 十指 *Shi zhi* Ten Directives
13. 重政 *Zhong zheng* Emphasize Governance
14. 服制像 *Fu zhi xiang* Images for the Regulation of Dress

15. 二端 *Er duan* Two Starting Points
16. 符瑞 *Fu rui* Signs and Omens
17. 俞序 *Yu xu* Yu's Postface

In contrast to the first group of chapter titles, most made up of two characters, the chapter titles of group 2, "Monarchical Principles," are uniformly three characters in length, and in ancient Chinese, they all rhymed, a feature unique to this group of chapters. But like those of the first group, these titles also describe the central themes of their respective chapters. One plausible explanation for the fact that these titles rhyme is that they formed a coherent group early on, perhaps in the Han, and the compiler incorporated them into the *Chunqiu fanlu* as a ready-made group.

GROUP 2: MONARCHICAL PRINCIPLES, CHAPTERS 18–22

18. 離合跟 *Li he gen* Departing from and Conforming to the Fundamental
19. 立元神 *Li yuan shen* Establishing the Originating Spirit
20. 保位權 *Bao wei quan* Preserving Position and Authority
21. 考功名 *Kao gong ming* Investigating Achievement and Reputation
22. 通國身 *Tong guo shen* Comprehending the State as the Body

In contrast to the first two groups, which exhibit a relatively uniform pattern of two- and three-character titles, the chapters of group 3, "Regulatory Principles," have titles ranging from two to four, six, and ten characters long. Chapters 23 and 25 have long titles, atypical of Han texts. The remaining chapter titles are two or four characters long, resembling the two-character titles of group 1 and the four-character titles characteristic of the cosmological chapters in groups 5 and 6. This variability suggests that the chapters in this group were probably brought together from disparate sources.

GROUP 3: REGULATORY PRINCIPLES, CHAPTERS 23–28

23. 三代改制質文 *San dai gai zhi zhi wen* The Three Dynasties' Alternating Regulations of Simplicity and Refinement
24. 官制象天 *Guan zhi xiang tian* Regulations on Officialdom Reflect Heaven
25. 堯舜不擅移湯武不專殺 *Yao Shun bu shan yi; Tang Wu bu zhuan sha* Yao and

Shun Did Not Presumptuously Transfer [the Throne]; Tang and Wu Did Not Rebelliously Murder [Their Rulers]

26. 服制 *Fu zhi* Regulations on Dress
27. 制度 *Zhi du* Regulating Limits
28. 爵國 *Jue guo* Ranking States

Group 4, "Ethical Principles," contains the most heterogeneous titles, varying in length from two to three, four, seven, and eleven characters. But once again, we see that titles of two and four characters in length are the most typical and that variations from this trend reflect variations in source-text. For example, the two titles that are identified as "official responses"—those of chapters 32 and 38—do not conform to the title lengths more typical of this collection.

GROUP 4: ETHICAL PRINCIPLES, CHAPTERS 29–42

29. 仁義法 *Ren yi fa* Standards of Humaneness and Righteousness
30. 必仁且智 *Bi ren qie zhi* The Necessity of [Being] Humane and Wise
31. 身之養莫重於義 *Shen zhi yang mo zhong yu yi* For Nurturing the Self Nothing Is More Important Than Righteous Principles
32. 對膠西 [i.e., 江都]王越大夫不得為仁 *Dui Jiaoxi* [*Jiangdu*] *Wang: Yue dafu bu de wei ren* An Official Response to the King of Jiangdu: The Great Officers of Yue Cannot Be Considered Humane[47]
33. 觀德 *Guan de* Observing Virtue
34. 奉本 *Feng ben* Serving the Root
35. 深察名號 *Shen cha ming hao* Deeply Examine Names and Designations
36. 實性 *Shi xing* Substantiating Human Nature
37. 諸侯 *Zhuhou* The Lords of the Land
38. 五行對 *Wuxing dui* An Official Response Regarding the Five Phases
39. [Title and text are no longer extant]
40. [Title and text are no longer extant]
41. 為人者天 *Wei ren zhe tian* Heaven, the Maker of Humankind
42. 五行之義 *Wuxing zhi yi* The Meaning of the Five Phases

47. The original chapter title indicates that this response was made to the king of Jiaoxi; we follow *Han shu* 56 in locating it in the court of Jiangdu.

The chapter titles of group 5, "Yin-Yang Principles," are mainly four characters long, and all are thematically based. Ten of the fourteen extant titles in this group are four characters long, two are two characters long, one is three characters long, and one is six characters long.

GROUP 5: YIN-YANG PRINCIPLES, CHAPTERS 43–57

43. 陽尊陰卑 *Yang zun yin bei* Yang Is Lofty, Yin Is Lowly
44. 王道通三 *Wang dao tong san* The Kingly Way Penetrates Three
45. 天容 *Tian rong* Heaven's Prosperity
46. 天辨在人 *Tian bian zai ren* The Heavenly Distinctions Lie in Humans
47. 陰陽位 *Yin yang wei* The Positions of Yin and Yang
48. 陰陽終始 *Yin yang zhong shi* Yin and Yang End and Begin [the Year]
49. 陰陽義 *Yin yang yi* The Meaning of Yin and Yang
50. 陰陽出入上下 *Yin yang chu ru shang xia* Yin and Yang Emerge, Withdraw, Ascend, and Descend
51. 天道無二 *Tian dao wu er* Heaven's Way Is Not Dualistic
52. 暖燠孰多 *Nuan ao shu duo* Heat or Cold, Which Predominates?
53. 基義 *Ji yi* Laying the Foundation of Righteousness
54. [Title and text are no longer extant]
55. 四時之副 *Si shi zhi fu* The Correlates of the Four Seasons
56. 人副天數 *Ren fu tian shu* Human Correlates of Heaven's Regularities
57. 同類相動 *Tong lei xiang dong* Things of the Same Kind Activate One Another

The chapter titles of group 6, "Five-Phase Principles," are uniformly four characters long, with the term "Five Phases" appearing in every title of this group. The uniformity of these titles extends to the principle of naming specific chapters; that is, all the titles are based on themes.

GROUP 6: FIVE-PHASE PRINCIPLES, CHAPTERS 58–64

58. 五行相生 *Wuxing xiang sheng* The Mutual Engendering of the Five Phases
59. 五行相勝 *Wuxing xiang sheng* The Mutual Conquest of the Five Phases
60. 五行順逆 *Wuxing shun ni* Complying with and Deviating from the Five Phases
61. 制水五行 *Zhi shui wuxing* Controlling Water by Means of the Five Phases
62. 制亂五行 *Zhi luan wuxing* Controlling Disorders by Means of the Five Phases

63. 五行變救 *Wuxing bian jiu* Aberrations of the Five Phases and Their Remedies
64. 五行五事 *Wuxing wu shi* The Five Phases and Five Affairs

The chapter titles of group 7, "Ritual Principles," are usually two characters long, with two exceptions. As in group 4, departures from the trend that typifies this group point to variations in the source-texts and setting. In addition, in the two exceptional titles—those of chapters 71 and 73—the third character functions as a marker of genre, in one case as an "official response" and in the other as a "hymn." All the titles describe the content of their respective chapters.

GROUP 7: RITUAL PRINCIPLES, CHAPTERS 65–76

65. 郊語 *Jiao yu* Sayings Pertaining to the Suburban Sacrifice
66. 郊義 *Jiao yi* The Principles of the Suburban Sacrifice
67. 郊祭 *Jiao ji* Sacrificial Rites of the Suburban Sacrifice
68. 四祭 *Si ji* The Four [Seasonal] Sacrificial Rites
69. 郊祀 *Jiao si* The Suburban Sacrifice
70. 順命 *Shun ming* Following Orders
71. 郊事對 *Jiao shi dui* An Official Response Regarding the Suburban Sacrifice
72. 執贄 *Zhi zhi* Presenting Gifts to Superiors
73. 山川頌 *Shan chuan song* Hymn to the Mountains and Rivers
74. 求雨 *Qiu yu* Seeking Rain
75. 止雨 *Zhi yu* Stopping Rain
76. 祭義 *Ji yi* The Principles of Sacrificial Rites

The chapter titles of group 8, "Heavenly Principles," are generally four characters long, with "Heaven" appearing prominently in all but one chapter title. The titles of three of the six chapters in this group are derived from the first characters of their opening lines: chapter 77, "Conform to Heaven's Way"; chapter 78, "The Conduct of Heaven and Earth"; and chapter 82, "The Way of Heaven Bestows." This method of naming chapters is unique to this group.[48]

48. The only other chapter to do so is the very first chapter of the *Chunqiu fanlu*, "King Zhuang of Chu." We agree with Su Yu that that title was not the original one in the collection and that the proper title should be "Fan lu" (Luxuriant Gems).

GROUP 8: HEAVENLY PRINCIPLES, CHAPTERS 77–82

77. 循天之道 *Xun tian zhi dao* Conform to Heaven's Way
78. 天地之行 *Tian di zhi xing* The Conduct of Heaven and Earth
79. 威德所生 *Wei de suo sheng* The Origins of Severity and Beneficence
80. 如天之為 *Ru tian zhi wei* In Imitation of Heaven's Activities
81. 天地陰陽 *Tian di yin yang* Heaven, Earth, Yin, and Yang
82. 天道施 *Tian dao shi* The Way of Heaven Bestows

As seen from the lists, the chapter titles of six of the eight groups of chapters in the *Chunqiu fanlu* usually are of similar lengths: most of group 1's chapter titles are two characters long; those of group 2 are three characters long; most of group 5's chapter titles are four characters long; all of group 6's chapter titles are four characters long; all but two of group 7's chapter titles are two characters long; and all but one of group 8's chapter titles are four characters long. The chapter titles of groups 3 and 4 are more varied in length, but aside from the few long titles, most of the chapter titles are two and four characters long. As suggested earlier, we believe that the chapter titles that are longer or shorter than is typical of each group may alert the prudent reader that they reflect different sources. It is no accident, for example, that the titles assigned to "official responses" found in different groups in the text depart from the title lengths typical of their group. We suspect that these chapter titles were added when the collection was compiled, because either the materials used by the editor had no titles (as would have been true, for example, of official documents) or the original titles had been lost.

The practice of naming a chapter based on its opening line, rather than its central theme, is the exception rather than the rule, occurring as it does in only four chapters: chapter 1, "King Zhuang of Chu"; chapter 77, "Conform to Heaven's Way"; chapter 78, "The Conduct of Heaven and Earth"; and chapter 82, "The Way of Heaven Bestows." We believe that the original titles of these chapters were lost and subsequently were replaced using this method.

A Proposed Stratification of the *Chunqiu fanlu*

Our close reading of the entire *Chunqiu fanlu* and our analysis of its eight groups of chapters, the chapters themselves, and the chapter sections brought us to the following conclusions.

The *Chunqiu fanlu* comprises highly disparate materials, of diverse authorship, written over a period of time extending from the mid–Western Han period (ca. 150–120 B.C.E.) through the Eastern Han period (25–220 C.E.) and perhaps somewhat beyond.

Some materials included in the *Chunqiu fanlu* probably were assembled as groups of texts sometime after the death of Dong Zhongshu in 104 B.C.E. and before the compilation of the *Chunqiu fanlu* as we know it. An example is group 1 (chapters 1–17), which consists of two well-defined subgroups (chapters 1–5 and 6–16) plus a *xu* postface by the otherwise unknown "Mr. Yu" that ties the group of chapters together.

The *Chunqiu fanlu* as a received text was assembled and edited by an unknown compiler not later than the early sixth century C.E. (the time of the earliest reference to the work with that title) and most likely during the fifth century C.E. The unknown compiler apparently tried to assemble and preserve all the materials that he could find that were in any way attributable to Dong Zhongshu, whether they were preexisting groups of chapters or individual chapters or chapter sections. He took a liberal view of his task, as the compilation includes some materials that diverge rather widely from Dong's views as described in the *Shiji* and the *Han shu*. Of course, we have no way of knowing what, if any, materials the unknown compiler may have examined and rejected as unworthy of inclusion in his work. The compiler did, however, consciously group materials together by theme.

The larger purpose behind the compilation of the *Chunqiu fanlu* appears to have been to preserve materials relating to the Gongyang Learning tradition of Confucianism, at a time when Confucian scholarship had been somewhat eclipsed in Chinese intellectual circles by Buddhism and religious Daoism.

The authorship of individual chapters and chapter sections can be ascribed, with more or less confidence, as follows:

- Works by Dong Zhongshu (ca. 150–120 B.C.E.)
    - Chapters 1–5
    - Chapter 30, section 2
    - Chapter 32
    - Chapter 71
    - Chapters 74–75
- Works by Dong Zhongshu or members of his immediate circle, including first-generation disciples (ca. 130–100 B.C.E.)
    - Chapters 6–16

- Chapter 23, sections 5–8, 14
- Chapter 28, sections 1–7
- Chapter 29
- Chapter 30, section 1
- Chapter 31
- Chapters 33–37
- Chapters 43–53
- Chapters 68–69
- Chapter 72, section 1
- Chapter 76
- Chapter 77, section 3

- Works by later followers of Dong Zhongshu (first century B.C.E.)
  - Chapter 17
  - Chapter 23, sections 1–2
  - Chapters 61–63
  - Chapter 70
  - Chapter 72
- Works by Western Han writers not directly associated with Dong Zhongshu (second and first centuries B.C.E.)
  - Chapters 18–22
  - Chapters 24–25
  - Chapter 26
  - Chapter 27
  - Chapter 28, sections 8A–8E
  - Chapter 38
  - Chapters 41–42
  - Chapters 55–57
  - Chapter 64
  - Chapter 73
  - Chapter 78A, section 1
  - Chapters 80A–81A
  - Chapter 82A, section 1
- Works by Eastern Han writers (25–220 C.E.)
  - Chapter 23, sections 3–4, 9–13, 15–16
  - Chapter 58
  - Chapter 60
- Works by post–Eastern Han writers (ca. third and fourth centuries C.E.)

Chapter 77, section 2
Chapter 78A, section 2

These attributions naturally involve some degree of uncertainty. We have assigned works unambiguously to Dong Zhongshu only when we felt quite sure that they were written by Dong himself. Distinguishing between works attributed to "Dong Zhongshu or members of his immediate circle" and "later followers of Dong Zhongshu," however, necessarily involved a certain amount of doubt, and assigning the many sections of two long and complicated chapters, 23 and 26, was fraught with difficulties. Some readers will undoubtedly come to different conclusions about different chapters and chapter sections.[49] The ones we list here represent our best judgment on the basis of a complete translation and intensive study of the text.

Some traditional scholars view the *Chunqiu fanlu* as being largely, if not entirely, the work of Dong Zhongshu. Other, more skeptical scholars dismiss the whole text as having little to do with Dong. Our view gives limited support to both positions. We believe that the text does indeed contain a substantial amount of material by Dong, his immediate disciples, and later followers of his tradition but that it also includes many chapters and chapter sections that clearly have little or nothing to do with Dong and his tradition. In the end, the *Chunqiu fanlu* provides a kind of moving picture of the development, evolution, and (perhaps one might say) dilution of the Gongyang Learning tradition from the years when Dong flourished in the middle decades of the Western Han period into the Period of Disunion when the text was compiled in its received form by an unknown scholar loyal to the memory of Dong Zhongshu.

About This Book

Methods of Translation

In our translation of the *Chunqiu fanlu*, we have followed the same principles established in our earlier translation of the *Huainanzi*, tailored to address the specific characteristics and challenges posed by the *Chunqiu fanlu*:

49. See, for example, the proposals for the stratification of the text in Arbuckle, "Restoring Dong Zhongshu"; and Loewe, *Dong Zhongshu*.

1. The translation must be as complete and as accurate as it is possible to make it, with all Chinese words accounted for and nothing added or paraphrased.
2. The translation must use standard, highly readable English, with no jargon or esoteric vocabulary and no resort to contrived syntax.
3. The translation must preserve the vital features of the Chinese original, such as parallel prose, verse, and aphoristic sayings.
4. Special attention must be paid to the formal characteristics of the chapter titles and chapter contents for guidance in assessing the source materials employed to compile the text and the particular circumstances that brought the collection's source materials into existence.
5. The text must be approached on its own terms, following the organization, content, and contours of individual chapters and the text as a whole.

Conventions

Chapters and Chapter Sections

The earliest references to the *Chunqiu fanlu* indicate that the work was divided into eighty-two chapters, the same arrangement followed in the extant work, with placeholders for the three chapters whose titles and contents have been lost to posterity. The original manuscript copy would have had either no punctuation or only minimal punctuation, with little or no indication of sentence and paragraph breaks, no differentiation of prose and verse, and no sections or other subdivisions within chapters. We have provided all these in our English translation. In general, we have followed the suggested punctuation and, less often, the paragraph breaks suggested by D. C. Lau, editor of the standard edition on which we have based our translation. We note our departures from Lau's punctuation and paragraph division only when they have a significant effect on how we construe the meaning.

We also have divided each chapter into sections, which, although not present in the original text, provide an important tool to enhance readers' understanding of the text and to facilitate cross-references. In referring to these sections, we follow a simple convention: in discussing a section within an individual chapter, we refer to "*section* x.y." So, for example, in a discussion of chapter 28, we might refer to "section 28.2." This draws the reader's attention to section 2 of the chapter under discussion. But when mentioning a section of a chapter other than the one under discussion, or in the context of a general discussion, we refer to *chapter* x.y; for example, in a discussion of chapter 22, we might refer to "chapter 19.2." This alerts the reader to turn to chapter 19, section 2, to find the comparison being made with chapter 22.

As we have defined them, the chapter sections are by no means arbitrary; instead, we have tried to follow breaks in the material itself. The section breaks are intended to show readers where essays, thematic or rhetorical subdivisions within essays, and essay fragments begin and end. This is critical in the *Chunqiu fanlu* because so many of its chapters contain more than one essay or essay fragment. In some instances, several essay fragments from originally separate essays addressing a common theme have been combined in a single chapter. Noting these features of the text will give readers a greater appreciation of the patchwork quality of many chapters by pointing to the various materials that have been stitched together to constitute—or perhaps reconstitute—many chapters in this collection, as well as illustrating the ways in which the poor condition of the collection shapes the reader's reception of the text.

Format and Typography

As is the case with many Han works, formal features such as parallel prose are important components of the *Chunqiu fanlu*'s rhetorical structure. Accordingly, we have been careful to translate parallel prose lines into parallel lines of English, indented and set line-for-line.

Words that do not appear in the Chinese text but are implied by the wording of the original or, in our judgment, are required to complete the sense of a phrase or sentence (taking care not to add anything that is not clearly implied by the text itself) are enclosed in square brackets.

Arrangement of Chapters and Appendices

As we noted earlier, the seventy-nine surviving chapters that constitute this work are divided into eight groups, and we have provided introductions to each group of chapters.

Notes have been kept to a necessary minimum and generally cover such matters as *textual emendations*, as when we disagree with the proposed changes of D. C. Lau, agree with the emendations of Su Yu or other commentators, or propose emendations of our own; *explanations of terms*, such as obscure words or characters used in unusual ways; *source lines* from the *Spring and Autumn* and *Gongyang Commentary*; *people and places* mentioned in the text whose importance requires a brief identification; *cross-references* in the text and references to comparable passages in early texts; and *explanations of obscure passages*, like historical anecdotes that cannot readily be understood without information supplementing the original text.

We also offer full translations (appendices A and B) of Dong Zhongshu's biographies from the *Shiji* and the *Han shu*, the two most important sources for his life. Throughout the book, references to the *Shiji* are cited as *SJ*, and references to the *Han shu* are cited as *HS*.

Translation Issues

Key Terms

DAO 道 The word *dao* is always translated as "the Way."

DE 德 In our translation of the *Huainanzi*,[50] we generally translated *de* as "potency" or "moral potency," in keeping with the eclectic and syncretic nature of that text. Here, reflecting the Confucian orientation of the *Chunqiu fanlu*, we translate *de* as "virtue."

E 惡 We translate *e* as "evil," "bad," "hateful," and "wrongdoing," according to context. *E* is often a paired antonym with *shan* 善, and *shan/e* yields meanings such as "good/evil," "good/bad," "admirable/hateful," "to like/to dislike," and "to accept/to reject." *E* also is sometimes paired with *mei* 美, with meanings like "beautiful//ugly," "excellent/execrable," and "to approve/to disapprove."

GONG 公, HOU 侯, BO 伯, zi 子, AND NAN 男 Following the long-standing convention, we translate these terms as "duke," "marquis," "earl," "viscount," and "baron," respectively, but with the understanding that they do not imply any influence or connotations of European feudal hierarchy.

JUNZI 君子 In the *Chunqiu fanlu*, *junzi* often refers specifically to Confucius as the putative author of the *Spring and Autumn*, and in those cases we translate the term as "the Noble Man" (capitalized). In other cases, *junzi* refers to other individuals distinguished by the nobility of their conduct, and in those instances, we translate the term as "a noble man" (lowercased).

50. Major et al., *Huainanzi*.

LI 理 — The word *li* has the basic meaning of "pattern"; the image is of the pattern of veins in a piece of jade. *Li* is often translated as "principle," but here, in order to avoid confusion with *yi* (righteous principle), we generally translate *li* as "inherent pattern."

QUAN 權 — The word *quan* has the basic meaning of "weight" (used in conjunction with a scale to weigh things). But in the *Chunqiu fanlu*, it often has the extended metaphorical meaning of "expediency," which we translate accordingly.[51]

REN 人 — Translated as "person" or "man," *ren* is used in a special way in the *Spring and Autumn* when the text avoids naming a person to emphasize that person's low (nonaristocratic) status or implicitly to express criticism of that person.[52] In such cases, we translate *ren* as "a man," as in "a man from Jin."

RU 儒 — For reasons already explained, and contrary to the current fashion, we translate *ru* as "Confucian," on the minimalist ground that all scholars who self-identified as *ru* regarded Confucius as a uniquely great teacher and sage and accepted as canonical a small number of texts—such as the *Spring and Autumn*, the *Odes*, and the *Documents*—that were closely associated with him.

SHU 數 — The word *shu* means "number." In the *Chunqiu fanlu*, it often has the extended meaning of "regularity," as in the cycle of the seasons or the motions of celestial bodies. In some cases, *shu* has the broader, metaphorical meaning of "norm," and we employ that translation where appropriate.

WU WEI 無為 — We consistently translate the term *wu wei* as "non-action," albeit recognizing that the Han-dynasty discourse makes clear that "non-action" is not the same as "doing nothing." Our "non-action" should be construed as "taking no purposive action," "non-striving," or "taking no action contrary to the Way," to cite a few other attempts to convey the essence of this important term.

YI 義 — This is a complicated term with many meanings, on a spectrum from "justice" to "significance." In the *Spring and Autumn*, *yi* almost

---

51. Griet Vankeerberghen, "Choosing Balance: Weighing (*quan* 權) as a Metaphor for Action in Early Chinese Texts," *Early China* 30 (2005/2006): 47–89. See also the discussion of *quan* in Victor H. Mair, trans., *The Art of War* (New York: Columbia University Press, 2007), xlv, 139n.20.

52. Van Auken, "Who Is a *rén* 人?" Van Auken translates *ren* as "someone."

invariably connotes both "righteousness" and "meaning." In our translation of the *Huainanzi*, we translated *yi* as "rightness," in keeping with the eclectic and syncretic nature of that text. Here, reflecting the Confucian orientation of the *Chunqiu fanlu*, we generally translate *yi* as "righteousness" or "righteous principle" and, where appropriate, as "meaning" or "justice."

YUE 曰 The word *yue* means "to say" or "said." In the *Chunqiu fanlu*, it often appears in the formula *wenzhe yue* 問者曰, "someone raising a question said," or *nanzhe yue* 難者曰, "someone raising an objection said." In many cases, the word *yue* stands alone, with no identified speaker. In some of those cases, we translate *yue* as "someone said"; but in pedagogical debate (a rhetorical form that appears frequently in chapters 1 through 5, for example), where the text that follows *yue* is clearly an authoritative response to a question or objection, we translate *yue* as "the answer is."

ZHU HOU 諸侯 This is a collective term for rulers of states in ancient China. Some authors translate *zhu hou* as "feudal lords," but we consistently translate the term as "Lords of the Land" in order to emphasize the uniqueness of the term and the sharpness of its focus.

Terms Not Translated

We have made every effort to avoid cluttering our pages with untranslated Chinese terms, but we nonetheless had to leave untranslated a number of words that simply have no good English equivalent:

- Some words pertaining to measurement, such as *li*, a linear distance equal to about one-third of a mile (about 500 meters), and *mu* (or *mou*), a measure of area equal to about one-sixth of an acre (about 0.067 hectare)
- Other words of linear measure, such as *ren*, *zhang*, and *pi*
- Words for units of weight, such as *jun* and *dan*
- The names of the five notes of the pentatonic scale: *gong*, *shang*, *jue*, *zhi*, and *yu*
- The names of some musical instruments, such as the *se* and the *qin*, often, but in our view inappropriately, translated as "lute" or "zither"
- The names of the ten Heavenly Stems and the twelve Earthly Branches and their sexagenary combinations
- Some technical terms, notably *qi*, which we sometimes render as "vital energy" but more often leave untranslated

Nonstandard Romanizations

In order to avoid confusion of terms that are spelled identically in romanized form, we use nonstandard romanizations to distinguish the following pairs of terms:

- The Zhou 周 dynasty and Djou 紂, the last king of Shang
- The Duke of Zhou 周公 and the duke of Jou 州公
- The state (and empire) of Han 漢 and the state of Hann 韓
- The state of Lu 魯 and the county of Luu 潞
- The state of Qi 齊 and the state of Qii 杞
- The state of Wei 魏 and the state of Wey 衛

Citations

Chinese Text

We take as our standard edition the work of D. C. Lau, *Chunqiu fanlu zhuzi suoyin* 春秋繁露逐字索引 (*A Concordance to the "Chunqiu fanlu"*), Chinese University of Hong Kong, Institute of Chinese Studies Ancient Chinese Text Concordance Series (Hong Kong: Commercial Press [Shangwu yinshuguan], 1992), cited as *CQFL*. When we accept Lau's emendations, we do so without comment, but when we depart from his text, we explain why in the notes. Our standard form of reference to this and other concordances in the ICS Ancient Chinese Text Concordance Series is to chapter/page/line in the form [10/83/19].

Our standard reference texts of the *Chunqiu fanlu* for collected commentaries are by Su Yu 蘇輿, *Chunqiu fanlu yizheng*春秋繁露義證 (Beijing: Zhonghua Shuju chuban, 1992), cited as Su Yu, *CQFLYZ*; Lai Yanyuan 賴炎元, *Chunqiu fanlu jinzhu jinyi* 春秋繁露今注今譯 (Taibei: Commercial Press, 1984), cited as Lai, *CQFLJZJY*; and Zhong Zhaopeng 鐘肇鵬, *Chunqiu fanlu jiaoshi* 春秋繁露校釋 (Jinan: Shandong youyi chubanshe, 1994), cited as Zhong, *CQFLJS*.

References to Other Classical Works

Classical works are usually referred to by standard divisions of chapter and verse, without reference to any particular edition—for example, *Odes* 96, stanza 2; *Analects* 1.3. Where an exact page and line reference is called for, unless otherwise indicated and whenever they are available, we cite editions of pre-Han and Han works in the ICS Ancient Chinese Text Concordance Series (all edited by D. C. Lau and published in Hong Kong by the Commercial Press). Citations take the form of the title plus chapter/page/ line—for example, *Liezi* 2/6/20.

We recognize that this translation and study of the *Chunqiu fanlu* will raise more questions and problems than we have been able to answer. Nonetheless, we hope that our work will serve as a springboard for a revival of scholarly attention to this fascinating and difficult collection of "Luxuriant Gems."

Group 1

Exegetical Principles

GROUP 1, "Exegetical Principles," generally describes the exegetical approaches and guiding principles of what later became known as "New Text Confucianism."[1] Followers of this tradition of scholarship, which we will henceforth refer to as Gongyang Learning, believed that Confucius wrote the *Spring and Autumn* as a record of "subtle terms embodying great principles" of praise and blame that he desired to bequeath to the world.[2] Dai Hong (fl. ca. 150 C.E.), whose description came to be accepted as authoritative, describes the transmission of the Gongyang Learning as having begun with Confucius's disciple Zixia 子夏 as an oral teaching transmitted through various descendants of the Gongyang family to Gongyang Shou 公羊壽, who, in turn, transmitted it to the Han scholar Huwu Zedu, the person identified as having

1. The concepts New Text and Old Text were important to Ming and Qing scholars working on Han materials, but they are not Han categories. The debate that was to become so important in this later period was not particularly relevant to Western Han scholastics. Thus what is conventionally referred to as Han New Text Scholarship we will more accurately refer to as Han Gongyang Learning. The competing Guliang Learning tradition, which we treat only in passing, also was part of what later became known as the "New Text School." See Michael Nylan, "The Chin wen / Ku wen Controversy in Han Times," *T'oung Pao* 80 (1994): 83–145; and Hans Van Ess, "The Old Text / New Text Controversy: Has the 20th Century Got It Wrong?" *T'oung Pao* 80 (1994): 146–70.
2. Liang Cai, "Who Said 'Confucius Composed the *Chunqiu*'? The Genealogy of the *Chunqiu* Canon in the Pre-Han and Han Periods," *History of China* 5, no. 3 (2010): 363–85; Joachim Gentz, "The Past as a Messianic Vision: Historical Thought and Strategies of Sacralization in the Early Gongyang Tradition," in *Historical Truth, Historical Criticism, and Ideology: Chinese Historiography and Historical Culture from a New Comparative Perspective*, ed. Helwig Schmidt-Glintzer, Achim Mittag, and Jörn Rüsen (Leiden: Brill, 2005), 227–54.

finally committed these teachings to writing during the reign of Emperor Jing (r. 157–141 B.C.E.).[3]

This first group of thematically linked discussions and essays consists of seventeen chapters, which differ markedly in the state of their preservation.

GROUP 1: EXEGETICAL PRINCIPLES, CHAPTERS 1–17

1. 繁露 *Fanlu* Luxuriant Gems (楚莊王 *Chu Zhuang Wang*, King Zhuang of Chu)
2. 玉杯 *Yu bei* Jade Cup
3. 竹林 *Zhu lin* Bamboo Grove
4. 玉英 *Yu ying* Jade Brilliance
5. 精華 *Jing hua* The Quintessential and the Ornamental
6. 王道 *Wang dao* The Kingly Way
7. 滅國 (上) *Mie guo (shang)* Annihilated States, Part A
8. 滅國 (下) *Mie guo (xia)* Annihilated States, Part B
9. 遂本消息 *Sui ben xiao xi* Waxing and Waning in Accord with the Root
10. 盟會要 *Meng hui yao* The Essentials of Covenants and Meetings
11. 正貫 *Zheng guan* The Rectifying Thread
12. 十指 *Shi zhi* Ten Directives
13. 重政 *Zhong zheng* Emphasize Governance
14. 服制像 *Fu zhi xiang* Images for the Regulation of Dress
15. 二端 *Er duan* Two Starting Points
16. 符瑞 *Fu rui* Signs and Omens
17. 俞序 *Yu xu* Yu's Postface

These chapters elucidate and extend the principles of the *Spring and Autumn* through the lens of the *Gongyang Commentary*, but they do so in different ways that have important implications for understanding the authorship and various source-texts used to compile the *Chunqiu fanlu*. We regard the *Chunqiu fanlu* as a posthumous collection of Gongyang Learning that includes Dong Zhongshu's

3. Su Yu, *CQFLYZ* 475–76. Note that this genealogy is hardly conclusive. Additional teachers and transmitters of the *Spring and Autumn* identified with the *Gongyang* tradition may be found in the *Gongyang Commentary*, in which no fewer than eight masters are cited by name. Chapter 17 of the *Chunqiu fanlu* also names additional teachers not mentioned in the *Gongyang Commentary* or in Dai Hong's preface. For a more detailed discussion of the early history of the *Gongyang* tradition, see Sarah A. Queen, *From Chronicle to Canon: The Hermeneutics of the "Spring and Autumn" According to Tung Chung-shu* (Cambridge: Cambridge University Press, 1996), 115–26.

interpretations and those of his disciples and later followers. As such, the collection documents the ways in which the tradition was transmitted during the Western Han after the *Gongyang Commentary* had been committed to writing during the reigns of Emperors Jing and Wu, continuing through a number of successive reigns. The materials in group 1 appear to predate Wang Mang's interregnum but would have remained authoritative through much of the Eastern Han until He Xiu 何休 (129–182 C.E.) stepped onto the interpretive stage to build on Dong's interpretations. Most important, they demonstrate how Han scholars working in this tradition used the *Spring and Autumn* to address the most pressing issues of their day.[4]

This first group of chapters divides naturally into two subgroups, chapters 1 through 5 and 6 through 17. They originally may have been separate collections of materials relating to Gongyang Learning that were amalgamated at some unknown later time.

Description of Chapters 1 Through 5

The first five chapters in the text contain the closest readings and the most detailed explications of the specific passages and the terminology that Confucius supposedly used to encode his moral evaluations of the affairs recorded in the *Spring and Autumn*.[5] The majority of passages in these chaptersfollow a uniform pattern of explication,[6] exhibiting a common question-and-answer format. Topics are taken up in a seemingly random fashion; in other words, they do not follow the order of the *Gongyang Commentary*, nor do they explain its principles in a linear or developmental sequence. These discussions typically consist of an exchange between an authoritative voice and other, less authoritative voices. The authoritative voice of the unnamed speaker is denoted by the simple expression "someone stated" (*huo yue* 或曰) or "it was stated" (*yue*). Sometimes,

4. For an alternative discussion of these chapters, see Gary Arbuckle, "Restoring Dong Zhongshu (BCE 195–115): An Experiment in Historical and Philosophical Reconstruction" (Ph.D. diss., University of British Columbia, 1991).

5. For a study and translation of chapters 1 through 6, see Robert Gassmann, *Üppiger Tau des Frühling-und-Herbst-Klassikers: Übersetzung und Annotation der Kapitel eins bis sechs*, Schweitzer Asiatische Studien Monographien 8 (Bern: Peter Lang, 1988); and Gary Arbuckle, "Some Remarks on a New Translation of the *Chunqiu fanlu*," *Early China* 17 (1992): 215–33.

6. Specifically, chapters 1.1, 1.2, 2.1, 2.2, 3.1, 3.2, 3.4, 3.5, 4.4, 4.7, 4.8, 4.9, 5.2, 5.3, and 5.6. (We use this system of reference throughout the book to refer to chapters and sections. For example, chapter 1.1 means chapter 1, section 1.)

especially when the authoritative voice answers a question or concludes a dialectical exchange, we gloss *yue* as "the answer is." This anonymous authoritative voice identifies the various principles of the *Spring and Autumn*, Confucius's subtle terminology, and the method of praise and blame informing that terminology. The interpretations of the *Gongyang Commentary* and claims regarding Confucius's use of terminology articulated by this authoritative voice are sometimes enhanced with flourishes from the *Odes*.[7] The other unidentified voices in these discussions, indicated by the set expressions "someone raising a question stated" (*wen zhe yue* 問者曰) and "someone raising an objection stated" (*nan zhe yue* 難者曰), either pose queries and conceptual difficulties in response to the claims articulated by the authoritative voice or challenge the consistency of claims put forth by the authoritative voice, a principle, or the application of a principle. These questions and challenges are answered in turn, and the dialogue ends when the authoritative voice enjoys the last word.

The topics addressed by the participants of the discussion follow neither a logical sequence nor a systematic exposition, although we would argue that this is neither the consequence of a badly damaged or misarranged text nor the outcome of the putative master's inability to present his theoretical claims systematically. Rather, it is indicative of the mode of instruction operative in these passages, one that is intentionally discursive and unmethodical. It is meant to inculcate an intuitive sense of the whole of Confucius's reform program laid out in the *Spring and Autumn* by means of a judicious sampling of its parts. The students, too, are expected to build on these examples, applying a method of radiating analogies to other similar entries in the text until they achieve a holistic sense of the *Spring and Autumn*.[8] As one passage explains,

> In discussing the undertakings of twelve generations, [the *Spring and Autumn*] comprehensively encompasses the Human Way and perfectly delineates the Kingly Way. Its standards are found throughout the 240 years [it discusses], reinforcing one another and constituting a variegated pattern. They are based on juxtaposition and contrast and do not simply follow a linear [path] from antiquity. For this reason, those who discuss the *Spring and Autumn* must collate and

7. The *Odes* are cited in this manner in chapters 1.2, 1.3, 1.4, 2.7, 3.1, 3.2, and 4.3.
8. This method of instruction was employed through the ages in the tradition of classical teaching known as "transmission of teachings by a master" (*shi cheng shi shuo* 師承師說). We thank David Pankenier for sharing his thoughtful insights concerning this method of instruction, which he personally witnessed while studying the *Gongyang Commentary* in Taiwan (1974–1977) under the tutelage of Aisingioro Yu-yun.

> thereby penetrate [its] standards and connect and thereby inquire into them. [They must] group together those that are comparable, match those that are categorically similar, scrutinize their connections, [and] pick out their omissions. Only then will the Way of Humankind be harmonized and the Kingly Way be established.[9]

The terminological subtleties and purposeful lacunae are the hidden signs to be connected to others similar in kind in order to gain a comprehensive knowledge of the world.

The mode of instruction operative in the first five chapters also is highly fluid and interactive. The master is ideally guided not only by the knowledge of the *Spring and Autumn* that he wishes to impart to his students but also by the queries and responses of those students, as well as their characters and temperaments. These factors shape the master's instructional approach at every turn. It is not limited to the *Spring and Autumn* but is indicative of how all the Six Arts should ideally be transmitted. As chapter 2.6, explains, "[T]hose who excel at providing instruction, having praised [their understanding of] the Way, will [then] pay cautious attention to [their pupil's] conduct. They will adjust the timing of their instruction, some earlier and others later, conferring on some students more while others less, adopting a fast or slow pace [according to the abilities of their students]."[10]

In addition to exemplifying a distinctive method of instruction, the first five chapters identify a number of substantive principles that explain precisely how Confucius encoded the *Spring and Autumn* with his ethical-political message for later generations of rulers. Accordingly, many passages discuss in great detail the terminology of the *Spring and Autumn*: the specific terms employed by Confucius to indicate praise and blame, his deliberate omission of certain events, the method he used to encode the *Spring and Autumn*, the causes of specific deviations from the standard terminology, as well as apparent terminological contradictions, contraventions, and inconsistencies across different entries of the *Spring and Autumn*.[11] Some typical examples are

---

9. *CQFL* 2/4/4–8; chapter 2.3. For other examples of this approach to teaching the student how to understand the *Spring and Autumn* by analogizing from one particular example to other cases until a larger sense of the whole is obtained, see chapters 1.3 and 2.7.
10. *CQFL* 2/4/25–26.
11. Joachim Gentz, "Language of Heaven, Exegetical Skepticism, and the Reinsertion of Religious Concepts in the *Gongyang* Tradition," in *Early Chinese Religion: Part One, Shang Through Han (1250 BC–220 AD)*, ed. John Lagerwey and Mark Kalinowski (Leiden: Brill, 2008), 813–38. Gentz points out that what is absent from the text is as significant as what is included.

> The *Spring and Autumn* employs terminology enabling what has already been clarified to be elided and what has not yet been clarified to be recorded explicitly. (chapter 1.1)

> The *Spring and Autumn* distinguishes twelve generations and treats them as three periods: Those that [Confucius] personally witnessed, those that he heard of from others, and those that he heard of through transmission by others. (chapter 1.3)

> When the *Spring and Autumn* [records] affairs that are the same, [it employs] terminology that is the same. (chapter 4.5)

> When the *Spring and Autumn* records events, it sometimes distorts the facts to avoid mentioning certain events. When the *Spring and Autumn* records people, it sometimes alters their names to conceal their identities. . . . Thus those who discuss the *Spring and Autumn* must master these terms that distort the facts and follow their twists and turns. Only then will they comprehend the events that it records. (chapter 4.9)

Through these discussions, students came to understand the implications of specific terms in the *Spring and Autumn* as well as the terminological trends that are key to understanding Confucius's ethical evaluations. These ethical evaluations amounted to a political template for the Han, one that addressed the most important issues of the day. Thus the focal point of many discussions—the praiseworthy or reprehensible actions of the regional Lords of the Land during the Spring and Autumn period—expressed the desire of the early Han rulers (particularly Emperors Jing and Wu) and the scholar-officials who spoke for them to resolve the urgent political challenges that regional lords posed to the early emperors of the Han.

The *Gongyang*'s position that Confucius wrote the *Spring and Autumn* as a specific response to the chaos created by the regional lords as they usurped the power and prerogatives of the enfeebled Heavenly kings of the Zhou, and that he saw his mission as one of reestablishing peace and harmony by restoring the realm's proper hierarchic order, must have resonated strongly in the Western Han era. The Han emperors were similarly challenged by regional lords who rose in rebellion or usurped various prerogatives of the Son of Heaven. These circumstances may have fostered the growth and appeal of Gongyang Learning.

At the very least, these very real concerns are the subtext for understanding the standards articulated in the exegetical chapters of the *Chunqiu fanlu*.

Based on their content and formal features, we concluded that these first five chapters represent instructional sessions between a *Gongyang* master and his disciples. The breadth and depth of the authoritative voice (possibly an officially recognized Erudite of the *Gongyang Commentary* to the *Spring and Autumn*) are typical of one who has mastered the corpus, in contrast to those who posit questions and objections. We might further speculate that this reflects the method of instruction used in the Imperial Academy, where Erudites were employed to give advanced classical training to recommended students. But the instructional milieu depicted here also could be a reflection of the methods of a private academy in which a master instructed his personal disciples. Whatever the case may be, it is distinct from the method of instruction Sima Qian identified with Dong Zhongshu when describing the transmission of his teachings as an Erudite under Emperor Jing: "During the reign of Emperor Jing, he became an Erudite. [From behind] a lowered curtain, he lectured to and recited for his disciples who in turn transmitted [his teachings] from those with greatest seniority to those with least seniority, so that some of his disciples never even saw his face."[12]

Whether this disparity reflects different contexts, and therefore different methods adopted by Dong Zhongshu to transmit his interpretations, or whether it indicates that the authoritative voice of the first five chapters could not be that of Dong Zhongshu cannot be determined without recourse to a wide variety of additional factors, which we will explore toward the end of this introduction. But whether or not that master was an Erudite, whether the context was an imperial or private academy, and whether or not the authoritative voice is that of Dong Zhongshu, these materials certainly are valuable for their ability to shed light on how Gongyang Learning was actually transmitted from a master to his disciples. They also illuminate how the interpretive principles and political ideals of Gongyang Learning developed during the Western Han to address the pressing political concerns of the day. This was after the *Gongyang Commentary* was committed to written form but long before He Xiu, building on Dong Zhongshu's theories, formulated his interpretations of the *Gongyang Commentary*, which, in turn, greatly influenced such prominent nineteenth-century New Text scholars as Liu Fenglu and Wei Yuan.

12. *SJ* 121/3127.

Description of Chapters 6 Through 17

The remaining twelve chapters of the "Exegetical Principles" group also elucidate the subtle language and great principles of the *Spring and Autumn* and address political concerns that reveal their Western Han origins. But they do not do so through instructional sessions in which multiple voices are present. Rather, these chapters instruct by means of prose essays in which the voice of a *Gongyang* master (or the voices of several masters) sets out foundational claims concerning the *Spring and Autumn*.

Chapter 6, "The Kingly Way," is a long, devolutionary historical narrative of a kind that became emblematic of *Gongyang* scholarship. It begins by establishing the critical terminological link between text and ideal by defining kingship with reference to the first character of the first entry of the *Spring and Autumn*. The formulaic phrase in the *Spring and Autumn* for the first year of a Lu duke is *Yuan nian, chun, wang zheng yue* 元年春王正月 (Origin [i.e., first] Year. Spring. The royal first month):

> Why does the *Spring and Autumn* value the Origin [year of each reign] and discuss it? The Origin means the beginning. [It means that] the foundation [must be] upright. The Way is the Kingly Way. [It means that] the king is the beginning of humankind. When the king is upright, the primal *qi* (*yuan qi* 元氣) will be harmonious and compliant, wind and rain will be timely, lucky stars will appear, and the yellow dragon will descend. When the king is not upright, then above there will be alterations in the heavens, and baleful *qi* will simultaneously appear.[13]

The Five Emperors and Three Kings realized this ideal of the Kingly Way. The text describes in idyllic terms the perfect unity and harmony between rulers and ruled. But the original utopian age was not to last, as the descendants of these early kings were unable to duplicate their perfected rulership. So began a slow and steady decline, beginning with the arrogant, reckless, extravagant, and harsh reigns of Jie and Djou, the last rulers of Xia and Shang, and ending with the reign of the Zhou Son of Heaven. The description of disunity and conflict that characterizes this later age provides a startling contrast to that of the Five

13. *CQFL* 6/14/27–29.

Emperors and Three Kings as described earlier. Confronted with these desperate times, Confucius tried to restore the Kingly Way by censuring the Zhou rulers in order to reverse the tide of history. This historical narrative provides the overarching framework in which to understand the examples of praise and blame and the ethical and political principles of rulership derived from them that together provide the template of ideal rule that constitute the remaining sections (6.2–6.9) of the chapter.

The ideal reign described in these sections is replete with a sacrificial system that reestablishes the proper hierarchy between the Son of Heaven and his Lords of the Land (6.2); rituals that, among other things, require the Lords of the Land to pay proper courtesy visits to the ruler's court (6.3); principles that condone Lords of the Land who act in hegemonic ways (6.4) or follow the principle of expediency (6.5) to preserve their state. Under normal circumstances, this was intended to curtail the authority of the Lords of the Land so that they would not arrogate to themselves powers that properly belonged to the Son of Heaven (6.2, 6.8, 6.9). These all were matters of urgent concern in the early years of the Han as the imperial blood relatives who were enfeoffed as Lords of the Land and kings challenged the powers and prerogatives of the Son of Heaven, particularly under Emperor Jing when regional rulers who were related to the Liu emperors rebelled in untoward numbers.

In addition to their concern with elucidating the proper conduct of the Lords of the Land and delimiting their power and authority in comparison with that of the Son of Heaven, the later sections of this chapter discuss the role of the other group of important shareholders in power: the ministers. The ideal reign envisioned in the *Spring and Autumn* also provides a code of conduct and describes the values that should guide them. By studying specific examples in the *Spring and Autumn*, the ruler and his ministers will understand how to follow the path of survival and avoid the path of destruction (6.6–6.9). Finally, and perhaps most important, the teachings of the *Spring and Autumn* enable the ruler to secure a position superior to those to whom he delegates authority. These include the Lords of the Land: the royal relatives enthroned as kings of the neofeudal kingdoms in the eastern part of the empire; the high bureaucrats appointed by the central court to govern the commanderies in the western part of the country and on the frontiers; and the ministers and advisers at the imperial court who rule the kingdom of ideas: the political notions, moral values, and scriptural techniques required by the Han emperors to legitimize their empire in the making. Section 6.10 ends on a note of realpolitik: "[T]here has never been a ruler who abandoned his political authority who was able to control the tendencies in the various states; there has never been a ruler who abandoned the distinctions between the honorable and the lowly who was able to preserve his political position."[14] Chapter 6 was not necessarily written as a single, continuous essay, and some of the later sections might have had an earlier existence as separate documents. But it seems clear that they were at least edited and assembled into a well-organized chapter in such a way that the later sections all built on and amplified the principles adduced in section 6.1.

The theme of survival and destruction continues into chapter 7, "Annihilated States, Part A," and chapter 8, "Annihilated States, Part B."[15] Echoing the historical narrative in chapter 6 that glorifies the unity of the utopian age of the Five Emperors and Three Kings and denigrates the disunity of the waning years of the Zhou dynasty, the introduction to chapter 7 explains that annihilation is the result of isolation. The text then offers as examples various kings of the *Spring and Autumn* and their most famous ministers—Duke Ling of Jin and Zhao Dun, King Helü of Wu and Wu Zixu, King Kun of Chu and his ministers Ziyu and De Chen, and the duke of Yu and Kong Zhiji. Those rulers who did not choose good ministers or those who sought to harm upright ministers inevitably were destroyed, while those who chose the right ministers and relied on them always survived. Moreover, as examples in chapter 8 demonstrate, when rulers are on the verge of destruction and no one comes to rescue them, one can discover the cause of their demise by examining their conduct in ordinary times before their states were faced with annihilation.

Chapter 9, "Waxing and Waning in Accord with the Root," continues the theme of destruction, focusing not on the annihilation of states and their causes but on the deaths of their rulers and the conduct that caused them. The chapter consists of two distinct parts that we believe could not originally have formed a single essay, so we have divided it into two sections. Although section 9.1 ostensibly serves as an introduction to the chapter, on close inspection, the messages

---

14. *CQFL* 6/18/24–25.
15. We believe these two chapters were originally one long essay that was later divided into chapters 7 and 8. Chapter 7 begins with an introduction that relates to the content of both chapters 7 and 8, whereas chapter 8 lacks an introduction. How this came to be the case is an intriguing question that once again brings us back to the highly speculative but attractive idea of an anonymous compiler attempting to reconstitute a text attributed to Dong Zhongshu by compiling and collating what he could find in circulation with an understanding that the putative text had a certain number of chapters he was trying to match. There are other examples later in the text in which an essay appears to have been divided and spread over two chapters. For example, chapters 11 and 12 probably were originally a single essay. See the lengthy discussion in chapter 11, note 1. Chapters 61 and 62 comprise material that is consecutive in *Huainanzi* 3 but is divided into two chapters in *CQFL*.

it conveys—"Heaven is cutting me off" and "there are certain situations that [the sage] is powerless to salvage"—do not match the many examples that follow in the chapter's second section. Section 9.2 cites the deaths of several rulers recorded in the *Spring and Autumn* and notes the bad choices they made and their failures to take the proper precautions. It suggests that the cause of their demise lay in their actions rather than in the notions of fate discussed in the first part of the chapter.

Probably because previous chapters already have given many examples of annihilated states and assassinated rulers, chapter 10, "The Essentials of Covenants and Meetings," turns to the reasons why Confucius was intent on documenting the various causes of such calamities:

> Although his highest intentions are difficult to convey, is it not the case that the Sage [Confucius] prized eradicating the world's misfortunes? Thus the *Spring and Autumn* attaches great importance to this subject and records the world's misfortunes in a comprehensive way. It takes as its root revealing the various causes of misfortune with the intention of eradicating misfortune in the world.[16]

The essay continues, in a spirit very much like that of Dong's memorials, that eradicating misfortune in the world is the prerequisite for human flourishing because only then can the ruler create an environment in which the people can be morally transformed. Depictions of Confucius as a sage whose mission was to eradicate wrongdoing in the world can be found in a wide range of Han sources, but the Gongyang Learning of the Western Han appears to have developed this notion of Confucius with the greatest elaboration. An example is the oft-repeated trope that Confucius took note of wrongdoing no matter how seemingly trivial or inconsequential it was to the uninitiated eye. In chapter 9, the liminal moment when the world plunged into new depths of turpitude, as the title and content suggest, came when the Lords of the Land arrogated to themselves the prerogatives of the Son of Heaven—a theme pertinent to the conduct of Lords of the Land and kings of the neofeudal kingdoms of the Western Han. The failure to eradicate this kind of wrongdoing, the essay argues, led eventually to the assassination of the thirty-six rulers and the destruction of the fifty-two states recorded in the *Spring and Autumn*. Thus the essay concludes by praising the efficacy of the *Spring and Autumn*:

16. *CQFL* 10/20/30–21/1.

> With a public-spirited heart, it relies on right and wrong to reward good and punish evil so that the enriching influence of the king spreads throughout the world. It begins by eradicating misfortune [and concludes] by rectifying the [grand] unity [of King Wen] so that all things are put in order. Thus it is said, "Great indeed are the designations of the *Spring and Autumn*! With two expressions, [praise and blame], it disciplines the world." This is what this expression means.[17]

In this way, Confucius cleared the moral ground for the kingly transformation he hoped to initiate.

The great principles of the *Spring and Autumn* are identified and categorized further in the next two chapters of this group: chapter 11, "The Rectifying Thread," and chapter 12, "Ten Directives." Chapter 11 opens by stating that the righteous principle of the *Spring and Autumn* can be understood in terms of "categories" and "directives." The remainder of the chapter expands on the notion of "six categories," leaving the "ten directives" to chapter 12. This chapter argues (as do other chapters in group 1) that the teachings of the *Spring and Autumn* are the key to the ruler's ability to achieve the moral transformation of the populace. That is because in these categories, "it is possible to apply [the *Spring and Autumn*] to every kind of human [situation] without confusing [what is proper to] its various classifications of human relationships." Having mastered the *Spring and Autumn*, the ruler can instruct the people and they will comply, because he now understands precisely how "to arouse those things that their Heaven-endowed natures cherish and to repress those things that their emotions despise."[18] The ruler is the paramount teacher of the *Spring and Autumn*. The essence of ruling well is teaching well; the essence of teaching well is mastering the *Spring and Autumn*; and the essence of understanding the *Spring and Autumn* is understanding human emotions and human nature. This, as the essay concludes, is the basis of governing well.

Chapter 12 continues the theme of chapter 11, and it seems likely that the two chapters once formed a single essay.[19] After defining the "ten directives" mentioned at the beginning of chapter 11, this chapter argues that the *Spring and*

17. *CQFL* 10/21/7–9.
18. *CQFL* 11/21/17, 19.
19. But in the ninth directive of chapter 12, the Mutual Production Sequence of the Five Phases, is read into the *Spring and Autumn*, a theoretical stance not generally seen in these early exegetical chapters of the *Chunqiu fanlu*. This might be explained as a later interpolation, or it could be taken as evidence that chapters 11 and 12 as a whole were compiled somewhat later than the other chapters in group 1.

Autumn is a comprehensive text: "In the *Spring and Autumn*'s record of 240 years, there is nothing that it fails to transmit, [despite] the vastness of the world or the extensiveness of alterations in human affairs." Its essential elements are boiled down to ten directives that "are what bind together all its affairs and are the source from which the king's transformative [influence] flows." As in chapter 11, this chapter concludes with a description of how these teachings of the *Spring and Autumn* will further the ruler's moral transformation of the populace. Perhaps because of its brevity and clarity and its apparently straightforward summary of the *Spring and Autumn*'s guiding principles, this chapter has attracted the attention of a surprising number of translators, making it one of the *Chunqiu fanlu*'s most widely known chapters.[20]

Chapter 13, "Emphasize Governance," is a ragbag chapter consisting of four unrelated fragments. Only the third fragment, in which the two characters that constitute the chapter title appear, is related to the emphasis on governance. Thus we have treated the four sections of the chapter as essentially independent units. Section 13.1 revisits the concept of the "Origin" discussed in the fragmentary statement that opens chapter 4.1, echoing its basic sentiment but expanding on that earlier discussion of the concept. Fragment 13.1 appears to be an introduction to a lost longer piece. As it now stands, it ends abruptly, raising questions whose answers have been lost. This fragment may very well be related to the opening sentence of chapter 4, as a number of commentators have suggested. But even if we accept that position, the essay still is incomplete.

Section 13.2, another essay fragment, maintains that the classifications and taxonomies of the *Spring and Autumn* determined by the sage Confucius were inspired first and foremost by his desire to discuss the ethical values of humaneness and righteousness and to clarify their principles. Once again, we find the insistence that the *Spring and Autumn* and the *Gongyang Commentary* are the "great root [of learning]." The reader is warned, however: "But if you fail to be diligent in applying your mind, [even though you act so as to] embitter

20. Translations of chapter 12 include those by Anne Cheng, *Étude sur le Confucianisme Han: L'élaboration d'une tradition exégétique sur les Classiques* (Paris: Collège de France, Institut des hautes études chinoises, 1985); Benjamin Elman, *Classicism, Politics, and Kinship: The Ch'ang-chou School of New Text Confucianism in Late Imperial China* (Berkeley: University of California Press, 1990); Fung Yu-lan, *A History of Chinese Philosophy*, vol. 2, *The Period of Classical Learning* (*From the Second Century B.C. to the Twentieth Century A.D.*), trans. Derk Bodde (Princeton, N.J.: Princeton University Press, 1953); Otto Franke, *Studien zur Geschichte des konfuzianischen Dogmas und der chinesischen Staatsreligion* (Hamburg: Friedrichsen, 1920); Joachim Gentz, *Das "Gongyang zhuan" Auslegung und Kanonisierung der "Frühlings und Herbstannalen (Chunqiu)"* (Wiesbaden: Harrassowitz, 2001); and Woo Kang, *Les trois théories politiques du Tch'ouen Ts'ieou interpretées par Tong Tchong-chou d'après les principes de l'école de Kong-yang* (Paris: Leroux, 1932).

your resolve and deplete your feelings, [it will be to no avail]. Even if your hair turns white and your teeth fall out, you still will not come up to the standards recorded [in them]."[21]

The essay fragment that constitutes section 13.3 appears to have originally been the introduction to a now-lost essay on the various forms of fate or destiny in relation to the vicissitudes of governance. Section 13.4, a fragment devoid of context, urges the ruler to create unity, promote goodness, and eradicate wrongdoing, and it praises the perspicacity of the *Spring and Autumn*.

As its title indicates, chapter 14, "Images for the Regulation of Dress," contends that clothing is as essential to adorning the body as food is to nourishing it and, furthermore, that correct clothing and accessories are crucial aspects of a ruler's potency. Those who adorn their bodies with their sword on the left, dagger on the right, knee pads in front, and *guan* cap on top embody the four directions symbolized by the Bluegreen Dragon, White Tiger, Vermilion Bird, and Dark Warrior, respectively. These symbols are the most splendid ornamentations of humankind because they correspond to the patterns of Heaven. Accordingly, it is fitting that they not adorn the dress of ordinary people indiscriminately but be reserved for those who possess special qualities: "Only those who are able to connect antiquity with the present and distinguish what is so from what is not so are able to dress in this manner." Implicitly, this should mean the Son of Heaven, as the symbolic vestments described here are correlated with the directions in such a way that they are correctly aligned only if the person is facing south—and the one who faces south is, of course, the ruler. But as the essay proceeds, we see that the person uniquely qualified to wear court dress adorned with such symbols is none other than Confucius, which makes perfect sense in the context of Gongyang Learning, as it envisions him as the uncrowned king of the *Spring and Autumn*.

The Dark Warrior is the principal symbol of this essay and, as the most martial of all symbols, paradoxically embodies the notion of the highest form of pacifism:

> Now the Dark Warrior's appearance is the fiercest and most awe inspiring. That its image occupies the rear,[22] but [its article of dress] occupies the [top of] the

21. *CQFL* 13/22/25.
22. The Dark Warrior (depicted as a snake entwined around a turtle) was the divine symbol of the north. It "occupies the rear"—that is, the northern quadrant—reflecting the orientation of the imperial throne, which always faced south. The southern gate of a city or a palace was referred to as the front gate, and the northern gate as the rear gate.

head [shows that] martiality at its utmost is not employed. The reason that the sage surpasses [others] is because even if he were to wish to follow [a policy of martiality], no occasion for it would arise. Those who are able to stop the enemy only after "grasping armor and helmet" [i.e., resorting to warfare] are certainly not those whom the sage prized.[23]

Confucius simply adorned himself with this potent figure of martiality, and the "intentions of the brave and martial were vitiated [when confronted by] his appearance." This pacific ideal of conquering without fighting also can be found throughout the *Spring and Autumn* in such examples as the righteousness of Kongfu, the prescience of Kong Zhiji, and the dragon-embroidered robe worn by King Wu.[24] The essay concludes: "How can it be the case that bravery must be proved in battle and slaughter before awesomeness [is established]? This is why the Noble Man [Confucius] attached greatest importance to his dress. Those who gazed at his dignified appearance could not help but exhibit such dignity. You must not fail to examine this matter in great depth!"[25]

The next two chapters, chapter 15, "Two Starting Points," and chapter 16, "Signs and Omens," turn to the subject of omens. This was another preoccupation of Gongyang Learning, how to decode the various portents, anomalies, signs, and omens recorded in the *Spring and Autumn*. Chapter 15 argues that the highest aspirations of the *Spring and Autumn* may be summarized as two essential distinctions: between the insignificant and significant and the hidden and manifest. These are the starting points for understanding the various anomalies recorded in the *Spring and Autumn*. If you can grasp the cause of events when they still are insignificant and hidden, then you will understand the reasons why Confucius recorded various anomalies and the significance of such records. These preliminary remarks serve to introduce the real point of the essay, which is that the time has come for the Han to reform the calendar, though presumably the auspicious sign that the dynasty has received the Mandate has not yet appeared.[26] An uncanny ability to anticipate how events would unfold

23. *CQFL* 14/23/10–12.
24. Kongfu was a high officer of the state of Song. His enemies realized that in order to overthrow the lord of Song, they first would have to assassinate Kongfu, which they did. Kong Zhiji was a minister of the state of Yu whose good advice, had it been heeded, would have saved the state from destruction. King Wu's robe was so awesome that on the battlefield, the soldiers of the Shang army laid down their weapons without a fight.
25. *CQFL* 14/23/15–16.
26. This issue is taken up by Emperor Wu when questioning Dong: "Where are the auspicious signs that the Mandate received by the [rulers of the] Three Dynasties now rests at the present time [with Us]?" (*HS* 56/2502).

when they were still insignificant and hidden informed Confucius's method of recording anomalies:

> Therefore [the *Spring and Autumn*] records eclipses, meteors, water monsters, mountains crumbling, earthquakes, great rainstorms in the summer, great hailstorms in the winter, descents of frost that [nevertheless] did not harm plants, lack of rain from the first month of the year to the seventh month in autumn, and cranes and mynahs nesting [in Lu]. The *Spring and Autumn* noted these occurrences as anomalies and used them to manifest the incipient stirrings of disorder. In this way what was [still] insignificant was not able to become significant and what was still hidden was not able to become manifest. Even if they were quite subtle, [they still were considered] the starting points [of events] and Confucius used them to verify [their outcomes].[27]

The essay concludes by insisting that Confucius recorded such anomalies in the hopes that the ruler would heed Heaven's warnings.

In chapter 16, "Signs and Omens," a badly damaged and fragmentary chapter with two sections, we find a moving account of undoubtedly the most important portent in the *Spring and Autumn*: the capture of a *qilin* in the western suburbs.[28] That event, recorded in the final entry of the *Gongyang Commentary*, is read here as the sign that both confirmed Confucius's symbolic reception of the kingly mandate and sanctioned his writing of the *Spring and Autumn*: that the writing of history is depicted as a responsibility and a privilege reserved solely for the Son of Heaven.

Chapter 17, "Yu's Postface," is the last of the *Chunqiu fanlu*'s first group of chapters.[29] These seventeen chapters clearly form a coherent unit, in effect a "book within a book," that the unknown compiler of the *Chunqiu fanlu* placed at the beginning of the larger and more diverse work. (As we pointed out earlier, the group 1 chapters themselves may be an amalgamation of two separate, early collections of Gongyang Learning, comprising chapters 1 through 5 and 6 through 16.) This impression is strengthened by the content of chapter 17, which reiterates a vision of Confucius commensurate with that of the first sixteen chapters of the text and which summarizes many of the themes that those chapters discuss, including Confucius's use of the *Spring and Autumn* to render

27. *CQFL* 15/23/25–24/1.
28. The *qilin* was a composite animal sometimes described as having the head of a dragon, the body of a lion, and the legs and feet of a goat. It was believed to appear only during eras of sagely government.
29. For another translation and analysis of chapter 17, see Gentz, *Das "Gongyang zhuan,"* 499–533.

judgments on history, the fate of rulers who ignored the lessons of history, the importance of relieving the misfortunes of the people, and the principle of criticizing great wrongdoing but taking a lenient stance toward minor transgressions.

The chapter's title indicates that it is a *xu*, a type of essay often attached to the end of multichapter works in early China to introduce and epitomize the preceding body of material. We believe that in fact, chapter 17 is a postface to what originally was a separate book made up of chapters 1 through 16, just as the final chapter of the *Huainanzi* serves as a postface to the twenty substantive chapters of that work, or as chapter 33 serves as a postface to the *Zhuangzi*. This is evident from its opening lines:

> When Zhongni [i.e., Confucius] composed the *Spring and Autumn*, he first plumbed the uprightness of Heaven to rectify the positions of the king and the nobles and the desires of the multitudinous people. Next he illuminated successes and failures and promoted the worthy and capable in expectation of a future sage. Thus he cited historical records, ordered past events, rectified right and wrong, and revealed his kingly mind. Now the events of the twelve dukes in the historical records all were events of a declining age. Consequently, Confucius's disciples had doubts about them. Confucius told them, "I rely on past events and apply my kingly mind to them because I consider that explaining things with abstract theories is not as good as the breadth and depth of past events for parsing and illuminating things."[30]

The essay proceeds to lay out a genealogy of Gongyang Learning, starting from Confucius and continuing through several of his most famous disciples—such as Zigong, Minzi, Kong Jianzi, Shizi, Zi Xian, Zengzi, and Zi Shi—citing how the teachings of each disciple contributed to the richness of the tradition. The author of the chapter uses each example to argue for the instrumental value of Gongyang Learning to successful rule, and he ends with one final appeal: "When the transforming influence of [*Spring and Autumn*] instruction flows forth, virtue and kindness will greatly permeate the people of the world, and they will conduct themselves as scholars and noble men and scarcely transgress at all." This effort to "sell the text" is reminiscent of the postface to the *Huainanzi*, which similarly argues for the importance of that work as the key to successful rule.

30. *CQFL* 17/24/15–18.

It is intriguing that this group of chapters ends with a self-identified postface (*xu*). Given that every chapter illuminates a critical aspect of the *Spring and Autumn* and so is tied to concepts and methods associated with Gongyang Learning, it appears that this first group of seventeen chapters is indeed a book within a book, or (to use a traditional Chinese bibliographical term) a *nei shu* (inner book), preserving the work's most important chapters. Did the compiler of the *Chunqiu fanlu* begin by incorporating into his collection a preexisting set of chapters attributed to Dong Zhongshu? And was this "inner book" the creation of a man named Yu, about whom we know nothing? We may never know, but the evidence is strongly suggestive. Whatever the case, the exegetical interpretations preserved in these chapters are best understood as Western Han expressions of Gongyang Learning with clear affinities and links to Dong Zhongshu and his disciples.

Issues of Dating and Attribution

Chapter Titles

We have argued that the literary form and exegetical approach of the first five chapters are different from those of the last twelve chapters of group 1, and this difference appears to carry over to the chapter titles for these subgroups. All the two-character titles of the first five chapters—assuming, as Su Yu does (and as we agree), that chapter 1 was originally called "Fanlu" (Luxuriant Gems)—are highly ornamental and propitious. Most (Jade Cup, Bamboo Grove, Jade Brilliance) evoke images associated with auspicious omens. In contrast, the titles of chapters 6 through 17 describe their central themes.

The titles of chapters 1 through 5 give us important clues to the dating and authenticity of the text. Han sources attribute three works to Dong Zhongshu. The *Shiji*'s "Biography of Confucian Scholars" attributes to him "Zai yi zhi ji" (Records of Disasters and Anomalies). The *Han shu*'s "Bibliographic Treatise" lists two additional works attributed to him: *Dong Zhongshu*, in 123 *pian*,[31] and *Gongyang Dong Zhongshu zhiyu* (*The Gongyang* [*Scholar*] *Dong Zhongshu*

31. A *pian* 篇 is a single bundle of bamboo strips (used for writing), approximately equivalent to an essay or a chapter of a book.

Judges Cases) in 16 *pian*. No reference to a text titled *Chunqiu fanlu* appears in any book, bibliography, or fragment that survives from the Han dynasty. The earliest reference to such a work dates from the Liang dynasty.

One important piece of the puzzle that does survive from the Han is Ban Gu's description of Dong's writings, in *Han shu* 56. There we find prominently listed several works whose titles are highly relevant to the first five chapters of the existing *Chunqiu fanlu*:

> Zhongshu's compositions all elucidated the meaning of the classical arts. Memorials submitted to the throne and items of instruction totaled 120 *pian*. His expositions of the successful and unsuccessful affairs of the *Spring and Autumn*, [in] such writings as "Heard and Promoted," "Jade Cup," "Luxuriant Gems," "Pure Brightness," and "Bamboo Grove," came to an additional several tens of *pian* amounting to more than a hundred thousand characters. All were transmitted to later generations. Selections from compositions relating to matters of the court at the time comprised additional *pian*.[32]

This description suggests that the five writings referred to by name circulated separately from the *Dong Zhongshu*. Moreover, "Jade Cup" and "Bamboo Grove" appear as the titles of chapters 2 and 3 in the *Chunqiu fanlu*. It is highly likely, as Su Yu suggests, that chapter 1 originally also had an auspicious title—"Luxuriant Gems"—that later was wrongly attached to the compendium as a whole. Consequently, chapter 1 would then have needed, and acquired, a substitute title.[33]

What are some of the possible implications? First of all, the *Chunqiu fanlu* simply cannot be the *Dong Zhongshu* renamed; the extant text is not long enough. (Remember that the *Dong Zhongshu* is described as having 123 *pian*.)[34] It still is possible, however, that *parts* of the *Dong Zhongshu* and the separate named writings may have been combined to form the *Chunqiu fanlu*. Surprisingly, scholars have not emphasized the fact that several of the seventy-nine extant chapter titles in the received text appear by name in *Han shu* 56. This is even more surprising because the content of those chapters, describing and evaluating the affairs chronicled in the *Spring and Autumn*, are absolutely consistent with Ban Gu's description.

32. *HS* 56/2525.

33. The argument for this position is laid out in detail in Gary Arbuckle, "The Works of Dong Zhongshu and the Text Traditionally and Incorrectly Titled *Luxuriant Dew of the Annals (Chunqiu fanlu)*," a source that unfortunately is no longer available.

34. For a discussion of the possibility that someone added the first five chapters to the *Chunqiu fanlu*, see Su Yu, *CQFLYZ* 1–31.

Historical Context

Can we date the materials in the first group by reading them with particular attention to their content, in an attempt to discover the contemporaneous concerns they address? Do the principles they posit as being essential to the *Spring and Autumn* point to a nexus of Han issues—scholastic or political—that we might identify to anchor these materials in their historical contexts? If so, working in the reverse direction—from the outside in, from the context to the text—can we establish a probable historical period during which such principles would have been relevant?

From our description of the content of individual chapters, several salient characteristics of this group become evident.

1. The authoritative voices that speak to disciples through the instructional sessions recorded in the first five chapters, and the prose essays in the latter eleven chapters, are those of one or more *Gongyang* masters.

2. With the exception of chapter 12, these chapters are virtually devoid of references to yin-yang or Five-Phase cosmology. This suggests that the words of the *Gongyang* master recorded in these chapters reflect an era when yin-yang or Five-Phase cosmology had not yet been incorporated into Confucian (*ru*) discourse. That, in turn, would indicate a date in the first half of the Western Han. This is not entirely probative, however, as such cosmological principles may simply have been irrelevant to the mode of exegetical activity that dominates these early chapters, preoccupied as they are with clarifying the terminology of the *Spring and Autumn* and the political ideals and actions that it condones or condemns. But even though the absence of references to cosmological theory in these chapters is not conclusive, this tendency contrasts markedly with later chapters of the *Chunqiu fanlu,* in which discussions of yin-yang and Five-Phase cosmology are quite prominent.

3. The principles that these discussions associate with the *Spring and Autumn* and highlight as keys to understanding and transmitting that text are directly and essentially relevant to issues that preoccupied the ruling elite in the Former Han period. These issues concerned the unity of the newly won empire, the role of ritual in its governance, the status and position of the Son of Heaven (who held the relatively new and distinctive title of "emperor"), and the conflict between the power of officials who were in the central administration and that of the royal relatives who ruled the empire's various marquessates and kingdoms.

As we explore further the relationship of the *Chunqiu fanlu*'s "Exegetical Principles" to these issues, we will not have to review all the examples in the early chapters of the text.[35] Instead, we will discuss one concern that illustrates the text's engagement with Western Han issues: the issue of the regional lords. Here—especially in the first five chapters of the *Chunqiu fanlu*—principles associated with the *Spring and Autumn* apply directly to issues that dominated the early years of the Han and engaged members of the elite as they worked through the implications of a unified empire.

The Han dynasty's founding Son of Heaven, Liu Bang (Emperor Gaozu), parceled out much of the eastern half of the empire to allies and royal relatives who ruled locally as kings in their semiautonomous territories. This was, in effect, a "return to normalcy." The Qin system of bureaucratic centralism would have struck many contemporaries as aberrant, and the time-honored Zhou system of domains ruled by aristocrats who owed fealty to the Son of Heaven would have represented the natural way to govern "all under Heaven." But this Han "neo-feudal" arrangement raised difficult questions: How much authority should the various lords and kings enjoy in their territories and in the newly unified empire as a whole? What would ensure that the power and authority of the Son of Heaven would be acknowledged as superior to that of the regional lords? What rituals should the Son of Heaven and the Lords of the Land perform to affirm that political hierarchy? How could the *Spring and Autumn* serve as a template for the Han? Finally, could the hegemonic lords of the Spring and Autumn period who took up arms to defend the Zhou Sons of Heaven serve as acceptable models for their Han counterparts when the emperor might call on them to put down rebellions and repel foreign incursions? These were vital questions for both the royal relatives who served in their various territories and the scholars and ministers at the central court who competed with them for authority. They were vital questions as well for the emperor, who needed to delegate a certain amount of power to both groups to support and legitimate his own claims to the throne, all while understanding that both groups threatened the very power he hoped to preserve. Where should the lines be drawn?

These questions preoccupied all who hoped to influence the course of early Han history and to shape the power they stood to enjoy as members of the

35. Many such passages are discussed in detail in Queen, *From Chronicle to Canon*. Those pertaining to later chapters will be explored in their respective group introductions. For the substantive principles identified and discussed in these early chapters, we refer the reader to this earlier study.

ruling class. Their views of the issues and the arguments they set forth differed, depending on the perch of power they occupied, be it that of the scholar-official class or the royal relative. For example, the *Xin shu* (*New Writings*), a compilation of memorials and essays attributed to the scholar-official Jia Yi—who was instrumental in pressing Emperor Jing to adopt firmer measures to restrain and limit the power of the regional lords—represents one end of the spectrum of argument.[36] The *Huainanzi*, compiled in the court of a regional lord, Liu An, king of Huainan (who was Emperor Jing's first cousin), represents the other end of the spectrum. The entire book assumes and argues for an empire divided into neofeudal kingdoms in which the regional lords would provide critical support to the emperor and his central administration.[37] The comments on the regional lords in the *Chunqiu fanlu* (especially in the first five chapters but also elsewhere in the text) are attempts to negotiate a position on this spectrum of opinion. Probably the clearest statement of the text's position comes in chapter 37, "The Lords of the Land," in which it is written:

> The sages of antiquity observed Heaven's intention to provide bountifully for the people, so when they faced south and ruled the world, they invariably brought universal benefit to their people. On account of things that were distant that their eyes could not see [and] things that were muffled that their ears could not hear, beyond one thousand *li* they parceled out the land and allocated its people to create states and establish overlords to enable the Son of Heaven to observe what he could not see [personally, and] perceive what he could not hear. With a court audience, the overlords were summoned and questioned. This is why the expression "Lords of the Land" (*zhuhou* 諸侯) resembles the expression "numerous servants" (*zhuhou* 諸候).[38]

The implication is clearly that as regional kings, the Lords of the Land have a role to play in the present day in service to the Son of Heaven. To understand and appreciate the various claims made in these texts, we need to briefly review the history of the regional lords in the Western Han.

36. See comments in the essays "Zongshou" 宗首, "Fanshang" 藩傷, "Fanqiang" 藩彊, "Dadu" 大都, "Dengqi" 等齊, "Yirang" 益壤, "Quanzhong" 權重, "Wumei" 五美, "Shenwei" 審微, and "Jieji" 階級.

37. For a discussion of the role of the regional lords in the *Huainanzi*, see Judson E. Murray, "The Liu Clan's 'Flesh and Bone: The Foundation of Liu An's Vision of Empire,'" 291–325, and Griet Vankeerberghen, "The Discourse About Lords (*zhuhou*) in the *Huainanzi*," 326–50, both in *The "Huainanzi" and Textual Production in Early China*, ed. Sarah A. Queen and Michael Puett (Leiden: Brill, 2014).

38. *CQFL* 37/48/4–6.

The Challenges of the Regional Lords

When he assumed the title of emperor of Han in 202 B.C.E., Liu Bang had no choice but to recognize as legitimate the various territories and kingdoms held by those who had helped him win victory.[39] There were ten such kingdoms, dominating the eastern part of the empire. They controlled a more extensive area, a larger population, and more natural resources than the commanderies under the direct control of the emperor. Thus the emperor's dilemma was how to recognize the claims of the powerful regional kings while asserting his own authority over the entire empire. In the event, the kings themselves proved refractory as one after another they rebelled and were crushed. By 196 B.C.E., all but one of the original kings had been defeated and eliminated. That did not mean an end to the kingdoms, however. Emperor Gaozu maintained them more or less intact but appointed his close relatives (brothers or sons) to serve as their kings, assuming that they and their descendants would remain loyal to the imperial throne. Michael Loewe describes the situation of the kingdoms:

> Each king presided over an administration which was a small-scale replica of the central government, with its chancellor, royal counsellor, and other functionaries. These officials were responsible for collecting taxes in the kingdom and for its defense; they were free, and even encouraged, to make their territories as productive as possible. The fealty of the kings to the emperor was marked by their obligation to render homage annually; they were also required to submit returns of the population of their territories and of the taxes which they had levied, a proportion of which they transmitted to the central government. Although they were responsible for raising and training armed forces, they were not entitled to mobilize them for active service without express orders from the central government.[40]

This proved to be a dangerously unstable system. The early Han emperors directly controlled less than half of the empire and relied on loyal kinsmen to

39. An excellent account of the relationship between the Han imperial realm and the territorial lords is found in Michael Loewe, "The Former Han Dynasty," in *The Ch'in and Han Empires, 221 B.C.–A.D. 220*, ed. Denis Twitchett and Michael Loewe, vol. 1 of *The Cambridge History of China* (Cambridge: Cambridge University Press, 1986), esp. 103–79. We relied extensively on this source in preparing the brief remarks presented here.

40. Loewe, "Former Han Dynasty," 126.

rule the rest on their behalf. Jia Yi (201–169 B.C.E.) and Chao Cuo (d. 154 B.C.E.) perceived the danger and urged Emperor Wen (r. 180–157 B.C.E.) to enact measures to reduce the kings' power. But relations between the emperors and the territorial kings continued to deteriorate; bonds of kinship, which in any case naturally weakened with the passing of generations, proved woefully insufficient to ensure the loyalty and support of the regional kings. In our view, this created the need to articulate a new ethical creed with which to bind the regional kings to the emperor, a need filled in part by the exegetical activities of *Gongyang* scholars working under Emperors Jing and Wu. Language in the *Spring and Autumn* that, according to the *Gongyang* interpretation, criticized the Lords of the Land and hegemons[41] during the Zhou era was seen as highly relevant to the system of kingdoms established by Emperor Gaozu. The accession of Emperor Wen is a case in point. Three possible candidates from the pool of royal relatives stood ready to assume the throne. One of them, Liu Xiang, king of Qi, was instrumental in ousting the politically powerful Lü family from the capital to clear the way, perhaps for his own enthronement. This, however, involved raising troops without obtaining the authority of the central government, an issue mentioned on numerous occasions in the first five chapters of the *Chunqiu fanlu*.

In the end, the king of Qi lost out to Liu Heng, king of Tai, who reigned as Emperor Wen. He and his successor, Emperor Jing, made a concerted effort to reinforce the authority of the central government and curtail that of the kings: "The reduction of the kingdoms was achieved partly by deliberate design, and partly by exploiting chance opportunities such as a king's rebellion or his death without a successor."[42] The early years of Emperor Jing's reign proved to be a disaster for the regional kings. In 154 B.C.E., the king of Wu and six other kings staged a concerted revolt against the imperial house. The nature of the rebellion is unclear, and it is entirely possible that the emperor and his advisers, with a vested interest in bringing the kingdoms' territory back under imperial control, may have provoked the rebellion to some extent, or they may have taken quick advantage of some supposed expressions of disloyalty by the kings. In any event, the revolt was defeated, the kings and their immediate families

41. The term "hegemon" translates the Chinese word *ba* 霸. It refers to a system, supposedly current during the Spring and Autumn period but known only from descriptions in later texts, in which the lord of one or another of the major states acted as "first among equals" to wield power on behalf of the Zhou kings, whose authority by then had greatly diminished.

42. Loewe, "Former Han Dynasty," 140.

were exterminated, and their kingdoms were variously split into smaller parts, reduced in size, assigned to new kings, or simply absorbed into the imperial domain. An important lesson was learned: no longer was the government content to cede important powers to the regional kings or to rely on them to protect against internal enemies or intruders. Proof that the central government wished to maintain its own supervision over areas that were potentially both vulnerable and subversive came when Emperor Jing introduced a change to the governmental structure of the territories: the status of their senior officials, *chengxiang* (chancellors), was lowered by a formal change of title to *xiang* (ministers), and they were directly appointed by the central government. All other senior posts in the kingdoms were abolished, and the number of their courtiers and counselors was substantially reduced.[43]

Soon after ascending the throne in 141 B.C.E., Emperor Wu introduced additional measures aimed at strengthening central control. He curtailed the power and perquisites of nobles who had been granted honors as rewards for services rendered to the state. Liu An, king of Huainan (and patron of the *Huainanzi*), was accused in 122 B.C.E. of harboring imperial ambitions. Subsequently, he committed suicide under duress, and the kingdom of Huainan was abolished. Similar fates awaited the other kings. By the end of Emperor Wu's reign, all the problematic kingdoms had been obliterated, and those that remained were politically and militarily neutralized. The status of the Lords of the Land was no longer a contested issue: time, imperial enmity, the reckless behavior of some of the regional kings, and the consequent absorption of most of the states into the imperial domain had rendered the question moot. Thus the prominence of issues concerning the Lords of the Land in the early chapters of the *Chunqiu fanlu* seems to provide a clear *terminus post quem* for dating those chapters.

Whose Voice or Voices?

This overview of early Western Han political history provides evidence that the materials preserved in the first group of chapters of the *Chunqiu fanlu* address concerns directly relevant to that history and so cannot be dated later than the reign of Emperor Wu.

43. Loewe, "Former Han Dynasty," 144.

Last in our discussion we turn to questions of authenticity. Whose, then, is the authoritative voice transmitting interpretations of the *Gongyang Commentary* to his disciples through the instructional sessions of the first five chapters? What is the relation between this singular authoritative voice that appears in chapters 1 through 5 and the seemingly multiple voices that find expression in chapters 6 through 17? These are critical questions for establishing the authenticity of these materials.

With regard to the first five chapters, the two most obvious candidates are Dong Zhongshu and Huwu Sheng. They are the two most prominent scholars who transmitted their teachings on the *Gongyang Commentary* as Erudites of the *Spring and Autumn* in the early years of the Western Han. As we pointed out earlier in this introduction, the *Shiji*'s "Biography of Confucian Scholars" describes Dong's activities under Emperor Jing.

Ban Gu's revised and expanded version of the "Biography of the Confucian Scholars" in the *Han shu* recapitulates the *Shiji*'s account of the career of Huwu Sheng and supplies additional information critical to understanding the relationship between Dong's and Huwu's scholarship:

> Master Huwu, whose name was Zidu, was a native of Qi. Having mastered the *Gongyang Commentary* to the *Spring and Autumn* during the reign of Emperor Jing, he became an Erudite. Together with Dong Zhongshu, he followed the same calling. The writings composed by Dong Zhongshu recognized the virtues [of Huwu's teachings]. When elderly, he returned to teach in Qi. Scholars from Qi who expounded on the *Spring and Autumn* revered and served Master Huwu. Gongsun Hong also received a good deal of instruction from him. When Dong Zhongshu became administrator to Jiangdu, he established a tradition of transmission of his own.[44]

Moreover, the teaching of both masters continued to dominate the court under Emperor Wu. As Sima Qian comments, "Discussions of the *Spring and Autumn* in Lu and Qi derived from Master Huwu; in Zhao they derived from Dong Zhongshu."[45]

The influence of these two masters is further confirmed by the historians' discussions of their disciples. Sima Qian describes Dong's disciples:

44. *SJ* 121/3127.
45. *SJ* 121/3127.

> Among Dong Zhongshu's disciples who achieved fame were Chu Da of Lanling, Yin Zhong of Guangchuan, and Lu Bushu of Wen. Chu Da became prime minister of Liang, while Lu Bushu became a chief secretary. He was given the imperial seals and sent as an envoy to settle legal affairs in Huainan, where he reprimanded the Lords of the Land for arbitrarily acting on their own authority and failing to report their actions to the central government, pointing out that such actions were not in accordance with the principles laid down in the *Spring and Autumn*. The emperor highly approved of both Chu Da and Lu Bushu. In addition to these, some hundred or more disciples of Dong Zhongshu achieved fame as palace counselors and attendants, masters of guests, and officials in charge of precedents. Dong Zhongshu's sons and grandsons all won high office because of their learning.[46]

Ban Gu's account expands the list of Dong's disciples, carrying the genealogy of transmission into the Eastern Han. After repeating the *Shiji*'s account of Chu Da and others, the *Han shu* continues,

> But only Yinggong preserved the master's teachings and did not stray from his example, remonstrating with the great officers on behalf of Emperor Yuan. He transmitted the master's teachings to Meng Qing of Donghai and Sui Meng of Lu. When Meng became a manager of credentials, he was tried and punished with execution for having expounded on [the meaning of] disasters and anomalies. He established a tradition of transmission of his own.[47]

The disciples mentioned in these accounts appear with varying frequency in both the *Shiji* and the *Han shu*, in the "Biographies of Confucian Scholars" and, in some cases, in other chapters as well. The *Han shu* mentions Yinggong of Dongping as having transmitted his tradition, in turn, to Meng Qing of Donghai and Sui Meng of Lu, thus making clear that the teachings of Dong Zhongshu enjoyed a direct line of transmission for at least several generations.[48]

46. *SJ* 121/3129.
47. *SJ* 121/3129.
48. For the biographies of Dong's disciples see Queen, *From Chronicle to Canon*, app. 2.

Conclusion

We conclude from all this material that the authoritative voice in chapters 1 through 5 could be that of either Huwu Sheng or Dong Zhongshu, but more likely the latter. We further suggest that the multiple voices in chapters 6 through 17 could well be those of some of the disciples mentioned earlier. Clearly it is not possible, based on the surviving sources, to prove definitively that the first five chapters represent the teachings of Dong Zhongshu, but we believe that it is most likely the case.

Although the absence of Five-Phase concepts and influence from the apocryphal texts points to an early Western Han date,[49] that alone does not provide enough information to choose between Huwu Sheng and Dong Zhongshu, because the two were near contemporaries. In addition, the ideas and arguments throughout the first five chapters of the *Chunqiu fanlu* are consistent with what we know of Dong Zhongshu and the ideas associated with him in other sources that survive from the Han.

This argument from content is strongly persuasive. The chapters exhibit a clear concern with resolving some of the most pressing issues that defined the reigns of Emperor Jing and Wu. Chief among them were the political challenges presented by the regional lords. These chapters address these challenges at every turn, and their suggested resolutions are consistent with Dong's memorials. But this is not the only subject addressed in the first five chapters that finds echoes in other writings attributed to Dong Zhongshu. The list is quite long and elaborate. For example, the depiction of Confucius and the vision of sagely transformation articulated in these chapters are consistent with those found in Dong's memorials. Moreover, their content corresponds to Dong's discussions of the *Spring and Autumn* preserved in his famous memorials, which also overlap in important ways with the handful of cases that have survived from Dong's legal work *Deciding Court Cases According to the Spring and Autumn* (*Chunqiu jue yu*).[50]

49. To that extent, we agree with the analysis of Arbuckle, "Works of Dong Zhongshu," but we do not agree that the first five chapters are most likely the teachings of Huwu Sheng. On this account, we do not find his arguments to be persuasive. We do not believe that identifying a handful of inconsistencies between the first five chapters of the *Chunqiu fanlu* and Dong's memorials provides sufficient evidence to question the traditional attribution of this text.

50. For a detailed discussion of these correspondences, see Queen, *From Chronicle to Canon*, chap. 6.

Finally, we believe that the titles of the *Chunqiu fanlu*'s first five chapters also point to associations with Dong Zhongshu. Of the extant seventy-nine titles, only those that appear in this first body of materials are attested in Han sources and attributed to Dong Zhongshu. Even though Ban Gu does not mention all the titles of the first five chapters, the sampling he presents suggests that all go back to Dong Zhongshu. As we stated earlier, the titles of the first five chapters—assuming "Fanlu" was the original title of chapter 1—share many features suggesting that they are closely linked to Dong Zhongshu.

But in what context and when? Over the course of his long career, Dong encountered numerous opportunities to expound on the great principles of the *Spring and Autumn*. His official biographies, however, point to several particularly propitious moments, the kinds of moments that capture the attention of the scribe, call forth the imagination of the biographer, tame the objections of the opponent, or quiet the confusion of the disciple.

As we have seen, Dong's official biographies paint a striking picture of him as an Erudite under Emperor Jing: "[From behind] a lowered curtain, he lectured to and recited for his disciples who in turn transmitted [his teachings] from those with greatest seniority to those with least seniority, so that some of his disciples never even saw his face." This image is all the more striking when we consider the first five chapters of the *Chunqiu fanlu*, in which a different teaching method appears to dominate. In contrast to the preceding image, in which the teacher is far removed from his disciples and there is no conversation, the instructional sessions preserved in the first five chapters are clearly bidirectional and the teacher is anything but sequestered. Moreover, those positing questions and raising objections are not doing so from a tabula rasa. Instead, they assume a certain degree of familiarity with and knowledge of the *Spring and Autumn*. What should we make of the discrepancy? If the teaching methods employed at court by Erudites were as formal as Dong's biographies depict, then the first five chapters can hardly record such instructions. What, then, could they be?

We have argued that the first five chapters preserve a book within a book and that they appear to be the records of doctrinal expositions of the *Gongyang Commentary* in varying degrees of completeness. Some consist of questions and answers concerning a single passage or a series of passages from the *Gongyang Commentary*, and others contain statements and rebuttals of specific points of interpretation. Seemingly multiple voices address the singular authorial voice of the *Gongyang* master, who casts wide his canonical net to capture a point or lend additional authority to a point with a flourish from the *Odes*, *Documents*, or utterances of Confucius himself. Are they records of discussions that Dong held with his closest disciples in more informal places and times? Or are they records of deliberations or debates in which Dong participated with other scholars conversant in the ways of the *Gongyang Commentary*, but less so than the master? Or perhaps they are what remain of all of these? The biographies mention some of these occasions, but no doubt they are only a sampling of what must have been a much larger pool of opportunity to expound on and discuss the *Spring and Autumn*. Although the context that occasioned the records of instruction in the first five chapters may be lost forever, some of the teachings of this singular *Gongyang* master of the early Han have fortunately survived.

Book 1, Part 1

CHAPTER 1

King Zhuang of Chu

Section 1.1

Why is it that in the case of King Zhuang of Chu killing Xia Zhengshu of Chen, the *Spring and Autumn* uses censorious language to express disapproval of his taking authority into his own hands to launch a punitive expedition,[1] but in the case of King Ling of Chu killing Qing Feng of Qi, [the *Spring and Autumn*] straightforwardly refers to him as a viscount?[2]

The answer is: King Zhuang of Chu's conduct was worthy, and Zhengshu's crime was grave. Looking to a worthy ruler to punish a grave crime always wins the approval of the people's hearts. If he were not censured, then who would understand that he violated the correct norm?[3] The *Spring and Autumn* often

1. Duke Xuan 7.11.5: "Winter. The tenth month. A man from Chu killed Xia Zhengshu of Chen." *Gongyang*: "This was the Viscount of Chu. Why was he designated 'a man' [i.e., a commoner]? He was censured. Why was he censured? [The *Spring and Autumn*] does not condone punitive expeditions abroad."
2. Duke Zhao 10.4.3.
3. In other words, Confucius referred to him with the noble rank of viscount and did not degrade him to commoner status, as in the case of King Zhuang of Chu. The *Gongyang Commentary* at Duke Zhao 10.4.3 asks:

> This was an attack on the state of Wu. Why, then, was Qing Feng of Qi taken captive? He was executed on behalf of [the ruler of] Qi. Why was he executed on behalf of [the ruler of] Qi? Qing Feng traveled to the state of Wu, and the [ruler of] Wu established a fief for him at Fang. Why, then, does [the *Spring and Autumn*] not say "they attacked Fang?" [The *Spring and Autumn*] does not permit the Lords of the Land taking authority into their own hands to launch punitive expeditions.

uses cases that deceptively appear permissible to reveal what is not permissible.[4] This is why

> Duke Huan of Qi was not allowed to take authority into his own hands to distribute territory by conferring land;[5]
> Duke Wen of Jin was not allowed to summon the king to pay court to him;[6]
> and King Zhuang of Chu was not allowed to take authority into his own hands to initiate a punitive expedition to sentence [a person from another state] to death.

These three undertakings were not permitted, so that what was permissible for the Lords of the Land could be inferred. This is why King Ling of Chu was designated a viscount when he punished [Qing Feng]. The terminology of the *Spring and Autumn* has many instances like this. Its language is terse, but its method is clear.

Someone raising a question said: [The *Spring and Autumn*] does not allow the Lords of the Land to take authority into their own hands to distribute territory. [This principle] reappears in the annihilation of Chen and Cai.[7] The *Spring and Autumn* does not allow the Lords of the Land to take authority into their own hands to initiate punitive expeditions. Why does this principle alone not reappear in the killing of Qing Feng?

The answer is: The *Spring and Autumn* employs terminology enabling what has already been clarified to be elided and what has not yet been clarified to be recorded explicitly. Now the principle that the Lords of the Land were not permitted to initiate a punitive expedition on their own authority certainly was already clear. However, Qing Feng's crime had not yet been revealed. Therefore, [the *Spring and Autumn*] designates [King Ling as] "viscount of Chu" [when he acted as] a hegemon[8] [in launching] the punitive expedition

4. An alternative rendering would take *de* 得 as interchangeable with *de* 德, yielding the following reading: "[The *Spring and Autumn*] often uses cases that deceptively appear virtuous to reveal what is not virtuous" (Su Yu, *CQFLYZ* 1).
5. Duke Xi 5.1.2.
6. Duke Xi 5.28.8.
7. Duke Zhao 10.8.9: "Winter. The tenth month. *Renwu*. Chu troops annihilated Chen." Duke Zhao 10.11.10: "Winter. The eleventh month. *Dingyou*. Chu troops annihilated Cai." Duke Zhao 10.13.5: "The marquis of Cai, Lu, returned home to Cai. The marquis of Chen, Wu, returned home to Chen." *Gongyang*: "These both were annihilated states. Why does [the *Spring and Autumn*] state that they returned home [to rule]? It does not condone the Lords of the Land distributing territory on their own authority."
8. The text is playing off the etymological affinity of *bo* 伯 and *ba* 霸. In attacking Qing Feng, King Ling assumed the authority of a hegemon (霸), which can be converted to the rank of earl (伯). By way of registering that King Ling's actions were only quasi-legitimate, the *Spring and Autumn* demotes him one rank from earl to viscount (*zi* 子). This is in contrast to the case of King Zhuang, who, for

[against Qing Feng]. [This was] to state clearly that death was the proper punishment [for Qing Feng's crime]. This was to seriously prohibit such crimes in the world. This is to say: When the conduct of a minister degrades the position of the ruler or wreaks havoc on the tenets of the state,[9] even if the minister does not usurp the throne or commit regicide, in every case the crime deserves the death penalty. To call attention to this, [the *Spring and Autumn*] speaks in this way. [1/1/5–13]

Section 1.2

The *Spring and Autumn* states: "Jin attacked Xianyu."[10] Why does it disparage Jin by putting it on a par with the Yi and Di tribes?[11]

The answer is: The *Spring and Autumn* honors propriety and values trustworthiness. Trustworthiness is more valuable than one's territory; propriety is more venerable than one's body. How do we know that this is so?

Boji of Song perished in a fire [to forestall] doubts of her propriety;[12]

Duke Huan of Qi gave up territory [to forestall] doubts of his trustworthiness.

The *Spring and Autumn* [judges them] worthies and elevates them to establish them as exemplary models for the world, as if to say: regarding trustworthiness and propriety, there is nothing to which propriety does not respond, there is nothing that trustworthiness cannot repay.[13] It is Heaven's norm. Now the ruler and ministers of Lu treated Jin [with the propriety] commensurate with

committing a similar act of *lèse-majesté*, was not named or accorded any rank at all. As the *Chunqiu fanlu* explains here, King Ling is sanctioned more mildly so as to make clear the gravity of Qing Feng's offense; that is, readers might not understand that Qing Feng in fact would have deserved to die if King Ling had been severely censured.

9. Emending *chen* 臣 to *ji* 己, following Liu Shipei, *Chunqiu fanlu jiaobu* 春秋繁露斠補, cited in Lai, *CQFLJZJY* 3, note 15.
10. Duke Zhao 10.12.10.
11. The *Spring and Autumn* typically refers to the Lords of the Land of the Central States by referencing the name of their state and their rank—for example, Chu zi (viscount of Chu). In this entry, only the name of the state appears. Without a rank, the named state is treated in the same way as the tribes or ethnic groups that were not regarded as Sinitic states and did not participate in the rituals of the Central States.
12. Duke Xiang 9.30.3: "The fifth month. *Jiawu*. There was a fire in Song. Boji of Song died." In what became a famous moral tale in ancient China, Lady Song Boji died in a fire because she refused to leave a burning building without a proper escort to preserve her chaste reputation. See Sarah A. Queen, "Beyond Liu Xiang's Gaze: Debating Womanly Virtue in Early China," *Asia Major* (forthcoming).
13. Emending *shi* to *xin*.

one who shared the identical surname,[14] but the ruler of Jin was devoid of pure motives. Not only did he fail to respond with propriety, but he frightened and worried Lu. How could he not be treated like one of the Yi and Di tribes?

During the rebellion brought about by Duke [Huan of Lu's] son, Qing Fu,[15] the state of Lu was endangered and on the verge of perishing. Duke Huan of Qi pacified the rebellion. The duke of Qi was no relative of Lu, and yet he still felt anxious for it. How is it that one who shared a surname with Lu attacked and tyrannized it?

An *Ode* declares:

> So small, the cooing dove,
> yet it flies aloft to Heaven.
> My heart bears sorrow's wounds
> as I think of my forefathers.
> At daybreak, when I cannot sleep,
> I cherish memories of my parents.[16]

All people possess such a heart. Now Jin did not, on the basis of their being relatives, feel [appropriate] anxiety for Lu but instead coerced and greatly oppressed Lu. In their hearts the people of Lu resented Jin for these actions, therefore [the *Spring and Autumn*] indicates their not being good by referring to them merely as "Jin." [Under the circumstances,] this language was mild indeed! [1/1/15–22]

Someone raising a question said: The state of Jin was detestable and could not be treated as kin. Duke [Zhao] went to Jin but did not dare enter its borders.[17]

---

14. From this point forward, the passage uses the pronoun *wo* (we/us/our) to denote Lu and the pronoun *ru* (you/your) to denote Jin. The author speaks as a member of the state of Lu or a descendant of that state.

15. For *Gongyang* discussions of Qing Fu, see the entries at Duke Zhuang 3.27.3 and 3.32.3; Duke Min 2.3, 4.1.1, 4.1.6, and 4.2.2; and Duke Xi 5.1.9. Qing Fu was the son of Duke Huan and the younger brother of Duke Zhuang. When Duke Zhuang died, his son Ban ought to have ascended the throne, but Qing Fu murdered him and set up Duke Min. Later he had Duke Min assassinated, and the people of Lu wanted to punish him with execution. Qing Fu fled to the territory of Ying. After Duke Xi ascended the throne, he asked the ruler of Ying to return Qing Fu to Lu, but Qing Fu committed suicide.

16. *Odes* 196, verse 1.

17. During the time of Duke Zhao of Lu, powerful subjects usurped the government. Duke Zhao thought to obtain assistance from abroad. Because Lu and Jin shared a surname, during the twenty-three years of his rule, Duke Zhao set out for Jin on seven occasions, but five times after reaching the Yellow River, he returned to Lu. In the twenty-fifth year of his rule, Duke Zhao of Lu attempted to assassinate the head of the Ji clan, whose leaders had long usurped the rights proper to the duke's house. He was unsuccessful and twice fled his state, but neither time did he meet with the ruler of Jin. He remained at the border and ultimately died there (Lai, *CQFLJZJY* 4–5).

Such are human emotions. Why then did the Noble Man [Confucius] feel shame and state that "the duke was ill"?[18]

The answer is: If evil falls on him without cause, a noble man is not ashamed of it. If on examining himself, he is without fault, why should he feel anxious? Why should he feel ashamed? It is what it is. In the present case, however, the *Spring and Autumn* expresses shame because Duke Zhao brought the situation upon himself. Instances of ministers usurping the authority of their rulers began with [the time of] Duke Wen and worsened in [the time of] Duke Zhao. The state suffered usurpations and gradually declined like a mountain being leveled, and yet the heart [of Duke Zhao] was devoid of fear or anxiety. He made plans lightly and wantonly punished other states. He defied the great rites [of matrimony] and took a woman who shared his surname as a wife.[19] He drew close to the unrighteous and valued those who took themselves lightly. There is a proverbial expression among the people that says: When the state is ordered, neighbors from all four sides come with congratulations; when a state is disordered, neighbors keep their distance. Thus when the Jisun [clan] usurped Duke Zhao's authority, none of the powerful states rectified the situation. Duke Zhao fled his state and wandered for eight years, returning [as a corpse] only after he died. He lost his life, and his sons were endangered. This is the most extreme difficulty that one can suffer. This noble man was not ashamed of his difficulties, but rather he felt shame for what had caused the duke to become destitute. Although Duke Zhao encountered these times, if he had not married a woman who shared his surname, how could things have come to this? Although he married a woman who shared his surname, if he had been able to employ Confucius to assist him, he likewise would not have come to this. The times were difficult and he ruled with laxity; his conduct was reckless and no one rescued the situation. These are the reasons why he became destitute.[20] [1/1/24–31]

18. In other words, why didn't Confucius simply state that the duke turned back because he feared approaching the bad ruler of Jin when such an emotional response is shared by all human beings alike?

19. Throughout Chinese history, the rites concerning marriage prohibited relatives who shared a surname from marrying each other. Nonetheless, even though the ducal houses of Lu and Wu shared a surname, Duke Zhao married several women from that state. See the "Fangji" chapter of the *Liji* and *Analects* 7.30.

20. Su Yu maintains that this passage belongs in the fourth section of chapter 3, "Bamboo Grove."

Section 1.3

The *Spring and Autumn* distinguishes twelve generations and treats them as three periods:

Those that [Confucius] witnessed, those that he heard of from others, and those that he heard of through transmission by others.

Those that he personally witnessed, constituted three generations;
those that he heard of from others, constituted four generations;
and those that he heard of through transmission, constituted five generations.
He witnessed the reigns of Ai, Ding, and Zhao.
He heard from others of the reigns of Xiang, Cheng, Wen, and Xuan.
And he heard through historical transmission of the reigns of Xi, Min, Zhuang, Huan, and Yin.
The [generations] that he witnessed [with his own eyes] constitute sixty-one years [541–480 B.C.E.],
those that he heard [with his own ears] constitute eighty-five years [626–542 B.C.E.],
and those that he heard through historical transmission constitute ninety-six years [722–627 B.C.E.].
[When speaking of] what he witnessed with his own eyes, Confucius veiled his terminology;
[when speaking of] what he learned from others, Confucius expressed sorrow for calamities;
[when speaking of] what he learned through historical transmission, Confucius stifled his compassion [and recorded events in full.

For this reason,

when the Ji clan was expelled [from the state of Lu], Confucius stated [only that a crowd assembled] to restore the rain-seeking ceremony. [Such was a case of] veiling his words.[21]

21. Duke Zhao 10.25.4: "Autumn. The seventh month. The first *Xin* day. We performed the grand rain-seeking sacrifice. The third *Xin* day. We again performed the rain-seeking sacrifice." *Gongyang*: "Why was the rain-seeking sacrifice performed again? The second reference to the rain-seeking sacrifice was not the rain-seeking sacrifice. Our lord gathered the people together to expel the head of the Ji clan."

When Zi Chi was killed, [Confucius] could not bear to record the day [of his death] and thereby expressed sorrow for the calamity.[22]

However, when Zi Ban died, he recorded the day *yiwei*, in this way stifling his compassion.[23]

The retraction or extension of his attention,
the detail or generality of his writing,

reflects these principles in every case. By understanding the manner in which he

treats as close what is close, as far what is far,
as intimate what is intimate, as distant what is distant,

I also understand how he

treats as noble what is noble, as base what is base,
as important what is important and as insignificant what is insignificant.

Likewise, I understand how he

treats as generous those who are generous and stingy those who are stingy,
as good those who are good and as bad those who are bad.

Furthermore, I understand how he

treats yang as yang, yin as yin,
white as white, and black as black.

All things have their matching counterpart.[24]

He pairs them;
he matches them;
he contrasts them;
he juxtaposes them.

Excellent indeed!

An *Ode* declares:

"Grave in deportment,
of reputation consistent,
without malice or hate,
following the way of all his peers."[25]

22. Duke Wen 6.18.6: "Winter. The tenth month. The viscount died." *Gongyang*: "'The viscount died.' To whom does this refer? It refers to Zi Chi. Why is the day not recorded? To conceal it. Why is it concealed? He was assassinated. In the case of assassinations, why is it not recorded? [Confucius] could not bear to mention it."
23. Zi Ban, son of Duke Zhuang of Lu, was assassinated in 662 B.C.E. The *Gongyang Commentary* does not record his death, so Su Yu relies on He Xiu's comments to Duke Yin to explicate Dong's reasoning.
24. For the notion of *he* 合 (matching), see chapter 53.
25. *Odes* 249, verse 3. See Arthur Waley, trans., *The Book of Songs: The Ancient Chinese Classic of Poetry*, ed., with additional translations, Joseph R. Allen (New York: Grove Press, 1996), 251.

This expresses my meaning. Hence the greatness of the principles of the *Spring and Autumn* lies in the fact that

> having grasped one of its starting points, you can broadly apply it;
> having observed what it approves and condemns, you can attain a rectifying model;
> having perceived its use of subtle words, you will understand how to stave off resentment.

For this reason,

> with regard to what is external, [the *Spring and Autumn*] points out the Way but is not obvious.
> With regard to what is internal, [*the Spring and Autumn*] veils but does not hide.
> With regard to what is honorable, the same principle holds true.
> With regard to what is worthy, the same principle holds true.

Here the *Spring and Autumn* distinguishes between internal and external, differentiating the worthy and the unworthy and ordering the honorable and humble.

> The righteous do not abuse their superiors;
> the wise do not endanger themselves.

Therefore,

> when [discussing] distant events, [Confucius] concealed them on account of his righteousness;
> when speaking of more recent events, [he] was careful of them on account of his wisdom.

[Confucius] employed caution and righteousness simultaneously; thus as the generations that he discussed moved even closer, his words accordingly grew more discreet. This is why he veiled his words when speaking of the times of Ding and Ai. Thus,

> if [Confucius's methods] were employed, then the world would be peaceful;
> if [his methods] were not employed, his person would [still] be secure.

Such is the Way of the *Spring and Autumn*. [1/2/1–13]

Section 1.4

The Way of the *Spring and Autumn* is to serve Heaven and emulate the ancients. For this reason,

> even though you are good with your hands, if you do not avail yourself of the compass and carpenter's square, you will not be able to draw a true square or circle;

even though you possess discerning ears, if you do not avail yourself of the six pitch pipes, you will not be able to establish the five notes;

even though you possess a knowledgeable mind, if you do not look to the Former Kings, you will not be able to pacify the world.

Such being the case, the Way bequeathed by the Former Kings is indeed the world's compass, carpenter's square, and six pitch pipes. Thus

those who are sagely emulate Heaven,

and those who are worthy emulate the sages.

This is the grand norm of the *Spring and Autumn*. If you hold to this grand norm, there will be order; if you disregard this grand norm, there will be chaos. This is the difference between order and chaos.

Now from what I have heard, there are not two Ways in the world. Thus, though sages differ in the manner in which they bring order to the world, they share the same principles. Because past and present are interconnected and interpenetrating, the former worthies transmitted their standards to later generations. Thus, with regard to contemporary affairs, the *Spring and Autumn* praises restoring the ancient ways and criticizes modifying the constant [norms], for it desires to emulate the Former Kings. Such being the case, I would interject one comment and say: "Those [who rule as] king must [still] reform the regulations."

Those who are self-deluded take this as their watchword, saying: "If the ancients are to be followed, why do the Ways of the Former Kings not comply with one another?" People of the current age are fooled by such hearsay, so they come to doubt the correct Way and instead trust perverse doctrines. This is truly worrisome. I would respond to them and say: Upon hearing that the leaders of the Lords of the Land shot [their arrows to] the "Fox Head" tune,[26] someone cut off a fox's head, hung it up, shot arrows at it, and asked, "Where is the music?" This is a case of hearing the name of something but failing to understand its corresponding reality.

Now what I mean when I say that a new king must reform the regulations is not that he changes the Way or alters its principles. Having received the Mandate of Heaven [to found a new dynasty], one rules under a surname different [from the preceding kings] and does so as a new king rather than perpetuating the practices of the preceding king. If he completely accords with the former

26. "Fox Head" was a tune sung at aristocratic archery competitions to gauge the amount of time a contestant had to shoot (i.e., the archer had until the end of the song to let fly his arrow). In classical Chinese, the phrase can be misunderstood as "the music produced by shooting the fox's head."

regulations and follows[27] the old pursuits without making any changes, this would be no different from ruling by perpetuating the practices of the preceding king. The ruler who has received the Mandate of Heaven is one whom Heaven has made preeminently manifest.

> One who serves a father follows his wishes;
> one who serves a ruler is faithful to his intentions;

and one who serves Heaven does the same thing. Now if Heaven has made [the reception of the Mandate] preeminently manifest and all affairs have been transferred, yet most remain unchanged, then [the reception of the Mandate] is neither manifest nor clear. This is not Heaven's will.

Therefore, the founder of a new dynasty must shift his place of residence, assume a new dynastic name and personal name, amend the day on which the [civil] year begins, and change the color of ceremonial garb—all for no other reason than that he dare not disobey Heaven's will and fail to make clear that it is he who has been made preeminently manifest. As for the great bonds, human ethics, the patterns of the Way, government order, educational transformation, habitual customs, and literary meanings: all these remain as before. How could one change them! Therefore the king reforms regulations in name but does not change the substance of the Way. Confucius said: "Was it not Shun who governed through non-action?"[28] He meant that Shun did nothing more than rule with the Way of Yao. Is this not the efficacy of the unchanging?

Someone raising a question said: If affairs[29] are changed to manifest Heaven's conferment of the Mandate, why is it necessary to compose new music?

The answer is: Music differs from these things. Regulations are changed in response to Heaven; music is composed in response to the people. The one who receives the Mandate is invariably the one in whom the people uniformly rejoice.[30] For this reason, regulations are changed at the beginning to manifest Heaven's Mandate, whereas new music is composed at the end[31] to reveal Heaven's achievements. He makes a pattern for the newly felt joy in the world, to harmonize the government, to inspire virtue. The king does not vainly compose

27. Emending *xiu* 修 to *xun* 循, following Liu Shipei, cited in Su Yu, *CQFLYZ* 17.
28. *Analects* 15.5.
29. "Affairs," here as earlier, refers to such phenomena as the dynastic title, the reign name, and the civil calendar.
30. The text is playing on the double meaning of 樂 as both "music" (*yue*) and "joy" (*le*).
31. Both here and later, "end" refers to the completion of the transfer of the Mandate. Other matters, such as changing the calendar and the dynastic title, are undertaken even before the departing dynasty has been overthrown, but new music is composed only after the new dynasty is securely in power.

music until accord and harmony have filled the world. Music is something that flourishes internally before finding expression externally. Responding to a well-ordered age, the ruler institutes ritual and composes music to perfect the age. Perfection means that root and branch, substance and form, are fully present. For this reason, those who compose music must return to what first brought joy to the people of the world and takes this as their root.

In the time of Emperor Shun, the people rejoiced in the manner in which he illuminated (*shao*) the undertakings of Yao. Therefore the *shao* music was composed. *Shao* means to illuminate.

In the time of Emperor Yu, the people rejoiced in the mutual succession of the Three Sages (Yao, Shun, and Yu). Therefore the *xia* music was composed. *Xia* means grand.

In the time of Emperor Tang, the people rejoiced in being rescued from distress and injury. Therefore the *hu* music was composed. *Hu* means to rescue.

In the time of King Wen, the people rejoiced when he raised troops and carried out a punitive attack [against the Shang]. Therefore the *wu* music was composed. *Wu* means to attack.

These four rulers were the same in that the world uniformly rejoiced in them, but the reason why the people uniformly rejoiced in their rule differed. The method for composing music is invariably to return to what constitutes the root of what brings the people joy. If the people do not find joy in the same things, then how can music not differ from age to age? This is why Yao composed the *shao*, Yu composed the *xia*, Tang composed the *hu*, and King Wen composed the *wu*. The four types of music differ in name, yet each complies with what first brought the people joy. [Thus] we see how [these compositions] turned out to be as they are.

An *Ode* declares:

> "King Wen received the Mandate of Heaven;
> he achieved his martial success.
> Having attacked Chong,
> he built his capital city at Feng."[32]

They rejoiced in his influence. Another *Ode* declares:

> "The king rose majestic in his wrath;
> he marshaled his troops."[33]

32. *Odes* 244, verse 2, adapted from James Legge, trans., *The She King, or, The Book of Poetry*, vol. 4 of *The Chinese Classics*, 2nd rev. ed. (1894; repr., Hong Kong: Hong Kong University Press, 1960), 461.
33. *Odes* 241, verse 5, adapted from Legge, *She King*, 453.

At that time, King Djou had lost the Way, and the Lords of the Land were in great chaos. The people rejoiced in King Wen's anger and so praised him in song. When the virtue of the Zhou [dynasty][34] had spread throughout the world, they returned to the root [of the joy] to compose music. It was called "Great Martiality" to indicate that what first brought joy to his people was his martial achievements. Thus music is composed at the end, but its name is derived from the beginning. This is the meaning of valuing the root.

Looking at the matter from this perspective, revising the calendar and the color of ceremonial garb are based on the ruler's receiving the Mandate and responding to Heaven, whereas the differences in ritual regulations and musical compositions are based on the ruler's responding to the stirrings in the peoples' hearts. The two diverge and yet return to unity. What accomplishes them is the same. [1/2/15–1/3/11]

34. Excising the character *ren* 人, following Lu Wenchao.

Book 1, Part 2

CHAPTER 2

Jade Cup

Section 2.1

The *Spring and Autumn* criticizes Duke Wen for making marriage plans during a mourning period.[1]

Someone raising an objection said: It is the practice of mourning not to exceed three years. Three years of mourning is [really] twenty-five months.[2] Now according to the Classic, Duke Wen married only in the forty-first month. At the time he married, there was no mourning; the prescribed period had already long since passed. Why, then, does the *Spring and Autumn* state that he made marriage plans during a mourning period?[3]

The title of this chapter may be related to what was believed to be an auspicious omen. The "Annals of Emperor Wen the Filial" in the *Shiji* reports:

> In the seventeenth year a jade cup was found bearing the inscription "Long Life to the Lord of Men." Because of this the emperor began to number the years of his reign over again, calling this year the "first year." He ordered that there be great feasting and drinking throughout the empire. In the same year it was discovered that the jade cup and the other signs and wonders reported by Xinyuan Ping were all frauds, and he was executed along with relatives to the third degree of kinship. (10/430; modified from Burton Watson, trans., *Records of the Grand Historian*, rev. ed. [New York: Columbia University Press, 1993], 1:304)

See also the reference to this incident in *SJ* 28/1381, "Treatise on the Feng and Shan Sacrifices"; and Watson, *Records of the Grand Historian*, 2:23.

1. Duke Wen 6.2.8: "Our lord's son Sui entered Qi to present silk [as a betrothal gift for the duke of Qi]." *Gongyang*: "[He was] criticized for making marriage arrangements during a mourning period."
2. "Three years mourning" really meant "mourning into the third year"—that is, two years plus one month.
3. The important distinction being made here seems to be between the actual wedding and the prewedding negotiations with the state of Qi. Although the wedding did not take place until after he mourning period was over, the embassy to negotiate the marriage fell within the mourning period.

Someone said: When the *Spring and Autumn* judges events, nothing is more important than intent. Now when planning a marriage, one must send silk [presents] as a betrothal gift. The month in which this silk was sent fell within the mourning period. This is why [the *Spring and Autumn*] refers to [this event] as "marrying during a mourning period." Furthermore, Duke Wen enacted the Xia sacrifice during the autumn and sent his betrothal gifts during the winter.[4] In each case, his mistake lay in having done these things prematurely. That the *Spring and Autumn* does not criticize the former [enacting the Xia sacrifice in autumn] but only the latter [betrothal gifts in winter] is certainly because the mourning period of three years is [meant to give adequate expression to] the emotional responses by those who are blood kin. In following custom, even if he was not able to [carry out the mourning period] to the end, he still should not have felt settled in his heart. Instead, he completely lacked the intention of mourning and, on the contrary, thought of marriage. This is something that the *Spring and Autumn* truly loathes, so it criticized [Duke Wen] merely for initiating [his marriage arrangements] before the three-year mourning period had expired and for "marrying during the mourning period." [The *Spring and Autumn*] makes no distinction between "before" and "after";[5] it slights him for lacking a human heart.

The *Spring and Autumn* bases its discussions of ritual on this type of example, for the most important aspect of ritual is one's intentions.

> When someone had respectful intentions and completely conformed to prescriptions, the Noble Man [Confucius] granted that such a person understood ritual.
>
> When someone had harmonious intentions and [produced] graceful tones, the Noble Man granted that such a person understood music.
>
> When someone had sorrowful intentions and constrained himself, the Noble Man granted that such a person understood mourning.

This is why [the *Spring and Autumn*] states: "[Ritual] should not be emptily applied." This refers to the emphasis on one's intention. The intention [of ritual] is the [inner] substance, while the objects [involved in ritual] are the [outward] form. The form [of ritual] manifests substance. Thus if substance does not abide

4. Duke Wen 6.2.6: "The eighth month. *Dingmao*. [We held] the Grand Service at the Grand Temple and promoted Lord Xi [in the ancestral ranking]."

5. In other words, the *Spring and Autumn* does not absolve the duke on the technical grounds that his actions did not fall within the proscribed period but instead scrutinizes his intent.

in the form, how will form give to that substance [an adequate] display? Only when both substance and form are complete can ritual be perfected. If practiced in isolation, neither form nor substance is worthy of its name.[6] Yet in a case in which it is impossible for both to be complete and one errs on one side, it then is better to have substance and lack form. Although [Confucius] would not grant that [such a person was] competent in ritual, he would still approve to some extent. [The entry] "Jie Helü came" is a case in point.[7] However, if one possesses [only] form and lacks substance, not only would [Confucius] not grant [that such a person was competent in ritual], but he also would disapprove to some extent. A case in point is [the entry] in which the *Spring and Autumn* says of the duke of [the small state of] Jou, "That same person came."[8]

Thus, in setting out the proper sequence of the Way, the *Spring and Autumn* places substance first and form afterward [and] gives primary position to the intention [of a person engaged in ritual] and secondary position to the external objects [of ritual]. This is why [Confucius] said:

> "Ritual they say! Ritual they say! Can mere jade and silk be called ritual?"[9]

From this one can infer that it also is proper to say:

> Government they say! Government they say! Can mere commands and orders be called government?[10]

[Confucius also said:]

> "Music they say! Music they say! Can mere bells and drums be called music?"[11]

From this one can infer that it also is proper to say:

> Mourning they say! Mourning they say! Can mere clothing and garments be called mourning?

6. The phrase *bu de wo er zhi ming* 不得我爾之名 literally means "cannot attain the names of 'me' and 'you.'" In other words, neither aspect of ritual is genuine without the other; they are codependent.
7. The *Gongyang Commentary* at Duke Xi 5.29.1 explains that this man was a ruler of the Yi and Di tribes who came to pay court respects to the Zhou court. The text replaces the standard term designating paying court respects (*chao* 朝) with the character meaning simply "to come" (*lai* 來). Although this ruler did not know the ritual form proper to paying court respects, the text suggests that he adopted an attitude appropriate to such a ritual.
8. Duke Huan 2.5.9: "Winter. The duke of Jou (州) entered Cao." *Gongyang*: "When a foreign envoy arrives [the *Spring and Autumn*] does not record it. Why does it record it in this instance? [The duke of Jou] passed through our state." Duke Huan 2.6.1: "The sixth year. Spring. The first month. That same person [i.e., the man referred to in the previous entry] came." The *Gongyang Commentary* explains that this indicates disapproval of the duke of Jou. The duke of Jou passed through the state of Lu and did not pay court respects to the ruler of Lu. His actions lacked propriety, so the *Spring and Autumn* does not record his title and his name.
9. The "jade and silk" are the external objects of ritual. The quotation is from *Analects* 17.11.
10. "Commands and orders" are the outward manifestations of government.
11. *Analects* 17.11.

Therefore when Confucius established the Way of a New King,[12] he made it clear that he valued intentions in order to return to harmony, and he revealed that he cherished sincerity in order to obliterate hypocrisy. It is because Confucius encountered the failings of the Zhou that he [expressed himself] in this way. [2/3/15–29]

Section 2.2

The standard of the *Spring and Autumn* is this: the people follow the lead of the ruler, and the ruler follows the lead of Heaven.

Someone said: Now the hearts of the people and the ministers cannot be without a ruler for a single day. They cannot be without a ruler for even a day, and yet for the three years of mourning [after the death of his father], the ruler's son is designated "son" because in the heart of the [new] ruler, it is not yet appropriate to assume his father's position. Is this not [a case in which] the people [must] follow the lead of the ruler?

[Someone said]: The heart of a filial son cannot stand to take up his father's position for three years, and yet after the first year of mourning has passed, he assumes the throne so as to accord with Heaven's cycle.[13] Is this not a case of the ruler following the lead of Heaven? Therefore to restrain the people while extending the ruler's authority [and] to restrain the ruler while extending Heaven's authority is an important principle of the *Spring and Autumn*.[14] [2/3/31–2/4/2]

12. This refers to a hermeneutical position, common in the Han and perhaps before, that in writing the *Spring and Autumn*, Confucius assumed the mantle of an "uncrowned king" 素王. This section of the *Chunqiu fanlu* specifically expounds on a historiographical principle derived from *Analects* 3.14: "The Zhou is resplendent in culture (*wen* 文). It reviewed [the legacy of the preceding] two dynasties. I follow the Zhou." Some Han scholars understood this to mean that successive dynasties naturally alternated between those that emphasized culture/form and those that emphasized substance. At *Analects* 3.14, Confucius thus declares that the Zhou had emphasized form and that his new dynasty would emphasize substance. Michael Loewe regards the tension between *wen* (pattern) and *zhi* (substance) as one of the principal themes of the *Chunqiu fanlu*, in *Dong Zhongshu, a "Confucian" Heritage, and the "Chunqiu fanlu,"* Brill China Studies, no. 20 (Leiden: Brill, 2011), 275–83. See also *SJ* 47/1936 and *Bohutong* 27, "San zheng" (Three Rectifications); and Tjan Tjoe Som, trans., *Po Hu T'ung: The Comprehensive Discussions in the White Tiger Hall* (Leiden: Brill, 1952), 2:551, 553.

13. Heaven's yearly course begins in spring and ends in winter. Therefore after the ruler dies, the new ruler must wait until the spring of his second year of mourning before assuming the throne. Until then, he is referred to only as the "son" (i.e., heir apparent) rather than by his prospective new rank as ruler.

14. *Yi* 義 may mean either "righteousness" or "meaning," and in the context of the *Spring and Autumn*, it almost invariably means both. We translate *yi* as "important principle."

Section 2.3

In discussing the undertakings of twelve generations, [the *Spring and Autumn*] comprehensively encompasses the Human Way and perfectly delineates the Kingly Way. Its standards are found throughout the 240 years [it discusses], reinforcing one another and constituting a variegated pattern. They are based on juxtaposition and contrast and do not simply follow a linear [path] from antiquity.

For this reason, those who discuss the *Spring and Autumn* must

collate and thereby penetrate [its] standards
and connect and thereby inquire into them.

[They must]

group together those that are comparable,
match those that are categorically similar,
scrutinize their connections, [and]
pick out their omissions.

Only then will the Way of Humankind be harmonized and the Kingly Way be established. If you are of the opinion that this is not true, then consider the standards that the Son of Heaven must wait a year before assuming the throne of his deceased father and that while a Lord of the Land mourns for three years within his fief, he refers to himself as "son" [and not according to his new rank and title].[15] Neither is present in the Classic,[16] and yet we cling to them as if they were no different from [those standards] that are present in the Classic. It is not that there is nothing to discriminate them. There is something that is discernible, and therefore the Classic securely preserves its omissions.[17] Therefore, if you are able to connect categories using comparison and can extrapolate[18] [from] omissions using critical reasoning, you will have greatly mastered the *Spring and Autumn*. [2/4/4–8]

15. In other words, they do not refer to the deceased ruler's son by his new rank and title for three years following his father's death.
16. Jing 經, that is, the *Spring and Autumn*.
17. That is, some standards are positively declared in the *Spring and Autumn* but others must be read between the lines.
18. *Fu* 付 literally means to "match" or to "tally." It translates as "extrapolate" in the sense that the reader must provide the positive standard to match the significant lacunae in the text.

Section 2.4

Human beings receive their destinies from Heaven. They possess a nature that approves of goodness and despises wrongdoing. They can nurture [their nature] but they cannot fundamentally change it. They can provide for it but they cannot dispense with it, just as they can make their body fat or thin but they cannot fundamentally alter it.

For this reason, even the worthiest of men can, for the sake of their ruler and parents, only contain and bridle their bad tendencies but cannot, for the sake of their ruler and parents, completely free themselves from bad tendencies. The *Documents* states: "When a ruler [acts in a manner] not [befitting] a ruler, eradicate his shortcomings." One serves one's parents in this way as well. Both are instances of the utmost loyalty and filial piety. If not the worthiest of men, how could one be like this? When a father fails to be a father, a son will fail to be a son. When a ruler fails to be a ruler, subjects will fail to be subjects.[19] [2/4/10–13]

Section 2.5

Duke Wen was not able to submit to the [proper period of] mourning and did not make timely sacrifices. Before three years of mourning had passed, he married, taking as his wife the daughter of a great officer, thereby debasing the ancestral temple.[20] He disordered the proper arrangement of the ancestors' tablets, thereby defying Duke Xi.[21] He was devoid of even one small instance of goodness, and his instances of grave wrongdoing were numerous.[22]

Thus the Lords of the Land did not conclude covenants with him,[23] and the great officers did not carry out his orders. This provides clear evidence that he

19. This passage appears to be intrusive and is not attributable to Dong Zhongshu. The subject that it addresses, the characteristics of human nature, is not in keeping with the rest of the chapter; moreover, its position on human nature is not congruent with Dong's known views on the subject. Su Yu (*CQFLYZ* 34) argues emphatically that these are not the words of Dong Zhongshu.

20. Duke Wen 6.4.2: "Summer. We received the wife [of the Jiang clan] in Qi." The *Gongyang Commentary* holds that the event was recorded in a cursory manner because the duke married a woman of a great officer's family, a rank too low to be a suitable match. In other words, no subject is given for the verb "to meet" (*ni* 逆).

21. By not according him his proper place in the ancestral temple.

22. Literally, four or five.

23. Emending *ming* 命 to *meng* 盟, following Su Yu, *CQFLYZ*; and Lai, *CQFLJZJY* 24.

was despised for his wrongdoing, the result being that his subjects acted disloyally. When he left his state, he was insulted abroad; when he remained in his state, his power was usurped from within. He was a ruler without position. Confucius said: "It has been four generations since government came under the control of the officers."[24] He is likely speaking of the time commencing with the rule of Duke Wen. [2/4/15–18]

Section 2.6

The Noble Man knew that those who occupy the throne cannot rely on hateful [measures] to win the people's submission.

For this reason, he compiled

the *Six Arts* to support and nurture them.

The *Odes* and *Documents* to order their intentions;

the *Rites* and *Music* to purify their loveliness;

and the *Changes* and the *Spring and Autumn* to clarify their understanding.

These six forms of learning all are great, yet each has its particular strength.

The *Odes* guides intentions; consequently it excels at inner substance.

The *Rites* moderates conduct; consequently it excels at outer refinement.

The *Music* extols virtue; consequently it excels at transformation through moral suasion.

The *Documents* records meritorious deeds; consequently it excels at affairs.

The *Changes* is rooted in Heaven and Earth; consequently it excels at [divinatory] techniques.

The *Spring and Autumn* rectifies right and wrong; consequently it excels at governing the people.

One can collectively attain their strengths, but one cannot take up one detail in isolation.[25]

Thus, if the ruler's study of them is

too detailed, his understanding will be obscured;

[if it is] too general, his successes will decrease.

---

24. *Analects* 16.3.

25. The idea here seems to be that the classics must be approached as a whole, not studied in isolation from one another.

These two shortcomings differ but are alike in leading to defeat,[26] so that setbacks will inevitably occur. One cannot fail to consider this. For this reason, those who excel at providing instruction,

having praised [their understanding of] the Way,
will [then] be cautiously attentive to [their pupils'] conduct.
They will adjust the timing of their instruction,
some earlier and others later,
conferring on some students more while others less,
adopting a fast or slow pace [according to the abilities of their students].
When quick they are not hurried;
when slow they do not struggle to keep up.

They conserve their students' actions and fill out their deficiencies. Therefore they do not exhaust their students' strength, yet their persons are greatly perfected. This is the meaning of "sagely transformation."[27] I have appropriated this method. [2/4/20–27]

Section 2.7

Why does the *Spring and Autumn* cherish subtle terminology? [It does so] because it values intentions. The *Spring and Autumn*

cultivates the principles of roots and branches,
comprehends the responses of alterations and consequences,
penetrates the intentions [that bring] life and death,
and traces the extremes of the human way.

For this reason, when the ruler is assassinated and the assassin is punished, it approves of [that] and records the event. If the assassin is not punished, the ruler is not recorded as having been "properly buried,"[28] and the assassin does not reappear [in later entries]. It does not record the burial [when the assassin is not punished] because it considers that there are no [true] ministers and sons.

26. Emending *bian* 貶 to *bai* 敗, based on the "Rong jing" chapter of Jia Yi's *Xin shu* (Su Yu, *CQFLYZ* 26).
27. *Sheng hua* 聖化. The passage draws heavily on the educational methods advocated by Jia Yi. Beginning with "the ruler," the passage parallels a passage in the "Rong jing" chapter of Jia Yi's *Xin shu*. See D. C. Lau, ed., *Xin shu zhuzi suoyin* 新書逐字索引 (*A Concordance to the "Xin shu"*), Chinese University of Hong Kong, Institute of Chinese Studies Ancient Chinese Text Concordance Series (Hong Kong: Commercial Press, 1994), 6.2/45/1–3.
28. The phrase *jun bu shu zang* 君不書葬 indicates that the specific term *zang* is not used when an assassinated ruler is buried.

The assassin [who is not apprehended] does not reappear [in later entries] because it considers it fitting that the assassin's line be extinguished.

Now Zhao Dun assassinated his ruler,[29] and four years later he reappears in another entry. This contravenes the usual phraseology of the *Spring and Autumn*. Past and present [*Gongyang*] scholars have found strange this [deviation from the norm of the *Spring and Autumn*] and raised a question, asking: This is a case of regicide. Why does [Zhao Dun] reappear [in a later entry]? This is like when it says [elsewhere],[30] "The assassin was not punished. Why is the ruler's burial recorded?" They ask: "Why is the burial recorded?" because it was not proper to record the burial, yet the burial is recorded. They ask: "Why does Zhao Dun reappear in a later entry?" likewise because it is not proper for him to reappear and yet he reappears. These two [exceptions] are interpenetrating, so they cannot but be parallel to each other.

[One might posit that] Zhao Dun reappears in a later entry to raise the question, so as to show that "not personally murdering his ruler" is not the same as "not deserving to be put to death." [Likewise,] one cannot say that it is not recorded that Duke Dao received a proper burial. The question is raised so as to show that "not completing an act of regicide" does not mean "not being guilty of a crime." If that were the case, the theories of the *Spring and Autumn* would be confused and who could emulate them?[31]

Therefore, if you connect their comparable points and evaluate what is true and false, although it may be difficult to distinguish right from wrong, you will discover that the meaning [of these two cases] is identical. Therefore if you connect, compare, and evaluate them, although it is difficult to distinguish right

29. Zhao Dun was a great officer of the Jin state. During the reign of Duke Xiang of Jin, he participated in governmental affairs. When Duke Xiang died, he helped establish Duke Ling on the throne. Duke Ling was an unprincipled ruler, and on several occasions Zhao Dun remonstrated with him. Duke Ling was about to assassinate Zhao Dun when Zhao Dun fled the state. Before he had crossed the border into another state, his brother Zhao Quan assassinated Duke Ling. Zhao Dun returned and established Duke Cheng on the throne. The historians of Jin recorded simply the following: "Zhao Dun of Jin assassinated his ruler Yi Gao." Duke Xuan 2.6: "Autumn. The ninth month. *Yichou*. Zhao Dun of Jin assassinated his ruler Yi Gao." For the discussion of Zhao Dun and Zhao Quan, see the *Gongyang Commentary* at Duke Xuan 7.6.1.

30. This question appears in Yin 1.11.4 (where it is introduced and explained), Huan 2.18.4, Xuan 7.12.1, Xiang 8.8.2 and 8.30.8, and Zhao 10.19.5. As the text farther down shows, it refers here to the parallel in Zhao 10.19.5.

31. The grammar and diction here are very convoluted, but the gist is this: the *Chunqiu fanlu* is refuting one possible interpretation of the Zhao Dun/Duke Dao anomaly, as the necessary parallelism between these two exceptional records would yield a moral paradox. If one posits that Zhao Dun reappears to demonstrate that he deserves execution despite his not having personally killed the duke, then one would have to hold that the record of Duke Dao's burial indicates that a failure to complete an act of regicide absolves one of a crime.

from wrong, you will discover that the righteousness [of these two cases] is identical.

Now the *Spring and Autumn*'s record of Zhao Dun[32] has no [*Gongyang*] commentary stating that Zhao Dun was punished with execution, and it has no [*Gongyang*] commentary stating that he was spared execution. If we discuss it on the basis of analogous entries recorded in the text, we will [be able to] judge according to standards. If we do not discuss it on the basis of analogous entries recorded in the text, we will make a perverse judgment. Now if we examine those entries that are analogous to [the case of] Zhao Dun, we will find that in every case, execution was not suitable. Why, then, punish Zhao Dun with execution? The *Spring and Autumn* raises hundreds of questions, and it supplies thousands of responses. In regard to the identical cases enumerated in the Classic, if you repeatedly cite entries and compare categories in order to reveal its clues, you will not ask unfounded questions, and you will always find an appropriate response from the commentary. For example, suppose there were a *Chunqiu* rule that rebels from abroad could not be punished and subsequently all such rebels reappeared in the text. If you then asked: "Why does he reappear in this entry?" there could be no more erroneous question than this. How could you expect to find a response to this question in the text? Therefore, because the text supplied a response, I know that the question raised [about Zhao Dun] was not erroneous. Because the question raised was not erroneous, I know that the case of [Zhao] Dun must be examined carefully. For cases bearing the name "patricide" but in reality not deserving incrimination, the *Spring and Autumn* already provides a precedent. Likewise, there are cases named "regicide" for which the punishment was not execution. Rather than rush to blame someone, it is best to ruminate at leisure. Moreover, there is a basis for my appraisal of Zhao Dun.

An *Ode* declares:

> "What other human beings possess in their hearts
> I can measure by reflection."[33]

This indicates that all events have their counterparts. By observing the external facts of an event, one can see what lies within. Now if we look into the actions of Dun to observe his heart, [we will find that] his original intention was not criminal. If we match and are faithful to them, [his actions] were not equivalent to regicide. We can also examine what Dun said when he called out to Heaven.

32. Duke Xuan 2.6.
33. *Odes* 198, verse 4.

If his heart were not sincere, then how was he able to act in that way? Therefore, if we follow [his intentions] from beginning to end, we will find that he did not intend to commit regicide. If he is to be labeled with a bad [deed], his error was not to go beyond the border [and absolve himself of allegiance]. His crime lay in not punishing the assassin, that is all. It is proper for a minister to punish an assassin on behalf of his ruler, just as it is proper for a son to taste medicine on behalf of his father. The son [Xu Zhi] did not taste [his father's] medicine, and consequently [Confucius] increased [the crime to] patricide. The minister [Zhao Dun] did not punish the assassin, and consequently [Confucius] increased [the crime to] regicide. The significance [of both omissions] was identical. This is how Confucius showed the world that to abandon the correct relations between ruler and minister and between father and son is an abomination as significant as this. Thus [the *Spring and Autumn*] considers that

> [the case of] Dun, who by not killing his ruler's assassin had committed regicide, was no different from
>
> [the case of] the son [Zhi], who by not tasting his father's medicine had committed patricide.

From this analogous example, we see that it was not suitable to execute Zhao Dun.

Someone raising a question said: [The *Spring and Autumn*] designates the event as regicide, but he was not executed. This judgment is difficult to fathom. It is not something that the majority of people can readily understand. Why does the *Spring and Autumn* clearly transmit the fact that Zhi's crime was pardoned but it does not transmit the fact that Dun was not put to death?

The answer is: The age was chaotic and righteousness was abandoned; men defied their rulers and did not act as ministers should. Those who committed regicide and overthrew their rulers were numerous, so [Confucius] made it clear that this great wrongdoing was punishable by death. Who else could speak to the punishment? Thus in the case of Zhao Dun of Jin and Gongzi Bi of Chu,[34] there are phrases that indicate that they were not executed, yet this was not openly transmitted because [Confucius] was not of a mind to make this obvious.

Someone raising a question said: When someone assassinates a ruler and the great ministers of state are present but unable to punish the assassin, this is not

34. Gongzi Bi was the third son of King Gong of Chu. King Ling was violent and unprincipled. When he attacked the state of Xu, Gongzi Qi murdered his heir apparent Lu and forced Gongzi Bi to become the king of Chu. King Ling committed suicide. Duke Zhao 10.13.2: "Summer. The fourth month. Gongzi Bi of Chu returned to Chu from Jin. He assassinated his ruler Qian in Gan Ke."

[what one may call] a unified state. When Duke Ling was murdered, Zhao Dun was abroad. To not be present [when a ruler is assassinated and to not punish the assassin] constitutes a lesser wrong than to be present [and not punish the assassin]. The *Spring and Autumn* criticizes those who are present but do not punish the assassin by not designating them as ministers.[35] It criticizes those who are not present and do not punish the assassin by labeling the act regicide. Why is the greater wrong treated lightly and the lesser wrong treated sternly?

Someone said: The Way of the *Spring and Autumn* is to observe what brings confusion to people and offer explanations to greatly enlighten them. Now Zhao Dun was a worthy, but he did not follow the principle [of punishing the assassin]. Everyone saw his goodness, but no one saw his crime. Thus because of his worthiness, the *Spring and Autumn* expressly associates him with this great evil and implicates him with strong criticism to cause people to think deeply and look into themselves, reflecting on the Way, so that they say, "Oh! The great duty of the ruler and minister and the Way of father and son indeed extend this far!" This is why the lesser wrong is criticized more heavily. Those from other states who do not punish assassins, people who are mere utensils, are they worth enumerating? [The *Spring and Autumn*] simply does not designate them as persons, and that is all. This is why the greater wrong is criticized less heavily. A tradition states: "Light for heavy, heavy for light." Isn't this what is referred to here? Thus

> it deceptively appeared that it was permissible to establish Gongzi Bi of Chu as the ruler;
>
> it deceptively appeared that when the ruler was assassinated, Zhao Dun was not responsible for punishing the assassin;
>
> and it deceptively appeared that when his father died from poisoning, it was not the fault of Xu Zhi.

This is why the *Spring and Autumn*, in dealing with people who do not understand evil, but who act complacently and improvidently, repeatedly criticizes and upbraids them. It is like using a straightening-frame to straighten out a crooked age. Unless the straightening-frame is stronger than [what is to be made] straight, it cannot be straightened. If you understand this, then you will have fully comprehended the meaning of the *Spring and Autumn*. [2/5/1–31]

35. The author believes that the *Spring and Autumn* omits their rank in order to indicate that they did not act as true ministers.

Book 2, Part 1

CHAPTER 3

Bamboo Grove

Section 3.1

The usual terminology of the *Spring and Autumn* grants that the Central States participate in proper ritual, but not the Yi and Di peoples. Why, on the contrary, is this [principle] contravened when it comes to the battle of Bi?[1]

1. Duke Xuan 7.12.3: "Summer. The sixth month. *Yimao*. Xun Lin Fu of Jin led troops to battle with the viscount of Chu at Bi. The Jin troops were defeated soundly." *Gongyang*: "A great officer is not equal to a ruler. Why does [the *Spring and Autumn*] here give the personal name and the family name [of Xun Lin Fu], thus making him an equal of the viscount of Chu? [The *Spring and Autumn*] here grants the correct use of ritual, not to Jin, but to the viscount of Chu."

The *Gongyang Commentary* explains that after the battle between Chu and Zheng, King Zhuang was reluctant to take the capital of Zheng. When his general urged him to take possession of the city, King Zhuang responded:

"In the days of old, one did not travel in the four directions unless one's bowls had been pierced [and destroyed] and one's furs had been eaten by grubs." Therefore the Noble Man [Confucius] stood firm on ritual while he considered profit to be of lesser concern. "I want the men of Zheng to admit their guilt; I do not desire their land. Not to pardon an enemy who has submitted is inauspicious. If I were to lead my people with inauspicious means, calamity would overtake me in no time at all." Eventually the troops of Jin who were sent to rescue Zheng arrived and requested a battle. King Zhuang gave his consent. General Zi Zhong remonstrated saying, "Jin is a great state. Your army has been fatigued for a long time. I beg you not to grant this [request]!" King Zhuang responded: "If I were to overawe the weak and avoid the strong, I would no longer keep my position in the realm." He ordered him to bring back the army and went to meet the intruders from Jin. The Jin army was soundly defeated. But when they suffered heavy casualties, King Zhuang lamented: "Alas, what crime is that of the people, that we two rulers cannot get on together?" He ordered [his commanding officers] to make the army withdraw and let the intruders from Jin escape. (Adapted from Göran Malmqvist, "Studies on the *Gongyang* and *Guliang* Commentaries," *Bulletin of the Museum of Far Eastern Antiquities* 43 [1971]: 184)

The answer is: The *Spring and Autumn* does not employ consistent terminology but rather

follows alterations [in circumstances]
by shifting [its phrasing].

Now if Jin changes and acts like the Yi and Di peoples, or conversely, if Chu changes and acts like a noble man, then it shifts its terminology to reflect these facts. When King Zhuang of Chu yielded to [the entreaties of the earl of] Zheng, he exhibited an inner beauty that was truly admirable.[2] The man of Jin [i.e., Xun Lin Fu] did not understand his goodness and wanted to attack him. What he wanted to rescue [i.e., Zheng] had already been spared, and yet he still wanted to provoke [Chu] into battle. This was to disparage the good-heartedness [of King Zhuang] and to slight his intention to spare the people [of Zheng]. This is why the *Spring and Autumn* degrades [the Jin general] and does not grant that he was equal to the worthy who engaged in proper ritual.

Earl Mu of Qin insulted Qian Shu, and he was soundly defeated.[3]
Duke Wen of Zheng slighted the masses and [had to] mourn his troops.[4]

The *Spring and Autumn* respects the worthy and values the people in this way. Therefore, although there were several hundred instances of battles, assaults,

2. The *Gongyang Commentary* explains that after King Zhuang of Chu defeated the earl of Zheng, the earl approached him and begged King Zhuang to take pity on him. Thereupon, King Zhuang ordered his troops to retreat.

3. Duke Xi 5.33.3: "Summer. The fourth month. *Xinsi*. A man from Jin together with the Jiang Rong peoples defeated Qin at Yao." *Gongyang*:

> Why does [the *Spring and Autumn*] use the term "Qin"? [To treat them as] the Yi and Di peoples. Why does [the *Spring and Autumn*] treat them as the Yi and Di peoples? The earl of Qin was about to launch a surprise attack on Zheng. Viscount Bai Li and Viscount Qian Shu remonstrated, saying: "Those who have launched a surprise attack against others from a distance of one thousand *li* have never failed to perish." The earl of Qin became furious and replied: "At your age it would take two arms to grasp round the trees on your graves. What do you know about warfare?" The troops departed. Viscount Bai Li and Viscount Qian Shu bid their sons good-bye and warned them, saying: "You will surely die. It will surely happen at the precipitous mountain cliffs at Xiao. That is where King Wen sheltered himself from wind and rain. We will collect your corpses there." The sons saluted their fathers in the military fashion and left. Viscount Bai Li and Viscount Qian Shu followed their sons and wept for them. The earl of Qin said angrily, "Why do you weep for my troops?" They replied: "We dare not weep for the troops of our lord. We weep for our sons."

The *Gongyang Commentary* goes on to explain that the Qin troops were defeated so badly that "not a single horse and not a single [chariot] wheel returned" (adapted from Malmqvist, "Studies on the *Gongyang* and *Guliang* Commentaries," 170).

4. Duke Min 4.2.5: "Zheng abandoned its troops." *Gongyang*: "Duke Wen despised the general of his forces, Gao Ke. He ordered him to lead troops to the border of the state and remain there. After much time had elapsed he did not instruct them to return. This was the way he abandoned his troops."

incursions, and attacks [in its 242 years of history], it recorded them all one by one, being grieved at the great extent of their destruction.

Someone raising a question said: [The *Spring and Autumn*] records battles and attacks in great detail. Why, then, are there no expressions indicating that it despised such battles and attacks?

The answer is:

[When the *Spring and Autumn* records] meetings and assemblies,
large states [are described as having] hosted small states;
[when the *Spring and Autumn* records] battles and attacks,
[states] mentioned later [are described as having] hosted the ones [mentioned] first.[5]

If the *Spring and Autumn* did not despise warfare, why would it place the state that initiated the aggression in an inferior position? This was an expression indicating its hatred of warfare.

Moreover, it also is a standard of the *Spring and Autumn* that renovations not be carried out in years of bad harvests.[6] The intention is to not inflict suffering on the people. If the *Spring and Autumn* despises causing the people to suffer, how much more is this the case of harming them. If the *Spring and Autumn* grieves at harming the people, how much more is this the case of killing them! Therefore it states: "Those who renovate the old during years of bad harvests are criticized; those who fortify a city during years of bad harvests are concealed."[7]

5. That is, the state that was attacked acted as the host and was mentioned second, whereas the state that attacked was mentioned first but was placed in the inferior position of being the guest. Duke Zhuang 3.28.1: "Spring. The royal third month. *Jiayin*. People from Qi attacked Wey. Wey together with people from Qi battled. People from Wey were utterly defeated." *Gongyang*:

[In records of] attacks, the day is not normally recorded. Why in this case is the day recorded? The attack occurred on the day the Qi troops arrived. [The *Spring and Autumn*] does not normally use the term "battle" in conjunction with the term "attack." Why in this case does [the *Spring and Autumn*] employ the term "attack"? The attack occurred on the day the Qi troops arrived. In [the *Spring and Autumn*] the attacker is represented as the guest and the attacked is represented as the host. Therefore [the *Spring and Autumn*] represents Wey as the host.

6. Duke Zhuang 3.29.1: "Spring. We renovated the Yan stable." *Gongyang*: "What does the phrase 'renovated the Yan stable' mean? It means that we repaired the old [stable]. [Repairs are not normally recorded]; why was it recorded here? To criticize. Why was [the duke] criticized? In years of bad harvests, one does not renovate."

7. Duke Zhuang 3.28.3: "Winter. We fortified the city of Mei. There was a great deficiency in the wheat crop." *Gongyang*: "Why does [the *Spring and Autumn*] first say: 'We fortified the city of Mei' and only then say: 'There was a great deficiency in the wheat crop'? It was in order to conceal the fact that a city was fortified during a year of bad harvest."

When the people are harmed in a small way, [the *Spring and Autumn*] despises this to a small degree.

When the people are harmed in a great way, [the *Spring and Autumn*] despises this to a great degree.

How great is the harm suffered by the people during warfare! Examine its intentions and observe its precepts, and you will discover that the *Spring and Autumn* despises those who rely on force rather than virtue and those who coerce and devastate the people, but it cherishes those who rely on humaneness and righteousness to win the submission of the people. An *Ode* declares:

"Spreading the virtue of his governance throughout the lands."[8]

This is what the *Spring and Autumn* considers to be praiseworthy.

If there are those whose virtue is not sufficient to bind to them those who are near and whose cultural achievements are not sufficient to attract those who are distant,

but who instead rely on warfare to accomplish these things, the *Spring and Autumn* will certainly deeply despise them because they lack righteousness.

Someone raising an objection said: When the *Spring and Autumn* records battles and attacks, it expresses disdain for some while praising others.

It despises deceitful assaults,
but it praises prearranged battles.[9]
It scorns those who attack during the mourning period,
but it glorifies those who avenge a grievance.

How, then, can you claim that the *Spring and Autumn* holds that there is no such thing as a righteous war and that it despises all wars, without exception?

The answer is: When the *Spring and Autumn* records calamities and anomalies, [even] though a plot of land contains a few stalks of wheat or rice, it still refers to such a plot as lacking wheat and rice. Throughout the vast territories and during the lengthy three hundred years that it describes, the instances of battles, punitive expeditions, invasions, and attacks cannot be counted, whereas there are only two instances of military revenge. How is this different from the plot of land that contains a few stalks but is referred to as lacking wheat and rice? This is not sufficient to challenge the *Spring and Autumn*; therefore I state that there are no righteous wars.

8. *Odes* 262, stanza 6. Translation follows Arthur Waley, trans., *The Book of Songs: The Ancient Chinese Classic of Poetry*, ed., with additional translations, Joseph R. Allen (New York: Grove Press, 1996), 281.
9. The expression is *pian zhan* 偏戰, denoting battles, whose dates and places are fixed by both sides in advance in accordance with ritual rules (Lai, *CQFLJZJY* 35, note 20).

If you do not accept that there are no righteous wars, then likewise you cannot accept that there are lands devoid of wheat and rice.

If you accept that there are lands devoid of wheat and rice, then you also must accept that there are wars devoid of righteousness.

In the case of prearranged battles, the *Spring and Autumn* praises the fact that [the two sides] arranged the battle in advance; it does not praise the battle. There is evidence that this is so. The *Spring and Autumn* loves the people, and warfare kills them. What pleasure does a noble man derive from killing what he loves? Thus in the case of prearranged battles, the *Spring and Autumn* [takes a] similar view, as it does in the case of the [Sinitic] states. When describing the state of Lu, it refers to [the other states as] external; when describing the Yi and Di peoples, it refers to [the other states] as internal.[10] Compared with a deceitful assault, a prearranged battle is considered righteous. Compared with [the alternative of] not fighting, a prearranged battle is not righteous. Therefore no alliance is better than an alliance, and yet there are references to praiseworthy alliances. No battles are better than engaging in battle, and yet there are references to praiseworthy battles. Within an unrighteous act, righteousness may dwell. Within a righteous act, unrighteousness may dwell. When the terminology cannot be explicit, in every case [the explanation] rests with the guiding principles [of the *Spring and Autumn*]. How could one who lacks a refined mind and penetrating thoughts understand this! An *Ode* declares:

"The flowers of the cherry tree, how they wave about!
It is not that I do not think of you, but your home is far away."

Confucius commented: "He did not really think of her. If he did, there would be no such thing as being far away."[11] From this, we see that you must observe its guiding principles and not take its words too literally. When you do not take its words too literally, you will head toward the proper path. [3/6/5–29]

Section 3.2

While acting as an envoy for his lord [King Zhuang of Chu], Commander Zi Fan disregarded his orders and informed the enemy of the true situation [in the ranks of the Chu army]. He complied with [the enemy's] request and achieved

10. That is, the frame of reference is the Sinitic (Xia 夏) polity; the *Spring and Autumn* changes its vocabulary to reflect the perspective of the circumstance being described.

11. These verses are not in the received text of the *Odes*; they apparently were part of an ode that has been lost. The entire passage, including both the verses (with a slight variation in wording) and Confucius's comment, is evidently copied from *Analects* 9.30.

peace with Song.[12] This is a case of usurping political authority inside your state while trading on the good reputation [of your lord] outside your state.

To usurp political authority is to slight the ruler;
to trade on the good reputation of your lord is to fail to be a minister.

Why, then, does the *Spring and Autumn* praise Zi Fan?

The answer is: Because Zi Fan possessed compassion rooted in empathy, he could not bear to starve the people of a single state or cause them to eat one another.

Those who extend their compassion are far-reaching in their greatness;
those who act humanely are spontaneous in their goodness.

Now Zi Fan revealed his [compassionate] heart and pitied the people of Song. He did not plan to disobey [his lord's commands]. Thus [the *Spring and Autumn*] glorifies this event.

Someone raising an objection stated: The standards of the *Spring and Autumn* dictate that

ministers must not shoulder the anxieties of the Lords of the Land,
and political power must not devolve into the hands of the great officers.

Zi Fan was a Chu minister, yet he pitied the people of Song. This is a case of shouldering the anxieties of the Lords of the Land. He did not report to his lord but made peace with the enemy. This is a case of political authority devolving into the hands of the great officers. The covenant at Ku Liang rested on trust between the great officers. The *Spring and Autumn* criticized this because the

12. Duke Xuan 7.15.2: "Summer. The fifth month. A man from Song and a man from Chu made peace." *Gongyang*: "Peacemaking between states of the Exterior is not normally recorded. Why in this case is it recorded? To glorify the fact that they achieved peace between themselves." The *Gongyang Commentary* goes on to explain in a lengthy narrative that while the *Spring and Autumn* employs censorious language (referring to the protagonists simply as "men"), because, by making peace, they usurped the prerogatives of their rulers, it ultimately expresses approval of their actions. To paraphrase: King Zhuang [of Chu] besieged Song. As the siege continued, both sides suffered from a lack of supplies. The two commanders, Zi Fan of Chu and Hua Yuan of Song, met for a parley. Instead of dissembling, as expected, Hua Yuan admitted that the people of the Song capital were in desperate straits. Zi Fan, impressed by this candor, revealed that his army had provisions to press the siege for only seven more days and promised to withdraw his troops if the siege was not successful by then. Ordered by King Zhuang to continue to press the attack nevertheless, Zi Fan requested leave to return home rather than break his promise. The king then abandoned the campaign. The narrative concludes, "The Noble Man glorified the fact that [the two commanders] achieved peace between themselves." Thus eschewing the strategy of wartime deception, two officers chose to speak honestly with each other as they recognized a mutual code of shared humanitarian values and sought to end the violence and bloodshed between the states of Song and Chu. Significantly, this is the single instance in the *Gongyang* in which Confucius "glorified" an action related to warfare: one that sought an end to it.

great officers usurped the respect due their lord.[13] [In the case of Zi Fan,] peace was concluded between the great officers [of Chu and Song], but the *Spring and Autumn* glorified this event. This is what causes me doubt. Moreover, it is a righteous principle of the *Spring and Autumn* to despise the minister who trades on the good reputation of his lord. Therefore, loyal ministers do not openly criticize their lords, hoping that the right conduct will emanate from the lord himself. The *Documents* states: "When you possess a good plan or counsel, enter the lord's palace and inform the ruler. Thereafter, when you are acting abroad in accordance with [these plans or counsel,] say, 'This plan, this counsel, is due to the virtue of my ruler.'"[14] This is a standard of a true minister. The good ministers of antiquity all served their ruler in this way. Now Zi Fan departed from his ruler only a short distance, yet he did not turn back to him; he could see King Zhuang of Chu, yet he did not report to him. Most people think that to resolve the problem between the two states [of Chu and Song], he could not help but act in this way. But why did he trade on the good reputation of his lord? This is what confuses me.

[Someone] stated [in response]: The Way of the *Spring and Autumn* certainly includes both constancy and flexibility. [It]

> employs flexibility in extraordinary circumstances
> and employs constancy in ordinary circumstances.

Each stays in its category and does not interfere with the other.

Now what the various masters recognize are the constancies of the world. Their righteousness is [like] a thunderclap.[15] The conduct of Zi Fan

---

13. Duke Xiang 9.16.2: "The third month. Our Lord met with the marquis of Jin, the duke of Song, the marquis of Wey, the earl of Zheng, the viscount of Ying, the viscount of Zhu, the earl of Xie, the earl of Ji, the viscount of Lesser Zhu at Xiaoliang. *Wuyin*. The great officers made a covenant." *Gongyang*:

    All the Lords of the Land were present here. Why then does [the *Spring and Autumn*] say "the great officers made a covenant"? Trust rested with the great officers. Why does it say "trust rested with the great officers"? In order to criticize the great officers in the world. Why criticize the great officers of the world? It was as if the ruler was irrelevant and ornamental.

14. *Documents*, "Jun chen" 君陳 (Lord of Chen) 6; James Legge, trans., *The Shoo King, or, The Book of Historical Documents*, vol. 3 of *The Chinese Classics*, 2nd rev. ed. (1894; repr., Hong Kong: Hong Kong University Press, 1960), 540.

15. That is, they are principles with which everyone agrees, just as all things respond alike to the clap of thunder.

responded to sudden change. His was the righteousness cultivated in a particular instance.

When the eyes are startled, the body loses its proper posture;
when the heart is startled, [some] matters are forgotten.

Such are the emotional responses of human beings. Penetrating bewildering emotions, the *Spring and Autumn* grasps a single act of goodness and does not exhaustively [describe] a person's mistakes. An *Ode* declares:

"He who plucks greens, plucks cabbage,
does not judge by the lower parts."[16]

This expresses my meaning. Now when Zi Fan went to observe the state of Song, he heard that people were eating one another. He was deeply startled and pitied them. He did not anticipate that the people of Song would be driven to such an extreme. It was because his heart was alarmed and his eyes were startled that he violated the propriety that applies under ordinary circumstances.[17] Propriety derives from humaneness. It refines one's inner substance and completes one's person. Now when [the Chu army besieged the capital of Song] and compelled the people to eat one another, their humaneness was greatly lost. How, then, could they exhibit propriety? When you are endeavoring to rescue the inner substance of humaneness, how can you think of the outer refinement of propriety?[18] Thus it is said: "One ought to be humane and not submit [to the demands of form]."[19] This expresses my meaning.

Regarding the terminology of the *Spring and Autumn*, there is what is referred to as lowly and what is referred to as lower than lowly. Now if there is the lower than lowly, so too is there the loftier than lofty. Submitting to a superior's demand is something that the *Spring and Autumn* esteems. However, when one sees people eating one another and one becomes startled and moves to save them while forgetting to submit [to one's ruler], this is the Way of the Noble Man that is loftier than submission. Therefore, when those who discuss the *Spring and Autumn* do not question the greatness of changing ancient precedents based on the constant righteousness governing usual circumstance, then righteousness will be proclaimed.

16. *Ode* 35, stanza 1. Waley, *Book of Songs*, 30.
17. The expression employed here is *chang li* 常禮. An alternative translation would be "the constant rites," as opposed to flexible or changeable rites. In this passage, *chang li* is synonymous with the expression *chang yi* 常義 (constant righteousness).
18. An alternative rendering would be: At that moment [Zi Fan was trying] to save the substance. How could he be moved by the form?
19. Zi Fan is faced with choosing between substance and form: acting for the sake of benevolence or out of duty to the orders of his ruler.

However, when one sees people eating one another and one becomes startled and moves to save them while forgetting to submit [to one's ruler], this is the Way of the Noble Man that is loftier than submission. Therefore, when those who discuss the *Spring and Autumn* do not, on account of the constant righteousness governing usual circumstances, question the righteousness of altering precedents, then righteousness can truly be judged. [3/7/1–20]

Section 3.3

The *Spring and Autumn* records the successes and failures of the world. It reveals what causes events to be as they are.

> Though deeply hidden, they are nevertheless made clear;
> without being [directly] transmitted, they are nevertheless recorded.

One must not fail to examine this. Now Mount Tai is quite large, but if you do not observe it, you will not see it. How much more is this the case of those things that are subtle and profound!

Therefore, examine the *Spring and Autumn* and compare the events of the past that it describes; carefully deduce the origins of events and observe their causes. A ruler who has realized his ambitions is a person who knows contentment. One must not fail to be cautious.

Duke Qing of Qi was a blood relative of Duke Huan of Qi, being his grandson.

> The puissance of his state was expansive and great.
> The strategic position of his territory was advantageous and beneficial.

He also inherited the accumulated prestige [of his grandfather's status] as a hegemonic leader, so he could realize his ambition to dominate the other Lords of the Land. For these reasons,

> it was difficult to compel the duke to attend interstate meetings and assemblies,
> while it was quite easy to cause him to feel proud and arrogant.

In the nine years that he was established on the throne, there is not a single confirmation that he participated in a meeting or an assembly. He was angered by the ambitions of Lu and Wey and he refused to follow the other Lords of the Land at Qing Qiu or Duan Dao.[20] In the spring [of the second year of Duke

20. In other words, he did not meet and sign covenants with the other Lords of the Land. No mention is made of his presence in the following two entries. Duke Xuan 7.12.6: "A man from Jin, a man from Song, a man from Wey, and a man from Cao assembled to make a covenant at Qingqiu." Duke Xuan 7.17.6: "*Jiwei.* Our Lord met with the marquis of Jin, marquis of Wey, earl of Cao, viscount of Zhu. They assembled to make a covenant at Duandao."

Cheng], he attacked Lu, entering the state from its northern border.[21] On his way home, he attacked the state of Wey, defeating its army at Xin Zhu.[22] At that time, the duke's mind was still filled with the glory of recent success so that when the great states paid him court respects, their messengers were insulted and treated rudely.[23] The states of Jin and Lu grew angry at [Duke Qing of Qi]. Internally, Jin and Lu gathered together their multitudes while externally they joined forces with the states of Cao and Wey. By supporting one another, these four states were able to utterly defeat Qi at An.[24] Consequently, they captured Duke Qing of Qi and decapitated Feng Choufu.[25] If we examine deeply the roots that caused Duke Qing of Qi to bring insult to his person, lose his state, and become the laughingstock of the land, we will discover that their beginnings may be traced to [the time when he] subdued the state of Lu and defeated the state of Wey. When he attacked Lu, Lu did not dare array troops to battle. When he attacked Wey, he soundly defeated it. Because he had achieved his ambitions and thought that there was no one in the world that could match him, he precipitated his own disaster. Therefore it is said: Those who achieve their ambition and are content must not fail to be alert. Here is the proof. From this time onward, Duke Qing was filled with fear and trepidation. He did not listen to music, drink wine, or eat meat.

---

21. Duke Cheng 8.2.1: "The second year. Spring. The marquis of Qi attacked our northern border."
22. Duke Cheng 8.2.2: "Summer. The fourth month. *Bingxu*. Sun Liangfu of Wey led troops and, together with Qi troops, battled at Xin Zhu. The Wey troops were soundly defeated."
23. Duke Cheng 8.2.4: "Autumn. The seventh month. The marquis of Qi sent Guo Zuo [as an envoy] to the army [of the allies]. *Jisi*. They made a covenant with Guo Zuo at Yuanlou." *Gongyang*:

    [The *Spring and Autumn*] does not normally represent the ruler as employing a great officer as an envoy. Why does [the *Spring and Autumn*] do so here? [The marquis of Qi] had escaped from captivity. Under what circumstances did he do so? The [enemy] army had surrounded the marquis of Qi. Xi Ke of Jin threw his halberd on the ground, withdrew hesitantly, saluted twice, and kowtowed in front of the horses [of the chariot of the marquis of Qi]. A certain Feng Choufu was spearman to the right in Duke Jing's chariot. His features resembled those of Duke Jing, and he also was dressed alike and had taken Duke Jing's place on the left side of the chariot. He ordered Duke Jing to fetch water to drink. Duke Jing brought the drinking water and went up [to Feng Choufu who] said: "Change this and bring me some clear water!" Duke Jing took advantage of the situation, escaped, and did not return. Feng Choufu said: "With the aid of the divine powers of the spirit of our land our ruler has already escaped." Xi Ke said: "What does the law prescribe for one who cheats [the commander of] the three armies?" [Feng Choufu] replied: "The law prescribes decapitation! Thereupon he had Feng Choufu decapitated." (Adapted from Malmqvist, "Studies on the *Gongyang* and *Guliang* Commentaries," 191)

24. Duke Cheng 8.2.3: "The sixth month. *Guiyou*. Jisun Xingfu, Cang Sunxu, Shusun Jiaoru, and Gongsun Yingqi led troops to join with Xi Ke of Jin, Sun Liangfu of Wey, and Gongzi Shou of Cao to do battle with the marquis of Qi at An. The Qi troops were utterly defeated." *Gongyang*: "The state of Cao had no great officers. Why, then, does [the *Spring and Autumn*] record [the name of] of Gongzi Shou of Cao? [Gongzi Shou of Cao] was worried about internal affairs [and so acted like a great officer]."
25. Feng Choufu deceived the commander of Jin to save his ruler and thereby committed the offense of "cheating the leader of the three armies." For Duke Cheng 8.2.4, see note 23.

Within the borders of his state, he showed affection for his people, asking about their illnesses and mourning at their burials.

Beyond the borders of his state, he was respectful of the Lords of the Land, submitting to convene with them and establish alliances.

In this way, he was able to preserve his person and bring peace and security to his state. This is a case in which

the roots of prosperity are born of anxiety

and the roots of calamity are born of contentment.

The causes of events are closely bound up with human beings. Is it possible not to contemplate them? [3/7/22–3/8/3]

Section 3.4

Feng Choufu sacrificed his life to save his ruler. Why does the *Spring and Autumn* not grant that he understood expediency? Choufu deceived [the state of] Jin, and Zhai Zhong complied with [the demands of] Song.[26] Both deviated

26. According to Duke Huan 2.11.4, the state of Song was so strong and Zheng so weak that Zhai Zhong could preserve his ruler's life only by complying with the king of Song's demand to put another in his place, meanwhile biding his time until he could restore his own ruler to the throne. If unsuccessful, Zhai Zhong would bring disgrace on his own person. Duke Huan 2.11.4: "The ninth month. A man from Song [i.e., the king of Song, not named so as to indicate the text's disapproval] seized Zhai Zhong of Zheng." *Gongyang*:

Who was Zhai Zhong? [He was] a minister of Zheng. Why is his personal name not recorded? [He was] worthy. In what respect was Zhai Zhong worthy? [The *Spring and Autumn*] considers that he understood expediency. Why does [the *Spring and Autumn*] consider that he understood expediency? In ancient times, the state of Zheng was located in Liu. The former earl of Zheng had gained the friendship of the duke of Gui. [The earl of Zheng] had illicit relations with the wife [of the duke of Gui], and consequently he took the state [of Gui] and moved his own court there, allowing Liu to lie waste. When Duke Zhuang died and was buried, [Zhai Zhong] was about to go and inspect Liu. On his journey he ventured into [the territory of the state of] Song. The ruler of Song seized him and spoke to him saying: "Expel Hu and establish Du as ruler for my sake!" If Zhai Zhong refused to obey his command, then [his lord (i.e., Hu)] would surely die, and the state of Zheng would surely perish. If he obeyed [his command], then his ruler would remain alive instead of dying, and his state would survive instead of perishing. If he could let developments play out for a time, Du could be expelled and Hu could be reinstated. If this could not be achieved, then [Zhai Zhong] would be disgraced, but the state of Zheng would still be preserved. Zhai Zhong was one of the men of antiquity who understood expediency. What is meant by the term *quan* 權 (to weigh or, here, expediency)? The term *quan* means that one acts contrary to the constant norms (*jing* 經) to ultimately achieve goodness. Expediency cannot be applied in cases other than those in which the life [of one's ruler] or the preservation [of one's state] is at stake. There are principles governing the application of expediency. The one who practices it may suffer personal losses, but no harm must come to others. A noble man does not kill others to save his own life, nor does he destroy [the states of] others to preserve his own [state]. (Adapted from Malmqvist, "Studies on the *Gongyang* and *Guliang* Commentaries," 106)

The story of Zhai Zhong also appears in chapter 6.6.

from what was correct to preserve their rulers. Moreover, what [Feng] Choufu accomplished was more difficult than what Zhai Zhong achieved. Why is Zhai Zhong shown to be worthy, and Choufu is shown to be wrong?

The answer is: The difficulty of distinguishing between right and wrong lies in [cases like] this. These cases, which are deceptively similar to one another but are not identical in their principles, cannot help but be investigated. When [a ruler] abdicated the throne to avoid trouble with his brother, the Noble Man treated such cases with deep respect.[27] When [a ruler] was captured and fled, the Noble Man treated such cases with deep condemnation. To save his ruler's life, Zhai Zhong placed him in that position that others respect. Thus the *Spring and Autumn* considers that he understood expediency and treats him as a worthy. To save his ruler's life, however, Choufu placed his ruler in that position that others disrespect. Thus the *Spring and Autumn* considers that he did not understand expediency and treats him in an abbreviated manner. The two ministers resemble each other in that both deviated from what was proper in order to save their rulers. But causing the ruler to be honored and causing the ruler to be disgraced are not identical with respect to inner principles. Thus in all cases in which human beings intervene, if they first deviate from what is proper but later achieve righteousness, the *Spring and Autumn* refers to this as hitting the mark of expediency.[28] Even if they are unsuccessful, the *Spring and Autumn* praises them.[29] This is the case with Duke Yin of Lu and Zhai Zhong of Zheng. However, if they first do what is proper but later deviate from what is proper, [the *Spring and Autumn*] refers to this as an abominable course. Even if they are successful, the *Spring and Autumn* does not cherish them. This is the case with Duke Qing of Qi and Feng Choufu. If a person must suffer a great insult to survive, his feelings will be bereft of joy. Therefore worthies do not act in this way. But the majority of people would have doubts about that. The *Spring and Autumn* [upholds a standard of] righteousness that most people do not understand and therefore doubt. Thus it instructs them in righteousness by stating: "If the state perishes and the ruler dies, this is proper." "What is proper" refers to what is proper with respect to the Heaven-conferred nature and destiny

27. This refers to Hu, the legitimate ruler of Zheng who, following Zhai Zhong's forced compliance with the duke of Song's demands, gave up the throne to his younger brother (see note 26).

28. The expression used here is *zhong quan* 中權. *Zhong* literally means "the center" or "the middle." When used as a verb, as in this case, it means "to hit the mark." It indicated a state of harmony and equilibrium, generally translated as "the mean." In this case, Zhai Zhong had achieved a perfect balance between the conflicting choices that the rapidly changing circumstances had presented to him.

29. Here again, the *Spring and Autumn* judges men's intentions, regardless of the external outcome of their actions.

of human beings. The Heaven-conferred nature and destiny of human beings enable them to practice humaneness and righteousness, to feel shame for what is shameful, and to not be like the birds and beasts that seek only to survive and benefit themselves. This is why the *Spring and Autumn* esteems what Heaven bestows and complies with the principles of human [nature]. It holds that those who occupy the highest positions must not suffer extreme disgrace or great slights, so when [a ruler] is captured [by an enemy], it cuts off the narrative about him. It also holds that those who suffer great disgrace may not be elevated to a position of high rank. Therefore suppose that a ruler loses his position of authority; then it no longer treats him as the ruler of a state. Even after the ruler returns to his state and resumes his position, the *Spring and Autumn* will not employ terms that designate him as ruler. How much more is this the case when a ruler suffers great dangers and is captured by others!

If we discuss this from the perspective of righteousness, we can confirm that [Duke Qing of Qi] was no longer the ruler of his state. If he was not the ruler of his state, then how can we say that Feng Choufu understood expediency? Choufu deceived the [Jin] forces,[30] committing a serious offense against the state of Jin. In allowing Duke Qing to escape, he disgraced the ancestral temple of the state of Qi. Thus, although his circumstances were quite difficult, the *Spring and Autumn* does not cherish him. If Choufu [had understood] the principles of righteousness, it would have been proper for him to say to Duke Qing: "You, my lord, have acted negligently and angered the Lords of the Land. You have lost all propriety. Today, after suffering such great disgrace, if you are unable to submit to death, this is shameless and will double your offenses. Please let us die together so that you will not disgrace the ancestral temple and slight the altar of grain [of the state of Qi]." If Choufu had acted in this way, although he would have given up his life, he still would have left behind an honorable reputation. In this instance, death was worthier than life. This is why, according to the Noble Man, choosing life and suffering disgrace does not compare with choosing death and achieving renown. This is what "proper" refers to here.

If we discuss this case from the perspective of standards, then Choufu is guilty of deceit and did not hit the mark of expediency. He was loyal but he did not hit the mark of righteousness. If you do not think that this is so, then look again at the *Spring and Autumn*. The *Spring and Autumn* arranges its terms in a particular order. When it places the word "king" between the word "spring" and the

30. Literally, the "Three Armies," a standard trope for the armed forces of a state.

word "rectify," is it not saying: If you show respect for Heaven above and you rectify the people below, then you can become a true king?

To praise good, despise the bad,
cherish renown, and loathe disgrace;

these proclivities cannot be engendered by human beings on their own accord; they are bestowed on human beings by Heaven. The Noble Man judged human beings based on what Heaven bestows on human beings. Thus from this perspective, Choufu was not loyal. What Heaven bestows on human beings enables them to possess a sense of shame. Those who possess a sense of shame will not suffer profound disgrace. There is no disgrace that surpasses a lord's losing his position of authority and being taken captive. Zeng Zi said: "If disgrace can be avoided, then avoid it. But when you cannot avoid it, then a noble man will look upon death as if returning home." Such comments were directed at men like Duke Qing. [3/8/5–27]

Section 3.5

The *Spring and Autumn* states: "Zheng attacked Xu."[31] Why does [the *Spring and Autumn*] express disapproval of [Duke Xiang of] Zheng and treat him as if he were no different from the Yi and Di peoples?

[Someone] stated: Marquis Wei of Su died and Zheng troops invaded Wey. This [is a case of] attacking [a state] in mourning. Zheng made a covenant with the other Lords of the Land at Shu. After the covenant was concluded and the Lords of the Land returned to their states, Zheng attacked Xu. This [is a case of] betraying a covenant.

To attack [a state] in mourning is unrighteous;
to defy an oath is untrustworthy.

[The ruler of Zheng] was untrustworthy and unrighteous. Consequently, [the *Spring and Autumn*] expressed great disapproval toward him.

Someone raising a question said: That ruler [Duke Xiang of] Zheng died and his son [Duke Dao] succeeded to the throne before a year had passed. The *Spring and Autumn* refers to [Duke Xiang's] son as the earl of Zheng and does not refer to him as a son.[32] According to the standards expressed [in the *Spring and Autumn*], what crime did he commit?

31. This is a reference to Duke Cheng 8.3.16. The entry refers only to the state of Zheng and does not mention the rank of Duke Xiang of Zheng, thereby expressing disapproval of his actions.
32. Duke Cheng 8.4.9.

The answer is: The regulations of the former kings dictate that for three years, no one must call at the gates of those who are [engaged in] the great mourning [for their parents]. This is to comply with their state of mind, which is not attuned to official duties. The *Documents* state: "Gao Zong grieved in a thatched hut and for three years did not speak a word."[33] This is an example of the righteousness of mourning. Even if [Duke Dao] were incapable of acting in this way, how could he, before [even] a year had passed since his father died, raise troops during the mourning period?! Because his gratitude [for his deceased father] was wanting and because he lacked the heart proper to a son, the *Spring and Autumn* would not again grant [Duke Dao] the designation of "son." It referred to him as "the earl of Zheng" to degrade him. Furthermore, the previous ruler, Duke Xiang, attacked [states] in mourning and defied covenants. Having committed numerous offenses against the Lords of the Land, their anger had not yet subsided, and their hatred for the state of Zheng had not yet dissipated. Having inherited his father's legacy, Duke Dao should have exerted himself to accomplish good deeds and thereby overturn [the bad legacy of his father]. But instead, he exacerbated them by attacking others without cause when he himself [should have been] in mourning [for his father].

The father attacked others while they mourned;
the son attacked others while he mourned.
The father was unrighteous toward others;
the son lacked gratitude toward his father,

thus transgressing against the Central States.
This was a case in which:

his father committed bad deeds in the past,
and he himself committed worse ones later.

Naturally, the Lords of the Land were angered and despised him. They met to discuss a united attack against the state of Zheng. Only then did [Duke Dao of] Zheng grow frightened and anxious. He abandoned Chu and convened and concluded a covenant at Gulao [with Jin, Qi, Lu, Song, and others].[34] Chu and the Central States united and attacked Zheng. Zheng was exhausted and annihilated, and Duke Dao lived out his life in misery. Tracing the outcome to the

33. Abbreviated from a passage in *Documents*, "Wu yi" 無逸 (Against Luxurious Ease) 5; Legge, *Shoo King*, 466.

34. Duke Cheng 8.5.7: "The twelfth month. *Jichou*. Our lord met with the marquis of Jin, the marquis of Qi, the duke of Song, the marquis of Wey, the earl of Zheng, the earl of Cao, the baron of Zhu, and the earl of Ji to assemble to make a covenant at Chonglao."

source, I find that he was defeated because he was unrighteous. He was like this because his heart was irreverent. Confucius said: "When guiding a state of a thousand chariots, approach your duties with reverence and be trustworthy."[35] He understood the importance of the causes of success and failure; therefore he was respectful and wary of them. Now the earl of Zheng lacked the gratitude proper to a son, and he did not make plans with care. He raised troops at an unsuitable time on one occasion, and he brought endless misery upon his state. This is something that he brought on himself. Therefore throughout his life, [the *Spring and Autumn*] does not refer to him as a "son" [to reveal how much] he had departed from righteousness. After he died, [the *Spring and Autumn*] does not record his burial, in order to reveal the fact that he was utterly lost. Thus I say: "If those who possess a state do not abandon righteousness when conducting themselves and do not disregard the times when initiating events, how could they come to such ends? [3/8/29–3/9/12]

35. *Analects* 1.5.

Book 3, Part 1

CHAPTER 4

Jade Brilliance

Section 4.1

[The *Spring and Autumn*] refers to the first [year of a ruler's reign] as the Origin [year] to emphasize the beginning.[1] To know one's intentions from the Origin is what the great person values and what the small person slights. [4/9/18]

Section 4.2

For this reason, the starting point of ordering a state lies with the rectification of names. When the rectification of names has prospered beyond five generations and five transmissions [of the *Spring and Autumn*], then good and bad will show their true form, and it can be said that the genuine nature [of good and

The title of this chapter may have drawn its inspiration from an event that was initially interpreted as an auspicious omen. "The Annals of Emperor Wen the Filial" of the *Shiji* (*SJ* 10/430) reports the following: "A man of Zhao named Xinyuan Ping, appearing before the emperor to report an unusual cloud formation he had seen, advised the emperor to set up temples to the Five Thearchs north of the Wei River. He requested that they excavate the [lost] cauldrons of Zhou which could be found where a 'jade-like brilliance' appeared" (modified from Burton Watson, trans., *Records of the Grand Historian*, rev. ed. [New York: Columbia University Press, 1993], 1:303).

1. This is a reference to the *Spring and Autumn*'s standard practice of noting the first year of each reign period with the special term "Origin year" (*yuan nian* 元年). Deviations from this usual pattern were taken to indicate a hidden judgment left by Confucius.

bad] has been grasped. This is not something that Zi Lu was able to perceive.[2] [4/9/18–19]

Section 4.3

When someone assumes the throne when it is not rightfully his, although he received it from the former ruler, the *Spring and Autumn* [considers this] perilous. Duke Mu of Song is a case in point.[3] When it is not rightfully his and he has not received it from the former ruler but, rather, has assumed it on his own

2. For the *Analects* discussion of Zi Lu and the rectification of names, see *Analects* 13.3. According to Su Yu, this thirty-six-character section of text beginning 是故 and ending 能見, which we designate as section 4.2, belongs in chapter 35. Su Yu also emends the first section of chapter 4 by moving two passages from chapters 13 and 15 to this location. The first passage, from chapter 13, states:

> Only a sage is able to link the myriad things to the One and to bind them to the Origin. If ultimately you do not reach and acknowledge the root from which [the myriad things] proceed, you cannot succeed in your endeavors. This is why the *Spring and Autumn* alters the first [year of each reign] and designates it the Origin [*yuan* 元] year. The word *yuan* is homophonous with the word *yuan* 原, [which means "source"]. It signifies that [the *Spring and Autumn*] follows the cycles [literally, ends and beginnings] of Heaven and Earth. Thus people are the only [creatures] whose lives have beginnings and ends but do not necessarily respond to the alterations of the four seasons. Therefore the Origin is the root of the myriad things, and the Origin of humans [likewise] lies therein. Where is [the Origin]? It existed before Heaven and Earth. This is why, although people are born of Heaven's vital energy and are endowed with Heaven's vital energy, it cannot [be said that] their vital energy is coextensive with the Heavenly Origin. The Heavenly Origin decrees, but people often defy Heaven's workings. Thus [an entry such as] "Spring. The [royal] first month" is meant to acknowledge the actions of Heaven and Earth and to continue the actions of Heaven and bring them to completion. The Way [of designating the Origin year] is to pair up [Heaven's decrees and human works] in mutual accomplishments and supportive enterprises. How is it that the Origin of Heaven and Earth is to be found here, and how does it operate in the human realm? [The *Spring and Autumn*] attaches much importance to those who can connect and acknowledge the inherent patterns of[Heaven's] will. (*CQFL* 13/22/13–18)

The second passage, from chapter 15, states:

> Therefore the sage alone is able to focus his attention on what is hidden and cause it to be manifest. This is why the Way of the *Spring and Autumn* is to rely on the profundity of the Origin to rectify the starting point of Heaven [i.e., the first month of the civil calendar]; to rely on the starting point of Heaven to rectify the government of the king; to rely on the government of the king to rectify the authority of the Lords of the Land; to rely on the authority of the Lords of the Land to rectify the administration within the borders [of the various states]. When these five are rectified, then [the sage-king's] transformative influence will greatly issue forth. (*CQFL* 15/23/23–25)

For the relevant commentaries, see Su Yu, *CQFLYZ* 67–71.

3. Duke Yin 1.3.7: "*Guiwei*. There was the burial (*zang* 葬) of Lord Mu of Song." *Gongyang*:

> When a burial takes place at the proper time and the day is given, this indicates that the performance of the burial was endangered. What danger was there? Duke Xuan spoke to [his younger brother who later became] Duke Mu saying: "My love for my son Yu Yi cannot match [my love for] you. Why should you not eventually become ruler?" Duke Xuan died, and Duke Mu succeeded the title. Duke Mu expelled his two sons, Bing [who later became] Duke Zhuang and Bo, who held the office of *zuo shi* 佐師. Eventually Duke Mu of Song handed over the state to Yu Yi.

accord, the *Spring and Autumn* [likewise considers this] perilous. King Liao of Wu is a case in point.[4]

However, if a ruler is able to practice goodness and win the support of the common people, the *Spring and Autumn* will not [consider this] perilous. Marquis Jin of Wey assumed the throne, and when he died, [the *Spring and Autumn*] recorded his burial [with the term *zang* reserved for a ruler]; he is a case in point.[5] In all three cases, it was improper for [these men] to succeed to the throne, but Duke Mu of Song received the throne from the former ruler and [the *Spring and Autumn*] designated it perilous, while Duke Xuan of Wey [the former marquis Jin of Wey] did not receive the throne from the former ruler, and it did not designate it perilous. From these examples, we can see that winning the hearts of the multitudes is considered the greatest security.

Now Duke Huan of Qi not only assumed the throne without receiving it from the former ruler, but he also helped another set himself up as ruler when it was not proper to do so. His crimes were weighty indeed. Nevertheless, having taken stock of his fearful anxieties, he respectfully promoted worthy men to compensate for [his crimes]. He knew that he must not defy the oaths he had sworn under compulsion to absolve himself [of his crimes]. Consequently, he became a worthy ruler and was recognized as a hegemon among the Lords of the Land. If Duke Huan of Qi had committed those bad deeds but had not carried out those good deeds, he would have been lucky to avoid being murdered. How could he have become a hegemon? Duke Huan of Lu forgot his troubles, and calamity befell him. Duke Huan of Qi worried about his troubles and established a meritorious reputation. From this, we can deduce that those who confront troubles but do not worry are unlucky but that those who confront troubles and worry deeply are lucky. The *Changes* states: "If you return

---

4. Duke Xiang 9.29.8: "The Viscount of Wu dispatched Zha to come on a friendly diplomatic mission." *Gongyang*:

   Helü said: "That the late ruler did not hand the state to his son but instead handed it to you, his younger brother, was entirely on account of you, Ji Zi. Shall we follow the instructions given by the late lord? If so, the state should properly belong to Ji Zi. Or shall we disobey the instructions of our former lord? If so, I am the one who should properly be set up as ruler." And so he sent Zhuan Zhu to kill Liao and then handed over the state to Ji Zi. Ji Zi declined the offer saying: "You assassinated my lord. If I were to receive the state as a gift from you, then I would become an accomplice in your rebellion. You killed my elder brothers. If I in turn were to kill you, then fathers and sons, elder brothers and younger brothers, would continue to kill one another in an endless sequence." Ji Zi then left Wu and went to Yanling. For the rest of his life he did not enter the state of Wu.

5. Duke Yin 1.4.7: "Winter. Men from Wey set up Jin [as their ruler]." *Gongyang*: "Why does [the *Spring and Autumn*] employ the term *li* (立, to set up)? The use of the term *li* (to set up) implies that it was not proper to set up Jin. [The *Spring and Autumn*] refers to 'men from Wey' to indicate that the multitudes set him up as ruler."

to the Way, how could you go wrong?"[6] This expresses my meaning. Although it is difficult for most people to return to the Way to eradicate wrongdoing, it is quite easy for the true ruler to do so. An *Ode* declares: "Virtue is light as a feather."[7] This describes how easy it is to do so. [4/9/21–4/10/5]

Section 4.4

"Our Lord viewed the fish at Tang."[8] What was the transgression?

[The answer is:] As a general rule, it is the nature of human beings to praise righteousness without exception. When people are unable to practice righteousness, however, it is because they are overcome by [the desire for] profit. Thus to the end of his days, the Noble Man [Confucius] did not speak of profit. He hoped that by not speaking of profit, he would shame those who did. By shaming them, he would obstruct its source. If [Confucius] expresses disdain for one who occupies the throne and arouses the great winds of moral transformation when that person even mentions the term "profit," how much more is this the case of those who seek profit. Therefore when the Heavenly King sent others to seek funds and gold, in every case [Confucius] considered them to be weighty transgressions and recorded them as such.[9] Now if one does not simply send envoys [to seek profit] but personally seeks it oneself, this is considered an even graver crime. In censoring such actions, why the expression "to view the fish?" It is analogous to the expression "to view the altar of the earth." They both are expressions that conceal grave transgressions.[10] [4/10/7–10]

6. *Changes*, hexagram 9 (*xiao chu* 小畜), first line.
7. *Odes* 260, verse 6.
8. Duke Yin 1.5.1: "Spring. Our lord viewed the fish at Tang." The *Gongyang Commentary* explains that the duke traveled a great distance to this city and, with a net, caught precious fish. The *Spring and Autumn* conceals his bad actions and states simply that he went "to view" the fish.
9. Duke Yin 1.3.4: "Autumn. The son of the Wu clan came to request funds." The *Gongyang Commentary* cites this case along with the very similar case of the earl of Mao (Duke Wen 6.9.1: "The ninth year. Spring. The earl of Mao came to request gold"), both of whom violated ritual propriety in two ways. First, each assumed his throne before a year had elapsed since the death of his father, and second, each traveled to Lu to request financial assistance (presumably to help defray expenses of the late rulers' funerals).
10. Duke Zhuang 3.23.3: "Summer. Our Lord went to Qi to view the Altar of the Earth." *Gongyang*: "Why was this recorded? It is in order to criticize. What was there to criticize? For a Lord of the Land to cross the borders [of his state] to view the Altar of the Earth violates ritual protocol."

Section 4.5

The *Spring and Autumn* records immutable rites and mutable rites.[11] Those instances in which your emotions are calm and your mind is settled are governed by immutable rites. Those instances in which your emotions are not calm and your mind is not settled, yet your Way remains unchanged, are governed by mutable rites.

For this reason, the *Spring and Autumn* does not refer to the host [i.e., bridegroom] when it records marriage ceremonies in accordance with immutable rites. But when no other wording is possible [because there is no male to whom the *Spring and Autumn* can refer], it refers to the bridegroom in accordance with mutable rites.[12]

[The *Spring and Autumn*] designates the Son of Heaven as king only after three years have passed [since the death of the former ruler], in accordance with immutable rites. But when the circumstances warrant, [the *Spring and Autumn*] designates him as king before three years have passed, in accordance with mutable rites.

The wife, having no duties beyond the border [of her state], accords with immutable rites. When a mother [crosses the border of her state] to choose a wife on behalf of her son or when a woman hastens [to cross the border] to bury her parents, this accords with mutable rites.

---

11. *Jing li* 經禮 are immutable rites, and *bian li* 變禮 are mutable rites that can be altered according to circumstance.

12. Duke Yin 1.2.5: "Ninth month. Lie Xiu of Ji came to receive a lady." *Gongyang*:

> Who was this Lie Xiu of Ji? He was a great officer of Ji. Why is he not referred to as an envoy? In the marriage ritual [the *Spring and Autumn*] does not refer to the host [i.e., the bridegroom]. To whom, then are references made? [The *Spring and Autumn*] refers to the paternal uncles, elder brothers, teachers, and friends. Why, then, is reference made to the bridegroom in the entry "The duke of Song sent Duke Xun Shou to come and present marriage gifts?" No other wording [of this entry] would have been possible. What does this imply? [The duke of Song] had no mother. [The marquis of] Ji, did he have a mother? The answer is: "he did." Since this is so, why does [the *Spring and Autumn*] not refer to his mother? The mother could not communicate [directly with the envoy]. The [*Spring and Autumn*] does not record the meeting of brides of [the Lords of the Land] of the Exterior. Why is this instance recorded? It is in order to reprimand. What was there to reprimand? [The *Spring and Autumn*] reprimands [the marquis of Ji] with unusual severity for this first recorded instance of a groom failing to meet his bride in person, on the grounds that Confucius particularly condemned those who instituted evil practices.

See also chapter 6, note 79.

Only after you have clarified which affairs exemplify immutable rites and which exemplify mutable rites will you understand the distinction between the insignificant and the significant and know [how to] weigh [and evaluate changing circumstances].

One raising an objection stated: When the *Spring and Autumn* [records] affairs that are the same, [it employs] terminology that is the same. If all four of these cases exemplify mutable rites, why does the *Spring and Autumn* record some as immutable and not record others as immutable?

[The answer is:] The *Spring and Autumn*

lays out the principles of its numerous affairs,
distinguishes its classes and categories,
differentiates the subtleties of its deceptive resemblances,
cultivates its roots and branches.

For this reason,

when stars fell, it referred to them with the term *yun*, "to fall";
when locusts swarmed, it referred to them with the term *yu*, "to rain."

The place from which each originated differed; one fell from the heavens while the other issued forth from the earth. Thus their respective terminology cannot be the same. Now all the four cases exemplify mutable rites and in this respect are identical. But those who initiated them differed; some were initiated by men and others were initiated by women. Their respective terminology cannot be identical. Thus the *Spring and Autumn* described some as immutable and others as mutable. [4/10/12–20]

Section 4.6

In the mind of Duke Huan [of Lu], there was no king;[13] therefore [the *Spring and Autumn*] did not record the term *wang*, "king."[14] In his mind, he desired the throne, therefore [the *Spring and Autumn*] recorded the expression *ji wei*,

13. Duke Huan of Lu did not recognize the authority of the Son of Heaven, so when the *Spring and Autumn* recorded the period in which he reigned, it did not use the term for king.
14. Duke Huan 2.1.2: "The third month. Our lord met with the earl of Zheng at Chui." He Xiu notes that in this entry, the *Spring and Autumn* does not use the usual terminology, "the king's third month" (*wang san yue*). The term "king" is omitted to criticize Duke Huan, who "did not recognize the king."

"to assume the throne."[15] It recorded that "he assumed the throne" to indicate that he assassinated the ruler who was his brother. It did not record the term "king" to indicate that he defied the Son of Heaven. This is why in the case of Duke Yin, [the *Spring and Autumn*] does not mention the term *li*, to be established as ruler.[16] In the case of Duke Huan, [the *Spring and Autumn*] does not mention the term *wang*, "king." It follows the intentions of Dukes Yin and Huan to reveal their undertakings. It follows the intentions of worthies to describe their righteousness; it follows the intentions of fools to manifest their wrongdoing. From this perspective, we see that what the *Spring and Autumn* praises is good and that what it does not praise is bad. You must not fail to examine both. [4/10/22–25]

15. According to the *Gongyang Commentary*, when a ruler was assassinated and a new ruler assumed the throne, it did not employ the phrase *ji wei* 即位 (to assume the throne). This terminological practice derives perhaps from the desire to express the sentiments of an heir apparent who would be reluctant to assume the throne of an assassinated father. But since Duke Huan intended to become ruler after assassinating his brother, the *Spring and Autumn* complies with his intentions and employs this phrase. Duke Huan 2.1.1: "Spring. The king's first month. Our lord assumed the throne." *Gongyang*: "The succession to the title [vacated by] an assassinated prince is not normally indicated by the phrase 'assumed the throne' [*ji wei*]. Why does [the *Spring and Autumn*] use this phrase here? [It is in order to indicate that the proceedings] were in accordance with Huan's desires." Note that the inclusion of the word "king" in this quotation from Duke Huan 2.1.1. seems to contradict without explanation the principle mentioned here in notes 13 and 14, that under some circumstances the word "king" is not used.

16. Duke Yin 1.1.1: "The Origin year. Spring. The king's first month." *Gongyang*:

> What is meant by the term "Origin year"? It is the first year of the ruler. What is meant by the term "spring"? It is the beginning of the year. To whom does the term "king" refer? It refers to King Wen. Why does [the *Spring and Autumn*] first mention the term "king" and then mention the term "first month"? It is the king's first month. Why does [the *Spring and Autumn*] use the expression "the king's first month?" It is in order to glorify the unity. Why does [the *Spring and Autumn*] not state that the duke "assumed the throne" (*jiwei*)? It is to give full expression to the duke's intention. Why so? The duke intended to pacify the state and restore it to Huan. Why restore it to Huan? Huan was the younger brother, but of nobler birth. Yin was the older, but of lower birth. The difference in their relative status was slight: of the people in the state, none knew [whom the late duke had elected as his successor.] Yin was grown up and also a worthy man. The great officers brought Yin forward and established him as ruler. If under these circumstances, Yin had rejected [their decision to] establish him as ruler, then he would have had no reassurance that Huan would be certain to be established as ruler. Furthermore, supposing that Huan were established as ruler, the great officers might have feared that they would be unable to assist so young a ruler. Therefore, that Yin allowed himself to be established as ruler was, for all intents and purposes, for the sake of Huan. Since Yin was grown up and a worthy man besides, why was it not proper for him to be established as ruler? The establishment of sons of the principal wife is based on seniority and not on considerations of worth; the establishment of sons [other than the sons of the principal wife] is based on nobility and not on seniority. In what respect was Huan nobler [than Yin]? His mother was nobler [than the mother of Yin]. Why should the fact that the mother was nobler make the son nobler? A son shares the nobility of his mother and a mother shares the nobility of her son. (Adapted from Göran Malmqvist, "Studies on the *Gongyang* and *Guliang* Commentaries," *Bulletin of the Museum of Far Eastern Antiquities* 43 [1971]: 69)

Section 4.7

The *Classic* states: "Du of Song assassinated his ruler Yu Yi."[17] The *Commentary* states that Ping, Duke Zhuang of Song, murdered him.[18] Why is it not possible to find this in the Classic itself?

The answer is: It is not the case that it does not appear in the Classic. Its appearance is subtle, and it is not sufficient to rely on other events that belong to the same category to grasp it. Consequently it is difficult to comprehend. The *Commentary* states: "Cang Sunxu and Xi Ke of Jin paid a courtesy visit to Qi on

17. Duke Huan 2.2.1: "Spring, The king's first month. *Wushen*. Du of Song assassinated his ruler, Yu Yi, and his great officer, Kongfu." *Gongyang*:

> What is implied by the term *ji* (meaning "and")? [It signifies that Kongfu] was implicated [and died for his lord]. [The *Spring and Autumn* records] many instances of regicide. Apart from this [Kongfu] were there no others who died for their lord? The answer is: there were [others]. If so, why was an entry made [only] in this case? [Kongfu] was worthy. In what respect was Kongfu worthy? Of Kongfu, it may be said that his righteousness was manifested in his outward appearance. Under what circumstances did his righteousness manifest itself in his appearance? Du was about to assassinate duke Shang (Yu Yi). As long as Kongfu remained alive, there would be no opportunity to assassinate Duke Shang. Therefore [Du] consequently first attacked Kongfu's residence. Duke Shang knew that once Kongfu were dead, he himself would have to die and therefore hurried to his rescue. Both died there. When Kongfu adjusted his appearance and took up his position in the court, no one dared to commit any fault or cause distress to his lord. Of Kongfu, it may be said that his righteousness manifested itself in his outward appearance. (Adapted from Malmqvist, "Studies on the *Gongyang* and *Guliang* Commentaries," 96)

18. Duke Yin 1.3.7: "*Guiwei*. They buried Lord Mu of Song." *Gongyang*:

> Why does [the *Spring and Autumn*] sometimes give and sometimes omit the day of the burial? In the case of a premature burial [i.e., a burial before the ritually correct amount of time had elapsed], the day is given to indicate that it was a hasty burial, while the omission of the day indicates that it was a negligent burial. In the case of burials that took place too late, the day is given to commiserate with him [i.e., the deceased], while the omission of the day indicates that it was impossible to perform the burial [within the stipulated period]. When a burial took place at the stipulated time, the omission of the day is the correct norm. When in such cases the day is given, this indicates that the performance of the burial was endangered. This [burial] took place at the stipulated time. What danger was there? Duke Xian [on one occasion] spoke to [his younger brother, who later became] Duke Mu, saying: "My love for [my son] Yu Yi is not as great as my love for you. Considering [the selection of my successor] head of the state and the ancestral temple, Yu Yi cannot match you. Why should you not eventually become ruler?" Duke Xian died, and Duke Mu succeeded to the title. Duke Mu expelled his two sons, Ping [who later became] Duke Zhuang, and Bo, who held the office of historian on the left, saying: "You are my sons, [but] we shall not meet again in life, nor shall we cry over each other in death." Yu Yi reported and said: "The reason why the late lord did not give the state to me but handed it to you, sir, was that he considered you more suited to be the head of the state and of the ancestral temple. Now you expel your two sons and intend to hand over the state to me, Yu Yi. This was not the intention of the late lord. If sons may indeed be expelled, then the late lord would have expelled me!" Duke Mu said: "It is indeed obvious that the late lord did not [intend to] expel you. My position here is that of a deputy." Eventually he handed over the state to Yu Yi. Ping [who later became] Duke Zhuang assassinated Yu Yi. Therefore, the Noble Man considered it [of] great [importance] that one conforms to the correct norm. It was Duke Xuan who caused the calamity in Song. (Adapted from Malmqvist, "Studies on the *Gongyang* and *Guliang* Commentaries," 77)

the same occasion."[19] But if you examine the *Classic*, there is no such record. This is subtle indeed! The *Spring and Autumn* does not record their expedition to conceal it. Similarly, the *Commentary* records Ping, Duke Zhuang of Song, but the *Classic* does not. By not recording the courtesy visit to Qi, [Confucius] concealed what caused him shame. By not recording that Duke Zhuang assassinated Yu Yi, [Confucius] concealed what he praised. Therefore, those who yield the throne are those who are praised by the *Spring and Autumn*. Duke Xuan of Song did not transmit the authority to rule to his son but gave it to his younger brother. Likewise, his younger brother did not give it to his son but returned it to his older brother's son. Although they did not hit the mark of this standard, in each case they yielded to the lofty; therefore [Confucius] could not reject them. The Noble Man [Confucius] concealed later instances of rebellion because of this. Thus when Duke Zhuang was assassinated, he implicated Du of Song, to preserve the praiseworthy intentions [of Duke Xuan and Duke Mu]. Here the *Spring and Autumn* also praised the good without exception.[20] If the

---

19. Duke Cheng 8.2.4: "Autumn. The marquis of Qi dispatched Guo Zuo to go to the troops. *Jiyou*. We made a covenant with Guo Zuo at Yuanlou." *Gongyang*:

On the day *jiyou*, they made a covenant with Guo Zuo at Yuanlou. Why did they not make a covenant with the army present, but at Yuanlou? On an earlier occasion Xi Ke and Zangsun Xu of Jin simultaneously had paid courtesy visits to Qi. Xiao Tong Zhizi (the daughter of Tongshu, lord of the state of Xiao), and the mother of the marquis of Qi [Lord Qing of Qi], climbed a ladder to spy on the guests, and found that one was lame and the other shortsighted. Then she made a lame man receive the lame guest and a shortsighted man receive the shortsighted guest. When the two great officers emerged from the court, they stood leaning on the gate and talked together. A long time passed before they finally took leave of each other. The people of Qi all said: "When the trouble starts, it is bound to be due to this!"

The two great officers returned to Jin. Together they led their armies and fought at the Battle of An, where the Qi army suffered a heavy defeat. When the marquis of Qi sent Guo Zuo to enter the army of the allied troops as an envoy, Xi Ke demanded: "Give us the Yan Vessel which formerly belonged to the marquis of Ji. Return the land that Qi has taken from Lu and Wey. Order the farmers to draw the field divisions from east to west! We must take the daughter of Tongshu of Xiao as hostage. Grant these demands and I shall let you go!"

Guo Zuo replied: "As to your request for the Xian Vessel, which formerly belonged to the marquis of Ji, I will agree. As to your request for the return of the land which we have taken from Lu and Wey, I also beg to agree. But to order our farmers to make the field divisions run east to west, that amounts to giving you the land of Qi. This daughter of Tongshu, lord of Xiao, is the mother of the lord of Qi! The mother of the lord of Qi is equal to the mother of the lord of Jin. I cannot agree to these two requests. I request leave to fight. If we are not victorious in the first battle, I request permission to fight a second battle. If we are not victorious in the second battle, I request permission to fight a third battle. If we are not victorious in the third battle, then the entire state of Qi shall belong to you. Why is it necessary to take the daughter of Tongshu of Xiao as your hostage?" [Guo Zuo] saluted twice and left him.

Xi Ke winked at the envoys from Lu and Wey. The envoys made a request on behalf of Guo Zuo, basing themselves on his statement. Thereafter Xi Ke agreed to this proposal. He caught up with Guo Zuo at Yuanlou and made a covenant with him there. (Adapted from Malmqvist, "Studies on the *Gongyang* and *Guliang* Commentaries," 192)

20. Emending *yi shan* 義善 to *shan shan* 善善, following Lai, *CQFLJZJY* 63, note 10.

Spring and Autumn had recorded simply that Duke Zhuang of Song usurped the position of rulership, then the loftiness of Duke Xuan and Duke Mu would have been destroyed, and no one would see their goodness.

Someone raising an objection stated: Why is it that when the *Spring and Autumn* conceals [bad deeds] committed by worthies, the *Commentary* discusses it, but when it conceals the deeds of Duke Xuan and Duke Mu, the *Commentary* does not discuss it?

The answer is: Duke Xuan and Duke Mu cannot be considered worthies. They accomplished good deeds, but they did not comply with the standard. Therefore they cannot be emulated, yet they cannot be rejected, either. If you reject them, then you have rejected their good intentions. If you emulate them, then you will harm the standards set down by the king. Therefore the *Spring and Autumn* neither rejects them nor records them. It reveals them through their intentions. Confucius said: If you set your will on humaneness, you will be free from wrong." This expresses my meaning. [4/10/27–4/11/6]

Section 4.8

[In referring to] vessels, [the *Spring and Autumn*] follows the name [of the original owner]. [In referring to] land, [it] follows [the name of the current] owner.[21] These are designated regulations, but the starting point of expediency also lies within. This must be examined.

Now although expediency runs contrary to the constant norms, it necessarily falls within the realm of acceptability. If it did not fall within the realm of acceptability, then if one were about to die or ultimately perish, he would not act. The duke's son Muyi exemplifies this principle. Therefore, when fathers, sons, older brothers, or younger brothers among the Lords of

21. Duke Huan 2.2.4: "Summer. The tenth month. We seized the great tripod of Gao at Song." *Gongyang*:

> Here [it is stated that] he took it from Song. Why, then, is it referred to as "the tripod of Gao"? [In referring to] vessels [one] follows the name [of the original owner]. [In referring to] land [one] follows the [name of the current] owner. [Why is this so?] Song first took possession of this tripod of Gao through an unrighteous deed. Therefore it was referred to as "the tripod of Gao." When it comes to land being given to someone, then it is not so. Ownership of land can be established in a single instant [by the act of taking the land in possession]. If so, may then the [act of] taking possession [of the land] be regarded as [equivalent to the establishment of full] ownership [of the land]? The answer is no. And why? [This is] like the king of Chu marrying his younger sister: at no time can such an act be allowed. (Adapted from Malmqvist, "Studies on the *Gongyang* and *Guliang* Commentaries," 97)

the Land assumed rulership when it was not proper to do so, the *Spring and Autumn* treated their states as if they were no different from states led by legitimate rulers.[22] Such states existed within the realm of acceptability. When, however, the ruler of Zheng took a wife from Ying and held that her grandson was to inherit the throne,[23] [the *Spring and Autumn*] stated: "A man from Ying annihilated Zheng."[24] For this did not fall within the realm of acceptability. Therefore when the Lords of the Land operated within the realm of unacceptability, [Confucius] referred to this as [a matter involving] "great virtue." Those possessing great virtue who did not overstep the bounds, [Confucius] designated "upright and normative." When the Lords of the Land operated within the realm of acceptability, [Confucius] referred to this as [a matter of] "small virtue." "Small virtue" means it is permissible to "come and go" [i.e., be less meticulous].[25] [The principle of] expedient adjustment to circumstance involves deception, but ultimately it supports the great norms. Therefore, the principles of the *Spring and Autumn* are extensive yet synoptic; they are detailed yet they revert back to a unified [ethical path].

Prince Mu Yi [of Song] submitted to his ruler's commands but ultimately did not turn over the state of Song [to Chu].[26] Zhai Zhong [of Zheng] already had turned his state over to [Du] but later transferred it [to Hu].[27] To his death,

22. Literally this reads "rulers who were properly established on the throne."
23. Emending *tong ju* 同居 to *sijun* 司君 and reading 司 as 嗣, following Yu Yue (Lai, *CQFLJZJY* 66, note 6).
24. Duke Xiang 9.6.5: "A man from Ying annihilated Zheng." The *Gongyang Commentary* does not comment. As the story goes, the ruler of Zheng selected a woman from the state of Ying to be his wife. He loved her dearly, but she bore him only a daughter. The daughter returned to the state of Ying when she married and subsequently bore a son. When the ruler of Zheng established his daughter's son on the throne, his legitimate heir fled to the state of Jin. Establishing as an heir the son of a daughter who has a different surname is the same as if the state had been destroyed, so the *Spring and Autumn* recorded that "a man from Ying annihilated Zheng."
25. *Analects* 19.11: "The Master said, '[In matters involving] great virtue, one must not overstep the bounds. [In matters involving] small virtue, it is permissible to come and go.'"
26. The *Gongyang Commentary* at Duke Xi 5.21.6 explains that the duke of Song and the viscount of Chu had agreed on an unarmed meeting. Prince Mu Yi, however, urged the duke of Song to prepare himself for an armed meeting because the ruler of Chu could not be trusted. Having already agreed to an unarmed meeting, the duke of Song vowed to take ultimate responsibility for what followed. When the duke went to the meeting, he was taken captive by Chu and held hostage. Consequently, the duke recognized Mu Yi as the de facto ruler and urged him to return and guard the state of Song. Seeing that the Song state already had a new ruler, even though the duke of Song was being held hostage, Chu released the duke of Song. The duke of Song proceeded to the state of Wey. Prince Mu Yi sought him out and reported that he had guarded the state for the sake of Duke Xiang. Thereafter he escorted him back to Song to reinstall him as the ruler.
27. Duke Huan 2.11.4: "The ninth month. A man from Song seized Zhai Zhong of Zheng." For the story of Zhai Zhong, see chapter 3, note 26.

Xun Xi of Jin would not heed the advice of [Li Ke].[28] Man Gu of Wey resisted [Kuai Kui] and would not allow him to return to [the state of Wey].[29] The actions of these four ministers differed, but their intentions were identical. Their righteousness was one. Mu Yi did not give away the state in order to preserve the ancestral temples, but Zhai Zhong gave away the state, likewise to preserve the ancestral temples. Xun Xi died to honor the commands of his former lord, and likewise Man Gu resisted [Kuai Kui] to honor the commands of his former lord. Although their actions opposed each other, what they accomplished was identical. Both Mu Yi and Zhai Zhong preserved the ancestral temples of their states, and both Xun Xi and Man Gu honored the commands of their former lords.

Someone raising an objection said: The actions of Prince Mu Yi and Zhai Zhong preserved [the state] and served the ruler. It therefore is permissible to praise them. Xun Xi and Man Gu, however, did not act in this way. Moreover, both those whom they wanted to support were men who should not have assumed the position of rulership. Why were they recorded as being righteous?

[The answer is:] It is a method of the *Spring and Autumn* not to record the accession of those who assume rulership when it is not proper for them to do so. When the great officers of a state supported them to become ruler, it recorded their accession. The *Spring and Autumn* recorded the accession because it did not approve of those great officers who supported illegitimate rulers; it did not record the accession because it approved of those who were able to become

---

28. Duke Xi 5.10.4: "Li Ke of Jin assassinated his ruler Zhaozi and his great officer Xun Xi." The *Gongyang* explains that Lord Xian of Jin, infatuated with his favorite consort Li Ji, murdered Shen Sheng, the son of his senior consort and therefore the legitimate heir, in order to secure the succession for Li Ji's son, Xi Qi. Although the great officer Xun Xi disapproved of these actions, he acceded to the dying Lord Xian's request to promote Xi Qi's succession. When another great officer, Li Ke, attempted to restore the legitimate line of succession, Xun Xi felt bound by his promise to the late ruler and refused to join in Li Ke's plot. Li Ke then instigated the murder of both the illegitimate ruler Xi Qi and his successor Zhaozi, as well as his loyal officer Xun Xi. Xun Xi is praised for his steadfast loyalty to Lord Xian despite the dubious status of the lord's successors.

29. Duke Ai 12.3.1: "In the third year, in spring, Guo Xia of Qi and Dan Man Gu of Wey led troops to besiege Qii." The *Gongyang* elaborates:

> Why did Guo Xia of Qi and [Dan] Man Gu of Wey lead troops to besiege Qii? It was a punitive expedition [to intervene in the succession of the rulers of Qii]. Why, in this instance, does [the *Spring and Autumn*] judge it to be a punitive expedition? [Dan] Man Gu [of Wey] received a command from Duke Ling [of Wey] to install Zhe. Relying on the resoluteness of Man Gu's sense of righteousness, [Duke Ling] was able to oppose [the state of Qii]. Who was this Zhe? He was the son of Kuai Kui. Why did Duke Ling not install Kuai Kui but installed Zhe? Kuai Kui acted contrary to the Way, so Duke Ling expelled Kuai Kui and installed [his son] Zhe. Then based on Zhe's righteousness, was it permissible to install him as ruler? The answer is: It was permissible. Why was it permissible? [The principle is:] Do not on account of your own father's commands shirk your kingly father's commands, and do not on account of your kingly father's commands shirk your own father's commands. The [commands] of the father devolve to the son. Do not, on account of family obligations, neglect the obligations to your ruler; do not, on account of the obligations to your ruler, neglect your family obligations. [Thus in all cases, the obligations] of the superior devolve to the subordinate.

rulers. Those who became rulers when it was not appropriate to do so were not correct. But if they became rulers and were embraced by the great officers, then the *Spring and Autumn* considered them to be correct. This is why the actions of Xun Xi and Man Gu were considered righteous. [4/11/8–21]

Section 4.9

Someone raised an objection concerning Ji of Ji, saying: "The standards of the *Spring and Autumn* dictate that great officers are not permitted to distribute land without the authorization of their lords."[30] He also said: "There is the righteous principle that the sons of lords do not flee their states."[31] He also said: "A noble man does not avoid difficulties that come from abroad."[32] Ji of Ji defied all three of these standards. How can he be considered worthy? A worthy minister would certainly not steal land and hand it over to the enemy; nor would he abandon his lord to avoid difficulties!

[The answer is:] A worthy would not do such things. For this reason, the *Spring and Autumn* makes a pretext of praising Ji of Ji to reveal that he would not act in such a way. Because Ji of Ji would not act in such a way, it is possible to discover that the marquis of Ji ordered him to take such actions. When the *Spring and Autumn* records events, it sometimes distorts the facts to avoid mentioning certain events. When the *Spring and Autumn* records people, it sometimes alters

30. Emending *yong di* 用地 to *zhuan di* 專地, following Lai, *CQFLJZJY* 82. Duke Zhuang 3.3.4: "Autumn. The third brother of [the marquis of] Ji, relying on [the territory of] Shi, entered into Qi." *Gongyang*:

> Who was this third brother of [the marquis] of Ji? The younger brother of the Yi of Ji. Why is he not referred to by his personal name? He was worthy. In what respect was he worthy? He took the penalty upon himself. Under what circumstances did he do so? Master Lu says: "He asked permission to perpetuate the five halls of the ancestral temple in order to preserve [the offerings for his] elder and younger sisters and paternal aunts." (Adapted from Malmqvist, "Studies on the *Gongyang* and *Guliang* Commentaries," 121)

He Xiu:

> The feud between Ji and Qi was unequally balanced, since Qi was great and Ji small. [The ruler of] Ji knew that [his state] was bound to be lost. Therefore he pledged [the city of] Shi and took on himself the guilt that his forefather had attracted vis-à-vis Qi [see Zhuang 4.4]. He asked permission to be the perpetuator of the five halls of the ancestral temple, wishing to sue [the city of] Shi to provide for the sacrifices whereby he would preserve his elder and younger sisters and paternal aunts. (Adapted from Malmqvist, "Studies on the *Gongyang* and *Guliang* Commentaries," 150)

31. Duke Xiang 9.29.8. The *Gongyang* illuminates this passage with a long and complex anecdote, whose gist is that the throne of Wu had become vacant because Ji Zi's cousi n, Helü, had assassinated the previous ruler in order to promote Ji Zi's succession. Although he had a legitimate claim to the throne, Ji Zi fled the state rather than succeed to the throne under those circumstances. See also note 4.

32. The *Gongyang Commentary* at Duke Zhuang 3.27.3 notes: "A noble man avoids internal difficulties. He does not avoid external difficulties."

their names to conceal their identities. Therefore it distorted the fact that Duke Wen of Jin realized his ambitions [when he summoned the Son of Heaven to a meeting with the other Lords of the Land] by recording "[The Son of Heaven went on] a hunt [north of the river]" to conceal this fact and to avoid mentioning that the king was summoned by his subject Duke Wen.[33] It distorted the rank of the viscount of Ying and referred to him as a commoner to avoid mentioning Duke Yin. It altered the name of Jing Fu and referred to him as Zhong Sun. It changed the name of the state called Sheng to [the city of] Cheng to avoid mentioning a great wrong.[34] Thus those who discuss the *Spring and Autumn* must master these terms that distort the facts and follow their twists and turns. Only then will they comprehend the events that it records. Now Ji of Ji received a command from his lord, but the *Classic* records that he "usurped the authority of his ruler" [and returned lands to Qi]. He lacked a reputation, but the words of the *Spring and Autumn*, [by not referring to him by name,] reveal him to be a worthy. These are examples of records that distort the facts. They must be examined. The *Spring and Autumn* invariably follows the intentions of those it wants to praise as worthy and unifies the terminology describing them to reveal their righteousness and praise their inner beauty. The marquis of Ji was a ruler whom the *Spring and Autumn* admired and respected. Thus when the *Spring and Autumn* judged his intentions to enter the state of Ji, it concealed the expressions indicating that he admitted his guilt and transferred them to Ji of Ji. Therefore, the one who sought to buy grain from the state of Qi was Duke Zhuang of Lu, but the *Spring and Autumn* uses terms to conceal this fact and states that it was Cang Sun Chen. The one who returned the city of Xi to the state of Qi was the marquis of Ji, but the *Spring and Autumn* uses terms to conceal this fact and states that it was Ji of Ji. Although the means by which it distorts the facts differ, the method of concealment is the same.

33. Emending the character *dai* 代 to *shou* 狩, following Lai, *CQFLJZJY* 82. In the twenty-eighth year of Duke Xi, Duke Wen of Jin "realized his ambitions" when he summoned the Son of Heaven to an assembly of the Lords of the Land north of the Yellow River and the king complied. For a subject to summon his ruler to an assembly did not accord with the rites. The *Spring and Autumn* concealed the truth of the matter and stated simply: "The Son of Heaven went on a hunt north of the [Yellow] River." Duke Xi 5.28.16: "The Heavenly King hunted at Heyang." *Gongyang*: "[The *Spring and Autumn*] does not normally record hunts, why in this instance does it do so? It does not condone the fact [that the duke] again summoned the Son of Heaven. Master Lu said: '[He was] mild to those nearby but trampled on distant lands.'"

34. It was a serious crime to attack blood relatives. Duke Zhuang 3.8.3: "Summer. Our troops, together with Qi troops, surrounded Cheng. Cheng fell to the Qi troops." *Gongyang*: "What was this Cheng? [It was the state of] Sheng. If so, why does [the Spring and Autumn] refer to it as Cheng? It is in order to conceal the fact that [we] extinguished [a state whose ruler had] the same clan name [as our ruler]" (adapted from Malmqvist, "Studies on the *Gongyang* and *Guliang* Commentaries," 127).

Someone raising an objection stated: If there is someone in a state whom the people wish to install [as ruler], he should strenuously decline and not listen to them. But if the state is perishing and the ruler dies [trying to save it], the *Spring and Autumn* considers this to be upright. Why, then, was the marquis of Ji considered worthy?

[The answer is:] The ruler of Qi was about to avenge a [long-standing] grievance [between the two states of Qi and Ji]. The marquis of Ji knew that he could not match the strength of Qi, but it was his intention to resist Qi. Thus he said to his younger brother [Ji of Ji]: "I preside over the ceremonies in the ancestral temple. If I am unable to avoid death, you must go to the city of Xi, admit your guilt to the ruler of Qi, and request that you be allowed to perpetuate the five halls of the ancestral temple so that our ancestors will be sure to receive their yearly offerings." Thereupon he led the people of his state into battle to defend the nine generations of Ji rulers [that had preceded him]. Duke Xiang of Qi tried to drive him out of the state of Ji, but the marquis of Ji would not flee. He implored him to return the city of Xi, but the marquis of Ji would not give up the city. Superior and inferior were of the same mind, and they died together. This is why the *Spring and Autumn* refers to "a grand exodus."[35] The *Spring and Autumn* deems worthy those who die for righteous causes and those who win the hearts of the populace. Therefore, by avoiding mention of it, it conceals the fact that the state of Ji was extinguished. Because it conceals this fact, it is possible to discover that it deemed the marquis of Ji worthy.[36] Because it deems the marquis of Ji worthy, it is possible to discover that his conduct hit the mark of humaneness and righteousness. [4/11/23–4/12/9]

35. Duke Zhuang 3.4.4: "The marquis of Ji made a grand exodus from his state."

36. The discussion follows the *Guliang*, not the *Gongyang Commentary*. The *Gongyang Commentary* maintains that the *Spring and Autumn* conceals the extinction of the Ji state, not for the sake of the marquis of Ji, but for the sake of the worthy Duke Xiang of Qi. It states:

> What is implied by the expression "grand exodus" (*da qu* 大去)? The Ji state was extinguished. Who extinguished it? The Qi state did. Why is this not stated? It is not stated to conceal the affair for the sake of Duke Xiang. [The *Spring and Autumn*] conceals [bad deeds] for the sake of the worthy. In what respect was Duke Xiang worthy? He acted in revenge. What was there to revenge? It was [the death of] a distant ancestor. Duke Ai was boiled to death in Zhou." The *Guliang Commentary* maintains that the *Spring and Autumn* concealed the extinction of the Ji state for the sake of the worthy marquis of Ji: The marquis of Ji was worthy and yet the marquis of Qi extinguished him. (Adapted from Malmqvist, "Studies on the *Gongyang* and *Guliang* Commentaries," 122)

Book 3, Part 2

CHAPTER 5

The Quintessential and the Ornamental

Section 5.1

The *Spring and Autumn* uses language cautiously. It is careful of how it designates human relationships and how it ranks the events [that it records].

For this reason, [when referencing] the Lesser Yi people, it says "to attack" but does not permit saying "to do battle." [When referencing] the Greater Yi people, it says "to do battle" but does not permit saying "to capture." [When referencing] the Central States, it says "to capture" but does not permit saying "to detain."[1] Each case has its respective terminology. [When referencing] the Lesser Yi, [the *Spring and Autumn*] avoids [terminology relevant to] the Greater Yi people and does not permit the term "to do battle." [When referencing] the Greater Yi people, the *Spring and Autumn* avoids [terminology relevant to] the Central States and does not permit the term "to detain."[2] [When referencing] the Central States, [the *Spring and Autumn*] avoids [terminology relevant to] the Son of Heaven and does not permit the term "to detain." In designating [categories of] human relationships, [the *Spring and Autumn*] prohibits conferring [inappropriate designations] and rejects terminology that

1. This is why in discussions of the Lesser Yi peoples, it uses the term *fa* 伐 (attack) but does not permit the term *zhan* 戰 (do battle). In discussions of the Greater Yi peoples, it uses the term *zhan* 戰 but does not permit the term *huo* 獲 (capture). In discussions of the Central States, it uses the term *huo* 獲 but does not permit the term *zhi* 執 (detain).

2. Duke Zhuang 3.10.5: "Autumn. The ninth month. Jing [Chu] defeated Cai troops at Shen. They went back with the marquis of Cai, Xianwu." *Gongyang*: "Why is it not stated that he was captured? [The *Spring and Autumn*] does not grant the Di and Yi peoples the right to capture [a ruler] of the Central States."

equates [rulers and] ministers. For this reason, when the great and the small do not exceed their rank and the eminent and humble follow [the moral obligations binding] their [respective] human relationships, this is the perfection of righteousness.[3] [5/12/13–16]

Section 5.2

What was the grand rain-seeking sacrifice? [It was] a drought sacrifice.[4]

Someone raising an objection stated: When there was a great drought, the rain-seeking sacrifice was performed to implore Heaven to send down rain. When there was a great flood, the drums were beaten to intimidate the [spirit of] the altar of the earth. The operations of Heaven and Earth arise from the yin and yang energies. Why is it that sometimes [the spirits were] supplicated while other times they were [intentionally] intimidated?

The answer is: When there is a serious drought, yang obliterates yin. When yang obliterates yin, [this] corresponds to the lofty restraining the lowly. This certainly is righteous. Thus even if the drought is quite severe, you pray and implore Heaven to send down rain and nothing more. Who would dare to do more?[5] A great flood is due to yin's obliterating yang. When yin obliterates yang, the lowly prevails over the lofty. Solar eclipses also are like this. Both are instances of the inferior defying the superior. Using the ignoble to injure the noble is to contravene proper regulations. Therefore the drums are beaten and [the spirit of the altar of the earth] is assaulted. It is coerced [by being bound with] with a vermilion silken cord because it lacked righteousness.[6] This also is

3. Emending *zheng* 正 to *zhi* 至.

4. Duke Huan 2.5.7: "We performed the Great Rain-seeking Sacrifice." *Gongyang*:

> What was the Great Rain-Seeking Sacrifice? [It was a] drought sacrifice. If so, why does [the *Spring and Autumn*] not mention the drought? When [the *Spring and Autumn*] mentions the Rain-Seeking Sacrifice, a drought may be inferred. When it mentions a drought, the Rain-Seeking Sacrifice may not be inferred. Why was [this entry] written? It was in order to record a calamity.

5. The recommendation to do nothing more than pray to Heaven when drought occurs contrasts markedly with the instructions for active intervention described in chapter 74, "Seeking Rain."

6. Duke Zhuang 3.25.3: "The sixth month. *Xinwei*. The first day of the month. The sun was eclipsed. We drummed and offered sacrificial animals at the altar of the earth." *Gongyang*: "One surrounded the altar of the earth with a red cord. Some say [that this was done] to coerce yin. Others say that because of the darkness, one feared lest people might violate the altar and that one therefore surrounded it [with a cord]." He Xiu comments: "The red cord was used on behalf of the altar of the earth to help aid yang suppress yin. Others say that it was to intimidate the altar of the earth" (Su Yu, *CQFLYZ* 87).

[an example of the idea expressed in the] *Spring and Autumn* that one does not fear a powerful opponent.[7] Therefore,

to distinguish clearly the proper positions of Heaven and Earth,

to rectify the proper sequences of yin and yang,

and in an upright manner instantiate this Way without fearing whatever difficulties may come your way; this is the perfection of righteousness. For this reason,

to threaten and assault the altar of the earth does not necessarily mean that one has failed to respect the spirits;

to drive out the Heavenly King does not necessarily mean that one has failed to respect a superior;[8]

to resist the commands of one's father does not necessarily mean that one has failed to serve one's father;

to cut off relations with one's mother does not necessarily mean that one has failed to be filial and generous.[9]

They are righteous as well. [5/12/18–25]

7. The saying derives from the narrative preserved in the *Gongyang Commentary* at Duke Zhuang 3.12.3, which commemorates the worthy Qiu Mu, who is killed when he fearlessly attempts to punish his lord's assassin, Wan of Song. The narrative concludes: "Of Qiu Mu it may be said that he did not fear a powerful opponent."

8. Duke Xi 5.24.4: "Winter. The Heavenly King left and resided in Zheng." *Gongyang*: "For the king there is no Exterior. How is it that here [the *Spring and Autumn*] speaks of 'leaving'? He was unable to care properly for his mother."

9. Duke Zhuang 3.1.2: "The third month. Our lady withdrew to Qi." *Gongyang*:

> What was implied by the term *sun* (孫, grandson)? "Sun" is the same as *sun* (孫 + radical 162; to withdraw). "Sun" is used of the Interior in order to conceal [the fact that she] fled. Our lady was definitely already in Qi. Why, then, does [the *Spring and Autumn*] state that she withdrew to Qi? [Duke Zhuang] thought of his mother. By entering the first month, [the *Spring and Autumn*] represents the ruler as present. The first event [recorded in the section of the *Spring and Autumn* relating to duke Zhuang] reveals his thoughts of his mother. Why is the spouse not referred to as lady Jiang? It is in order to degrade her. Why degrade her? She participated in the assassination of the duke. Under what circumstances did she do so? The spouse slandered the duke before the marquis of Ji, alleging that the duke had said: "Tong is not my son, but the son of the marquis of Ji." The marquis of Ji became angry. [On one occasion when] the marquis of Ji drank wine with him, he ordered Prince Pengsheng to escort him when he left. When he was about to mount his carriage, [Pengsheng] broke his backbone and thereby killed him. To think of one's mother is something of which [the *Spring and Autumn*] approves. Why does [the *Spring and Autumn*] degrade [her in this context in which Duke Zhuang is said to] think of his mother? [Under the circumstances,] [the *Spring and Autumn*] does not allow [Duke Zhuang] to think of his mother. (Adapted from Göran Malmqvist, "Studies on the *Gongyang* and *Guliang* Commentaries," *Bulletin of the Museum of Far Eastern Antiquities* 43 [1971]: 117)

Section 5.3

Someone raising an objection said: It is a standard of the *Spring and Autumn* that "a great officer has no [authority] to initiate an undertaking."[10] [But] it states [elsewhere]: "If on a journey abroad, it is possible to benefit one's state, then it is permissible [for a great officer] to act without authorization."[11] It also states [elsewhere]: "It was on account of his lord's order that he left [the state of Jin to attack Qi], but whether to advance or retreat lies within the jurisdiction of a great officer."[12] And it further states: "When a great officer hears of a parent's death while traveling abroad for one's lord, he proceeds slowly and does not return [hastily]."[13] Now the *Spring and Autumn* states: "[A great officer] has no [authority] to initiate an undertaking," but it also states: "It is permissible for [a great officer] to act without authorization." It states: "Whether to advance or retreat lies within the jurisdiction of the great officer," but elsewhere it states: "[A great officer] proceeds slowly and does not return [hastily]." It appears that these statements contradict each other. What is their meaning?

The answer is: Each one of these four principles applies to a particular circumstance. If you grasp the particular circumstance pertinent to each principle, then

10. The term *sui shi* 隨事 appears at Duke Huan 2.8.6: "The duke of Zhai came [to Lu and from there he] proceeded to meet the [future] queen in Ji." *Gongyang*:

> What is implied by the term *sui*? It means to initiate an undertaking (*sheng shi* 生事). Since a great officer has no [authority] to initiate an undertaking, why does [the *Spring and Autumn*] use the term *sui*? [He] completed his mission with our assistance. Under what circumstances did he do so? [The Son of Heaven had instructed him] to make the state of Lu serve as a go-between. If this could be, he would subsequently, and in accordance with [our mediation,] go forward and meet the bride [in Ji].

He Xiu states that *sheng* means "to initiate." It is an expression meaning "to take sole charge of a matter" (adapted from Malmqvist, "Studies on the *Gongyang* and *Guliang* Commentaries," 104). Lai Yanyuan (*CQFLJZJY* 75, note 1) states that *sui shi* means to engage in one undertaking as a consequence of another undertaking.

11. This dictum appears in the *Gongyang Commentary* at Duke Zhuang 3.19.3.

12. Duke Xiang 9.19.9: "Shi Gai of Jin led a force and invaded Qi. When he had arrived at Gu, he heard of the death of the marquis of Qi and returned." *Gongyang*:

> Why does the *Spring and Autumn* record that he returned? It is terminology that indicates praise. Why is he praised? In order to glorify the fact that he did not conduct a punitive attack during a time of mourning. This was a case of receiving orders from the ruler to conduct a punitive attack on Qi. Why, then, does [the *Spring and Autumn*] glorify the fact that he did not conduct a punitive attack? It was on account of his lord's order that he left [the state of Jin to attack Qi], but whether to advance or retreat lies within the jurisdiction of a great officer.

13. Duke Xuan 7.8.2: "Summer. The sixth month. Duke [Zhuang's] son, Sui, went to Qi. Only after he arrived at Huang did he return." *Gongyang*: "Why does [the *Spring and Autumn*] state that only after he arrived at Huang did he return? He proceeded hastily. Why indicate that he returned with haste? In order to criticize him. Why criticize him? When a great officer hears of a parent's death while traveling abroad for one's lord, he proceeds slowly but does not return [hastily]."

they all will be correct. If you lose sight of the particular circumstances of each event, then they all will be incorrect. The *Spring and Autumn* certainly possesses constant principles of righteousness. But there also are [righteous principles] adapted to changing circumstances. To "have no authority to initiate an undertaking" refers to ordinary times of peace and security. "It is permissible to act without authorization" refers to times of relieving danger and eradicating harm. "Whether to advance or retreat lies within the jurisdiction of a great officer" refers to [times when a great officer] leads an army and employs officers. "A great officer proceeds slowly and does not return [hastily]" refers to not harming the honorable on account of one's relatives and not opposing the public good because of private interests.[14] This is to say, when [a great officer] is about to achieve his personal aims, he is mindful of these precepts. Therefore, when [the great officer] Gongzi Jie received orders to accompany the wife of a man from Chen to Zheng and he initiated an undertaking while on the road by following Duke Huan of Qi and establishing an alliance, the *Spring and Autumn* did not judge him to be wrong. It held that he took these actions to rescue Duke Zhuang from danger. Gongzi Sui received orders to travel to the capital as a messenger. While on route, he initiated an undertaking at Jin. The *Spring and Autumn* judged his actions to be wrong. It held that at that time Duke Xi was not in danger. Therefore, when there is danger and [a great officer] does not act without authorization to rescue [his lord], the *Spring and Autumn* states that he is disloyal. When there is no danger and [a great officer] initiates an undertaking without authorization, this is a case of slighting one's lord. Therefore, although these two officers each initiated an undertaking, the *Spring and Autumn* judged one to be right and the other to be wrong. Their righteousness corresponded accordingly. [5/12/27–5/13/8]

Section 5.4

With the talents of a worthy prime minister and with the resources of a large state, Duke Huan of Qi ruled for five years, but he was unable to win the allegiance of a single Lord of the Land. At the meeting at Ke, he concluded a covenant with Duke Zhuang of Lu and exhibited his deep trustworthiness.[15]

14. A great officer should not abandon the duties that his lord has bestowed on him on account of the death of a parent. The obligations due one's ruler must take precedence over obligations due one's kin. In other words, one should not obstruct public matters on account of private affairs.
15. Duke Zhuang 3.13.4.

Within a year, all the rulers of the neighboring states came to pledge their allegiance to Qi. These were the interstate meetings at Zhuan and You.[16] From that time forward for the next twenty years, through this lengthy period of time, Duke Huan still was not able to unify all the Lords of the Land. But when it came to the matter of rescuing the states of Xing and Wey,[17] he exhibited the righteous principle of preserving those who are on the verge of extinction and continuing the bloodline of those who are about to perish. The following year, all the rulers of distant states came to pledge their allegiance to Qi. These were the meetings at Guanzi and Yanggu.[18] Therefore it is said:

> "In drawing close those who are near, do not rely on words;
> in attracting those who are distant, do not rely on envoys."[19]

Duke Huan of Qi is the proof! From this time forward, however, Duke Huan of Qi grew arrogant regarding his accomplishments. He became haughty and self-satisfied and failed to cultivate his virtue. Consequently, when the state of Chu destroyed the state of Xuan, he did not feel alarmed. When the state of Jiang and the Huang led a punitive expedition against the state of Chen, he did not move to rescue them. He harmed the people of other states. He detained their great officers. He did not relieve the suffering in the state of Chen but instead upbraided Chen for failing to provide a route [when he needed to cross that state].[20] He did not allow the state of Zheng to find peace and security again. Instead he employed troops to tyrannize that state. He had not yet completed his meritorious undertakings, but his heart already was content. Therefore [Confucius] said: "Guan Zhong was indeed a vessel of small capacity."[21] He was referring to these events. From this time forward, the state of Qi gradually declined and numerous states rose up in rebellion against it. [5/13/10–16]

---

16. Duke Zhuang 3.14.4 and 3.15.1.
17. Duke Min 4.1.2.
18. Duke Xi 5.2.4: "The marquis of Qi, the duke of Song, a man from Jiang, and a man from Huang made a covenant at Guan." Duke Xi 5.3.5: "In autumn, the marquis of Qi, the duke of Song, a man from Jiang, and a man from Huang held a meeting at Yanggu." *Gongyang*:

    This was a great meeting. Why does [the *Spring and Autumn*] use a minimizing expression? Duke Huan said: "Do not dam up [the rivers in] the valleys! Do not hoard grain! Do not substitute [the true heir] in order to set up [another] son! Do not raise a concubine to the rank of a wife!" (Adapted from Malmqvist, "Studies on the *Gongyang* and *Guliang* Commentaries," 162)

19. This aphorism also appears in the "Xingshi" chapter of the *Guanzi*, 1.2/33/6.
20. Duke Huan of Qi wanted to pass through Chen when he attacked the state of Chu. Chen had not yet agreed that his troops could return through the state when Duke Huan of Qi captured Yuan Taotu.
21. *Analects* 3.22. Translation follows D. C. Lau, trans., *The Analects* (Harmondsworth: Penguin, 1979), 70.

Section 5.5

When settling cases, the *Spring and Autumn* consistently deduces the motives [informing the accused] based on the facts. When the intent is evil, it does not wait for the evil intent to come to fruition in an evil deed before passing judgment. The initiator of an evil deed receives the heaviest penalty. [Those whose intentions] are originally upright are judged with a light penalty.

For this reason, the crime of Feng Choufu warranted decapitation,[22] but it was not proper to capture Yuan Taotu.[23] Ji Zi of Lu banished Qingfu, while Ji Zi of Wu pardoned Helü.[24] In these four cases, the crimes were identical, but the judgments differed because the basis [of their intentions] differed.[25] When the leader of an army was deceived, in one case [the accused] died and in the other case [the accused] did not die. When the ruler was assassinated, in one case [the accused] was punished, and in another case [the accused] was not punished. When settling cases, one must be cautious! If the decision in a legal case is correct, then correct principles will be further clarified, and moral education will be enhanced. If the decision in a legal case is incorrect, then correct principles will be obscured, and the populace will be misled. [The legal process] will oppose [the influences] of moral education. Education is the root of government. Litigation is its branches. The realms over which each has jurisdiction differ, although they are employed to the same end. They must comply with one another. Therefore the Noble Man [Confucius] attached much importance to them. [5/13/18–23]

Section 5.6

Someone raising an objection to the matter involving the state of Jin stated: It is a standard of the *Spring and Autumn* that a lord who has not yet passed the first

22. According to the *Gongyang Commentary* at Duke Cheng 8.2.4, Feng Choufu of Qi intentionally deceived the leader of the Jin forces in the hope that Duke Jing would escape from the enemy surrounding them. After the duke fled, Choufu was decapitated for the offense of deceiving the commander of the three armies. This case also is discussed in *CQFL* 3.4.

23. See note 20.

24. The *Gongyang Commentary* at Duke Min 4.2.3 explains that Ji Zi of Lu did not execute the assassin Qingfu but banished him. Ji Zi reduced the punishment because the two men were relatives. The *Gongyang Commentary* at Duke Xiang 9.29.8 explains that Ji Zi of Wu pardoned Helü for assassinating his elder brother in a succession crisis. According to the *Gongyang Commentary*, Ji Zi did not want to set a poor example for his subjects. He states: "You killed my elder brother. If I in turn were to kill you, then fathers and sons, elder brothers and younger brothers, would continue to kill one another in an endless sequence."

25. There are really two pairs of identical cases discussed here. Both Yuan Taotu and Feng Choufu were said to have cheated the commander of an army, while Qingfu and Helü assassinated their lords.

year of mourning for his father is referred to as "a son."[26] This practice accords with the usual sentiments of the heart. Why, then, when Li Ke assassinated Xi Qi, did the *Spring and Autumn* avoid this usual terminology and instead refer to him as "the lord's son"?[27]

The answer is: I have heard that the *Odes* lacks a single comprehensive explanation; the *Changes* lacks a single comprehensive prognostication; and the *Spring and Autumn* lacks a single comprehensive term.[28] The terminology employed by the *Spring and Autumn* follows changing circumstances and righteous principles and thereby uniformly reveres Heaven's Way.[29] When a humane person records the calamities that befall a blood relation, it certainly is appropriate to use a different method to describe these events. The ruler of Jin had the same surname as [the one who prepared] the *Spring and Autumn*.[30] Now the plot of Lady Li brought about the assassination of three rulers. These were events that caused everyone in the world to grieve. If you consider the matter based on her actions, her actions will blind you to what she desired, which was to establish her sons [as rulers], and you will not discover the calamity [she initiated]. The *Spring and Autumn*, abhorring the possibility of being blinded by her actions, abandoned its usual terminology and referred [to the ruler of Jin] as "the lord's son" and nothing more. It used this terminology as if to say to Xi Qi: "How regrettable! The son of a lord of a great state should find it sufficient to be wealthy and honored! Why must you usurp the throne of your elder brother and bring the state to such ruin?" The *Spring and Autumn* records terms that expressed [Confucius's] grief. Thus in his grief was something that caused him even greater grief. It was the assassination of those who were not guilty. Shen Sheng, Xi Qi, and Zhuo Zi were such persons. In an evil deed was an even greater evil. To bring about one's own assassination after having set oneself up as ruler does not compare with a subject's assassinating one's ruler. The son of Duke [Huan] of Qi, Shang

26. The point is that a son who has recently lost a father is so grieved that he cannot stand to assume the deceased ruler's title immediately. This notion appears in two earlier discussions.

27. Li Ke was a great officer in the service of Duke Xian of Jin. He was also the tutor of Duke Xian's heir apparent, Shen Sheng. Xi Qi was Duke Xian's son by his concubine Lady Li. Lady Li wanted to establish her son Xi Qi on the throne, so she had Shen Sheng killed. When Duke Xian died, Xi Qi assumed the position of ruler, but he was assassinated by Li Ke. Consequently, Lady Li's second son, Zhuo Zi, assumed the position of ruler. But he also was assassinated by Li Ke. See Duke Xi 5.9.6.

28. In other words, there is no single explanation to account for all the poems in the *Odes*; no single grand prognostication to account for all that the *Changes* predict; and no single term to cover all the affairs in the *Spring and Autumn*.

29. Emending *ren* 人 to *tian* 天, following Lu Wenchao (Lai, *CQFLJZJY* 82). An alternative rendering would be: "Whether following along with changing circumstances or righteous principles, they uniformly revere Heaven's Way."

30. The *Spring and Autumn* is a chronicle of the state of Lu. Both the state of Lu and the state of Jin were established by relatives of the Zhou kings, and they shared the surname Qiang.

Ren, was such a person.[31] Thus the Jin calamity was painful, and the Qi calamity was weighty. The *Spring and Autumn* expresses sorrow toward what is painful and anger toward what is weighty. Therefore it [did not refer to Xi Qi of Jin as a "son"] in order to avoid terminology designating one who inherits the position of ruler. It [referred to the son of Duke Zhao of Qi as "Lord She"] to bestow on him the designation of one who already has assumed the throne. It reveals these matters in the details of its terminology. [5/13/25–5/14/5]

Section 5.7

People of antiquity had a proverb that said: "If you do not know what is to come, observe what has gone before."[32]

Now as a discipline to be studied, the *Spring and Autumn* informs us of what has gone before to illuminate what is to come. However, its terminology embodies the subtle principles of Heaven and consequently is difficult to comprehend.[33] Therefore, if you do not investigate its terminology, the *Spring and Autumn* will remain silent as if it does not contain a thing. If, however, you investigate its terminology, there will be nothing that it does not contain. Therefore, when studying the *Spring and Autumn*, if you grasp one clue and enumerate and link it to others; and if you observe one omission and expand and connect it to others, then you will gain complete knowledge of the world.

Duke Xi of Lu assumed the position of rulership during a time of rebellion. He knew to trust and employ Ji Zi. When Ji Zi was alive, there was not a single rebellious minister in the state of Lu, and beyond the borders there were no Lords of the Land who came to invade the state of Lu. For twenty years, the state was peaceful and calm. But after Ji Zi died, the state of Lu could not resist

31. Shang Ren was the son of Duke Huan of Qi. When Duke Zhao of Qi died, Shang Ren set up Duke Zhao's son She as the ruler of Qi. Before one year passed, Shang Ren assassinated She, whom he had set up as ruler.

32. This is possibly an unattributed apothegm borrowed from the "Xingshi" (Conditions and Circumstances) chapter of the *Guanzi* (*Guanzi* 1.1; W. Allyn Rickett, trans., *Guanzi: Political, Economic, and Philosophical Essays from Early China* [Princeton, N.J.: Princeton University Press, 1985], 1:83). Su Yu (*CQFLYZ* 96) adds,

> Those who would question the present should investigate the past. Those who do not understand what is to come should look at what has gone before. Handling of the myriad affairs may lead in different directions, but they all return to a common goal. From ancient times to the present it has always been so.

33. As Su Yu (*CQFLYZ* 96) explains:

> Heaven does not speak, and the four seasons follow their course. The sage embodies Heaven and sets forth words but cannot exhaust Heaven's intentions. This is what is meant by the expression "The pure subtleties of the heart/mind cannot be spoken of. The subtleties of words cannot be captured in writing." To read the *Spring and Autumn*, one must investigate its subtleties and examine its words and, from the many particulars, extrapolate what is similar. This is why some say the *Spring and Autumn* values repetition.

invading its neighboring states and was compelled to request reinforcements from the state of Chu.

Now it is not the case that Duke Xi suddenly became an unworthy ruler, but his state declined and became ever more endangered. Why? It was because there was no Ji Zi [to assist him any longer]. Since this was the case in the state of Lu, we know that other states also were like this. Since other states were like this, we know that the entire world was like this. This is what is meant by the expression connecting and threading together.

Therefore, although the world is quite large and the expanse between antiquity and the present is quite long, you can rely on this method to reason things through. Thus when worthy men are appointed to office, we deduce that the ruler will be honored and the state will be secure. When unworthy men are appointed to office, we deduce that the ruler will be slighted and the state will be endangered. For ten thousand generations, this will hold true without a doubt. The *Changes* state: "A tripod with bent legs will overturn the cooked rice [inside]." "A tripod with bent legs" symbolizes appointing unworthy men. "Will overturn cooked rice" symbolizes the overthrow of a state. This is why from antiquity to the present, we have never heard of a ruler appointing unworthy men and his state not being overthrown.

Therefore I examine the *Spring and Autumn*, observe those who succeed and those who fail, embrace the various causes of success and failure in former ages, and discover that the states that employed worthies were the states that prospered. If the ruler's wisdom was not sufficient to recognize who was worthy, then there was no chance for his state. As for those rulers who could recognize worthies but who did not employ them, in the worst cases their states were destroyed, and in the best cases their states were endangered.

Why were they like this? Do you think that Duke Zhuang did not know that Ji Zi was worthy? If he did not know that Ji Zi was worthy, then why did Duke Zhuang summon Ji Zi to pass on the state to him when the duke was sick and about to die? Do you think that Duke Shang did not know that Kongfu was worthy? Then how did Duke Shang know that if Kongfu died, he also would die and consequently hasten to rescue him from death? The wisdom of these two rulers was sufficient to recognize a worthy, but they hesitated and could not commit themselves, and so they were unable to employ them. Therefore, Duke Zhuang of Lu became endangered, and Duke Shang of Song was murdered. If Duke Zhuang had employed Ji Zi earlier, and if Duke Shang of Song had appointed Kongfu sooner, they still would have been able to bring prosperity to the neighboring states, not to mention avoiding assassination. But in the end they were killed. This causes me great remorse and regret. [5/14/7–21]

Book 4, Part 1

CHAPTER 6

The Kingly Way

Section 6.1

Why does the *Spring and Autumn* value the Origin [year of each reign] and discuss it?

The Origin means the beginning. [It means that] the foundation [must be] upright.

The Way is the Kingly Way. [It means that] the king is the beginning of humankind.

When the king is upright,

the primal *qi* will be harmonious and compliant,
wind and rain will be timely,
lucky stars will appear,
and the yellow dragon will descend.

When the king is not upright, then above there will be alterations in the heavens, and baleful *qi* will simultaneously appear. [6/14/27–29]

When the Five Emperors and Three Kings governed, [no one in] the world dared harbor [a distinction] between the mind of the ruler and [that of] the people. [The rulers] taxed [the land] one part out of ten. They

taught [the people] with love;
and moved them with sincerity.

There was

respect for the elderly,
affection for relatives,
and reverence for the honorable.

[They] did not take the people from their seasonal [tasks], and they did not employ them for more than three days a year. The households of commoners could provide sufficiently for their members. There were no hardships arising from resentment and anger, nor troubles arising from [inequities] between the strong and the weak. There were no people who were slanderous or envious [of others]. People cultivated virtue and found beauty in the good. With hair unbound and eating whatever came to hand, they wandered freely. They did not covet wealth or nobility. They were ashamed of doing wrong and did not transgress.

Fathers did not [have to] mourn their sons;
older brothers did not [have to] mourn their younger brothers.
Poisonous insects did not sting;
wild animals did not strike;
fierce beasts did not butt.

Thus Heaven sent down sweet dew on their behalf.

Vermilion grasses came to life;
sweet springs issued forth;
winds and rains were timely;
excellent millet flourished.

The male and female phoenix and the *qilin*[1] wandered in the suburbs. The prisons were empty. [The rulers] depicted [the crimes of criminals on their] clothing, and the people did not transgress.[2] The four Yi tribes[3] sent envoys to visit the court. The people's emotions were perfectly simple and unadorned. [The rulers] performed

the Jiao sacrifice to Heaven,
and the Si sacrifice to Earth.

They sacrificed to the mountains and rivers in accordance with their ranks. In the proper season, they performed

the Feng sacrifice at Mount Tai
and the Shan sacrifice at Liangfu peak.

1. It was believed that phoenixes (*fenghuang* 鳳鵝) and *qilins* 麒麟 appeared only during the reigns of sages. The phoenix was a fabulous bird, somewhat resembling a peacock or a pheasant; the *qilin* was a composite beast (often wrongly translated as "unicorn"), sometimes depicted as having the body, legs, and horns of a goat and the head and tail of a lion.
2. The reference here is to the practice of symbolic punishments. The rulers of the well-governed age of the Five Emperors and Three Kings employed the more humane practice of symbolic punishments instead of mutilating punishments.
3. That is, non-Chinese peoples from all four directions.

They established the Hall of Light.[4] They performed the ancestral sacrifices to the former emperors so that their ancestors accompanied Heaven. The Lords of the Land from throughout the world, each in accordance with their official duty, came to sacrifice. They first presented what their fiefs had provided. [They stood] adorned in ritual cap and gown before [the ruler's] more remote ancestors in the ancestral temple and then before their less remote ancestors. Such are the rewards of virtue and kindness and the recompense for reverencing the Origin.[5] [6/14/27–6/15/6]

Both Jie and Djou were descendants of sage-kings, [yet] they were arrogant and reckless. They constructed extravagant palaces and spacious parks. They

> indulged in endless permutations of the five colors;
> pushed to the extreme the crafts of ornamental materials;
> set snares for the feet of wild animals;
> sapped the resources of the mountains and lakes;
> dined on disgusting kinds of animals;
> stole the people's food and property;
> constructed high lookout towers with elaborately ornamented carving;
> exhausted the labors of the craftsmen [who worked with] gold, jade, bone, and ivory;
> made abundant feather and fur adornments;
> and eradicated the alterations of black and white.[6]

They

> punished harshly and murdered recklessly to control their subordinates;
> listened to the melodies of Zheng and Wey;
> satiated their desires in the side palaces;[7]
> and penned tigers, rhinoceroses, [and other] ornamental and colorful beasts

with the aim of viewing such rarely seen specimens.

They

> made hills of the lees of grain [from making fermented drinks]
> and made lakes of wine.

They did not care for the orphaned or the poor. [Djou]

> murdered sages and worthies and cut out their hearts,

---

4. The hall of light (*mingtang* 明堂) was a special building in which the ruler performed monthly and seasonal sacrifices.
5. Duke Yin 1.1.1 explains: "What is the Origin Year? It is the lord's first year."
6. The meaning of this phrase is unclear. It may refer to ignoring the proper distinction between day and night, and specifically to having sex in the daytime.
7. These were the apartments that housed the women.

burned people alive and savored the odor,[8]

cut open the womb of a pregnant woman to see the developing [fetus].

He cut off the feet of those crossing the ford in the morning and inspected their toes. Djou killed Mei Bo and pickled him. He punished the wife of Marquis Gui and took her jewels.[9] He exploited [the people] without cease, so that [the resources and the wealth of] the world were utterly exhausted. The officials were terrified, and no one dared give their sincere [opinions], so Djou considered himself worthier day by day.

The Zhou raised troops to surprise [the troops of Yin] at the ford at Meng. Eight hundred Lords of the Land united to attack Djou, who lost his dominion over the world. The *Spring and Autumn* treated [this event] as a warning and stated: "The altar of Bu was visited by fire."[10]

When the [House of] Zhou declined, the Son of Heaven grew feeble and weak, and

the Lords of the Land overpowered the government;

the great officers usurped power in their states;

and the functionaries usurped power in their counties.

Consequently, [the Son of Heaven] could not implement the properly measured regulations or emulate the rituals [of King Wen].[11] The Lords of the Land turned their backs in rebellion, and none offered tribute or sent envoys to [the court of the Son of Heaven].

Ministers murdered their rulers,

sons murdered their fathers,

and the sons of concubines murdered the eldest sons of the legal wives.

[The Son of Heaven] could not unify [moral] principles. Instead, states attacked one another and enlarged their territories. The powerful threatened one another with force, and [the Son of Heaven] could not control them.

The powerful overcame the weak,

the majority violated the minority,

and the rich bullied the poor.

---

8. This is a reference to the ancient punishment called *paolao* 炮烙. A prisoner was forced to walk on a beam of metal that was coated with oil and kept hot by a fire below. The prisoner often fell off the slippery beam to perish in the fire (Lai, *CQFLJZJY* 91).

9. Su Yu adds from the *Shiji*, "The Annals of Yin": "The women of the nine rulers were not fond of sex. Djou was angered by this and killed them."

10. Duke Ai 12.4.8.

11. Duke Wen 6.9.1 emphasizes perpetuating King Wen's regulations and rituals.

These tendencies multiplied without end. Subordinates usurped the [authority] of their superiors, and their superiors could not stop them. There were eclipses, shooting stars like rainstorms, rains of locusts, and landslides.

In summer heavy rains fell;
in winter heavy snows fell.

Five stones fell [from the sky] in Song, and six herons flew backward.[12] Frost fell without killing the grass. Plum and prune trees bore fruit.[13] In the first month [of spring] there was no rain, and [the drought] continued until the seventh month in autumn.[14] There were earthquakes.[15] Mount Liang collapsed and obstructed the flow of the [Yellow] River for three days.[16] During the day, the [sky turned] dark.[17] A comet appeared in the east; becoming oppositional, it was located in [the constellation] Great Indicators.[18] Mynah birds came [to Lu] and built nests.[19]

The *Spring and Autumn* took these events to be anomalous and used them to reveal the incipient stirrings of chaos and rebellion. Confucius

illuminated successes and failures
and distinguished the lofty and the lowly

to return to the foundations of the Kingly Way. He censured the Heavenly King[20] to usher in [an era of] Great Peace. He condemned wrongdoing, criticizing its slightest manifestation, no matter how small or large.

---

12. Duke Xi 5.16.1: "In the sixteenth year, in spring, in the king's first month, on the day *wushen*, on the first day of the month, there fell stones over Song, five pieces. In the same month, six herons flew backward and passed the capital of Song." *Gongyang*:

    Why does [the *Spring and Autumn*] first state that they fell and only thereafter that they were stones? [The entry] "there fell stones" is a record of what was heard. A rumbling noise was heard. On inspection they were found to be stones. . . . [The entry] "six herons flew backward" is a record of what was seen. On inspection they were found to be six. On closer inspection they were found to be herons. On a prolonged inspection, they were found to be flying backward.

    These were famous portents, supposedly witnessed by many people. The same portents are alluded to in chapters 33.4, 35.3, and 36.1.

13. Duke Xi 5.33.12.
14. Duke Wen 6.10.4 and 6.13.4.
15. Duke Wen 6.9.12; Duke Xiang 9.16.5; Duke Zhao 10.19.3 and 10.23.9; Duke Ai 12.3.2.
16. Duke Cheng 8.5.4.
17. Duke Cheng 8.16.6.
18. Duke Ai 12.13.10; Duke Zhao 10.17.5. A *pei* 孛 is a comet in opposition—that is, lined up with the Earth and the sun—often without a visible tail. The Great Indicators (*da chen* 大辰) refer to the lunar lodge Heart (*xin* 心, lodge no. 5), the pole star, and the lunar lodge Alignment (*shen* 參, lodge no. 21), which together define a particular arc across the sky. See Joseph Needham, *Science and Civilisation in China*, vol. 3, *Mathematics and the Sciences of the Heavens and the Earth* (Cambridge: Cambridge University Press, 1959), 250, 431.
19. Duke Zhao 10.25.3.
20. This title refers to the Son of Heaven of the Zhou dynasty.

There was no instance of goodness too small for him to praise,
no instance of wrongdoing too minor for him to eradicate.
He promoted good
and condemned the bad

in his desire to cut off [wrongdoing] at its root and nothing more. [6/15/8–22]

Section 6.2

[Thus] When the Heavenly King sent the administrator Xuan to accompany with presents the funerals of Duke Hui [of Lu] and Zhongzi, [Confucius] censured the envoy for not arriving in time for the funeral ceremony.[21]

When the Heavenly King attacked Zheng, [Confucius] criticized him [for attacking a state that] shared his surname.[22]

When [the Lords of the Land] called a meeting with the king's heir apparent [Shou Zhi], [Confucius] criticized [the king's] weakness.[23]

When the duke of Cha came [to Lu and from there] proceeded to meet the [future] queen [in Ji], [Confucius] criticized the king for lacking propriety.[24]

[He] censured [the king for sending] Jiafu to request carriages[25] when a son of the Wu family and the earl of Mao came [to Lu] to request money contributions,[26] when the king sent men to rescue Wey,[27] and when, the king's troops having been defeated at Mao, Wey and the Heavenly King did not supply succor [but left [Zhou] to reside in Zheng.[28]

When the king killed his maternal uncle[29] and when the king's household rebelled, he was unable to meet with those who came from abroad.[30] When Zhou was divided into the eastern and western territories, the Son of Heaven was unable to maintain his preeminence in the world. He summoned the marquis of Wey and could not make him come.[31] He sent Zitu to chastise Wey but

21. Duke Yin 1.1.4.
22. Duke Huan 2.5.6.
23. Duke Xi 5.5.4.
24. Duke Huan 2.8.6.
25. Duke Huan 2.15.1.
26. Duke Yin 1.3.4; Duke Wen 6.9.1.
27. Duke Zhuang 3.6.1.
28. Duke Cheng 8.1.6; Duke Xi 5.24.4.
29. Duke Xiang 9.30.4.
30. Duke Zhao 10.22.7.
31. Duke Huan 2.16.5.

could not stop [the duke of Wey's disobedience].[32] He attacked Zheng but could not [make Zheng] submit.[33] Wuhai's destructiveness was extreme, but he could not punish him.[34]

The Lords of the Land were able to carry out a great rebellion, killing and murdering without cease. The lower officials coerced their superiors and usurped the prerogatives of the Son of Heaven. Among the Lords of the Land, the strong established their authority, and the weak states were destroyed. Three times Jin attacked Zhou.[35] Jin fought with the forces of the king at Gu Rong and soundly defeated them.[36] The Rong attacked the earl of Fan at Chu Hill and carried him back with them.[37] The Lords of the Land resented and despised one another. They dispatched troops to attack one another and destroyed one another's ancestral temples and altars of the soil. [The king] could not bring them under control. Ministers and sons were so overbearing that they murdered their rulers and their fathers.

The [Son of Heaven's] models and standards were abandoned, so that they were never to be used again. His awe-inspiring martiality was eradicated, so that it was never to be realized again. Thus Zheng and Lu exchanged their territory,[38] and Duke Wen of Jin twice summoned the Son of Heaven.[39] Duke Huan of Qi called a meeting with the king's heir apparent.[40] Without proper authorization from the king, he enfeoffed [the Lords of the Land of] Xing, Wey, and Ji.[41] [Duke Huan of Qi] swept across the Central States hoping to establish himself as king over the entire world. The [duke of] Lu employed eight rows of dancers,[42]

32. Duke Zhuang 3.6.2.
33. Duke Huan 2.5.6.
34. Duke Yin 1.2.3.
35. For the three attacks against Zhou, see Duke Xuan 7.1.11, Duke Cheng 8.1.5, and Duke Zhao 10.23.4.
36. Duke Cheng 8.1.5.
37. Duke Yin 1.7.5.
38. Duke Huan 2.1.4 records that the earl of Zheng borrowed the fields of Xu in exchange for a jade disk. The *Gongyang Commentary* explains that the "fields of Xu" indicated a city where the dukes of Lu rested when they paid court visits to the Son of Heaven. It was called the "fields of Xu" to conceal the fact that Lu had taken possession of land belonging to the Royal House of Zhou. As long as there was a Son of Heaven, the Lords of the Land were not granted the authority to monopolize land. The fact that Lu had taken over this land indicated that this particular standard limiting their prerogatives had been abandoned because the Zhou no longer had the authority to enforce it.
39. Duke Xi 5.28.9 and 5.28.16 indicate that the duke twice summoned the Son of Heaven during this year and that this behavior violated ritual protocol. The entries indicate that the Son of Heaven had certainly lost whatever authority he had enjoyed because of his martial powers.
40. Duke Xi 5.5.4.
41. When each of these states was attacked and each was destroyed, Duke Huan of Qi helped their rulers rebuild their capitals (Duke Xi 5.1.2; Duke Min 4.1.2; Duke Xi 5.14.1).
42. Duke Yin 1.54.

performed the Wang sacrifice to Mount Tai,[43] the Jiao sacrifice to Heaven, and the Si sacrifice to Earth as if he were the Son of Heaven.[44] For these reasons, thirty-two rulers were assassinated, and fifty-two states were annihilated. This happened because evils were not eradicated when they still were trifling matters. [6/14/27–6/16/5]

Section 6.3

The *Spring and Autumn* upholds [the following] principles:

The Son of Heaven sacrifices to Heaven and Earth.

The Lords of the Land sacrifice to the altars of the grain and soil.

The various mountains and rivers that are not in their territories do not receive sacrifices.[45] When a Son of Heaven occupies the throne,

the Lords of the Land are not authorized to [exert absolute] rule in their territories;[46]

they are not authorized to enfeoff subjects;[47]

they are not authorized to detain the great officers of the Son of Heaven;[48]

they are not authorized to have anyone dance to the music of the Son of Heaven,[49]

they are not authorized to transmit the poetry of the Son of Heaven,

they are not authorized to enjoy the honors of the Son of Heaven.

Rulers who are relatives [of the king] must not plot rebellion. If they do, they must be executed.[50]

Great officers do not inherit titles and ranks.[51]

Great officers are not authorized to disregard the commands of their lord.[52]

When establishing heirs [i.e., the sons of the principal wife], seniority takes precedence over worthiness.

When establishing the sons [of other than the principal wife], nobility takes precedence over seniority.[53]

43. Emending *bei* 北 to *wang* 望, following Su Yu, *CQFLYZ* 112. For the Wang sacrifice, see Duke Xi 5.31.3.
44. Duke Xi 5.31.3.
45. Duke Xi 5.31.3.
46. Duke Huan 2.1.3.
47. Duke Xi 5.1.2.
48. Duke Yin 1.7.5.
49. Duke Yin 1.5.4.
50. Duke Zhuang 3.32.3.
51. Duke Zhao 10.31.6.
52. Duke Wen 6.14.17.
53. Duke Yin 1.1.1.

When establishing wives, they consider the principal wife and not the concubine.[54]

The Son of Heaven does not employ relatives of his mother or wife as officials.[55]

The Son of Heaven cherishes those who are near to attract those who are distant. Thus he never fails to promote those who are near in order to summon those who are distant.

Therefore the *Spring and Autumn* treats

the state [of Lu] as the interior and the central states of the Lords of the Land as the exterior;

the central states of the Lords of the Land as the interior and those of the Yi and Di tribes as the exterior.[56]

This is the meaning of "beginning from what is near." [6/16/7–12]

Section 6.4

When the Lords of the Land came [to the state of Lu] to pay a court visit, they received praise [in the *Spring and Autumn*]:

Yifu, [the ruler of] Zhulou, is referred to by his appellation;

[the rulers of] Teng and Bi are referred to as marquises;

[the great officers of] Xing are called "men";

and Helü, [the ruler of] Jie, is called by his personal name.[57]

Departures from within [the state of Lu] are termed *ru*, "to travel to."

When the Lords of the Land came [to the state of Lu], it was called *chao*, "to pay a court visit."

When the great officers came [to the state of Lu], it was called *bin*, "a friendly diplomatic visit."[58]

These expressions signify the Kingly Way.

[The *Spring and Autumn*] criticizes wrongdoing, no matter how insignificant or significant the transgression. Thus

the Lords of the Land are not authorized to raise troops on behalf of a commoner;

they are not authorized to detain a great officer of the Son of Heaven.

If they do, their crime is considered the same as [as that by] one who had initiated a punitive expedition against another state. Therefore,

54. Duke Xi 5.8.3.
55. Duke Huan 2.2.5.
56. Duke Cheng 8.15.11.
57. For these examples of praise, see Duke Yin 1.1.2 and 2.11.1, Duke Zhuang 3.23.5, and Duke Xi 5.29.1.
58. Duke Yin 1.11.1.

[when the Rong] captured Fan Bo, [Confucius] said that he had been "attacked."

[When the duke] presented eight rows of dancers, [Confucius] avoided the term "eight" and said "six" rows of dancers.

When Zheng and Lu exchanged their territory, [Confucius] avoided the term "to exchange" and said "to borrow."

When Duke Wen of Jin summoned the Son of Heaven for the second time, [Confucius] avoided the term "to summon" and said the king had "a court reception."

When Duke Huan of Qi revived [the states of] Xing, Wey, and Ji, [those events] did not appear in the *Spring and Autumn*.

In his heart [Confucius] approved of their conduct, but because they violated the standards, he [expressed] disapproval. The task of ending disorder is not an obligation appropriate to the Lords of the Land. [It is the prerogative of the Son of Heaven.] [6/16/14–18]

Section 6.5

According to the righteous principles of the *Spring and Autumn*:

ministers who do not punish those who murder their ruler are not [true] ministers;

sons who do not take revenge on their fathers' enemies are not [true] sons.

Thus the *Spring and Autumn* records that Zhao Dun was punished with execution. Since the murderer was not apprehended, it does not record the burial of the assassinated ruler. This is a criticism directed at the minister. [Similarly,] when Xu Shizi did not taste [his father's] medicine, the *Spring and Autumn* recorded that he was executed for having murdered his father.

The duke's son Bi of Chu was compelled to become ruler and thus could not avoid being implicated in the death [of King Ling].

Duke Huan of Qi and Duke Wen [of Jin] distributed territory to others [without authorization from the Son of Heaven], and they summoned the Son of Heaven to meetings. They attacked those who were rebellious, reestablished lineages that had been cut off, and revived states that had perished. They invaded and attacked those Lords of the Land who sought cross alliances, and they often acted as if they were the rulers. Thus [the *Spring and Autumn*] states: Duke Huan of Qi rescued the Central States, expelled the Yi and Di tribes, and eventually subjugated Chu. He conducted himself as if he were the Son of Heaven.

Duke Wen of Jin twice summoned the Son of Heaven. In each case, the *Spring and Autumn* does not criticize these men but, rather, praises them for governing the Lords of the Land, honoring and serving the Son of Heaven, and submitting to the House of Zhou. The *Spring and Autumn* approved of them as hegemons. This is what is called "to disapprove in one's thoughts but not to disapprove in one's speech." [6/16/18–23]

Section 6.6

When Duke Yin of Lu assumed the throne on behalf of [Duke] Huan;[59]
when Zhai Zhong expelled Hu and established Du;[60]
when Qiu Mu, Kongfu, and Xunxi died to preserve their honor;[61]
and when the duke's son Mu Yi would not agree to the demands of Chu;[62]

These all are examples in which in every case

they grasped [the principle of] expediency and preserved their states;
they practiced the righteous principle of rectifying their age and defended their sincere intentions.

The *Spring and Autumn* delighted in their righteousness and consequently, in every instance, revealed their conduct. This is what is called "restoring uprightness."

---

59. Duke Yin of Lu was the son of Duke Hui of Lu and the elder brother of Duke Huan of Lu. Duke Hui died, and according to the rites, Duke Huan, who was born of the principal wife of Duke Hui, should have inherited the throne. But because Duke Huan still was young and Duke Yin was older and capable, the great officers of Lu established Duke Yin on the throne. Duke Yin intended to yield the throne to Duke Huan once he attained adulthood (Duke Yin 1.1.1).

60. A long narrative in the *Gongyang Commentary* praises Zhai Zhong for knowing how to exercise expediency. The story describes how the ruler of Song (referred to as "a man of Song," denoting the *Spring and Autumn*'s disapproval) seized Zhai Zhong and tried to coerce him to expel Hu, the rightful heir to the throne of Zheng, and replace him with his younger brother, a contender for the throne named Du. The narrative explains:

> If Zhai Zhong refused to obey his command then his lord [i.e., Hu] would surely die, and the state of Zheng would surely perish. If he obeyed [his command], then his lord would remain alive instead of dying, and his state would survive instead of perishing. If he could let developments play out for a time, Du could be expelled and Hu could be reinstated. If this could not be achieved, then Zhai Zhong would be disgraced, but the state of Zheng would still be preserved. Zhai Zhong was one of the men of antiquity who understood expediency. (Duke Huan 2.11.4)

For a complete translation of this passage, see chapter 3, note 26.

61. Three narratives commemorate these three ministers as worthies who gave up their lives pursuing their lords' assassins. Qiu Mu lost his life in a particularly grisly manner when he sought to punish his lord's assassin Nangong Wan of Song. Kongfu Jia died defending his lord from the assassin Hua Du. Xunxi died protecting his lord from an assassin so as not to break a promise made with his former lord (Duke Zhuang 3.12.3; Duke Huan 2.2.1; Duke Xi 5.10.4).

62. For the story of Gongzi Mu Yi, see Duke Xi 5.21.6.

When the Yi and Di tribes and the peoples of Zhulou, Mou, and Ge, on account of the death of the Heavenly King, performed the *chao* and *bin* ceremonies, [the *Spring and Autumn* described them as deserving] punishment.[63]

When there was a murder of an heir apparent or a younger son [by the ruler's principal wife], [the *Spring and Autumn*] made a direct reference to the lord to make clear that there had been a departure from [the principle of] showing affection toward relatives.[64]

When Ji Zi of Lu pardoned [Jingfu's crime] and Ji Zi of Wu ceded [rulership of] the state [to Helü], [the *Spring and Autumn*] made clear their generosity in showing affection toward relatives.[65]

When a gatekeeper assassinated Viscount Yuji of Wu, [the *Spring and Autumn*] made it evident that a person punished with mutilation should not be [allowed to] approach [the ruler].[66]

When Earl Kun Yuan of Cheng perished at the meeting [held by Duke Xiang], [the *Spring and Autumn*] concealed the murder. This was because [Confucius] was distressed by the usurpation by powerful ministers of their ruler's authority, which made the ruler unable to practice goodness.[67]

When men from Wey murdered Zhouxu[68] and men from Qi killed Wu Zhi,[69] [the *Spring and Autumn*] made clear the righteous relationship between ruler and minister and the uprightness of preserving the state.

When the people of Wey established Jin [as their ruler], [the *Spring and Autumn*] praised him for having obtained the support of the multitudes.

When the ruler himself was in command, [the *Spring and Autumn*] did not use the term "to lead troops" [to manifest] the righteous principle of valuing one's ruler.[70]

[*The Spring and Autumn* recorded] "The first month the duke was in Chu." This means that when the subject contemplates the ruler, in his thoughts the subject cannot [bear to] be without a ruler for even a day.[71]

63. Because of their "barbarian" status, they were not authorized to conduct such ceremonies.
64. Duke Xi 5.5.1.
65. Duke Xiang 9.29.8.
66. In antiquity, criminals who had suffered the punishment of mutilation often were put to work as gatekeepers.
67. Duke Xiang 9.7.9.
68. Duke Yin 1.4.6.
69. Duke Zhuang 3.9.1.
70. Duke Yin 1.5.3.
71. Duke Xiang 9.29.1.

[The *Spring and Autumn*] criticizes those who did not follow orders. Contemplating [the return of] the treasures of Wey, it took the just imprisonment [of those involved] to be fair.[72]

[The *Spring and Autumn*] noted when the city of Cheng was surrounded and when on the day *jia wu* arms were dedicated [in the temple] in order to distinguish the crimes of coercion. This was its method of criticizing the intention.[73]

[The *Spring and Autumn*] noted

when [Duke Xiang] renovated and altered the southern gate [of the capital],[74]

when [Duke Zhuang] carved the rafters of [Duke Huan's] temple and painted its pillars red,[75]

when [Duke Ding] built a crenellated gate with two side towers,[76]

when [Duke Zhuang] built three towers [in the space of one year], and when he renovated his stables.[77]

[The *Spring and Autumn*] criticized the arrogance of these men and their lack of compassion toward the people below. Therefore when Cang Sunchen requested leave to buy grain from Qi, Confucius said: "When a noble man governs a state, he invariably procures provisions for three years. If he requests to buy grain after only one year of harvest, he has failed in his responsibilities as a ruler."[78] [This exemplifies the principle of] punishing with execution the initiator of an offense, [thus, by deterring others,] reducing punishments, eradicating wrongdoings, and demonstrating disdain toward the initiator [of the wrongdoing.][79] [6/16/25–6/17/3]

Section 6.7

When the great officers made a covenant at Shanyuan, [the *Spring and Autumn*] criticized the officers for usurping the authority of the government.[80] Yet when

72. Supplying the negative *bu*, following Su Yu, *CQFLYZ* 120. The next sentence is related to Duke Zhuang 3.6.5: "Winter. A man from Qi came to return the treasures of Wey."
73. Duke Zhuang 3.8.2.
74. Duke Xi 5.20.1.
75. Duke Zhuang 3.24.1 and 3.23.8.
76. Duke Ding 11.2.4.
77. Duke Zhuang 3.31.1 and 3.29.1.
78. Duke Zhuang 3.28.4.
79. The *Gongyang Commentary* at Duke Xi 5.17.2 states: "When the Noble Man expressed loathing for evil he disdained it at its initiation; when he expressed praise for goodness, he found joy in its conclusion." For other occurrences of the expression *ji shi* (疾始), see Duke Huan 2.7.1 and Duke Yin 1.4.1, where the *Gongyang Commentary* claims that Confucius expressed disdain for the initiation of an attack by fire and the capture of a town.
80. Duke Xiang 9.30.9.

the Lords of the Land gathered together to meet and when a worthy led the meeting, [Confucius praised them for] esteeming the worthy.[81] The *Spring and Autumn* records the slightest faults in order to return to the Kingly Way. [Yet] it follows antiquity in valuing trustworthiness [and in their dealings with one another], making verbal contracts and nothing more. They had no need to make use of sacrificial pledges and then to complete a covenant. Thus [the *Spring and* Autumn] states: "The marquis of Ji and the marquis of Wey pledged each other at Pu." The *Commentary* adds: "In ancient times, no covenants were made; [men] made verbal contracts and withdrew."[82] [6/17/3–6]

Section 6.8

Boji of Song said: When a woman goes out at night, unless her guardian is [by her side], she does not descend [from] her quarters.[83]

It is said: In ancient times, when the Duke of Zhou subdued the eastern states, the western states grew resentful.[84]

Duke Huan [of Qi] said: "Do not dam up [the rivers in] the valleys. Do not hoard grain. Do not set up [another] son in place of [the true heir]. Do not raise a concubine to the rank of wife."[85]

Duke Xiang of Song said: "Do not beat drums [as a signal] to attack an enemy who has not yet formed his formations. Do not distress others."[86]

King Zhuang [of Chu] said: "In ancient times, unless one's food bowls were worn through and one's skin [garments] were worm eaten [i.e., under conditions of extreme poverty], one did not leave [one's state to invade another]. Therefore, the noble man stands firm on ritual while he scorns profit. What I want is for the men [of Zheng to admit their guilt]. I do not want their land. Not to pardon an enemy who has submitted is inauspicious. The strong should not abuse the weak."[87]

Duke Qing of Qi mourned the dead and cared for the injured [following the battle of Ke.][88]

81. That is, Duke Huan of Qi and Duke Wen of Jin.
82. Duke Huan 2.3.2.
83. Duke Xiang 9.30.3.
84. Duke Xi 5.4.4. They were resentful because they felt neglected by the sagely Duke of Zhou, who made them wait to be subdued.
85. Duke Xi 5.3.5.
86. Duke Xi 5.22.4.
87. Duke Xuan 7.12.3.
88. Duke Cheng 8.8.1.

When Kongfu, with an upright appearance, took up his position in the court, no one dared commit any fault or cause distress to his lord.[89]

Guo Zuo of Qi would not dishonor the command of his lord and ultimately won respect for the duke of Qi.[90]

In such cases, the *Spring and Autumn* follows the external appearance [of such men's actions] in order to reveal their [inner] substance. Following the [external] appearance in order to reveal the [inner] substance also reveals the reasons that lead men to lose their states.

The viscount of Luu desired to align himself with the propriety and righteousness of the Central States and set himself apart from the Yi and Di tribes. But he never achieved alignment with the Central States, and so he perished.[91]

King Fuchai of Wu bullied the state of Yue. He made the ruler [of Yue] his subject and took the ruler's wife as his concubine. Ultimately he brought about his own destruction. His ancestral temples were razed, and his altars of the soil and the grain were destroyed. This certainly was painful. The aged king [Fuchai] drowned himself at Xi. This certainly was regrettable.

[Duke] Ling of Jin's conduct violated propriety. He ensconced himself in a high tower and shot pellets at his ministers. He amputated the limbs of criminals and butchered men, leaving their bodies [to rot]. He revealed the plans of Yang Chufu and caused his death.[92] Distressed by the remonstrances of Zhao Dun, he attempted to murder him. In the end, he was murdered by Zhao Dun.[93]

Duke Xian of Jin's conduct contravened correct principles. He murdered his legal heir Shen Sheng, and, because of [the influence of his] concubine Li, established her sons Xi Qi and Zhuo Zi [as rulers]. Both were assassinated, and the state was thrown into great chaos.[94] Four generations passed before the state was settled, but then it was almost destroyed by Qin. These disasters may be traced to the rise of the concubine Li.

King Ping of Chu's conduct lacked restraint. He murdered the father and elder brother of Wu Zixin. When Duke Zhao of Cai paid him a court visit, [King Ping] demanded that Duke Zhao give him his coat, but the duke did not give it to him. [King Ping subsequently detained him.] The king of Wu held that King Ping of Chu was wrong. Consequently he raised an army, fought Chu, and

89. Duke Huan 2.2.2.
90. Duke Cheng 8.2.4.
91. Duke Xuan 7.15.3.
92. Duke Wen 6.6.8.
93. Duke Xuan 7.6.1.
94. Duke Xi 5.10.4.

soundly defeated it. The ruler of Wu went to live in the house of the Chu ruler, and the great officers of Wu resided in the houses of the great officers of Chu. The ruler of Wu took the Chu ruler's mother as his wife. These things were brought about by the covetous and violent attitude [of King Ping of Chu].[95]

Duke Wan of Jin's conduct assaulted the Way. He executed those who were innocent. In one morning, he murdered three great ministers.[96] By the following year, all his subjects feared him, and [the people of Jin] murdered him.[97]

Marquis Tuo of Chen behaved licentiously in Cai. A man from Cai murdered him.[98] In ancient times when Lords of the Land left their states, they always were accompanied by the left and right [wings of their armies]. They prepared themselves with [these two] armies[99] to be prepared for the unexpected. But the marquis of Chen was irresponsible and traveled among the people by himself, and so he died among the commoners. [His actions] deeply contradicted the conduct [appropriate to] one who rules others. [6/17/4–21]

Duke Min of Song was boastful in front of his wives, and his heart was filled with jealousy. [On one occasion] while playing chess with his great officer Wan, Wan praised Duke Zhuang of Lu, saying: "Of all the Lords of the Land in the kingdom, only the sovereign of Lu is suited to be the ruler!" Duke Min grew jealous of his comments and said to himself, "This [Wan] was a prisoner." [Turning to Wan, he said:] "You were a prisoner there, [and so you praise the sovereign of Lu]. What do you know about the virtue or evil of the sovereign of Lu?" Wan became furious, struck Duke Min, and broke his neck. That [outcome] was due to the error of playing chess with one's minister. In ancient times the people's lord occupied the yin [position, i.e., he was quiescent] while his ministers occupied the yang [position, i.e., they were active]. Consequently, their positions were distinguished, making clear [the difference between] the lofty and the base. When [Duke Min] sat opposite his minister to play chess and placed his wives at his side, he lost the distinction between ruler and minister. This led Wan to praise another state and deride the intentions of Duke Min. When Duke Min played chess with Wan, he lost the proper status due to a ruler and disgraced himself by setting his wives at his side and being boastful in front of them. He was solely responsible for precipitating his own death.[100] The commentary to the *Spring*

95. Duke Ding 11.4.13.
96. Duke Cheng 8.17.12.
97. For the killing of the lord of Jin, see Duke Cheng 8.18.2.
98. Duke Huan 2.6.3.
99. An army (*shi* 師) consisted of 2,500 men.
100. Duke Zhuang 3.12.3.

and Autumn states: "A great officer does not match his ruler."[101] It did so to avoid this kind of coercion. [6/17/21–27]

[The ruler of] Liang worked his people incessantly until his people could not endure it. He organized people of neighboring fields into groups of five families. If one family fled, those remaining in the [other four of the] five family groups were executed as punishment. His people said: "Those who are first to flee are fortunate, and those who are last to flee are punished." One who acts as the ruler of a state ought to cause his people

> to be filial toward their fathers and mothers;
> to comply with their elders;
> to preserve grave mounds and tombs;
> and to make offerings at the temples of the ancestors;

so that from age to age and generation to generation, they sacrifice to the ancestors. But the ruler of Liang sought wealth and still did not feel satisfied. He practiced penalties and punishments like a commander who would not be defeated; he murdered and killed his people as if slaughtering animals, causing his people to be grieved and resentful. Like a fish that rots and perishes, the state of Liang was exhausted and depleted. Thus the *Spring and Autumn* states: "Liang was destroyed."[102] "Was destroyed" refers to self-destruction. It was not that others destroyed Liang. [6/17/27–30]

The duke of Yu coveted wealth. Regardless of the trouble it caused, he loved to treat his ears and please his eyes. He received jade and a team of Qiu horses from the state of Jin and consequently granted the Jin army a right of way through his state [to attack Guo]. But on their way back, the Jin army destroyed [the state of] Yu. The ancestral temples were ruined; the sacrifices at the altars of the soil and grain ceased; and the duke died without a burial. These [calamities] were brought on by the duke of Yu's greediness. Thus the *Spring and Autumn* enumerates these events to illustrate [the principle] that affairs do not occur without reason and that treasures are not given up without a cause.[103]

> Those that go abroad from within will not go forward without a companion;
> those that arrive from abroad will not stop without a host.

Such are the proper responses to greed. [6/17/30–6/18/3]

King Ling of Chu overpowered [the states of] Chen and Cai.[104] He intended to expand his territory by means of brute force without considering

101. Duke Xi 5.28.5.
102. Duke Xi 5.19.6.
103. Duke Xi 5.3.1.
104. For the destruction of Chen and Cai, see Duke Zhao 10.8.9 and 10.11.10.

the [consequences of his] conduct. Fixated on what he found beautiful, he exhausted the labors of the common people. For in the Qian river in the state of Chu, there lived a female ghost. When the river was emptied of water, she would appear, and when it was filled with water, she would disappear. [On account of this ghost,] King Ling demanded corvée labor from everyone in the country [to construct the Qian River Tower]. In three years' time, the tower was still not completed, and the people of Chu had grown resentful.[105] Duke Ling of Chu once again exhibited his cruel and tyrannical heart and murdered his innocent minister Cheng Ran.[106] The people of Chu became outraged. In the end, the duke's son Qi Zhi compelled King Ling and his son [the crown prince] to commit suicide, and [Qi Zhi] assumed the position of ruler.[107]

When the minister of water does not depart from the rivers and streams,
When the director of agriculture does not depart from the fields and the soil,

the people will love one another. Was [the chaos in Chu] not due to the fault of being overly ambitious? [6/18/3–6]

Duke Zhuang of Lu lusted after palaces and chambers. Within a single year, he erected earthen platforms three times.[108] His wife had illicit relations with his two younger brothers.[109] Younger brother and elder brother, son and father, murdered each other. Consequently, the lineage of the state was cut off, and there was no one to inherit the throne. [Duke Huan of] Qi revived the state [by setting up Duke Xi of Lu].[110] [The chaos in Lu] was created by the licentious conduct of [Duke Zhuang's] wife. [Thus we see that] when elevating a concubine to [the rank of] a wife, one cannot fail to be cautious!

These all are examples of internal defeats brought about by [a ruler's] self-importance and his giving free rein to his every whim. Having shown that self-importance brings about defeat, still there remain [cases in which] upright remonstrations were presented but not put into action. In the end, all those [who did not use upright remonstrations] always suffered destruction.

[Thus] Ji of Cao remonstrated with his ruler [Duke Xi], saying: "The people of Rong are numerous and unrighteous. Do not try to resist them on your own." His ruler did not heed his advice, and in the end he was killed by men from Rong.[111]

105. Duke Zhao 10.13.2.
106. Duke Zhao 10.12.6.
107. Duke Zhao 10.13.2.
108. For the entries that document the construction of these three earthen platforms, see Duke Zhuang 3.31.1, 3.31.3, and 3.31.5, translated in chapter 8, note 11.
109. The illicit relations between Duke Zhuang's wife Ai Jiang and his younger brothers Prince Qing Fu and Prince Ya are reported in Duke Zhuang 3.27.3.
110. Duke Min 4.2.3.
111. Duke Zhuang 3.24.6.

Wuzi Xu warned King [Fuchai] of Wu that Yue would inevitably rise again [from its defeat by Wu.] The king of Wu did not heed his advice but instead murdered Wuzi Xu. Nine years later, Yue destroyed the state of Wu.[112]

Duke Mu of Qin wished to send troops to launch a surprise attack on the state of Zheng. Boli [Ziyu] and Jianshu remonstrated, saying: "No one has yet to make a surprise attack from a distance of a thousand *li* without perishing." Duke Mu did not heed their warnings, and ultimately his army was soundly defeated [by the state of Jin] in Xiao. Not a single horse or a single [chariot] wheel returned.[113]

The ruler of Jin requested an access route from the ruler of Yu [allowing their army to pass through Yu to invade the state of Guo.] The duke of Yu agreed. Gong Zhiji warned: Without lips, the teeth freeze. [The relations between Yu and Guo are like those of the lips to the teeth.] They protect each other without having to show generosity toward each other. Now the army of Jin requests an access route through Yu to attack Guo. You must not agree to their request." The duke of Yu did not heed his advice. Yu ultimately perished at the hands of the state of Jin.[114] [6/18/6–13]

Section 6.9

The *Spring and Autumn* makes clear that the path of survival and destruction can be observed.

[Thus] having observed the [fire] at the altar of Bu, you will understand the punishment of arrogance.[115]

Having observed the exchange of territories [between Lu and Zheng], you will understand that Lords of the Land do not possess the right to enfeoff.

Having observed Duke Huan of Qi, Duke Wen of Jin, Duke Xiang of Song, and King Zhuang of Chu, you will understand the merit of employing worthies and respecting superiors.

Having observed Duke Yin of Lu, Zhai Zhong, Shu Wu, Kongfu, Xun Xi, Qiu Mu, Ji Zi of Wu, and the duke's son Muyi, you will understand the efficaciousness of loyal ministers.

112. The narrative describing Wuzi Xu and King Fuchai of Wu in the *Gongyang Commentary* differs from the preceding description (Duke Ding 11.4.13).
113. See the long narrative at Duke Xi 5.33.3.
114. Note the earlier discussion of the duke of Yu in this section (Duke Xi 5.2.1).
115. In this section, the author recapitulates twenty-three lessons gleaned from the *Spring and Autumn* discussed earlier in the essay that will enable a ruler to restore the Kingly Way. The examples not discussed earlier are cited in the following two notes. These constitute only a small minority of the cases and may very well point to the possibility that parts of the essay were lost during the long centuries of transmission.

Having observed the conduct of the duke's son Bi of Chu, you will understand the principles of a true minister and the righteous principle of sacrificing your life for your state.

Having observed the viscount of Luu, you will understand the failures of a ruler who lacks the assistance of a worthy and makes policy decisions on his own.

Having observed the events of Duke [Xiang] of Lu in the state of Chu, you will understand the proper gratitude that a minister exhibits toward his lord.

Having observed [that Duke Ling of Jin divulged] the secret message [of Yang Chufu], you will understand that loyal principles may be cut off.

Having observed [that the state of Lu presented eight rows of dancers] and that the *Spring and Autumn* concealed this fact] and recorded that there were six rows of dancers, you will understand the distinctions between superior and inferior.

Having observed Boji of Song, you will understand the trustworthiness of a chaste woman.

Having observed King Fuchai of Wu, you will understand [the fate of] a strong state that tyrannizes a weak one.

Having observed the conduct of Duke Xian of Jin, you will understand the mistake of defying correct principles and engaging in licentiousness.

Having observed King Zhao of Chu attack Cai, you will understand that those who are unrighteous are repaid.

Having observed that Duke Wen of Jin recklessly executed innocent men, you will understand the retribution of violent acts.

Having observed Tuo of Chen and Min of Song, you will understand the folly of jealousy and licentiousness.

Having observed that the duke of Yu suffered the destruction of Liang, you will understand the bankruptcy of those who covet material possessions and distort the laws.

Having observed King Ling of Chu, you will understand the hatefulness of causing the people to suffer.

Having observed Duke Zhuang of Lu erecting towers, you will understand the faults of extravagance and recklessness.

Having observed Marquis Shuo of Wey, you will understand the crime of failing to respond to a summons.[116]

116. Duke Huan 2.16.5. See chapter 7, note 3.

Having observed the capture of Fan Bo, you will understand that capturing Fan Bo defied the laws pertaining to one's superior.[117]

Having observed Xi Que of Jin lead a punitive expedition against the Zhulou, you will understand the criticisms that a minister who seeks his fortune will receive.

Having observed Prince Hui of Lu, you will understand ministers who spy out the intentions of their rulers.

Having observed the institution of hereditary ministers, you will understand the failures brought about by the devolution of power. [6/18/13–23]

Section 6.10

Therefore, the enlightened king examines what is dark and murky [and] listens to what has no sound. Like Heaven, he covers the world, and like Earth, he supports it. Thus all the rulers of the myriad states in the world will try to fulfill their obligations to the utmost. The one who receives the Mandate will not expose himself to his ministers below. This is the perfection of wisdom. Thus

> if the path that the ruler follows is identical with those of his ministers, he will not be able to lead them;
>
> if his emotions are identical to those of his ministers, he will not be able to direct them.

These are the teachings [of the *Spring and Autumn*]. Considering it from this perspective,

> there has never been a ruler who abandoned his political authority who was able to control the tendencies in the various states;
>
> there has never been a ruler who abandoned the distinctions between the honorable and the lowly who was able to preserve his political position.

Therefore the Noble Man treated these matters with extreme caution. [6/18/23–25]

117. The capture of Fan Bo does not appear in the earlier discussion. Duke Yin 1.7.5. reports that during the winter of the seventh year of Duke Yin's reign, the Heavenly King ordered the great officer Fan Bo to come to the capital on a mission of friendly inquiry but that en route he was taken captive by the Rong. Confucius used the term *fa* (to attack) rather than *zhi* (to capture) to glorify the event in order to draw attention to the righteous principle that forbids people belonging to the Yi and Di to capture people from the Central States.

Book 5, Part 1

CHAPTER 7

Annihilated States, Part A

Section 7.1

The king is one toward whom the people move;
the ruler is one who does not lose his following.[1]

Thus one who can cause the myriad people to flock to him and one who can gain a following throughout the world will be unmatched in the world. In the *Spring and Autumn*, [instances of] the assassination of rulers [number] thirty-six and the annihilation of states [number] fifty-two.[2] [Of these,] the small states of meager virtue had not paid courtesy visits or sent friendly emissaries to other states, and the large states did not attend meetings with or assemblies of other Lords of the Land.

Battling alone, they did not defend one another.
Living isolated, they did not unite a following.

Thus when they encountered difficulties, no one rescued them, and consequently they were annihilated. Not only are dukes, lords, and great officers like this. There is nothing that lives between Heaven and Earth with shallow roots

1. Both lines contain puns: between "king" (*wang* 王) and "move toward" (*wang* 往), and between "ruler"(*jun* 君) and "following" (in the sense of "constituency," *qun* 群). These paranomastic definitions of "the king" and "the ruler" are not unique to the *Chunqiu fanlu*. They appear to have been popular during the Han, and similar definitions are found in such texts as the *Hanshi waizhuan*, *Bohutong*, and *Chunqiu yuanming bao*. For these examples, see Su Yu, *CQFLYZ* 133. The idea that people will flock to live in the kingdom of a worthy ruler is especially associated with Mencius.
2. Emending 失國之君三十六亡國之君五十二 to 弑君三十六亡國五十二 and supplying 春秋 at the head of the sentence, as suggested by Su Yu. For the references to the assassination of thirty-six rulers and the annihilation of fifty-two states, see Zhong, *CQFLJS* 214–15, notes 4 and 5.

that can withstand fierce winds or violent rains. Whether their demise is sudden or gradual, they will surely suffer annihilation.

> When Marquis Shuo of Wey served Duke Xiang of Qi, the world grew anxious.[3]
> When [the states of] Yu and Guo combined their strength, [Duke] Xian of Jin was distressed by it.[4]

Zhao Dun of Jin was a lone knight, with not a foot or an inch of land or a single person in his entourage; yet Duke Ling, who possessed the honor and power bequeathed to him by his hegemonic ancestors, [feared him and] wanted to kill him. Although [Duke Ling] used every kind of artifice and utmost deceit, with deceit overflowing and his strength fully employed, [nevertheless] the calamity that [eventually] fell on his own person was great. Zhao Dun's heart [was such that] had he been the ruler of [even] a small state, who would have been capable of destroying him?[5]

Thus, Wu Zixu [also] was a lone knight. He left Chu, sought out Helü, [king of Wu], and was able to fulfill his ambition in Wu.[6] If the person whom a ruler entrusts is truly the right person, then who will be able to resist him?

> When King Kun of Chu entrusted his state to Zi Yu and De Chen, the world feared them.[7]
> When the duke of Yu entrusted his state to Kong Zhiji, Duke Xian of Jin grew apprehensive of him.[8]

---

3. Duke Huan 2.16.5. *Spring and Autumn*: "In the eleventh month, Shuo, marquis of Wey, left his state and fled to Qi." *Gongyang*:

   Why does [the *Spring and Autumn*] refer to Shuo, marquis of Wey, by his personal name? It was in order to cut him off [from his lineage]. Why cut him off? He committed a crime against the Son of Heaven. How did he commit a crime against the Son of Heaven? Charged to defend Wey, Shuo was not even capable of employing a small band of men to do so. He traveled [beyond the borders of his state] to the northern side of Mount Dai in Qi. [There] he established a dwelling place and did not submit to punishment.

4. Duke Xi 5.2.3. A long narrative in the *Gongyang Commentary* relates that Duke Xian of Jin suffered a nightmare in which the states of Yu and Guo appeared. When the minister Xun Xi guessed at the cause of Duke Xian's distress, the duke took him into his confidence and revealed both his desire to attack the states of Yu and Guo and his concern that it would be impossible to invade one of these states without the other coming to the rescue, making it a challenge for him to succeed in his plans. Xun Xi assuaged his anxieties by suggesting a stratagem that the duke supported. Xun Xi carried out his scheme, and Duke Xian annihilated Yu and Guo.
5. For the story of the rapacious Duke Ling of Jin and worthy minister Zhao Dun, see Duke Xuan 7.6.1. The *Gongyang* narrative states that Zhao Dun of Jin failed to punish his lord's assassin and so must be held culpable for assassinating his lord. The *Gongyang* narrative, however, reads against the grain of the *Spring and Autumn*, underscoring Lord Ling's treacherous conduct toward his ministers, his endeavors to kill Zhao Dun, Zhao Dun's dramatic escape, and his return to install the future ruler (Lord Cheng).
6. For the anecdote describing Wu Zixu's meteoric rise to power under King Helü of Wu and his successful attempt to "fulfill his ambition" to avenge his father's wrongful death, see Duke Ding 11.4.14.
7. Duke Xi 5.28.4. He Xiu's commentary explains that Zi Yu and De Chen were two arrogant and haughty ministers of Chu who repeatedly urged their ruler to invade the Central States (Su Yu, *CQFLYZ* 134).
8. See the narrative at Duke Xi 5.2.3 mentioned in note 4.

[But]

When King Kun of Chu killed De Chen, the world disregarded him.

When the duke of Yu did not make use of Kong Zhiji, Duke Xian of Jin destroyed him.

[Whether or not a ruler employs the right person is] the source of survival and destruction. [The ruler] must not fail to understand this.

The Lords of the Land found themselves increasingly taking up arms and, [when defeated], ran away and fled, so that it reached the point that their states were on the verge of destruction and no one rescued them. Such outcomes may be deduced from their conduct in ordinary times. Duke Yin's replacing Duke Huan is what people refer to as a matter of "prudent survival."[9] But when Wuhai was ordered to lead troops to annihilate Ji,[10] inside the state of Ji there were no ministers who would remonstrate, and outside the state there were no Lords of the Land who would rescue Ji. The state of Zai was destroyed for the same reasons. When the states of Song, Cai, and Wey united and attacked [Zai], [the earl of] Zheng relied on their strength and annexed [Zai].[11] There is no difference between this and leaving precious jewels unguarded in the street. Whoever discovers them will surely take them. Deng and Gu lost their land and paid court respects to Duke Huan of Lu. Was it not fitting that they lost their territory?[12] [7/19/5–17]

9. In other words, Yin assumed the throne as regent for Huan to ensure the survival of Lu.

10. Duke Yin 1.2.3.

11. Duke Yin 1.10.6.

12. Duke Huan 2.7.2. The point seems to be that the rulers of Gu and Deng should not have paid court respects to a duke who had assassinated his brother in order to assume the throne.

Book 5, Part 2

CHAPTER 8

Annihilated States, Part B

Section 8.1

The reason why the marquis of Ji was destroyed was [due to] nine generations of revenge. Words spoken one morning [by a former marquis of Ji] endangered one hundred generations of [his] descendants. Thus [the *Spring and Autumn*] states: "[The marquis of Ji] made a grand exodus [from his state]."[1]

"A man from Wey invaded Sheng."[2]

"[A man] Zheng entered Sheng."[3]

"Qi troops besieged Sheng."[4]

Three times [the state of Sheng] was attacked by powerful armies. In the end, [the state] was destroyed, and no one attempted to rescue it. Where were those on whom the state relied?

---

1. The *Gongyang Commentary* explains that the *Spring and Autumn* conceals the true facts of the event in consideration of Duke Xiang's worthiness. Duke Xiang of Qi annihilated Ji to avenge the wrongful death of a former Qi lord who had been slandered nine generations earlier by a former Ji lord. The *Commentary* explains:

   Even after a hundred generations, avenging an offense [against an ancestor] is condoned. Is it condoned with regard to [the head of a] household? It is not condoned. Why, then, in the case of [the head of] a state, is it condoned? The lords of a state are one body. The shame of the former rulers is the shame of the current ruler; the shame of the current lord is the shame of the former rulers. (Duke Zhuang 3.4.4; see also the earlier reference to Zheng in chapter 4.8)

2. The text reads Cheng 成, but the *Gongyang Commentary* at Duke Zhuang 3.8.3 explains that Cheng actually signifies the state of Sheng 郕.
3. Duke Yin 1.10.7.
4. Duke Zhuang 3.8.3.

Duke Huan of Qi wanted to implement the Hegemonic Way. When Tan proceeded to defy his orders, [the Qi army] destroyed [Tan], and [the viscount of Tan] fled to Ju.[5] [The viscount of Tan] would not serve a great state, so [he ended up] serving a small one.

The reason why the earl of Cao battled to the death to defend his throne was that none of the Lords of the Land relieved his distress.[6] [This was because] on the numerous occasions when Duke Huan of Qi summoned the Lords of the Land together at You, although Cao was a small state, it did not once attend.

Lu was a large state, but Duke Zhuang did not attend the meeting at You. Consequently, men of the Rong [people] attacked to the west of the Ji River.[7] From this incident, one can see that Lu was isolated and alone and no one came to its rescue. At this time, the great officers [of Lu] disregarded the orders of their lord and took it upon themselves to rescue other states in danger.

In the twenty-seventh year of Duke Zhuang's reign, Duke Huan of Qi called a meeting at You, and the ruler of Wey did not attend.[8] The following year Duke Huan grew angry and soundly defeated Wey.[9] When he attacked the Mountain Rong [people], Duke Huan displayed the Rong banners and spoils of war to boast to the Lords of the Land.[10] Meanwhile, [Duke Zhuang] of Lu constructed three earthen platforms in the space of a single year.[11]

> Rebellious ministers rose up three times within the state[12]
> while the Yi and Di armies destroyed [Wey] from without.

The sprouts of Wey's destruction lay in their missing the meeting at You, and the source of the chaos [in Lu] lay in relatives deceiving one another.

5. Duke Zhuang 3.10.6: "Winter. The tenth month. Qi troops annihilated Tan. The viscount of Tan fled to Ju." *Gongyang*: "Why did [the *Spring and Autumn*] not say he went abroad? His state had been annihilated so there was no place that could be considered 'abroad.'"
6. Duke Zhuang 3.24.6.
7. Duke Zhuang 3.18.2.
8. Duke Zhuang 3.27.2.
9. Duke Zhuang 3.28.1.
10. Duke Zhuang 3.31.4.
11. Duke Zhuang 3.31.1: "Spring. We constructed an earthen platform at Lang." *Gongyang*: "Why was this entry made? In order to criticize. What was there to criticize? It was near the place where the people did their washing." Duke Zhuang 3.31.3: "We constructed an earthen platform at Xue." *Gongyang*: "Why was this entry made? In order to criticize. What was there to criticize? It was too far away from the capital." Duke Zhuang 3.31.5: "Autumn. We constructed an earthen platform at Qin." *Gongyang*: "Why was this entry made? In order to criticize. What was there to criticize? It was too close to the capital." These platforms also are mentioned in chapter 6.8.
12. Duke Zhuang 3.32.3 and 3.32.5; Duke Min 4.2.3. All three entries record a death, using a word reserved for members of a ruling house. In each case, the *Gongyang Commentary* ascribes the death to assassination.

[The ruler of] Xing never met with Duke Huan of Qi.[13] He also had a clandestine attachment to Jin. But when the duke of Jin was captured at Hann, the ruler of Xing turned his back on Jin and attended the interstate meeting in Huai.[14] When Duke Huan of Qi died, Shu Diao and Yi Ya rose up in rebellion. The ruler of Xing joined forces with the Di people to attack [Wey], whose ruler shared the same clan name, and annexed [part of] it. Given that the ruler of Xing conducted himself in this manner, even if other states wanted to draw near to him, how could they? In the end, this ruler was destroyed by a member of the same surname group. [This is what the *Spring and Autumn* records as] "Marquis Hui of Wey destroyed the state of Xing."[15]

When Duke Huan of Qi called the meeting at You, the duke of Wey did not attend. This angered Duke Huan, and he attacked Wey. However, when the Di people destroyed Wey, Duke Huan of Qi was sorrowful and [re]established the Duke of Wey. In the covenant of Ge, Duke Zhuang of Lu threatened [Duke Huan regarding] the lands of Wenyang.[16] However, when [Duke Zhuang of Lu] died, Duke Huan [helped] establish [his rightful heir].[17] The rulers of Xing and Ji never paid a courtesy call on Duke Huan of Qi, but when their states suffered destruction, he sent Lords of the Land [to their assistance] and reestablished them. Because Duke Huan of Qi cared for others in this way, how could he not be considered a true hegemon![18] Therefore the *Spring and Autumn* praised him for shouldering the anxieties of the world. [8/19/21–8/20/1]

13. Duke Xi 5.16.5.
14. Duke Xi 5.15.13.
15. Duke Xi 5.25.1.
16. Duke Zhuang 3.13.4.
17. Duke Zhuang 3.32.3; see note 12.
18. For a somewhat fanciful account of Duke Huan's rise to power (with the aid of his statesman Guan Zhong), see *Guanzi*, book 7, chapter 18 (Da Kuang 大匡); and W. Allyn Rickett, trans. *Guanzi: Political, Economic, and Philosophical Essays from Early China* (Princeton, N.J.: Princeton University Press, 1985), 1:293–311.

Book 5, Part 3

CHAPTER 9

Waxing and Waning in Accord with the Root

Section 9.1[1]

When Yan Yuan died, the Master [i.e., Confucius] said: "Alas! Heaven has caused me this loss!" When Zi Lu died, the Master said: "Alas! Heaven is cutting me off!" When a *qilin* was captured in a royal hunt in the west, Confucius said: "My Way has come to an end! My Way has come to an end!"[2] Three years later, he passed away. From these events, we see that successes and failures are decreed by Heaven. The sage knows this and [also that] there are certain situations that he is powerless to salvage. Such events are decreed [by Heaven]. [9/20/5–7]

The title of this chapter does not fit the content of section 9.1, but it does pertain to the rhetorical aims of section 9.2. Ling Shu (cited in Su Yu, *CQFLYZ* 137) cites several passages from other works that are relevant to this chapter title. The first is a commentary to the "You Tong" (Mystical Union) *fu* preserved in the *Wen Xuan*, which states: "In every instance, people's actions accord with their fate. People's fate is preordained by the spirits. Therefore signs and omens precede it. Nevertheless, its realization also lies with people's activity or passivity. Heaven's Mandate protects the good and brings calamity to the evil. It does not miss the mark." The *Li shu* states: "The Yellow Emperor established the Five Phases and initiated their waxing and waning." The *Cheng yi* states: "When yang is generated, it is waxing; when yin dies, it is waning." Our sense is that the title corresponds well to section 9.2. Just as Heaven causes yin and yang to wax and wane during particular seasons of the yearly cycle, so the ruler's power waxes and wanes in accordance with his conduct in concert with the great foundation or root of all his activities: Heaven. The source of a state's survival or destruction, blessings or disasters, can be traced to the conduct of its ruler and the extent to which he follows active or passive policies in accordance with Heaven.

1. Just before citing Ling Shu (see the preceding note), Su Yu points out that the text of section 9.1 appears not to correspond to the chapter title. We agree with his view that 9.1 is a text fragment lacking context and probably belongs in chapter 16, "Signs and Omens" (Su Yu, *CQFLYZ* 137).
2. Duke Ai 12.14.1. For the *qilin*, see the introduction to group 1, note 28.

Section 9.2[3]

Before the death of Duke Xian of Jin, Duke Huan of Qi called a meeting at Kuiqiu and gathered [his allies] together twice in one year.[4]

Before Duke Xiao of Qi had been dead for [even] a year, Duke Xi of Lu sought military aid [from Chu] and occupied the Qi territory of Gu.[5]

Relying on his power to intimidate, Duke Wen of Jin summoned the Son of Heaven to meet with the Lords of the Land twice in a single year.[6] A year before Duke Wen of Jin died, the heart of Duke Xi of Lu became divided, and he began to serve Qi. By the [end of the] reign of Duke Wen [of Jin], the state of Lu no longer served the state of Jin.[7]

A year before Marquis Bang of Qi [i.e., Duke Zhao of Qi] died, Duke Wen of Lu traveled to the state of Jin [to conclude a covenant]. The marquis of Wey and the earl of Zheng did not make the appropriate plans in advance before concluding covenants with Duke Wen.[8] Once the Marquis Bang of Qi passed away, the Lords of the Land consequently met with [Zhao Dun,] the great officer of Jin at Xincheng.[9]

Duke Zhao of Lu served the state of Chu; [therefore] the men of Jin would not allow [Duke Zhao] to enter [their state].[10] When the ruler of Chu became powerful enough to realize his ambitions, he summoned the Lords of the Land for an interstate meeting twice in a single year, violently attacked Wu, killed the rebellious minister [Qing Feng] on behalf of the state of Qi, and proceeded to annihilate the state of Li.[11] The state of Lu relied on the power of Chu and destroyed the state of Zeng.[12] The following year, Duke Zhao of Lu entered Jin and did not encounter resistance when crossing the Yellow River.[13] [Thus] a year

3. Commensurate with the chapter title, this section relates the waxing and waning of power among the various lords to their conduct in interstate relations. But note that some commentators suggest that the content of section 9.2 belongs with the title of chapter 10, "The Essentials of Covenants and Meetings."
4. Duke Xi 5.9.2.
5. Duke Xi 5.26.8: "Our Lord attacked Qi with Chu troops and took Gu."
6. Duke Xi 5.28.10 and 5.28.17.
7. Duke Xi 5.28.8.
8. Duke Wen 6.12.6 and 6.13.8.
9. Duke Wen 6.14.4.
10. Duke Zhao 10.4.2.
11. Duke Zhao 10.4.4, 10.4.5, and 10.4.6.
12. Duke Zhao 10.4.7.
13. Duke Zhao 10.2.4: "Winter: Our Lord went to Jin. But he reached the Yellow River and then returned." *Gongyang*: "Why does the Text record 'But he reached the Yellow River and then returned'? He did not dare enter [the state of Jin]." According to He Xiu, Duke Zhao of Lu heard that Jin wanted to capture him, so when he came to the Yellow River, he did not dare enter the state of Jin. In the fourth year of his reign, Lu occupied Zeng, and subsequently Duke Zhao successfully invaded Jin.

before Duke Zhao of Jin died, [Duke Zhao of Lu] no longer encountered any resistance [from Jin].

There was disorder in the state of Chu. A minister assassinated the ruler.[14] The Lords of the Land met at Pingqiu to plan the execution of this rebellious minister of Chu.[15] Duke Zhao of Lu did not participate in the alliance, and his great officer [Jisun Yin] was taken captive.[16] At Jifu, the state of Wu utterly defeated the six states of the Chu alliance.[17] Duke Zhao of Lu traveled to Jin and was greatly humiliated. The *Spring and Autumn* concealed this fact on his behalf and stated instead that he had fallen ill.

From these events, we see that when you act in concert [with other states], you cannot rely solely on them. When you serve [other states], you cannot be unwary of them. This also is the essence of a state's preservation or destruction, glory or humiliation.

Three years before King Zhuang of Chu died, the state of Jin vanquished the Lu clan, the Shen clan, and the Liu clan of the Red Di.[18]

Two years before Viscount Shen of Chu died,[19] Zheng surrendered [to Jin] at the meeting of Xiaoyu.[20]

[The year that Duke Diao of Jin died] and two years before Viscount Zhao of Chu died, Chu joined with the states of Chen and Cai to attack and soundly defeat Zheng.[21] The following year, Chu Jian of Chu met with the Lords of the Land and extended [the territory of] the Central States.[22] The year after he died,[23] the rulers of the various Sinitic states [of the Central Plains] traveled to Chu to pay court respects.[24] Viscount Zhuan of Chu succeeded [Viscount Zhao of Chu], but he died after [ruling for only] four years. Yet the state of Chu was not occupied by the ruler of another state. On the contrary, it became more prosperous and powerful, and the Central States could not match it. Why was this the case? It was because Viscount Zhao of Chu exceeded in ability all

14. Duke Zhao 10.13.3.
15. Duke Zhao 10.13.4 and 10.13.5.
16. Duke Zhao, 10.13.7; Lai, *CQFLJZJY* 128.
17. Duke Zhao 10.23.7.
18. Duke Xuan 7.15.3: "Jin troops annihilated the Lu Clan of the Red Di." See also Duke Xuan 7.16.1.
19. Emending "three" to "two" years, following Liu Shipei (Lai, *CQFLJZJY* 129, note 17). Viscount Shen of Chu was King Gong of Chu, and he was the son of King Zhuang of Chu. His *ming* was Shen. He died in the thirteenth year, ninth month, of Duke Xiang's reign.
20. Duke Xiang 9.11.4.
21. Duke Xiang 9.26.9.
22. Duke Xiang 9.27.2.
23. Emending *sannian* 三年 to *mingnian* 明年, following Liu Shipei (Lai, *CQFLJZJY* 129, note 23).
24. Duke Xiang 9.29.1.

the [other] Lords of the Land. Everyone in the world who despised their rulers brought their complaints to him and availed themselves [of his aid]. Whenever [lit., four or five times] he sent forth his armies, his troops always were numerous and those he fought were few, [so] whenever he attacked, [the enemy] was defeated. He developed his righteousness to the fullest.

Four to five years before King Kang of Chu died, the Central States were no longer united. The armies of Qi, Jin, Lu, and Wey had dispersed to guard their respective territories. Powerful states attacked weaker ones. The Lords of the Land met again at Chenyi.[25] The ruler of Qi did not attend. Wu lay to the south of Chu, but two rulers had been assassinated [there].[26] The Central States lay to the north of Chu, but the great officers of Qi and Wey assassinated their rulers.[27] Qing Feng coerced his ruler and revolted against his state. The great officer of Wey, She Wu, and his followers united their forces. Wei Heng took possession of Chenyi and deceived [Sun] Linfu [of Wey]. [Sun Linfu] took possession of Jie and rose up in rebellion. Duke Ping of Song murdered the heir apparent, and the state of Lu suffered a devastating famine.

The conduct of the rulers of the various states of the Central Plains corresponded to the conduct of states on the verge of destruction. Between the reigns of Duke Wen and Duke Huan of Lu, five rulers were assassinated within five years. Duke Ling of Jin sent the great officer [Zhao Dun] to meet with the other Lords of the Land at Feilin. Clasping their hands to their breasts and bowing low, there was not a single Lord of the Land at the meeting who dared not send troops [to help Jin]. [They were constrained by the lord of Jin,] just as "the marsh has its banks."[28] [9/20/9–26]

25. Duke Xiang 9.24.8.
26. Duke Xiang 9.25.10 and 9.29.9.
27. Duke Xiang 9.25.2 and 9.26.1.
28. This is an allusion to *Ode* 58, verse 6: "The Qi River has its shoreline, the marsh has its banks."

Book 5, Part 4

CHAPTER 10

The Essentials of Covenants and Meetings

Section 10.1

Although his highest intentions are difficult to convey, is it not the case that the Sage [i.e., Confucius] prized eradicating the world's misfortunes? Thus the *Spring and Autumn* attaches great importance to this subject and records the world's misfortunes in a comprehensive way. It takes as its root revealing the various causes of misfortune with the intention of eradicating misfortune in the world. What do I mean?

Only when the world is free of misfortune can human nature become good.

Only when human nature can become good will the transformative influence of purity and honesty flow forth.

According to the *Gongyang Commentary*, covenants initiated by the Lords of the Land violated ritual protocol and were considered a major source of political turmoil, leading to the demise and destruction of many rulers and their states. Thus in attempting to eradicate evil in the world and restore the Kingly Way, Confucius targeted instances of interstate covenants as particularly problematic. *The Gongyang Commentary* at Duke Huan 2.3.2 explains: "In ancient times there were no covenants. One made a verbal contract and withdrew." As for meeting and assembling, Duke Zhuang 3.4.4 explains: "In ancient times, the Lords of the Land participated in matters of meeting and assembling with other Lords of the Land. In accordance with the Way of Chao and Bin, their official addresses invariably mentioned the former lords when they greeted one another."

The record on interstate meetings is more complicated. Even though the *Gongyang Commentary* seems not to approve of them in general, because the Lords of the Land were not supposed to cross their borders except to pay a court visit to the Son of Heaven when summoned, some Lords of the Land are praised for the manner in which they conducted themselves during an interstate meeting. This appears to be one of those instances of Confucius's "seeing good in evil" discussed elsewhere in the *Chunqiu fanlu* (Lai, *CQFLJZJY* 237, note 1). But note that Zhong Zhaopeng cites He Xiu's commentary to support the blanket condemnation of covenants and meetings. While it is clear from the preceding example that the *Gongyang* expresses overt disapproval of interstate covenants, its disapproval of interstate meetings appears to be embedded in the choice of terminology when these records appear.

Only when the transformative influence of purity and honesty flows forth will the Kingly Way prosper and ritual and music flourish.

The heart of the matter lies here.

A tradition states: "When the Lords of the Land assembled together and concluded covenants, the Noble Man said: This is a case of the generals taking the lead in order to restore their states."[1] By this means, the Noble Man expressed sorrow for the world, considering that misfortunes had already amounted to the assassination of thirty-six rulers and the destruction of fifty-two states. [This happened] because evil had not been eradicated when it was still quite insignificant. His terminology itself conveyed this [sorrow]. Thus I say [the *Spring and Autumn*]:

establishes principles to illuminate the distinction between the lofty and humble;
strengthens the trunk and weakens the branches to illuminate duties great and small;
differentiates conduct that appears deceptively similar to illuminate the righteous principles of rectifying the age;
selects various people with the intention of assigning to them praise or blame, to rectify those who stray from correct ritual practice;
never fails to praise goodness, no matter how insignificant
and never fails to condemn evil, no matter how trifling,
[in order] to enhance moral beauty [in the world];
differentiates the worthy and foolish to illuminate the honorable;
cherishes those who are near and attracts those who are distant, starting with his own state [of Lu] and [extending to] encompass the world;
and designates human relationships and ranks the events [that it records][2] so that they do not depart from their respective principles.

With a public-spirited heart, it relies on right and wrong to reward good and punish evil so that the enriching influence of the king spreads throughout the

1. Emending *junzi xiu guo yue: ci jiang shuai wei ye* 君子修國曰: 此將率為也 to *ci jiang shuai wei xiu guo ye* 此將率為修國也, as suggested by Yu Yue and cited in Su Yu, *CQFLYZ* 141.

2. The same expression *ming lun deng wu* 名倫等物 appears at the beginning of chapter 5.1: "The *Spring and Autumn* uses language cautiously. It is careful of how it designates human relationships and how it ranks the events [that it records]."

world. It begins by eradicating misfortune [and concludes] by rectifying the [grand] unity [of King Wen] so that all things are put in order. Thus it is said, "Great indeed are the designations of the *Spring and Autumn*! With two expressions, [praise and blame], it disciplines the world." This is what this expression means. [10/20/30–10/21/9]

Book 5, Part 5

CHAPTER 11

The Rectifying Thread

Section 11.1

The *Spring and Autumn* is the root of the great righteous principles [that bring order to the world] that we refer to as the "six categories" and "ten directives."[1] From this it follows that [the six categories] invoke Heaven's starting points,

It is difficult to convey the meaning of the title of this essay, *zhengguan* 正貫, in a single English rendering because it simultaneously denotes the upright stroke of a Chinese graph, a set of principles that rectify the myriad affairs of the world, and the actions of rectifying and connecting. The expression functions as a metaphor for the king. Dong Zhongshu explains, "The ancients who created language, employed three [horizontal] strokes and connected them through the center [with a single upright stroke] to constitute the designation." The three horizontal strokes symbolize Heaven, Earth, and humankind. The upright stroke binds them together to symbolize the king. Confucius said: "The one that threads together the three is the king." Thus the title echoes the (spurious but widely accepted) etymology of the character for "king," which, in turn, hints at the functions of the true king as the thread that connects and thereby rectifies the human and heavenly realms. The expression that occurs at the end of this chapter, *san shi dang zhong* 三示當中, appears to be a somewhat garbled expression of this idea as well (Lai, *CQFLJZJY* 135).

The title also resonates with an important passage from the "Tianlun" chapter of the *Xunzi*:

> What has remained unchanged throughout [the reigns of] the Hundred Kings is sufficient to be regarded as the connecting thread of the Way (*dao guan* 道貫). If with each rise and each fall, you respond with this connecting thread and pattern [yourself in accordance with] this connecting thread, there will be no disorder. If you do not know the connecting thread, you will not know how to respond to changing circumstances. The great, essential matter of this connecting thread has never ceased to be. Thus, disorder is produced by mistakes concerning it; order by exhaustive application of its every detail. Hence, with regard to what is good when judged by the standard of the Way, follow what perfectly coincides with the Way; what departs from it by bits and fractions should not be done; and what is utterly contrary to it should be treated as the gravest of errors. (*Xunzi zhuzi suoyin* 17/82/20–22; John Knoblock, *Xunzi: A Translation and Study of the Complete Works* [Stanford, Calif.: Stanford University Press, 1994], 3:21)

1. The essay that constitutes this chapter must be incomplete, as it refers to "categories" and "directives" in the *Spring and Autumn* but what follows is limited to "categories" and does not touch on "directives." The next chapter, however, spells out the "ten directives" of the *Spring and Autumn*. We support

displaying and circulating them through concrete examples, and connecting and comprehending their inherent patterns, so that the changing circumstances of affairs are reflected in its terminology.

Therefore, it

[explains] what causes the aspirations of some to succeed while others fail, thereby differentiating the beginnings of the honorable and the base;

assesses whether the sources of criminal acts are deep or shallow and assigns appropriate punishment according to the laws, thereby distinguishing those who should die and those who should live;

establishes righteous principles and ranks the proper hierarchy of the lofty and the lowly, thereby clarifying the duties of ruler and minister;

records the methods of the world's worthies to elucidate where the righteous principle of deference resides, thereby revealing [their efforts] to restore uprightness;[2]

does not shy away from dark and hidden matters but draws near them and examines them in detail, thereby [comprehending] the inexhaustible responses of the myriad things.[3]

Therefore, it is possible to apply [the *Spring and Autumn*] to every kind of human [situation] without confusing [what is proper to] its various classifications of human relationships. For this reason, you must clearly [understand] how appropriately it [maintains] its unity in applying [its principles]. Therefore

only when you understand its temperament will you be able to nourish its aims;

only when you understand its voice will you be able to promote its essence;

only when you understand its conduct will you be able to follow its forms;

and only when you understand its affairs[4] will you be able to distinguish its sentiments.

Zhong Zhaopeng's contention that the materials preserved in chapters 11 and 12 originally constituted a single essay. Accordingly, the first part of the essay enumerates the "six categories" of the *Spring and Autumn*, and the second half of the essay turns to the "ten directives." We, therefore, emend the phrase *liuzhi* 六指 to *shizhi* 十指 to match the title and content of chapter 12, "Ten Directives." We believe reading these two chapters as one essay restores the materials preserved in chapters 11 and 12 to a form that more closely resembles the original essay. Note that there are other instances in which a single essay is divided into two parts to constitute two separate chapters, as if our unknown compiler/editor had a limited amount of material available to reconstitute a work that he believed must consist of eighty-two chapters. For Zhong's comments, see *CQFLJS* 249, note 1.

2. For the expression *fuzheng* 復正 (restoring uprightness), see also *CQFL* chapter 6, section 6.6 [6/16/26].
3. Some editions have here *wanbian* 萬變 (myriad alterations) instead of *wanwu* 萬物.
4. In *CQFLJZJY*, Lai glosses the graph *wu* 物 as *shi* 事.

Therefore [the ruler]
leads and the people comply;
moves and the people follow.
This is because he knows
to arouse those things that their Heaven-endowed natures cherish
and to repress those things that their emotions despise.
Being like this,
although his words are restrained, his speech will certainly resonate widely;
although his undertakings are modest, his achievements will certainly be great.
His voice and profuse transformative powers will move through living things,
spreading and infusing their inherent patterns.
His virtue will fill Heaven and Earth,
and spirit illumination will come to rest and accumulate [in his person].

As he takes [various] actions simultaneously without tiring, [his renown] will spread [everywhere within] the Four Seas, and the people will sing his praises. The *Documents* state: "When the eight musical tones are harmonized and none encroach on one another, spirits and humans attain harmony."[5] This expresses my meaning.

Thus only when you understand human emotion and human nature can you conduct a discussion about how to govern. Otherwise, even though you exert yourself, you will not succeed. Even if [you stay] awake from dawn until nightfall, exhausting your mind with contemplation, you will not understand how to govern, and you will be rejected by the world. [Even some of] those who connected the three realms [of Heaven, Earth, and humankind], Confucius judged to be wrong. How, then, could [such rulers] have fully understood the proper principles of governing? [11/21/13–24]

5. *Documents*, "Shun dian" (The Canon of Shun) 24; James Legge, trans. *The Shoo King, or, The Book of Historical Documents*, vol. 3 of *The Chinese Classics*, 2nd rev. ed. (1894; repr., Hong Kong: Hong Kong University Press, 1960), 48.

Book 5, Part 6

CHAPTER 12

Ten Directives

Section 12.1

In the *Spring and Autumn*'s record of 240 years, there is nothing that it fails to transmit, [despite] the vastness of the world or the extensiveness of alterations in human affairs. Although this is so, the essential elements of its broad outline [consist] of ten directives. These ten directives are

> what bind together all its affairs
> and are the source from which the king's transformative [influence] flows.

To hold up [for scrutiny] the alterations of human affairs and show which ones are weighty is one directive.

To reveal from whence the alterations of human affairs arise is one directive.

To follow the causes of the alterations of human affairs and master them is one directive.

To strengthen the trunk and weaken the branches and to magnify the roots and minimize the twigs is one directive.

To distinguish the deceptively similar and differentiate [things that appear to belong to] the same category is one directive.

To discuss the righteousness of the worthy and talented and distinguish the various strengths of their abilities is one directive.

To show affection toward those who are close and to attract those who are distant and to identify with what the common people desire is one directive.

Having inherited the refinement of the Zhou, to revert to simplicity is one directive.

To take as Heaven's starting point that Wood generates Fire and Fire constitutes summer is one directive.[1]

To take as humanity's[2] starting point examining how those who merit criticism are punished and investigating what brings on anomalies and portents is one directive.

By describing the alterations of human affairs and by illuminating their significance, the one hundred surnames will find security.

By revealing from whence arise the alterations of human affairs, success and failure will be illuminated.

By following the causes of the alterations of human affairs and mastering them, affairs will be rectified at their source.

By strengthening the trunk and weakening the branches and by magnifying the roots and minimizing the twigs, the distinction between ruler and subject will be clarified.

By distinguishing the deceptively similar and by differentiating [things that appear to belong to] the same category, right and wrong will become manifest.

By discussing the righteousness of the worthy and talented and differentiating them according to the strength of their abilities, the hierarchy of officials will be properly ordered.

By having inherited the refinement of Zhou and reverting to simplicity, the responsibility of [kingly] transformation will be accomplished.

By showing affection toward those who are close and attracting those who are distant and by identifying with what the common people desire, humaneness and compassion will become prominent.

By Wood generating Fire and Fire constituting summer, the inherent patterns of yin and yang and the four seasons will follow one another in orderly sequence.

By examining how those who merit criticism are punished by investigating what brings on anomalies and portents, what Heaven desires will be realized.

If you bring together these precepts and promote them, humaneness will [radiate] outward, and righteousness will arrive. The enriching influence of

1. This reference may signify a preference for the Fire phase. The tendency to identify the dynasty with Fire began with Wang Mang's interregnum (9–23 C.E.) between the Western and Eastern Han dynasties. This chapter outlines ten directives of the *Spring and Autumn*; chapter 11 mentioned "six directives," which we emended to "ten" on the basis of this chapter. See chapter 11, note 1.

2. Reading *tian* 天 as *ren* 人, as suggested in *CQFL* 22, note 1.

your virtue will broaden and expand, spreading and overflowing within the Four Seas. Yin and yang will be harmoniously balanced, and none of the myriad things will fail to conform to its inherent patterns. All those who explicate the *Spring and Autumn* use these directives and [take them] as their standards. [12/21/28–12/22/9]

Book 5, Part 7

CHAPTER 13

Emphasize Governance

Section 13.1

Only a sage is able to link the myriad things to the One and to bind them to the Origin. If ultimately you do not reach and acknowledge the root from which [the myriad things] proceed, you cannot succeed in your endeavors. This is why the *Spring and Autumn* alters the first [year of each reign] and designates it the Origin [*yuan* 元] year.[1] The word *yuan* is homophonous with the word *yuan* 原, [which means "source"]. It signifies that [the *Spring and Autumn*] follows the cycles [literally, ends and beginnings] of Heaven and Earth. Thus people are the only [creatures] whose lives have beginnings and ends but do not necessarily respond to the alterations of the four seasons. Therefore the Origin is the root of the myriad things, and the Origin of humans [likewise] lies therein. Where is [that Origin]? It existed before Heaven and Earth. This is why, although people are born of Heaven's vital energy and are endowed with Heaven's vital energy, it cannot [be said that] their vital energy is coextensive with the Heavenly Origin. The Heavenly Origin decrees, but [people] often defy Heaven's actions. Thus [an entry such as] "Spring. The [royal] first month" is meant to acknowledge the actions of Heaven and Earth and to continue the actions of Heaven and bring them to completion. The Way [of designating the Origin year] is to pair up [Heaven's decrees and human works] in mutual accomplishments and supportive enterprises. Is that not to say in effect to return to the Origin of Heaven

1. The formulaic phrase in the *Spring and Autumn* for the first year of a Lu duke is *Yuan nian, chun, wang zheng yue* 元年春王正月 (Origin [i.e., first] Year. Spring. The royal first month).

and Earth? How is it that the Origin of Heaven and Earth is to be found here, and how does it operate in the human realm? [The *Spring and Autumn*] attaches much importance to those who can connect and acknowledge the inherent patterns of [Heaven's] will. [13/22/13–18]

Section 13.2

Those who can discuss the [various] categories of birds and beasts are not those with whom the sage desires to converse. The sage desires to discuss humaneness and righteousness and lay out their inherent patterns. He knows their divisions and classes, their categories and distinctions, and threads together those that fit together. The sage clarifies things that have been investigated by means of righteousness, so that there will be no instances of deceptive resemblance [between things]. This, and only this, is what the sage prizes. If this were not the case, and the sage

> adhered to the terminology of the multitude
> and saw things from the perspective of the multitude,

then lax words would be spoken, and that would give rise to doubts, impeding those who are advancing [in their learning]. This is what the noble man most deeply despises.

Why would one act like that? The daylight hours are not sufficient to satisfy the thoughts of a sage; they continue into the evening hours. Having contemplated the myriad affairs of the world, they come down to humaneness and righteousness. When speaking of it from this perspective, we say that you must practice [humaneness and righteousness] yourself if you are to attain them. Therefore I say: "Indeed! If one is to instruct others, can one fail to be cautious?" Righteousness derives from the *Classic* [i.e., the *Spring and Autumn*]. The *Classic* and the [*Gongyang*] *Commentary* are the great root [of learning]. But if you fail to be diligent in applying your mind, [even though you act so as to] embitter your resolve and deplete your feelings, [it will be to no avail]. Even if your hair turns white and your teeth fall out, you still will not come up to the standards recorded [in them]. [13/22/20–25]

Section 13.3

When human beings are first born, they [already] have their great destiny. This is [incorporated in] their physical substance. There is, as well, a changeable destiny that endures during one's life span. This destiny [is contingent on] governance.

If governance is not equitable, then people will develop vexed and angry intentions. If it happens that you are in the midst of danger and hardship, in accordance with the times things may go smoothly or adversely. [One who possesses] spirit illumination accepts this. [Whether your destiny] tallies with a life cut short or a life in full also varies according to one's [fated] life span. Because things are inequitable in this way, one cannot help but investigate them. When investigating them, one finds that the weightiest [factor] is [taking] governance as the root. [13/22/25–27]

Section 13.4

Bring [all things] together to create unity. Promote righteousness and eradicate wrongdoing. Cut off [wrongdoing] at its root and disseminate [righteousness]. Such actions resemble those of [Kings] Tang and Wu, although they also differ. Tang and Wu used them to order [the populace] by returning to [the practices of] antiquity. The *Spring and Autumn* illuminates success and failure, distinguishes the lofty and the base, and is rooted in Heaven. It explains what caused kings to lose their authority over the world and what enabled the Lords of the Land to disorder the world. It also explains [the cases of] those who ultimately grasped [proper principles] and returned to them. Thus it is said: "[The *Spring and Autumn*] is extensive and illuminating, discriminating and deep." [13/22/29–13/23/1]

Book 6, Part 1

CHAPTER 14

Images for the Regulation of Dress

The reason that Heaven and Earth generate the myriad things is in order to nourish human beings. Therefore,

> what can be consumed is used to nourish the body;
>
> what invokes awe is used to adorn and clothe [the body].

This is what makes ritual flourish.

> That the sword [is worn] on the left is to imitate the Bluegreen Dragon.[1]
>
> That the knife [is worn] on the right is to imitate the White Tiger.[2]
>
> That the knee pads[3] [are worn] in the front is to imitate the Vermilion Bird.[4]
>
> That the cap [is worn] on the head is to imitate the Dark Warrior.[5]

These four are humankind's most splendid ornamentations. Only those who are able to connect antiquity with the present and distinguish what is so from what is not so are able to dress in this manner.

Now the Dark Warrior's appearance is the fiercest and most awe inspiring. That its image occupies the rear,[6] but [its article of dress] occupies the [top of]

---

1. In early Chinese cosmology, the Bluegreen Dragon was the divinity or emblem of the east.
2. The White Tiger was the divinity or emblem of the west.
3. This refers to leather knee pads worn to protect the knees while kneeling during sacrificial rituals.
4. Reading *niao* 鳥 for *wu* 烏. The Vermilion Bird was the divinity or emblem of the south.
5. The Dark Warrior, a composite image of a snake coiled around a turtle, was the divinity or emblem of the north. See John S. Major, "New Light on the Dark Warrior," *Journal of Chinese Religions* 13–14 (1985/1986): 63–86.
6. Reading *hou* 後 (rear) for *you* 右 (right). If the knee pads are worn "in front," their paired opposite, the Dark Warrior, must occupy the rear. The text also specifies that the knife is worn "on the right." The orientation implied in this passage reflects a king's-eye view of the world: the ruler's ceremonial throne always faced south, so east would be on the king's left, west on his right, south in front of him, and north to the rear. The southern gate of a city was always known as the "front gate," and the northern gate as the "rear gate."

the head [shows that] martiality at its utmost is not employed. The reason that the sage surpasses [others] is because even if he were to wish to follow [a policy of martiality], no occasion for it would arise. Those who are able to stop the enemy only after "grasping armor and helmet" [i.e., resorting to warfare] are certainly not those whom the sage prized. The Noble Man manifested this in his dress. The intentions of the brave and martial were vitiated [when confronted by] his appearance. Therefore,

civility and virtue are prized;
awesomeness and martiality are subordinated.

This is the means by which the world perpetually [will] remain whole.

In the *Spring and Autumn*, how is this expressed? The righteousness of Kong Fu was manifest in his appearance, and so rebellious ministers did not dare act out their depravity.[7] Kong Zhiji [presided] in Yu, so Duke Xian [passed many] sleepless [nights].[8] Duke Li of Jin grew powerful, so [the great officers of] the Central States [were murdered one after the next], and their bleeding corpses lay around without cease.[9] King Wu conquered Yin wearing his dragon-embroidered robe and crown with his tablet in his girdle, so the tiger-fierce soldiers [of Yin] laid down their swords.

How can it be the case that bravery must be proved in battle and slaughter before awesomeness [is established]? This is why the Noble Man [Confucius] attached greatest importance to his dress. Those who gazed at his dignified appearance could not help but exhibit such dignity. You must not fail to examine this matter in great depth! [14/23/5–16]

7. Duke Huan 2.2.1. The *Gongyang Commentary* explains that because of Kong Fu's awesome deportment, Minister Du of Song did not dare carry out his plan to assassinate his lord, Duke Shang of Song. He therefore assassinated Kong Fu first and then killed Duke Shang.
8. Duke Xi 5.2.3. The *Gongyang Commentary* refers to the well-known story of how Duke Xian of Jin bribed the lord of Yu for safe passage across Yu territory for the Jin army. After conquering the small state of Guo, Jin extinguished the state of Yu. The point here is that the lord of Yu unwisely accepted the bribe, despite the good counsel of his minister Kong Zhiji.
9. Duke Cheng 8.17.12: "Jin killed their great officers Shi Ji, Shi Chou, and Shi Zhi." Duke Cheng 8.18.1: "Spring. The royal first month. Jin killed their great officer Xiu Tong." The *Gongyang Commentary* does not comment on these entries.

Book 6, Part 2

CHAPTER 15

Two Starting Points

Section 15.1

The highest aspirations of the *Spring and Autumn* [can be expressed as] two starting points. If you do not understand where these two starting points arise, you will not be able to begin to assess the portents and anomalies [recorded in the *Spring and Autumn*]. [These starting points are:]

the distinction between the insignificant and significant,

and [the distinction between] the hidden and manifest.

If you look into the causes of events when they have not yet reached their starting point, then you will certainly understand how insignificant events transform into significant events and how events that were hidden become manifest. Only a sage is able to understand events before their auspicious or inauspicious qualities have taken shape. This is to say that even if you wish to follow [the appropriate responses to such portents], you will not know where they arose.[1]

Therefore, when a [dynasty-founding] king receives the Mandate, he alters the month with which the calendar begins. He does not go along with the [previous dynasty's] calculations but departs [from them]. [But he also] must [base his] calculations on [the calendar of] the previous dynasty, and [in that sense he] accepts it.[2] This is "the principle of conferring and accepting."

1. Su Yu (*CQFLYZ* 146) believes that these twelve characters, beginning with *sui* and ending with *ye* (雖欲從之微末由也已此之謂也), contain errors and should be excised from the text.
2. Here *ying* 迎 means "to calculate"; *lai* 來 refers to the dynasty before the one that currently holds the Mandate.

Therefore the sage alone is able to focus his attention on what is hidden and cause it to be manifest. This is why the Way of the *Spring and Autumn* is

to rely on the profundity of the Origin to rectify the starting point of Heaven [i.e., the first month of the civil calendar];

to rely on the starting point of Heaven to rectify the government of the king;

to rely on the government of the king to rectify the authority of the Lords of the Land;

and to rely on the authority of the Lords of the Land to rectify the administration within the borders [of the various states].

When these five[3] are rectified, then [the sage-king's] transformative influence will greatly issue forth.

Therefore [the *Spring and Autumn*] records eclipses, meteors, water monsters, mountains crumbling, earthquakes, great rainstorms in the summer, great hailstorms in the winter, descents of frost that [nevertheless] did not harm plants, lack of rain from the first month of the year to the seventh month in autumn, and cranes and mynahs nesting [in Lu]. The *Spring and Autumn* noted these occurrences as anomalies and used them to manifest the incipient stirrings of disorder.

In this way what was [still] insignificant was not able to become significant

and what was [still] hidden was not able to become manifest.

Even if they were quite subtle, [they still were considered] the starting points [of events], and Confucius used them to verify [their outcomes]. This is why I value the subtle and emphasize beginnings. This is also why I despise those who predict portents and anomalies in advance, but only [when they occur do they] take action to secure [their realms from] the danger, misfortune, and chaos that follow in their wake. This is not something for which the *Spring and Autumn* expresses admiration. On the contrary, the *Spring and Autumn* brings up these anomalies and considers them as points of departure because [Confucius] hoped that this would cause [the ruler] to heed Heaven's reprimands and be awed by Heaven's majesty so that

within, it would move his heart and intentions,

and without, it would find expression in his actions.

[It would cause him to] cultivate his person and understand goodness of heart so as to return to the Way. If you do not value the subtle and emphasize beginnings, how will you be able to cautiously predict the conclusion of events and deduce their outcomes? [15/23/20–15/24/4]

3. The "five" are the Origin (i.e., first year), the first month, the royal government, the government of the Lords of the Land, and the local administration.

Book 6, Part 3

CHAPTER 16

Signs and Omens

Section 16.1

There are events that cannot be brought about by human effort but that happen spontaneously. Just such an event was the capture of the *qilin* in the royal hunt in the west, which tallied with [Confucius's] receiving Heaven's Mandate. Consequently, [Confucius] availed himself of the distinction between the proper and improper affairs [recorded] in the *Spring and Autumn* to illuminate the righteous principle of reforming regulations to unify governance under the Son of Heaven. He accepted the worries of the world as his own and labored to eradicate what brought misfortune to the world. He wanted to transmit [the teachings of] the Five Thearchs of high antiquity and attain [the virtue of] the Three Kings of later ages in order to comprehend the Way of the One Hundred Kings and to follow the cycles of Heaven.[1] With extensive knowledge of the subtle proofs of success and failure, he investigated the various manifestations of fate and portents. He plumbed the principles of things to develop fully what is suitable to the emotions and nature, thereby extending Heaven's prosperity.[2] [16/24/8–11]

1. We translate the Chinese word *di* 帝 as "thearch" in reference to mythical, semidivine, cultural heroes and "sage-rulers" like Lord Millet (Hou Ji) and the Divine Farmer (Shen Nong). The four characters *tian zhi zhong shi* 天之終始 mean literally "the ends and beginnings of Heaven."
2. It also would be possible to read *tian rong* 天容 (Heaven's prosperity) as *tian rong* 天榮 (Heaven's glory).

Section 16.2

The numerous officials gaze in unison from different paths.

The task of unifying them lies with the ruler.

The task of leading them rests with the ministers.[3] [16/24/11]

3. These sixteen characters do not belong with the essay that precedes them. Our translation is tentative because of this lack of context. Qian Tang also has suggested that these characters do not belong here but did not know where they originally belonged (Lai, *CQFLJZJY* 148).

Book 6, Part 4

CHAPTER 17

Yu's Postface

Section 17.1

When Zhongni [i.e., Confucius] composed the *Spring and Autumn*, he first plumbed the uprightness of Heaven to rectify the positions of the king and the nobles[1] and the desires of the multitudinous people.[2]

Next he

illuminated successes and failures
and promoted the worthy and capable

in expectation of a future sage. Thus he

cited historical records,
ordered past events,
rectified right and wrong,
and revealed his kingly mind.[3]

1. We follow Su Yu's (*CQFLYZ* 159) emendations, reading *tan* 探 as an error for *yuan* 援 and relocating *zheng* 正 before *wang* 王. At the most literal level, this sentence refers to the linguistic structure of the passage that begins the reign period of each duke in the *Spring and Autumn*: "The first year. Spring. The royal first month." "The first year. Spring" refers to the starting point of the Heavenly cycles that define the seasons of the year. Thus in the *Chunqiu fanlu*'s discussions of the *Spring and Autumn*'s records, *duan* 端 (as in *tianduan* 天端 [Heaven's starting point]) is, in effect, synonymous with *yuan* 元 (Origin). According to the *Gongyang* tradition, one can rectify wrongdoing in the world only by returning to the beginning of affairs. Thus one anticipates the outcome of events based on their incipient germinations, just as one determines the correct punishment for a crime based on the motivations that initiated an affair.
2. Translating *yu* 欲 (desires), following Su Yu (*CQFLYZ* 158) and Lau.
3. Following Su Yu (*CQFLYZ* 159), who emends *gong* 公 to *xin* 心.

Now the events of the twelve dukes in the historical records all were events of a declining age. Consequently, Confucius's disciples had doubts about them. Confucius told them, "I rely on past events and apply my kingly mind to them because I consider that explaining things with abstract theories is not as good as the breadth and depth of past events for parsing and illuminating things."[4]

[The disciples] Zigong, Minzi, and Kong Jianzi discussed [Confucius's] parsings and thereby were able to assist the rulers of their states. His parsings touched on the assassination of rulers, the annihilation of states, and those who fled and failed to defend their altars of the grain and soil. They explained that these events came to pass because these rulers did not understand the Way, having failed to read the *Spring and Autumn*. Thus it was that Zixia of Wey said: "Those who rule a state must not fail to study the *Spring and Autumn*. If they do not study the *Spring and Autumn*, they will lack the means to observe the dangers that surround them and will not understand the state's 'great handle of authority,' which is the chief responsibility of the ruler."[5]

Thus some rulers lost their states through coercion or impoverishment, and others were assassinated while still on their thrones. [Such evils] did not coalesce in a single day.[6] If you could perpetuate the standards of the *Spring and Autumn* and practice its Way, would this not give you the power to rid the world of such calamities? This would approach the virtue of Yao and Shun. Thus it was that Shizi said: "Their merit extended to their sons and grandsons, resplendently illuminating one hundred generations. [Among] the virtues of the sage-king, none is more beautiful than magnanimity." Thus it was that Zi Xian[7] said: "The *Spring and Autumn* spoke in detail about [the affairs of] its own [state (i.e., Lu)] and in general outline about [the affairs of] other [states]. It took account of [the affairs of] its own state and extended [its principles to] the entire world.

As for the Way of the *Spring and Autumn,*

if you comprehend it in to a great degree, you will become a king;
if you comprehend it to a lesser degree, you will become a hegemon."

Thus it was that Zengzi and Zi Shi effusively praised the marquis of Qi for pacifying the Lords of the Land and honoring the Son of Heaven. The Way of hegemons and kings is rooted in humaneness. Humaneness is the heart of

4. A more elaborate rendition of this quote appears in the "Grand Historian's Preface" (Taishi gong) to the *Shiji*. See Su Yu's discussion at *CQFLYZ* 159.
5. A similar quotation attributed to Master Dong appears in the "Grand Historian's Preface" (Taishi gong) to the *Shiji*. See Su Yu's discussion at *CQFLYZ* 160.
6. Restoring the character *fei* 非 before *yi* 一, following Liu Shipei (Su Yu, *CQFLYZ* 159).
7. Emending *yu* 予 to *zi* 子, following Yu Yue (Su Yu, *CQFLYZ* 161).

Heaven. Therefore [the text] ranked them in accordance with their Heavenly heart.

In the great matter of loving the people, nothing is greater than being mindful of their misfortunes and making preparations to defend against them. Thus when Chai realized its aims in Wu and when Lu realized it aims in Qi, the *Spring and Autumn* did not report such events. Therefore it disparaged them by stating:

> "People who are angry with you cannot be brought near."
>
> "A state that despises you cannot be tamed."
>
> "A state you have pillaged cannot be made to have enduring affection for you."

All these admonitions defend against misfortune; they begin with the intention of eradicating misfortune on behalf of the common people. If your love for the people does not well up, then you ultimately will perish. This is why the *Spring and Autumn* explained that King Ling of Chu and Duke Li of Jin were assassinated while on their thrones. Their inhumanity led to these consequences. Therefore [the *Spring and Autumn*] praised Duke Xiang of Song because he did not endanger his people. He felt that to abandon the Way to defeat others did not compare with holding fast to the Way and being defeated. The *Spring and Autumn* honored him because he tried to transform the habits and customs of his people and thereby perfect the transformative influences of the king. Thus it was that Zi Xia said, "The *Spring and Autumn* emphasizes the people. All its numerous criticisms are based on this."

> Those who were extravagant and wasteful angered and enraged the people;
>
> those who were violent and cruel injured and harmed the people.

Ultimately they all suffered personal calamity. Thus Zi Chi spoke of [the *Spring and Autumn* entries that record] Duke Zhuang of Lu erecting [three] earthen platforms,[8] painting the pillars [of Duke Huan's temple] red, and carving its rafters.[9] [He also spoke of] the punishments [enacted by] Duke Li of Jin that revealed his oppressive intent. None [of these rulers] were able to live out their natural life spans.

When the ruler is extravagant and his punishments are harsh, [it shows] a lack of sympathy within himself. Yet he demands perfection from others. Therefore, in case after case, [one must] use the *Spring and Autumn* to

> accord with the feelings of others
>
> and pardon their minor transgressions.

8. Duke Zhuang 3.31.1, 3.31.3, and 3.31.5. See chapter 8, note 11.
9. Duke Zhuang 3.23.8 and 3.24.1.

Moreover, the [*Gongyang*] *Commentary* clarifies [this principle when it] states, "The Noble Man [expressed leniency] in his terminology."[10]

[In the *Spring and Autumn*,] Confucius featured successes and failures and illustrated victories and defeats. He loathed the fact that [he lived in] an age of inhumanity in which the world had lost the substance of the Kingly Way. Thus [Confucius]

accorded with the feelings of others
and pardoned their minor transgressions.

Moreover, the [*Gongyang*] *Commentary* clarifies [this principle when it] states, "The Noble Man [expressed leniency] in his terminology."

Confucius said: "I rely on past events and apply my kingly mind to them." [Thus he]

availed himself of [recorded] positions and titles to rectify human relationships
and relied on [recorded] successes and failures to illuminate compliance and disobedience."

Thus

what he admired was the conduct of Dukes Huan and Wen, who ultimately succeeded;
what he loathed was the conduct of chaotic states that ultimately were defeated.

Therefore he began by discussing the gravest crimes, the assassination of rulers and the annihilation of states, and he ended by discussing pardoning the slightest crimes. That is, he began with the coarse and unrefined and ended with the refined and subtle. When the transforming influence of [*Spring and Autumn*] instruction flows forth, virtue and kindness will greatly permeate the people of the world, and they will conduct themselves as scholars and noble men and scarcely transgress at all. This indeed is also the implication of the criticism [that Confucius directed at] "those with two [personal] names."[11] [17/24/15–17/25/6]

10. Typically, the *Gongyang* claims that the burial of a duke is recorded in the *Spring and Autumn* only when the traitor who committed regicide had been punished. But on some occasions, Confucius showed leniency. For example, in the record of Duke Ling of Chen's burial, *Spring and Autumn*, Duke Xuan 7.12.1 states: "They buried Duke Ling of Chen." The *Gongyang* explains: "The ones who punished this traitor were neither [the duke's] ministers nor his sons. Why then does the [*Spring and* Autumn] say 'they buried Duke Ling of Chen'? The Noble Man [expressed leniency] in his terminology. Chu had already punished [the traitor]. Even though the duke's ministers and sons wanted to punish him they had no way of doing so." For other expressions of the Noble Man's leniency, see Duke Huan 2.18.4 and Duke Xiang 9.30.8.

11. Duke Ding 11.6.4: "Summer. Jisun Si and Zhongsun Heji went to Jin." Duke Ding 11.6.7: "Jisun Si and Zhongsun Ji led troops and surrounded Yun." *Gongyang*: "This was Zhongsun Heji. Why was he referred to as Zhongsun Ji? In order to criticize [the fact that he had] two personal names. It was not in accordance with propriety." In other words, the author argues here that the criticism of two names is a concrete example of a minor or insignificant transgression.

Group 2

Monarchical Principles

On the whole, the five chapters of group 2, "Monarchical Principles," express an intellectual viewpoint quite different from those of group 1.[1] Those chapters were based on close readings of the *Spring and Autumn*, whereas these chapters are made up of essays and essay fragments that mention neither the *Spring and Autumn* nor any other texts of the Confucian canon.[2] The ideal ruler described in these chapters is not defined by the praise-and-blame methodology of the *Spring and Autumn* but instead is crafted from different raw materials and embodies different ideals and practices, as their titles suggest.

GROUP 2: MONARCHICAL PRINCIPLES, CHAPTERS 18–22

18. 離合根 *Li he gen* Departing from and Conforming to the Fundamental
19. 立元神 *Li yuan shen* Establishing the Originating Spirit

---

1. These chapters are often called the "Huang-Lao chapters," a term that Sarah A. Queen also used in *From Chronicle to Canon: The Hermeneutics of the "Spring and Autumn" According to Tung Chung-shu* (Cambridge: Cambridge University Press, 1996). But we now feel that it is better to avoid that term, because there is no consensus on what "Huang-Lao" signifies and not enough evidence to settle the issue. See the section "Issues of Dating and Attribution" and the discussion in John S. Major, Sarah A. Queen, Andrew Seth Meyer, and Harold D. Roth, trans. and eds., *The "Huainanzi": A Guide to the Theory and Practice of Government in Early Han China* (New York: Columbia University Press, 2010), 27–32.
2. Although we recognize that the "Confucian canon" had not yet stabilized during the Western Han, it is clear that Han scholars in the *ru* tradition were generally closely associated with the *Documents*, the *Spring and Autumn*, the *Odes*, the *Changes*, and the *Rites*.

20. 保位權 *Bao wei quan* Preserving Position and Authority
21. 考功名 *Kao gong ming* Investigating Achievement and Reputation
22. 通國身 *Tong guo shen* Comprehending the State as the Body

The influences at work in these chapters include Laozi's emptiness and nonpurposive action; Shen Buhai's technique of assessing officials by comparing their official titles with their actual performances; Han Feizi's notion of impartial rewards and punishments, as well as his ideal of a remote and mysterious ruler visible to his subjects only through the actions of his ministers; Mozi's emphasis on elevating the worthy; and Guanzi's techniques of inner cultivation. They consequently employ a number of technical terms that do not generally appear in other chapter groups of the *Chunqiu fanlu* or, when they do appear, carry decidedly different meanings from those found here. These terms include *shen* (spirit or spiritlike), *ming* (brilliant), *wuwei* (non-action), and *jing* and *jing qi* (quintessence and quintessential *qi*).[3] Moreover, political techniques are recommended for their efficacy alone, as their legitimacy derives from their ability to preserve the power and authority of the ruler and nothing more. Although humaneness, righteousness, and other moral values appear in these chapters, they do not have an especially privileged status. Such characteristics distinguish these writings from other materials in the *Chunqiu fanlu*, and they raise compelling and challenging questions concerning their provenance, dating, and authorship.

Description of Individual Chapters

Chapter 18, "Departing from and Conforming to the Fundamental," prescribes the roles of the ruler and his ministers in accordance with their respective correlates: Heaven and Earth. Although separate, with each performing its proper duties, they ultimately form a unity, fitting together like two halves of a tally: "Heaven elevates its position yet sends down its manifestations; conceals its form yet reveals its light."[4] These Heavenly activities generate the pairs of contrasting

3. Queen, *From Chronicle to Canon*, 87, table 5, and the detailed discussion of the distinctive characteristics and technical vocabulary of these chapters on 85–91.
4. *CQFL* 18/25/10.

qualities of being spiritlike (dark and mysterious) yet brilliant (bright and clear), and honorable (revered) yet humane. The ruler emulates these qualities of Heaven:

> For this reason, he is deeply hidden within; that is what makes him spiritlike; he is widely observant without; that is what makes him brilliant. He relies on the multitudinous worthies; that is what makes him enjoy success; he does not weary himself with tasks; that is what makes him honorable. He universally loves the multitudinous living things, not using [his personal] joy or anger [as the basis for] rewards and punishments; that is what makes him humane.[5]

When the ruler implements such techniques, he "takes holding to 'no action' to be his Way, and takes holding to 'no self' to be his treasure."[6] This enables him to rely completely on his officials, whose activities are likened to the ruler's feet, which do not move; his mouth, which does not speak; and his mind, which does not scheme.

The second half of the chapter has suffered damage, and portions of the original essay have been lost. What remains describes the roles of the ministers, who complement the Heavenly characteristics of the ruler by taking Earth as their model. Just as the Way of Earth "exposes its form and reveals its true nature,"[7] so that its qualities may be discerned and judged, the ministers are to value trustworthiness and fully manifest their true nature so that likewise the ruler is able to discern and judge them. When such techniques of bureaucratic control are implemented, the essay concludes, the Way of the King will be "awe inspiring and faultless."[8]

A second, longer, and more complete recension of this essay is found near the end of the *Chunqiu fanlu* in chapter 78, "The Conduct of Heaven and Earth" (in Su Yu's reconstructed version, which we endorse).[9] Chapters 18 and 78 are the first of several pairs of linked chapters that appear throughout the text. We call these "linked chapters" because they have a common topic, parallel passages, and numerous similarities of wording. Their common features suggest that they are interrelated in some fashion. For example, they might be two recensions of

5. *CQFL* 18/25/12–14.
6. *CQFL* 18/25/14.
7. *CQFL* 18/25/16–17.
8. *CQFL* 18/25/19.
9. See the discussion of chapter 78A.1 in the introduction to group 8, "Heavenly Principles."

an originally identical essay or perhaps two distinct essays, one of which reworks an earlier original.[10]

Chapter 19, "Establishing the Originating Spirit," brings together materials of varying degrees of completeness from no fewer than six essays. We designate them as sections 19.1 through 19.6 to indicate that they are largely independent of one another. We believe that these six essays or essay fragments were collected into a single chapter given the descriptive title "Establishing the Originating Spirit" because they address a common theme: the ruler's spirit or spiritlike qualities. But they appear to do so in different ways and with different aims. Section 19.1 begins by asserting that the ruler is "the origin of the state," but in contrast to the activist interpretation of this concept that appears in Dong Zhongshu's memorials (collected in his biography in the *Han shu* and translated in appendix B of this book), here the concept is defined as follows: "Uttering words and initiating undertakings, he is the axial mechanism of the myriad things. The operation of the axial mechanism is the trigger of honor and disgrace. If it errs in the smallest degree, a team of horses cannot put it right again."[11] To avoid error, the ruler is advised to cultivate a non-active and quiescent state: "His will resembles [the stillness of] dead ashes; his body resembles [the emptiness of] abandoned clothing; he calms his quintessence and nourishes his spirit."[12] Still and silent, not only will the ruler not err but he will remain beyond the judgment and possible manipulation of his ministers. He occupies the optimal position to judge the ministers, which he does "by relying "on the internal to verify the external, . . . the insignificant to verify the significant, and so without fail will ascertain the true reality of things." The section concludes by referring to this technique of rulership as "opening and closing." This expression is found in a number of early texts, such as the *Laozi* and *Guanzi*.[13] The following passage

10. Other "linked chapters" include 38/42 and 35/36, discussed in the introduction to group 4, "Ethical Principles."
11. *CQFL* 19/25/24–25.
12. *CQFL* 19/25/25.
13. *Daodejing* 10: "When the gates of Heaven open and shut, can you keep to the role of the female?" *Guanzi* 69, "The Art of Fiscal Management" (Cheng ma shu), begins:

> Duke Huan questioned Guanzi saying, "Youyu implemented planned fiscal management. I wish to do the same. How do I go about it?" "States involved in warfare," replied Guanzi, "concentrate their efforts on building city walls and moats. Consequently, they invariably fail to make proper use of their land. On the other hand, states that adhere to the Kingly Way act in accordance with the seasons." "What do you mean by 'in accordance with the seasons?'" "Issue orders setting a standard price [for grain] and maintain control over land utilization and policies affecting people. In this way, opening and closing the gates to wealth will lie entirely in the hands of the ruler on high, and there will be no need to seek it directly from the people."

from the *Huainanzi*, however, best illuminates how the expression functions as a metaphor for the ruler's critical role in governance:

> Thus to have the benefit of positional advantage means that what you hold is very small but what you manage is very large; what you guard is very compact, but what you control is vast. Thus a tree trunk ten [hand] spans [in circumference] can support a roof weighing a thousand *jun*,[14] and a key five inches long can control the opening and closing [of a door]. How can this small amount of material be sufficient for the task? The position they occupy is the important thing.[15]

This seemingly arcane expression about "opening and closing" compares the ruler to the key of a door; that is, the ruler controls his ministers as the key controls the door. What the ruler wields is very small, but his positional advantage makes it very powerful. With the key, the ruler can open the door to observe and assess the conduct of his ministers yet remain closed off to them as he keeps himself secluded and mysterious. Since they cannot see him, he is forever beyond the reach of their possible machinations.

Section 19.2, one of only two sections in this group of chapters that promotes the sorts of Confucian virtues and policies readily identified with Dong Zhongshu,[16] depicts the ruler as the revered "root of the state," possessing spiritlike qualities that give him the ability to transform his people below. As the root of the state, the ruler must serve the three great roots of the myriad things—Heaven, Earth, and humankind. These, in turn, are identified with filial piety and fraternal love, food and clothing, and ritual and music. The three are intimately interconnected: "The three assist one another just as the hands and feet join together to perfect the body; it is not possible to dispense with one of them."[17] Ignoring any one of the three roots spells inevitable social chaos and

---

The chapter concludes,

> If you are able to take charge of the four seasons, control the opening and closing of the gates of wealth, and your people do not move away, it will provide a stability similar to placing a square object on the ground. This is what is meant by the art of planned financial management. (W. Allyn Rickett, trans., *Guanzi: Political, Economic, and Philosophical Essays from Early China* [Princeton, N.J.: Princeton University Press, 1998], 2:365, 367)

14. A Han *jun* 鈞 weighed about sixteen pounds, so the weight of the roof described here is about eight tons.
15. Major et al., *Huainanzi*, 9.26, 326. This may have been a popular proverb in the Han, as similar lines appear in the *Shuoyuan* and in the *Wenzi*. Compare also *Huainanzi* 10.23: "It takes a carpenter to frame up a door, but without a foot-long door latch, you cannot close it securely" (358).
16. See also the summary of chapter 22.
17. *CQFL* 19/26/2–3.

disaster for the ruler. Thus a brilliant ruler and worthy lord respectfully attends to the three roots by promoting these decidedly Confucian policies. By doing so, his government will take on the characteristics of a family: the people will be like sons and brothers, not daring to act on their own authority; the ruler will be like a parent, not having to rely on grace to demonstrate his love for the people or on sternness to command them. And like children who cannot bear to leave their parents, should the ruler fall on hard times and be forced to relinquish his throne, "the people will strap their children on their backs and follow him."[18] This is because there is simply nothing better than virtue for administering the state: "It is sweeter than cake or honey and firmer than glue or lacquer."[19]

Section 19.3 begins by claiming that the ruler is "the authentication of the state." He occupies a position of leadership but does not use its strategic advantage. What remains of this essay is only a fragment, however; it breaks off before it can fully develop its opening claims, and its conclusion is missing.

Section 19.4, another essay fragment, returns to the ruler's qualities of being honorable and spiritlike and recalls chapter 18 but describes the ruler somewhat differently. Here, being honorable is the means by which the ruler effects his policies, and being spiritlike is the means by which he extends his transforming influence. To achieve these desired qualities, the ruler must employ worthies and unify their minds.

Section 19.5 similarly advocates recruiting worthy men and unifying their minds but justifies these policies through yet another set of correlations drawn between Heaven and the sage: "[T]he Way of Heaven strives to make its quintessence flourish; the sage strives to make his worthies numerous.... Only after unifying its yang can [Heaven] extend its spirit; only after unifying their minds can [the sage] extend his achievements."[20]

The last section of this chapter, 19.6, also promotes the ruler's spiritlike qualities and encourages him to prize and emulate them. In contrast to the arguments made earlier in the chapter, here the ruler's spiritlike qualities are identified with his mysterious and unfathomable qualities. Like the spirits, he cannot be apprehended through sight or hearing. The chapter contends that these qualities are

18. This phrase recalls the story of King Danfu of high antiquity, who was followed into exile by the entire population of his state. There are many versions of the story. See *Zhuangzi* 28 in Victor H. Mair, trans., *Wandering on the Way: Early Tales and Parables of Chuang Tzu* (Honolulu: University of Hawai'i Press, 1997, 285–86); *Lüshi chunqiu* 21.4 in John Knoblock and Jeffrey Riegel, trans., *The Annals of Lü Buwei: A Compete Translation and Study* (Stanford, Calif.: Stanford University Press, 2000), 557–58; and Major et al., *Huainanzi* 12.15, 451.

19. *CQFL* 19/26/12.

20. *CQFL* 19/26/20–23.

advantageous for the ruler because they enable him to stand beyond the discernment and judgment of others. Thus the ruler resides in yin, occupying a hidden position, but he is yang because his status is superior to that of his ministers. His ministers reside in yang because they occupy an exposed position, but they are yin because their status is inferior to that of their ruler.

Chapter 20, "Preserving Position and Authority," consists of three short essays that recommend different techniques closely associated with the *Hanfeizi*. Section 20.1, from which the title of the chapter is taken, aims to preserve the ruler's position and authority in relation to his people. It argues that the successful ruler does so by building on the intuitive preferences of the people—that is, what they love and what they hate.[21] This ensures that the ruler will be authoritative and awesome. In turn, these qualities enable the ruler to impose prohibitions and regulations on the populace, rewarding what they love and prohibiting what they hate. This will safeguard his strategic advantage and place of honor above those over whom he governs. By thus manipulating the preferences of the common people, the ruler can encourage and awe the people and thereby regulate them in order to preserve his position and authority as the supreme source of power in the world.

Section 20.2 pairs power and fearsomeness as the ruler's defining characteristics. It contends that those qualities must not be shared with or delegated to others under any circumstances, as this will inevitably lead to chaos and rebellion. Power is the basis on which the ruler subjugates his people, and authority is the means by which he rectifies his ministers.

Section 20.3 emphasizes the ruler's non-active and quiescent qualities, maintaining that these are the true wellsprings of his power. "Silent and voiceless, quiescent and formless," the ruler takes "the ministers' speech as his voice" and "the ministers' tasks as his form." The ruler, "with an empty mind and in a quiescent state," is perfectly positioned to listen to and observe the metaphorical echoes and shadows of his ministers and thereby implement rewards and punishments by assessing their actual performance against the official titles they hold: "The lord clings to their titles and investigates their true substance in order to assess their actual performance."[22] This will ensure an impartial basis for bestowing rewards and imposing punishments. That will inspire the ministers to maintain the various distinctions in their duties and compete to advance their meritorious deeds

21. A similar argument is made in *Huainanzi* 20.10 (Major et al., *Huainanzi*, 804).
22. *CQFL* 20/27/27.

while the ruler is carried along by their achievements. This, the essay concludes, is a technique of governance that spontaneously extends the lord's strength.

As the title suggests, chapter 21, "Investigating Achievement and Reputation," enumerates various strategies to test bureaucratic personnel. Because of the radical discontinuities in its content, we have divided the chapter into four sections. Whether these four segments of text were once part of a much longer continuous essay from which substantial portions have been lost over the centuries, or whether the compiler of the text simply collected four fragments on the subject of how best to assess the merit of officials as a basis for rewards and punishments, is now impossible to ascertain. The first and most complete section, 21.1, uses the Way of Heaven to describe the theoretical underpinnings of an examination system that tests officials in order to establish appropriate rewards and punishments, not in accordance with the longevity of their tenure in office or based on their noble rank (their main qualification for office), but determined by the merit they have accumulated in their service to the government: "The Way of Heaven accumulates and collects an abundance of quintessence in order to be radiant; the sage accumulates and collects an abundance of excellence in order to be meritorious."[23] Therefore, just as the sun and moon must depend on the radiance of quintessence to generate their brilliance, the sage must rely on the merit of many acts of goodness by his officials to generate an age of Great Peace. He must assess his positional advantage, establish his authority, adapt to the current situation, and institute standards of righteousness. In doing so, the ruler must follow the natural tendencies of the situation to bring benefit to the world, as "the spring *qi* engenders the vegetation," and to eradicate wrongdoing, as "the rivers and streams flow into the sea."[24] It does not matter if he departs from the practices of former sages, because although sages possess "different methods, their virtue is the same." The best way, however, to bring benefit to and eradicate harm in the world is to establish a clear system of evaluation: "Investigate the merit [of the officials] and demote or promote them; examine the affairs [that they have managed] and employ or dismiss them. . . . Reward those who have merit; punish those who commit crimes."[25] When such a system is established, the distinction between worthy and unworthy officials is not determined by empty reputation but by an official's record of actual performance.

23. *CQFL* 21/28/5.
24. *CQFL* 21/28/7–8.
25. *CQFL* 21/28/10–12.

The remaining three sections of this chapter describe a more detailed program for implementing these ideals. Section 21.2 addresses how much time should be spent testing officials of varying ranks and how often they should be assessed. It distinguishes high-ranking from low-ranking officials and recommends that more time be devoted to high-ranking officials. Accordingly, as one moves up the three ranks of government described in this section—from the Lords of the Land, through the provincial governors, to the Son of Heaven—officials are tested monthly, seasonally, and annually. Section 21.3 lists which factors should be considered when testing officials: degree of nobility, salary, duties, length of service, achievements, merits, and faults. These determine how officials should be ranked. Section 21.4, which, like the preceding section, has suffered considerable textual damage and can be translated only tentatively, discusses in greater detail the re-rating of officials. As we discuss at length later, this material may express the views Dong Zhongshu and his disciples.

Chapter 22, "Comprehending the State as the Body," once again argues that the best state is one that promotes worthy men to staff its bureaucracy. Like chapter 19.2, it evokes associations that are consistent with the known views of Dong Zhongshu, although it couches those associations in a matrix of self-cultivation that is not quite like anything found in works that unquestionably can be attributed to him. In this chapter, promoting worthies is viewed not as the basis for enhancing the ruler's power but as the basis for spreading Virtue throughout the realm. The essay justifies this political ideal by making analogies of the body to the state not seen in previous chapters. For instance, those who regulate their bodies consider accumulating quintessence—the purest form of *qi*—as their treasure, just as those who regulate the state consider accumulating worthies—the purest men—as their Way. Those who wish to accumulate pure *qi* must do so by emptying their mind and stilling their body; those who desire to acquire worthy men must do so by humbling and abasing themselves. The quintessential *qi* that enables the adept to achieve enlightenment and longevity is analogous to the worthy men who enable the sagely ruler to extend his Virtue and achieve Great Peace.

Issues of Dating and Attribution

We have suggested that the chapters in this group share characteristics that distinguish them from other chapters in the text. They generally do not promote

Confucian norms, and they do not draw on the authority of the *Spring and Autumn* to justify the political techniques they recommend. Techniques are presented as desirable and legitimate that efficaciously preserve and promote the ruler's power, authority, and strategic advantage. Nowhere else in the *Chunqiu fanlu* is the ruler advised (as in the *Hanfeizi*, for example) to embody non-active, quiescent, and spiritlike qualities as a defensive strategy to shield him from encroaching ministers. Nowhere else in the text is he advised (as in the *Mozi*) to promote the worthy in order to bring benefit and eradicate wrongdoing, or (as with Shen Buhai) to reward and punish officials impartially by "demanding that the substance of their performance accord with their title." Nowhere else in the *Chunqiu fanlu* is there such a heightened and unabashed concern to secure the ruler's unrivaled power, awesome authority, and strategic advantage. And nowhere else in the text is there such a pervasive use of the vocabulary of inner cultivation, which is associated most notably with the *Guanzi* and *Huainanzi*.

The political techniques recommended in these chapters also appear foreign to those promoted by Dong Zhongshu in writings of unquestioned authenticity that have survived from the Han, such as those preserved in *Han shu* 56. But the corpus of authentic Western Han writings is not very large, and much of what has survived dates from the reign of Emperor Wu. This has led some scholars, including Sarah Queen, to entertain the possibility that chapters 18 through 22 preserve materials that are best understood as expressions of the syncretic stream of political thought that enjoyed imperial patronage during the formative years of the Han. These currents of thought might include Daoism as defined by the Han historians Sima Tan and Sima Qian in their famous essay on the "Six Traditions,"[26] as well as the poorly understood and much debated tradition known as Huang-Lao, "the teachings of the Yellow Emperor and Laozi."[27] Although the early Han emperors summoned Confucian scholars to the central court to take up posts as Erudites, just as Dong Zhongshu was summoned under Emperor Jing, imperial patronage before the time of Emperor Wu was granted mainly to adepts identified with Huang-Lao techniques. The *Shiji* and *Han shu* record that numerous officials and politically prominent figures studied Huang-Lao doctrines and practiced Huang-Lao techniques. Indeed, some of the clearest and most unambiguous indications of official support for Huang-Lao practitioners dates from the reign of Emperor Jing, and many of Dong's associates were identified with Huang-Lao learning. In the Huang-Lao atmosphere of Emperor

26. *SJ* 130.
27. For a more detailed discussion of this issue, see Queen, *From Chronicle to Canon*, 85–91.

Jing's court, the Confucian Erudite Dong Zhongshu might have trimmed his sails to the prevailing winds and written in a Huang-Lao vein himself. But there is no evidence that he did so and some evidence that he did not.

Ban Gu's biography of Dong Zhongshu in the *Han shu* recounts that during this time, Dong "first transmitted his interpretations of the *Spring and Autumn* according to the *Gongyang* tradition" and embraced his teaching and scholarly agenda with such dedication that "scholars regarded him as a teacher to be respected." Thus in a period dominated by Huang-Lao, Dong appears to have been actively transmitting his own interpretations of the *Spring and Autumn* to an ever-widening group of disciples and winning a reputation for doing so among the most prominent scholars in the capital.[28] We see no reason to doubt that he remained steadfast in his advocacy of Gongyang Learning.

In our work on the *Chunqiu fanlu*, we have generally avoided the term "Huang-Lao" and instead have designated chapters 18 through 22 as the "Monarchical Principles" group. We believe that the term "Huang-Lao" has not been helpful as an analytical rubric for dealing with early Han materials. Despite a flurry of scholarly activity and debate over the question of Huang-Lao in the 1990s and the early 2000s,[29] no scholarly consensus has emerged about exactly which doctrine(s) were associated with Huang-Lao and which (if any) received or archaeologically recovered texts should be classified as Huang-Lao works. We therefore wonder not whether chapters 18 through 22 are a "Huang-Lao group" but why these chapters are included in the *Chunqiu fanlu*.

As we noted earlier, of the chapters in this group, chapter 19.2 and chapter 22 are the most consonant with what we know from reliable sources about the teachings of and policies advocated by Dong Zhongshu. One can imagine him crafting an essay promoting the kinds of Confucian virtues and rituals described

28. For another discussion of the Huang-Lao issue, see Gary Arbuckle, "Dong Zhongshu and Huang-Lao," a source that unfortunately is no longer available.

29. For example, Hsiao Kung-ch'uan, *A History of Chinese Political Thought*, trans. F. W. Mote (Princeton, N.J.: Princeton University Press, 1979), 570–82; Charles Le Blanc, *Huai-nan Tzu: Philosophical Synthesis in Early Han Thought: The Idea of Resonance (Kan-ying) with a Translation and Analysis of Chapter Six* (Hong Kong: Hong Kong University Press, 1985), 4–8; John S. Major, *Heaven and Earth in Early Han Thought: Chapters Three, Four, and Five of the "Huainanzi"* (Albany: State University of New York Press, 1993), 8–14; Harold D. Roth, *The Textual History of the "Huai-nan Tzu,"* Monograph no. 46 (Ann Arbor, Mich.: Association for Asian Studies, 1992), 13–19; Tu Wei-ming, "The Thought of Huang-Lao: A Reflection on the *Lao Tzu* and *Huang Ti* Texts in the Silk Manuscripts of Ma-wang-tui," *Journal of Asian Studies* 39 (1979): 95–100; Randall Peerenboom, *Law and Morality in Ancient China: The Silk Manuscripts of Huang-Lao* (Albany: State University of New York Press, 1993); Robin D. S. Yates, *Five Lost Classics: Tao, Huang-Lao, and Yin-Yang in Han China* (New York: Ballantine Books, 1997); Mark Csikszentmihalyi, "Emulating the Yellow Emperor: The Theory and Practice of Huang-Lao, 180–141 B.C." (Ph.D. diss., Stanford University, 1994); Wang Aihe, *Cosmology and Political Culture in Early China* (Cambridge: Cambridge University Press, 2000), 184–85.

in chapter 19.2. Similarly, one can envision him arguing, as in chapter 22, that the ruler must be humble and self-abasing if he hopes to attract worthy men to serve him so that he may extend his virtue and usher in an age of Great Peace. (In contrast, the overt emphasis on inner cultivation that pervades chapter 22 seems atypical of Dong's known views, and the concept of Great Peace, though pervasive in Han political discourse, is not especially associated with Dong.) Even though there is no proof, and no prospect of proof, that Dong Zhongshu was the author of these essays, they could have been written by him or some member of his immediate circle.

In addition to chapter 19.2 and chapter 22, portions of chapter 21 have some points in common with Dong's known views. In general, chapter 21 is concerned with the proper recruitment of officials, and Dong wrote at length about that issue in one of his memorials to Emperor Wu. He contends that the later kings of the Three Dynasties, in contrast to the earlier thearchs,[30] followed different policies because it was necessary to rectify the faults they inherited from their predecessors. Likewise in the present, Emperor Wu ought to adopt policies that will rectify the faults of his Han predecessors. Chief among them is the sorry state of official recruitment, which, Dong insists, is surely the source of the anomalies that plague Emperor Wu's reign:

> Currently the governors of the commanderies and prefects of the provinces are the teachers and leaders of the common people. They are the ones who have been commanded to propagate transformation [among the common people]. Thus if the teachers and leaders are not worthy, then the virtue of the ruler will not be proclaimed, and his benevolent and saturating [moral influence] will not flow forth. . . . This is why yin and yang are out of step and noxious *qi* fills and chokes the heavens so that the numerous forms of life rarely reach maturity and the common people have yet to find relief.[31]

The solution, Dong argues, is thoroughgoing reform:

> In antiquity, those who were deemed meritorious were ranked in accordance with the degree to which officials fulfilled the responsibilities of their assigned posts and not in accordance with the length of time they served. . . . Nowadays,

30. We translate the Chinese word *di* 帝 as "thearch" in reference to mythical, semidivine, cultural heroes and "sage-rulers" like Lord Millet (Hou Ji) and the Divine Farmer (Shen Nong).

31. *HS* 56:2511–12.

> the circumstances are not the same. Officials earn various honors according to their seniority, so the longer their tenure in office is, the higher their post will be. This is why the honest and the corrupt are mixed together and the worthy and degenerate are confused, and their true abilities are not yet ascertained. . . . Do not consider the longevity of an official's tenure to be meritorious, but, rather, give priority to substantiating and testing an official's worthiness and ability. Assess their capabilities and appoint them to office; appraise their virtue and determine their rank, and then the honest and the corrupt will follow distinct paths and the worthy and foolish will occupy different posts.[32]

This acerbic and cutting response analyzing the Liu family's hiring policies testifies vividly to the lengths to which Dong would go to express his disapproval of policies emanating from the emperor. The chapter's suggestion that "those who recommend unworthy men should be punished" is a strong critique of the favoritism and nepotism prevalent at the imperial court. Based on this evidence, Dong Zhongshu was a brave man and an engaged and astute adviser. The detailed procedures outlined here for recommendation and recruitment of officials testifies to Dong's strong interest in this subject and the extent to which he grounds his policy reforms on an understanding of history. On the basis of this analysis, we conclude that at least some of the passages in (the textually damaged) chapter 21 may have been written by Dong Zhongshu or one or more of his immediate disciples.

The remaining essays in this group offer a different scenario. It is not likely that Dong Zhongshu could have written any of them, as they recommend political techniques and ideas that contradict everything we know about his interests and beliefs. They support the unrivaled power of the ruler. They depict a ruler who cares for neither the material well-being of his people nor their moral grounding. They are decidedly suspicious of the ministers who staff the bureaucracy, often assuming that these officials present the most serious political threats to the ruler. These essays also do not justify the political techniques they recommend based on the authority of either the Confucian canon or Heaven, the usual strategies adopted by Dong Zhongshu to promote his political ideals, and they have little or nothing to say about Humaneness, Righteousness, or other Confucian virtues.

32. *HS* 56: 2512–13.

Moreover, just as there is no reason to think that these chapters were written by Dong Zhongshu or any member of his circle, there also is no reason to think that they were written by a single individual. These chapters present different perspectives on power and position, as well as different means to achieve them. They present varied and inconsistent strategies to legitimize the political techniques that they recommend. Some, as is the case with the three essays in chapter 20, imply that the ability to secure the ruler's power and position requires no justification; royal authority by definition is seen as being good. Other chapters, such as 18 (and its alternative version, chapter 78.1), draw on cosmic models to justify the policies they recommend. In addition, these chapters' views of such crucial issues as rewards and punishment, non-action, and the need for the ruler to have spiritlike qualities are inconsistent. Finally, these chapters employ a distinctive vocabulary of technical terms, quite different from the vocabulary of most of the rest of the *Chunqiu fanlu*.

Why, then, are these chapters in this text? They are most similar not to other chapters of the *Chunqiu fanlu* but to texts classified as *za* (miscellaneous, eclectic, syncretic) works in the bibliographic treatise of the *Han shu* and later official histories—such as the *Lüshi chunqiu*, the *Guanzi*, and the *Huainanzi*. Possibly, the essays in these chapters somehow *acquired* associations with the name of Dong Zhongshu, despite their divergence from his known works and views and for reasons that we now cannot fathom. We may, then, imagine that the unknown compiler of the *Chunqiu fanlu*, eager to collect in one volume everything that he could lay his hands on that was in any way associated with Dong, dutifully included them in his compilation.

Book 6, Part 5

CHAPTER 18

Departing from and Conforming to the Fundamental

Section 18.1

Heaven
　　elevates its position yet sends down its manifestations,
　　conceals its form yet reveals its light.
　　It elevates its position; that is what makes it honorable.
　　It sends down its manifestations; that is what makes it humane.
　　It conceals its form; that is what makes it spiritlike.
　　It reveals its light; that is what makes it brilliant.
Therefore
　　to position oneself as honorable yet practice humaneness,
　　to conceal one's form[1] yet reveal one's light,
is the conduct of Heaven.

Therefore one who would rule others emulates the conduct of Heaven. For this reason,
　　he is deeply hidden within; that is what makes him spiritlike;
　　he is widely observant without; that is what makes him brilliant.

Although Su Yu maintains that the title of this chapter, "Li he gen" 離合根, does not correspond to the contents, we believe that it does, at least to some extent. Like all the chapter titles in the "Monarchical Principles" group of chapters, the title is three characters long and begins with a verb. The subject of the chapter is the roles of the ruler and his ministers. The ruler is depicted as a sage who emulates Heaven's fundamental norms: he is honorable, humane, spiritlike, and brilliant, but also deep and mysterious. In choosing ministers and assigning them tasks, the ruler must assess their abilities and gauge the degree to which they depart from or conform to the fundamental.

1. We have emended *shen* 神 to *xing* 形 to make it consistent with its earlier parallel.

He relies on the multitudinous worthies; that is what makes him enjoy success;
He does not weary himself with tasks; that is what makes him honorable.
He universally loves the multitudinous living things, not using [his personal] joy or anger [as the basis for] rewards and punishments; that is what makes him humane.

Therefore one who would rule others
takes holding to "no action" to be his Way,
takes holding to "no self" to be his treasure.

Established in the position of no action, he avails himself of officials completely prepared for service.

His own feet do not move, but his assistants guide him forward.
His own mouth does not utter, but his master of ceremonies assists him by speaking.
His own mind does not scheme, but his multitudinous officials exert themselves to do what is needed.

Therefore no one observes him act, and yet his achievements are brought to fruition. This is how one who rules others emulates the conduct of Heaven.

One who would serve as minister to another emulates the Way of Earth, which
exposes its form
and reveals its true nature
in order to manifest [itself] to others so that [whether]
high or low,
difficult or easy,
firm or pliable,
hard or soft,
fertile or barren,
beautiful or ugly,
in every case [its terrain] may be discerned and judged. Therefore the suitability or unsuitability of its form may be discerned and judged.

One who would serve as minister to another is like the Earth in valuing trustworthiness and fully manifesting his true nature to the ruler so that the ruler may, in this case too, discern and judge him. Consequently, the Kingly Way will be awe inspiring and faultless. One who would serve as minister to another constantly reveals his true nature and uses his strength to the utmost and so manifests his shortcomings and capabilities, thereby enabling the ruler to employ him according to his talent. He is like the Earth that constantly reveals its true nature. Accordingly, the suitability of his form may [also] be discerned and judged.[2] [18/25/10–20]

2. Su Yu adduces *Guanzi*, book 1, chapter 5, "Sheng ma" 乘馬 (On Military Taxes): "When the ruler initiates an undertaking, the ministers do not dare lie about their lack of ability. The ruler knows his ministers, and the ministers know that the ruler knows them. Thus no minister will dare fail to exert himself to the utmost." Compare W. Allyn Rickett, trans., *Guanzi: Political, Economic, and Philosophical Essays from Early China* (Princeton, N.J.: Princeton University Press, 1985), 1:123. *Guanzi*, book 10, chapter 1, "Jun chen shang" 君臣上 (Ruler and Ministers, Part 1), states: "When an enlightened ruler promotes his subordinates, he is fully aware of their shortcomings and capabilities." Further, from "Jun chen xia" 下 (Ruler and Ministers, Part 2): "The ruler who possesses the Way clings to the fundamentals; the prime minister clings to the essentials; and the great officers cling to the laws to shepherd the multitudinous ministers. The multitudinous ministers expend their wisdom and use their strength to the utmost in serving their superior." Compare Rickett, *Guanzi*, 1:405, 415–16; and Su Yu, *CQFLYZ* 171–72. For the translation of the chapter title, "Sheng ma," as "On Military Taxes," see Rickett, *Guanzi*, 1:114–15.

Book 6, Part 6

CHAPTER 19

Establishing the Originating Spirit

Section 19.1[1]

One who is lord over others is the point of origin of the state. Uttering words and initiating undertakings, he is the axial mechanism of the myriad things. The operation of the axial mechanism is the trigger of honor and disgrace. If it errs in the smallest degree, a team of horses cannot put it right again. For this reason, one who would rule others is

attentive of the fundamental,
careful of the beginning,
respectful of the trivial,
careful of the subtle.
His will resembles [the stillness of] dead ashes;
his form resembles [the emptiness of] abandoned clothing.

He

calms his quintessence
and nourishes his spirit.[2]

1. Traditional commentators generally divide this chapter into two sections. However, material from no fewer than six different essays appears to comprise this chapter, combined here because of their common theme. Accordingly, when translating this chapter we have divided it into six sections.
2. Quintessence (*jing* 精) and spirit (*shen* 神) are important technical terms found in a number of essays devoted to nourishing the vital energy. The terms date from the fourth to the second century B.C.E.; examples are found in the *Lüshi chunqiu*, *Guanzi*, and *Huainanzi*. The quintessence, or quintessential *qi*, is the purest and most concentrated form of vital energy (*qi*). The spirit, which is the animating force of a living being, is composed of *qi* in a highly ethereal and dynamic state. For extended discussions of both terms, see John S. Major, Sarah A. Queen, Andrew Seth Meyer, and Harold D. Roth, trans. and eds., *The "Huainanzi": A Guide to the Theory and Practice of Government in Early Han China* (New York: Columbia University Press, 2010), 877, 885–87.

He is quiet and non-active.

Stilling his form, he does not cast a shadow;
silencing his voice, he does not emit a sound.

With an empty mind, he descends [to consult with] his officials, observing the future by scrutinizing the past.

He deliberates with the numerous worthies
and inquires into [the opinions of] the multitudes.[3]

[Thus he]

apprehends their hearts
and comprehensively understands their feelings;

He

investigates their likes and dislikes
to verify whether they are loyal or treasonous.

He examines their past conduct and verifies it against their present conduct. He assesses to what extent their collective accomplishments derive from former worthies. He dispels their grievances and observes the causes of their disputes. He distinguishes their factions and clans and observes the men they esteem. He relies on his position to govern others and uses harsh measures to make his reputation. As days pile up and time accumulates, what effort will not reach fruition?

He

can rely on the internal to verify the external,
can rely on the insignificant to verify the significant,

and so without fail will ascertain the true reality of things. This is to practice "opening and closing." [19/25/24–29]

3. Su Yu (*CQFLYZ* 167) cites the following relevant passage from the "Jun chen shang" (Ruler and Ministers, Part 1) chapter of the *Guanzi*:

> Listened to individually, the people are fools; listened to collectively, the people are sagelike. Even if he possesses the virtue of a Tang or Wu, the ruler will always cleave to the opinions of people in the marketplace. This is why an enlightened ruler follows the hearts of the people, finds security in their sentiments, and proceeds from a consensus.

Compare W. Allyn Rickett, trans., *Guanzi: Political, Economic, and Philosophical Essays from Early China* (Princeton, N.J.: Princeton University Press, 1985), 1:410.

Section 19.2

One who is lord over others is the root of the state. When administering a state, there is nothing more crucial to its transformation than reverence for its root. If the root is revered, the ruler will transform like a spirit. If the root is not revered, the ruler will have no means to unite others. Having no means to unite others, even if he institutes strict punishments and heavy penalties, the people will not submit. This is called "throwing away the state." Is there any greater disaster than this?

To what, then, does "root" refer? I answer: Heaven, Earth and humankind are the root of all living things.

> Heaven engenders them;
> Earth nourishes them;
> humankind perfects them.
> Heaven engenders them with filial piety and fraternal love;
> Earth nourishes them with food and clothing;
> humankind perfects them with ritual and music.

The three assist one another just as the hands and feet join together to perfect the body: it is not possible to dispense with one of them.

> Without filial piety and fraternal love, they will lose the means to be engendered;
> without food and clothing, they will lose the means to be nourished;
> without rites and music, they will lose the means to be perfected.

When all these three are lost, the people will resemble wild deer,

> each person following his own desires,
> each household establishing its own customs.
> Fathers will not be able to command their sons,
> rulers will not be able to order their ministers.

Even though the ruler enjoys possession of his walled city and outlying environs, it will be known as an "empty citadel." Under such circumstances, the ruler is left to find repose with only a clod of earth for his pillow.

> No one has endangered the ruler, yet he has endangered himself;
> no one has destroyed the ruler, yet he has destroyed himself.

This is what is called "a punishment that follows from the nature [of what came before]." When a punishment that follows from the nature [of what came before] arrives, even if he hides himself in a stone vault or barricades himself in a narrow pass, he still cannot escape it.

The enlightened ruler and worthy lord necessarily finds credence in this. For this reason, he respectfully and carefully attends to the three roots. He

performs the Suburban Sacrifice with the utmost reverence,
dutifully serves his ancestors and deceased father,
promotes and makes manifest those who exhibit filial piety and fraternal love,
displays and delineates [what is meant by] filial conduct.

These are the means by which he serves the root of Heaven.

He

takes up the plow handle and tills the soil,
plucks the mulberry leaves and nourishes the silkworms,
reclaims the wilds and sows the grain,
opens the frontiers, and provides sufficient food and clothing.

These are the means by which he serves the root of Earth.

He

establishes the imperial university and village schools;
cultivates filial piety, fraternal love, respect, and deference;
enlightens [the people] with the transformative powers of education;
moves [the people] with rites and music.

These are the means by which he serves the root of humankind.

When the ruler serves these three roots,

the people will be like sons and brothers not daring to act on their own authority;
the ruler will be like a parent not needing to rely on grace to demonstrate his love for the people or on sternness to command the people.

Should he take up residence in the wilds without a roof over his head, it will surpass living in a palace. Under such circumstances, the ruler will now find repose on a peaceful pillow.

No one has aided him, but he has made himself strong;
no one has comforted him, but he has made himself peaceful.

This is known as "a reward that follows from the nature [of what came before]." When a reward that follows from the nature [of what came before] arrives, even if he relinquishes the throne, abandons the state, and leaves the country, the people will strap their children on their backs and follow him as their ruler, so that he, too, will be unable to leave them. Therefore, when the ruler relies on virtue to administer the state, it is sweeter than cake or honey and firmer than glue or lacquer. This is why sages and worthies exert themselves to revere the root and do not dare depart from it. [19/25/29–19/26/13]

Section 19.3

One who is lord of others is the authentication of the state. He cannot take the lead. He is moved by others and only then responds. Therefore, although he occupies a position of leadership, he does not enact the strategic advantage of leadership.[4] Although he does not occupy a position of conciliation, he considers conciliation a virtue. Because he constantly uses his subordinates to the fullest, he consequently is able to secure his position of supremacy. [19/26/13–14]

Section 19.4

The way to instantiate the state lies in being honorable and spiritlike.

Being honorable is the means by which [the ruler] effects his policies;
being spiritlike is the means by which [the ruler] extends his transforming influence.

Therefore

if he is not honorable, he will not awe;
if he is not spiritlike, he will not transform.

Now

desiring to be honorable lies in employing worthies;
desiring to be spiritlike lies in unifying minds.

When worthies are established as the legs and arms of the ruler, he will be honorable and awe inspiring, and his state will be secure. When unified minds support one another, the ruler's transforming influence will be spiritlike. No one will observe how he acts, but his merit and virtue will be perfected. This is what I mean by "honorable" and "spiritlike." [19/26/16–19]

Section 19.5

Heaven accumulates an abundance of quintessence to make itself robust;
the sage accumulates an abundance of worthies to make himself strong.
Heaven arrays the sun, moon, and stars to make itself radiant;
the sage arrays ranks and emoluments to make himself manifest.

4. By remaining still and allowing his ministers to initiate affairs, the ruler is better positioned to verify whether their acts bring benefit or harm to the state.

The means by which Heaven becomes robust is not the strength of one quintessence;

the means by which the sage becomes strong is not the virtue of one worthy.

Therefore,

the Way of Heaven strives to make its quintessence flourish;

the sage strives to make his worthies numerous.

Striving to make its quintessence flourish, [Heaven] unifies its yang;

striving to make his worthies numerous, [the sage] unifies their minds.

Only after unifying its yang can [Heaven] extend its spirit;

only after unifying their minds can [the sage] extend his achievements.

For this reason, the technique to establish one's governance consists of prizing the attainment of worthy men and unifying their minds. [19/26/20–23]

Section 19.6

One who would be lord over others must prize being spiritlike. The spirits

cannot be apprehended through sight;

cannot be apprehended through hearing.

For this reason,

though you listen, you will not hear their voices;

though you look, you will not see their forms.

Their voices cannot be heard, so no one apprehends their echoes;

their forms cannot be seen, so no one apprehends their shadows.

No one apprehends their shadows, so there are no means to see whether they are crooked or straight.

No one apprehends their echoes, so there is no means to see whether they are clear or turbid.

Neither crooked nor straight, their achievements cannot be apprehended and thwarted.

Neither clear nor turbid, their reputations cannot be apprehended and measured.

"Not seeing their forms" does not mean that no one sees their forms advancing and stopping. It means that no one sees how they advance or stop.

"Not hearing their echoes" does not mean that no one hears their summons and commands. It means that no one hears how they summon and command.

What is not seen or heard is said to be dark and hidden.

Because he can be dark, he is bright.

Because he can be hidden, he is manifest.
Being able to be [both] dark and hidden, he is called "spiritlike."
The lord of others
prizes residing in darkness yet making his position illustrious;
dwelling in yin yet facing yang;
loathes others observing his true nature yet desires to know the minds of others.
For this reason, the one who would be lord over others
clings to thoughts that have no source;
effects affairs that have no starting point;
takes without seeking;
inquires without asking.

When I take without seeking, it is beneficial to me. When others yield without giving, their efforts are for naught. When I inquire without asking, I am spiritlike. When others respond without being aware, they reveal their true nature. Therefore, I question others to the end of my days, but they do not know to whom they respond. I take from others to the end of my days, but they do not know to whom they have given up [their goods]. I become increasingly enlightened, whereas others do not know what they have lost. Therefore, the one who is minister to another resides in yang while being yin; one who is lord over others resides in yin while being yang.[5] The Way of yin esteems the form and expresses the true nature [of things]. The Way of yang has no starting point and prizes being spiritlike.[6] [19/26/23–27]

5. In other words, the minister is yang because he occupies an exposed position, but he is also yin because his status is inferior to that of the ruler. The ruler is yin because he occupies a hidden position, but he is yang because his status is superior to that of his ministers.
6. The Way of yin corresponds to the minister, and the Way of yang, to the ruler.

Book 6, Part 7

CHAPTER 20

Preserving Position and Authority

Section 20.1

When the people do not have something they love, the lord will lack the means to make use of authority.
When the people do not have something they hate, the lord will lack the means to make use of dread.
Without the means to make use of authority
and without the means to make use of dread,

the lord will lack the means to prohibit and to regulate. [If the lord] lacks the means to prohibit and to regulate, both [lords and common people] will have comparable weight and equal positional advantage. Thus [the lord] will lack the means to be honored. Therefore when a sage governs a state, he follows the nature and disposition of Heaven and Earth, from which derive the benefits pertaining to the orifices and apertures [of the human body]. He thereby

establishes regulations concerning the lofty and the base,
makes distinctions between the noble and the mean.

He establishes official ranks and emoluments, [so that they]

benefit from the five flavors,
prosper from the five colors,
and are aroused by the five notes,

thus gratifying their eyes and ears.

He personally leads

the pure and the impure to shine forth in distinguishing their substances,
the glorious and disgraceful to excel in exposing each other,

and thereby moves their hearts.

[The lord] strives to cause the people to be ordered by what they love. Only after the people have something they love will the lord be able to win them over and encourage them. Therefore he establishes rewards to encourage them. When the people have something they love, there inevitably will [also] be something they hate. Only after there is something they hate will the lord be able to instill dread in them. Therefore he establishes punishments to instill dread in them. When the lord possesses the means to encourage the people and to instill dread in them, he will be able to regulate them. Regulating them means

[he] regulates what they love;
for this reason, he encourages them with rewards that are not excessive.
[he] regulates what they hate;
for this reason, he instills dread in them with punishments that are not excessive.
If what they love is abundant, [the lord] will have created [too much] happiness;
if what they hate is excessive, [the lord] will have created [too much] fear.
If he creates [too much] fear, the ruler will lose his authority, and there will be mutual resentment throughout the world.
If he creates [too much] happiness, the ruler will lose his power, and there will be mutual harm throughout the world.[1]

Therefore when a sage regulates the people, he

enables them to have desires but does not exceed the proper limits;
he enables them to be honest and simple but does not eliminate their desires.

When [both] not having desires and having desires reach a sufficiency, the Way of the Lord has been attained. [20/27/5–15]

Section 20.2

That by which a state comes to be a state is power;
that by which a lord comes to be a lord is fearsomeness.

Therefore

power must not be shared;
fearsomeness must not be delegated.
If power is shared, [the lord] will lose his grace;

1. The locus classicus for the expressions "to create happiness" and "to create fear" is the "Great Plan" chapter of the *Documents*:

> Only the sovereign can create happiness; only the sovereign can create fear; only the sovereign [can confer] jade and food rations. The minister should not create happiness, create fear, or confer jade and food rations. If the ministers should create happiness, create fear, or confer jade and food rations, it would inflict injury on the [noble] families and inflict disaster on the state.

if fearsomeness is delegated, [the lord] will lose his authority.
If he loses authority, the lord will be demeaned;
if he loses grace, the people will scatter.
If the people scatter, the state will become chaotic;
if the lord is demeaned, his ministers will rebel.

For this reason, one who would rule others

must resolutely preserve his power to subjugate his people;
must resolutely maintain his authority to rectify his ministers.
Sounds may be compliant or contrary, but they must be either clear or turbid;[2]
forms may be pleasing or hateful, but they must be either crooked or straight.

Therefore

when the sage listens to sounds, he distinguishes the clear from the turbid;
when he observes forms, he differentiates the crooked from the straight.
He must know the clear in the turbid;
he must know the turbid in the clear.
He must see the crooked in the straight;
he must see the straight in the crooked.
There is no sound too small for him to detect;
there is no form too small for him to appraise.
He does not let what is obvious becloud what is hidden;
he does not let what is abundant obscure what is scarce.

In each instance, he responds to affairs and arrives at the appropriate response. When black and white are distinguished clearly, the people will know what to reject and what to follow. When they know what to reject and what to follow, it is possible to achieve order. This [should] be taken as the standard. [20/27/15–22]

Section 20.3

One who would be lord over others

establishes his position in non-action;
effects his instruction by non-speech.
Silent and voiceless,
quiescent and formless,

2. The meaning of *qing* 清 and *zhuo* 濁 ("clear" and "turbid," respectively) as technical terms of music is often uncertain. In some contexts, they appear to mean simply "high notes" and "low notes"; in other contexts, they may signify "tempered" and "untempered" scales. For further discussion, see John S. Major, Sarah A. Queen, Andrew Seth Meyer, and Harold D. Roth, trans. and eds., *The "Huainanzi": A Guide to the Theory and Practice of Government in Early Han China* (New York: Columbia University Press, 2010), 931.

he clings to the sourceless One and is the wellspring of the state.

He

accords with the state as if it were his own body;

accords with the ministers as if they were his own mind.

He takes

the ministers' speech as his voice;

the ministers' tasks as his form.

Where there is a voice, there inevitably is an echo;

where there is a form, there inevitably is a shadow.

When

the voice emerges from within,

the echo responds from without.

When

the form is established above,

the shadow reflects from below.

Echoes may be clear or turbid;

shadows may be crooked or straight.

The response of an echo is not a singular voice;

the reflection of a shadow is not a singular form.

Therefore, one who would rule with an empty mind and in a quiescent state

astutely listens to their echoes,

brilliantly observes their shadows,

and thereby practices the standards of rewards and punishments. When practicing rewards and punishments,

if the echo is clear, the one who has engendered this clarity is honored;

if the echo is turbid, the one who has engendered this turbidity is demeaned;

if the shadow is straight, the one who has engendered the straightness is promoted;

if the shadow is crooked, the one who has engendered the crookedness is demoted.

The lord clings to their titles and investigates their true substance in order to assess their actual performance.

Rewards are not bestowed groundlessly;

punishments are not inflicted heedlessly.

For this reason, the numerous ministers are governed according to the distinctions in their duties. Each serves with respect and vies to advance his meritorious deeds to manifest and extend his reputation, whereas he who rules others can be carried along in their midst. This is the technique to spontaneously extend [the ruler's] strength. The sage relies on this method. Therefore

the accomplishments emanate from the ministers;

the reputation reverts to the lord. [20/27/22–29]

Book 7, Part 1

CHAPTER 21

Investigating Achievement and Reputation

Section 21.1

The method of investigating the merit [of an official] is to investigate what he has amassed.

The Way of Heaven accumulates and collects an abundance of quintessence in order to be radiant;

the sage accumulates and collects an abundance of excellence in order to be meritorious.

Therefore

the brilliance of the sun and moon is not [due to] the radiance of a single [ray of] quintessence;

the Great Peace summoned by the sage is not [due to] the merit of a single [act of] excellence.

That from which brilliance is born cannot be [a single] source;

that from which excellence is born cannot be [a single] starting point.

Weigh the positional advantage and establish your authority;

adapt to the situation and institute [standards of] righteousness.

Therefore,

the way the sage brings benefit to the world is like the way the spring *qi* engenders vegetation.

Each grows small or large in accordance with its inborn [nature] and measures up to its greater or lesser [vitality].

The way the sage eradicates wrongdoing in the world is like the way the rivers and streams flow into the sea.

Each complies with the inherent potential of the land and is directed to the south or the north.

Therefore,

although their paths are different, their destinations are the same.[1]

[Likewise, although sages possess] different methods, their virtue is the same.

Their inclination to promote benefit and eradicate wrongdoing is one.

For this reason,

the essence of bringing benefit lies in achieving it, not in whether it is much or little;

the essence of eradicating wrongdoing lies in expelling it, not in whether it is to the south or the north.

Investigate the merit [of the officials] and demote or promote them;

examine the affairs [that they have managed] and employ or dismiss them.

With regard to those who have brought increase, call them "selfless";

with regard to those who have not brought increase, call them "troublesome."

Grab hold of their reputation and evaluate their actual performance. Do not accept empty words.

Reward those who have merit;

punish those who commit crimes.

Reward generously those whose merit is are abundant;

punish heavily those whose crimes are abundant.

[If there are some] who are unable to accomplish anything, do not reward them, even if they have a reputation for worthiness;

[If there are some] who do not neglect their official duties, do not punish them, even if they have a reputation for stupidity.

Rewards and punishments must be used in accordance with [each person's] actual performance, not in accordance with his reputation. When [the distinction between] the worthy and the stupid is determined by actual performance and not by externalities, then

right and wrong cannot be confused;

happiness and anger cannot be excessive;

villainous and rebellious men cannot be troublesome;

and all the myriad things will achieve their proper place. This being the case, the numerous officials will strive to the utmost to carry forth their duties and will vie to advance their merit. [21/28/5–14]

1. The phrase *yi kong er tong gui* 異孔而同歸 paraphrases the well-known proverb *shutu tonggui* 殊途同歸 (different roads, same destination).

Section 21.2

The method to examine and test [officials]:

> important ones at a measured pace,
> unimportant ones quickly,
> high ranking ones slowly,
> low-ranking ones swiftly.
> Lords of the Land monthly conduct tests in their states;
> provincial governors seasonally conduct tests in their provinces, four tests comprising one examination.
> The Son of Heaven annually tests the empire, three tests comprising one examination.

From start to finish, an official must undergo three examinations and then may be promoted or demoted. He is given a formal pronouncement called a "rating." [21/28/16–17]

Section 21.3

The way to examine and test [an official] is to

> collate his rank [of nobility] and emolument,
> summarize the duties [of his post],
> reckon his length of service,
> and set out his accomplishments,

[in order] to calculate his merits and weigh his faults. Take what is abundant to cancel what is scanty; consider his reputation [in the light of] ascertainable facts. First privately [i.e., in a closed session of court] establish his ranking, first of all comparing him with two or three [groups], in order [to grade him in the] upper, middle, or lower [subrank], and thereby to examine [his suitability] for employment or dismissal. After that, in a public [session of court,] gather [the candidates] and, in accordance with their [earned] designation, pronounce them accepted or dismissed. [In determining whether] to increase or decrease [their emoluments] by more or less, there should be a clear standard and order of ranking. [Establish] nine ranks, laid out as three times three, so that each rank has an upper, middle, and lower [subrank]. Level one is the highest; level five is the middle; and level nine is the lowest. Most officials revert to the middle rank; those who are superior to the middle rank receive [the highest rank]; those who are inferior to the middle rank are demoted. Those who receive [the highest rank] are few; they [are assigned to] the first rank and rewarded. Among those who reach the fourth rank, those who are demoted are more numerous; they are [assigned to] the fourth rank as a diminution. Among those who reach the first rank, their movement is contrariwise. Three times four is twelve, so when the ranking is completed, one apprehends the entire ranking [scheme] to demote or promote them. Time after time, each has his own ranking; each follows his assigned position. In order to comprehensively arrive at the numbers, there is an initial re-rating, [then] [a second], then [a third], and [next] a fourth re-rating, [so that] in each case no one fails [to be assigned to] his [proper] grade. This, too, is using the complete rating [scheme] to demote or promote them. [21/28/19–25]

Section 21.4

There is an initial re-rating; this is called the "second upgrading." There are a next [second], next [third], and fourth re-rating; this is called the "third upgrading." Nine years is a term in [any given] grade. If [there are those who] attain an additional nine, at the same time they are purged [after?] six, being dismissed in a third [re-]grading. Six and six, they attain their level. At the same time, the middling among them attain three; they are comprehensively purged. At the same time, three and three are [re-]rated. Those who attain six at the same time attain one rating.

This is the "four [re-]ratings." Demotions are [handled in] the same way.[2] [21/28/27–29]

2. This section, which appears to be a continuation of section 21.3, is very obscure and is likely to have become textually corrupted in the course of transmission. The standard commentaries agree that the sense of the passage is difficult to discern. Our translation is an attempt to render the word-by-word sense of the text as it now stands, but we do not pretend that it conveys any coherent meaning.

Book 7, Part 2

CHAPTER 22

Comprehending the State as the Body

Section 22.1

The purest of *qi* is quintessence.
The purest of men are worthies.
Those who regulate their bodies take the accumulation of quintessence as a treasure.
Those who regulate the state take the accumulation of worthies as the Way.
The body takes the mind as its foundation.
The state takes the lord as its ruler.
When quintessence accumulates at the foundation, the blood and *qi* support each other.
When worthies accumulate around their ruler, superiors and inferiors restrain each other.
When the blood and *qi* support each other, the embodied form has nothing to cause it suffering.
When superiors and inferiors restrain each other, the one hundred officials each obtain their proper place.
Only when the embodied form is free from suffering can it achieve tranquillity.
Only when the one hundred officials each obtain their proper place can the state achieve security.
Those who desire to acquire quintessence must empty and still their forms.
Those who desire to acquire worthies must humble and abase themselves.
Where the form is still and the mind empty is where quintessential *qi* collects.
Where rulers are humble and self-abasing is where humane worthies serve.

Therefore,

those who regulate their bodies strive to grasp emptiness and stillness to acquire quintessence;

those who regulate the state strive to fully develop their humility and self-abasement to acquire worthies.

Those who can acquire quintessence achieve enlightenment and longevity.

Those who can acquire worthies widely extend their virtue and their states achieve Great Peace. [22/29/1–9]

Group 3

Regulatory Principles

THE SIX chapters of group 3, "Regulatory Principles," prescribe regulations that the ruler should implement in governing his realm and managing his bureaucracy, specifically the changes that the founding ruler of a new dynasty should make to show that he has been invested with the Mandate of Heaven. They cover a wide range of issues, from ritual matters such as the proper day for the start of the civil calendar year and the color of court vestments, to administrative issues such as determining (on numerological grounds) the number of officials in various positions and how they should be selected, to hierarchical considerations such as regulations for the appropriate clothing for people of different ranks of society and how much wealth each rank should enjoy.

GROUP 3: REGULATORY PRINCIPLES, CHAPTERS 23–28

Description of Individual Chapters

Chapter 23, "The Three Dynasties' Alternating Regulations of Simplicity and Refinement," is extremely long.[1] It contains the *Chunqiu fanlu*'s most elaborate and complex discussions of the regulations that a dynastic founder should follow at the beginning of his reign. Adopting a question-and-answer format—a literary device commonly found in Western Han writings—it describes a series of specific ritual regulations to be observed by the ruler upon receiving the Mandate of Heaven. The regulations are determined by correlating the current dynasty with a number of different historical cycles and numerological schemes identified as the "Three Sequences" (*san tong* 三統), "Three Rectifications" (*san zheng* 三正), "Five Inceptions" (*wu duan* 五端), and "Four Models" (*si fa* 四法). We have divided the chapter into sixteen sections, each either containing one question and its response or following some other perceptible break in the chapter's content.

The chapter begins in section 23.1 on an ostensibly simple note, with a canonical reference to the first entry in the *Spring and Autumn* and its corresponding *Gongyang* explanation: "The *Spring and Autumn* states: 'The king's first month.' The [*Gongyang*] *Commentary* states: 'To whom does "the king" refer? It refers to King Wen. Why [does the *Spring and Autumn*] first mention "the king" and then mention "the first month"?' The king rectified the month."[2] The sense of this passage depends on a play on words. As a noun phrase, *zheng yue* 正月 means "the first month," but as a verb–noun construction, it means "to rectify the month." This introduces the main point of this whole long, multi-sectioned chapter: that the founding king of a new dynasty makes many ritual changes, including designating a new first month to begin the civil calendar, to demonstrate that he is the new holder of the Mandate of Heaven. In this case, we are told that the king is King Wen, founder of the Zhou dynasty, and that he

1. Readers will want to compare our translation of chapter 23 with that of Michael Loewe, *Dong Zhongshu, a "Confucian" Heritage, and the "Chunqiu fanlu,"* Brill China Studies, no. 20 (Leiden: Brill, 2011), 317–34. We have found Loewe's introduction to his translation (291–317) and the heavy annotation of the translation itself to be very helpful and to offer fine examples of how the content of the *Chunqiu fanlu* can repay meticulous and minute study. Our translation and his generally agree, the differences being mainly stylistic rather than substantive. Our principal difference with Loewe is that he regards chapter 23 as a unified work with a single author ("the author of *pian* no. 23 . . ." [315]) and as probably dating to the late first century C.E. ("composed as an account of the discussions held in 79 CE" [309]), whereas we see the chapter as an amalgam of sixteen sections written by different authors over a long period of time. The implication of our view is that the chapter was assembled, from thematically related but chronologically disparate materials, at some point during or after the later part of the Eastern Han dynasty.

2. *CQFL* 23/29/13–14.

"rectified" the month (that is, he designated a new first month of the civil calendar) at the beginning of his reign as the Son of Heaven.

In section 23.2, the simple formulaic expression "the king's first month" canonically justifies the chapter's subsequent prescriptions for a dynastic founder to change such symbolic hallmarks of his dynasty as the calendar, the color of the court dress, the music to be composed or performed at court, and the rituals to be observed. All these changes unite the empire and demonstrate that the surname of the ruling household has been changed and that the founder of the new dynasty has not displaced a legitimate sovereign but has received the Mandate of Heaven. The ruler thus creates specific categories to venerate Heaven.

After this opening reference to the canon, section 23.3 raises a question that moves the discussion into more elaborate theoretical territory: How precisely does the ruler "revise regulations and create benchmarks"? He must look back to preceding dynasties to match his own regulations with the appropriate sequences, designated by cycles of three, four, and five. The Three Sequences are symbolized by the three colors white, red, and black and are exemplified by the three rulers King Tang of the Shang, King Wu of the Zhou, and the "New King" or "New Royal Dynasty" (*xin wang* 新王) of the *Spring and Autumn*. It is interesting that here the Zhou dynasty is considered to have become defunct at the end of what we know as the Western Zhou period and that the Spring and Autumn period is regarded as a new dynasty that, given the overall political-historical stance of the *Chunqiu fanlu*, we may identify with Confucius, the "uncrowned king." The reigns of these dynastic founders are correlated with colors, as shown in table 1.

Section 23.4 summarizes and extends this discussion, emphasizing the Three Rectifications (which seems to be another name for the Three Sequences) to determine the first month of the civil calendar and the appropriate color and directional correlates following from that. The sequence begins with black, continues with white and then red, and then repeats the sequence. Black begins the year with the month *yin* (the third astronomical month) in the east-northeast, to which the handle of the Northern Dipper points; the sun and the (new) moon are in the lunar lodge Encampment.[3] White begins the year with the month *chou* (the

3. For the twenty-eight lunar lodges, see John S. Major, Sarah A. Queen, Andrew Seth Meyer, and Harold D. Roth, trans. and eds., *The "Huainanzi": A Guide to the Theory and Practice of Government in Early Han China* (New York: Columbia University Press, 2010), app. B, 922. Another list, in which the translations of some of the lodge names differ from this, is in Nathan Sivin, *Granting the Seasons: The Chinese Astronomical Reform of 1280, with a Study of Its Many Dimensions and an Annotated Translation of Its Records* (New York: Springer, 2009), 292–94. See also the richly annotated translation of relevant passages in *SJ* 27, the "Treatise on the Celestial Offices" (Tian guan shu 天官書), in David W. Pankenier, *Astrology and Cosmology in Early China: Conforming Earth to Heaven* (Cambridge: Cambridge University Press, 2013), 461–72.

TABLE 1

	White Sequence	Red Sequence	Black Sequence
Ruler	King Tang of Yin	King Wu of Zhou	Confucius
Dynastic name	Changed Xia to Yin	Changed Yin to Zhou	Changed Zhou to Spring and Autumn
Statutory color	White	Red	Black
Closest dynasty	Xia	Yin	Zhou
More remote dynasty	Yu (Shun)	Xia	Song (remnants of Yin)
Demoted to thearch	Tang (Yao)	Yu (Shun)	
Colored-coded thearch	Shen Nong as red	Xuan Yuan as yellow	
Royal city	Built north of Luo River	Built at Feng	
Name of palace	Yin	Cai	
Type of music	Huo	Wu	Airs of Shao and Wu
Ritual regulations	Simple rituals (*zhi*)	Refined rituals (*wen*)	Simple rituals (*zhi*)

second astronomical month) in the north-northeast, to which the handle of the Northern Dipper points; the sun and the (new) moon are in the lunar lodge Emptiness. Red begins the year with the month *zi* (the first astronomical month) in the north, to which the handle of the Northern Dipper points; the sun and the (new) moon are in the lunar lodge Ox Leader. The relevant dynasties again are taken to be Shang, Zhou, and the "New Royal Dynasty" of the *Spring and Autumn*; the regulations for each are shown in table 2.

The description of the Three Sequences and their respective Three Rectifications concludes with some interesting recommendations. It contends that the ancient rulers enacted these reforms at the beginning of their reigns upon receiving the Mandate and that they performed the Suburban Sacrifice with the express intention "to announce [the accession of the new dynasty] to Heaven, Earth, and the numerous spirits." Having performed this sacrifice, they presented offerings to their distant and recent ancestors and then proclaimed their accession throughout the empire: "The Lords of the Land received [the proclamation of the new statutory color and beginning of the civil year] in their ancestral temples. They then announced it to their spirits of the land and grain, to the ancestors, and to the spirits of mountains and streams in their respective

TABLE 2

	Black Sequence	White Sequence	Red Sequence
Sun and moon on first day of year	Located in Encampment	Located in Emptiness	Located in Ox Leader
Dipper on first day	Points to *yin* (ENE)	Points to *chou* (NNE)	Points to *zi* (N)
Heaven's *qi*	Begins to permeate things	Begins to cause things to shed coverings	Begins to cause things to move
Ritual color	Black	White	Red
Court clothing	Black	White	Red
Pendants of official caps	Black	White	Red
Imperial chariots	Black	White	Red
Imperial horses	Black	White	Red
Imperial cords carrying seals of office	Black	White	Red
Imperial headdresses	Black	White	Red
Imperial flags	Black	White	Red
Precious jades	Black	White	Red
Animals for suburban sacrifice	Black	White	Red
Horns of these sacrificial animals	Shaped like an egg	Shaped like a silk cocoon	Shaped like a chestnut
Location of capping ceremony	Performed at the eastern steps (of the main hall)	Performed at the platform (of the main hall)	Performed in the side chamber (of the main hall)
Location of marriage ceremony	Groom meets bride in the courtyard (of ancestral temple)	Groom meets bride at the platform (of ancestral temple)	Groom meets bride at the door (to eastern side of ancestral temple)
Location of funeral ceremony	Deceased encoffined above the eastern steps (leading to main hall)	Deceased encoffined between columns (on platform of main hall)	Deceased encoffined above the western steps (leading to main hall)
Sacrificial animal	Black	White	Red
Sacrificial offering	Liver	Lung	Heart
Musical instruments	Made of black materials	Made of white materials	Made of red materials
First division of day	Set at daybreak	Set at dawn	Set at midnight
Court rectification	Set at daybreak	Set at dawn	Set at midnight

territories. Only then were the movements and responses of the various officials united."[4]

The next section, 23.5, begins by linking the Three Sequences to a concept designated as the Five Inceptions. The Five Inceptions are associated with the founders of the Three Dynasties (the Xia, Shang, and Zhou), in contrast to the Three Sequences, which are associated with the rulers of the Shang, Zhou, and the idealized dynasty of the uncrowned king envisioned in the *Spring and Autumn*. All are said to have unified the world by grasping the essentials of the Five Inceptions, which enabled them to rectify the regulations pertaining to court audiences so that each ranked participant, moving downward and outward from the center (Son of Heaven, Lords of the Land, great ministers and officials, neighboring tribes, and those from distant lands), donned clothing distinctive of their rank relative to that of the Son of Heaven.

Section 23.6 is a fragment that explores the implications of two meanings of the word *zheng* 正: "first" (as in "first month") and "to rectify." Section 23.7 then returns to the theme of 23.4, discussing in greater detail how the Spring and Autumn period corresponds to a "new royal dynasty" and thus requires the alteration of the (red) symbolic emblems of the preceding Zhou dynasty to correspond to the Black Sequence. This section also introduces more remote eras of dynastic history, specifying the proper titles of the predynastic rulers, dynastic kings, and their descendants, as well as the necessity of preserving their descendants by bestowing the appropriate territories on them.

The next few sections (23.8–23.14) consist of questions and answers on points raised earlier about how the *Spring and Autumn* alters the titles of the preceding dynastic kings and predynastic thearchs so that each corresponds to a "new royal dynasty." Returning to a point made in section 23.7, section 23.8 asks: If descendants of the former kings were called dukes, why does the *Spring and Autumn* not follow this rule consistently, instead referring to the lord of Qii as a viscount in one instance and an earl in another? Section 23.9 explains why the Yellow Thearch stands at the head of the sequence of the Five Thearchs. Section 23.10 asks why, if "thearch" is an honorable designation, are the descendants of the "thearchs" given small states rather than large ones. This section introduces the principle guiding how descendants of the previous rulers are be treated. As they recede into the past, their noble titles

4. *CQFL* 23/30/14–15.

move down the hierarchy (through seventeen steps: Three Royal Dynasties, Five Thearchs, and Nine Sovereigns), and their states grow smaller. Finally, they drop off the ladder of hierarchy altogether and revert to commoner status:

> Therefore, even though they are eventually reduced to the status of commoner and are cut off from their territory, their positions in the ancestral temple and sacrificial offerings still are set forth in the liturgies of the Suburban Sacrifice, and they are honored at the sacrifice at Mount Tai. Thus it is said: "Reputation and name, *hun* and *po*, disperse into emptiness. Extreme longevity has no bounds."[5]

Section 23.10 also points out that in some cases, the Three Royal Dynasties leave unchanged the regulations of the preceding dynasty and, in others, revert to precedents from dynasties that are two, three, four, five, and nine cycles back. The next section, 23.11, asks why in certain respects the ruler should revert to the regulations of a previous dynasty after two cycles and in other respects he should revert after four. The answer to this question has been lost.

Section 23.12 explains that the "new royal dynasty" represented in the *Spring and Autumn* had three grades of noble rank, in contrast to the Zhou, which had five grades. This section follows the *Gongyang Commentary* in correlating the three grades with duke, marquis, and earl/viscount/baron. In contrast, section 23.13 associates the three grades with Heaven, Earth, and humankind.[6]

Section 23.14 describes in great detail the correlation of the three grades with the Heaven, Earth, and humankind sequence. The resulting Four Models move through four archetypes of governance and then repeat.

1. Those who take Heaven as their support emulate Shang and rule as kings.
2. Those who take Earth as their support emulate Xia and rule as kings.
3. Those who take Heaven as their support emulate Simplicity and rule as kings.
4. Those who take Earth as their support emulate Refinement and rule as kings.

These four sequences correspond to the characteristics and regulations presented in table 3.

5. *CQFL* 23/31/6–7. This comment, more than any other, points to an Eastern Han date for at least portions of the chapter, because we know that it was not until the Eastern Han that scholars became concerned with correlating the current dynasty with the Nine Sovereigns of early antiquity.
6. *CQFL* 23/31/9–10.

TABLE 3

	Shang/ Heaven	Xia/ Earth	Simplicity/ Heaven	Refinement/ Earth
Type of *qi*	Retiring yang	Advancing yin	Retiring yang	Advancing yin
Honor and affection	Show affection toward relatives	Honor the honorable	Show affection toward relatives	Honor the honorable
Abundance of	Humaneness and simplicity	Righteousness and moderation	Simplicity and love	Propriety and refinement
Succession to throne	Passes to king's son	Passes to king's grandson	Passes to king's son	Passes to king's grandson
Treated generously	King's younger brothers from same mother	Sons of earlier generation	King's younger brothers from same mother	Sons of earlier generation
Concubine who bears king's son	Gains an honorable position	Does not gain an honorable position	Gains an honorable position	Does not gain an honorable position
Capping	Son given new name by father	Son given new name by mother	Son given new name by father	Son given new name by mother
Marriage	Husband and wife sit opposite each other	Husband and wife sit together	Husband and wife sit opposite each other	Husband and wife sit together
Funeral	Husband and wife buried separately	Husband and wife buried together	Husband and wife buried separately	Husband and wife buried together
Tablets of deceased	Husband and wife occupy separate positions	Wife follows that of husband, together	Husband and wife occupy separate positions	Wife follows that of husband, together
Aristocratic rank	Three grades	Five grades	Three grades	Five grades
Emoluments	Two grades	Three grades	Two grades	Three grades
Suburban temple	Circular	Square	Circular inside and oval outside	Square inside and rectangular outside
Hall of light	Circular	Square	Circular inside and oval outside	Square inside and rectangular outside
Sacrificial implements	Round	Square	Oval	Cross-shaped
Jade	Nine *fen* thick	Eight *fen* thick	Seven *fen* thick	Six *fen* thick
Silk	Five strands	Four strands	Three strands	Two strands
Ceremonial dress	Flared at the upper garment	Flared at the lower garment	Front lapels are elongated	Rear lapels are elongated

	Shang/ Heaven	Xia/ Earth	Simplicity/ Heaven	Refinement/ Earth
Ceremonial cap	Tall and circular	Lowered in front and raised in back	Circular	Rippled and hanging loosely
Imperial carriage	Dignified	Humble	Dignified	Humble
Model of emulation	How Heaven arranges its constellations	How Earth arranges its form	How Heaven arranges its constellations	How Earth arranges its form
Bells	Four bells suspended in rack	Two bells suspended in rack	Four bells suspended in rack	Two bells suspended in rack
Music	Cai drums	She drums	Cheng drums	Xian drums
Dance	Xi dance in circular pattern	Mao dance in square pattern	Xiyue dance in oval pattern	Wang dance in rectangular pattern
Sacrifices	First present hair and blood, then perform music	First present a cooked sacrifice, then perform music	First perform the sound of jades, then present a cooked offering	First present a cooked offering, then perform music
Rectify punishments by	Extending principle of concealing faults	Following standards of Heaven	Extending principle of concealing faults	Following standards of Heaven
Relatives	Extend principle of avoidance to relatives		Extend principle of avoidance to relatives	
Feng and Shan performed	At the summit of the mountain	At the base of the mountain	At the left side of the mountain	At the right side of the mountain

Section 23.15 discusses the origins of the Four Models, tracing them to the era of the thearchs. This implies that they are more ancient than the Three Sequences observed by King Tang of the Shang and later exemplary rulers. In the Four Models scheme, Shun is identified with Heaven and Shang; Yu, with Earth and Xia; King Tang of the Shang, with Heaven and Simplicity; and King Wen of the Zhou, with Earth and Refinement. The attributes of each of these rulers are described to demonstrate how in turn they correlated with Heaven and Earth. Section 23.16 explains how the respective surnames of the ruling clans of these dynasties were selected.

Chapter 24, "Regulations on Officialdom Reflect Heaven," contains five sections. We believe that the chapter originally consisted of the first section only and that the later sections originally were bits of commentary that at some point were erroneously incorporated into the chapter. We should point out that the text of section 24.1 in the *Chunqiu fanlu* is identical to a passage in the "Kingly Regulations" of the *Classic of Rites*.[7] It maintains that the bureaucracy of the Son of Heaven consisted of 120 offices, divided into four ranks, with each rank consisting of officials whose total number was a multiple of three: the three dukes, nine ministers, twenty-seven great officers, and eighty-one senior functionaries. It proposes that the former kings of antiquity employed regulations to ensure that the number and ranking of their offices and the selection of their officials accorded perfectly with the "great warp of Heaven." Thus this ancient administration, with its numerology of fours and threes, was the perfect human image of Heaven's annual course, mirroring Heaven's four seasons, each consisting of three months: "According completely with Heaven's numbers to assist in [the conduct of] human affairs signifies that government carefully attends to the Way. These 120 officials were the means by which the former kings conducted themselves in accordance with the correct Way."[8] Just as the first, second, and third month of each of the four seasons has its distinctive characteristics, the upper, middle, and lower class of officials of each of the four tiers of officials has its distinctive qualities. Just as Heaven has its four permutations, human talent has its four selections: "The sagely person constitutes one selection; the noble person constitutes one selection; the good person constitutes one selection; [and] the upright person constitutes one selection."[9] Section 24.1 concludes: "It is only the sage who can [similarly] fully utilize the permutations of humankind and harmonize them with those of Heaven, thereby establishing the affairs of the king."[10] We believe that this concluding statement marks the end of the essay that originally constituted this chapter.

The next two sections, 24.2 and 24.3, are related commentarial intrusions that develop in new directions ideas put forth in the opening essay. Several features suggest that this is the case. First is the expression "What is meant by X (*he wei* 何謂 X)?" This is a classic formulaic expression often used in commentaries to unpack a particularly recondite concept or develop a previously mentioned concept in new directions. Second, these sections contain repetitions,

7. See chapter 24, note 1. This official hierarchy may have been associated in the Han imagination with the Xia dynasty. In the "Way of the Ruler" chapter of the *Shuoyuan* (*Garden of Persuasions*), these titles appear in a passage in which Tang, the first ruler of the Shang, questions his minister Yi Yin. But in chapter 24.1, it is associated with the former kings in general.

8. *CQFL* 24/32/21–22.

9. This scheme differs from the nomenclature and procedures outlined in chapter 28, which divides officials into four categories: talented, eminent, prominent, and brave.

10. *CQFL* 24/32/29.

contradictions, and novelties not present in 24.1. Section 24.2 asks, "What is meant by 'the great warp of Heaven'?" In 24.1, this expression was defined as a year of four seasons of three months apiece. In contrast, the expression here is defined as an elaborate numerology based on three and ten:

> There are the three commencements [sunrise, noon, and sunset] that complete one day; the three days that complete a *gui* [three-day period]; the three *xun* [ten-day periods] that complete a month; the three months that complete a season; the three seasons that complete the achievements [of the year].[11] The cold, warm, and tepid are the three [types of temperature] that complete [the vitality of living] things. The sun, moon, and stars are the three [types of celestial bodies] that complete [the phenomenon of] light. Heaven, Earth, and humankind are the three [types of entities] that complete [the perfection of] virtue.[12]

This list of examples demonstrates that "completing one with three" is emblematic of Heaven's great warp. To create official regulations, then, the recommendation is to follow this one-to-three ratio for the four ranks of the bureaucracy. Accordingly, "three dukes constitute one selection; three ministers [for each duke] constitute one selection; three great officers [for each minister] constitute one selection; [and] three senior functionaries [for each great officer] constitute one selection." Thus section 24.2 maintains the basic pattern of threes and fours seen in 24.1 but augments it with a numerology of three, four, twelve, and ten: "For this reason, taking three [men] to constitute a selection derives from Heaven's warp; taking four to constitute a round [of selections] derives from Heaven's seasons; taking twelve to constitute a cohort derives from the year's measuring points; arriving at ten cohorts and stopping derives from Heaven's starting points."[13]

Building on this conclusion, section 24.3 asks, "What is meant by 'Heaven's starting points'?" The ten starting points of Heaven are Heaven, Earth, humankind, yin, yang, Fire, Metal, Wood, Water, and Earth. They constitute a cohort, and each cohort takes twelve officers at a time to correspond to the twelve months of the year. The text goes on to play with the numbers three, four, ten, and twelve, creating additional Heavenly correlations to arrive in various ways

11. The "three seasons" mentioned here are spring, summer, and fall. Winter is a season of quiescence—literal "hibernation"—and so plays no role in the "achievements of the year." See chapter 43.1, which explores at length the concept of a ten-month "year" dominated by the power of yang.
12. *CQFL* 24/33/1–2.
13. *CQFL* 24/33/4–6.

at the number 120. That this can be done in several different ways is taken as evidence for the correctness and numerological power of "Heaven's numbers."

Section 24.4 is a brief fragment of a numerological essay or passage of commentary that once again discusses Heaven's numbers. Here the emphasis is on how human beings surpass all other living things in their ability to discover the significance of Heaven's numbers. Using the kind of macrocosm/microcosm imagery found in many Han texts, it correlates three, four, and twelve, identified as the numbers of Heaven, with the human body and with the regulations of officialdom:

> The body has four limbs, and each limb has three divisions. Three times four is twelve. When these twelve divisions support one another, the embodied form is established. Heaven has four seasons, and each season has three months. Three times four is twelve. When these twelve months receive one another, the yearly cycle is established. The officials have four selections, and each selection has its three men. Three times four is twelve. When these twelve officers support one another, the tasks of government are implemented.[14]

This brief statement concludes by urging the reader to examine the many and subtle human correspondences with Heaven.

Section 24.5 continues the Heavenly numerology of the preceding sections, expressed in its own arcane terminology. It discusses the annual cycle of the four seasons of three months each, and here the year is identified as a "pattern of Heaven and Earth," encompassing "Heaven's four selection times"—that is, seasons. The four selection times of Heaven—spring for Lesser Yang, summer for Greater Yang, autumn for Lesser Yin, and winter for Greater Yin—are further divided into beginning, middle, and ending periods (months). In accordance with this Heavenly sequence, the former kings established their four selections of officials. Nothing in this section is particularly new except for the special terminology that it employs; otherwise, it is not much more than a restatement of points already made in sections 24.2 through 24.4.

The title of chapter 25, "Yao and Shun Did Not Presumptuously Transfer [the Throne]; Tang and Wu Did Not Rebelliously Murder [Their Rulers]," refers to two short sections that were likely combined in this chapter by the *Chunqiu fanlu*'s compiler because both address the topic of dynastic change. Moreover, dynastic change is relevant to all the chapters in this group, as it is the momentous

14. *CQFL* 24/33/17–21.

historical event that triggers the various regulatory reforms discussed in other chapters in this group. Here two theoretical positions concerning how dynastic succession occurs—the abdication of good rulers and the violent overthrow of evil rulers—are challenged on the grounds that rulership is ultimately bestowed by Heaven and not determined by men.

Section 25.1 takes up the dynastic succession of the two exemplary sage-kings of legendary antiquity, Yao and Shun, revered for giving priority to virtue over blood. Each passed over his own sons to bequeath the throne to the most virtuous man in the kingdom. The first section of this chapter challenges this interpretation. Taking as its point of departure the opening lines of the *Classic of Filial Piety* that equate serving one's father with serving Heaven, the essay argues that Yao and Shun did not presume to transfer the throne to other men, but instead it was the work of Heaven.

Section 25.2 also addresses dynastic succession but uses King Tang and King Wu as the subject of discussion. The question is whether they established the Shang and Zhou dynasties by legitimate means—receiving the Mandate of Heaven—or by illegitimate means—committing regicide. The topic is addressed in a dialogue or debate between two unnamed parties. The reader apparently enters the debate in medias res, as the opening lines are responding to an assumed prior challenge to the view—explicitly identified as "Confucian"—that Tang and Wu were "the utmost worthies and greatest sages" in history:

> They hold that [these men] perfected the Way, [comprehensively] investigated righteousness, and epitomized [moral] beauty. Thus they rank them equal to Yao and Shun, designate them "sage-kings," and take them as their models of emulation. Now if you consider Tang and Wu to have been unrighteous, then, sir, which kings of what generations, would you designate as "righteous"?[15]

The respondent, apparently baffled by the question and unable to answer, is immediately barraged with a second question that challenges him to respond: "If you do not know, do you mean that [all] those who have ruled have been unrighteous? Or do you mean that there have been righteous rulers but that you are not familiar with them?"[16] The respondent replies with the example of the Divine Farmer (Shen Nong). This is immediately challenged. The commencement of the Divine Farmer's reign, the interlocutor points out, did not

15. *CQFL* 25/34/6–8.
16. *CQFL* 25/34/8–9.

coincide with the beginning of the world; therefore, his reception of the Mandate of Heaven, like that of Tang and Wu, must have involved replacing a prior ruler. This action is further justified by means of several interrelated principles of the Mandate of Heaven. Heaven establishes kings not on behalf of rulers but on behalf of the people; "Therefore if his virtue is sufficient to bring security and happiness to the people, Heaven bestows [the Mandate] on him; if his evil is sufficient to injure and harm the people, Heaven withdraws [the Mandate] from him."[17] This clearly indicates that neither the bestowal nor the withdrawal of the Mandate is permanent. The performance of the Suburban Sacrifice and the change in dynastic surname mark the transfer of power from one dynastic house to another and underscore the critical fact that rulership is, as in the first argument of the chapter, ultimately a gift bestowed by Heaven, not a political prerogative transmitted from one man to another. Thus in every case Tang and Wu, and the seventy-two later kings who also chastised the unrighteous, simply punished those from whom Heaven had already withdrawn the Mandate. They did not commit regicide.[18]

These principles, the argument continues, have existed for eternity. If one condemns Tang and Wu for attacking Jie and Djou, then the Han conquest of Qin is to be condemned equally. Those who use these arguments do not understand Heaven's principles or understand the *Gongyang* principle of concealment: "It is a matter of propriety that a son conceals his father's evil. Now if you were ordered to chastise others and you believed [the order] to be unrighteous, then you ought to conceal it for the sake of your state. How could it be appropriate [to use the order] to slander [your state]? This is what we call 'With one statement, two errors.'"[19] Moreover, having lost the allegiance of their people, Jie and Djou no were longer kings in the true sense of the word. Thus executing them could not be regicide.

Chapter 26, "Regulations on Dress," deals with sumptuary regulations: "Let clothing be regulated according to gradations in rank. Let wealth be spent according to gradations in salaries."[20] The scope of the chapter is greater than that suggested by its title. Regulations are proposed not only for clothing but also for buildings, domesticated animals, retainers, boats and vehicles, and armor and weapons and not only for the living; mortuary items for the dead are included as well. The chapter concludes with a catalog of sumptuary regulations

17. *CQFL* 25/34/11.
18. This position reflects *Mencius* 1B:8.
19. *CQFL* 25/34/18.
20. *CQFL* 26/34/24.

for various social ranks, from the Son of Heaven down to the lowest echelons of society: artisans, merchants, traders, and criminals.

Chapter 27, " "Regulating Limits," consists of five sections, all of which appear to have been included in this chapter because they embrace the notion that sage-rulers must establish regulations in order to maintain social order. Section 27.1 begins by quoting a well-known teaching attributed to Confucius: "Do not worry about poverty; worry about inequality."[21] The text then explains that excesses of either poverty or wealth give rise to the most extreme of human emotions, desperation and haughtiness, which, in turn, give rise to two of the greatest social ills: thievery and violence. The sage consequently creates regulations to limit the extremes of wealth and poverty to enable rich and poor to live peacefully with each other and to enable the ruler to govern with ease. The current state of affairs is quite different, however:

> The present age has abandoned regulations [that set] limits so that each person indulges his or her desires. When desires have no limits, then the vulgar act without restraint. When this tendency persists without end, the powerful people worry over insufficiencies above; the little people fear starvation below. Thus the wealthy increasingly covet profit and cannot act righteously; the poor daily disobey prohibitions and cannot be stopped. This is why the present age is difficult to govern.[22]

The next section, 27.2, consists of a statement attributed to Confucius and two citations from the *Odes*, all of which advocate setting limits on the material benefits enjoyed by the wealthy and powerful so that something is left for the weaker members of society, such as commoners and widows. This is the canonical basis for the conduct of the nobleman: "Therefore when the gentleman serves in office, he does not farm; when he farms, he does not fish; he eats what is in season and does not strive for delicacies."[23] The section closes with a rebuttal by an unnamed person who maintains that this principle is not sufficient to restrain the common people; they still will risk their lives competing for material benefits.

While section 27.1 argues that the sage sets limits based on people's emotional responses, and 27.2 justifies them on the basis of treating the common people

21. *Analects* 16.1.
22. *CQFL* 27/35/5–10.
23. *CQFL* 27/35/13

fairly (backed by the authority of Confucius), section 27.3 argues that the sage looks to Heaven when creating regulations and limits. It quotes what may have been a popular proverb of the time: "Heaven does not bestow things in duplicate; what has horns is not permitted to have upper [incisor] teeth.[24] Therefore those who already possess what is great cannot possess what is small."[25]

Section 27.4 observes that one characteristic of sages is their capacity for forethought. The sage eliminates deceptively insignificant and trivial affairs by guarding against them early on, in the same way that levees and dikes guard against floods. Thus he "promulgates regulations and limits; he promulgates ritual restrictions." This claim is supported by a closing citation from the *Documents* proposing that if the ruler pays attention to the status markers of the nobility, they will respond with reverence.

Section 27.5 turns to the ways in which regulations that set limits affect sumptuary laws. Simple clothing was first created to satisfy the physical needs of humans, to protect their bodies from the elements. But once people began to dye and ornament clothing, it became a means to order society hierarchically. Different colors and types of decoration illuminated the distinction between superior and inferior so that social order could be maintained. But if sumptuary regulations are not promulgated and enforced, the text warns, chaos will ensue. The section concludes with a brief reference to the different garments worn by the various ranks of society in ancient times: the Son of Heaven, the Lords of the Land, the great officers, and the common folk.

Chapter 28, "Ranking States," is a long chapter that we have divided into eight sections (the last of which is divided into five subsections). The chapter falls neatly into two parts: the first made up of sections 28.1 to 28.7, and the second, subsections 28.8A through 28.8E. Both parts outline idealized schemes of administrative organization, both of which differ markedly from those proposed in chapter 24, "Regulations on Officialdom Reflect Heaven."[26] The titles of officials, their numbers, and their ranks are not the same in these two chapters. In chapter 24, the idealized bureaucracy derives its justification from Heaven, and the rank and number of its officials are patterned on Heaven's annual cycle. But in chapter 28, the idealized bureaucracy is based on the authority of the *Spring and Autumn* read through the filter of the *Gongyang Commentary*. It describes

24. A version of this saying also appears in *Huainanzi* 4.11.

25. *CQFL* 27/35/15.

26. We consulted a detailed study of this chapter by Gary Arbuckle, "Ideals of Administration: The Structures Proposed in 'Appanages and States,' Chapter 28 of the Present *Chunqiu fanlu* Collection," a source that unfortunately is no longer available.

the bureaucracy of the Son of Heaven, as in chapter 24, as well as the administrations of different types of states, described as large, small, and dependent. It also touches on a range of topics not addressed in chapter 24.

Section 28.1 compares the Zhou dynasty and the era of the *Spring and Autumn*. The five-grade ranking system of the Zhou (duke, marquis, earl, viscount, baron), with its three classes of officers, is seen as an expression of the emphasis on outer refinement that is said to have characterized the Zhou. The ranking system of the *Spring and Autumn* is quite different. The three dukes of the Son of Heaven and the king's descendants designated as dukes comprise one grade; rulers of large states designated as marquises comprise one grade; and rulers of small states designated as earls, viscounts, and barons combine to comprise one grade. The system thus has three grades and two classes of officers, which is seen as an expression of the Spring and Autumn "dynasty's" emphasis on inner simplicity. This alternating scheme of inner simplicity and outer refinement is mentioned in Dong's memorials, a point to which we will return in our discussion of issues of dating and attribution. Section 28.2 specifies the terminology used in the *Spring and Autumn* to refer to the four grades of dependent states. Section 28.3 specifies the size of the territories controlled by the Son of Heaven, dukes and marquises, earls, viscounts and barons, and various ranks of dependent states. They range from a realm one thousand *li* square for the Son of Heaven to a realm ten *li* square for the least of the dependent states.[27]

Section 28.4 describes the ranking system employed in the *Spring and Autumn* to refer to nobles of various grades. There are five ranks below the Son of Heaven: the three dukes, great officer, junior great officer, functionary, and junior functionary. Section 28.5, interestingly, contends that the reference to five ranks in the previous section was in fact a criticism because it departed from the ancient practice of observing four ranks: senior minister, junior minister, senior functionary, and junior functionary. This section also shows how the *Spring and Autumn* refers in comparative terms to high officials of states of various sizes, so that, for example, a great officer of a small state is referred to in the same terms as a junior minister of a middling state. Finally, it specifies the categorical rankings for officials with outstanding merit and virtue. Section 28.6 uses a macrocosm/microcosm argument to show how the grades and numbers of officials of the Son of Heaven and the Lords of the Land are modeled on Heaven. Section 28.7 deals in numerological terms with the "Three Armies" (the conventional term for the armed forces of a state), describing the number of conscripts enlisted by

27. A *li* is equal to about one-third mile, or about 500 meters.

various levels of nobility and how the armies were supported. Sections 28.8A through 28.8E describe the size of territories allocated to the five grades of rulers (the Son of Heaven, dukes and marquises, earls, viscounts and barons, and dependent states), their associated land usage, armies, and populations; and the numbers, ranks, and salaries of their bureaucracies. These subsections repeat one another exactly, differing only in the rank of the various rulers and the numbers and grades appropriate to the administrations of each rank.

The first half of the chapter, sections 28.1 through 28.7, depicts the ranking system of this idealized empire by marshaling copious references to specific entries in the *Spring and Autumn* followed by their attendant *Gongyang* explications. The second half of the chapter, sections 28.8A through 28.8E, does not refer to the *Spring and Autumn* in making its arguments. Instead, its ranking system clearly parallels the *Mencius* and the "Royal Regulations" chapter of the *Classic of Rites* and introduces some details not included in those sources. The two halves of chapter 28 deal with idealized schemes of administrative organization but differ in important ways and probably originally were separate essays by different authors.

Issues of Dating and Attribution

Like other groups of chapters in the *Chunqiu fanlu* and of the text overall, group 3, "Regulatory Principles," assembles different materials of diverse origins. Several of its chapters or chapter sections are likely to date from around the lifetime of Dong Zhongshu and may be his work, but other chapters are almost certainly by others.

Chapter 23, "The Three Dynasties' Alternating Regulations of Simplicity and Refinement," contains very disparate materials. Some of the chapter's sections are very unlikely to have been written by Dong Zhongshu or anyone in his immediate circle, but Dong could plausibly have been the author of some of the other sections. As can be seen from our summary description, section 23.10 is a complex discussion of historical cycles based on numerological calculations involving the numbers two, three, four, five, and nine. The cycles in this section do not correspond to those described in the first group of *Chunqiu fanlu* chapters (group 1, "Exegetical Principles") or in Dong's memorials. On the contrary, in Dong Zhongshu's third memorial to Emperor Wu and in the first group of *Chunqiu fanlu* chapters, which contains the materials most closely associated with the historical Dong Zhongshu, he lays out a different theory of historical cycles. True, the concept of altering regulations upon the reception of the Mandate is discussed in chapter 1.5 and in Dong's third memorial, but the details of those discussions differ markedly from those described in chapter 23. Furthermore, writings dating to the reigns of Emperors Jing and Wu (when Dong Zhongshu flourished) do not generally trace the rulers of remote antiquity back beyond the Three Kings and Five Thearchs. Instead, the chapter's reference to the Nine Sovereigns reflects the rhetoric of the era of Wang Mang or the early Eastern Han. The elaborate Red, White, and Black Sequences described in sections 23.3 and 23.4 are unlike anything found in the authentic writings of Dong Zhongshu. Although to some extent they reflect principles already in the "Yue ling" (Monthly Ordinances) calendars of the late Warring States period and early Han, as presented here they seem more like a reflection of the concerns of the Wang Mang interregnum and the Eastern Han period. To that extent, we agree with the Japanese scholar Harada Masaota, who concluded that these sections of chapter 23 were not written by Dong and could not have been written earlier than the Eastern Han, based on their affinities with the *Bohutong* and *Chunqiu Gongyang zhuan Heshi jiegu.*[28]

The references to the *Spring and Autumn* in sections 23.1 and 23.2 seem superficially not to be out of character for the genuine writings of Dong Zhongshu. But section 23.2 clearly advises making comprehensive changes in regulations at the founding of a dynasty, whereas in one of his memorials to Emperor Wu, Dong quotes Confucius as saying, "'Was it not Shun who ruled by taking no action?' He simply altered the first month of the year and changed the color of court dress to comply with the Mandate of Heaven, that's all. In the remaining matters of governance, he completely followed the Way of Yao. Why would he have changed anything else?" But then Dong points out that dynastic founders did in fact make some changes in their predecessors' practices while retaining others.[29] The emphasis in 23.13 on "simplicity and refinement" (which we find also in chapter 28.1) is consistent with Dong's known opinions. In addition, the idea of Confucius as the "uncrowned king" of the Spring and Autumn period, reflected in section 23.7, was dear to Dong's heart, as seen in one of his memorials to Emperor Wu:

28. Sarah A. Queen, *From Chronicle to Canon: The Hermeneutics of the "Spring and Autumn" According to Tung Chung-shu* (Cambridge: Cambridge University Press, 1996), 81. Loewe also stresses the affinity of chapter 23 with the *Bohutong*, in *Dong Zhongshu*, 309.

29. *HS* 56/2518–19.

> When Confucius was writing the *Spring and Autumn*, he entered the terms *zheng* and *wang* at the beginning of the first entry and related them to the myriad affairs of governance, thus revealing the writings of an uncrowned king. Viewed from this perspective, there is indeed only one thread binding together the thearchs and kings, yet the difference between toiling away and remaining idle is due to the different ages that rulers happen to live in. And so Confucius also said: "The *wu* is the ultimate in beauty but not quite in goodness." This is what he meant.[30]

Thus we conclude that chapter 23, not surprisingly, contains diverse materials of strikingly different date and authorship, only some sections of which could plausibly be regarded as the work of Dong Zhongshu or his immediate circle of disciples.

Like the numerology of section 23.10, the numerological description of the ideal bureaucracy found in chapter 24 is uncharacteristic of the known works of Dong Zhongshu, though it was not necessarily written much later than his own lifetime. Similarly, the content of chapter 25 also is not characteristic of Dong's writings. In his comments at the close of chapter 25, Su Yu, the Qing scholar and commentator of the *Chunqiu fanlu,* states that this chapter could not have been written by Dong Zhongshu. He gives several reasons for his position. For example, he argues that even though Dong deeply despised the Qin, this chapter accepts that the Zhou dynasty was appropriately replaced by the Qin. When discussing punitive expeditions, scholars of the *Spring and Autumn* always held up King Wen's punishment (of Djou) for veneration and paired it with King Tang's punishment (of Jie). Here, however, Kings Tang and Wu are cited together and compared with the Qin conquest of Zhou and the Han conquest of Qin. The "Biography of the Confucian Scholars" in the *Shiji* records that Yuan Gu and Master Huang had a debate in front of Emperor Jing on the subject. It is possible that chapter 25 preserves a longer portion of that debate, of which the *Shiji* quotes only a small part. Su Yu concludes that the evidence dates the chapter to the reign of Emperor Jing but does not link it to Dong Zhongshu. We concur with this assessment.

Chapter 26 probably predates Dong but is compatible with his views:

> Your servant has heard that sumptuary regulations and the ornamental black and yellow insignia were the means to distinguish the lofty from the base [and to] differentiate the noble from the mean in order to encourage the Virtuous. Thus in the *Spring and Autumn*, the first things to be regulated by those who received

30. *HS* 56/2509.

> Heaven's Mandate were the change in the first month of the year and the alteration of the color of court dress to respond to Heaven. Nonetheless, the regulations concerning palaces and dwellings and flags and banners were as they were because they were based on particular models. Thus Confucius said: "Extravagance leads to insubordination; frugality leads to stubbornness."[31] Frugality is not the Mean when it comes to the regulations of a sage.[32]

Chapter 27, which consists of five short sections, has many parallels in the "Fangji" chapter of the *Liji*. The fragments in this chapter read as a pastiche that is not overtly at odds with Dong Zhongshu's views but that might not be confidently ascribed to him without stronger evidence. A partial exception is that both sections 27.1 and 27.3 deal with the equitable distribution of resources. This shared theme links the two sections, each roughly echoing positions taken by Dong in his third memorial to Emperor Wu.

As we noted earlier, chapter 28 has two distinct halves. The ideal bureaucracy and system of government organization described in the first half derives its authority from the *Spring and Autumn* and so is linked, at least in that sense, with the *Gongyang* Erudite Dong Zhongshu. The scheme proposed in the second half, sections 28.8A through 28.8E, is an elaboration of ideas found in *Mencius* 5B.2 and in the "Royal Regulations" chapter of the *Liji*. Except for a general Confucian orientation, there is nothing particular in that half of the chapter to evoke the views of Dong. We assume that the unknown compiler of the *Chunqiu fanlu* included in his edition the materials that make up both halves of chapter 28 because he thought that they were in some way linked to Dong or one of his followers or that at least they could be taken (contradictions and all) to represent Dong Zhongshu's views on government organization.

---

31. *Analects* 7.35.
32. *HS* 56/2509.

Book 7, Part 3

CHAPTER 23

The Three Dynasties' Alternating Regulations of Simplicity and Refinement

Section 23.1

The *Spring and Autumn* states: "The king's first month." The [*Gongyang*] *Commentary* states: "To whom does 'the king' refer? It refers to King Wen. Why [does the *Spring and Autumn*] first mention 'the king' and then mention 'the first month'? The king rectified the month."[1] [23/29/13–14]

Section 23.2

Why [does the text] say "the king rectified the month"?[2] The answer is: One who is a king must receive the Mandate and, only then, reigns. One who is a king must

revise the first month of the year,
change the color of [official] dress,
regulate rituals and music,

Su Yu (*CQFLYZ* 184) has suggested that the current title is a conflation of two earlier titles, *sandai gai zhi* 三代改制 and *sandai zhi wen* 三代質文, listed in the Southern Song encyclopedia *Yuhai* 玉海 (*Jade Sea*).

1. This is a play on words: the expression *zheng yue* 正月 means "first month," but the word *zheng* by itself can also mean "to rectify."
2. Duke Yin 1.1.1. The distinction made between the *Spring and Autumn* and the *Gongyang Commentary* is not typical of most chapters of the *Chunqiu fanlu*.

to unite[3] the empire into one. By changing the surname of the [ruling household], it is made clear that [the king] has not succeeded another person's line but that he himself has received [the Mandate] of Heaven.[4] The king receives the Mandate and, only then, reigns. He rectifies the month [that serves as the first month of the year] to respond to the change [in Heaven's Mandate]. He creates benchmarks to venerate Heaven.[5] Therefore [the text] refers to it as "the King's first month." [23/29/14–16]

Section 23.3

How does one who is a king revise regulations and create benchmarks? The answer is: He matches the twelve colors [correlated with the twelve months of the year]. He calculates by various methods to rectify the color [for his dynasty]. Counting backward by three and then beginning again, he omits anything that precedes the three [earlier dynasties]. As for the Five Thearchs, each thearch took one color as the most important. [Thus] complying with the number five, one [counts a sequence of five] and then repeats. [With respect to] ritual and music, for each [the king] uses a standard so that it matches what is appropriate. [In that case,] one complies with the number four, [counting by four] and then beginning again. [In these ways, the ruler] variously establishes the name of the state, shifts his residence, alters the titles of the various offices, regulates ritual, and creates music.

Thus when Tang [the Victorious] received the Mandate and reigned, in response to Heaven he altered [the name] Xia and created the name Yin. [In accordance with] the times, he established the White Sequence [as the statutory color]. [He considered] the Xia dynasty to be closest [to him] and [understood] Yu [Shun] to be more remote. [Accordingly,] he demoted Tang [Yao], designating him as Thearch Yao. He took Shen Nong to be the Red Thearch. [Tang the Victorious] built the royal city on the north bank of the Luo River and named the corresponding palace Yin. He created the music of Huo and made regulations for simple rituals to venerate Heaven.

3. The word *tong* 統 appears frequently in this chapter and presents a challenge to the translator. One of the chapter's rhetorical strategies is to play on two of the several meanings of *tong*. Our practice is to take *tong* as "to unify" when it is used as a verb and as "sequence" when it is used as a noun, with some exceptions as demanded by context.
4. A similar topic is mentioned at *HS* 56/2510.
5. Since the entire paragraph is about Heaven (*tian*) and there is no prior mention of Earth (*di*), we have treated the character *di* as excrescent.

Thus when King Wen received the Mandate and reigned, in response to Heaven he altered [the name] Yin and created the name Zhou. [In accordance with] the times, he established the Red Sequence [as the statutory color]. [He considered] the Yin dynasty to be closest [to him] and [understood] the Xia dynasty to be more remote. [Accordingly,] he demoted Yu [Shun], designating him as Thearch Shun. King Wen took Xuan Yuan to be the Yellow Thearch. He pushed Shen Nong further back to become one of the nine [archaic] sovereigns. He built the royal city at Feng and named the corresponding palace Cai. He created the music of Wu and made regulations for refined rituals to venerate Heaven.

When King Wu received the Mandate and reigned, he built the royal city at Hao. He made regulations for the five grades of nobility. He created the music of Xiang and continued the refined rituals of King Wen to venerate Heaven.

When the Duke of Zhou assisted King Cheng, who received the Mandate and reigned, he built the royal city at Luoyang, brought to completion the regulations of Kings Wen and Wu, and created the music of Shao to venerate Heaven. He enfeoffed the descendants of King Tang of Yin at Song and named their city Yi to demonstrate that Heaven alters [the Mandate of those] who defy Heaven. Thus the Mandate of the Son of Heaven is not constant. Heaven rewards only those who are virtuous.[6]

Therefore, when the *Spring and Autumn,* responding to Heaven, brought up the affairs of the new royal [dynasty], [in accordance with] the times it established the Black Sequence [as the statutory color]. It entrusted [the functions of] the [new] king to the state of Lu, esteemed the color black, and demoted Xia. [It considered] the Zhou to be closest and the Song [i.e., the remnant state of Shang/Yin] to be more remote. In music, it was considered suitable to draw near the Shao [Airs of Shun] and the Wu [Airs of Zhou].[7] Thus in order to draw near Shun Yu, in music they regulated what was appropriate to the Shang. It combined into one the ranks of earl, viscount, and baron. [23/29/16–28]

Section 23.4

What, then, are the general contours of this theory? The answer is: The Three Rectifications [of the three sequential colors] begin with the Black Sequence.

6. Emending *wei qing shi de* 唯慶是德 to *wei de shi qing* 唯德是慶, following Su Yu, *CQFLYZ* 187.

7. Both Shun and Zhou belong to the Red Sequence, so the Spring and Autumn period (Black Sequence) can be considered the successor and heir of both.

On the first day of the year, the sun and new moon stand in [the lunar lodge] Encampment, and the Dipper establishes [i.e., points to] *yin* [east-northeast as the first month of the civil calendar]. Heaven's all-embracing *qi* then first begins to permeate and transform things, [causing] buds of growth [to] appear. The [ritual] color is black.

Therefore, the clothes formally worn at court are black; the pendants on official caps are black; the imperial chariots are black; their horses are black. The cords that carry the great seals [of the officials], and their headdresses, are black; the flags are black; the great precious jades are black; and the animals used in the Suburban Sacrifices are black. The horns of these animals are egg shaped. The ceremony of capping [that takes place when a youth comes of age] is performed at the eastern steps [of the main hall]. In the marriage ceremony, [the groom] goes to meet [the bride] in the courtyard [of the ancestral temple of her home]. In the funeral ceremony, the deceased is encoffined above the eastern steps [leading to the main hall]. The sacrifice uses a black male [animal]. The sacrificial offering is the liver. The musical instruments are made of black materials.

The laws do not punish those who are pregnant or those who have just given birth. In this month, there are no executions. In accordance with the first month, punishments are set aside while virtue is promoted. The ritual vessels preserve the memory of the two [preceding] royal [dynasties]. [This sequence] is close to the Red Sequence; therefore the first division of the day is set at daybreak. At daybreak the court rectifies [matters].

What about the establishment of the White Sequence? The answer is: When the White Sequence is established, on the first day of the year the sun and new moon stand in [the lunar lodge] Emptiness.[8] The Dipper establishes [i.e., points to] *chou* [north-northeast as the first month of the civil calendar]. Heaven's all-embracing *qi* then first causes living things to shed their coverings and transform. They begin to bud. The [ritual] color is white. Therefore, the clothes formally worn at court are white; the pendants on official caps are white; the imperial chariots are white; and their horses are white. The cords that carry the great seals [of the officials], and their headdresses, are white; the flags are white; the great precious jades are white; and the animals used in the Suburban Sacrifices

8. *Xu* 虛, eleventh of the twenty-eight lunar lodges; sometimes also translated as "Tumulus."

are white. The horns of these animals are shaped like a silk cocoon. The ceremony of capping is performed at the [platform in front of] the main hall. In the marriage ceremony, [the groom] goes to meet [the bride] at [the platform in front of] the main hall [of her family's ancestral temple]. In the funeral ceremony, the deceased is encoffined between the columns [on the platform of the main hall]. The sacrifice uses a white male [animal]. The sacrificial offering is the lungs. The musical instruments are made of white materials.

The laws do not punish those who are pregnant or those who have just given birth. In this month, there are no executions. In accordance with the first month, punishments are set aside while virtue is promoted. The ritual vessels preserve the memory of the two [preceding] royal [dynasties]. [This sequence] is close to the Black Sequence; therefore the first division of the days is set at dawn. At dawn the court rectifies [matters].

What about the establishment of the Red Sequence? The answer is: When the Red Sequence is established, on the first day of the year the sun and new moon stand in [the lunar lodge] Ox Leader. The Dipper establishes [i.e., points to] *zi* [north as the first month of the civil calendar]. Heaven's all-embracing *qi* then first comes forth and transforms things, and these things begin to move. The [ritual] color is red. Therefore, the clothes formally worn at court are red; the pendants on official caps are red; the imperial chariots are red; and their horses are red. The cords that carry the great seals [of the officials], and their headdresses, are red; the flags are red; the great precious jades are red; and the animals used in the Suburban Sacrifices are red. The horns of these animals are shaped like chestnuts. The ceremony of capping is performed in the side chamber [of the main hall]. In the marriage ceremony, [the groom] goes to meet [the bride] at the door [to the eastern side of the ancestral temple of her home]. In the funeral ceremony, the deceased is encoffined above the western steps [leading to the main hall]. The sacrifice uses a red male [animal]. The sacrificial offering is the heart. The musical instruments are made of red materials.

The laws do not punish those who are pregnant or those who have just given birth. In this month, there are no executions. In accordance with the first month, punishments are set aside while virtue is promoted. The ritual vessels preserve the memory of the two [preceding] royal [dynasties]. [This sequence] is close to the White Sequence; therefore the first division of the day is set at midnight. At midnight the court rectifies [matters].

The righteous principle of altering the first month arose from venerating the Origin. In ancient times, those who were kings received the Mandate and then reigned. They altered the regulations, titles and designations, and the first month [of the calendar year]. Once the color of clothes [worn at court] had been determined, [the king] performed the Suburban Sacrifice to announce [the accession of the new dynasty] to Heaven, Earth, and the numerous spirits. He offered sacrifices to his distant and nearer ancestors and then proclaimed [the accession of their dynasty] throughout the empire. The Lords of the Land received [the proclamation of the new statutory color and beginning of the civil year] in their ancestral temples. They then announced it to their spirits of the land and grain, to the ancestors, and to the spirits of mountains and streams in their respective territories. Only then were the movements and responses of the various officials united. As for the alternations of the Three Sequences, neither the Yi and Di tribes who lived near [the Central States] nor the more distant states promulgated them. It was a matter for the Central States alone. That being so, the Three Dynasties inevitably used the Three [Sequences] to administer the world.[9] [23/29/28–23/30/15]

Section 23.5

It is said: "The Three Sequences and the Five Inceptions are the basis for transforming the Four Quarters [of the world]." When Heaven begins to withdraw [the Mandate from the old dynasty] and begins to bring forth [the new dynasty], Earth necessarily waits [passively] at the center. For this reason, the Three Dynasties necessarily occupied the Central States. Emulating Heaven and revering the root, they grasped the essentials of the Five [Inceptions] to unify the world and received the Lords of the Land at court audiences. Therefore they used the righteous principle of rectifying [the rituals of] court audiences, [so that] the Son of Heaven donned clothing purely the color appropriate to the current sequence; the Lords of the Land donned clothing appropriate to the current sequence, but their embroidered hems and sashes were differently colored; the great ministers

9. The text is problematic at this point. Su Yu (*CQFLYZ* 195–96) believes that a character is missing before *tianxia* 天下 and suggests supplying the character *tong* 統. Given the sentence's grammatical structure, we would expect to find a verb at this position. We therefore follow Su Yu's recommendation to supply *tong* but recognize that the choice of this particular verb is highly speculative.

and officials wore caps whose crowns corresponded to the color of the current sequence; the neighboring Yi [tribes] wore caps whose tassels corresponded to the color of the current sequence; and those from distant lands donned clothing appropriate to court audiences held in their respective states in order to manifest the righteousness of the Heavenly sequences. [23/30/15–18]

Section 23.6

In regard to what is called "Unifying the Three Rectifications," "first" [as in "first month"] [also] means "to correct." [Heaven's] sequences bring the [yin and yang] *qi* into operation, to which all things respond and thus are made correct. When the sequences are correct, everything else is correct. What is vital to the entire year is [the starting point of] its first month. To emulate the Way of Rectification is

to correct the root and the branches respond,
to correct the inside and the outside responds.

Then, as movements and activities are initiated or stopped, there will be nothing that does not follow [an orderly sequence] in its transformations. This may be called Emulating the First [month]. Thus the Noble Man said: "King Wu resembled the first month [of the civil year]." [23/30/18–21]

Section 23.7

The *Spring and Autumn* states: "The earl of Ji came to pay a court visit to the ruler of Lu."[10] The descendants of the king are called dukes; why, then, is the ruler of Ji referred to as an "earl"? [With regard to those who came before,] the *Spring and Autumn* considers the Xia to be the most remote; it preserves the [descendants of] Zhou as the most recent; and it considers the Spring and Autumn era] to correspond to a new royal [dynasty]. [23/30/21–22]

How does the Spring and Autumn [era] correspond to a new royal [dynasty]? The answer is: The method of the king must be to rectify titles. The most remote [predynastic] kings are designated as "thearchs." One grants land to their descendants for small states and allows them to pray and offer sacrifices there. Next, one preserves the descendants of the two [former] royal [dynasties], [granting

10. The earl of Ji's visits to the Lu court are recorded in identical language four times in the *Spring and Autumn*: Duke Zhuang 3.27.6, Duke Wen 6.12.2, Duke Cheng 8.4.3, and Duke Cheng 8.18.9.

them land for] large states, permitting them to wear their own color of clothing, practice their own rituals and music, and be treated as guests when they come to court. Thus at the same time, those who are designated as "thearchs" number five, and those who are designated as "royal [dynasties]" number three, in order to reflect the Five Inceptions and penetrate the Three Sequences. This is why the royal dynasty of the Zhou

extended their veneration back to Shen Nong, taking him to be one of the Nine Sovereigns [of high antiquity];

altered the title of Xuan Yuan, designating him as the Yellow Thearch;

preserved the titles of Thearch Zhuan Xu, Thearch Gao, and Thearch Yao;

showed the remoteness of Yu[11] by giving him the name Shun and calling him Thearch Shun;

and endowed the descendants of the Five Thearchs with small states [to enable them to offer sacrifices to their forebears].

Coming down [to later times,] they

preserved the descendants of Yu [the Great] of Xia in the state of Ji

and preserved the descendants of Tang of Shang in the state of Song.

[Each was granted land for a state of] one hundred *li* square and was given the rank and title of duke. Both [dukes] were allowed to wear the clothing proper to their dynasty, to carry out their ritual and music, and [were granted the right to be] recognized as "formerly royal guests" when they appeared at court.

When the Spring and Autumn [era] carried forth the matter [of creating] the new royal [dynasty], it altered the regulations of the Zhou, [changed] its regulations to correspond to the Black Sequence, and considered the people of the Yin and Zhou to be the descendants of the former kings. It [treated] the Xia as remote and changed the title of Yu [the Great], calling him Thearch Yu. It granted land to his descendants for a small state. Thus the answer is: [taking] the Xia as remote and preserving the Zhou is to take the Spring and Autumn [era] as a new royal [dynasty]. [23/30/22–29]

Section 23.8

[That the *Spring and Autumn*] does not refer to the marquis of Ji as a duke is to show that he is not the same as the descendants of the [two former] royal

11. Not Yu 禹 the Great, tamer of the great flood, but Yu 虞, clan name of the sage-king Shun.

[dynasties]. Why, then, does the *Spring and Autumn* on one occasion refer to him as "viscount" and on another as "earl"? To show that he was already designated as [the ruler of] a small state. [23/30/29–30]

Section 23.9

Why was the Yellow Thearch the first [to be granted] a posthumous title[12] while the [other] four Thearchs were [granted] posthumous titles [only later]? The answer is: With the titles of the thearchs, [the number] five must be preserved. With the era of the thearchs, priority is given to Heaven's [five] colors. The designations run to five and revert back [to the first color]. For the royal dynasty of the Zhou, Xuan Yuan came at the head of the [sequence of] Heaven's color designations. He therefore was referred to as the Yellow Thearch. The designation as thearch is honorable, while posthumous titles [in general] are humble. This is why [the remaining] four thearchs were [granted] posthumous titles only later. [23/30/30–23/31/2]

Section 23.10

"Thearch" is an honorable designation. Why, then, are the thearch's descendants awarded small states? The answer is:

> Those who are remote [in time] have honorable titles but smaller territories;
> those who are close [in time] have humble titles but larger territories.

This is the principle guiding those who are close and those who are remote. Therefore, for those [who would be] kings, [there are]

> certain respects in which they do not change [their regulations from those of the preceding dynasty];
> certain respects in which they should revert [to those of an earlier dynasty] after [a cycle of] two;
> certain respects in which they should revert after [a cycle of] three [dynasties];
> certain respects in which they should revert after [a cycle of] four;
> certain respects in which they should revert after [a cycle of] five;
> certain respects in which they should revert after [a cycle of] nine.

12. In other words, early on he became known by the posthumous title "Yellow Thearch" rather than by his given name, Xuan Yuan, whereas the other four of the Five Thearchs became known by their posthumous color titles only later.

By this, they illustrate that they comprehend Heaven and Earth, yin and yang, the four seasons, the sun and moon, the stars and planets, the mountains and rivers, and human relationships. Those whose virtue accords with that of Heaven and Earth are called sovereigns and thearchs. Heaven protects them and considers them to be like sons, thus they are called Sons of Heaven.

Thus when a sagely ruler is alive, he is referred to as the Son of Heaven.

When he dies, he is shifted and preserved as [one of the rulers of] the Three Royal Dynasties.

When he is demoted and [this title] is discarded, he becomes [one of the Five Thearchs]. When he descends to [the rank] of a vassal state, he is demoted to become [one of the] Nine Sovereigns.

When he descends to the most extreme [position], he becomes a commoner.

[This is] one way of referring to the "Three Eras." Therefore, even though they are eventually reduced to the status of commoner and are cut off from their territory, their positions in the ancestral temple and sacrificial offerings still are set forth in the liturgies of the Suburban Sacrifice, and they are honored at the sacrifice at Mount Tai. Thus it is said: "Reputation and name, *hun* and *po*,[13] disperse into emptiness. Extreme longevity has no bounds." [23/31/2–7]

Section 23.11

Why is it said that [in certain respects the ruler] reverts to a sequence after two, but in other respects he repeats a sequence after four? [Response is missing.] [23/31/7–8]

Section 23.12

Why does the *Spring and Autumn* refer to Hu of Zheng by his given name? The *Spring and Autumn* states: "The ranks of earl, viscount, and baron are one. This terminology is not a criticism." Why are they considered one? The answer is: The Zhou had ranks of five grades. The Spring and Autumn [era] had three grades. [23/31/8–9]

13. The *hun* (ethereal soul) and *po* (material soul) were embodied in living humans. Although the *hun* departed at the moment of death, the *po* was interred along with the corpse of the deceased.

Section 23.13

What three grades did the *Spring and Autumn* recognize? The answer is: Those who rule as king take as their regulations [in sequence]:

one Shang;
one Xia;
one Simplicity;
one Refinement;
[those who follow] Shang and Simplicity take Heaven as their support;
[those who follow] Xia and Refinement take Earth as their support;
the Spring and Autumn [era] takes humankind as its support.

Thus there are three grades [corresponding to Heaven, Earth, and humankind]. [23/31/9–10]

Section 23.14

Those who take Heaven as their support emulate Shang and rule as kings. Their Way is that of recessive yang. They show affection toward those who are close and possess an abundance of humaneness and simplicity. Therefore, the succession [to the throne] passes to the son, and [the heir's] younger brothers from the same mother are treated generously. A concubine [who bears the king] a son gains an honorable position thereby. At the marriage and capping ceremonies, [at the latter] the son is given his new name by the father; [at the former, the groom and bride first] do not glance at each other, [but later] husband and wife sit opposite each other [on different mats] when eating [their first meal].

At the funeral service, [husband and wife] are buried separately, and when sacrifices are made to them, pork fat is the first thing offered. [In the ancestral temple, the tablet of the deceased] husband and wife occupy separate positions on the left and right sides.

Regulations [rank] aristocrats into three grades; emoluments [divide] officials into two grades.

They establish a suburban temple and hall of light that are circular. Their rooms are lofty, majestic, and sumptuously circular. They use sacrificial implements that are round and jades that are nine *fen* thick, with [cords braided from] five strands of white and multicolored silk. Ceremonial dress is flared at the upper garment; ceremonial caps are tall and circular. The royal bell-carriage is dignified, with a canopy mimicking the phenomena of the heavens, and with four suspended bells.

When music is played, the drums are set out in a row. Dancers brandish decorated wands; their dance flows in a circular pattern. [In sacrificing,] they first present the hair and blood [of the sacrificial animal] and, only then, perform music.

When rectifying punishments, they follow the principle of concealing faults; many exceptions are made for [royal] relatives. They perform the Feng and Shan sacrifices from the summit [of the mountain.]

Those who take Earth as their support emulate Xia and rule as kings.

Their Way is that of advancing yin. They honor those who are honorable and possess an abundance of righteousness and moderation. Accordingly, the succession [to the throne] passes to the [king's] grandson, and sons of [the earlier] generation are treated generously. A concubine [who bears the king] a son does not gain an honorable position thereby. At the marriage and capping ceremonies, [at the latter] the son is given his new name by his mother; [at the former the groom and bride first] do not glance at each other, [but later] husband and wife sit together [on the same mat] when eating [their first meal together].

At the funeral service, [husband and wife] are buried together, and when sacrifices are made to them, cooked [food] is the first thing offered. [In the procession to the ancestral temple, the tablet of the deceased] wife follows that of the husband, [after which the tablets are] arranged [separately] on the left and right sides.

Regulations [rank] aristocrats into five grades; emoluments [divide] officials into three grades.

They establish a suburban temple and hall of light that are square. Their rooms are low and austerely square. They use sacrificial implements that are square and jades that are eight *fen* thick, with [cords braided from] four strands of white silk. Ceremonial dress is flared at the lower garment; ceremonial caps are lowered in the front and raised in the back. The royal bell-carriage is humble, mimicking the way in which Earth arranges its forms, and with two suspended bells.

When music is played, the drums form an array. Dancers brandish oxtails; their dance flows in a square pattern. They first present a cooked sacrifice and, only then, perform music.

In rectifying punishments, they follow the standards of Heaven.[14] They perform the Feng and Shan sacrifices at the base of the mountain.

Those who take Heaven as their support emulate Simplicity and rule as kings. Their Way is that of recessive yang. They show affection toward those who are close and possess an abundance of simplicity and love. Therefore, the succession [to the throne] passes to the son, and [the heir's] younger brothers from the same mother are treated generously. A concubine [who bears the king] a son gains an honorable position thereby. At the marriage and capping ceremonies, [at the latter] the son is given his new name by his father; [at the former the groom and bride first] do not glance at each other, [but later] husband and wife sit opposite each other [on different mats] when eating [their first meal together].

At the funeral service, [husband and wife] are buried separately, and when sacrifices are made to them, grain is the first thing offered. [In the ancestral temple, the tablet of the deceased] husband and wife occupy separate positions on the left and right sides.

Regulations [rank] aristocrats into three grades; emoluments [divide] officials into two grades.

They establish a suburban temple and hall of light that are circular inside and oval outside. Their rooms resemble interconnecting circles and ovals. They use sacrificial implements that are oval and jades that are seven *fen* thick, [with cords braided from] three strands of white silk. The front lapels of the ceremonial dress are elongated; ceremonial caps are circular. The royal bell-carriage is dignified, with a canopy perfectly mimicking the phenomena of Heaven, and with four suspended bells.

When music is performed, the drums are arranged on racks. Dancers brandish feathered flutes; the dance flows in an oval pattern. They first perform music on the jade chime stones and, only then, present a cooked offering.

In rectifying punishments, they follow the principle of concealing faults, and many exceptions are made for [royal] relatives. They perform the Feng and Shan sacrifices at the left side of the mountain.

---

14. A line of text is apparently missing here.

Those who take Earth as their support emulate Refinement and rule as kings. Their Way is that of advancing yin. They honor those who are honorable and possess an abundance of propriety and refinement. Therefore, the succession [to the throne] passes to the [king's] grandson, and sons of [the earlier] generation are treated generously. A concubine [who bears the king] a son does not gain an honorable position thereby. At the marriage and capping ceremonies, [at the latter] the son is given his new name by his mother; [at the former the groom and bride first] do not glance at each other, [but later] husband and wife sit together [on the same mat] when eating [their first meal together].

At the funeral service, [husband and wife] are buried together, and when sacrifices are made to them, liquor made from glutinous millet is the first thing offered. [In the procession to the ancestral temple, the tablet of the deceased] wife follows that of the husband, [after which the tablets are] arranged [separately] on the left and right sides.

Regulations [rank] aristocrats into five grades; emoluments [divide] officials into three grades.

They establish a suburban temple and hall of light that are square inside and rectangular outside. Their rooms repeat one another in a rectangular shape. They use sacrificial implements that are cross shaped and jades that are six *fen* thick, with [cords braided from] two strands of white and multicolored silk. The rear folds of the ceremonial dress are elongated; the ceremonial caps are rippled; and both front and back hang loosely. The royal bell-carriage is humble, mimicking the way in which Earth arranges its forms, and with two suspended bells. When music is performed, the drums are suspended on stands. The dancers brandish shields and spears; the dance flows in a rectangular pattern. They first present a cooked offering and, only then, perform music.

In rectifying punishments, they follow the standards of Heaven [and no exemptions are made for royal relatives]. They perform the Feng and Shan sacrifices from the right side[15] of the mountain. [23/31/10–23/32/2]

Section 23.15

These four models were cultivated throughout antiquity and originated with the former thearchs. Thus the Four Models [Shang, Xia, Simplicity, and Refinement] are like the four seasons:

15. The text says "left side" here, but that is certainly an error; symmetry requires "right side" in this passage.

When the cycles are spent, they begin anew;
when the cycles reach their end, they return to their root.

All these four are modeled on Heaven.[16] Heaven confers its auspicious Mandate, giving the models of kingship to those who are sages. The [sagely] nature and [Heavenly] Mandate took form in our ancestors and became ever more manifest when they became kings and lords.

Thus when Heaven was about to confer [the Mandate] on Shun, taking Heaven as his support and emulating Shang, [Shun] became king. His ancestors were granted the surname Yao. When it came to Shun, his form and upper body were large and his head was round. He had two bright pupils in his eyes. By nature, he was adept at understanding Heaven's patterns, and he was pure in his filial piety and tenderheartedness.

When Heaven was about to confer the Mandate on Yu, taking Earth as his support and emulating Xia, [Yu] became king. His ancestors were granted the surname Si as their clan name. When it came to Yu, he was born out of his mother's back. His body was elongated, and he was long in the foot. He had a limping gait, leading with his left foot and dragging his right foot, exhausting his left foot while easing his right foot. By nature, he excelled at traveling. He was well versed in geography and understood the properties of water.

When Heaven was about to confer the Mandate on Tang, taking Heaven as his support and emulating Simplicity, [Tang] became king. His ancestors were granted the surname Zi as their clan name. Qi's mother swallowed the egg of a swallow and gave birth to Qi.[17] Qi was born out of his mother's breast. By nature, he excelled at human relationships. When it came to Tang, his body was fat and short. He walked with a stiff left foot and an agile right foot, so that his right foot was exhausted while his left foot remained in ease and comfort. By nature, he excelled [at understanding] the Heavenly radiances.[18] His inner substance was easygoing, and he was pure and benevolent.

When Heaven was about to confer the Mandate on King Wen, taking Earth as his support and emulating Refinement, [Wen] became king. His ancestors were granted the surname Ji as their clan name. Hou Ji's mother Jiang Yuan stepped on Heaven's footprint and gave birth to Hou Ji.[19] Hou Ji grew up at Tai and propagated the five grains. When it came to King Wen, his body was robust

16. This statement contradicts the preceding passage, which sets out a ritual schedule modeled alternately on Heaven and Earth.
17. Qi was Tang's first ancestor.
18. The meaning of *tian guang* 天光 is unclear; presumably it refers to celestial portents of some kind.
19. Hou Ji [Lord Millet] was King Wen's first ancestor.

and tall. He had four nipples and broad feet. By nature, he excelled at topography. [23/32/4–12]

Section 23.16

Thus the thearch [Shun] ordered Yu and Gao to discuss the surname [to be adopted by the dynasty].

Recognizing that the virtue of the Yin dynasty [corresponded to] the virtue of yang, they consequently took "Zi" to be the surname [of the Yin]. Recognizing that the virtue of the Zhou dynasty [corresponded to] the virtue of yin, they consequently took "Ji" to be the surname [of the Zhou]. Thus when the Yin reigned, they altered the script, taking the male [radical] to write their surname "Zi"; when the Zhou reigned, they took the female [radical] to write their surname "Ji." Thus in each case, the Way of Heaven is to act in accordance with its categories. How would one who is not a sage be able to understand this? [23/32/12–14]

Book 7, Part 4

CHAPTER 24

Regulations on Officialdom Reflect Heaven

Section 24.1

The king regulates the offices. With the three dukes, nine ministers, twenty-seven great officers, and eighty-one senior functionaries, a total of 120, his hierarchy of officials is complete.[1] I have heard that the standards adopted by the sage-kings were modeled on the great warp of Heaven,[2] which completes each season with three months and each year with four [seasonal] revolutions, so the regulations of the offices are as they are. This is the standard.

That three men constitute the first selection [of officials] is a standard derived from the fact that three months constitute one season. That four such selections are made, and no more, is a standard derived from the fact that with the four seasons, [the year] is brought to its conclusion. The three dukes are the means by which the king supports himself. With three [months], Heaven completes [each

Chapters 24 and 28, though both are in group 3, present different models of ideal imperial government.

1. These offices correspond to those listed in the "Wang zhi" (Regulations of the King) chapter of the *Liji*. See James Legge, trans., *Li Chi: Book of Rites*, ed. Ch'u Chai and Winberg Chai (New Hyde Park, N.Y.: University Books, 1967), 1:209–48. Zheng Xuan held that they were the regulations of the Xia Dynasty. The "Jun dao" (Way of the Lord) chapter of the *Shuoyuan* lists these official titles in a passage in which Tang, the first ruler of Shang, questions his minister Yiyin. The *Shuoyuan* passage suggests that this system may well have been attributed to the Shang dynasty. Translations of official titles follow Charles O. Hucker, *A Dictionary of Official Titles in Imperial China* (Stanford, Calif.: Stanford University Press, 1985), 399, 176, 465, 596, respectively. See Su Yu, *CQFLYZ* 214.
2. *Tian zhi da jing* 天之大經. *Jing* (warp) is a metaphor for the basic structure of the universe. It is found in other Han-era texts; for example, the title of *Huainanzi* chapter 8, "Ben jing" (The Basic Warp). The warp of a textile not only provides its basic structure but also allows the cloth to emerge onto the loom over time as the weaver adds weft threads to the warp. Thus the metaphorical image here has implications of both space and time.

season]; with three [dukes], the king supports himself. When he establishes the number [three], that brings things to completion as his foundation, and four times repeats it, then the ruler can be free from error.[3] According completely with Heaven's numbers to assist[4] in [the conduct of] human affairs signifies that government carefully attends to the Way.[5] These 120 officials were the means by which the former kings conducted themselves in accordance with the correct Way. For this reason,

the Son of Heaven assisted himself with the three dukes;
[each of] the three dukes assisted himself with three ministers;
[each of] the [nine] ministers assisted himself with three great officers;
[each of] the [twenty-seven] great officers assisted himself with three senior functionaries.

There is [a multiple] of three men in [each] selection, repeated four times. [Thus] from the "Way of Three" is derived the government of the world. So also Heaven's four repetitions are derived from the three [months] that make up each season, thus ending and beginning the yearly cycle. There is one yang but three [months in each] spring; does this not accord with there being three [months in each] season? Heaven repeats this four times so that its numerical pattern is identical.

Heaven has its four seasons, and [each] season comprises three months;
the king has his four [rounds of] selections, and [each] selection comprises [a multiple of] three officials.

For this reason, the first, second, and third month of each season constitute the various characteristics[6] of each season, just as the upper, lower, and middle class of officials constitute the various characteristics of each selection of officials. With four selections, the ruler stops, for he has exhausted the various human characteristics. Human talent must have its four selections, just as Heaven's seasons must have its four permutations.

The sagely person constitutes one selection;
the noble person constitutes one selection;
the good person constitutes one selection;
the upright person constitutes one selection.

---

3. See note 10.
4. There is an implicit play on words here; *can* 參 means "to assist" but also can be a synonym for *san* 三 (three).
5. The significance of arranging Heaven's numbers for participation in [human] affairs is that government should be conducted with careful attention to the yearly course of Heaven.
6. *Qing* 情.

Those who exist below these grades are not worthy of being selected.

Within the four [rounds] of selections, each has its own criteria. For this reason, Heaven selects the four seasons, brings them to completion with the twelve [months], and the Heavenly permutations are fully utilized.[7] It is only the sage who can [similarly] fully utilize the permutations of humankind and harmonize them with those of Heaven, thereby establishing the affairs of the king. [24/32/16–29]

Section 24.2

What is meant by "the great warp of Heaven"? There are

the three commencements [sunrise, noon, and sunset] that complete one day;

the three days that complete a *gui* [three-day period];[8]

the three *xun* [ten-day periods] that complete a month;

the three months that complete a season;

the three seasons that complete the achievements [of the year].[9]

The cold, warm, and tepid are the three [types of temperature] that complete [the vitality of living] things.

The sun, moon, and stars are the three [types of celestial bodies] that complete [the phenomenon of] light.

Heaven, Earth, and humankind are the three [types of entities] that complete [the perfection of] virtue.

From this we see that to complete one with three is the great warp of Heaven. One takes the great warp of Heaven to create the Heavenly regulations. Therefore,

with ritual, three [instances of] yielding constitute one sequence;

with officials, [multiples of] three men constitute one selection.

Three dukes constitute one selection;

three ministers [for each duke] constitute one selection;

three great officers [for each minister] constitute one selection;

three senior functionaries [for each great officer] constitute one selection.

7. Emending the sentence to read *tian xuan si shi, zhong shi er er tian bian jin yi* 天選四時終十二而天變盡矣, following Su Yu, *CQFLYZ* 216.

8. *Gui* 規 normally means "compass" (i.e., an instrument for drawing circles), but here has the special meaning of "a period of three days."

9. The "three seasons" mentioned here are spring, summer, and fall. Winter is a season of quiescence—literal "hibernation"—so plays no role in the "achievements of the year."

These four selections, each with their three officers, respond to Heaven's seasons, each with its three months. For this reason,

taking three [men] to constitute a selection derives from Heaven's warp;
taking four to constitute a round [of selections] derives from Heaven's seasons;
taking twelve to constitute a cohort derives from the year's measuring points;
arriving at ten cohorts and stopping derives from Heaven's starting points. [24/32/29–24/33/6]

Section 24.3[10]

What is meant by "Heaven's starting points"? The answer is: Heaven has ten starting points. With [these] ten, the starting points come to an end and that is all.

Heaven constitutes one starting point;
Earth constitutes one starting point;
yin constitutes one starting point;
yang constitutes one starting point;
Fire constitutes one starting point;
Metal constitutes one starting point;
Wood constitutes one starting point;
Water constitutes one starting point;
Earth constitutes one starting point;
humankind constitutes one starting point.

With these ten starting points, [we reach] completion. They are Heaven's constants. Heaven's constants are completely expressed by the number ten. The king receives these ten starting points from Heaven, and they constitute the measure of one cohort. Each cohort, for each starting point, takes twelve [officers] at a time, just as Heaven completes each year with twelve months. The numbers of Heaven are ten; the measuring points of the year are twelve. The measuring points of the year regulate the numbers of Heaven. With twelve, the numbers of Heaven are completely expressed. Thus ten years are completed with 120 months. [Likewise,] the cohorts for each of the ten starting points are completed

10. Section 24.3 builds on the numerology of three and four introduced in section 24.2, in which four rounds of selection in multiples of three yield a grand total of 120 officials. Section 24.3 complements this 3 × 4 numerology by pointing out that 120 is 10 × 12. The fact that the grand total comes out the same in both cases would have struck a Han numerologist as a strong argument for the correctness of this ritual procedure for selecting officials.

with 120 officers. Each corresponds to Heaven. Three chosen officers complete [a group called] "Prudently Selected Officials."[11] Therefore,

eighty-one senior functionaries constitute twenty seven [groups of] "Prudently Selected Officials" and support twenty seven great officers;

twenty seven great officers constitute nine [groups of] "Prudently Selected Officials" and support nine ministers;

nine ministers constitute three [groups of] "Prudently Selected Officials" and support three dukes;

three dukes constitute one [group of] "Prudently Selected Officials" and support the Son of Heaven.

The Son of Heaven accumulates forty [groups of] "Prudently Selected Officials" in order to constitute the four selections. With each selection comprising one [group of] three "Prudently Selected Officials," all correspond to Heaven's constants. For this reason, using the four selections to count them,

each selection totals thirty men.
Three times four is twelve, [for a total of] 120 men.
This, too, corresponds to Heaven's constants.

Using the ten starting points to count them,

ten starting points total forty [groups of] "Prudently Selected Officials."
Each [group of] "Prudently Selected Officials" has three men.
Three times four is twelve, [for a total of] 120 men.
This, too, corresponds to Heaven's constants.

Using the subordinates of the three dukes to count them,

the subordinates of one duke total forty men.
Three times four is twelve, [for a total of] 120 men.
This, too, corresponds to Heaven's constants.

Thus

when disaggregated and named, they are called the 120 officials;
when selected and honored, they are called the twelve "Seniors."

Thus although their designations are numerous, nothing compares with calling them "the four selections of the twelve 'Seniors.'" Nonetheless, when they are divided up and counted, each has its proper correspondence, and none fails to hit the mark of Heaven's constants. [24/33/6–17]

11. The word *shen* 慎, usually a verb meaning "to act with care," appears here in an unusual sense, as a noun meaning "a group of three officials allocated to a higher official." The use of this term may also involve a play on words, with *can* 參 in its meaning of "three."

Section 24.4

For seeking out the subtleties of Heaven's constants, none compares with humankind.

> The body has four limbs, and each limb has three divisions.
> Three times four is twelve.
> When these twelve divisions support one another, the embodied form is established.
> Heaven has four seasons, and each season has three months.
> Three times four is twelve.
> When these twelve months receive one another, the yearly cycle is established.
> The officials have four selections, and each selection has its three men.
> Three times four is twelve.
> When these twelve officers support one another, the tasks of government are implemented.

Based on these examples we see that

> the constants of Heaven;
> the body of humankind;
> the regulations of officialdom

support and affect one another. There are many human correspondences with Heaven of this kind, but they are quite subtle. They must be examined. [24/33/17–21]

Section 24.5

The pattern of Heaven and Earth is to allocate the permutations of a single year to make four seasons. The four seasons also constitute Heaven's four selection times. Therefore,

> spring is the selection time of the Lesser Yang,
> summer is the selection time of the Greater Yang;
> fall is the selection time of the Lesser Yin;
> winter is the selection time of the Greater Yin.

Within these four selection times, each has its beginning, middle, and ending [months]. [Thus] there are selection times within selection times. Hence within a year there are four seasons, and within a season there are the three spans [of time]. These are the sequences of Heaven. Human beings are generated by Heaven, and consequently they embody Heaven's sequences. Hence they also exhibit greatness and pettiness, generosity and meanness. [Such is] the *qi* of human beings. The former kings accorded with the *qi* of human beings to distinguish such permutations thereby creating the four selections [of officials]. For this reason,

> the posts of the three dukes correspond to the selection of sagely men;
> the posts of the three ministers correspond to the selection of noble men;
> the posts of the three great officers correspond to the selection of good men;
> the posts of three senior functionaries correspond to the selection of upright men.[12]

They distinguished them according to their permutations and thereby created the four selections [for office]. Each selection established three officials, just as Heaven distinguishes the permutations of the year and thereby creates the four seasons, in each of which there are three [monthly] divisions. Heaven thus completes the year by harmonizing the selections of the four seasons with those of the twelve [monthly] divisions. [Likewise,] the ruler smooths out the mutual relationship between the four ranks of selections and the twelve officials [who fill them], thus attaining the perfection [of the Way]. Only when the Way extends to the realm of perfection can the [ruler] avail himself of the moral beauty of Heaven and Earth. [24/33/21–28]

12. Emending *zhi* 直 to *ren* 人, based on the preceding lines and the opening passage of the essay.

Book 7, Part 5

CHAPTER 25

Yao and Shun Did Not Presumptuously Transfer [the Throne]; Tang and Wu Did Not Rebelliously Murder [Their Rulers]

Section 25.1

Why could Yao and Shun presume to transfer [rulership of] the world [from one to the other]? The words of the *Classic of Filial Piety* state: "If you serve your father with filial piety, then you will serve Heaven brilliantly." Serving Heaven and serving one's father are ritually identical. Now if a father bestows a responsibility on his son, the son will not presume to bestow it on someone else. People's hearts are all like this. Now the king is also Heaven's son. Thus when Heaven gave the world to Yao and Shun, they received the Mandate of Heaven and ruled the world. Being [Heaven's] sons, how could they presume to transfer to others the responsibility they received from Heaven? Heaven illuminated the Way of being a son by not giving Yao and Shun the authority to pass on the throne. It follows beyond doubt that Yao and Shun did not personally transmit the world [to someone else] and [did not] presume to transfer [the throne] to someone else.[1] [23/34/3–6]

The phrase *bu zhuan* 不專 appears often in the *Chunqiu fanlu* in the sense of "to act without proper authorization from one's superior." That meaning applies here also, but the specific sense of this chapter title is (as the content of the chapter argues) that Tang and Wu, the respective founders of the Shang and Zhou dynasties, were not acting as rebels when they overthrew the existing Xia and Shang dynasties because they already had been granted Heaven's Mandate to rule.

1. The unstated essence of the argument here is that the transfer of the throne was made by Heaven itself, not by Yao and Shun on their own authority.

Section 25.2[2]

Confucians consider Tang and Wu the utmost worthies and greatest sages. They hold that [these men] were ones who

perfected the Way,
[comprehensively] investigated righteousness,
and epitomized [moral] beauty.

Thus they rank them as equal to Yao and Shun, designate them "sage-kings," and take them as their models of emulation. Now if you consider Tang and Wu to have been unrighteous, then, sir, which kings of what generations would you designate as "righteous"?

[That person] said: I do not know.

[I replied:] If you do not know, do you mean that [all] those who have ruled have been unrighteous? Or do you mean that there have been righteous rulers but that you are not familiar with them?

[The person] replied, Shen Nong [was one such].

I responded to this by saying: Did Shen Nong become the Son of Heaven simultaneous with the inception of Heaven and Earth? Or was there someone he replaced?[3] What if you approved of the ruler whom Shen Nong replaced but you took exception and disapproved of the rulers whom Tang and Wu replaced? How could that be? Moreover, when Heaven gives birth to the people, it is not for the sake of kings; when Heaven establishes kings, it is done on behalf of the people. Therefore

if his virtue is sufficient to bring security and happiness to the people, Heaven bestows [the Mandate] on him;
if his evil is sufficient to injure and harm the people, Heaven withdraws [the Mandate] from him.

An *Ode* declares:

They were subdued by the Zhou.
Heaven's Mandate is not permanent.

2. The issues raised in this section also were addressed in a formal debate between Dong Zhongshu and Master Huang during the reign of Emperor Jing. This debate is recorded in *SJ* 121/3122–23. See also Sarah A. Queen's translation in *From Chronicle to Canon: The Hermeneutics of the "Spring and Autumn" According to Tung Chung-shu* (Cambridge: Cambridge University Press, 1996), 18.

3. The character *fa* 伐 (to chastise, attack, or conquer) appears here and in several other sentences later in this section. We follow the reading proposed by Lu Wenchao and Su Yu (*CQFLYZ* 220), both of whom emend it to read *dai* 代 (to replace or substitute). Su Yu bases his emendation on *SJ* 121. In either case, the implication is of a violent replacement or overthrow.

The officers of Yin, great and petty,
offered libations in the capital [of Zhou].[4]

This means that Heaven's bestowal or withdrawal of the Mandate is not constant. Thus there is the Feng sacrifice on top of Mount Tai, the Shan sacrifice below Liangfu Peak, and the change of clan name when there is a [new] king. Those whose virtue resembled that of Yao and Shun numbered seventy-two men. Kingship is bestowed by Heaven. As for those whom the kings replaced, they are in every case those from whom Heaven had withdrawn [the Mandate]. Now you have held that only Tang and Wu's attack on Jie and Djou was not righteous but that there were seventy-two kings who also conquered others. If I extend your argument to its conclusion, then you would hold that all of the seventy-two kings were unrighteous.

Thus,

the Xia being without the Way, the Yin replaced them;
the Yin being without the Way, the Zhou replaced them;
the Qin being without the Way, the Han replaced them.

Those with the Way replace those without the Way. This is the principle of Heaven. It has existed since ancient times. How could this principle begin with Tang and Wu? If you condemn Tang and Wu for chastising Jie and Djou, then you also must condemn Qin for chastising Zhou, and Han for chastising Qin.[5] It is not simply that you do not know Heaven's principles. You also do not understand the propriety dictating human relationships. It is a matter of propriety that a son conceals his father's evil. Now if you were ordered to chastise[6] others and you believed [the order] to be unrighteous, then you ought to conceal it for the sake of your state. How could it be appropriate [to use the order] to slander [your state]? This is what we call "With one statement, two errors." The term "ruler" designates one who controls the orders. Orders put actions into effect, and prohibitions stop them. Now Jie and Djou sent orders throughout

4. *Odes* 235, verse 5.
5. Supplying "and Han for replacing Qin," following Lu Wenchao and Su Yu, *CQFLYZ* 221.
6. Here we retain the word *fa* 伐 (chastise [i.e., to attack in a righteous fashion; see note 3]).

the empire, but the people did not carry them out; they sent out prohibitions throughout the empire, but the people were not stopped by them. In what sense were they able to cause the empire to submit? If they truly were not able to cause the empire to submit, how can you say that Tang and Wu rebelliously murdered [their rulers]?[7] [23/34/6–20]

7. Since they were not kings in the true sense of the word, the men who killed them could not have committed regicide.

Book 7, Part 6

CHAPTER 26

Regulations on Dress

Section 26.1[1]

Let clothing be regulated according to gradations in rank.
Let wealth be expended according to gradations in salaries.
Let there be restraints governing food and drink.
Let there be regulations governing garments and clothes.
Let there be gradations governing dwellings and halls.
Let there be quotas governing animals and retainers.
Let there be prohibitions governing boats and chariots, armor and weapons.

In life, let there be distinctions governing carriages and official caps, clothing and positions, honors and salaries, and fields and dwellings. In death, let there be gradations in coffins, shrouds, and tombs.

Even if someone possesses worthy capabilities or a handsome physique, let him not dare wear clothing that does not befit his rank.

This text also appears in the *Guanzi*. See W. Allyn Rickett, trans., *Guanzi: Political, Economic, and Philosophical Essays from Early China* (Princeton, N.J.: Princeton University Press, 1985), 1:108–9.

1. The first eleven characters of the chapter are problematic and have been omitted from this translation. They read 率得十六萬國三分之則各. They do not appear in the *Guanzi* version of the text. Su Yu (*CQFLYZ* 221–22) quotes the earlier commentator Qian Tang, who suggests that characters are missing from these opening sentences and that their content is not commensurate with the text that follows. The first nine characters resemble very closely a line from chapter 28 [28/37/13], which reads 率得十六萬口三分之 ([This farmland] could sustain a population of 160,000. [This population] was divided into three [groups]). The doubtful opening sentence of chapter 26 thus could be an intrusive repetition from chapter 28.

Even if someone possesses a wealthy household and extensive property, let him not spend wealth that exceeds his salary.

Let the clothing of the Son of Heaven be decorated with insignia.

Do not permit the Principal Wife to wear informal dress when at a banquet and when at the ancestral temple.[2]

Do not permit the generals and great officers to wear informal dress when at a banquet, at the ancestral temple, or at an audience.

Limit the official administrators and instructed functionaries to [wearing] decorations on their belts and on the hems [of their robes].

Never let the common people dare to wear mixed colors.

Never let the various artisans, merchants, and traders dare to wear fox and raccoon [fur].

Never let [criminals] who have undergone castration and people who have undergone mutilation as punishment dare to wear silk, [wear] black and red [clothes in place of the usual ones made of undyed [hemp], or ride horses.

These are what are called "regulations of dress." [26/34/24–29]

---

2. We have emended the text at this point, following and revising Su Yu's reconstruction as follows: 夫人不得以燕［服］餐，以廟。將軍大夫不得以燕［服］餐，以廟，［以］朝，官吏命士至於帶緣. For Rickett's reconstruction, see *Guanzi*, 1:109; for Su Yu, see *CQFLYZ* 224.

Book 8, Part 1

CHAPTER 27

Regulating Limits

Section 27.1

Confucius said: "Do not worry about poverty, worry about inequality."[1] Therefore where

there is accumulation and excess,
there is shortage and deficiency.
Great wealth gives rise to haughtiness;
great poverty gives rise to desperation.
Desperation gives rise to thievery;
haughtiness gives rise to violence.[2]

These are the emotional propensities of the majority of human beings. The sage establishes rules based on the emotions of the majority of human beings and observes from whence disorder arises. This is why the sage regulates the Way of Humanity by distinguishing superior and inferior.

He ensures that the wealthy have sufficient means to reveal their nobility and [are not enriched] to the point of haughtiness.

1. *Analects* 16.1. The received version of the *Analects* reads 不患貧而患不安 (Do not worry about poverty, worry about unrest).
2. A similar claim appears in the "Fangji" (Records of the Dikes) chapter of the *Liji*. See *Liji* 30.2; James Legge, trans., *Li Chi: Book of Rites*, ed. Ch'u Chai and Winberg Chai (New Hyde Park, N.Y.: University Books, 1967), 2:284–85. The chapter discusses the various ways in which rites serve to restrain the people. It appears to be a debate between those who argue that they are an adequate means to restrain the populace and those who doubt their efficacy.

He ensures that the poor have sufficient means to nourish their lives and are not
[impoverished] to the point of desperation.[3]

The sage uses this [principle] to establish limitations and harmonize the rich and the poor. This is why resources are not lacking and superior and inferior are at peace with each other. Consequently, it is easy to govern. The present age has abandoned regulations [that set] limits so that each person indulges his or her desires. When desires have no limits, then the vulgar act without restraint. When this tendency persists without end,

the powerful people worry over insufficiencies above;
the little people fear starvation below.

Thus

the wealthy increasingly covet profit and cannot act righteously;
the poor daily disobey prohibitions and cannot be stopped.

This is why the present age is difficult to govern. [27/35/5–10]

Section 27.2

Confucius said: "The noble man does not use up material benefits, so there is something left for the common people."[4] An *Ode* declares:

"There are some handfuls left behind,
here are some ears left unharvested:
they are for the benefit of the widows."[5]

Therefore

when the gentleman serves in office, he does not farm;
when he farms, he does not fish;

he eats what is in season and does not strive for delicacies.[6]

A great officer does not sit on sheep skin;
a functionary does not sit on dog skin.

An *Ode* states:

3. The "Fangji" states this proposition in the negative: "Therefore when the sage regulates wealth and nobility, the sage allows the people's wealth to be insufficient to make them haughty and their poverty to be insufficient to make them desperate" (*Liji* 30.2; Legge, *Li Chi*, 2:284–85).
4. *Liji* 30.36, "Fangji"; Legge, *Li Chi*, 2:296.
5. *Odes* 212, verse 3.
6. Dong makes a similar claim in his memorials: "[W]hen the gentleman serves in office, he does not farm" (*HS* 56/2521).

Gathering turnips, gathering radishes,
you do not take the lowermost parts.
Your reputation is flawless;
[the people] will stay with you until death."[7]

[Rejoinder]: If you rely on this [principle] to restrain the people, some people still will neglect righteousness and vie for material benefits, thereby forfeiting their lives.[8] [27/35/12–15]

Section 27.3

Heaven does not bestow things in duplicate; what has horns is not permitted to have upper [incisor] teeth.[9] Therefore, those who already possess what is great are not permitted to possess what is small. This is Heaven's norm. Now if Heaven does not allow those who already possess what is great to compete with those who [possess what is] small, how can human [rulers] allow it! Therefore, the enlightened sage creates regulations [setting] limits that reflect Heaven's various activities. He does not allow those who receive generous salaries to encroach on those who enjoy few material benefits or compete with them to enhance their livelihoods. This is Heaven's principle.[10] [27/35/15–17]

7. *Odes* 35, verse 1.
8. This section of eighty-five characters mirrors a portion of the "Fangji" chapter of the *Liji*. See *Liji* 30.32–33; Legge, *Li Chi*, 2:296–97. *CQFL* attributes the first citation to Confucius; *Liji*, to "the Master." Sections of the *Liji* chapter typically begin with a claim concerning the rites and end with a rebuttal, as if it were a record of a debate, as Jeffrey Riegel has noted in "The Four 'Tzu Ssu' Chapters of the *Li Chi*: An Analysis and Translation of the *Fang Chi*, *Chung Yung*, *Piao Chi*, and *Tzu I*" (Ph.D. diss., Stanford University, 1978), 110–15.
9. This statement appears to be based on the actual observation of the dentition and horns (or lack thereof) of domestic animals like horses, swine, cattle, and sheep. A similar saying appears in *Huainanzi* 4.11.
10. The seventy-four characters that begin with "Heaven does not bestow things in duplicate" and end with "Heaven's principle" roughly follow a section of Dong's third memorial to Emperor Wu (*HS* 56/2521). It appears to be a poorer recension of the argument presented in the *Han shu* memorial. *HS* 56/2521 reads:

    Those households that receive official salaries should live off their salaries and nothing more. They should not compete for their livelihood with the common people, for only then will there be an equal distribution of material benefits and adequate provision for the common households. These are the principles of exalted Heaven and the Way of remote antiquity. They are what the Son of Heaven should find suitable to imitate to create his regulations and what the officials should follow as their practice.

    The theme of equitable distribution ties this section of the memorial to chapter 27.1.

Section 27.4

In general, the sources of various disorders are events that appear deceptively insignificant and trivial but that gradually mature and develop until they are quite significant. The sage points out the deceptive and identifies the trivial. He cuts off trivialities and does not permit ambiguities and so guards against them early on. The Way of the sage corresponds to the category of levees and dikes.

He promulgates regulations and limits;
he promulgates ritual restrictions.

Therefore,

nobility and lowliness have gradations;
garments and clothing are regulated;
court audiences are [conducted according to] ranks;
and districts and townships have gradations.

Hence the people possess a sense of yielding and do not compete. This is how the sage unifies them.[11] The *Documents* states: "If you bestow chariots and ceremonial garb on them, who will dare not yield, who will dare not respond with reverence?"[12] This expresses it. [27/35/19–22]

Section 27.5

Clothing was first produced to cover and warm the body. But when clothing is dyed in the five colors or ornamented with insignia, it is not in order to express feelings that arise from muscle and flesh, blood and *qi*. It is for the purpose of honoring the honorable, respecting the worthy, and distinguishing clearly the relationship between superior and inferior. It allows educational measures to be quickly put into effect and moral transformation to be easily perfected. It is done to create order.

Now if you discard regulations and limits and allow people to follow their desires, satisfying their inclinations, and following them without end, then you will greatly disrupt human relations and waste material resources. You will lose sight of the purpose for which insignia and colors were originally intended.

11. Compare this passage with the "Fangji" chapter of *Liji* (Legge, *Li Chi*, 2:285).
12. *Documents*, "Yi ji," paragraph 7; James Legge, trans., *The Shoo King, or, The Book of Historical Documents*, vol. 3 of *The Chinese Classics*, 2nd rev. ed. (1894; repr., Hong Kong: Hong Kong University Press, 1960), 3:84–85.

If the obligations between superior and inferior are not distinguished, then the positional advantage [of the one] will not be sufficient to regulate [the other]. Consequently, they will suffer bitterly from disorder. If there is no limit to the material possessions they desire, their potential [of the lowly] will not be sufficient to satisfy [the demands of the higher-ups]. Accordingly, they will suffer bitterly from poverty. Now if you desire

to transform disorder to order,
to transform poverty to wealth,

you cannot fail to revert to regulations and limits.

In ancient times,

the Son of Heaven [always] wore ornamented garments,
[whereas] the Lords of the Land wore them [only] on ritual occasions.
The great officers [always] wore ceremonial robes,[13]
whereas their functionaries wore them [only] on ritual occasions.

The common people wore unadorned clothing. This is the broad outline. [27/35/24–29]

13. Commentators describe the *lu* 褖 robe as being black with a red embroidered hem.

Book 8, Part 2

CHAPTER 28

Ranking States

Section 28.1

The *Spring and Autumn* states: "[Our lord] met with [the royal] minister, the Duke of Zhou." It also states: "Our lord met with the marquis of Qi, duke of Song, earl of Zheng, baron of Xu, and viscount of Sheng."[1] Moreover, it says: "For the first time we presented six [rows of] feather dancers."[2] The [*Gong-yang*] *Commentary* says: "The three dukes of the Son of Heaven are designated as dukes, and the descendants of the kings are designated as dukes. As for the rest, the rulers of large states are called marquises, and the rulers of small states are called earls, viscounts, and barons."[3] In general, there were these five grades. Thus the ranks of the Zhou dynasty consisted of five grades with officers in three classes. There was more outer refinement and less inner simplicity. The *Spring and Autumn* had [ranks of] three grades, combining "earl," "viscount," and "baron" in one rank, and its officers had two classes. There was less outer refinement and more inner simplicity. [28/36/3–6]

1. Duke Xi 5.9.2.
2. Duke Yin 1.5.1
3. Duke Yin 1.5.1.

Section 28.2

The *Spring and Autumn* says: "Jing."[4] The [*Gongyang*] *Commentary* says: "[Being referred to by] clan is not as good as being referred to as 'a man'; being referred to as 'a man' is not as good as being referred to by personal name; being referred to by personal name is not as good as being referred to by style.[5] As a general rule, [in the *Spring and Autumn*] these four grades [are] designated [as] "dependent states." All the Three Dynasties upheld these terms. [28/36/6–7]

Section 28.3

This being so, what kinds of divisions and ranks were there in the various territories? The answer is, the boundaries of the lands were as follows: the Son of Heaven [had a territory] one thousand *li* [square]; dukes and marquises [had a territory] one hundred *li* [square]; earls [had a territory] seventy *li* [square]; and viscounts and barons [had a territory] fifty *li* [square]. With the dependent states, [persons] designated by a style [had a territory] thirty *li* square; [persons] designated by a personal name [had a territory] twenty *li* square; [persons] referred to as "men" or by their clan name [had a territory] ten *li* square. [28/36/7–9]

Section 28.4

The *Spring and Autumn* mentions: "[the royal] minister, the Duke of Zhou." The [*Gongyang*] *Commentary* explains: "[He was one of the] three dukes of the

4. The full reference at Duke Zhuang 3.0.5 reads: "Autumn, ninth month. Jing [Chu] defeated Cai troops at Shen and brought back [as prisoner] Xianwu, marquis of Cai."
5. The full reference in the *Gongyang Commentary* at Duke Zhuang 3.10.5 reads:

> Why is there a reference to "Jing"? It was the name of one [of the nine] regions. [To be referred to by] region is not as good as by state; by state is not as good as by clan (*shi* 氏); by clan not as good as by the designation "a man" (*ren* 人); by designation as "a man" not as good as personal name (*ming* 名); by personal name not as good as by style (*zi* 字); by style not as good as official title. Why is Xianwu, marquis of Cai, here referred to by his personal name? In order to disown him. Why disown him? He was captured. Why is this fact not stated? [The *Spring and Autumn*] does not grant the Yi and Di tribes the right to capture [a ruler of] a central state. (Adapted from Göran Malmqvist, "Studies on the *Gongyang* and *Guliang* Commentaries," *Bulletin of the Museum of Far Eastern Antiquities* 43 [1971]: 130; see also Newell Ann Van Auken, "Who Is a *rén* 人? The Use of *rén* in *Spring and Autumn* Records and Its Interpretation in the *Zuǒ*, *Gōngyáng*, and *Gǔliáng* Commentaries," *Journal of the American Oriental Society* 131, no. 4 [2011]: 555–90)

Son of Heaven."[6] [The *Spring and Autumn* records:] "The earl of Cai arrived." The [*Gongyang*] *Commentary* explains: "[Who was this earl of Cai?] [He was a] great officer of the Son of Heaven."[7] [The *Spring and Autumn* mentions:] "The [royal] minister Zhu Bo Jiu." The [*Gongyang*] *Commentary* states: "He was a junior great officer."[8] [The *Spring and Autumn* mentions:] "Shi Shang." The [*Gongyang*] *Commentary* explains: "He was a functionary of the Son of Heaven."[9] The *Spring and Autumn* records: "The king's man." The [*Gongyang*] *Commentary* states: "It was a case of avoiding his name. He was a junior functionary."[10] These references total five ranks. [28/26/9–12]

Section 28.5

The *Spring and Autumn* states: "create the Three Armies." The [*Gongyang*] *Commentary* states: "Why was this recorded? In order to criticize. What was there to criticize? In ancient times [there were the four ranks of] senior minister, junior minister, senior functionary, and junior functionary."[11] Now as for these four ranks: the great officer of a small state shared a rank equal to that of the junior minister of a middling state; the great officer of a middling state shared a rank equal to that of the junior minister of a large state; the junior great officer of a large state shared a rank equal to that of a junior functionary of the Son of Heaven. There were a total of twenty-four grades and eight levels of compensation.

> Those with great merit and virtue received greater rank as a functionary;
> those with less merit and virtue received lesser rank as a functionary.
> Those with great talent held a great official position;
> those with small talent held a small official position.

When official posts accord with ability, it is the perfection of governance. Thus

6. Duke Xi 5.9.2.
7. Duke Yin 1.1.6.
8. The full citation reads: "The Celestial King dispatched the minister Zhu Bo Jiu to come on a friendly diplomatic visit" (Duke Huan 2.4.1).
9. Duke Ding 11.14.9.
10. Duke Xi 5.8.1.
11. Duke Xiang 9.11.1.

one man in ten thousand men was designated "talented";
one man in one thousand was designated "eminent";
one man in one hundred men was designated "prominent";
and one man in ten was designated "brave."[12]

The [designations] brave, prominent, eminent, and talented did not contravene one another. Consequently, governing the world was [as easy as] rolling a ball in the palm of one's hand. [28/36/12–17]

Section 28.6

On what were the numbers of the various departments of the Son of Heaven and Lords of the Land modeled? The answer is: The departments of the Son of Heaven were divided into right and left, with five grades totaling 360 men,[13] in imitation of the number of days in Heaven's yearly cycle, with the color symbols of the five grades corresponding to the five seasons. The assistant generals numbered seven, and senior and junior ministers totaled 280 men in the image of the Heavenly Court. This was double the number for the Lords of the Land.

The outer assistants for the Lords of the Land were divided into four grades, totaling 120 men, in imitation of the numbers corresponding to the six nodal points of the four seasons. Their assistant generals and senior and junior functionaries numbered sixty, imitating the numbers of days and the chronograms.[14]

Why do the assistants consist of three groups of three and then repeat? The answer is: Each season is completed in three months, and the great Chronogram constellation consists of three stars.

Why do the ranks of the Lords of the Land consist of five grades? The answer is: They imitate the numbers of Heaven and Earth. The five officials are likewise. [28/36/17–21]

12. For another description of these types of men, see John S. Major, Sarah A. Queen, Andrew Seth Meyer, and Harold D. Roth, trans. and eds., *The "Huainanzi": A Guide to the Theory and Practice of Government in Early Han China* (New York: Columbia University Press, 2010), 819–20. See also the additional passages in *Shuoyuan*, *Lüshi chunqiu*, and *Heguanzi* mentioned in Su Yu, *CQFLYZ* 237–38.

13. Although the text has "363," we suspect this must originally have read "360," a number sometimes used to approximate the days of the year. It corresponds to the twenty-four solar periods of fifteen days each of the solar agricultural calendar and also to six sexagenary day-cycles. The number 360 also has the advantage in this passage of being divisible by both two and five, to account for "left and right, in five grades."

14. In this passage, the word "days" (*ri* 日) refers to days designated by the Ten Heavenly Stems, while the word "chronograms" (*chen* 辰) refers to days designated by the Twelve Earthly Branches. A full cycle (six repetitions of the Heavenly Stems and five repetitions of the Earthly Branches) yields a sexagenary period, sixty days.

Section 28.7

This being so, how were the numbers for the officials and subofficials divided and allocated? The answer is: The Lords of the Land of the large states had four armies. Such were the ancient regulations. Among them, one army was meant to guard the royal family.

Why was the total number of the conscript armies three? The answer is: A large state with a population of 160,000 established three conscript armies.

What is the explanation for this? The answer is: [The ruler] used the well field as a standard to calculate. Each square *li* made one "well"; each well consisted of nine hundred *mu* and was used for calculating the population. [Each] square *li* sustained eight households; every household had one hundred *mu*, which fed [a minimum of] five people. The best farmers,[15] cultivating one hundred *mu*, fed nine people; the next best, eight people; the next best, seven people; the next best, six people; the next best, five people.[16] Those who were even more inferior [produced] proportionate results, so that one hundred *mu* fed three people. [In that case,] one square *li* of land fed twenty-four people, and ten square *li* fed 240.[17]

A square ten *li* [on a side] makes 100 square *li*, which can sustain 2,400 people; a square one hundred *li* [on a side] makes 1,000 square *li*, which can sustain 24,000 people. A square 1,000 *li* [on a side] makes 10,000 square *li*, which can sustain 240,000 people.[18]

15. "Nongfu 農夫," as in the *Mencius* and *Liji* parallels.
16. *Mencius* 5B.2 states: "What a farmer got was what he reaped from a hundred *mu* of land, the allocation of each man. With an allocation of a hundred *mu*, a farmer could feed nine persons, eight persons, seven persons, six persons, or five persons, according to his grading as a farmer" (D. C. Lau, trans., *The Book of Mencius* [Harmondsworth: Penguin, 1970], 152).
17. It is interesting that all subsequent calculations are based on this minimal level of productivity.
18. The arithmetic here is wrong: a square that is one hundred *li* on a side actually makes ten thousand square *li*. Similarly, a square that is one thousand *li* on a side makes one million square *li*, not, as stated, ten thousand.

[The ruler] in standard [practice] divided [this land] into thirds and set aside one-third for walls and moats, inner walls and watchtowers, halls and houses, gates and lanes, streets, roads, and markets, government offices and bureaus, gardens and parks, hedges and stockades, terraces and fishponds, and groves and gardens.[19] [Thus] there was [a remainder] of sixty-six plots of good land in each [area of] ten *li* square. This additional [area of] square *li*, [amounting to] sixty-six [hundredths of the total], was designated as [farmland] that sustained a population of 160,000. Dividing this into thirds, each third contained 53,333 people, of whom the adult [males] made up the Three Armies. This applied to dukes and marquises. [28/36/21–29]

Section 28.8A

The territory of the Son of Heaven was one thousand *li* [square], that is, one hundred parcels of one hundred *li* square [i.e., in both calculations, one million square *li*.] [In this case] also, one-third was put aside [for nonagricultural use]. [Thus] there were sixty-six parcels of [agricultural] fields, [each] one hundred *li* square. This additional [area of] ten-*li*-square [parcels, amounting to] sixty-six [hundredths of the total], was designated as [farmland] that could sustain a population of 16,000,000. Dividing this by nine, each group had 1,777,777 persons, which [formed the basis of] the capital's nine conscript armies. Three of the capital's conscript armies were meant to defend the royal family.

Thus the Son of Heaven established [his household as follows:] One queen; one elder consort; consorts of the center, left, and right; four concubines; and three ladies of excellence. He established one heir apparent, three dukes, nine ministers, twenty-seven great officers, eighty-one senior functionaries, and 243 junior functionaries. There also were seven senior ministers, twenty-one junior ministers, sixty-three senior functionaries, and 189[20] junior functionaries.

19. Lai Yanyuan (*CQFLJZJY* 217, note 40) cites Lu Wenchao, who suspects that the two characters *chuan cai* 椽采 are erroneous and that perhaps the text should read "something along the lines of groves and gardens" 林麓菜之類.

20. The existing text has "129." This must be a mistake for "189," since the text here is multiplying by three as it works down the ranks.

The royal queen appointed one grand mentor, one grand mother, three uncles, and three aides. The elder consort [was attended by] four concubines and three ladies of excellence; each had her respective tutor. The heir apparent had a greater and a lesser mentor,[21] three senior commandants, and three junior commandants.[22]

The officers who entered [the palace] to take up office as lodging guards of the Son of Heaven were comparable to the junior functionaries. The junior functionaries were taken from the lower numbers of the senior functionaries. The personal guards of the royal queen consisted of senior and junior attendants, each numbering five. The heir apparent; center, left, and right consorts; and four concubines were provided with senior and junior attendants, each numbering five. The three ladies of excellence were each provided with five men. The guardians of the heir apparent's concubines and his officers followed the regulations for dukes and marquises.

The mentors of the empress had senior and junior scribes, each numbering five men; the three uncles each had senior and junior scribes, each numbering five men; and the junior uncles each had five scribes. The grand mentor to the heir apparent had senior and junior scribes, each numbering five men; the lesser mentor to the heir apparent also had five scribes; three senior commandants and three junior commandants also had scribes, each numbering five. The three dukes had senior and junior scribes, each numbering five men; the minister had senior and junior scribes, each numbering five men; the great officers had senior and junior scribes, each numbering five men; the senior functionaries had senior and junior scribes, each numbering five men; the scribes of the senior and junior ministers and the senior and junior offices also each numbered five. The [scribes for the] underlings of the ministers, great officers, and senior functionaries numbered three. [28/36/29–28/37/12]

21. Following the emendation of Su Yu, *CQFLYZ* 243.
22. Following the emendation of Su Yu, *CQFLYZ* 243.

Section 28.8B

Accordingly, the territory of dukes and marquises was one hundred *li* square, with one-third of the land put aside [for nonagricultural use]. [Thus] in each parcel that was ten *li* square, sixty-six [parcels] were designated as agricultural land. This additional [area of] square *li*, [amounting to] sixty-six [hundredths of the total] was designated as [farmland] that could sustain a population of 160,000. This [population] was divided into three [groups] to [form the basis of] the three conscript armies of a large state, [thus] establishing it as a large state.

[The dukes and marquises appointed] one principal wife, one elder consort, one consort of the left and one of the right, three concubines, and two ladies of excellence. [They] appointed one heir apparent, three ministers, nine great officers, twenty-seven senior functionaries, and eighty-one junior functionaries. [They] established one heir apparent and three ministers. There also were five plenipotentiary great officers who established senior and junior functionaries.

The position of the senior minister was comparable to the senior functionary of the Son of Heaven, with [an annual salary of] eight hundred bushels.[23] The junior ministers received [an annual salary of] six hundred bushels; senior functionaries received [an annual salary of] four hundred bushels; and junior functionaries received [an annual salary of] three hundred bushels. The principal wife appointed one maternal mentor, three uncles, and three aides. The elder consort and the consorts of the left and right [each were attended by] three concubines and two ladies of excellence, each with their respective mentors and guardians. The heir apparent appointed a senior mentor and an aide.

The officers [designated as] guards of the lodgings of the honorable were [variously] of comparable rank to the senior ministers [of the Son of Heaven], of whom there were three, to the junior ministers, of whom there were six, and to the senior and junior functionaries with appropriate numbers [according to] senior or junior [status].

The personal guards of the principal consort consisted of senior and junior attendants, five of each. The elder consort and the left and right consorts were

23. We use the word "bushels" as an approximate translation of the Chinese unit of dry measure *dan* 石 (pronounced this way only in this usage, otherwise pronounced "*shi*"). It corresponds to a basketful of grain, and in the early Han period a *dan* weighed approximately sixty-five pounds.

provided with senior and junior attendants, five of each. The two ministers were each provided with attendants, five for each.

The senior mentor to the heir apparent had senior and junior scribes, five of each; the aides had five scribes each. The three ministers, nine great officers, and senior functionaries each had five scribes. The junior functionaries each had five scribes. The plenipotentiary great officers and senior and junior functionaries each had five scribes. The [scribes for the] underlings of the ministers were two in number. These are the regulations for dukes and marquises. Worthy men of the rank of duke and marquis became regional overlords, who were presented with a battle-ax and a halberd and were furnished with one hundred "Brave as Tigers" [guards]. [28/37/12–21]

Section 28.8C

Accordingly, the earls' territory was seventy *li* [square]. Seven times seven is forty-nine [making a total area of 4,900 square *li*]. One-third of the land was put aside [for nonagricultural use]. Land for agricultural use was established as twenty-eight parcels, [each] ten *li* square. This additional [area of] ten *li* square [parcels], amounting to] sixty-six [hundredths of the total] was designated as [farmland,] which sustained a population of 109,212, constituting the three conscript armies of a medium state, [thus] establishing it as a medium state.

[Earls appointed] one principal consort, one elder consort, one consort of the left and one of the right, three ladies of excellence, and two grandsons. [They] established one heir apparent, three ministers, nine great officers, twenty-seven senior functionaries, eighty-one junior functionaries, and five plenipotentiary great officers, with five senior functionaries and fifteen junior functionaries.

The position of the senior minister was comparable to the junior minister of a large state with [an annual salary of] six hundred bushels. The junior ministers received [an annual salary of] four hundred bushels; senior functionaries received [an annual salary of] three hundred bushels; junior functionaries received [an annual salary of] two hundred bushels. The principal consort appointed one maternal mentor, three uncles, and three aides. The elder consort, consort of the left and of the right, three concubines, and two ladies of excellence each had their respective mentors and guardians. The heir apparent had a senior mentor.

The officers [designated as] guards of the lodgings of the honorable were [variously] of comparable rank to the senior ministers [of the Son of Heaven], of whom there were three, to the junior minister, of whom there were six, and to the senior and junior functionaries with appropriate numbers [according to] senior or junior [status]. The personal guards of the principal consort consisted of senior and junior attendants, five of each. The elder consort and consorts of the left and of the right were provided with senior and junior attendants, five of each. The two ministers were each provided with attendants, five for each.

The senior mentor to the heir apparent had senior and junior scribes, five of each. The three ministers, nine great officers, and senior functionaries each had five scribes. The junior functionaries each had five scribes. The plenipotentiary great officers and senior and junior functionaries each had five scribes. The [scribes for the] underlings of the ministers were two in number. [28/37/21–29]

Section 28.8D

Accordingly, the territory of viscounts and barons was fifty *li* [square]. Five times five is twenty-five, [making a total area of 2,500 square *li*]. Land for agricultural use was established as ten *li* [square] [parcels amounting to] sixty-six [hundredths of the total] to sustain a population of forty thousand, which constituted the three conscript armies of a small state, thus establishing it as a small state.

[Viscounts and barons appointed] one principal consort, one elder consort, one consort of the left and of the right, three ladies of excellence, and two grandsons. [They] established one heir apparent, three ministers, nine great officers, twenty-seven senior functionaries, eighty-one junior functionaries, five plenipotentiary great officers, five senior functionaries, and fifteen junior functionaries.

The position of the senior minister was comparable [in rank] to the junior minister of a medium state, with [an annual salary of] four hundred bushels. The junior ministers received [an annual salary of] three hundred bushels; senior functionaries received [an annual salary of] two hundred bushels; junior functionaries received [an annual salary of] one hundred bushels.

The principal consort appointed one maternal mentor, three uncles, and three aides. The elder consort, consorts of the left and of the right, three concubines, and two ladies of excellence each had their respective mentors and guardians. The heir apparent had a senior mentor.

The officers [designated as] guards of the lodgings of the honorable were of comparable rank to the senior ministers, of whom there were three, and to the junior ministers, of whom there were six.

The personal guards of the principal consort consisted of senior and junior guards, five of each. The elder consort and consorts of the left and of the right were provided with senior and junior attendants, five of each. The two ministers were each provided with attendants, five for each.

The senior mentor to the heir apparent had senior and junior scribes, five of each; the aides had five scribes each. The three ministers, nine great officers, and senior functionaries each had five scribes. The junior functionaries each had five scribes. The plenipotentiary great officers and senior and junior functionaries each had five scribes. The [scribes for the] underlings of the ministers were two in number.

These were the Zhou regulations. The *Spring and Autumn* combined earl, viscount, and baron into one grade. [28/37/29–28/38/6]

Section 28.8E

Accordingly, the territory of a dependent state whose ruler was referred to by his style was thirty *li* [square].[24] Three times three is nine; [thus the area of the state was nine hundred square *li*]. One-third of the land was put aside [for non-agricultural use]. Land designated for agricultural use, in parcels ten *li* square,

24. *Mencius* 5B.2 explains:

> The territory under the direct jurisdiction of the Son of Heaven was one thousand *li* square, under a duke or a marquis one hundred *li* square, under an earl seventy *li* square, while under a viscount or baron it was fifty *li* square, totaling four grades. Those who held territories under fifty *li* square had no direct access to the king. They had to affiliate themselves to a Lord of the Land and were known as "dependent states."

> Note that the size of the territories for each rank mentioned in the *Mencius* match those of the *Chunqiu fanlu* but that the number of grades do not. *Mencius* 5B.2 explains: "The Son of Heaven constituted one rank; duke constituted one rank; marquis constituted one rank; earl constituted one rank; and baron and viscount were combined to constitute one rank for a total of five grades." But this section of the *Chunqiu fanlu* account combines duke and marquis into one rank and baron and viscount into one rank, making four grades in this passage (Son of Heaven, duke and marquis, earl, and baron and viscount).

amounted to six[-ninths of the total], designated as sustaining a population of 14,400, which constituted the three conscript armies.

[The ruler appointed one] principal wife for the [head of the] lineage, two secondary wives, one heir apparent, one steward, one aide, one functionary, and five ranked functionaries. The steward [was comparable in rank to] the junior minister of a viscount or baron, with [an annual salary of] three hundred bushels. The principal wife of the [head of the] lineage had her mentors and guardians. She had three attendants; the secondary wives each had two. The heir apparent had one mentor. The officers [designated as] guards of the lodgings of the lord were comparable [in rank] to the senior minister and junior minister [of a viscount or baron], of whom there were one of each, with comparable numbers of seniors and juniors. The mentor of the heir apparent had senior and junior scribes, five all together.[25]

The territory of a dependent state whose ruler was referred by his personal name[26] was half[27] of the size of a dependent state whose ruler was referred to by his style. Nine halved [is 4.5; therefore the area of the state was 450 square *li*]. One-third was put aside [for nonagricultural use]; thus there were three [hundred] parcels of [agricultural] fields. This was designated [as being able to sustain] a population of 7,200. The heir apparent was comparable to a steward with [an annual salary of] two hundred bushels.

The ruler of a dependent state of the lowest order had a territory one-fourth that [of a ruler who was referred to by his style]. It was divided into thirds, [with a total area of] 22.5[28] parcels [of land of ten square *li*]. One third was set aside [for nonagricultural use]. Thus of land designated as [agricultural] fields, there was one fewer ten-square-*li* field than the fifteen [such] fields[29] designated

25. We have followed Lu Wenchao, who suggested that the three characters 下良五 are erroneous or corrupt, so we have not translated them (Lai, *CQFLJZJY* 219, note 76).
26. Treating the character 善 as excrescent, following Yu Yue (Lai, *CQFLJZJY* 219, note 77).
27. Although some commentators have claimed that this statement is incongruous with claims made at the outset of the chapter regarding the territorial allotment of dependent states, in fact the two claims are quite compatible. A ruler named for his style had 900 square *li*. Half of that is 450 square *li*, which is what our text has for a ruler called by his personal name. "Half" must refer to the area of the territory, not to the dimension of one side of it. So in the final cut, the territory is halved again, to 225 square *li*. The numbers all work out as they should. See Yu Yue's comments in Lai, *CQFLJZJY* 219, note 77.
28. Reading "22.5" for "25."
29. We make a conjectural reconstruction of these two lines following the logic of the mathematics to keep the claims made here mathematically consistent.

[as being able to sustain] a population of 3,600. The heir apparent was comparable to a steward with [an annual salary of] one hundred bushels. There were five scribes. The principal wife of the [head of the] lineage had personal guards;[30] the heir [apparent] had underlings.[31] [28/37/29–28/38/13]

30. Emending *shiwei* 仕衛 to *yuwei* 御衛, based on earlier occurrences. Su Yu (*CQFLYZ* 248) suggests instead "officers who [took up office] as lodging guards of the lord" (*shi suwei junzhe* 士宿衛君者).

31. Lu Wenchao notes that the text has fallen away from this point in the essay. For Su Yu's reconstruction, see *CQFL* 38, note 9.

Group 4

Ethical Principles

GROUP 4, "Ethical Principles," consists of twelve chapters that discuss typically Confucian themes such as humaneness, righteousness, wisdom, the rectification of names, and filial piety. With the exception of the last three chapters, which are closely associated with the *Classic of Filial Piety,* they develop these ethical principles in conjunction with the *Spring and Autumn,* demonstrating how that text, often through specific illustrations, supports and illuminates them. These chapters appear to have been grouped together by the *Chunqiu fanlu*'s compiler or perhaps by an earlier editor whose work the compiler adopted on the basis of content (Confucian ethical principles) and classical grounding (*Spring and Autumn*, *Classic of Filial Piety*).

GROUP 4: ETHICAL PRINCIPLES, CHAPTERS 29–42

29. 仁義法 *Ren yi fa* Standards of Humaneness and Righteousness
30. 必仁且智 *Bi ren qie zhi* The Necessity of [Being] Humane and Wise
31. 身之養莫重於義 *Shen zhi yang mo zhong yu yi* For Nurturing the Self, Nothing Is More Important Than Righteous Principles
32. 對膠西 [i.e., 江都] 王越大夫不得為仁 *Dui Jiaoxi* [*Jiangdu*] *Wang: Yue dafu bu de wei ren* An Official Response to the King of Jiangdu: The Great Officers of Yue Cannot Be Considered Humane
33. 觀德 *Guan de* Observing Virtue
34. 奉本 *Feng ben* Serving the Root
35. 深察名號 *Shen cha ming hao* Deeply Examine Names and Designations

36. 實性 *Shi xing* Substantiating Human Nature
37. 諸侯 *Zhuhou* The Lords of the Land
38. 五行對 *Wuxing dui* An Official Response Regarding the Five Phases
39. [Title and text are no longer extant]
40. [Title and text are no longer extant]
41. 為人者天 *Wei ren zhe tian* Heaven, the Maker of Humankind
42. 五行之義 *Wuxing zhi yi* The Meaning of the Five Phases

Description of Individual Chapters

Chapter 29, "Standards of Humaneness and Righteousness," consists of a single essay that discusses how the *Spring and Autumn* uses these central virtues of the Confucian tradition to bring order to the self and society at large: "What the *Spring and Autumn* brings order to is others and the self. The means by which it brings order to others and the self is humaneness and righteousness. It employs humaneness to pacify others and righteousness to correct the self."[1] But in contemporary society, people pervert and misapply these two virtues, using humaneness to enrich themselves and righteousness to oppress others. This, the essay argues, is the main reason why the *Spring and Autumn* devotes so much attention to clarifying the meaning and application of these virtues. It does so by setting clear standards that demonstrate that humaneness "lies in loving others, not in loving the self" and that "righteousness lies in correcting the self, not in correcting others."[2] Moreover, the ability to censure others does not qualify as righteousness, and the ability to love oneself does not qualify as humaneness. Several examples demonstrate this point: Duke Ling of Jin was filled with self-love but failed to love others; in contrast, Duke Zhuang was an exemplar of humaneness, for he worried over the most distant in the land. King Ling of Chu may have punished the rebels of Chen and Cai, but he failed to rectify his own person, and thus the *Spring and Autumn* did not consider him a standard of righteousness. These distinctions are critical to ordering the self and society at large. Thus, the essay concludes, the ruler's self-rectification is paramount. This conclusion explains the methodology of praise and blame in the *Spring and Autumn*: "The *Spring and Autumn* censures the faults of those above and pities

1. *CQFL* 29/38/17.
2. *CQFL* 29/38/20–21.

the hardships of those below. It does not call attention to minor transgressions external [to the ruler], but when they reside in [the ruler] himself, it records and condemns them."[3] The ruler must ponder these standards of humaneness and righteousness. If not, even if he possesses the Way of the Sages, he will fail to understand the meaning of the *Spring and Autumn*.

Chapter 30, "The Necessity of [Being] Humane and Wise," consists of two unrelated sections. Section 30.1 is an essay that defines humaneness and wisdom and their relationship to each other. The opening paragraph shares interesting parallels with section 9.30 of the *Huainanzi*'s chapter 9, "The Ruler's Techniques," although the *Huainanzi* passage describes humaneness and wisdom differently: "In human nature nothing is more valuable than Humaneness; nothing is more urgently needed than Wisdom. Humaneness is used as the basic stuff; Wisdom is used to carry things out."[4] In contrast, chapter 30 of the *Chunqiu fanlu* states: "Humaneness is the means to love all human beings, and wisdom is the means to rid them of harm."[5] Neither humaneness nor wisdom is identified with the basic substance of a human being, but both are means or methods to improve the human community. Such an approach is consistent with Dong Zhongshu's views of human nature expressed in his memorials that, for example, define human nature as "the unadorned character of the basic substance," a topic we will turn to in greater detail later. The remaining discussion amplifies these initial claims by describing the various attributes associated with humaneness and wisdom.

The brief passage that constitutes section 30.2 is about natural disasters and bizarre events initiated by Heaven. It characterizes natural disasters as Heaven's warnings and bizarre events as Heaven's threats and maintains that natural disasters always precede strange events and are less ominous. It interprets both as confirmation of Heaven's humane concern and argues that by these means it is possible to observe Heaven's will. Although natural disasters and bizarre events should be feared, they should not be despised, as they express Heaven's desire to rescue the ruler from his errors and save him from doing wrong. Thus, the passage concludes, "If a sagely ruler or worthy lord still delights in receiving the reproofs of his loyal ministers, then how much more should they delight in receiving Heaven's warnings."[6]

3. *CQFL* 29/39/20.
4. John S. Major, Sarah A. Queen, Andrew Seth Meyer, and Harold D. Roth, trans. and eds., *The "Huainanzi": A Guide to the Theory and Practice of Government in Early Han China* (New York: Columbia University Press, 2010), 338.
5. *CQFL* 30/40/8–9.
6. *CQFL* 30/41/3–4.

One commentator has suggested that section 30.2 would be more appropriate as part of chapter 15, "Two Starting Points," which also discusses anomalies in conjunction with the *Spring and Autumn* and in relation to the ruler's transgressions.[7] This is an attractive suggestion, as the passage clearly seems out of place here and bears little relation to the discussion of humaneness and wisdom in section 30.1.

Chapter 31, "For Nurturing the Self, Nothing Is More Important Than Righteous Principles," develops an important distinction concerning self-cultivation that Mencius made some two centuries earlier, between the greater aspects of personhood (*dati* 大體) and the lesser aspects of personhood (*xiaoti* 小體):

> Gongduzi asked: "We all are men. Why, then, are some great men while others are small men?" Mencius replied: "Those who follow the greater aspects of their person become great men; those who follow the lesser aspects of their person become small men." Gongduzi then asked: "How is it that some follow the greater aspects of their person while others follow the lesser aspects of their person?" Mencius replied: "The faculties of hearing and sight are unable to think and so can be misled by external things. When one thing interacts with another, it leads one another astray, that's all. The faculty of the mind is thought. If it does think, it will find the answer. If it does not think, it will not find the answer. This is what Heaven has bestowed on us. If you seek to establish yourself relying on the greater aspects of your person, then the lesser aspects of your person will not displace them. This is what makes a person a great man and nothing more."[8]

Taking this famous dictum as its starting point, chapter 31 affirms that material benefits and righteous principles equally are gifts from Heaven but that their purposes are different: "[M]aterial benefits to nourish the body; righteous principles to nourish the heart."[9] In addition, righteous principles are more important than material benefits, as borne out in the following argument: "When people amply possess righteous principles but sorely lack material benefits, though poor and humble, they may still bring honor to their conduct, thereby cherishing their persons and rejoicing in life."[10] In contrast, "When people amply possess material benefits but utterly lack righteous principles, though exceedingly wealthy, they are insulted and despised. If their misdeeds are

7. *CQFLYZ* 262.
8. *Mencius* 6A.15.
9. *CQFL* 31/41/10.
10. *CQFL* 31/41/12–13.

excessive, their misfortunes are serious. If they are not executed for their crimes, they [nevertheless] are struck down by an early death. They can neither rejoice in life nor live out their years."[11] Nonetheless, people typically forget this fact. Forgetting righteous principles, they lust after material benefits. Disregarding inherent principles and following hateful ways, they not only harm themselves but endanger their families as well. In contrast, the sage perfectly embodies righteous principles, manifesting them in his virtuous conduct and instructing the people through his personal example. Through his personification of righteous principles, he can move others:

> Having moved others, he can transform them. Having transformed them, he can glorify their conduct. Having transformed and glorified their conduct, laws are not disobeyed. When laws are not disobeyed, punishments are not employed. When punishments are not employed, the virtue of Yao and Shun is achieved. This is the Way of Great Governance. The former sages transmitted and received it in succession. Thus Confucius said: "Who can go out without using the door? Why, then, does no one follow the Way?"[12]

The essay concludes that this is the Way of Great Governance. If the ruler fails to follow this course of action, even though he may institute severe and harsh punishments, it will serve only to harm the people he rules and compromise his power and positional advantage.

Chapter 32, "An Official Response to the King of Jiangdu: The Great Officers of Yue Cannot Be Considered Humane," also addresses the subject of humaneness. In this case, the topic is raised during an exchange between the imperial kinsman Liu Fei, who reigned as King Yi of Jiangdu, and Dong Zhongshu, who at the time was serving as the kingdom's administrator. (A second recension of the official document recording the exchange is preserved in the *Han shu*'s "Biography of Dong Zhongshu," affirming its close association with Dong. The original chapter title indicates that this response was to the king of Jiaoxi, but we follow *Han shu* 56 in assigning it to the court of Jiangdu.) The dialogue between the king and the administrator reflects the unsettled political situation of Emperor Wu's reign. Part of the imperial realm was under the emperor's direct control, and part was divided into kingdoms ruled by imperial relatives. On several occasions, some of these neofeudal lords rebelled against the imperial throne, and

11. *CQFL* 31/41/13–14.
12. *CQFL* 31/41/23–25.

the empire also had to contend with incursions of the nomadic Xiongnu, who from time to time attacked across the northern frontier from their homeland in the distant steppes. Some of the regional kings and military officials who took up arms to defend the emperor may have seen themselves as fitting the mold of the hegemons of the Spring and Autumn period, wielding political and military power on behalf of the Son of Heaven. Others may simply have been trying to curry favor with an emperor who was not averse to crushing the neofeudal kingdoms and incorporating their territory into the imperial domain.

Chapter 32 provides testimony to the relevance and appeal of the hegemonic system for at least some of the Han regional kings. The king of Jiangdu initiates a dialogue concerning one of the five famous hegemons of the Spring and Autumn period,[13] the king of Yue, and his worthy ministers. The king of Jiangdu himself was a devoted military man who had rallied to defend the imperial throne during the Rebellion of the Seven Kingdoms in 154 B.C.E. and who at the time was contemplating taking up arms once again to fight the Xiongnu. Querying Dong Zhongshu, who had already established his reputation as an incorruptible scholar, the king asks a leading question: Were King Goujian of Yue and his two most trusted ministers exemplars of humaneness, even though they went to war to defend their ruler? Clearly the king expected an affirmative answer, one that by implication would endorse his own credentials for humaneness. Typical of his uncompromising character, Dong was unwilling to cede the point. His answer was unambivalent: the kingdom of Yue lacked even one humane man, he said, much less three. Why so? Dong explained that the hegemons relied on treachery and force rather than humaneness and righteousness: "Compared with other Lords of the Land, the Five Hegemons were worthy; compared with the sages, how can they be considered worthy? They were but coarse stone to polished jade."[14]

Chapter 33, "Observing Virtue," and chapter 34, "Serving the Root," develop the cosmic aspects of virtue and ritual in ways reminiscent of the works of Xunzi. Chapter 33 begins by situating human virtue in the larger context of cosmic virtue. That is, not only do we form one body with the universe but our virtue derives from Heaven and Earth as well: "Heaven and Earth are the root

13. The Five Hegemons were identified in various ways. Duke Huan of Qi (r. 685–643 B.C.E.) is generally recognized as the first hegemon, and Duke Wen of Jin (r. 636–628 B.C.E.) as the second. One list continues with Duke Xiang of Song (r. ca. 650–638 B.C.E.), Duke Mu of Qin (r. ca. 650–621 B.C.E.), and King Zhuang of Chu (r. 613–591 B.C.E.). Other lists omit Duke Xiang of Song and Duke Mu of Qin and substitute either King Helü of Wu or King Fuchai of Wu, and King Goujian of Yue.

14. *CQFL* 32/42/11.

of the myriad things, the place from which our first ancestors emerged. . . . The Way of ruler and minister, father and son, and husband and wife derive from Heaven and Earth."[15] To observe the "vast and limitless" Virtue of Heaven and Earth, the text avers, we need only contemplate how the subtle wording of the *Spring and Autumn* ranks all who appear in its pages in accordance with this cosmic virtue. Numerous examples demonstrate this general claim, spelling out the different patterns of notation in the *Spring and Autumn* and making explicit their relevance to the virtue of specific actors.

Section 33.3 discusses the rules said to be observed in the *Spring and Autumn* for referring to foreign peoples and blood relatives. Contact with foreigners apparently is regarded as embarrassing for the Sinitic states, and therefore the *Spring and Autumn* downplays such instances. Conversely, the chapter's author gives special attention to blood relations, citing examples in which the *Spring and Autumn* sets aside its usual terminology because of blood ties, literally "sharing the same surname." During the Han, these claims may have been especially relevant to foreign relations, on the one hand, and rank, precedence, and subordination in the imperial Liu clan, on the other.

The opening section of chapter 34, "Serving the Root," cites the most important attributes of the rites: they "connect Heaven and Earth; embody yin and yang; [and] are punctilious about host and guest."[16] Heaven, Earth, and humanity each have quintessential counterparts reflecting their abiding virtue: the sun and moon are the quintessence of Heaven; mountains are the quintessence of Earth; and the Son of Heaven is the quintessence of humanity. But what promises to be a compelling essay on ritual and its relation to the virtues of the three realms quickly breaks down. The remaining four sections of this chapter are disparate fragments brought together in patchwork fashion, perhaps because of their references to the *Spring and Autumn*.

Chapter 35, "Deeply Examine Names and Designations," and the closely related chapter 36, "Substantiating Human Nature," develop a position on human nature close to that of Xunzi. Indeed, these two chapters share much with the *Xunzi*, particularly the ideas set forth in *Xunzi* 22, "On the Correct Use of Names," and 23, "[Human] Nature Is Bad." Like the *Xunzi*, these two chapters of the *Chunqiu fanlu* define human nature as what is inborn and natural, and contend that human nature cannot be considered good because goodness is a virtue acquired through education. They also develop Xunzi's ideas about

15. *CQFL* 33/42/16–18.
16. *CQFL* 34/43/21.

language in three important ways: they emphasize the cosmic origins of language, they associate his rectification of names with the *Spring and Autumn*, and they use the rectification of names and draw on the *Spring and Autumn* to develop a position on the inherent qualities of human nature.

Chapters 35 and 36 share many parallel passages and arguments, which has led some scholars to conclude that chapter 36 is an abbreviated version or a synopsis of chapter 35 and thus is the later of the two essays. We believe the reverse to be more likely: the shorter chapter 36 is actually the earlier of the two essays on human nature, and chapter 35 amplifies and develops it. Not only does chapter 35 contain passages that also appear in chapter 36, but chapter 35 also develops these positions in novel ways. The rectification of names, for example, is given a cosmological basis in chapter 35, and nature and emotions are related to yin and yang only in chapter 35. Since the arguments of chapter 36 are encompassed by chapter 35, our discussion of chapter 35 will introduce both chapters.

Chapter 35, "Deeply Examine Names and Designations," has four sections. Each addresses the rectification of names but for different purposes. Section 35.1 introduces the rectification of names as the starting point of social order and posits that the rectification of names itself originates with Heaven and Earth. Thus, the argument continues, when the sages created language, they were simply imitating what was already inherent in the patterns of the cosmos itself. Therefore, names and designations are ultimately "the means by which the sage communicates Heaven's intentions." The sage does so by availing himself of the two essential categories of language, names and designations, which serve complementary but distinct functions: names denominate, and designations generalize. As the numerous examples that follow demonstrate, all things in the universe possess an inherent name and designation. Thus, this short essay concludes, "For this reason, when each affair complies with its name and each name complies with Heaven, the realms of Heaven and humankind are united and become one."[17] This is another manifestation of the Way of Virtue.

Section 35.2 continues this in-depth examination of names and designations, using orthographic (visual) and aural puns to explore the range of meanings connoted by two related terms: *wang* 王 (king) and *jun* 君 (lord). By analyzing these two terms, the section leads the reader to understand how, in the *Spring and Autumn*'s theory of language, they are imbued with inherent virtue. Section 35.3 returns to the sage's use of names, emphasizing that the sage employs

17. *CQFL* 35/45/2–3.

names to authenticate things—that is, to distinguish what is so from what is not so. This claim concerning the rectification of names serves as a preamble to the heart of the essay, a discussion of human nature. The author believes that the question of nature is mired in confusion, which he proposes to clarify. He does so in section 35.3 (and an analogous paragraph in chapter 36) through a critique of Mencius, who asserted that human nature is inherently good because it contains the starting points of virtue. Even though, like Mencius, the author of this critique associates the word "nature" (*xing* 性) with "what is inborn" (*sheng* 生), his understanding of this basic stuff (*zhi* 質), which constitutes a person's nature, is much closer to the position adopted by Xunzi. Human nature, as with Xunzi, is the natural and uncultivated stuff with which one is born. Furthermore, goodness, as with Xunzi, is achieved through education. Therefore, says the author of section 35.3, to identify human nature with goodness is to misunderstand and misrepresent its reality: "If we search for the basic substance of 'nature' in the name 'good,' is it capable of hitting the mark?"[18]

What, then, are the spontaneous qualities that one possesses at birth and that define the basic substance called "nature"? To answer this question, the author analyzes the closely related term *xin* 心, which means both "heart" and "mind," arguing that the heart/mind acts to restrain human nature. If nature were inherently good, would it require such restraint? The word "body" is thought to be closely related to Heaven. Like Heaven, which possesses two aspects of *qi* manifested in yin and yang, the body possesses two aspects of nature manifested as greed and humaneness. Moreover, just as Heaven places controls on yin and yang, a person must restrain his emotions and desires. This assertion emphasizes Heaven's control of yin (which, as we will see in group 5, "Yin-Yang Principles," is strongly identified with negative qualities) and therefore a person's need to restrain his greed and other negative mental states.

Accordingly, rather than viewing education as Mencius envisioned it—as a process of developing the inchoate sprouts of goodness that are present at birth as part of human nature—goodness is presented here as a human achievement, not as the development of an inherent human quality. This is shown in the final term examined in the essay, the designation *min* 民 (common people), which, the author asserts, is derived from the term *mian* 眠 (eyes closed). Our eyes, the author continues, are closed in sleep and only when we awaken can we see. Analogously, the common people are ignorant and depraved and only when they are given an education can they become good.

18. *CQFL* 35/45/24.

In a slight semantic shift, the essay next associates the sleeping person with the nature (*xing*) and the emotions (*qing* 情) mutually conferred by Heaven and Earth. Humans partake of both nature and emotions. Those who claim that human nature is good do not account for the emotions: "Therefore the sage [Confucius] never referred to the nature as good because it would have violated the [meaning of the] name. A person has a nature and emotions, just as Heaven has yin and yang. To speak of one's basic substance without mentioning one's emotions is like speaking of Heaven's yang without mentioning its yin."[19] The essay concludes by pointing out that its discussion of human nature does not refer to the highest or the lowest type of person but to average people. Like an egg that awaits incubation to become a chicken and a silk cocoon that awaits unwinding and spinning to become silk thread, ordinary people must await education to become good: "The people receive from Heaven a nature that is not yet capable of being good, and they humbly receive from the king the education that will complete their nature."[20]

Section 35.4 refutes the Mencian position once again, but from a slightly different perspective. This last section consists of an exchange (real or imagined?) between two people. The exchange is initiated by the phrase "[Suppose] someone says," and then this unnamed "someone" raises the notion of "sprouts of goodness." A long discussion follows, introduced by the words "[I] would say in response." The respondent attempts to settle the debate as to whether human nature is inherently good by turning to the subject of "goodness" as a standard in the teachings of Mencius and Confucius. He maintains that Mencius and Confucius differed radically in the ideals of goodness they espoused and that Mencius was wrong and Confucius was right. Mencius's position is described as follows: "[Human] nature contains the sprouts of goodness. Children love their fathers and mothers so are better than birds and beasts. In this sense, [their nature] is called good. This is Mencius's notion of goodness."[21] In contrast, Confucius's position is described as having a much more rigorous idea of goodness:

> Therefore Confucius said, "A good man is not mine to see. If I saw a man who possessed constancy, I would be content. . . ."[22] If simply activating the sprouts of goodness that make one better than birds and beasts may be called goodness, why did Confucius maintain that he never saw such a person? . . . The nature

19. *CQFL* 35/46/11–12.
20. *CQFL* 35/46/14–15.
21. *CQFL* 35/46/22–23.
22. *Analects* 7.26.

> of the myriad commoners is better than that of birds and beasts but it cannot be called good.[23]

Mencius's notion of goodness embodied the lowest ideal of the term, and Confucius's represented the highest. What Confucius called goodness "was not easy to match," whereas what Mencius called goodness was simply a matter of "being better than the birds and the beasts." The passage concludes:

> Mencius looked below to find the substance [of goodness] in comparison with what birds and beasts do and therefore said that nature is inherently good. I look above to find the substance [of goodness] in comparison to what the sages did, and therefore I say that nature is not yet good. Such a standard of goodness surpasses nature, just as the sages surpass this standard of goodness. The *Spring and Autumn* attaches importance to the origins of things. Therefore it is meticulous with regard to the correct use of names. If the name is not traced to its beginning, how can you say whether the nature is not yet good or inherently good?[24]

The stance of chapter 36 on nature and goodness—and so, by extension, the stance of the entire group—is to reject the Mencian position in favor of more stringent views resembling those of Xunzi.

The very brief chapter 37, "The Lords of the Land," states that great sages of antiquity observed Heaven's cycles because they understood that although Heaven does not speak, its intentions to benefit and sustain the people are evident in those cycles. Therefore, when the sages faced south to rule the world, they invariably brought universal benefit to their people. Because what they could see and what they could hear were limited, they parceled out lands to be ruled by overlords who were established as their eyes and ears. Using a play on words, the essay defines "Lords of the Land" (*zhuhou* 諸侯) as "numerous servants" (*zhuhou* 諸候), making clear that although the king delegates power to the lords, the proper hierarchical relationship between ruler and nobles must be respected. Despite being projected back into antiquity, the relevance of this definition to the neofeudal kings of the Han is obvious: they exist only to serve the Son of Heaven. This was a timely message in the era of Emperors Jing and Wu. Faced with interminable problems with the regional kings during the first

23. *CQFL* 35/46/23–27.
24. *CQFL* 35/47/3–5.

century or so of Western Han rule, the emperors would very likely have welcomed an ideological justification for doing away with them.

The last three extant chapters in this group—chapter 38, "An Official Response Regarding the Five Phases"; chapter 41, "Heaven, the Maker of Humankind"; and chapter 42, "The Meaning of the Five Phases"—all discuss the virtue of filial piety. Chapters 38 and 42 link filial piety to the Mutual Production Sequence of the Five Phases, and chapter 41 quotes extensively from the *Classic of Filial Piety*.[25]

Section 38.1 purports to be an official exchange between "Master Dong of Wencheng" and "King Xian of Hejian." As the chapter title, "An Official Response Regarding the Five Phases," implies, this chapter is ostensibly (though not necessarily) an official account of the exchange between the king and the master, duly reported to the central court. Section 38.2, a brief interpretive passage on the *Classic of Filial Piety*, very likely migrated from chapter 41 to chapter 38 at some point during the long transmission of the text. Because it shares many formal features with the materials collected in the second part of chapter 41, we will discuss it in conjunction with that chapter.

In the opening lines of section 38.1, King Xian of Hejian initiates a dialogue with "Master Dong" (possibly a fictional version of Dong Zhongshu) by requesting an explication of a passage from the *Classic of Filial Piety*. The passage defines filial piety as "Heaven's Warp and Earth's Righteousness." What does this mean?[26] Master Dong responds in two steps. He explains Heaven's Warp in terms of the Mutual Production Sequence of the Five Phases, which he also associates with the five seasons and their five characteristic activities, to yield the correlations presented in table 1. Although the Five Phases are said to exemplify the five forms of human conduct, filial piety is the sole virtue discussed in the first part of Master Dong's response, consistent with the question he was asked. In the Mutual Production Sequence, each phase engenders the next; that is, the next phase receives what the previous one has engendered. Master Dong interprets this as a cosmic template for the father–son relationship. In this reading, filial piety exemplifies the Way of Heaven because each phase in turn is the cosmic expression of the "father conferring and the son receiving."

25. Or we might say more cautiously, chapter 41 contains passages that are parallel to the received *Classic of Filial Piety*. Although chapter 38 quotes the *Classic of Filial Piety* by name, it is not certain that it existed in its received form when these chapters were written.

26. *CQFL* 38/48/10.

TABLE 1

Phase	Wood	Fire	Earth	Metal	Water
Season	Spring	Summer	Midsummer	Autumn	Winter
Activity	Germination	Growth	Nourishing	Harvesting	Storing

In the second part of his response, Master Dong explains Earth's righteousness first as an analogy to the weather: even though Earth is the source of wind and rain, it confers the merit for these achievements on Heaven, as exemplified in the expressions "Heavenly rain" and "Heavenly wind." Earth's service to Heaven, characterized by "diligence and hard work," in turn provides the cosmic template for "great loyalty," the proper service offered by subordinates to their superiors.

Master Dong's response then turns to Five-Phase analogies, and he reiterates, again in accordance with the Mutual Production Sequence, that Earth is the son of Fire. But this part of the response emphasizes the special status of Earth in relation to the Five Phases and its subordinate status to Heaven: "Thus subordinates serve superiors, just as Earth serves Heaven. . . . Earth is the son of Fire. Of the Five Phases, none is more noble than Earth."[27] But despite Earth's special status, it plays only a minor role in the seasons (which, in the second part of the essay, consist of only the four conventional seasons, in contrast to the earlier five): "Earth's relation to the four seasons is that there is nothing that it commands, and it does not share in the accomplishments and reputation of Fire."[28] This last enigmatic statement is explained in a later chapter,[29] which makes clear that nothing can impede Fire's potent yang:

> [The phase] Earth resembles "earth" [meaning "soil"]. Earth rules righteousness [as Heaven rules humaneness]. . . . Although [the phase] Earth dwells in the center, it also rules for seventy-two days of the year, helping Fire blend, harmonize, nourish, and grow. Nevertheless, it is not named as having done such things, and all the achievement is ascribed to Fire. Fire obtains it and thereby flourishes.

27. *CQFL* 38/48/19–20.
28. *CQFL* 38/48/20.
29. It is explained in a passage that we, following Lau (*CQFL* 43/51/8–23), locate in chapter 43 (where we designate it as 43.2) but that Su Yu proposes to move to chapter 44. This passage, which now reads as a fragment that has lost its moorings, may originally have been part of either chapter 38 or chapter 42.

> [Earth's] not daring to take a share of the merit from its father is the ultimate in the perfection of filial piety. Thus both the conduct of the filial son and the righteousness of the loyal minister are modeled on Earth. Earth serves Heaven just as the subordinate serves the superior.[30]

Finally, the nobility of Earth is reaffirmed in relation to its correlates among the five tones, five flavors, and five colors: "The righteousness of the loyal minister and the actions of the filial son are derived from Earth. Earth is the most noble of the Five Phases, and nothing can augment its righteousness, [just as] of the five tones, none is more noble than *gong*; of the five flavors, none is more noble than sweetness; of the five colors, none is more luxuriant than yellow."[31]

Chapter 42, "The Meaning of the Five Phases," repeats many of the arguments that appear in chapter 38.1. The phases are listed in the Mutual Production Sequence, called here the "Heavenly endowed sequence," which is said to embody the father–son relationship. Heaven is identified with filial piety and Earth with loyalty, two of the five modes of virtuous conduct. Here, too, Earth enjoys a special status in relation to the Five Phases. The phases are correlated with the seasons and directions in the standard ways: Wood-spring-east; Fire-summer-south; Earth-[no season]-center; Metal-autumn-west; and Water-winter-north. Earth is not correlated with any particular season (unlike in chapter 38.1, which employs the alternative strategy of positing a special season of "midsummer" for Earth); instead, its influence is distributed over all the four natural seasons. The emphasis of the Five-Phase reasoning in chapter 42 is entirely on ethical issues, foregrounded in filial piety. The ruler, ritually facing south, conforms to the influences and activities of the phases according to the correlations shown in table 2. As presented here, the relationships between Wood and Fire and between Metal and Water are interesting and unusual. When Wood is born, its lesser yang is nurtured by the greater yang of its successor, Fire; when Metal is born, its demise is both hastened and mourned by its successor, Water. With these specific correlations defined, the remainder of the essay expands on the special status of Earth as the "Heavenly Fructifier," the "arms and legs of Heaven." Just as the four flavors—sourness, saltiness, acridness, and bitterness—could not perfect their respective tastes without the ruling flavor of sweetness (as was already affirmed in chapter 38), the four seasonal phases could not accomplish their respective functions

30. *CQFL* 44/52/11–15.
31. *CQFL* 38/48/20–22.

TABLE 2

Mutual Production Sequence	Wood	Fire	Earth	Metal	Water
Location of the Five Phases	Left	Front	Center	Right	Rear
Activities of the Five Phases	Wood is born and nurtured by Fire	Fire delights in Wood and nourishes it with yang	Earth serves Heaven by fully expressing its loyalty	Metal dies and is buried by Water	Water over-comes Metal and mourns it with yin
Correlate activities of sons	Missing?	Nourish their fathers as Fire . . .	Serve their lord as Earth . . .	Missing?	Bid their fathers farewell in death as Water . . .
Dwelling	Eastern quarter	Southern quarter	Center	Western quarter	Northern quarter
Governs	*qi* of spring	*qi* of summer	All seasons, just as all phases rely on Earth to accomplish their functions	*qi* of autumn	*qi* of winter

without the assistance of the ruling phase, Earth: "Sweetness is the root of the Five Tastes; Earth is the ruler of the Five Phases."[32]

In its current form, chapter 42 does not explicitly subordinate Earth to Fire. But it originally may have done so, as in chapter 38. The passage that we just quoted—"Earth dwells in the center, . . . helping Fire blend, harmonize, nourish, and grow" but "is not named as having done such things, and all the achievement is ascribed to Fire"[33]—places Earth in the role of the loyal minister, wielding great power but selflessly subordinating himself to the great yang authority of the ruler. The chapter concludes by once again correlating Earth with the virtue of loyalty. This emphasis on loyalty is a distinctive feature of chapters 38 and 42.

The similarity in the structure and content of the arguments presented in chapters 38 and 42 suggests that they are closely related, and both chapters also

32. *CQFL* 42/50/19.
33. *CQFL* 44/52/13–14; Su Yu places this passage in chapter 43; we follow Lau, who locates it in chapter 44.

share important features with chapters 43 and 44. Both chapters 38 and 42 develop the cosmic implications of filial piety and loyalty celebrated in the *Classic of Filial Piety* by establishing clear links to the Mutual Production Sequence of the Five Phases. As we shall see, these distinctive features provide important clues to the dating and attribution of these chapters.

Chapters 39 and 40 no longer exist.

Chapter 41, "Heaven, the Maker of Humankind," also has important links to the *Classic of Filial Piety*. The title of the chapter derives from its opening lines, which assert the categorical unity of Heaven and humanity: "What gives birth cannot make human beings. The maker of human beings is Heaven. The humanness of human beings is rooted in Heaven. Heaven is also the supreme ancestor of human beings. This is why human beings are elevated to be categorized with Heaven."[34] Section 41.1 discusses the human correlates of Heaven, supplying many examples that will be elaborated in group 5, "Yin-Yang Principles." The task of the ruler, the passage concludes, is to husband these Heaven-endowed aspects of the self.

Section 41.2 similarly draws on the *Classic of Filial Piety* to lend authority to its statements. This section consists of three short passages (four, if we include a short passage now located in chapter 38.2 that probably was originally part of section 41.2). Each has a number of identical formal features, and each begins with a short saying introduced by the formulaic phrase "a tradition states" (*zhuan yue* 傳曰), an expression often used in the *Chunqiu fanlu* and other Han texts to introduce lore transmitted orally through the generations.[35] The saying is then briefly explained, beginning with a term or phrase repeated from the opening saying. The explication concludes with a citation from the *Classic of Filial Piety* marked off with the standard "Thus it is said" (*gu yue* 故曰).[36] A typical example is the following:

OPENING SAYING

> A tradition states: "The Son of Heaven alone receives orders from Heaven; the world receives orders from the Son of Heaven; a single state receives orders from its lord."

34. *CQFL* 41/49/11.
35. For example, the numerous instances in *Hanshi waizhuan*.
36. See the numerous examples in chapters 1, 4, 5, 7, and 8.

EXPLICATION

If the lord's orders comply [with Heaven], the people will have cause to comply with his orders; if the lord's orders defy [Heaven], the people will have cause to disobey his orders.[37]

CONCLUDING CANONICAL REFERENCE

Thus it is said: "When the One Man enjoys blessings, the myriad commoners will rely on it."

This expresses it.[38]

The formal features employed here and in chapter 38.2 follow a pattern of explication seen most prominently in the *Hanshi waizhuan*,[39] the only significant difference being that the explications of oral sayings in that text close with citations from the *Classic of Odes* rather than the *Classic of Filial Piety*. There is no doubt, however, that these three chapters—38, 41, and 42—appear at this point in the text because of their common aim to explicate various aspects of filial piety and that their focus on a key Confucian virtue supports their identification as part of group 4, "Ethical Principles."

Issues of Dating and Attribution

The chapters of group 4 preserve quite diverse materials. Their dates, and the authorship of these chapters and their sections, can be assigned with varying degrees of certainty. Some (chapters 30.2 and 32) are unquestionably the work of Dong Zhongshu; we know that because the same materials have been preserved in other Han sources that identify Dong as their author. Others (chapters 35 and 36)

37. This quotation also appears in the "Biaoji" (Record of Uprightness) chapter of the *Liji*. See James Legge, *Li Chi: Book of Rites*, ed. Ch'u Chai and Winberg Chai (New Hyde Park, N.Y.: University Books, 1967), 2:347.
38. *CQFL* 41/49/20–21.
39. "Master Han's Supplementary Disquisitions on the *Classic of Odes*" (ca. 150 B.C.E.), by Han Ying (ca. 200–120 B.C.E.).

may confidently be attributed to Dong because they are similar in spirit to statements on the same subject ascribed to him in Han sources or because they are highly consistent with Han descriptions of his thought. Several chapters in this group (29, 30, 31, 33, 34) may reasonably be ascribed to Dong Zhongshu or his disciples, but without direct evidence of their authorship, because they are broadly consistent with what we know about Dong's teachings.

On the other end of the spectrum, we find materials that almost certainly are not by Dong Zhongshu or anyone in his immediate circle. Chapter 41 represents an exegetical tradition grounded in the *Classic of Filial Piety*; no independent contemporary source links Dong's teachings to that text. The formal character of chapter 38 leads us to believe that it is a forgery, and both it and the closely related chapter 42 address themes that did not arise in Han political discourse until well after Dong Zhongshu's lifetime.

Han shu 56, "The Biography of Dong Zhongshu," provides corroborating evidence that several chapters (and one section) in this group are by Dong Zhongshu: chapters 30.2, 32, 35, and 36. For example, in his memorial to Emperor Wu, Dong Zhongshu grounds his omenology in the *Spring and Autumn* and in Confucius's authorial intentions. In addition, Dong's memorial states, "When a state is about to suffer a defeat because [the ruler] has strayed from the proper path, Heaven first sends forth disastrous and harmful [signs] to reprimand and warn him. If the [ruler] does not know to look into himself [in response], then Heaven again sends forth strange and bizarre [signs] to frighten and startle him."[40] The language and spirit of the brief passage on anomalies that constitutes chapter 30.2 is nearly identical to these passages from Dong's memorials. Consider, for example, "Natural disasters are Heaven's warnings; bizarre events are Heaven's threats. If Heaven warns [the ruler] and he does not acknowledge [these warnings], then Heaven will frighten him with threats."[41] Given that 30.2 so closely resembles arguments in Dong's first memorial to Emperor Wu, preserved in *Han shu* 56, and that it also contains the kind of formulaic language known to have been used in memorials, petitions, and letters to the throne, we believe this to be an excerpt from the original memorial to Emperor Wu. The small differences between the two documents are probably simply the result of typical editorial decisions made by Ban Gu when he quoted the memorial in "The Biography of Dong Zhongshu."

40. *HS* 56.2498.
41. *CQFL* 30/40/24.

Chapter 32, preserving an official exchange between King Yi of Jiangdu and Dong Zhongshu, also is quoted in *Han shu* 56, attesting to its early provenance and the reliability of its attribution to Dong Zhongshu. The formulaic writing of the document also indicates beyond question that it is a contemporary record of an official communication. This communication must have been sent to the imperial court, where it was read and then stored in the imperial archives. Thus it would have been available years later to Ban Gu, who included it in his biography of Dong Zhongshu.[42] Furthermore, the opening line of chapter 32 refers to Dong's official title, administrator. Dong Zhongshu served Liu Fei, who reigned as King Yi of Jiangdu, in that capacity for several years beginning in the mid-130s B.C.E., enabling us to date the document with reasonable accuracy.[43] We also can match the document's political agenda to events occurring at that time. Although on the surface, chapter 32 is a discussion of humaneness and its relationship to hegemonic rule, in reality it is a coded discussion of the mounting challenges posed by the Xiongnu, who threatened China's northern frontier. The *Shiji* reports: "In the fifth year of the Yuanguang era (130 B.C.E.), when the Xiongnu were invading and plundering Han territory in great numbers, [Liu] Fei submitted a letter [to Emperor Wu] requesting permission to attack the Xiongnu, but the throne did not grant permission."[44] In chapter 32, the humiliations suffered by King Goujian of Yue at Guiji, when his army was surrounded and defeated by the army of King Fuchai of Wu, allow Dong Zhongshu to argue, using veiled language, against Liu Fei's enthusiasm for leading an attack on the Xiongnu. This grounding in historical events provides additional corroboration that chapter 32 was written by Dong Zhongshu himself.[45]

Chapters 35 and 36 address human nature, a topic on which thinkers during the Warring States period expressed a range of strong opinions and which continued to attract great interest among Han intellectuals. Its continued importance is hardly surprising, given the demand for well-educated, morally upright officials to staff the burgeoning bureaucracy of the Han Empire. Human nature also pertained to the question of the education of the emperor himself and his

42. *HS* 56.2523.
43. For the dating of Dong's service to King Yi, see Sarah A. Queen, *From Chronicle to Canon: The Hermeneutics of the "Spring and Autumn" According to Tung Chung-shu* (Cambridge: Cambridge University Press, 1996), 25–26.
44. *SJ* 59.2096.
45. For a detailed analysis of the content of this document, see Sarah A. Queen, "The Rhetoric of Dong Zhongshu's Imperial Communications," in *Facing the Monarch: Modes of Advice in the Early Chinese Court*, ed. Garret Olberding, Harvard East Asian Monographs (Cambridge, Mass.: Harvard University Press, 2013), 189–96.

designated heir. Influential scholars from Lu Jia, Jia Yi, Liu An, Liu Xiang, and Yang Xiong in the Western Han to Ban Gu, Wang Chong, Xu Shen, Wang Fu, and Xun Yue in the Eastern Han, offered their views concerning human nature. Dong Zhongshu was no exception. Indeed, the content of these essays, with their polemical edge and combative claim that contemporary discussions on human nature are hopelessly mired in confusion, indicates that they were written as contributions to a robust and flourishing discourse on the topic.

The earliest surviving testimony to Dong's views on human nature beyond the *Chunqiu fanlu* come from his memorials preserved in *Han shu* 56. There we find a discussion of human nature wholly consonant with that of chapters 35 and 36 of the *Chunqiu fanlu*: left to their own devices, human beings are incapable of becoming good; they are wholly reliant on the transformative influences of moral instruction initiated by the sage-king.

The distinction between the nature and the disposition made in this chapter also appears in chapter 35: "A person has a nature and emotions just as Heaven possesses yin and yang. To speak of one's basic substance without mentioning one's emotions is like speaking of Heaven's yang without mentioning its yin." Chapter 36 likens human nature to raw materials and claims: "What Heaven does stops with the cocoon, hemp, and rice plant. Using hemp to make cloth, the cocoon to make silk, the rice plant to make food, and the nature to make goodness—these all are things that the sage inherits from Heaven and advances. They are not things that the unadorned substance of the emotions and the nature is able to achieve."[46]

Further evidence comes from the works of Wang Chong. His essay "The Basic Nature" echoes an essay on human nature by Dong Zhongshu, who was said to have appraised the theories of Mencius and Xunzi. Wang Chong portrays Dong as associating the disposition and nature with yin and yang:

> Dong Zhongshu surveyed the writings of Sun [Xunzi] and Mengzi and created a theory about the disposition and the nature. He said, "The great constancy of Heaven consists of yin and yang; the great constancy of humankind consists of the disposition and the nature. The nature is born of yang and the disposition is born of yin. Yin qi is base and yang qi is humane." Those who say that the nature is good are those who look at yang; those who say it is bad are those who look at yin.[47]

46. *CQFL* 36/47/14–15.
47. Wang Chong, "Ben Xing," in *Lunheng* 13/38/8–10.

Wang Chong appears to be describing Dong's views accurately, for these correlates are likewise found in chapter 35, which argues that the *qi* of both humaneness and greed coexist in the body:

> Now if I use the name "mind" to apprehend the true character of human beings, then I must conclude that the truth about human beings is that they possess both greed and humaneness. The *qi* of humaneness and greed coexist in the self. . . . Heaven [imposes] prohibitions pertaining to yin and yang; the self [observes] restraints on the emotions and desires. In this respect, it is identical to the Way of Heaven. . . . What Heaven restricts is also restricted in the body. . . . One must understand that if the Heaven-bestowed nature is not supplemented by education, it ultimately cannot be restrained.[48]

Thus we find that chapters 35 and 36 of the *Chunqiu fanlu* are consistent with all surviving contemporaneous claims about Dong's theory of human nature.

Chapter 38, "An Official Response Regarding the Five Phases," purports to be an official exchange between King Xian of Hejian and Dong Zhongshu, but the discerning reader will recognize that it is problematical. First, the document is devoid of any of the formulaic expressions of humility that were required in communications to the throne. In responding to the questions raised by King Xian, the so-called Master Dong from Wenchang makes no use of the self-effacing prostrations or expressions that typically preface a response from a subordinate to a superior, such as "Your humble servant" and "knocking his head and bowing." We could hypothesize that such language was edited out of the document, but why would any editor do that and so portray Dong as committing an almost treasonous ritual affront? A comparison with the two other "official responses" preserved in the text, chapters 32 and 71, makes the deficiencies of chapter 38 glaringly apparent. Second, an encounter between Dong Zhongshu and the king of Hejian seems unlikely. Liu De, the son of Emperor Jing by his concubine Lady Li, was appointed as King Xian of Hejian in the second year of Emperor Jing's reign, 155 B.C.E., and he remained in this post for the next twenty-six years until his death in 129 B.C.E.[49] Liu De was an important patron of Confucian learning. He made great efforts to attract scholars to his court and to collect copies of precious pre-Qin texts for his library, which rivaled that of the capital.

48. *CQFL* 35/45/29–32.

49. *SJ* 59/2093; *HS* 2410; Steven van Zoeren, *Poetry and Personality: Reading, Exegesis, and Hermeneutics in Traditional China* (Stanford, Calif.: Stanford University Press, 1991), 83.

He is reported to have done much to promote the *Zuo Commentary*, the *Rites of Zhou*, and texts associated with the Mao interpretations of the *Odes*. There is no evidence that he would have been interested in the views of Dong Zhongshu, a proponent of the *Gongyang Commentary*. Third, the reference to "Master Dong from Wencheng" in an official document is equally odd and suspicious. The two official exchanges preserved in chapters 32 and 71 refer to Dong by his full name and his official titles (the administrator of Jiangdu and the former administrator of Jiaoxi, respectively). Su Yu surmises that the place-name "Wencheng" (温成) could be a mistake for "Changcheng" (昌成), the name of one of the counties in Dong's native place, the kingdom of Guangchuan (廣川). But the identification of Dong Zhongshu with this otherwise unknown "Master Dong of Wenchang" seems quite tenuous. In addition, the definition of righteousness used in this supposed official document departs significantly from other teachings about righteousness identified with Dong Zhongshu. Recall that chapter 29 maintains, for example, that righteousness refers to the self and is the means to correct the self. All these considerations suggest that chapter 38, if it indeed was supposed to be the work of Dong Zhongshu, is a forgery.

A final point supports that conclusion and speaks to the probable late date of chapter 38 and the closely related chapter 42. The subordination of the phase Earth to the phase Fire peculiar to these two chapters (and to the fragment about Fire and Earth that is currently numbered 43.2 but that may originally have been part of chapter 38 or of chapter 42) indicates that those chapters could not have been written by Dong Zhongshu or anyone in the early generations of his disciples. Rather, these chapters express a form of highly politicized Five-Phase rhetoric that dates them to the time of Wang Mang. In our introduction to group 6, "Five-Phase Principles," we write at length about the polemics associated with the Mutual Production Sequence of the Five Phases that took hold in elite circles toward the end of the Western Han. We note here only that Wang Mang used the Five-Phase theories to support his claim to be the legitimate heir to the Han. Wang Mang identified the ruling power of the Han dynasty as Fire and his own Xin dynasty with the power of Earth; just as Fire peacefully and naturally produces Earth as ashes, so did the Han give way to the Xin. Here we find the key to the emphasis on loyalty in chapters 38 and 42. It is completely consistent with the arguments that scholars loyal to Wang Mang may have used to demonstrate Wang Mang's own "great loyalty" to the ruling house of Liu and his filial devotion as the "son" and heir to the former Han rulers. These chapters therefore are best understood as potent political arguments cloaked in cosmological language that clearly postdate Dong Zhongshu.

Summing up, all the chapters in this group address, in one way or another, issues relating to virtues highly esteemed by Confucian scholars during the Western Han. But they represent a range of dates and authorship. Chapters 29 through 37 are likely to be the work of, or closely associated with, Dong Zhongshu and his circle; chapter 41 seems atypical of Dong's teachings and exegetical interests; and chapters 38 and 42 are both late in time and alien to Dong Zhongshu's tradition.

Book 8, Part 3

CHAPTER 29

Standards of Humaneness and Righteousness

Section 29.1

What the *Spring and Autumn* brings order to is others and the self. The means by which it brings order to others and the self is humaneness and righteousness. It uses humaneness to pacify others and righteousness to correct the self. For this reason, "humaneness" is a term that refers to others, and "righteousness" is a term that refers to the self. The *Spring and Autumn* speaks in these terms to differentiate them.

The relationships between humaneness and others and between righteousness and the self must be scrutinized thoroughly. Most people, however, do not scrutinize them, so they use "humaneness" to treat themselves generously while using "righteousness" to treat others coercively. When their applications are reversed [in that way] and their principles are transposed, [the two terms] will rarely fail to create confusion. Thus even though no one wants confusion, deep-seated confusion will predominate. On the whole, people are in the dark about the distinction between the self and others, so they fail to understand where humaneness and righteousness reside. For this reason, the *Spring and Autumn* creates standards[1] of humaneness and righteousness. The standard of humaneness lies in loving others, not in loving the self. The standard of righteousness lies in correcting the self, not in correcting others. If we do not correct ourselves,

1. No single English word captures the many connotations of the term *fa* 法 used here. The *fa* of humaneness and righteousness are at once standards of perfection, models of emulation, and methods for cultivating humaneness and righteousness.

even if we are capable of correcting others, [the *Spring and Autumn*] will not grant that this is righteousness. If others are not the recipients of our love, even though we are replete with self-love, [the *Spring and Autumn*] will not grant that this is humaneness.

In ancient times, Duke Ling of Jin murdered his chief cook so he could get [someone] more skilled [at preparing his] food and drink,[2] and he shot pellets at his ministers to indulge his whims. He certainly was filled with self-love, but [the *Spring and Autumn*] did not grant that he was someone who secured the skill of others because he did not love others. If he were disposed to love the common people, [extending] downward [even] to birds, beasts, and swarming insects, there would be nothing that he failed to love. But since he did not love others, how could he be called "humane"? "Humaneness" is the term that designates loving others.

[When Duke Xi pursued the Chu army to] Sui,[3] the [*Gongyang*] *Commentary* did not use any terms that would magnify the event [in praise.] Yet [when Duke Zhuang] pursued [the Rong tribe] on his own initiative [before they had invaded his state],[4] the [*Gongyang Commentary*] praised him for worrying about those who were far away. [The *Spring and Autumn*] does not praise those who move to save a situation when troops have already invaded. It praises those who make advance preparation before troops have arrived. It praises those who preemptively save others from calamities.

If one moves to rescue a situation early and preemptively, then calamities will have no source from which to arise, and the world will be free from them. To observe the movement of events and awaken preemptively to their initial stirrings so as to eradicate disorder and prevent calamity when it has not yet taken shape—such is the intent of the *Spring and Autumn* and the acme of brilliance. Short of the wisdom of a Yao or Shun, who understood the root of propriety, who could match this?

Therefore, preventing calamities preemptively is the true expression of brilliance. Duke [Zhuang] worried about those who were far away, so the *Spring and Autumn* praised him. It recorded in great detail its praise for the [duke's] intent to worry about those who were far away so that [everyone] between Heaven and Earth would celebrate his humaneness. Short of the virtue of the Three Kings, who [embodied] the quintessence of selecting worthies, who could equal this?

2. The chef is said to have spoiled a dish of bear's paws by cooking them improperly; the duke then impulsively had him executed.

3. See *Gongyang Commentary* at Duke Xi 5.26.2.

4. See *Gongyang Commentary* at Duke Zhuang 3.18.2.

Therefore, using wisdom to illuminate what lies in the future and humaneness to attend generously to the distant, is love: the more distant, the more worthy; the nearer, the less estimable. Thus

the love of the king extends to the four tribes;[5]
the love of the hegemon extends to the Lords of the Land;
the love of the secure [ruler] extends to those within his territory;
the love of the imperiled [ruler] extends to his dependents and aides;
and the love of the [ruler] bereft [of his state] extends only to his person.

Although one who is isolated might achieve the position of Son of Heaven or Lord of the Land, he will not be able to employ a single person from among the officials or the common people. This being the case, even if no one destroys him, he will self-destruct. Thus the *Spring and Autumn* does not state: "Liang was attacked." Rather, it states: "Liang perished."[6] For in fact, the love of the ruler extended only to his person. Thus I say: Humaneness means loving others; it does not consist of loving the self. This is the standard.

Righteousness does not refer to rectifying others but to rectifying the self. When there are chaotic times and depraved rulers, everyone aspires to rectify others. Yet how can this be called "righteousness"? In ancient times, King Ling of Chu punished the rebels of Chen and Cai,[7] and Duke Huan of Qi put a stop to the crimes of Yuan Taotu.[8] It was not that [these rulers] were unable to rectify others but that the *Spring and Autumn* did not praise them. It did not consider them to be righteous because they had not rectified their own persons yet simply hastened to benefit [themselves personally].[9]

Helü was able to rectify the difficulties between Chu and Cai, but the *Spring and Autumn* withheld the expression "righteous" because he had not rectified his own person.[10] Luzi was not able to rectify any of the Lords of the Land, yet the *Spring and Autumn* granted that he possessed righteousness because he had rectified his own person.[11] Thus I say: Righteousness lies in rectifying the self; it does not lie in rectifying others. This is the standard.

5. That is, the various non-Sinitic peoples who surrounded the Central States on all four sides.
6. Duke Xi 5.19.6.
7. Duke Zhao 10.8.9 and 10.11.3.
8. Duke Xi 5.4.1. In the "Treatise on the Five Phases" of the *Han shu*, under the entry that records an eclipse in the fifth year of Duke Xi, Dong Zhongshu explains the cause of the anomaly: "Zhongshu considered that Duke Huan of Qi was not upright within his own person, and yet abroad he captured a great officer of Chen" (不內自正而外執陳大夫) (Su Yu, *CQFLYZ* 253).
9. Following Lu Wenchao and Su Yu (*CQFLYZ* 253), we have emended the four characters *qu li er ye* 趨利而也 to *qu li er yi* 趨利而已 and relocated them here.
10. Duke Ding 11.4.13.
11. Duke Xuan 7.15.3.

Now if we lack [some trait] but look for it in others, or if we have [some trait] and yet criticize it in others, this is something that no one will find acceptable; it is contrary to principles. How could this be called righteousness? Righteousness means that appropriateness resides in the self. Only when appropriateness resides in the self can one describe it as "righteousness." Thus the term "righteousness" combines [the concept of] the self and [the concept of] appropriateness in a single word. From this perspective, the term "righteousness" refers to the self. Thus I say: To act and attain righteousness means getting it by yourself; to act and lose righteousness means losing it by yourself. People who are fond of righteousness are said to like themselves, whereas people who are not fond of righteousness are said to dislike themselves. Having considered [the issue] from this perspective, it is clear that righteousness refers to the self. Thus righteousness differs from humaneness.

Humaneness refers to what is directed away [from the self];
righteousness refers to what is directed toward [the self].
Humaneness magnifies what is distant;
righteousness magnifies what is near.
Love of others is called humaneness;
appropriateness of the self[12] is called righteousness.
Humaneness governs others;
righteousness governs the self.

Thus I say: "Humaneness [refers to] others; righteousness [refers to] the self." This is what is meant.

The Noble Man sought out the distinction between humaneness and righteousness to bring order to the interactions between others and the self. Only then could the Noble Man distinguish between the internal and the external and determine compliance and deviance. For this reason, the Noble Man brought order to the internal by reverting to proper principles to rectify the self, relying on propriety to encourage good fortune. He brought order to the external by extending his compassion to ever widening circles of activity, relying on generous regulations to embrace the multitudes. Confucius said to Ranzi: "Those who bring order to the people first enrich them and only afterward provide them with education."[13] [Confucius] spoke to Fanji and said: "Those who bring order to their persons first encounter difficulties and only afterward reap

12. Emending *yi zai wo* 義在我 to *yi zai wo* 宜在我, following Liu Shipei (Su Yu, *CQFLYZ* 254).
13. *Analects* 13.9.

[the benefits]."[14] I understand these passages to mean that with regard to bringing order to the self and bringing order to others, the sequence followed is not the same. An *Ode* declares:

"Give us drink. Give us food.
Teach us. Instruct us."[15]

To first provide them with food and drink and then educate and instruct them refers to bringing order to others. Another *Ode* exclaims:

"*Kan kan*, he carves the wheel spokes. . . .
Indeed that noble man
does not eat the food of idleness."[16]

First the task and only afterward the repast; this refers to bringing order to the self.

The *Spring and Autumn* censures the faults of those above and pities the hardships of those below. It does not call attention to minor transgressions external [to the ruler], but when they reside in [the ruler] himself, it records and condemns them. "Minor transgressions outside [the state of Lu] are not raised, but [ones that pertain to] the person [of the ruler] are recorded and condemned." Now in these six examples, [the *Spring and Autumn*] uses [the term] "humaneness" to [refer to] bringing order to others; it uses [the term] "righteousness" [to refer] to bringing order to the self. "Criticize the self generously and censure others sparingly."[17] This expresses it. Moreover, the *Analects* already has articulated this principle, but others have failed to consider it. It states: "The noble man assails evil in his own person but does not assail evil in others."[18] Not to assail others' evil: Is this not the most generous kind of humaneness? By oneself to assail [one's own] evil: Is this not the perfection of righteousness? How does this differ from the expression "humaneness constitutes others; righteousness constitutes the self"?

Thus to declare one's own evil is called fact;
to declare others' evil is called slander.
To search in the self is called generosity;
to search in others is called stinginess.
To censure the self for the sake of perfection is called clarity;
to censure others for the sake of perfection is called stupidity.

14. *Analects* 6.22.
15. *Odes* 230, verses 1–3.
16. *Odes* 112, verse 2. These lines are not continuous in the *Ode* itself.
17. *Analects* 15.15.
18. *Analects* 12.21.

Therefore,

to rely on the standards for ordering the self to order others means the ruler is not lenient;

to rely on the standards for ordering others to order the self means lacking the proper reverence in carrying out ritual propriety.

If the ruler is not reverent in applying propriety, he will compromise his conduct, and the people will not respect him.

If the ruler is not lenient, he will compromise his generosity, and the people will not feel affection for him.

If the people do not feel affection for him, they will not trust him.

If they do not respect him, they will not revere him.

If those above defy these two principles of governance and implement them in a biased way, those below will condemn them. Is it possible not to deliberate the proper place of humaneness and righteousness? Now,

if the eyes do not look, they will not see;

if the mind does not deliberate, it will not apprehend.

Though possessing the greatest delicacy in the world, if you do not taste it, you will not know its excellence.

Though possessing the utmost Way of the sages, if you do not discuss it, you will not understand its meaning. [29/38/17–29/39/28]

Book 8, Part 4

CHAPTER 30

The Necessity of [Being] Humane and Wise

Section 30.1

Nothing is more pressing than [being] humane;
nothing is more urgent than [being] wise.
To fail to be humane yet to possess courage, strength, talent, and ability is to be crazy yet brandish a sharp sword;
to fail to be wise yet to possess discrimination, cleverness, reserve, and eloquence is to be blind yet mount a fine steed.

Thus, those who are neither humane nor wise yet possess talent and ability will use that talent and ability to support their degenerate and unruly hearts and to sustain their dissolute and offensive conduct. This will amply suffice to increase their transgressions and intensify their offenses.

Their strength will suffice to conceal transgressions;
their eloquence will suffice to perpetrate deceits;
their cleverness will suffice to confuse the foolish;
their discrimination will suffice to gloss over mistakes;
their determination will suffice to avoid punishments;
their harshness will suffice to stave off criticisms.

This is not a matter of being without talent or ability but of using them unsuitably and applying them inappropriately.

Those with malign intentions must not be placed in positions of advantage;
those made of lesser stuff must not be given sharp implements.

What the *Analects* calls "not knowing others" likely refers to not knowing how to distinguish these different types of people.[1]

To be humane but unwise is to love but fail to discriminate;
to be wise but inhumane is to know but fail to act.

Thus,

humaneness is the means to love humankind;
wisdom is the means to rid them of harm.[2]

What does "humane" mean? It means that those who are humane earnestly and sincerely love others and are respectfully and harmoniously uncontentious; their likes and dislikes accord with the norms of human relationships. They are without

hurtful and malicious feelings,
hidden and evasive intentions,
envious and jealous dispositions,
impressionable and anxious desires,
dangerous and prejudicial endeavors,
perverse and disobedient conduct.

Consequently,

their hearts are expansive;
their aims are just;
their dispositions are harmonious;
their desires are regulated;
their endeavors are simple;
their conduct matches the Way.

Thus, those who are able to be like this—just, simple, harmonious, principled, and uncontentious—are called "humane."

What does "wise" mean? [It means] speaking in advance of [an event] and later having [that event] transpire. Now when people are inclined or disinclined toward a particular course of action, they generally rely on their wisdom to

1. *Analects* 20.3.
2. For a discussion of this passage, see the introduction to group 4. The question of human nature is explored in greater detail in chapter 36. It also arises in Dong's third memorial to Emperor Wu, where he defines the nature of a living creature as its "unadorned substance" (*zhipu zhi wei xing* 質僕之為性) (*HS* 56/2515; see appendix B).

evaluate it first; only then do they implement it. If they evaluate correctly, what they set out to do will be achieved.

Their actions will be suitable;
their affairs will be appropriate;
their conduct will be efficacious;
their name will be praised;
their persons will enjoy many benefits and will be free from calamities;
their good fortune will extend to their sons and grandsons;
and their virtue will cleave to the multitudes.

Kings Tang and Wu were such people. But if people evaluate incorrectly, what they set out to do will not be achieved.

Their actions will not be suitable;
their affairs will not be appropriate;
their conduct will not be efficacious;
their name will be insulted;
harm will come to them personally;
their sons will be cut off, and they will have no descendants.

Kings Jie and Djou were such people. Thus I say: "Nothing is more urgent than wisdom."

The wise discern calamity and fortune from a distance and know benefit and harm early on.

When things [first] stir, they know the course of their transformations;
when incidents [first] arise, they know their outcomes.

They observe beginnings and know their ends.

When they say something, no one dares refute it;
when they establish something, no one can disregard it;
when they undertake something, no one can disregard it.
From start to finish, there are no contradictions;
from beginning to end, everything has its category.
When thinking about something, they think it over;
when they implement it, no one can impugn it.

Their words are

few but sufficient,
concise but instructive,
simple but apposite,
sparing but complete.
When few, no one can add to them;
when numerous, no one can abridge them.

Their actions perfectly coincide with the norms of human relationships;
their words perfectly suit the task at hand.

Those who are like this are called "wise." [30/40/1–21]

Section 30.2[3]

Regarding their broad and general classification, when things in Heaven and Earth undergo abnormal alterations, they are called "bizarre events." Lesser anomalies are called "natural disasters."[4] Natural disasters always are the first to arrive, only then do bizarre events follow.

Natural disasters are Heaven's warnings;
bizarre events are Heaven's threats.

If Heaven warns [the ruler] and he does not acknowledge [these warnings], then Heaven will frighten him with threats. An *Ode* declares:

"We stand in fear of Heaven's threats."[5]

Very likely this [*Ode*] refers to this.

Concerning the source of natural disasters and bizarre events, ultimately they are caused by the faults of the ruling family of the state. When the faults of the ruling family of the state have just begun to become apparent, Heaven sends disaster and destruction to warn and inform them. If after being warned and informed, [the ruling family of the state] does not know to change, then Heaven manifests uncanny and bizarre events to startle and terrify them. If after being startled and terrified, [the ruling family of the state] still does not know to fear and dread [Heaven], only then will death and extinction overtake them. From this we can see that Heaven's will is humane and that Heaven does not desire to harm others.[6]

[Your servant] respectfully notes that natural disasters and bizarre events are the means to observe Heaven's will.[7] The will of Heaven desires some things and

3. Some commentators, like Zhong Zhaopeng (*CQFLJS* 469, note 22), believe that this section has migrated from chapter 15 and so relocate it to that chapter.

4. Natural disasters serve as serious warnings to a ruler but are less ominous than such bizarre events as the birth of cattle with monstrous deformities. This is because natural disasters, albeit destructive, remain within the natural order, whereas bizarre events are a perversion of that order.

5. *Odes* 272.

6. This section of chapter 30 resembles a passage from *HS* 56/2498–9, the "Biography of Dong Zhongshu" (see appendix B).

7. The expression *jin an* 謹按 (respectfully notes) occurs at the beginning of this sentence and marks this text as part of an official document, as this term was frequently used in memorials, petitions, and letters to the throne. It also occurs in Dong's memorial to Emperor Wu. For additional examples of this formulaic expression, see Enno Giele, *Imperial Decision-Making and Communication in Early China: A Study of Cai Yong's "Duduan"* (Wiesbaden: Harrassowitz, 2006), 70, 114, 127 140, 141, 142, 143, 167, 223, 240.

does not desire other things. As for Heaven desiring some things and not desiring other things,

> when people look inward to examine themselves, they will appropriately find confirmation in their hearts;
>
> when they look outward to observe affairs, they will appropriately find verification in their states.

Thus to discern Heaven's will, look to natural disasters and bizarre events. Fear them but do not despise them, and thereby consider that Heaven desires to rescue [the ruling family of the state] from error and save it from doing wrong. Therefore Heaven relies on them to warn [the ruling family].

According to the standards of the *Spring and Autumn*, when rulers altered the ancient ways or changed the norms and Heaven responded with natural disasters, these states were said to be "fortunate states." Confucius said: "Heaven brings fortune to those who fail to be good, by repeatedly criticizing their faults." Moreover, King Zhuang [of Chu] declared: "Heaven does not bring forth natural disasters; Earth does not bring forth prodigies." Then he prayed to the mountains and rivers, saying: "Is Heaven about to destroy me? It does not announce my faults or criticize my crimes." From this we see that Heaven's disasters arise in response to human transgressions, and bizarre events are clearly to be feared. This is how Heaven hopes to save [a ruler who has transgressed]. This alone is what the *Spring and Autumn* takes to be fortunate. This is why King Zhuang of Chu prayed to and beseeched Heaven. If a sagely ruler or a worthy lord still delights in receiving the reproofs of his loyal ministers, then how much more should they delight in receiving Heaven's warnings. [30/40/23–30/41/4]

Book 9, Part 1

CHAPTER 31

For Nurturing the Self, Nothing Is More Important Than Righteous Principles

Section 31.1

In giving birth to people, Heaven sustains them by giving birth to righteous principles[1] and material benefits:

Material benefits to nourish their bodies; righteous principles to nourish their hearts.

If the heart does not obtain righteous principles, it cannot be joyful;

if the body does not obtain material benefits, it cannot be secure.

Righteous principles are the heart's nourishment;

material benefits are the body's nourishment.

With regard to the body, nothing is more exalted than the heart.

With regard to nurture, nothing is more important than righteous principles.

The current title reads: "For Nurturing the Self, Emphasize Righteous Principles" 身之養重於義. We follow the *Huangshi richao* (*Daily Reflections of Master Huang*) in emending the title by supplying *mo* following *yang* and preceding *zhong* to yield the reading 身之養莫重於義: "For Nurturing the Self, Nothing Is More Important Than Righteous Principles." This conforms to a sentence that appears early in the essay: "With regard to the body, nothing is more exalted than the heart; with regard to nurture, nothing is more important than righteous principles" (體莫貴於心,養莫重於義). The commentator Hu Sijing aptly notes that this essay develops Mencius's idea that "those who nurture the lesser [aspects of their] person become petty men; those who develop the greater [aspects of their] person become great men" (養小體為小人,養大體為大人) (Su Yu, *CQFLYZ* 263).

1. The word *yi* 義 has no single English equivalent. We translate it as "righteous principles" because that is its primary meaning throughout the text, particularly in the early chapters in which the *Spring and Autumn* is identified with a number of righteous principles. Here we distinguish *yi* as the "righteous principles" derived from a proper reading of Confucius's esoteric message in the *Spring and Autumn*, from *li* 理,, the principles or inherent patterns in things generally conceived. *Yi* also carries the following broad range of meanings: righteousness, morality, moral principles, justice, a sense of what is right or appropriate, and duty or dutifulness.

For nourishing and sustaining people, righteous principles are more important than material benefits. How do we know this to be true? When people amply possess righteous principles but sorely lack material benefits, though poor and humble, they still may bring honor to their conduct, thereby cherishing their persons and rejoicing in life. Those like Yuan Hui, Ceng [San], and Min [Sun] exemplify this.[2] When people amply possess material benefits but utterly lack righteous principles, though exceedingly wealthy, they are insulted and despised. If their misdeeds are excessive, their misfortunes are serious. If they are not executed for their crimes, they [nevertheless] are struck down by an early death. They can neither rejoice in life nor live out their years. People who are punished with execution or die prematurely exemplify this.

Now those who possess righteous principles, although poor, are able to find joy in themselves, but those who utterly lack righteous principles, although wealthy, are not able to preserve themselves. I rely on such examples to substantiate the claim that for nourishing and sustaining the people, righteous principles are more important than material benefits and more beneficial than wealth. But [ordinary] people are incapable of knowing this, so they constantly get it backward; they all

forget righteous principles and lust after material benefits,
disregard inherent principles and follow evil ways,

thereby harming themselves and endangering their families. It is not that they personally intend to be disloyal [to their families] but that this is a matter their knowledge is incapable of understanding.

Now if you hold dates in one hand and gold in the other and show them to a child, a child will certainly choose the dates and not the gold. Similarly if you hold a catty of gold [in one hand] and ten thousand pearls [in the other] and show them to an uncouth savage, the uncouth savage will certainly choose the gold and not the pearls. Thus when it comes to people and things, it is easy to comprehend what is unimportant but difficult to grasp what is really important. Now given that material benefits are unimportant and righteous principles are important, is it not strange that people seek material benefits and disregard righteous principles? They certainly must be in the dark on this point. The sage strives to illuminate righteous principles and to shed light on that about which people are in the dark so that consequently people will not fall into the trap [of evil]. An *Ode* declares:

"Show me how to manifest the conduct of virtue."[3]

2. These men were disciples of Confucius.
3. *Odes* 288.

This expresses it.

The former kings manifested virtue in order to instruct the people. The people were joyful and sang of this virtue, giving rise to odes;[4] they were pleased and transformed it,[5] giving rise to customs. Thus

> without being commanded [to act], they took it upon themselves to act;
> without being prohibited [from acting], they took it upon themselves to stop.

They followed the intentions of their superiors, and it was not necessary to coerce them. It was as if their actions came naturally. Thus it is said: The sage is one who moves with Heaven and Earth and transforms with the four seasons. It amounts to nothing other than that. His manifestation of righteous principles is profound; therefore he can move others.

> Having moved others, he can transform them.
> Having transformed them, he can glorify their conduct.
> Having transformed and glorified their conduct, laws are not disobeyed.
> When laws are not disobeyed, punishments are not employed.
> When punishments are not employed, the virtue of Yao and Shun is achieved.

This is the Way of Great Governance. The former sages transmitted and received it in succession. Thus Confucius said: "Who can go out without using the door? Why, then, does no one follow the Way?"[6]

Now if you do not instruct by manifesting virtuous conduct, the people will be in the dark about righteous principles and will not be able to be enlightened; they will be confused about the Way and will not be able to disentangle [their confusion]. If you try to use great severity and cruelty to compel their rectitude, you will simply harm and injure Heaven's people and compromise your power to rule. Your positional advantage will not be realized. Zhongni [i.e., Confucius] said: "When a state possesses the Way, though it might implement punishments, there would be no one to punish. When a state does not possess the Way, though it might slaughter the people, it will not be possible to subdue them." This speaks about [the difference between] those who possess the Way and those who do not, and [between] those who instruct the people by manifesting virtuous conduct and those who do not. [31/41/10–27]

4. The reference here is to sung compositions broadly construed, not limited to the classic collection known as the *Classic of Odes*.

5. The meaning here is that people transformed the exalted sagely virtue into local customs appropriate to their needs.

6. *Analects* 6:17.

Book 9, Part 2

CHAPTER 32

An Official Response to the King of Jiangdu

The Great Officers of Yue Cannot Be Considered Humane

Section 32.1

A directive [from the king of Jiangdu] to the administrator [Dong Zhongshu] stated: [There was] Great Officer [Fan] Li, Great Officer [Wen] Zhong, Great Officer [Shi] Yong, Great Officer Gao, and Great Officer Che Cheng. The king of Yue, together with these five great officers, made a plan to attack [the state of] Wu. After they destroyed Wu, they [considered themselves] avenged for the humiliation they had suffered at Guiji. Ultimately, [the king of Yue] became a hegemon. Fan Li left the state; Wen Zhong died there. I, the Orphaned One,[1] [i.e., the king of Jiangdu] consider that both these two great officers were worthy men. Confucius said: "There were three humane men [during] the Yin [dynasty]."[2] Now considering the worthiness of the king of Yue and the capabilities of Fan Li and Wen Zhong, I, the Orphaned One, submit that there also were three humane men in Yue. What is your opinion? As Duke Huan [of Qi] handed off his questions to Guan Zhong, so do I, the Orphaned One, hand off mine to you.

In the title, emending *Jiaoxi* 膠西 to *Jiangdu* 江都, based on the introduction to this exchange preserved in *HS* 56/2523.

The exchange alluded to in the subtitle, with some editorial variations, also is preserved in Ban Gu's "Biography of Dong Zhongshu" in *HS* 56. See appendix B and *HS* 56/2523–24. For the biographical details of Dong's service in Jiangdu, see Sarah A. Queen, *From Chronicle to Canon: The Hermeneutics of the "Spring and Autumn" According to Tung Chung-shu* (Cambridge: Cambridge University Press, 1996), 25–26.

1. "The Orphaned One" is a conventional term of self-reference used by rulers. A ruler ascends the throne only after his father's death.
2. *Analects* 18.1.

Dong Zhongshu prostrated himself and bowed twice. He [then] said: Zhongshu's knowledge is petty and his learning superficial. They do not suffice to decide this. Nonetheless, when a king has a question for his servant, his servant does not dare but do his utmost to respond, for [such are the rules of] propriety.

Your servant Dong Zhongshu has heard that in earlier times, the duke of Lu asked Liuxia Hui: "I wish to attack Qi. What do you think?" Liuxia Hui responded: "That is not permissible." Liuxia Hui returned home with a worried expression and said: "I have heard that when [the ruler] is going to attack another state, he does not question those who are humane. Why were these questions directed at me?" [Liuxia Hui] was ashamed merely to have been asked about this. How much more would that be the case if it had come to the point of hatching a treacherous scheme to attack [the kingdom of] Wu?[3] The inappropriateness of such a scheme is clear. Looking at the question from this perspective, [the kingdom of] Yue fundamentally lacked even one humane man, much less three. A humane man is one who

> corrects his Way but does not calculate what benefits that will bring him;
> adheres to principles without hurrying after success.

[Devoted to non-action, though practices and customs are greatly transformed by him: such a man can be called both humane and sagely. The Three Kings[4] were of that sort.][5] The righteousness of the *Spring and Autumn* honors trustworthiness and censures deceit. To deceive others to achieve victory, even if successful, is not something a noble man would do. This is why even a five-foot-tall[6] [i.e., young] boy who [lodges in] the gate of [i.e., follows the teachings of] Confucius is ashamed to mention the Five Hegemons. In their use of deceit to achieve their accomplishments, they simply were engaging in treachery. Therefore, they are not worthy of being mentioned in the gate of the great Noble Man. Compared with other Lords of the Land, the Five Hegemons were worthy; compared with the sages,[7] how can they be considered worthy? They were but coarse stone to polished jade. Your servant Dong Zhongshu [again] prostrates himself and bows twice, [to acknowledge] having been heard.[8] [32/41/31–32/42/12]

3. By analogy, this shows the inappropriateness of Yue's scheme to attack Wu.
4. Various possibilities for the Three Kings are Yao, Shun, and Tang, or Tang, Wen, and Wu.
5. The text in brackets does not appear in the recension of this response preserved in *HS* 56/2523–24.
6. The Han "foot" (*chi* 尺) was about nine modern inches long, so a "five-foot-tall boy" would be three feet, eleven inches, tall in modern terms—a very young boy.
7. We accept Lau's emendation of *ren* 仁 to *sheng* 聖.
8. This claim is interesting, given the numerous references to and discussions of the hegemons in the first part of the text.

Book 9, Part 3

CHAPTER 33

Observing Virtue

Section 33.1

Heaven and Earth are the root of the myriad things, the place from which our first ancestors emerged. Vast and limitless, their Virtue is radiant and brilliant. Their days and years accumulate and increase, long enduring and boundless. Heaven sends forth the acme of brilliance and makes known the numerous categories [of things]. [Thus] nothing that is hidden fails to be illuminated. Earth sends forth the acme of darkness, [but] what the stars and sun make bright, it does not dare darken. The Way of ruler and minister, father and son, and husband and wife, derive from Heaven and Earth.

[Thus in accordance with] the Great Rites of Mourning [following the death of the ruler, his] loyal son does not dare assume [his father's] position for three years.[1] When he does assume his position,

he invariably acknowledges the late ruler;
he invariably acknowledges his late ancestors;

for he does not dare covet [this position of] utmost respect. All the numerous rites honored [in the *Spring and Autumn*] are listed under "the months";

the months are listed under "the seasons";
the seasons are listed under "the rulers";

1. This is the standard "three years' mourning" period (actually twenty-five months) (*Gongyang Commentary* at Duke Wen 6.9.1).

the rulers are listed under "Heaven."

Those rejected by Heaven, the world will not support.

Jie and Djou exemplify this [righteous principle of the *Spring and Autumn*].

The heirs of one whom the king has punished and cut off [from the line of succession] cannot be restored to his position. The heir apparent of Cai[2] and Feng Choufu[3] exemplify this [righteous principle of the *Spring and Autumn*].

The [king's] sons and grandsons are not permitted to continue relations with those whom the king and father have cut off [from the line of succession]. Duke Zhuang of Lu not being allowed to think of his mother[4] and Che of Wey dismissing his father's orders[5] exemplify this [righteous principle of the *Spring and Autumn*].

Therefore, if you receive the Mandate and all within the seas follow you, it will be like

the numerous stars turning to the North Star[6]

and flowing water returning to the sea.

How much more is this true of those who live amid Heaven and Earth and pattern themselves after the bearing and conduct of their founding ancestor and predecessors and who follow their Ultimate Virtue and appropriate their appearance, amassing a reputation of respect and honor. This is what the sage regards as honorable. [33/42/16–23]

---

2. Duke Xiang 9.30.2: "Summer. The fourth month. The heir apparent of Cai, Ban, assassinated his ruler, Gu." Duke Zhao 10.11.3: "Summer. The fourth month. *Dingsi*. The viscount of Chu, Jian, lured the marquis of Cai, Ban, and killed him at Chen." Duke Zhao 10.11.10: "Winter. The eleventh month. *Dingyou*. Chu troops annihilated Cai. They seized the heir apparent, You, and returned back with him. They offered him as a sacrificial victim."

3. Feng Choufu was a great officer of Qi. Duke Cheng 8.2.4: "The sixth month. *Guiyou*. Jisun Xingfu, Cang Sunxu, Shusun Jiaoru, and Gongsun Yingqi led troops to join with Xi Ke of Jin, Sun Liangfu of Wey, and Gongzi Shou of Cao to do battle with the marquis of Qi at An. The Qi troops were utterly defeated."

4. Duke Zhuang 3.1.2: "The third month. Our lady withdrew to Qi." *Gongyang*:

   > Why is the spouse not referred to as Lady Jiang? In order to degrade her. Why degrade her? She participated in the assassination of the duke. . . . To think of one's mother is something of which [the *Spring and Autumn*] approves. Why does [the *Spring and Autumn*] degrade her [in this context, in which Duke Zhuang is said to] think of his mother? [Under the circumstances, the *Spring and Autumn*] does not allow [the duke] to think of his mother. (Adapted from Göran Malmqvist, "Studies on the *Gongyang* and *Guliang* Commentaries," *Bulletin of the Museum of Far Eastern Antiquities* 43 [1971]: 117)

5. Wey Che was Duke Chu of Wey 衛初公, the grandson of Duke Ling of Wey and the son of Kuai Kui. Because Kuai Kui was violent and immoral, Duke Ling expelled him from the state and established his son, Che, as heir apparent in his place. When Duke Ling died, Kuai Kui hoped to return to Wey and inherit the throne, but Wey Che honored his grandfather's command and resisted his father's orders (Lai, *CQFLJZJY* 247–48, note 15). For these events, see Duke Ai 12.3.1.

6. See also *Analects* 2.1: The Master said, "He who exercises government by means of his virtue may be compared to the north polestar, which stays in one place while the numerous stars turn toward it."

Section 33.2

The Utmost Virtue of Tai Bo[7] equaled that of Heaven and Earth. On behalf of Tai Bo, the High Thearch abrogated the customary [rules of succession],[8] changed the surname [of the ruling clan], and took [Tai Bo] as a son. Yielding to his Utmost Virtue, those who lived within the seas embraced him and gave their allegiance to him. [Yet] Tai Bo three times declined [when offered the throne] and did not dare assume that position. Bo Yikao [i.e., the eldest son of King Wen] knew that the people's hearts were divided, so he declined the throne and withdrew. [His conduct] was in accord with spirit illumination.

When one who possesses Utmost Virtue receives the Mandate, the martial and brave and the eminent and lofty will return to him like the spokes of a wheel to its hub. The eminent among them will be ranked as dukes and marquises, and those below them will become ministers and great officers. How fine they will be, each ranked in accordance with his virtue!

Thus, although [the ruler of] Wu and Lu shared a surname, at the meeting of Zhongli, [the *Spring and Autumn*] did not permit [the ruler of] Wu to be ranked and designated as ruler.[9] [The ruler of] Wu was [designated] differently from [the ruler of] Lu, even though he met with him. This was because of his conduct, [which resembled that of] the Yi and Di [tribes].

At the battle of Jifu, [the ruler of] Wu was not permitted to perform the rites along with [the rulers of] the Central States.[10] But when it came to [the ruler of Wu's] conduct at Boju[11] and Huang Chi,[12] it changed [for the better] and reverted to the Way. Only then was he ranked and not set apart from the Central States.

At the meeting of Shaoling, the ruler of Lu was present, but [the *Spring and Autumn*] did not grant him the title of "presider," in order to avoid mentioning

7. *Analects* 8.1 states: "The Master said: 'Tai Bo may be said to have achieved Utmost Virtue. Three times he declined [when he was offered the throne].'" According to the traditional genealogy of the Zhou royal house, Tai Bo was the uncle of King Wen.
8. Normally the throne devolved to a son of the ruler's principal wife.
9. The ruler of Wu is unnamed and last in the following entry. Duke Cheng 8.15.13: "Winter. The eleventh month. Shusun Jiaoru met with Shi Shi of Jin, Gao Wujiu of Qi, Hua Yuan of Song, Sun Linfu of Wey, Gongzi Jiu of Zheng, and a man from Zhu who together met with Wu at Zhongli."
10. Duke Zhao 10.23.7: "*Wuchen*. Wu defeated Dun, Hu, Shen, Cai, Chen, and Xu troops at Jifu."
11. Duke Ding 11.4.16: "Winter. The eleventh month. *Gengwu*. The marquis of Cai, on behalf of the viscount of Wu, did battle with a man from Chu at Boju. The Chu troops were utterly defeated." Note that the Chu ruler is disparaged by being referred to simply as "a man."
12. Duke Ai 12.13.3: "Our lord met with the marquis of Jin and the viscount of Wu at Huang Chi."

Duke Huan of Qi.[13] When Duke Huan of Lu had occupied the throne for thirteen years, the states of Qi, Song, Wey, and Yan raised troops and headed eastward. The states of Ji, Zheng, and Lu joined forces to repel them. The *Spring and Autumn* recorded the day of the battle after [recording the meeting with Ji and Zheng] but because Lu was not permitted to set the date of the battle on its own authority, it avoided mentioning the lord of Ji and Duke Li of Zheng.[14] [33/42/23–33/43/2]

Section 33.3

In the standard terminology of the *Spring and Autumn,* the Yi and Di tribes are not permitted to perform the rites along with the rulers of the Central States.[15] At the battle of Bi, the Yi and Di tribes reverted to the Way, yet the *Spring and Autumn* did not permit [it to be mentioned] that they participated in the rites of the Central States. [In this case,] it was in order to avoid mentioning King Zhuang of Chu.[16]

The states of Xing and Wey shared the same surname as the state of Lu. When men of the Di [tribe] destroyed them, the *Spring and Autumn* employed the principle of concealment in order to avoid mentioning Duke Huan of Qi, [who was unable to save them].

It was appropriate that the *Spring and Autumn* was like this. When describing those who were both virtuous and related by blood, it would place first those who were related by blood. Thus with regard to the sons and grandsons of the Zhou,

> when ranking blood relations, King Wen was given first preference;
> when ranking the four seasons, spring was given first preference;
> when ranking the twelve months, the first month was given first preference;

13. Duke Xi 5.4.5: "Qiuwan of Chu came to make a covenant at the place where the troops were and made a covenant at Shaoling."
14. Duke Huan 2.13.2: "*Jisi.* We did battle with the marquis of Qi, the duke of Song, the marquis of Wey, and a man from Yan." Duke Huan 2.13.3: "The Qi troops, Song troops, Wey troops, and Yan troops were utterly defeated." Again, the *Spring and Autumn* disparages the Yan ruler by calling him simply "a man."
15. In other words, the *Spring and Autumn* uses different language to record the performance of rites by rulers of the Central States and rulers of peripheral "barbarian" states.
16. Duke Xuan 7.12.3: "Summer. The sixth month. *Yimao.* Sun Linfu of Jin led troops to do battle with the viscount of Chu at Bi." Duke Xuan 7.12.4: "The Jin troops were utterly defeated."

when ranking the virtuous, showing affection toward relatives was given first preference;

when ranking the twelve dukes of Lu, Dukes Ding and Ai were given first honors.

The state of Wey belonged to the Sinitic states,[17] but [in the *Spring and Autumn*'s account of] the meeting of Shan Dao, Wey alone was given precedence as a state of the interior, because the state of Wey shared a surname with us [i.e., with the dukes of Lu].[18]

The state of Wu belonged to the states of the Yi and Di tribes, but [in the *Spring and Autumn*'s account of] the meeting of Zha, Wu alone was given precedence as a state of the interior, because [its rulers] shared a surname with us [i.e., with the dukes of Lu].[19]

Annihilated states number more than fifty [in the *Spring and Autumn*], but precedence was given only to those that belonged to the Sinitic states.[20]

The states of both Lu and Jin were Sinitic states, but when criticizing those who took a double surname, their rulers alone were placed first and implicated.[21]

The earl of Cheng and the viscount of Xiang ought to have been cut off, but they alone are not mentioned by name, because they shared a surname with us and were our relatives.[22]

Those who fled abroad were numerous, but when brothers [born of the same mother as the ruler] left the state, the *Spring and Autumn* singled them out for great opprobrium because they forgot their mothers and turned their backs on their flesh and blood.[23]

---

17. Literally, "[states] that belong to the [land of] Xia"—that is, states in the tradition of the Three Dynasties of Xia, Shang, and Zhou.
18. Duke Xiang 9.5.4: "Zhongsun Mie and Sun Linfun of Wey met with Wu at Shan Dao."
19. Duke Xiang 9.10.1: "Spring. Our lord met with the marquis of Jin, the duke of Song, the marquis of Wey, the earl of Cao, the viscount of Ying, the viscount of Zhu, the viscount of Teng, the earl of Xu, the earl of Ji, the viscount of Lesser Zhu, and the heir apparent of Ji, Guang. They met at Zha."
20. Duke Yin 1.2.3: "Wuhai led troops to enter Ji." *Gongyang*:

    Who was this Wuhai? He was Ran Wuxiu. Why does [the *Spring and Autumn*] omit his surname? In order to degrade him. Why degrade him? In order to criticize this first instance of the annihilation [of a state]. Was this actually the first instance of annihilation? There were instances before this. Since this is so, why, then, is this noted as the first instance? In order to mark it as the first. Why should it be marked as the first? It was the first instance in [the period covered by the *Spring and Autumn*]. This was an instance of annihilation. Why does the text use the term *ru* 入 (to enter)? When the interior is involved, avoidance is made of great evils. (Adapted from Malmqvist, "Studies on the *Gongyang* and *Guliang* Commentaries," 73)

21. Duke Ding 11.6.8: "Jisun Si and Zhongsun Ji led troops to surround Yun."
22. Duke Wen 6.12.1; Duke Xi 5.20.2.
23. Duke Zhao 10.1.4; Duke Xiang 9.20.7.

Those who exterminated other [states] were not [always] cut off, but when the marquis of Wey exterminated [a state whose rulers] shared his surname, he alone was cut off, because he had slighted his founding ancestors and forgotten his predecessors.[24] [33/43/2–10]

Section 33.4

With relatives of equal status, [the *Spring and Autumn*] begins with those who are nearest. The establishment of sons of the principal wife is based on seniority.[25] The mother follows the son's nobility and is placed first.

On the day *jiaxu* [or] on the day *jichou*, Marquis Bao of Chen died.[26] [Confucius] recorded what he saw and did not discuss what was obscure to him. "Five falling stones in Song, six herons flying backward."[27]

What his ears heard he noted;
what his eyes observed he recorded.
Some things he perceived only slowly;
and some things he perceived in great detail.

In every case, he recorded events in the order in which he personally experienced them.

His descriptions of the propriety governing meetings, covenants, court visits, and friendly diplomatic visits also were like this.[28] [Thus] although the covenants entered into by the Lords of the Land were numerous, Yifu alone was said to have "gradually advanced."[29] When Duke Xi of Zheng approached

24. Duke Xi 5.25.1.
25. *Gongyang Commentary* at Duke Yin 1.1.1: "The establishment of sons of the principal wife is based on seniority and not on considerations of worth; the establishment of sons [other than sons of the principal wife] is based on nobility and not on seniority" (adapted from Malmqvist, "Studies on the *Gongyang* and *Guliang* Commentaries," 69).
26. *Jiaxu* and *jichou* are the eleventh and twenty-sixth days, respectively, of the sexagenary cycle. Duke Huan 2.5.1: "Why was his death recorded on two [alternative] days? [He became] mad. On the day *jiaxu* he disappeared; on the day *jichou* he was found dead. The Noble Man [Confucius] was in doubt about this and therefore recorded his death on two [alternative days]" (adapted from Malmqvist, "Studies on the *Gongyang* and *Guliang* Commentaries," 100).
27. Duke Xi 5.16.1. Also see chapter 6.1, note 12; chapters 35.3 and 36.1.
28. Supplying *meng* 盟 after *hui* 會, following Ling Shu (Lai, *CQFLJZJY* 250, note 55).
29. Duke Yin 1.1.2: "Our lord and Yifu of Zhu made a covenant at Mie." *Gongyang*:

> Who was this Yifu? The ruler of Zhu. Why is he referred to by his personal name? It was his style. Why does the [*Spring and Autumn*] refer to him by his style? In order to praise him. Why praise him? He is praised because he made a covenant with the duke. Those who made covenants with the duke were already numerous. Why, then, is praise indicated in this case alone? [The *Spring and Autumn*] based itself on that for which he could be praised and consequently praises him. Under what circumstances may he here be represented as worthy of praise? He gradually advanced. (Adapted from Malmqvist, "Studies on the *Gongyang* and *Guliang* Commentaries," 70)

from distant lands to meet with us but was murdered on his way, the *Spring and Autumn* extended his intentions and said that he "went to the meeting."[30] When the viscount of Luu broke with the [Yi and] Di tribes and turned toward [the Central States,] so that [his state] was destroyed, the *Spring and Autumn* referred to him as a "viscount" to commemorate his intentions.[31]

At the meetings of Baolai, Shouzai, Huang Chi,[32] Qianshi, and Cao, the marquis of Chen, and the earl of Zheng left us [i.e., Lu], and the *Spring and Autumn* stated that they "fled and returned home."[33]

When the earl of Zheng remained in his locale and did not come [to the meeting of Tao], the *Spring and Autumn* stated that he "requested an alliance."[34]

When the marquis of Chen was the last to arrive [at the meeting of Jianshi], the *Spring and Autumn* stated that he "went to the meeting."[35] When a man from Ju was suspicious of us, [the *Spring and Autumn*] censured him and referred to him as "a man."[36]

The Lords of the Land attended audiences with the Lu dukes on numerous occasions, but only the rulers of Teng and Pi were referred to as marquises.[37]

When the duke of Jou treated us disrespectfully, [the *Spring and Autumn*] stripped him of his rank and sobriquet.[38]

---

30. Duke Xiang 9.7.9: "Our lord met with the marquis of Jin, the duke of Song, the marquis of Chen, the marquis of Wey, the earl of Cao, the viscount of Qu, and the viscount of Zhu at Wey. The earl of Zheng, Kuanyuan, went to the meeting, but he had not yet seen the Lords of the Land."
31. In other words, following his intentions to serve the state of Lu, the *Spring and Autumn* ranks him as a "viscount" as if he held rank in the state of Lu.
32. Several editions, including the Lau concordance, have Chi 池 rather than Tao 洮, and we follow this emendation. The meeting at Huang Chi is noted at Duke Ai 12.13.3. For the various editions in which this character occurs, see Lai, *CQFLJZJY* 4998, note 16.
33. Duke Yin 1.8.7; Duke Xi 5.5.4; Duke Ai 12.13.3; Duke Xi 5.28.8; Duke Xiang 9.7.9.
34. Duke Xi 5.8.1: "Eighth year: Spring. The royal first month. Our Lord met with the [Zhou] king's man, the marquis of Qi, the duke of Song, the marquis of Wey, the baron of Xu, the earl of Cao, and the heir apparent of Chen, Kuan, to make a covenant at Tao. The earl of Zheng requested to make a covenant." *Gongyang*: "What is meant by the term 'requested to make a covenant'? It means that he remained in his locality yet requested to participate."
35. Duke Xi 5.28.8: "Fifth Month. *Guichou*. Our lord met with the marquis of Jin, the marquis of Qi, the duke of Song, the marquis of Cai, the earl of Zheng, the viscount of Wey, and the viscount of Ju to make a covenant at Jiantu. The marquis of Chen went to the meeting."
36. Duke Yin 1.8.7: "The ninth month. *Xinmao*. Our lord and a man from Ju made a covenant at Baolai." *Gongyang*: "Why did the duke make a covenant with a man of low rank? In using the term *ren* (a man) [the *Spring and Autumn*] follows [the rule for instances when there is] no doubt of the correct identification" (adapted from Malmqvist, "Studies on the *Gongyang* and *Guliang* Commentaries," 84).
37. Duke Yin 1.11.1.
38. Duke Huan 2.6.1. "Spring. The first month. He came." This refers to the duke of Jou 州公 mentioned in the preceding entry, where it states: "The duke of Jou went to Cao." *Gongyang*:

    What is meant by the expression "He came"? It is the same as saying: "That man came." To whom does this refer? It refers to the duke of Jou. Why does [the *Spring and Autumn*] use the phrase *shi lai* 寔來? In order to express disregard for him. Why so? He treated us in a disrespectful manner. (Adapted from Malmqvist, "Studies on the *Gongyang* and *Guliang* Commentaries," 101)

The states of Wu and Chu were the first to come on a friendly diplomatic mission, so [the *Spring and Autumn*] portrayed them as worthies.[39] [When Duke Yuan of Song died at] Quji and [Gongzi Shou of Cao participated in] the battle of An,[40] because they were the first to show concern for us, [*the Spring and Autumn*] portrayed them as deserving of veneration.[41] [33/43/10–17]

39. Duke Xiang 9.29.8: "The viscount of Wu sent Zha on a friendly diplomatic visit." *Gongyang*:

> In the case of the state of Wu, [the *Spring and Autumn*] does not normally record its ruler or its great officers. Why does it do so here? In order to represent Ji Zi [i.e., Ji Zha] as worthy. In what respect what he worthy? He yielded the position of ruler of his state. (Adapted from Malmqvist, "Studies on the *Gongyang* and *Guliang* Commentaries," 198)
>
> Duke Zhuang 3.23.4: "A man from Jing came on a friendly diplomatic visit." *Gongyang*: "Why was the term 'a man' used in reference to Jing? It was the first time Jing was able to [send someone on a] friendly diplomatic visit."

40. Duke Cheng 8.2.1: "The marquis of Qi attacked our northern border." Duke Cheng 8.2.3: "The sixth month. Jisun Hangfu, Cang Sunxu, Shusun Qiaoru, and Gongsun Yingqi led troops to join with Xi Ke of Jin, Sun Liangfu of Wey, and Gongzi Shou of Cao to do battle with the marquis of Qi at An. The Qi troops were utterly defeated." *Gongyang*: "Cao had no great officers. Why, then, does the text record Gongzi Shou as one such? He showed concern for the interior [i.e., the state of Lu]."

41. Duke Zhao 10.25.8.

Book 9, Part 4

CHAPTER 34

Serving the Root

Section 34.1

The rites
 connect Heaven and Earth;
 embody yin and yang;
 are punctilious about host and guest.
They put in order
 the honorable and dishonorable,
 the noble and base,
 and the great and small.
They differentiate
 the inner and outer,
 the distant and near,
 and the new and old.

They model themselves on what abounds in virtue; the myriad things model themselves on what is widespread, numerous, and long lasting. Of all things that exist in the heavens and [serve as] counterparts of Heaven, none is greater than the sun and the moon, for they extend the radiant brilliance of Heaven and Earth, and there is nothing they fail to illuminate. Among the stars, none is greater than the Great [Celestial] Mark Points;[1] the Constant

1. Duke Zhao 17.X: "There was a comet at the Great [Celestial] Mark Point." *Gongyang Commentary*:

 Why did the text state that the comet was at the Great [Celestial] Mark Point? It was because it appeared at the Great [Celestial] Mark Point. What is the Great [Celestial] Mark Point? It is the asterism Great Fire. Great Fire constitutes a Great [Celestial] Mark Point; Halberd constitutes a Great [Celestial] Mark Point; and Northern Asterism constitutes a Great [Celestial] Mark Point.

Stars of the Northern Dipper;[2] the Departmental Stars, which number three hundred;[3] the Guardian Stars, which number three thousand;[4] [and the constellations] Great Fire with its sixteen stars,[5] Halberd with its thirteen stars, Northern Dipper with its seven stars, and the constant stars[6] of the twenty-eight lunar lodges.[7] These asterisms resemble the milfoil plant with its hundred stalks that all derive from a single root, and the tortoise that lives for a thousand years and is treasured by the people. This is why all the Three Dynasties in succession used them to resolve doubts.

With regard to the things that receive the embodiment of Earth, none compares with the mountains.

Of people who obtain a preponderance of Heaven's bounty, none compares with the Son of Heaven, who has received Heaven's Mandate.

Moving down the ranks to dukes, marquises, earls, viscounts, and barons, the hearts of all within the Four Seas rest with the Son of Heaven, and all the people who reside within his borders are governed by his Lords of the Land.

An eclipse of the sun or moon announced impending misfortune for [the ruler] who failed to practice Heaven's Way. When a comet was seen in the east,[8] in the Great [Celestial] Mark Points,[9] or entering the Northern Dipper,[10] [or] when the constant stars were not visible,[11] [or] when earthquakes occurred; when Liang Mountain[12] and Sha Lu [Hill] collapsed,[13] when catastrophic fires visited Song, Wey, Chen, and Zheng,[14] and when kings, dukes, and great officers committed usurpation or regicide, the *Spring and Autumn* always recorded such events, considering them to be [portentous] bizarre events. [But the *Spring*

2. We treat the repeated four characters *Bei Dou chang xing* 北斗常星 as excrescent, following Su Yu and other commentators.
3. *Bu xing* 部星 appears to refer to the stars that correspond to the bureaucrats in the various departments of the Central Office of the Five Heavenly Offices.
4. *Wei xing* 衛星 appears to refer to the stars corresponding to the Northern, Southern, Eastern, and Western Offices.
5. We treat the character *er* 二 as excrescent, following Lai, *CQFLJZJY* 256, note 7.
6. We treat the characters *jiuci* 九辭 as interpolations, following Su Yu, and so omit them here (Lai, *CQFLJZJY* 256, note 9).
7. Following Su Yu (*CQFLYZ* 277), we treat the seven characters *duo zhe xiu er shi ba jiu* 多者宿二十八九 as garbled and erroneous and so omit them here.
8. Duke Ai 12.13.10: "A comet was seen in the east."
9. Duke Zhao 10.17.5: "There was a comet in Tai Chen."
10. Duke Wen 6.14.6: "There was a comet that entered the Northern Dipper."
11. Duke Zhuang 3.7.2: "The constant stars were not visible."
12. Duke Cheng 8.5.4: "Mount Liang collapsed."
13. Duke Xi 5.14.3: "[The hill at] Sha Lu collapsed."
14. Duke Zhao 10.18.2: "There were fires in Song, Wey, Chen and Cheng."

and Autumn] does not mention when the general sort of stars came out resplendently, or torrential rains, or when high or low ground uniformly subsided, or when the common people of a state died, and it does not resolve doubtful matters relating to plants.[15] [34/43/19–30]

Section 34.2

Only with the names of fields and cities does the *Spring and Autumn* generally disclose the name of the owner.[16] When a lord raised troops for battle, the *Spring and Autumn* does not refer to the statesman by name; when a statesmen led an army, the *Spring and Autumn* does not refer to the army; when a lord was injured or captured, the *Spring and Autumn* does not mention the defeat of the army.

Confucius said: "It is Heaven that is great, and it was Yao who modeled himself on it."[17] Those who model themselves on the Way of Heaven are great. Confucius also said: ""Lofty was he in his successes."[18] Here Confucius explains that Yao revered Heaven, so his achievements met with success.[19] [Dukes] Huan of Qi and Wen of Jin did not respect the House of Zhou and were incapable of becoming hegemons; sages of the Three Dynasties who did not model themselves on Heaven and Earth were incapable of becoming kings. Looking at things from this perspective, it is possible to understand the nobility of Heaven and Earth. [34/43/30–34/44/4]

Section 34.3

Deep-flowing water cannot be fathomed;
the utmost venerableness commands boundless respect.

For this reason, whatever Heaven bestows, even if catastrophic and harmful, [the *Spring and Autumn*] records and treats as important, for its respectful

15. The meaning of the last phrase in this sentence—*bu jue yi yu zhong cao mu ye* 不決疑於衆草木有也—is obscure.
16. Duke Zhao 10.1.6: "Names of localities and objects follow the language of the Central States. Names of cities and persons follow the language of the owner."
17. *Analects* 8.19; D. C. Lau, trans., *The Analects* (Harmondsworth: Penguin, 1979), 94.
18. *Analects* 8.19; Lau, *Analects*, 95.
19. Emending *da* 大 to *tian* 天, following Su Yu.

submission [to Heaven] knows no bounds. The temple of Yi Bo being struck by lightning is an example.[20]

Heaven sends no erroneous anomalies;
Earth shakes and moves to [convey] portents.

When there were those whom the Son of Heaven executed or [whose lineages he] cut off, and [when there were] armies that he defeated, even when they departed from the Way, the *Spring and Autumn* did not dare omit such events. It was that cautious. Thus, [the *Spring and Autumn*] records many instances of armies departing for battle but does not record them returning. But [the entry] "[Our] army and the army of Qi besieged Cheng. Cheng surrendered to the army of Qi"[21] is the sole instance [that mentions that the army] returned. In this instance, the lord's [action] was forced by a foreign state,[22] and he had no choice but to attack, so [the *Spring and Autumn*] spoke of the incident in a forthright matter. But when it came to other instances of raising troops, they all were considered to be the consequence of their lord's shortcoming. But if [the *Spring and Autumn*] stated that the army was not to blame, this would amount to a minister or son not accepting the blame for his lord's or his father's crime. There is no greater crime than being disloyal or unfilial. [34/44/4–8]

Section 34.4

What is most brilliant illuminates without limit;
what is most dark conceals without limit.

Now the *Spring and Autumn*, basing itself on the history of Lu, discusses the righteous principles of kingship.

It degrades in rank Dukes Yin and Huan, treating them as distant ancestors;
it venerates Dukes Ding and Ai, treating them as recently deceased parents.
[Their] utmost honor: how lofty!
[Their] utmost glory: how illustrious!
In the foundations and earthworks they erected,
in the enrichment and moistening [of croplands] they received,

their orderly perfection was without limit.

In former times they were constant in their regularities.
For ten years they [lived as] neighbors.

20. Duke Xi 5.15.10.
21. Duke Zhuang 3.8.2.
22. The ruler of Qi forced Duke Zhuang of Lu to besiege Cheng.

Recluses [dwelling] near their tumuli [experienced] lofty enlightenment. [34/44/8–11]

Section 34.5

The great states of Qi and Song met each other; the *Spring and Autumn* did not state that it was a "meeting."
The lord of an insignificant state carried out the funeral rites; [the *Spring and Autumn* not only] recorded it but [also] wrote about it in great detail.
[With regard to] the ruler of the distant Yi [tribe], [the *Spring and Autumn* treated him as being] in [the Central States], not outside [them].[23]
At this time, Lu [recognized] no borders. [Whenever] the Lords of the Land collaborated in a punitive expedition against Duke Ai, [the *Spring and Autumn* always] states "[a punitive expedition against] us."
Zhulou Biwo[24] and Zhulou Jue[25] were [referred to by the *Spring and Autumn* as] great officers. They were not close relations [of the dukes of Lu].[26] It was because of their proximity that [the *Spring and Autumn*] treated them in that fashion. That makes it evident.
Duke Yin and Huan were [treated by] the *Spring and Autumn* as people from former times. [But in the first year of Duke Yin,] when Yi, [the son of Duke Yin,] led troops and died, [the *Spring and Autumn*] did not record the date. [When Duke Huan and others held] a meeting at [Gui]ji, [the *Spring and Autumn*] stated that they "settled the chaos in Song."[27] [Because it happened

23. This is another reference to "Viscount Lu."
24. Duke Xiang, 9.23.3: "Summer. Biwo of Zhu came fleeing." *Gongyang*: "What is meant by Zhulou Biwo?"
25. Emending the text following Lu Wenchao, we treat *shuqi* 庶其 as excrescent and supply *jue* 決 after *Biwo* 鼻我 (Lai, *CQFLJZJY* 258, notes 52, 53).
26. Emending *wuyi qin* 無以親 to *wuqin* 無親, following Lu Wenchao (Lai, *CQFLJZJY* 258, note 54).
27. Duke Huan 2.2.3: "The third month. Our lord met with the marquis of Qi, the marquis of Chen, and the earl of Zheng in Ji, to settle the chaos in Song." *Gongyang*:

> [With regard to] the interior, avoidance is made of great evils. Why does [the *Spring and Autumn*] refer to it explicitly here? [It was a] distant event. [The author of the *Spring and Autumn* used] different expressions [for the three periods of the *Spring and Autumn*, which were distinguished as follows: the period] that he had witnessed personally, [the period] that he knew through direct oral tradition, and [the period] that he knew through the indirect transmission of tradition. [Duke] Yin also [belonged to the most] distant [period of the *Spring and Autumn*]. Why were [evil matters] avoided on account of [Duke] Yin? [Duke] Yin was worthy, but [Duke] Huan was mean. (Adapted from Göran Malmqvist, "Studies on the *Gongyang* and *Guliang* Commentaries," *Bulletin of the Museum of Far Eastern Antiquities* 43 [1971]: 96)

in a remote period,] Confucius treated it as distant. At the meeting of Huang Chi, [the *Spring and Autumn*] used vocabulary that indicated two earls.[28] Its terminology does not regard them as external states. [Because this occurred in a period closer in time to Confucius,] he treated it as close and [belonging to] the interior. [34/44/11–15]

28. Duke Ai 12.13.3: "Our lord had a meeting with the marquis of Jin and the viscount of Wu at Huang Chi." For the relevant *Gongyang* passage, see Lai, *CQFLJZJY* 358, note 57.

Book 10, Part 1

CHAPTER 35

Deeply Examine Names and Designations

Section 35.1

The starting point for bringing order to the world lies in carefully distinguishing what is important. The starting point for distinguishing what is important lies in deeply examining names and designations. Names are the chief markers of general principles. Record the meanings of these chief markers, and by scrutinizing what lies at the heart of the matter, right and wrong can become known, deviance and compliance will become self-evident, and their workings [will allow you to] penetrate Heaven and Earth.

> The rectification of right and wrong derives from deviance and compliance;
> the rectification of deviance and compliance derives from names and designations;
> and the rectification of names and designations derives from Heaven and Earth.

Heaven and Earth [themselves] create the general idea of names and designations. The ancient sages shouted in imitation[1] of Heaven and Earth, and this was called a "designation." They cried out to put their orders into practice, and this was called a "name."[2] "Name" means "to call out" and "to order"; "designation" means "to shout" and "to imitate." What is shouted in imitation of Heaven and Earth is a designation. What is called out and gives orders is a name. Although

1. The text here makes a play on the words *xiao* 謞 (shout) and *xiao* 效 (imitate).
2. Again, this is a play on the words *ming* 鳴 (cry out), *ming* 命 (orders), and *ming* 名 (name).

names and designations have different sounds, they share one root: both are things that are called out and penetrate Heaven's will.

> Heaven does not speak but [nevertheless] causes people to communicate its intentions;
> Heaven does not act but [nevertheless] causes people to realize its centrality.

Names are the means by which the sage communicates Heaven's intentions. They must be deeply scrutinized.

A ruler's receiving the Mandate [shows that he] is the one in whom Heaven's intention is placed. Thus those who are designated "Son of Heaven" should look upon Heaven as their father and serve Heaven by following the path of filial piety. Those designated "Lords of the Land" should carefully oversee what has been granted to them by the Son of Heaven. Those designated as "great men" should fortify their loyalty and trust, esteem propriety and righteousness, and cause their goodness to surpass the standards of the common man so that it is sufficient to transform them. A "functionary" [means "one who] performs a function."[3] The "common people" [means] "eyes closed in sleep."[4] A "functionary" does not attend to transforming others. He can be directed to perform his duties and obey his superiors and nothing more. The five designations [of functionaries] are intrinsically commendable, each with its respective duty. If there are departures from these designated duties, these departures can be given names.

Names aggregate to form distinctions; distinctions make up the whole. Names denominate distinctions and separations, departures and individuations. Designations generalize and summarize. Names are particular and distinguishable. "Distinguishable" refers to the peculiar qualities of things. "To generalize" means to point out the overall qualities of things. To scrutinize means to comprehensively distinguish things. To generalize means simply to point out what is most important.

[For example,] there is a single designation for presenting offerings to ghosts and spirits. That designation is *ji* [meaning "to sacrifice"]. But specific names are associated with the designation "sacrifice." In spring, it is called "Ci"; in summer, it is called "Yue"; in autumn, it is called "Shang"; and in winter, it is called "Peng."[5]

3. The text here makes a play on the words *shi* 士 (functionary) and *shi* 事 (function).
4. This is a play on the words *min* 民 (common people) and *mian* 瞑 (eyes closed in sleep). The significance of this is explained later in the chapter.
5. These four sacrifices are described in depth in chapter 68, "The Four [Seasonal] Sacrificial Rites."

There is a single designation for hunting animals. That designation is *tian* [meaning "to hunt"]. But distinct names are associated with the designation *tian*. In spring it is called "Miao"; in autumn, "Sou"; in winter "Shou"; and in summer, "Xian." None [of these terms] fails to hit the mark of Heaven's intent.

There is not a single thing that does not have a general designation. And there is not a single designation that does not have a specific name as [these examples] illustrate. For this reason, when each affair complies with its name and each name complies with Heaven, the realms of Heaven and humankind are united and become one.

In identity, their inherent principles interpenetrate one another;
In activity, they supplement one another;
in compliance, they endow one another.

Such is the Way of Virtue. An *Ode* declares:

"For crying aloud in this way,
I have reason, I have justification."[6]

This expresses it. [35/44/21–35/45/4]

Section 35.2

If we deeply examine the general meaning of the designation *wang* [meaning "king,"] [we will find in it] five associated meanings: *huang*, *fang*, *kuang*, *huang*, and *wang*.[7] Combining these five associated meanings produces the single word *wang*, meaning "king."

[The designation] *wang* [meaning "king"] denotes *huang* [meaning "august."]
[The designation] *wang* [meaning "king"] denotes *fang* [meaning "properly aligned."]
[The designation] *wang* [meaning "king"] denotes *kuang* [meaning "correct."]
[The designation] *wang* [meaning "king"] denotes *huang* [meaning "yellow."][8]
[The designation] *wang* [meaning "king"] denotes *wang* [meaning "to move toward."]

6. *Odes* 192, verse 6.
7. The terms used here are *wang* 王 (king), *huang* 皇 (august), *fang* 方 (properly aligned), *kuang* 匡 (correct), *huang* 黃 (yellow), and *wang* 往 (to move toward). In early Chinese, all these words rhyme. Moreover, three of the five contain the character element *wang* 王, and one other (*fang*) closely resembles *wang* in early Han orthography.
8. In Five-Phase theory, the color yellow denotes the center and therefore is associated with the ruler.

Thus,

if the intentions of the king do not denote what is grand and exalted, then his Way cannot be upright and properly aligned.

If his Way cannot be upright and properly aligned, then his virtue cannot be correct and comprehensive.

If his virtue cannot be correct and comprehensive, then his ornaments cannot be yellow.

If his ornaments cannot be yellow, then the four corners of the empire cannot move toward him.

If the four corners of the empire cannot move toward him, he will not be complete in his kingship.

Thus it is said:

There is nothing Heaven does not cover;
there is nothing Earth does not support.
The winds carry forth his orders and make singular his awesomeness;
the rains pour forth his bounty and make equitable his virtue.

Such are the techniques of the king.

If we deeply examine the general meaning of the designation *jun* [meaning "lord,"] [we will find in it] five associated meanings: *yuan*, *yuan*, *quan*, *wen*, and *qun*.[9] Combining these five designations produces the single word *jun*, meaning "lord."

[The designation] *jun* [meaning "lord"] denotes *yuan* [meaning "origin."]
[The designation] *jun* [meaning "lord"] denotes *yuan* [meaning "source."]
[The designation] *jun* [meaning "lord"] denotes *quan* [meaning "expediency."]
[The designation] *jun* [meaning "lord"] denotes *wen* [meaning "genial."]
[The designation] *jun* [meaning "lord"] denotes *qun* [meaning "the multitude."]

Thus,

if the intentions of the lord do not match up to the origin, his actions will lack a foundation.

If his actions lack a foundation, his undertakings will not succeed.

If his undertakings do not succeed, he will not be comparable to the source.

If he is not comparable to the source, he will abandon personal responsibility [for his undertakings].

If he abandons personal responsibility [for his undertakings], his transformation [of the people] cannot be realized.

9. The terms given here are *jun* 君 (lord), *yuan* 元 (origin), *yuan* 原 (source), *quan* 權 (expediency), *wen* 溫 (genial), and *qun* 群 (the multitude). Again, in early Chinese, these words rhyme, giving force to this argument.

If his transformation [of the people] cannot be realized, he will use expedient measures to adapt [to circumstances].
If he uses expedient measures to adapt [to circumstances], he will depart from the appropriateness of centrality and suitability.
If he departs from the appropriateness of centrality and suitability, his Way will not be just, and his virtue will not be kindly.
If his Way is not just and his virtue is not kindly, the people will not feel close or secure.
If the people do not feel close or secure, they will disperse and lose their cohesion.
If the people disperse and lose their cohesion, [he] will not be complete in his lordship. [35/45/6–18]

Section 35.3

Names are born of authenticity. If [a name] is not authentic, it cannot be regarded as an [appropriate] name. Names are the means by which the sage authenticates things. Names are the means to verbalize authentically. Therefore, when something becomes the brunt of numerous criticisms for being obscure, if in each case you revert to what is authentically so, what was obscure will become obvious.

If you wish to distinguish the crooked from the straight, nothing compares to stretching out the marking cord;[10]
if you wish to distinguish what is so from what is not, nothing compares to its name.

Names discriminate what is so from what is not so, just as the marking cord discriminates the crooked from the straight. If you investigate names and their corresponding realities and observe whether they depart from or coincide with one another, the true facts of "so" and "not so" cannot be misrepresented.

The present age is confused about nature,[11] and those who discuss it diverge in their opinions. Why do they not simply return to the name "nature" itself? Doesn't the name "nature" denote "what is inborn"? If the spontaneous qualities

10. The "marking cord" (*sheng* 繩) is a device consisting of a hollow box containing ink-soaked fibrous material, a string arranged to run through the ink box and be inked by it, and a reel or another device to control the string. It is used to mark a straight line (for example, to indicate where to cut a plank or stone). Han texts often used this as a metaphor for correctness.

11. "Nature" here is *xing* 性, meaning "the qualities intrinsic to a person, creature, or thing," and here is punned with *sheng* 生, "what is inborn." ("Nature" here does not imply "the natural world.")

that one possesses at birth are called "nature," then "nature" is the basic substance. If we search for the basic substance of "nature" in the name "good," is it capable of hitting the mark? Since it is not capable of hitting the mark, then why do you still say that the basic substance is good? The term "nature" cannot be separated from the basic substance. If it is separated from the basic substance so much as a hair's width, it already will have ceased to be the "nature." One must not fail to examine this.

The *Spring and Autumn* examines the inherent principles of things to rectify their names. It names things according to what is authentically so without erring so much as the tip of an autumn hair.[12] Hence, when naming "falling stones," it mentions the number five last, and when naming "herons flying backward," it mentions the number six first.[13] The sage was this meticulous in rectifying names. "The noble person is never careless in his speech."[14] The phrasing of the "five stones" and "six herons" exemplifies this.

What restrains[15] the various evils within and does not allow them to find expression without is the mind. Therefore as a name, "mind" is associated with "to restrain." If human beings were endowed with *qi* that was free from depravities, what would the mind need to restrain? Now if I use the name "mind" to apprehend the true character of human beings, then I must conclude that the truth about human beings is that they possess both greed and humaneness. The *qi* of humaneness and greed coexist in the self.[16]

> The name "self" derives from "Heaven."
> Heaven has its dual manifestation of yin and yang;
> the self also has its dual nature of greed and humaneness.
> Heaven [imposes] prohibitions pertaining to yin and yang;
> the self [observes] restraints pertaining to emotions and desires.

In this respect, it is identical to the Way of Heaven. Therefore, the motions of yin are not permitted to interfere with spring and summer, and the darkness of the moon's disk is regularly overwhelmed by the brilliance of the sun, whether completely or partially. If Heaven restricts yin in this way, how can a person fail to reduce his desires and restrain his emotions in response to Heaven? What Heaven restricts is also restricted in the self. Therefore I say that the self

12. A hair of the winter undercoat of animals is very small and fine when it first begins to emerge from the skin; hence "the tip of an autumn hair" became a cliché in classical Chinese denoting anything extremely small.
13. Duke Xi 5.16.1; chapter 6.1, note 12. The same portents are alluded to in section 35.3 and chapter 36.1.
14. *Analects* 13.1.
15. *Ren* 栣 (to restrain).
16. *Shen* 身 ("body" or, by extension, "the self").

resembles Heaven. But to restrict what Heaven restricts is not to restrict Heaven. One must understand that if the Heaven-bestowed nature is not supplemented by education, it ultimately cannot be restrained.

If we examine [the principle that] what is authentically so makes names, [then if we look at] the time before education [has been accomplished], how can we hastily say that "the nature" is like this? Thus, the nature is comparable to a rice plant, as goodness is comparable to a rice kernel. A rice kernel emerges from a rice plant, but a rice plant cannot be considered entirely the same as a rice kernel. Likewise, goodness emerges from the nature, but the nature cannot be considered entirely the same as goodness. Goodness and a rice kernel are things that human beings extend from Heaven and bring to completion beyond Heaven's sphere. They do not lie within the sphere of what Heaven does. What Heaven does arrives at a certain point and stops. What lies within this sphere is called the Heaven-bestowed nature. What lies beyond this sphere is called human endeavor. [Human] endeavor is external to the nature, but the nature cannot fail to complete itself in virtue.

The designation "common people" is derived from [the designation] "eyes closed in sleep." If the nature is inherently good, why would the term "eyes closed in sleep" be used to designate the "common people"? The reason the common people are discussed [in this way] is because without support and assistance, they will sink into depravity and become dissolute. How can this be [called] good? Nature resembles the eyes. In sleep, the eyes are closed and there is darkness. Only after awaking does one see. Before awaking, we can say that one possesses the basic substance for seeing, but we cannot say that a person sees. Now it is the nature of the myriad commoners to possess a basic substance that has not yet awakened, just like a sleeping person who has not yet awakened. It is only after undergoing education that [the basic substance] becomes good. When they have not yet awakened, we can say that they possess the basic substance [to become good], but we cannot yet say that they are good. It is roughly comparable to the eyes being closed in sleep and awakening. If we carefully examine this with a calm mind, the point becomes evident. The nature resembles closed eyes that have not yet awakened. This is what Heaven has done. Imitating what Heaven has done, a designation is made. Thus we refer to it as "common people." And the term "common people" certainly resembles [the term] "eyes closed in sleep."[17]

17. This is a pun, as explained in note 4.

If we follow names and designations to plumb their inherent principles, we will apprehend them. This is how the rectification of names and designations proceeds in Heaven and Earth. What Heaven and Earth give birth to are designated "the nature" and "the emotions." The nature and the emotions are mutually conferred, constitutive of a single sleeping person. The emotions also are [part of] the nature. If you claim that the nature is inherently good, how will you account for the emotions? Therefore, the sage [Confucius] never referred to the nature as good because it would have violated the [meaning of the] name. A person has a nature and emotions just as Heaven has yin and yang. To speak of one's basic substance without mentioning one's emotions is like speaking of Heaven's yang without mentioning its yin. Such empty assessments will never be accepted.

The word "nature" does not refer to the highest or the lowest but to the nature of the average person. It resembles a silk cocoon or an egg:

An egg awaits incubation to become a chicken;
a silk cocoon awaits unwinding to become silk;
and the nature awaits education to become good.

This is called "authenticating [what is given] by Heaven."

Heaven provides the common people with a nature that possesses the basic substance [to become good] but that is not yet capable of being good. Consequently, it establishes a king on their behalf to make it good. Such is Heaven's intention. The people receive from Heaven a nature that is not yet capable of being good, and they humbly receive from the king the education that will complete their nature. The king supports Heaven's intention and considers it his responsibility to complete the people's nature. Now those who investigate the true character of the basic substance and claim that the people's nature is inherently good negate Heaven's intention and disregard the king's duty. If the nature of the myriad common people were inherently good, what responsibilities would the king shoulder when receiving Heaven's Mandate? To establish an erroneous name and consequently abandon one's solemn responsibility and violate the great Mandate is not to use words in an exemplary way.

According to the terminology of the *Spring and Autumn*, when an internal affair depends on something external, it discusses the affair from the external perspective. Now since the nature of the myriad commoners depends on external education before it can become good, goodness corresponds to education and does not correspond to the nature. If you equate it with the nature, many difficulties will arise, and you will miss the essence of the term. "We can rely on ourselves to succeed in our endeavors without the worthies and sages"—the highly respected people of our time mistakenly propagate such a theory, but that is not the *Spring and Autumn*'s technique for employing terminology. The Noble Man avoided language that has no standards and theories that have no proof. How could one consider using them? [35/45/20–35/46/20]

Section 35.4

[Suppose] someone says, "[Human] nature contains the sprouts of goodness, and the heart contains the basic substance of goodness. How can they fail to be good?"

[I] would say in response, "This is not so. A cocoon contains [potential] silk, but a cocoon is not silk. An egg contains a [potential] chicken, but an egg is not a chicken. These analogies being true, what doubt can there be?"

Heaven gives birth to human beings in accordance with a grand norm,[18] so those who discuss nature should not differ in their opinions. Yet some claim that nature is inherently good,[19] and others claim that it is not yet good. This is because they intend different meanings when they use the word "good."

[Human] nature contains the sprouts of goodness. Children[20] love their fathers and mothers so are better than birds and beasts. In this sense, [their nature] is called good. This is Mencius's notion of goodness.

Only those who follow the Three Bonds and the Six Skeins[21] comprehend the underlying principles of the Eight Starting Points,[22] practice loyalty and faithfulness, love widely, broaden their generosity, and cherish ritual propriety may be called good. This is the sage's [i.e., Confucius's] notion of goodness. Therefore

18. Emending *liu jing* 六經 to *da jing* 大經, following Su Yu, *CQFLYZ* 303.
19. Emending *ye* 也 to *yi* 已, following Su Yu (*CQFLYZ* 303), based on the numerous prior instances of the phrase *yi shan* 已善 in opposition to *wei shan* 未善.
20. Emending *dong* 動 (to move) to *tong* 童 (child), following Su Yu, *CQFLYZ* 303. The emendation is based on *Mencius* 7A.15:

> What a man is able to do without having to learn it is what he can truly do; what he knows without having to reflect on it is what he truly knows. There are no young children who do not know loving their parents, and none of them when they grow up will not know respecting their elder brothers. Loving one's parents is benevolence; respecting one's elders is righteousness. What is left to be done is simply the extension of these to the whole Empire. (D. C. Lau, trans., *The Book of Mencius* [Harmondsworth: Penguin, 1970], 184)

21. Emending *wuji* 五紀 (five skeins) to *liuji* 六紀 (six skeins). *Wuji* is very unusual and likely to be erroneous (Su Yu, *CQFLYZ* 303–4). Chapter 29 of the *Bohutong* (Sangang liuji 三綱六紀 [The Three Bonds and Six Skeins]) explains that the Three Bonds refer to the relationship between ruler and subject, father and son, and husband and wife, whereas the Six Skeins denote a (male) person's relationships with his paternal uncles, older and younger brothers, other kinsmen, mother's brothers, teachers and elders, and friends.
22. The "Eight Starting Points" cannot be clearly identified.

Confucius said, "A good man is not mine to see. If I saw a man who possessed constancy, I would be content."[23] From this point of view, we see that what the sage called goodness is not easy to match. What he termed goodness was not a matter of being better than birds and beasts. If simply activating the sprouts of goodness that make one better than birds and beasts may be called goodness, why did Confucius maintain that he never saw such a person? Even being much better than birds and beasts does not suffice to be called good, just as being more intelligent than herbs and trees does not suffice to be called wise. The nature of the myriad commoners is better than that of birds and beasts, but it cannot be called good.

The word "goodness"[24] derives from the sage [Confucius]. What the sage decreed, the world must consider correct. One corrects the time of dawn and dusk by observing the North Star; one corrects suspicions and doubts by observing the sage. The sage held that in an age in which there was no true king and in which the common people were not educated, no one could match [true] goodness. This is precisely how difficult it is to match this goodness. Thus, to claim that the nature of the myriad commoners can match this goodness without exception is simply wrong. Thus, if evaluated in comparison with the nature of birds and beasts, the nature of the multitudinous commoners is good. But if evaluated in comparison with the goodness of the Way of humankind, the nature of the common people generally will fall short of it. Thus I will accept that the nature of the myriad commoners is better than that of birds and beasts, but I will not accept that the nature of the myriad commoners is what the sage called good. My evaluation of what the word "nature" designates differs from that of Mencius. Mencius looked below to find the substance [of goodness] in comparison with what birds and beasts do and therefore said that nature is inherently good. I look above to find the substance [of goodness] in comparison with what the sages did, and therefore I say that nature is not yet good. Such a standard of goodness surpasses nature, just as the sages surpass this standard of goodness. The *Spring and Autumn* attaches importance to the origins of things. Therefore it is meticulous with regard to the correct use of names. If the name is not traced to its beginning, how can you say whether the nature is not yet good or inherently good? [35/46/20–35/47/5]

23. *Analects* 7.26.
24. Emending *zhi* 知 (knowledge or wisdom) to *shan* 善 (goodness), following Su Yu, *CQFLYZ* 304.

Book 10, Part 2

CHAPTER 36

Substantiating Human Nature

Section 36.1

Confucius said: "When names are not correct, speech will not comply."[1] Now if you state that the nature is already good [at birth], is that not like saying that [people] should not be educated and should follow their natural tendencies? And also that it does not comply with the Way of Governance? Moreover, the term ["nature"] refers to the substance [of the nature] and the substance refers to [the nature] unadorned.[2]

When [the unadorned nature] has not been educated, how can it suddenly become good? Goodness resembles the rice kernel, and nature resembles the rice plant.

> Although the rice plant begets the rice kernel, the rice plant still cannot be called a rice kernel.
>
> Although the nature begets goodness, the nature still cannot be called good.

1. *Analects* 13.3:

   When names are not correct, what is said will not sound reasonable; when what is said does not sound reasonable, affairs will not culminate in success; when affairs do not culminate in success, rites and music will not flourish; when rites and music do not flourish, punishments will not fit the crimes; when punishments do not fit the crimes, commoners will not know where to put hand and foot. Thus, when the gentleman names something the name is sure to be usable in speech, and when he says something this is sure to be practicable. The thing about the gentleman is that he is anything but casual where speech is concerned. (D. C. Lau, trans., *The Analects* [Harmondsworth: Penguin, 1979], 118)

2. 且名者性之實.實者性之質也. Note that the *Shuowen* defines the character *zhi* 質 in terms of the character *pu* 樸, meaning "simple, unadorned, or unembellished" (*Shuowen jiezi zhu* 281).

The rice kernel and goodness are what people inherit from Heaven and complete externally. They do not lie inside the sphere of what Heaven does internally. What Heaven does arrives at a certain point and stops.

What lies inside [this sphere] is called Heavenly.
What lies outside [this sphere] is called kingly education.

Kingly education lies outside the nature, but the nature must not fail to follow it. Therefore I say that the nature possesses the stuff of goodness but that it still cannot be called good. Who would dare argue differently, given that its inner substance is like this?[3]

What Heaven does stops with the cocoon, hemp, and rice plant.

Using hemp to make cloth,
the cocoon to make silk,
the rice plant to make food,
and the nature to make goodness—

these all are things that the sage inherits from Heaven and advances. They are not things that the unadorned substance of the emotions and the nature is able to achieve. Thus they cannot be called "the nature."

One corrects [the time of] dawn and dusk by observing the North Star;
one corrects suspicions and doubts by observing the sage.

Whatever was named by the sage [Confucius], the world must consider correct. Delving into the words of the sage, we find that originally he said nothing about nature being good, but there is [the statement] "A good man is not mine to see."[4] If the myriad commoners were by nature already capable of being good, how is it possible [that Confucius] could not observe any good people? Looking into the meaning of Confucius's statement, he must have considered that goodness is very difficult to match. Yet Mencius held that by their very nature, all the myriad commoners were capable of matching it. He was mistaken.

The nature of the sagely person cannot be termed [human] nature in general, just as the nature of [people who are] "mere utensils" cannot be termed [human] nature in general.[5] The term ["human] nature" [denotes] the nature of the average person. The nature of the average person is like a cocoon or egg.

An egg depends on being incubated for twenty days before it can become a chicken;
a cocoon depends on being unwound in boiling water before it can become silk thread;

3. Emending *mei* 美 to *yi* 異, following Lu Wenchao (Su Yu, *CQFLYZ* 311).
4. *Analects* 7.26. The same passage is cited in chapter 35.
5. For the expression *dou shao zhi ren* 斗筲之人, indicating people who are, like *dou* and *shao* vessels, mere utensils limited to containing what is placed into them, see *Analects* 13.20.

and [human] nature depends on being gradually steeped in education and admonition before it can become good.

Goodness is the outcome of education and admonition. It is not something that can be achieved by the unadorned basic substance. Hence one cannot say it is the nature.

[When referring to] the nature, one should be aware of what it denotes. It is what arises without being dependent on anything else. It is what people themselves possess at birth. What goodness naturally comes from is education and admonition alone; it is not from the nature. Hence,

a rice kernel emanates from the rice plant, but the rice plant cannot be called a rice kernel;

jade emanates from an unpolished stone, but an unpolished stone cannot be called jade;

and goodness emanates from the nature, but the nature cannot be called good.

If you consider this so for the vast majority of comparable things in the world, but not so for the nature, how can [this principle] not penetrate [all] categories [alike]? The nature of an egg is still not able to make a chicken; the nature of a cocoon is not still not able to make silk; the nature of hemp is still not able to make cloth; and the nature of the rice plant is still not able to make a rice kernel.

The *Spring and Autumn* distinguishes the inner principles of things to rectify their names. A name and its referent each must accord with what is true.

True to its meaning,
true to its character,

only then is it considered a [correct] name. Hence, when designating "falling stones [in Song]," the *Spring and Autumn* mentioned the number five last, and when designating [herons] flying backward, it mentioned the number six first.[6] For this reflected the true situation. In the sage's speech, there was simply no place for casual remarks.[7]

[Human] nature refers to the Heaven-endowed substance in its unadorned state. Goodness refers to the transformation produced by kingly education. Without the basic substance, kingly education could not transform, and without kingly education, the unadorned substance could not become good. If you rely on the basic substance to apply the name "goodness" to human nature,[8] the name will not be correct; consequently, it will not be accepted. [36/47/9–28]

6. Duke Xi 5.16.1. See also chapter 6.1, note 12, and chapters 33.4 and 35.3.
7. A slight variation on the concluding remark of *Analects* 13.3: *sheng ren* 聖人 substituted for *junzi* 君子.
8. Emending *zhi er bu yi shan xing* 質而不以善性 to *zhi er ming yi shan xing* 質而明以善性, following Liu Shipei (Lai, *CQFLJZJY* 275, note 8).

Book 10, Part 3

CHAPTER 37

The Lords of the Land

Section 37.1

To give birth to, to nurture, to nourish, and to grow;
to bring to completion and bring to life anew;
to bring to the end and begin again:
These endeavors are the means by which [Heaven] benefits and sustains the people without cease. Even though Heaven does not speak, Heaven's intention to provide sufficiently for the people may be observed. The sages of antiquity observed Heaven's intention to provide bountifully for the people, so when they faced south and ruled the world, they invariably brought universal benefit to their people. On account of
things that were distant that their eyes could not see [and]
things that were muffled that their ears could not hear,
beyond one thousand *li*[1] they parceled out the land and allocated its people to create states and establish overlords to enable the Son of Heaven
to observe what he could not see [personally, and]
perceive what he could not hear.
With a court audience, the overlords were summoned and questioned. This is why the expression "Lords of the Land" resembles the expression "numerous servants."[2] [37/48/3–6]

1. A territory one thousand *li* square, centered on the capital city, was supposedly reserved as the royal domain.
2. This plays on the aural and graphical similarity of *zhu hou* 諸侯 (Lords of the Land) and *zhu hou* 諸候 (numerous servants).

Book 10, Part 5

CHAPTER 38

An Official Response Regarding the Five Phases

Section 38.1

King Xian of Hejian questioned Master Dong of Wencheng, saying: "*The Classic of Filial Piety* states: 'Filial piety is Heaven's Warp and Earth's Righteousness.'[1] What does this mean?"

[Master Dong] responded: "Heaven has Five Phases. [They are] Wood, Fire, Earth, Metal, and Water.

Wood gives birth to Fire;
Fire gives birth to Earth;
Earth gives birth to Metal;
Metal gives birth to Water.

1. The "Three Talents" (San Cai 三才) chapter of the *Classic of Filial Piety*. The full text reads:

Zengzi said, "How profound is the greatness of filial piety!" The Master replied, "Yes, filial piety defines the constancy of Heaven, the righteousness of Earth, and the conduct of Humankind. Heaven and Earth invariably pursue a constant course and people imitate them. Imitate the brilliant luminaries of Heaven and accord with the advantages afforded by Earth, and you will accord with the world. Consequently your teachings, without being severe, will be successful, and your government, without being rigorous, will secure perfect order. The former kings saw how education could transform the people. Thus they gave first priority to extending love widely, and none of the people neglected their parents. They proclaimed virtue and righteousness, and the people roused themselves to practice them. They went before them with reverence and yielding courtesy, and the people did not contend. They directed them with rites and music, and the people were harmonious and well disposed. They showed them what they loved and what they despised, and the people understood their prohibitions. An *Ode* proclaims:

How awe inspiring you are, Grand-Master Yin!
The people all look up to you." (*Odes* 191, verse 1)

Water makes winter;
Metal makes autumn;
Earth makes midsummer;
Fire makes summer;
Wood makes spring.
Spring governs birth;
summer governs growth;
midsummer governs nourishment;
autumn governs harvesting;
winter governs storing away.

Storing away is what winter achieves.

Thus,

what fathers engender, their sons cultivate;
what fathers cultivate, their sons nurture;
what fathers nurture, their sons perfect.

What fathers accomplish is received and accepted by their sons, who continue to carry it forth. They do not dare fail to carry things forth in accordance with their father's intentions, doing their utmost to constitute the Human Way. Thus, the Five Phases exemplify the five [forms of] human conduct. From this perspective, we see that the father conferring and the son receiving is the Way of Heaven. Thus it is said: 'Filial piety is Heaven's Warp.' This is what the statement means."

The king responded: "Excellent! Now that I have heard your explanation regarding the phrase 'Heaven's Warp,' I would like to ask about the phrase 'Earth's righteousness.' "

[Dong] responded: "Earth sends forth clouds to produce rain and arouses *qi* to generate wind. Wind and rain are generated by Earth, but Earth does not dare claim merit for such achievements. Rather, it confers such merit on Heaven. Thus they are named as if they emanated from Heaven's *qi* and so are called Heavenly winds and Heavenly rains. No one refers to them as earthly winds or earthly rains. Diligence and hard work rest with Earth, while the reputation for such achievements resides with Heaven. If not for those who have achieved the pinnacle of righteousness, who could practice such a thing?

"Thus subordinates serve superiors, just as Earth serves Heaven. Such conduct may be called 'great loyalty.' Earth is the son of Fire. Of the Five Phases, none is more noble than Earth. Earth's relation to the four seasons is that there is nothing that it commands, and it does not share in the accomplishments and reputation of Fire.[2]

Wood designates spring;
Fire designates summer;
Metal designates autumn,
Water designates winter.

The righteousness of the loyal minister and the actions of the filial son are derived from Earth. Earth is the most noble of the Five Phases,[3] and nothing can augment its righteousness, [just as]

of the five tones, none is more noble than *gong*;
of the five flavors, none is more noble than sweetness;
of the five colors, none is more luxuriant than yellow.

This is what is meant [by the expression] 'filial piety is Earth's righteousness.'"
The king responded: "Excellent!" [38/48/10–22]

Section 38.2[4]

"Clothing and comportment are the means to delight the eyes;
Sonorous words and apt responses are the means to delight the ears;
Likes and dislikes, rejecting and following, are the means to delight the mind."

Therefore the noble man's

clothing is suitable and his comportment is reverent, so he delights the eyes.
His words are principled and his responses are agreeable, so he delights the ears.

His love of humaneness is ample and his hatred of shallowness is far reaching. He follows good men and avoids evil ones, so his mind is happy.[5]

2. See the nearly identical claim in chapter 44.2.
3. Chapter 42 also argues that the phase Earth enjoys special status, claiming that it is "the ruler of the Five Phases."
4. Lau includes the following passage in this location but notes that Su Yu, following Zhang Huiyan, suggests moving the eighty-five characters of this passage to the end of chapter 41, where other interpretive passages relating to the *Classic of Filial Piety* are collected.
5. Chapter 1 of *Hanshi waizhuan* and the "Xiuwen" chapter of the *Shuoyuan* contain rough parallels. The *Hanshi waizhuan* and *Shuoyuan* parallel each end with a quotation from the *Odes*.

Thus it is said:

> His conduct and thought can bring joy;
> his comportment and deportment are worthy of contemplation.[6]

This expresses it. [38/48/24–27]

6. This couplet is quoted from the chapter "Sheng Zhi" 聖治 (Sagely Government) in the *Classic of Filial Piety*, in which a somewhat longer version of this passage reads:

   When [the ruler] does not reside with goodness but always with what is injurious to virtue, though he achieves [his will], the noble man does not give him his approval. It is not so with the noble man. His speech and thought can be spoken; his conduct and thought can bring joy; his virtue and righteousness can be honored; his creations and initiatives can be imitated; his comportment and deportment are worthy of contemplation; his movements in advancing or retiring all are according to the proper rule. In this way, he elicits respect, and his advances and retreats can be measured; and in this manner he cleaves to the people. This is why his people both revere and love him, imitate and become like him. Thus he is able to perfect his virtuous instruction and implement governmental commands.

Book 10, Part 5

CHAPTER 39

[Title and text are no longer extant.]

Book 10, Part 6

CHAPTER 40

[Title and text are no longer extant.]

Book 11, Part 1

CHAPTER 41

Heaven, the Maker of Humankind

Section 41.1

What gives birth cannot make human beings. The maker of human beings is Heaven. The humanness of human beings is rooted in Heaven. Heaven is also the supreme ancestor of human beings. This is why human beings are elevated to be categorized with Heaven.

> Humans' form and frame transform with Heaven's regularities and so become complete;
> humans' blood and *qi* transform with Heaven's will and so become humane;
> humans' virtue and conduct transform with Heaven's principles and so become righteous.
> Humans' likes and dislikes transform with Heaven's warmth and coolness;
> humans' happiness and anger transform with Heaven's heat and cold;
> humans' endowment and life span transform with Heaven's four seasons.

Human beings at birth possess the responses of happiness, anger, sorrow, and joy, which [correspond to] the categories of spring, autumn, winter, and summer:

> Happiness is spring's response;
> anger is autumn's response;
> joy is summer's response;
> sorrow is winter's response.

Heaven's correlates lie in human beings. The emotions and nature of human beings include what is received from Heaven. Thus I say: "Endowment" is the designation for what is received from Heaven.

For those who govern humankind, no Way is clearer than husbanding [the aspects of] the self that [derive from] Heaven, just as they issue forth from Heaven. In causing them to issue forth, [the ruler] must, with the utmost effort, respond to Heaven's sending forth the four seasons. Thus there is nothing to be added to the governance of Yao and Shun. "One might be enriched or impoverished; one might be allowed to live or be executed; but one cannot be made to rebel."[1] Thus it is said:

> "If not [in accordance with] the Way, do not act;
> if not [in accordance with] the standard, do not speak."[2]

This expresses it. [41/49/11–18]

Section 41.2

A tradition states:

> the Son of Heaven alone receives orders from Heaven;
> the world receives orders from the Son of Heaven;
> a single state receives orders from its lord.

> If the lord's orders comply [with Heaven], the people will have cause to comply with his orders;
> if the lord's orders defy [Heaven], the people will have cause to disobey his orders.[3]

Thus it is said: "When the One Man enjoys blessings, the myriad commoners will rely on it."[4]

1. The "Biaoji" (Record of Uprightness) chapter of the *Liji* states: "The Master said: In serving one's lord, one can be ennobled or disgraced, one can be enriched or impoverished, one can be allowed to live or be executed, but one cannot be made to rebel" (James Legge, trans., *Li Chi: Book of Rites*, ed. Ch'u Chai and Winberg Chai [New Hyde Park, N.Y.: University Books, 1967], 2:346–47). Rebellion is apparently treated here as an individual act of will, not something that can be imposed on a person externally.
2. The "Ministers and Great Officers" (Qing Dafu) chapter of the *Classic of Filial Piety*.
3. This quotation also appears in the "Biaoji" chapter of the *Liji*. See Legge, *Li Chi*, 2:347.
4. This citation appears in chapter 2, "The Son of Heaven" (天子), in the *Classic of Filial Piety*. There the citation is used to demonstrate that if the Son of Heaven exhibits the utmost love and reverence toward his parents, he will be instrumental in teaching his people the virtue of filial piety:

   The Master said, "He who loves his parents will not dare (incur the risk of) being despised by others; he who reveres his parents will not dare (incur the risk of) being condemned by others. When the love and reverence (of the Son of Heaven) is fully developed in serving his parents, his virtuous instruction will affect all his people and will circulate to all [who reside] within the four seas. Verily, this is the filial piety of the Son of Heaven." *The Punishments of the (Marquis of) Fu* states: "When the One Man enjoys blessings, the myriad commoners will rely on it."

This expresses it.[5]

A tradition states: "Government has three starting points:

If father and son are not affectionate, extend their love and kindness;

if the great officials are not harmonious, make reverent and compliant their propriety;

if the hundred surnames[6] are not peaceful, strengthen their filial piety and brotherly love."

"Filial piety" and "brotherly love" are the means to pacify the hundred surnames. "To strengthen" means to compel them to practice filial piety and brotherly love so that they will personally be transformed.

The regularities of Heaven and Earth cannot rely solely on cold and heat to complete the year. There must be spring, summer, autumn, and winter.

The Way of the Sage cannot rely solely on harshness and compulsion to perfect his governance. There must be transformation and education.

Thus it is said:

"To give first priority to loving without discrimination is to teach them by means of humaneness.

That a noble man does not value things that are difficult to obtain is to teach them by means of righteousness.

That even the Son of Heaven must have something that he reveres is to teach them by means of filial submission.

To invariably place others first is to teach them by means of brotherly love."

Thus severity and coercion are not sufficient by themselves to be relied on, but is not the merit of transformative education great indeed?

A tradition states:

"Heaven engenders them;
Earth completes them;
the sage educates them."

---

5. Su Yu (*CQFLYZ* 319) believes that this passage belongs in chapter 70, "Following Orders," in which the topic of the passage is discussed more generally. But we believe that it belongs here for reasons stated in the introduction and that chapter 70 simply develops the ideas expressed here in greater detail.

6. The text implicitly makes a distinction here between *min* 民, the common people, and *bai xing* 百姓, the class of people who have surnames (and recognized ancestors) and thus participate in the ritual life of the state.

The lord is the people's mind;
The people are the lord's body.
In what the mind finds pleasing, the body invariably finds security;
what the lord finds pleasing, the people invariably follow.

Thus the lord and the people revere filial piety and fraternity and are fond of propriety and righteousness. They value humaneness and uprightness and scorn wealth and profit. When the utmost effort is devoted by superiors to implementing parental kindness, the people perceive it; [thus] happiness is engendered among those below. Thus it is stated: "The former kings saw that education could transform the people."[7] This expresses it. [41/49/20–41/50/2]

7. See the passage from the "Three Talents" (San cai 三才) chapter of the *Classic of Filial Piety*, quoted in chapter 38, note 1.

Book 11, Part 2

CHAPTER 42

The Meaning of the Five Phases

Section 42.1

Heaven has Five Phases:
    The first is Wood;
    the second is Fire;
    the third is Earth;
    the fourth is Metal;
    the fifth is Water.
    Wood is the beginning of the Five Phases;
    Water is the end of the Five Phases;
    Earth is the middle of the Five Phases.
This is their Heavenly endowed sequence.
    Wood gives birth to Fire;
    Fire gives birth to Earth;
    Earth gives birth to Metal;
    Metal gives birth to Water;
    Water gives birth to Wood.
This is their father–son relationship.
        Wood dwells on the left;
        Metal dwells on the right;
        Fire dwells in the front;

Water dwells in the rear;
Earth dwells in the center.[1]

This is their father–son sequence. [The phases] receive from and distribute to one another. Therefore,

Wood receives Water;
Fire receives Wood;
Earth receives Fire;
Metal receives Earth;
Water receives Metal.
Those that confer all are fathers;
those that receive all are sons.

To constantly rely on the father to direct the son is the Way of Heaven. Therefore,

once Wood is born, Fire nurtures it;
once Metal dies, Water buries it.
Fire delights in Wood and nourishes it with yang;
Water overcomes Metal and mourns it with yin;

Earth's [managing the] affairs of Fire fully expresses its loyalty. Thus the Five Phases [exemplify] the conduct of the filial son and loyal minister. The "Five Phases" as an expression resembles the "five [modes of virtuous] conduct," does it not?[2] That is the very reason why they are so named. The sage understands this and therefore increases his love and diminishes his sternness. He generously nourishes the living and cautiously bids farewell to the dead and so follows the regulations of Heaven. If sons,

in nourishing their fathers, can resemble Fire delighting in Wood;
in bidding their fathers farewell in death, can resemble Water overcoming Metal;
in serving their lords, can resemble Earth revering Heaven,

they may be called "men of [virtuous] conduct."

With the operations of the Five Phases, each follows its [respective] sequence;
with the offices of the Five Phases, each fulfills its [respective] capabilities.

Thus

Wood dwells in the eastern quarter and governs the *qi* of spring;
Fire dwells in the southern quarter and governs the *qi* of summer;

1. The perspective outlined here is that of a south-facing Son of Heaven: Wood (east) is on his left; Metal (west) is on his right; Fire (south) is in front of him; Water (north) is behind him; and Earth is the throne he is sitting on.
2. This is a play on two pronunciations of the character 行: *wuxing*[2] 五行 (five phases) and *wuxing*[4] 五行 (five [modes of] conduct).

Metal dwells in the western quarter and governs the *qi* of autumn;
Water dwells in the northern quarter and governs the *qi* of winter.

Hence

Wood governs giving birth, while Metal governs killing;
Fire governs heat, while Water governs cold.

[Thus]

to employ others by invariably relying on their respective sequence;
to appoint others by invariably relying on their respective ability,

is Heaven's regularity.

Earth dwells in the center and is called the Heavenly Fructifier.[3] Earth serves as the arms and legs of Heaven. Its potency is variegated and beautiful and cannot be named in accordance with the activities of any single season. Thus, there are Five Phases but four seasons, because Earth encompasses them all.[4] Even though Metal, Wood, Water, and Fire each have their respective functions, if they did not rely on Earth, their respective functions could not be established, just as sourness, saltiness, acridness, and bitterness could not perfect their respective tastes if they did not rely on sweetness.

Sweetness is the root of the Five Tastes;
Earth is ruler of the Five Phases.

Earth's ruling the Five Phases is analogous to the Five Tastes that would not achieve perfection without the sweetness they possess. Therefore among the actions of the sage, nothing is nobler than loyalty. This refers to the virtue of Earth.

The greatest human office is not named for the particular function it performs.
The minister exemplifies this.
The greatest Heavenly office is not named for what it gives birth to.
Earth exemplifies this. [42/50/6–21]

3. In using this expression, we follow "The Correspondence of Man and the Numerical Categories of Heaven," in *A Source Book in Chinese Philosophy*, trans. and comp. Wing-Tsit Chan (Princeton, N.J.: Princeton University Press, 1965), 280.

4. Note that chapter 42 seeks to harmonize the "Five Phases" with "four seasons" by arguing that "Earth" stands above the other phases, acting as the force that coordinates the other four. In contrast, in chapter 38, the "Five Phases" are harmonized with the "four seasons" by the addition of a midsummer season, which is identified with Earth. In the first case, the strategy is to subtract one phase to achieve a one-to-one correlation between seasons and phases. In the second, the strategy is to add one season to establish a one-to-one correlation between phases and seasons.

Group 5

Yin-Yang Principles

GROUP 5, "Yin-Yang Principles," contains fifteen thematically linked chapters that generally (though not exclusively) describe Heaven's Way in terms of yin-yang and four-seasons cosmology. The chapter titles vary in length from two to six characters, with three- and four-character titles predominating.

GROUP 5: YIN-YANG PRINCIPLES, CHAPTERS 43–57

43. 陽尊陰卑 *Yang zun yin bei* Yang Is Lofty, Yin Is Lowly
44. 王道通三 *Wang dao tong san* The Kingly Way Penetrates Three
45. 天容 *Tian rong* Heaven's Prosperity
46. 天辨在人 *Tian bian zai ren* The Heavenly Distinctions Lie in Humans
47. 陰陽位 *Yin yang wei* The Positions of Yin and Yang
48. 陰陽終始 *Yin yang zhong shi* Yin and Yang End and Begin [the Year]
49. 陰陽義 *Yin yang yi* The Meaning of Yin and Yang
50. 陰陽出入上下 *Yin yang chu ru shang xia* Yin and Yang Emerge, Withdraw, Ascend, and Descend
51. 天道無二 *Tian dao wu er* Heaven's Way Is Not Dualistic
52. 暖燠孰多 *Nuan ao shu duo* Heat or Cold, Which Predominates?
53. 基義 *Ji yi* Laying the Foundation of Righteousness

54. [Title and text are no longer extant]
55. 四時之副 *Si shi zhi fu* The Correlates of the Four Seasons
56. 人副天數 *Ren fu tian shu* Human Correlates of Heaven's Regularities
57. 同類相動 *Tong lei xiang dong* Things of the Same Kind Activate One Another

Many of the chapter titles refer specifically to cosmology (incorporating expressions such as "yin-yang," *tian dao* [the Way of Heaven], and *tian shu* [Heaven's regularities]), and all are linked by common content. The chapters propose cosmic cycles and patterns to be emulated by the ruler, prescribing his emotions, actions, and policies in accordance with the yin-yang characteristics of the seasons throughout the year.

Most of these chapters[1] adhere to an unusual cosmic model in which the power of yang is much stronger and more active than that of yin, and yang is cosmologically dominant for much more than half the year.[2] This cosmology is based on a decimal numerology derived from the ten Heavenly Stems, in which sets of ten, ten-day periods add up to artificial "seasons" of one hundred days each. Three such seasons allocate five-sixths of the year (five of six sexagenary day-cycles, for a total of three hundred days) to yang, and only one-sixth of the year (one sexagenary day-cycle) to yin. Yin and yang move around the horizon at an equal rate of speed and in opposite directions during the year, with yang moving clockwise and yin moving counterclockwise. Their positions at any given time are described by the directions correlated with the twelve Heavenly Branches. The two are together at the winter solstice (the first astronomical month, designated by the Earthly Branch *zi* and correlated with the north), in which yin is the dominant force and yang is hidden. Yang then moves clockwise to emerge in the northeast while yin moves counterclockwise to go into hiding in the northwest. Yang is dominant from month 3 (branch *yin*, east-northeast), and yin goes into hiding in month 11 (branch *xu*, west-northwest). Yang dominates the east (Wood, spring), south (Fire, summer), and west (Metal, autumn);

1. Especially chapters 43 through 53. As we note in our comments on specific chapters, chapters 55 through 57 describe the movements of yin and yang in accordance with a more conventional cosmological model.
2. The description of the movements of yin and yang in these chapters assumes an "emperor's-eye" view of the world, with south at the top of the page (or another visualization), north at the bottom, west to the right, and east to the left. See the opening lines of chapter 47:

   Yang *qi* first emerges in the northeast and moves toward the south to assume its [dominant] position. It then circles westward and withdraws in the north, where it stores itself away for repose. Yin *qi* first emerges in the southeast and moves toward the north, where it likewise assumes its [dominant] position. It then circles westward and withdraws in the south, where it hides itself away for rest. (*CQFL* 47/54/12–13)

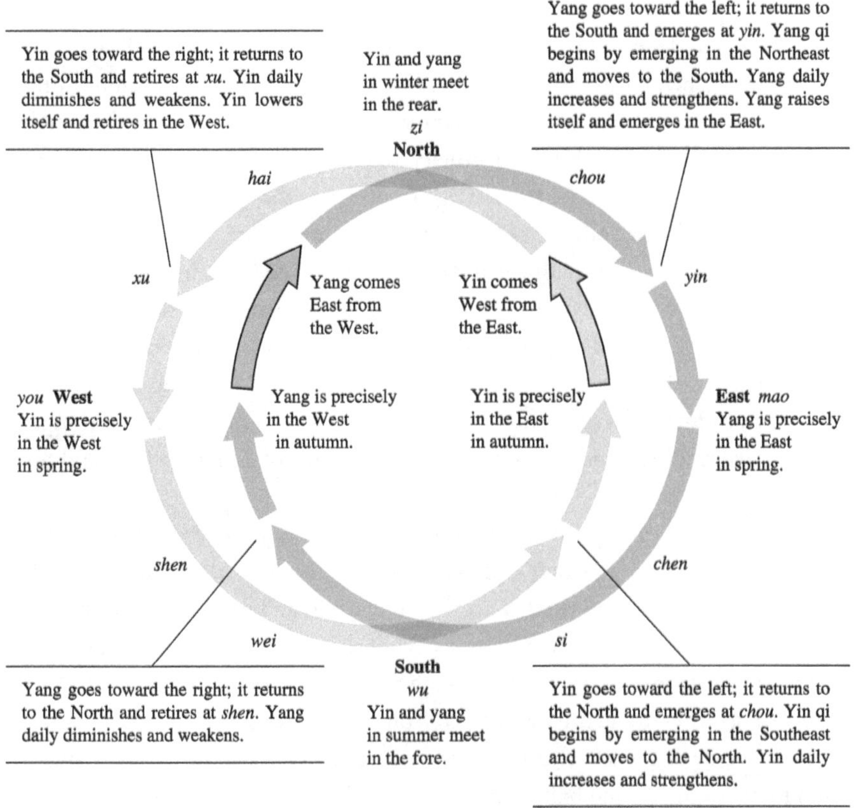

Motions of yin and yang as understood in the *Chunqiu fanlu*. (Redrawn from Fung Yu-lan, *A History of Chinese Philosophy*, vol. 2, *The Period of Classical Learning (From the Second Century* B.C. *to the Twentieth Century* A.D.*)*, trans. Derk Bodde [Princeton, N.J.: Princeton University Press, 1953], 28. Reproduced by permission of Princeton University Press)

yin plays no role in those directions/seasons. Yin and yang reach their maximum separation at the spring and autumn equinoxes. When yang is in the east, yin is hidden in the west; when yang is in the west, yin is hidden in the east. The two forces converge at the summer solstice (south, Fire), but yin is wholly hidden at that time and yang reaches its maximum force; yin is inactive when the phase Fire is active, as shown in the figure.

Despite some differences in the particulars of their cosmic schemes, most of the chapters in this group are based on this distinctive and otherwise unknown model and elaborate on the implications of its novel features. The chapters uniformly privilege the yang aspects of Heaven's Way over its yin counterparts. This strong preference for yang over yin is used in some chapters to justify and promote a general argument that in ruling the state, beneficence should predominate over punishment. These chapters seem to be aimed at mitigating such abuses of royal power as arbitrary cruelty and outright despotism. Other chapters use the yin-yang model to privilege the ruler as the wielder of yang power and therefore the embodiment of goodness, in contradistinction to his subordinates, who are identified with yin and evil. While linked by their yin-yang focus, these chapters were not necessarily written by the same person; their variability at the level of fine detail suggests multiple authors at work. At the same time, all these chapters share a yang-oriented ideological stance, indicating that even if they are products of several authors, they still are within the bounds of a single intellectual tradition and perhaps represent the views of a single master and his disciples.

The complex conception of the cycles of yin and yang envisioned in this group of chapters is strikingly different from the more usual scheme found in, for example, chapter 3 of the *Huainanzi*. There, yin and yang move around the horizon circle in tandem (on opposite sides of the circle but moving in the same direction) over the course of a year. Yang achieves accretion in the first half of the year, gaining in quantity and force from the winter solstice to the summer solstice, while at the same time yin undergoes recision, decreasing in quantity and force. In the second half of the year, it is the reverse: yang diminishes from the summer solstice to the winter solstice while yin increases. Yin and yang thus form a zero-sum pair, with the proportions of yin and yang shifting daily throughout the year but always adding up to a full complement of *qi*. This is the scheme envisioned in the familiar *taiji* 太極 diagram of yin and yang, showing two tadpole-like figures intertwined in a disk,[3] with yang and yin each dominating its half of the year. In contrast, in the scheme proposed in the *Chunqiu fanlu*, the cosmic system is almost totally dominated by yang.

The two most striking characteristics of these chapters of the *Chunqiu fanlu* are their unusual cosmological model and their strong preference for yang over yin. This cosmological stance is used to support a highly androcentric and patriarchal vision of society. To this extent, they all are at one extreme of yin-yang opinion. The opposite extreme is represented by the *Laozi*, which exhibits a

3. There is, however, no evidence for the *taiji* diagram itself until the Tang dynasty, many centuries later.

very strong preference for yin (and its embodiments, such as water and the valley spirit).[4] The middle ground is occupied by texts like the *Guanzi* (which contains Warring States material but may have been compiled in the early Han period) and the *Huainanzi* (139 B.C.E.), which tend to treat yin and yang in fairly neutral terms as complementary cosmic forces moving in tandem throughout the year. These texts show only a mild preference for yang (fructifying, growing, beneficent) over yin (ripening, harvesting, severe). It thus is interesting to see the *Chunqiu fanlu* employing cosmological arguments in support of patriarchy, hierarchy, and androcentrism.

All the chapters in group 5 incorporate the understanding, apparently ubiquitous and universally believed in early China, that yang governs the first half of the year—spring and summer—and that yin is at its height during the winter. But these chapters go beyond that common understanding to propose that yang also dominates autumn and, overall, plays by far the greater role in the annual cycle of seasons, with yin relegated to a small expanse of time and a wholly subordinate role.[5]

Many of these chapters comprise what must have been originally separate materials, as indicated by marked shifts in subject matter that cannot be explained by positing lacunae in continuous essays. Different editions of the text respond to these discontinuities with varying arrangements of the materials within individual chapters. As with earlier chapters, we follow D. C. Lau's edition, with frequent reference to Su Yu's editorial suggestions.

Description of Individual Chapters

Chapter 43, "Yang Is Lofty, Yin Is Lowly," has three sections and takes its title from the first of them. Section 43.1 emphatically privileges yang over yin and proposes an elaborate numerological scheme to support that notion. The sages of antiquity are said to have modeled themselves on "the great number of Heaven," which is identified here as the number ten. This chapter introduces the distinctive calendar in which ten periods of ten days each make up a sort of extended season (completely different from the natural seasons determined by

4. See, for example, *Laozi* 6, 8, 28, 61, 66, 78.
5. Fung Yu-lan gives an extensive analysis of yin and yang in the *Chunqiu fanlu*, in *A History of Chinese Philosophy*, vol. 2, *The Period of Classical Learning (From the Second Century B.C. to the Twentieth Century A.D.)*, trans. Derk Bodde (Princeton, N.J.: Princeton University Press, 1953), 7–31.

the solstices and equinoxes, which have an average length of ninety-one and five-sixteenth days), with ten months (three one-hundred-day "seasons") making up the yang portion of the year. The three hundred days of the yang portion of the year amount to five *ganzhi* sexagenary cycles as determined by paired (yang) Heavenly Stems and (yin) Earthly Branches. But the scheme presented here is described entirely as ten, ten-day "weeks," not sexagenary cycles. (The Earthly Branches play no role in this calendar except to designate the directions associated with the twelve months of the year.) In the annual calendar, yang is dominant for five-sixths of the year, and yin is relegated to a single sixty-day period (for cosmological purposes, the year is approximated as 360 days). Yin is discounted as a normal seasonal part of the year and treated almost as a taboo topic: "[Such] is the righteous principle of not being permitted to enumerate yin."[6] Yin is associated here not only (as usual) with darkness, quiescence, femaleness, and so on but explicitly with inferiority and evil. Thus, the text asserts, "[W]e observe how to honor yang and denigrate yin."[7]

In accordance with its annual cycle of three one-hundred-day periods, section 43.1 describes yang as determining the activities of the cosmos's other constituents as it makes its annual circuit of the horizon. As presented in this chapter, the movements of yin and yang do not specify, but also are not inconsistent with, the complex scheme just described and later elaborated in chapter 48. This model's separation of yin and yang provides the intellectual foundation for the emphasis found in this and the other chapters of the group on the movements and power of yang almost to the exclusion of the influence of yin.

The numerology of this chapter may be related to the stem-and-branch cycle as well as the "river chart" (*he tu* 河圖), an esoteric diagram believed to have emerged magically from the Yellow River.[8] The river chart, too, is based on the numerology of ten and serves to integrate yin and yang with the Mutual Production Sequence of the Five Phases. Whether or not the river chart plays any conceptual role in the cosmology of section 43.1, the text does hint at some esoteric calendrical lore: "Hence, when counting the days, do so according to the mornings and not the evenings; when counting the years, do so according to the yang [i.e., odd] and not the yin [i.e., even] years."[9] The denigration of yin is

6. *CQFL* 43/51/3.
7. *CQFL* 43/51/2.
8. John S. Major, "The Five Phases, Magic Squares, and Schematic Cosmography," in *Explorations in Early Chinese Cosmology*, ed. Henry Rosemont Jr., JAAR Thematic Studies, vol. 50, no. 2 (Chico, Calif.: Scholars Press, 1984), 133–66, esp. 149–52.
9. *CQFL* 43/51/2–3.

then traced to the *Spring and Autumn* with some brief illustrations. The essay concludes with some of the most extreme androcentric claims of the entire text, insisting that yang dominates yin invariably and in all respects.

Section 43.2 straightforwardly correlates the seasons (and their attendant qualities of warming and cooling) with the emotions of happiness, anger, sorrow, and joy. Note, though, that these emotional states are different from those (love, hatred. happiness, and anger) in chapters 44 and 45.

Section 43.3, a very short fragment, emphasizes that rulers should emulate Heaven in honoring yang and distancing themselves from yin. The chapter concludes with a clear lesson: "Punishment cannot be employed to perfect the age, just as yin cannot be employed to complete the year. Those who constitute government by employing punishment are said to defy Heaven. This is not the Way of the True King."[10]

The first section of chapter 44, "The Kingly Way Penetrates Three," opens with perhaps the most often cited and best-known claim attributed to Dong Zhongshu, the famous triadic vision of rulership from which the chapter title is derived:

> When the ancients invented writing, they drew three [horizontal] lines that they connected through the center [by a vertical stroke] and called this "king." These three lines represent Heaven, Earth and humankind, and the line that connects them through the center unifies their Way. Who, if not a [true] king, could take the central position between Heaven, Earth, and humankind and act as the thread that joins and penetrates them?[11]

The essay proceeds to explain how the king acts on Heaven's behalf. As the "thread that joins and penetrates" all three realms, the king's actions on Heaven's behalf must emulate Heaven's seasons, Heaven's commands, Heaven's numbers, Heaven's Way, and Heaven's will, all of which are notions developed further in other chapters in this group. Heaven is identified with the "perfection of humaneness," and the four seasons are "Heaven's instruments" for realizing Heaven's intention to "nourish and complete" things. Just as Heaven (unless

---

10. *CQFL* 43/51/23–25. A similar argument appears in chapter 43 and in one of Dong's memorials to Emperor Wu. See *HS* 56/2502.
11. This became the accepted, though demonstrably false, etymology of the character *wang* 王. For example, the *Shuowen jiezi* (ca. 100 C.E.) states: "Dong Zhongshu said: 'When the ancients invented writing, they drew three [horizontal] lines that they connected through the center [by a vertical stroke] and called this king'" (chapter 7.1, note 1).

disrupted by external perturbations) sends forth warmth, coolness, heat, and cold in a timely fashion to ensure the transformations of the four seasons and a good harvest, so, by analogy, in order to realize righteousness and bring about a well-ordered age, the ruler must express his likes, dislikes, happiness, and anger in conformity with the four seasons.

Section 44.2 returns to the analogous categories of good harvests, which correspond to orderly ages, and bad harvests, which correspond to disorderly ages. The essay concludes by stating that only when the ruler's four emotional states (likes, dislikes, happiness, and anger, as in 44.1) correspond to righteousness—as Heaven's four climatic variables correspond to their respective seasons—can it be deemed that he "becomes a counterpart of Heaven." This phrase (*can tian* 參天) explicitly recalls the query that begins this essay: "Who, if not a [true] king, could take the central position between Heaven, Earth, and Humankind and act as the thread that joins and penetrates them?" In this way, sections 44.1 and 44.2 are neatly tied together both conceptually and semantically.

Section 44.2 uses Five-Phase reasoning to extend the notion that "the superior is good and the inferior is bad" in the context of yin-yang cosmology. In our introduction to group 6, "Five-Phase Principles," we note that theorists who tried to coordinate the Five Phases with the four seasons basically had two choices, either to create an unnatural fifth "season" assigned to Earth or to regard Earth as applying in some general way to all four seasons but having no season of its own. Section 44.2 tries to find a middle ground:

> Although [the phase] Earth dwells in the center, it also rules for seventy-two days of the year, helping Fire blend, harmonize, nourish, and grow. Nevertheless, it is not named as having done such things, and all the achievement is ascribed to Fire. Fire obtains it and thereby flourishes. [Earth's] not daring to take a share of the merit from its father[12] is the ultimate in the perfection of filial piety. Thus both the conduct of the filial son and the righteousness of the loyal minister are modeled on Earth. Earth serves Heaven just as the subordinate serves the superior.[13]

12. According to the Mutual Production Sequence of the Five Phases, Fire gives birth to Earth (fire produces ashes). Therefore, their relationship is analogous to that of father and son, so that Earth, "serving Fire" and "uniting its merit with Fire," is exemplary of filial piety. The calendrical scheme of five "seasons" of seventy-two days, implied here, is also found in the *Huainanzi* 3.22 and *Guanzi* 41. For contrasting Five-Phase arguments, see also chapters 38 and 42.

13. *CQFL* 44/52/13–15.

In this conception, Heaven and Earth and yang and yin endorse a patriarchal society and the transcendent value of filial piety: "Although Earth is the counterpart to Heaven, it does not mean that they are equal. . . . Things categorized as evil ultimately are yin, whereas things categorized as good ultimately are yang."[14]

This section also reverts to the point made in 43.1 that the lord is never designated as evil and the minister is never called good, arguing that in the *Spring and Autumn*, "in every case goodness is associated with the ruler and evil is associated with the minister." (Note that this claim completely opposes the spirit of group 1, "Exegetical Principles," which discusses in depth several cases of worthy ministers and evil rulers in the *Spring and Autumn*. The argument made in these yin-yang chapters also directly opposes the spirit of Dong Zhongshu's memorials, in which he criticizes the emperor's policies.) Section 44.2 ends with a series of short statements contrasting the attributes of yin and yang, always to the detriment of yin.

Chapter 45, "Heaven's Prosperity," one of the shortest chapters in the entire work, consists of two essay fragments, of 171 and 47 characters, respectively, both addressing themes discussed in chapter 44. In fact, the language and topoi of the fragments are so close to those of chapter 44 that they may originally have been part of that essay. Section 45.1 returns to the ruler's four emotional states (love, hatred, happiness, and anger) to reiterate the argument of chapter 44: "The sage observes Heaven and acts. This is why he carefully chooses the appropriate occasion for [displaying] love, hatred, happiness, and anger, wishing to harmonize with Heaven, which will not send forth warming, cooling, chilling, and heating if it is not the appropriate season."[15] Section 45.2 defines the virtue of righteousness in terms of timeliness, another subject addressed in chapter 44: "When the ruler is happy or angry, he must not fail to be timely. [Those feelings] are permissible in their time, and in their time they are righteous."[16] We conclude, therefore, that the juxtaposition of these two essay fragments making up the current chapter 45 is highly problematic. It is more likely, we believe, that whatever essay was titled "Heaven's Prosperity" has long been lost and that what has been substituted for the lost chapter in transmitted editions of the *Chunqiu fanlu* is text that has migrated from its original location as part of the content of chapter 44.

14. *CQFL* 44/52/15–18.
15. *CQFL* 45/53/11–12.
16. *CQFL* 45/53/15–16.

Chapter 46, "The Heavenly Distinctions Lie in Humans," marks a notable shift from the prose essays of the previous yin-yang chapters to a literary form seen predominantly in the first five chapters of the *Chunqiu fanlu*: the question-and-answer format. In those earlier chapters, the anonymous questioner is sometimes identified with the formulaic expression "Someone raised an objection saying" (*nan zhe yue* 難者曰), and the anonymous respondent is denoted by the simple verb "[someone] stated" (*yue* 曰) or sometimes is merely implied.[17] In chapter 46, the text consists of a single question and its answer. The unknown inquirer, "raising an objection," asks: "In regard to the meeting of yin and yang, during the course of one year they have two encounters. They encounter each other in the southern quarter at the midpoint of summer, and they encounter each other in the northern quarter at the midpoint of winter. Winter is [dominated by] the *qi* of mourning for [the destruction of] things. Why, then, do [yin and yang] meet there?"[18]

The lengthy and detailed answer—which deals with both yin-yang cosmology and the Five-Phase correlates Wood/east/spring, Fire/south/summer, Metal/west/autumn, and Water/north/winter—takes up the rest of the chapter and includes features that appear to be unique to the *Chunqiu fanlu*. That is, it envisions yin moving counterclockwise and yang moving clockwise over the course of the year, as described earlier. This theory is merely hinted at here but is developed in detail in later yin-yang chapters, which we will analyze beginning with chapter 48. In common with many other Warring States and early Han cosmological texts, the chapter speaks of Lesser and Greater Yin (autumn and winter) and Lesser and Greater Yang (spring and summer).[19] For example, we find the statement "Thus, Lesser Yang in accordance with Wood arises and assists spring's generating; Greater Yang in accordance with Fire arises and assists summer's nourishing; Lesser Yin in accordance with Metal arises and assists autumn's completing; Greater Yin in accordance with Water arises and assists winter's storing away."[20] In addition, the four emotional states to be correlated with Heaven's seasons are identified as happiness, anger, joy, and sorrow. These are the same as the emotional states found in 43.2 but differ from the "love, hate, happiness, and anger" cited in chapter 44. Finally, the chapter links the four emotional

17. For a discussion of the significance of this literary genre in the *Chunqiu fanlu*, see the introduction to group 1, "Exegetical Principles."
18. *CQFL* 46/53/20–21.
19. These terms also appear in *CQFL* 48, 49, and 52.1.
20. *CQFL* 46/53/22–24.

states with the cosmological characteristics of the four seasons in a way that is somewhat different from that in the earlier yin-yang chapters:

> Likewise, without the *qi* of happiness, how could Heaven warm and thereby engender and nourish in spring? Without the *qi* of anger, how could Heaven cool and thereby proceed to kill[21] in autumn? Without the *qi* of joy, how could Heaven disperse yang and thereby nourish and mature in summer? Without the *qi* of sorrow, how could Heaven arouse yin and thereby seal up and store away in winter?[22]

It is striking that the cosmological processes associated with the four seasons here are treated in a relatively neutral fashion, that "engendering and nourishing" and "nourishing and maturing" (and so on) are taken to be natural processes in the annual round of waxing and waning of yang *qi*. Nevertheless the chapter also affirms the yang-centric approach of the other yin-yang chapters: "[Y]in is yang's assistant. Yang is the master of the year."

Consisting of only 167 characters, chapter 47, "The Positions of Yin and Yang," is the shortest of the yin-yang chapters. In its current form, it appears to be fragmentary. But it is consistent with chapter 46 and can be seen as an introduction to the complex description of the movements of yin and yang found in chapter 48. In fact, it is not clear why chapters 47 and 48 were divided, as the two can be read as a single continuous document. Chapter 47 picks up on chapter 46's description of the annual round of yin and yang, adding the detail that yang is "above" (i.e., in Heaven) in its half of the year and "below" (presumably in the subterranean Yellow Springs) during the autumn and winter, whereas yin is sequestered "below" in the spring and summer, emerging only in the autumn and winter. The chapter emphasizes the contrasting qualities of yin and yang—chilling and heating, emergence and withdrawal, and so on—and concludes again with a statement strongly privileging yang over yin: "Heaven uses yang and does not use yin. It loves accretion and abhors recision."

The title of chapter 48, "Yin and Yang End and Begin [the Year]," is echoed in the first line of the essay: "Heaven's Way ends and begins anew."[23] This short essay contains a fairly full description of the *Chunqiu fanlu*'s distinctive vision of the annual circuit of yin and yang, adumbrated in some of the earlier chapters

21. Following Ling Shu's edition, which here reads *jiu sha* 就殺 (Zhong, *CQFLJS* 600, note 20).
22. *CQFL* 46/53/29–30.
23. *CQFL* 48/54/23.

of the yin-yang group. Yin and yang meet twice a year, at the winter and summer solstices, and they are separated farthest apart twice a year, at the spring and autumn equinoxes. The movements of yin and yang are described as reciprocal ("there is never a time when yin and yang do not divide up [the whole year] and [keep their respective portions] separate from each other"),[24] but yang is seen as dominating cosmic processes throughout the three seasons of spring, summer, and autumn. Even in autumn, when yin might be expected to dominate, "Lesser Yin flourishes but is not permitted to use autumn to accompany Metal."[25] (In fact, in this scheme, the movements of yin and yang put yin at the eastern side of the horizon during autumn, so yin is quite literally not in a position to affect Metal.) If one assumes (and nothing in this chapter contradicts this) that these movements of yin and yang take place in the framework of the denary seasonal scheme of chapter 43, then here yang would dominate the year not only during spring, summer, and autumn but in the beginning and ending weeks of winter as well, for three hundred days, or five sexagenary day-cycles. Yin would dominate only during a single sexagenary day-cycle centered on the winter solstice, when yang is hidden away or occluded and the force of the dominant yin is producing quiescence and torpor. The chapter's concluding paragraphs, on the effects of yang in autumn, affirm that the scenario described conforms to the proper relationships, constant norms, and expediencies inherent in the Way of Heaven.

As do earlier chapters in this group, chapters 49, 50, and 51 stress this dominance of yang. All three chapters begin by claiming that the defining characteristic of Heaven's Way (stated somewhat differently in each chapter) is the singular manner in which it employs yin and yang. The opening line of chapter 49, "The Meaning of Yin and Yang," states: "The constancy of Heaven's Way is for there to be one yin and one yang."[26] But the two are not equal; the chapter reiterates that yang dominates three seasons of the year and yin, only one. Yang is privileged in what might be termed a metaphysical sense; yang is explicitly identified with life and yin, with death. Lesser and Greater Yin are correlated with the ruler's emotional states, as in chapters 43 and 44. Heaven's Lesser Yin is correlated with humankind's Lesser Yin and sternness, and Heaven's Greater Yin is correlated with humankind's Greater Yin and mournfulness. Chapter 49 reiterates the familiar associations of emotional states (in the form in which they are given in chapter 43) with the four seasons. The ruler once again is urged to

24. *CQFL* 48/54/23.
25. *CQFL* 48/55/1.
26. *CQFL* 49/55/7.

unify his person with Heaven and employ things as Heaven does. Accordingly, he must ensure that he uses beneficence more generously than punishment, just as yang exceeds yin.

Chapter 50, "Yin and Yang Emerge, Withdraw, Ascend, and Descend," similarly opens by stating: "In the grand design of Heaven's Way, things that are mutually opposed are not permitted to emerge together. Such is the case with yin and yang." Here, again, we see the *Chunqiu fanlu*'s distinctive yin-yang scheme in action, the two "emerging" and "withdrawing" in different places and moving in opposite directions around the horizon circle. The remainder of the chapter supports this opening assertion cosmologically by tracing the movement, directionality, and location of yin and yang in each of the four seasons and at the solstices and equinoxes. The locations of yin and yang are specified in terms of "positions," which denote the cosmological locations of the twelve calendar months around the horizon. The reciprocal movements of yin and yang around the horizon circle can be plotted as pairs of Earthly Branches, with meeting points at *zi* (the winter solstice) and *wu* (the summer solstice). In all these yin-yang chapters, this scheme gives the greater share of the year to yang, from the first month of spring through the last month of autumn. But the emphasis of this chapter is cosmological, describing the movements of yin and yang without reference to the moral and metaphysical characteristics emphasized in other chapters of the yin-yang group and without any notable preference for yang over yin. This, again, is the kind of small but significant difference that may indicate that this group of chapters derives from members of a coherent—but not uniform—intellectual lineage rather than a single author.

Like chapters 49 and 50, chapter 51, "Heaven's Way Is Not Dualistic," states: "In Heaven's constant Way, things that are mutually opposed are not permitted to arise simultaneously. Therefore Heaven's Way is said to be singular. What is singular and not dualistic is Heaven's conduct. Yin and yang are mutually opposed."[27] The chapter goes on to reiterate the now familiar circulation of yin and yang. Heaven's Way is characterized as "not dualistic" (despite there being two cosmic forces, yin and yang) because the movements of yin and yang are always reciprocal and yang is privileged over yin. The point of the chapter seems to be that the ruler should emulate this singular quality of Heaven's Way. The chapter spells out its advice to the ruler in detail, closing with a passage from the *Odes*:

27. *CQFL* 51/56/9.

> Therefore, to be constantly unitary and not destructive is Heaven's Way. . . . [If you try to] draw a square with one hand while [trying to] draw a circle with the other hand, you will not be able to complete either of them. . . . This is why the noble man disdains two and honors one. . . . An *Ode* declares: "The High God is close at hand; do not be double-minded."[28] These are the words of one who understands Heaven's Way.[29]

The first section of chapter 52, "Heat or Cold, Which Predominates?" also begins with a claim concerning Heaven's Way. Here, however, the focus is on how Heaven sends forth yang and yin, warming and cooling to engender and complete the myriad things of the world. Both are necessary, but as in previous instances, this chapter argues that Heaven clearly privileges yang over yin and the respective warmth and coolness they generate to carry out the transformations of the year. The text asks the reader to consider Heaven's activities from the first through the tenth month of the year, calculating the positions of yin and yang and asking whether warm or cold days are more numerous. One will discover that "[o]nly when the ninth month of autumn arrives does yin begin to be more abundant than yang."[30] At this time, Heaven sends down cold and frost to bring living things to completion. Like chapter 51, section 52.1 closes with a flourish from the *Odes* to support its conclusion.

Section 52.2, whose subject departs markedly from that of section 52.1, takes up the topic of Yu's flood and Tang's drought, arguing that they were caused by human emotional energy and were not the products of the "constant regularities of Heaven" (and therefore were not baleful portents). When Yao died, this passage argues, the people's mourning created so much yin energy that a flood ensued and Yu was called on to subdue it. Similarly, the tyrant Jie, last ruler of the Xia, created so much baleful yang energy that the reign of his virtuous conqueror Tang was marred at first by a great drought. This brief section tries to uphold the good reputations of Yu and Tang, and to do so, it must explain how such great sages encountered disasters when they ruled. It seeks to demonstrate beyond any doubt that the disasters associated with their reigns were not caused by their personal transgressions. Thus the section concludes: "Both [Yu and Tang] happened to encounter an untoward alteration [of seasonal *qi*]. These disasters were not caused by the transgressions of Yu or Tang. Do not, if you

28. *Odes* 236, verse 7.
29. *CQFL* 51/56/17–23.
30. *CQFL* 52/56/31.

happen to encounter an untoward alteration of *qi*, have doubts about the constancies of everyday life. In this way, what you wish to preserve will not be lost, and the correct way will become increasingly manifest."[31]

Chapter 53, "Laying the Foundation of Righteousness," develops the notion that "all things invariably possess counterparts."[32] Each pair of complements in the world—whether superior or subordinate, right or left, front or back, outside or inside, joy or anger, cold or heat, morning or evening—has its counterpart in the fundamental pairing of yin and yang. This holds true for the relations between ruler and minister, husband and wife, and father and son, all of whom also derive their righteousness from the Way of yin and yang. In keeping with the yang-centric bias of earlier chapters in the yin-yang group, section 53.1 maintains: "There are no places where the Way of yin circulates alone. At the beginning [of the yearly cycle], yin is not permitted to arise by itself. Likewise, at the end [of the yearly cycle], yin is not permitted to share in [the glories of] yang's achievements. Such is the righteous principle of 'joining.'"[33] Compare chapter 48: "[T]here is never a time when yin and yang do not divide up [the whole year]"; that is, both are always present at all times. But as chapter 47 stresses, "Heaven employs yang and does not employ yin." Thus as section 53.1 concludes, the minister joins his achievements to the lord, son to father, wife to husband, yin to yang, and Earth to Heaven.

The four sections that make up the remainder of chapter 53 appear to be fragments of essays that once were more complete. Section 53.2 continues the theme of paired opposites: some officials are promoted, some demoted, and so on. Section 53.3 returns to the theme of the annual reciprocal movements of yin and yang, in every case emphasizing the priority of yang. Section 53.4 is a fragment on the subject of seasonal warmth and coolness. Section 53.5 raises once again the notion of "Heaven's numbers" and the fundamental role of the ten-day "week" in calculating the periodicities of yin and yang.

Chapter 54 is an empty vessel; both its title and its content have been lost. Presumably, it once consisted of yet another essay on the subject of yin and yang.

As we have seen, despite their differences in detail, chapters 43 through 53 are based on the *Chunqiu fanlu*'s distinctive cosmological model of the opposite and reciprocal movements of yin and yang around the horizon, and most, if not all, of these chapters seem to accept (or at least are compatible with) the

31. *CQFL* 52/57/10–11.
32. *CQFL* 53/57/15.
33. *CQFL* 53/57/20–21.

denary division of the year into three one-hundred-day yang "seasons" (equivalent to five sexagenary day-cycles) plus one sixty-day yin "season" (equivalent to one sexagenary day-cycle). Chapters 55 through 57, in contrast, maintain a basic focus on yin and yang but seem to depart, each in its own way, from the model proposed in the earlier chapters.

Chapter 55, "The Correlates of the Four Seasons," returns to the theme of the four seasons, their activities, and their human correlates: "The sage correlates himself with Heaven's conduct to create his policies. . . . [Thus] gifts, rewards, penalties, and punishments must be promulgated in accordance with the appropriate occasion, just as warmth, heat, coolness, and cold must issue forth in accordance with the appropriate season." With these correlative claims established, the chapter concludes by asserting that this is precisely why the *Spring and Autumn* criticized those instances in which gifts, rewards, penalties, and punishments were not implemented on the proper occasions. In marked contrast with chapters 43 through 53, this chapter is entirely in the spirit of the "Yue ling" (Monthly Ordinances) calendar, various versions of which (*Lüshi chunqiu, Liji, Huainanzi*) were in circulation during the Western Han. The seasonal attributes found in these—spring germination, summer growth, autumn harvest, and winter storage—match the content of chapter 55. In addition, the annual movement of yin and yang—going in tandem from winter to summer and back again, yang waxing as yin wanes and vice versa—implied in the chapter matches the cosmological model found in the "Yue ling" calendar.

Chapter 56, "Human Correlates of Heaven's Regularities," details the noble qualities of humankind, derivative of its cosmic parents Heaven and Earth: "Of the living things born of the vital essence of Heaven and Earth, none is nobler than human beings. Human beings receive their destiny from Heaven, and therefore they surpass [the lesser creatures] that must fend for themselves." That is, only human beings can match Heaven and Earth. This is demonstrated in the remainder of the chapter, which describes in detail the macrocosm/microcosm heavenly correlates of the human body, employing a kind of reasoning about the relationship between Heaven and the human body widely encountered in such late Warring States and Western Han texts as the *Lüshi chunqiu* and *Huainanzi*.

Chapter 57, "Things of the Same Kind Activate One Another," develops further the theme that concludes chapter 56, the mutual resonance among things in the universe that are categorically alike. It repeats the example, found in a number of early texts, of musical resonance. The essay marshals a wide array of examples, many based on yin and yang, to demonstrate this principle of resonance. It touches on the practice of rainmaking: "Those who understand this, when wishing to bring forth rain, will activate yin, causing yin to arise; when wishing to stop rain, will activate yang, causing yang to arise." The questions of "seeking rain" and "stopping rain" are explored at length in chapters 74 and 75 of group 7, "Ritual Principles." Dong Zhongshu himself achieved a considerable reputation for his ability to cause rain to fall or to stop falling during the time he served as administrator of Jiangdu.

This brief review of the chapters in group 5 demonstrates that despite the fragmented and disarranged quality of some, these chapters do constitute a cohesive unit. We believe that whoever compiled the *Chunqiu fanlu* brought these materials together in this order precisely because they deal with the great Han theme of cosmology, expressed primarily as the complementarity of yin and yang in the transformations of the four seasons. In a few chapters (especially 43, 46, and 48), the yin-yang focus is augmented by the use of Five-Phase categories, particularly the directions (east, south, west, and north) and the seasons (correspondingly, spring, summer, autumn, and winter). In general, the phase Earth is ignored in these correlations, with its identification with the center assumed but not emphasized. This degree of Five-Phase analysis is only to be expected, as the seasons and the directions are among the most basic of the correlates of the Five Phases. Indeed, it would have been difficult for any Western Han intellectual to discuss yin-yang and the annual cycle of the seasons without reference to those basic correlates. But the focus of these chapters is clearly on yin and yang.

As the two basic types of *qi* employed by Heaven in managing the myriad processes of the phenomenal world, yin and yang make it possible to analyze the transformations of the four seasons. How this is accomplished is the second important organizing theme, addressed in chapters 43 to 53. Furthermore, all the chapters in the group argue that in the workings of the natural world, Heaven always privileges yang over yin. This cosmological claim has important political implications, because the way in which Heaven employs yin and yang provides a model for how the human ruler is to employ beneficence and punishment. Just as Heaven gives priority to yang over yin, so must the ruler favor beneficence over punishment. The first of two different but complementary arguments proceeds from the perspective of quantity (chapters 49 and 53)—that is, the portion of the year dominated by yang versus yin. The second line of reasoning argues from the perspective of location and direction (chapters 43, 46, 47, 48, 50, 51, and 53), maintaining that the reciprocal movements of yin and yang (by which yin is hidden for most of the year) demonstrate Heaven's preference for beneficence over punishment. The remaining chapters (44, 45, and 49) develop the notion of "adapting to the seasons," describing how the general qualities of the four seasons—for example, the coolness of autumn or the heat of summer—prescribe the ruler's activities.

Issues of Dating and Attribution

These chapters appear to be part of a conversation, or debate, over the nature of yin and yang and the exact mechanisms of their operation, a debate that originated in the mid-third century B.C.E. with such texts as the *Lüshi chunqiu*. It continued in the first century of the Western Han dynasty, especially during the reigns of Emperor Jing (r. 157–141 B.C.E.) and Emperor Wu (r. 141–87 B.C.E.), when such issues were a matter of widespread interest and dispute.[34] The position staked out in these chapters is yang centric and takes a strongly negative view of yin. It stands in stark opposition to the yin-biased *Laozi* and takes issue with the moderate stance exemplified by such texts as the *Guanzi* and *Huainanzi*. The androcentric and patriarchal stance of the *Chunqiu fanlu*'s yin-yang chapters is compatible with, and adds a cosmological dimension to, views inherent in the hierarchical and highly moral image of the ideal society envisioned in the works of Confucius and his earlier followers.

To reiterate, chapters 43 through 53 in the *Chunqiu fanlu* propose a novel and otherwise unknown understanding of the movements and periodicities of yin and yang. The very distinctive yin-yang theory presented in these chapters is strikingly different from the more usual view (found, for example, in *Huainanzi* 3 and other *Huainanzi* chapters) and did not become generally accepted during the Western Han or later. This argues for its being the view of a single individual or a small group of like-minded individuals whose lineage of transmission failed.

Was that individual Dong Zhongshu? Or was that group Dong Zhongshu and his disciples? There is good evidence that Dong's own views of yin-yang cosmology were quite similar to some of those expressed in the *Chunqiu fanlu*'s yin-yang chapters. Consider, for example, this passage from one of Dong's memorials, quoted in the *Han shu*:

34. Aihe Wang, *Cosmology and Political Culture in Early China* (Cambridge: Cambridge University Press, 2000), 185–90; A. C. Graham, *Disputers of the Tao: Philosophical Argument in Ancient China* (LaSalle, Ind.: Open Court, 1989), 330–40.

> The most important aspect of Heaven's Way is yin and yang. Yang corresponds to beneficence; yin corresponds to punishment. Punishment presides over death; beneficence presides over life. Thus yang always takes up its position at the height of summer, taking engendering, nurturing, nourishing, and maturing as its tasks. Yin always takes up its position at the height of winter, accumulating in empty, vacuous, and useless places. From this perspective, we see that Heaven relies on beneficence and does not rely on punishment. Heaven causes yang to emerge, circulate, and operate above the ground to preside over the achievements of the year. Heaven causes yin to retire and prostrate itself below the ground, seasonally emerging to assist yang. If yang does not obtain yin's assistance, it cannot complete the year on its own. Ultimately, however, it is yang that is noted for completing the year. Such is Heaven's intent.[35]

In addition, the *Yantie lun* (*Debates on Salt and Iron Monopolies*, 81 B.C.E.) testifies to Dong's interest and expertise in understanding phenomena by means of yin-yang and four-seasons cosmology:

> The origins [of anomalies] the administrator of Jiangdu Master Dong deduced from the mutual succession of yin and yang and the four seasons. The father begets it, the son nourishes it, the mother completes it, and the son stores it away. Therefore
>
> spring [presides over] birth and corresponds to humaneness;
> summer [presides over] growth and corresponds to beneficence;
> autumn [presides over] maturation and corresponds to righteousness;
> winter [presides over] concealment and corresponds to propriety.
>
> This is the sequence of the four seasons and what the sage takes as his model. One cannot rely on punishments to complete moral transformation. Therefore, one extends moral education.[36]

In the passage just quoted from the *Han shu*, Dong's statements to Emperor Wu show that by around 140 B.C.E., Dong was employing the authority of Heaven, manifested in the workings of its yin and yang *qi*, to make very specific political arguments. He contended that how Heaven employs the two basic forms of cosmic *qi*, yin and yang, provides a compelling model of rulership. Correlating punishment and beneficence with yin and yang, respectively, Dong urged the

35. *HS* 56/2502.
36. *Yantie lun* 9.6/67/15–17; *Yantie lun jiezhu* 382.

emperor to order his empire by means of moral authority rather than coercive punitive laws. Thus a comparison of the contents of *Chunqiu fanlu*'s chapters 43 through 53 with the known views of Dong Zhongshu on yin-yang and the four seasons makes it quite plausible that he was the author of some of those chapters. Some, but probably not all. For example, while he would have had no quarrel with the idea that ministers are yin to the ruler's yang, we regard it as unlikely that Dong—who had a long and successful bureaucratic career—would have stated categorically (as in chapter 44.2) that "in every case, goodness is associated with the ruler, while evil is associated with the minister." That statement, as we have pointed out, is quite at variance with the view of the relationship between ruler and minister found in the first five chapters of the *Chunqiu fanlu*—chapters closely associated with Dong Zhongshu himself. Moreover, considered as a group, these yin-yang chapters display small but significant differences in wording and technical details. In our view, this makes it unlikely that all these chapters were written by the same person.

Our considered opinion is that these chapters as a whole may indeed represent the views of Dong Zhongshu and one or more of his disciples, albeit with some puzzling contradictions. Beyond that we cannot go. It is unlikely, pending the discovery of definitive evidence, that the authorship of these chapters can be assigned to anyone with complete confidence.

Compared with chapters 43 through 53, chapters 55 through 57 are much more conventional and do not seem to represent Dong Zhongshu's distinctive views of yin and yang as we have identified them. Chapter 55 takes a standard Wood/Fire/Metal/Water view of the seasons/directions/phases and the governmental policies associated with them (gifts/rewards/severity/punishments). Chapter 56 deals in conventional macrocosm/microcosm principles like those found in many Western Han texts. Finally, chapter 57 is framed in terms of standard resonance theory, including the very common example that if you pluck one tuned string, another similarly tuned string nearby will respond. The fact that this chapter also mentions rainmaking by activating yin and rain-halting by activating yang is only weak evidence for an association with Dong, despite his reputation as a rainmaker, because it comes in the context of much other routine resonance theory.

It is hard to see what specific associations with Dong Zhongshu our "anonymous compiler" would have seen in chapters 55 through 57 to induce him to include them in the *Chunqiu fanlu*. They are not incompatible with chapters 43 through 55, but they represent more conventional yin-yang views with which

Dong Zhongshu may have agreed but which are not particularly associated with him. Again, it is possible that these chapters represent the work of one or more of Dong's disciples and were included in the text for that reason. We conclude that taken as a whole, the yin-yang chapters seem to be a fair representation of the cosmological views of Dong Zhongshu and his followers.

Book 11, Part 3

CHAPTER 43

Yang Is Lofty, Yin Is Lowly

Section 43.1

Heaven's great numbers conclude with ten periods of ten days.

The ten-day period: for everything between Heaven and Earth, ten suffices to initiate them.

The ten-day period: for everything that achieves birth and growth, ten suffices to complete them.

Ten is where Heaven's regularities come to a halt. The sages of antiquity, in accordance with the place where Heaven's regularities come to a halt, created numbers to record things.[1] [In recording things,] when they reached [the number] ten, they began anew. The common people through the ages transmitted this practice but did not know enough to investigate its origins.

If you know enough to investigate its origins,
you will observe the place where Heaven's regularities begin.
If you observe the place where Heaven's regularities begin,
you will know the place where honor, dishonor, compliance, and deviation lie.
If you know the place where honor, dishonor, compliance, and deviation lie,
the true nature of Heaven and Earth will become evident,

and the true substance[2] of the sage will emerge.

---

1. The argument here makes use of two senses of the word *shu* 數, its common meaning of "numbers" and its extended meaning of "regularities." Here we translate as one or the other according to context, but in the Chinese original, both meanings are present with variable emphasis.
2. Reading *bao* 寶 as *shi* 實, following Su Yu, *CQFLYZ* 324.

Thus, yang *qi* avails itself of the first month to begin to emerge from the earth, engendering and nourishing [things] above [its surface]. Arriving at the point when its achievements necessarily are brought to completion, ten months have accrued. Human beings likewise are engendered in ten months, matching the number of Heaven. Thus,

with ten months, the Way of Heaven is brought to completion,
and with ten months [of gestation,] humans likewise are brought to completion,

thus matching the Way of Heaven. Hence, yang *qi*

emerges in the northeast and withdraws in the northwest,
comes out in the first month of spring and expires in the first month of winter.

All things respond to this cycle.

When yang begins to emerge, things likewise begins to emerge.
When yang begins to prosper, things likewise begin to prosper.
When yang begins to decline, things likewise begin to decline.
Things follow yang and so emerge and withdraw;
numbers follow yang and so begin and end;
the rectification of the Three Kings[3] followed yang and so arose anew.

From this we observe how to honor yang and denigrate yin.[4] Hence,

when counting the days, do so according to the mornings and not the evenings;
when counting the years, do so according to the yang [i.e., odd] and not the yin [i.e., even] years.

[Such] is the righteous principle of not being permitted to enumerate yin.

For this reason, when the *Spring and Autumn* discussed the marriage ceremony, it mentioned the duke of Song but did not mention the mother of the marquis of Ji.[5] It was proper for the mother of the marquis of Ji to be referred to indirectly but not mentioned, whereas it was not proper for the duke of Song to be referred to indirectly but not mentioned. To mention yang and not to mention yin accords with what the Way of Heaven regulates.

3. In other words, when Kings Yu, Tang, and Wen rectified the first month of the calendars of the Xia, Shang, and Zhou dynasties, they supposedly followed yang. It is unclear what aspect of their rectification the author is referring to here. The *Bohutong*, chapter 27 ("San zheng" 三正 [The Three Rectifications]), states: "The Hsia took the first month of spring as the correct [beginning of the year]; the Yin took the last month of winter as the correct [beginning of the year]; the Chou took the middle month of winter as the correct [beginning of the year]" (Tjan Tjoe Som, trans., *Po Hu T'ung: The Comprehensive Discussions in the White Tiger Hall* [Leiden: Brill, 1952], 2:550).
4. This same argument appears in chapter 46.
5. See *Gongyang Commentary* at Duke Yin 1.2.5.

> Although a husband may be from the humble class, he is considered yang in every case.
> Although a wife may be from the noble class, she is considered yin in every case.
> All things in the yin [category] are likewise to be considered yin.
> All things in the yang [category] are likewise to be considered yang.
> All those in superior positions are considered yang by their subordinates;
> all those in subordinate positions are considered yin by their superiors.

Yin resembles [the word] "to sink."[6] Whence its name? Whence its content? Both combine and unite in yang. [Yin] expends all its strength but [still] subordinates its achievements [to yang]. Hence, [yin] sends forth the clouds and initiates the rains [but] invariably directs them to fall from Heaven.[7] Hence they are called "Heaven's rain." [Yin] does not dare hold the place from whence it emanates. The superior is good; the inferior is evil. When you promote goodness and demote evil, those who are bad receive [goodness], but those who are good do not receive [evil]. [43/50/25–43/51/8]

Section 43.2[8]

As for the expressions of happiness, anger, sorrow, and joy and warmth, coolness, heat, and cold, their substance is of a single category.

> Happy *qi* is warming and corresponds to spring;
> angry *qi* is cooling and corresponds to autumn;
> joyful *qi* is Greater Yang and corresponds to summer;
> sorrowful *qi* is Greater Yin and corresponds to winter.

These four [aspects of] *qi* are what Heaven and humankind identically possess. They are not something that humankind can accumulate [on its own]. Therefore [humankind] can regulate these four [aspects of *qi*,] but it cannot stop them altogether.

---

6. *Chen* 沉 (to sink).
7. Reading *xia* 下 as *tian xia* 天下, following Su Yu (Zhong, *CQFLJS* 579, note 10).
8. There is some debate concerning how to apportion material between this chapter and chapter 44. Su Yu (*CQFLYZ* 330), who follows the earlier commentator Zhang Huiyan, argues that this passage, beginning with "the expression of happiness, anger, sorrow, and joy" and ending with "humankind appropriates [these models] from Heaven" (*CQFL* 43/51/8–23), belongs in chapter 44 below the phrase "Heaven has cold and heat. "We followed the Lau version.

When they are regulated, there is compliance;
when they are stopped, there is chaos.

Human beings are born of Heaven, and they derive their [various] transformations from Heaven:

Happy *qi* derives from spring;
joyful *qi* derives from summer;
angry *qi* derives from autumn;
sorrowful *qi* derives from winter.

[These are] the heart's four [aspects] of *qi*.

In response, each of the four limbs has its proper position. That the heating and chilling of the four seasons cannot shift is similar to the limbs of the body:

When the limbs of the body shift and change their positions, it is called a "deformed person";
when chilling and heating shift and change their positions, it is called "a disastrous harvest";
when happiness and anger shift and change their positions, it is called "a chaotic age."

The enlightened king

rectifies his happiness to correspond to spring;
rectifies his anger to correspond to autumn;
rectifies his joy to correspond to summer;
rectifies his sorrow to correspond to winter.

Superior and inferior emulate this and thereby appropriate the Way of Heaven:

Spring *qi* is loving;
autumn *qi* is stern;
summer *qi* is joyful;
winter *qi* is sorrowful.
Loving *qi* is for giving birth to things;
stern *qi* is for bringing completion to things;
joyous *qi* is for nourishing life;
sorrowful *qi* is for mourning death.

This is Heaven's will. This is why

the warming of the summer *qi* is the means by which Heaven is loving and produces things;
the cooling of the autumn *qi* is the means by which Heaven is stern and completes things;
the heating of the summer *qi* is the means by which Heaven is joyous and nourishes things;

the chilling of the winter *qi* is the means by which Heaven is sorrowful and stores away things.
Spring governs giving birth;
summer governs nourishing;
autumn governs reaping;
winter governs storing.
With life, its joy is entirely devoted to nourishing;
with death, its sorrow is entirely devoted to storing.[9]

Hence
the conduct of the four seasons is the Way of the father and son;
the will of Heaven and Earth is the righteousness of the ruler and minister;
the patterns of yin and yang are the models of the sage.
Yin is the *qi* of punishment.
Yang is the *qi* of bounty.
Yin begins in autumn.
Yang begins in spring.
Chun [meaning "spring"], as a term, resembles *chun* [meaning "to move"].[10]
Qiu [meaning "autumn"], as a term, resembles *qiu* [meaning "mournful"].[11]
Chun [meaning "to move"] [implies] an attitude of happiness and joy.
Qiu [meaning "mournful"] [implies] an expression of sadness and sorrow.

For this reason,
spring is happiness;
summer is joy;
autumn is sadness;
winter is grief;

grief [means] death, but joy [means] life. To nourish spring in summer and store up autumn in winter constitutes the will of the great man. For this reason,
he puts love first and sternness behind;
he rejoices in life and mourns death.

This accords with Heaven, and humankind appropriates [these models] from Heaven. [43/51/8–23]

9. We deleted the excrescent phrase *wei ren zi zhe ye* 爲人子者也 (Those who are sons).
10. *Chun* 春 (spring) and *chun* 偆 (to move).
11. *Qiu* 秋 (autumn) and *qiu* 湫 (mournful).

Section 43.3[12]

[Heaven] emphasizes accretion and deemphasizes recision.[13] This is why human rulers

draw near to what Heaven draws near to,
moves away from what Heaven moves away from,
increase what Heaven increases,
and decrease what Heaven decreases.

This is why Heaven's regularities

esteem yang and do not esteem yin,
strive for accretion and do not strive for recision.

Punishment cannot be used to perfect the age, just as yin cannot be used to complete the year. Those who constitute government by using punishment are said to defy Heaven. This is not the Way of the True King.[14] [43/51/23–25]

12. This section is the same in the Lau, Su Yu, and Lai Yanyuan editions.
13. *De* 德 and *xing* 刑 are paired opposites. For *de* as "accretion" or accumulation, and *xing* as "recision" or paring away, see John S. Major, Sarah A. Queen, Andrew Seth Meyer, and Harold D. Roth, trans. and eds., *The "Huainanzi": A Guide to the Theory and Practice of Government in Early Han China* (New York: Columbia University Press, 2010), 122–24. The text here plays this specialized meaning of *de* and *xing* against their more usual meanings of "reward" and "punishment" or "benefit" and "harm."
14. A similar argument appears in one of Dong's memorials to Emperor Wu. See *HS* 56/2502 and, in this volume, appendix B.

Book 11, Part 4

CHAPTER 44

The Kingly Way Penetrates Three

Section 44.1

When the ancients invented writing, they drew three [horizontal] lines that they connected through the center [by a vertical stroke] and called this "king."[1] These three lines represent Heaven, Earth, and humankind, and the line that connects them through the center unifies their Way. Who, if not a [true] king, could take the central position between Heaven, Earth, and humankind and act as the thread that joins and penetrates them? Therefore the king acts only on Heaven's behalf.

> He extends Heaven's seasons and brings them to completion.
> He emulates Heaven's commands and circulates them among the people.
> He emulates Heaven's numbers and employs them when initiating affairs.
> He brings order to Heaven's Way and uses it when promulgating laws.
> He brings order to Heaven's will and returns to humaneness.

The beauty of humaneness rests with Heaven. Heaven is humane. Heaven

> protects and shelters the myriad things,
> transforms and engenders them,
> nourishes and completes them.

1. This describes the character *wang* 王 (king). See chapter 7, note 1.

Its affairs and achievements are limitless. When it reaches the end, it begins again. All that [Heaven] supports, it bequeaths to humankind. If we examine Heaven's intentions, we will see that it is inexhaustibly and boundlessly humane.

Human beings receive their destiny from Heaven. Human beings derive their humaneness from Heaven and thereby are humane. Therefore human beings receive as [part of] their destiny the Heaven-venerated relationships of father and elder brother, son and younger brother.

> They possess hearts that are loyal, trustworthy, kind, and virtuous.
>
> They possess conduct that exhibits propriety, righteousness, honesty, and conciliation.
>
> They possess knowledge that recognizes what is right and wrong, what complies with and what deviates from [Heaven].

Their refinement and principles are manifest and abundant, their knowledge broad and extensive. It is the Way of humankind alone that is able to connect with Heaven.

> It is the intention of Heaven to constantly love and confer benefit.
>
> It is the task [of Heaven] to nourish and bring to maturation.

Spring, autumn, winter, and summer all are Heaven's instruments for this. Similarly,

> it is the intention of the king to constantly love and confer benefits to all under Heaven.
>
> It is the task of the king to bring peace and contentment to the age.

His love, hatred, happiness, and anger all are instruments for this. Thus the ruler's love and hatred, happiness, and anger, are equivalent to the spring, summer, autumn, and winter of Heaven. Heaven combines warming, cooling, heating, and chilling to alter, transform, complete, and achieve things.

> When Heaven sends forth these four in a timely manner, there are good harvests;
>
> when Heaven sends forth these four in an untimely manner, there are poor harvests.

[Likewise,]

> when the ruler sends forth [his] four [temperaments] in accordance with righteousness, the age is well ordered;
>
> when he sends forth [his] four [temperaments] and they are not in accordance with righteousness, the age is disordered.

Therefore to order the age and to improve the harvest are of the same category. And to bring disorder to the age and to spoil the harvest are of the same category. From this, we see that the inner principles of humankind correlate with Heaven's Way. [44/51/30–44/52/11]

Section 44.2[2]

Heaven has cold and heat.[3] [The phase] Earth resembles "earth" [meaning "soil"].[4] Earth rules righteousness [as Heaven rules humaneness]. Thus in the *Spring and Autumn*, the lord is not designated evil, and the minister is not designated good. In every case, goodness is associated with the ruler, and evil is associated with the minister. The righteousness of the minister is comparable to earth ["soil"]. Thus,

those who are the ministers of others observe how earth ["soil"] serves Heaven;
those who are the sons of others observe how [the phase] Earth serves Fire.

Although [the phase] Earth dwells in the center, it also rules for seventy-two days of the year, helping Fire blend, harmonize, nourish, and grow. Nevertheless, it is not named as having done such things, and all the achievement is ascribed to Fire. Fire obtains it and thereby flourishes. [Earth's] not daring to take a share of the merit from its father[5] is the ultimate in the perfection of filial piety. Thus both the conduct of the filial son and the righteousness of the loyal minister are modeled on Earth. Earth serves Heaven just as the subordinate serves the superior. Although Earth is the counterpart to Heaven, it does not mean that they are equal. Thus, if you draw out the essence of Heaven and Earth and turn over [in your mind] the categories of yin and yang in order to distinguish the principles of compliance and deviation, where could you point to a place where they are not to be found? They lie in [the distinction between] superior and subordinate, great and small, strong and weak, worthy and foolish, and good and evil. Things categorized as evil ultimately are yin, whereas things categorized as good ultimately are yang.

Yang constitutes accretion;
yin constitutes recision.

Recision is the opposite of accretion, yet it complies with accretion and so in the end belongs to the category of expediency. Although it is called expediency, in every case it is brought to completion by constant norms.[6] Thus,

2. The Su Yu and Lai Yanyuan editions include at this point the lines found at 43/51/8–23 in the Lau edition (beginning with "As for the expressions of happiness, anger, sorrow, and joy" and ending with "humankind appropriates these models from Heaven"). See chapter 43.2.
3. This appears to be a stray sentence that does not fit with what either precedes or follows it.
4. The phase Earth is *tu* 土; earth as "soil" is *di* 地.
5. According to the Five-Phase scheme of mutual production, Fire gives birth to Earth, and therefore their relationship is analogous to that of father and son. Note here that the strategy to exempt correlating the phase Earth with the seasons differs again from chapters 38 and 42. Here "Earth" serving "Fire" and "uniting its merit with Fire" is the exemplar of filial piety. The calendrical scheme of five "seasons" of seventy-two days, implied here, is also found in *Huainanzi* 3.22 and *Guanzi* 41.
6. Emending *jie zai quan cheng* 皆在權成 to *jie yi jing cheng* 皆以經成, following Su Yu, *CQFLYZ* 327.

yang moves in compliance [with Heaven's Way];
yin moves contrary to [Heaven's Way].
To move contrariwise yet to be in compliance is yang;
to move compliantly but to be contrary is yin.[7]

Thus

Heaven uses yin for expediency;
Heaven uses yang as its constant norm.[8]
Yang emerges and [moves] southward;
yin emerges and [moves] northward.
Constant norms are used at the height [of the yearly cycle];
expediency is used at its final stage.

From this, we see that Heaven manifests its constant norms while it conceals its expediency. Heaven places accretion first and recision afterward. Thus it is said:

Yang is Heaven's accretion;
yin is Heaven's recision.
Yang *qi* warms;
yin *qi* chills.
Yang *qi* confers;
yin *qi* takes away.
Yang *qi* is humane;
yin *qi* is violent.
Yang *qi* is generous;
yin *qi* is stingy.
Yang *qi* is loving;
yin *qi* is hateful.
Yang *qi* gives birth;
yin *qi* kills.

Thus,

yang always occupies a full position and is active at the height [of the yearly cycle];
yin always occupies a hollow position and is active at its final stage.

This is the meaning of why Heaven

loves humaneness and moves close to it,
despises the vicissitudes of violence and keeps its distance from it,
and makes much of accretion and slights recision.

---

7. Supplying the three characters *zhe, yang ye* 者陽也, following Su Yu, *CQFLYZ* 327.
8. The distinction here between *quan* 權 and *jing* 經 also appears in group 1, "Exegetical Principles."

It gives priority to the constant norms and places expediency behind;
it honors yang and denigrates yin.

Thus in the summer, yin withdraws and resides below and is not permitted to play a part in the activities of the harvest. In the winter, it emerges and resides above, relegated to the vacuous wastes. During the season of nourishment and maturation, it lies submerged below. It is set apart at a distance and not permitted to take up the activities of yang. During the season of idleness, it is brought up to the vacuous wastes and is made to fill the secondary role of arranging and guarding [the activities of] shutting up and stopping up. These all are instances of Heaven drawing near to yang and keeping its distance from yin. [44/52/11–26]

Section 44.3

The ruler of humankind occupies a position [at the fulcrum] of life and death and, together with Heaven, grasps the positional advantage of alteration and transformation. Nothing fails to respond to Heaven's transformations. The transformations of Heaven and Earth are like the four seasons.

When the winds of what they love blow, there is warming *qi*, and giving birth becomes general;
when the winds of what they hate blow, there is cooling *qi*, and killing becomes general;
when the winds of what they find joy in blow, there is heating *qi* and nourishment and growth;
when the winds of what angers them blow, there is chilling *qi* and sealing and closing off.
The ruler employs his love, hatred, happiness, and anger to change habits and customs;
Heaven employs warming, cooling, heating, and chilling to transform the grasses and trees.
When happiness and anger are timely and proper, then the harvest will be good;
When they are untimely and improper, then the harvest will be bad.

Heaven, Earth, and the ruler are one. Nonetheless, the ruler's love, hatred, happiness, and anger [must correspond to] Heaven's warming, cooling, chilling, and heating. [The ruler] cannot [help] but examine their proper locations and exhibit [love, hatred, happiness, and anger] accordingly. Thus

when it should to be hot but it is cold or when it should be cold but it is hot, invariably there will be a bad harvest;

> when the ruler should be happy but is angry or when he ought to be angry but is happy, invariably there will be a disorderly age.

This is why the ruler must ensure that he is careful of what is stored [inside him] and regulates what is within [himself].

He must ensure that his love, hatred, happiness, and sorrow invariably correspond to righteousness and only then let them issue forth; just as warming, cooling, heating, and chilling invariably correspond to their respective seasons and only then issue forth. When the ruler grasps this and does not lose it, ensuring that his love, hatred, happiness, and anger will never once fall short [of what is proper], just as spring, autumn, winter and summer will never once be excessive, it can be said that he "participates in Heaven." What deeply stores up these four [seasons and emotions] and does not allow them to issue forth recklessly may be called heavenly. [44/52/26–44/53/6]

Book 11, Part 5

CHAPTER 45

Heaven's Prosperity

Section 45.1

Heaven's Way

has sequences and is thereby timely;
has measures and is thereby regulated;
alters but has constancy;
reverts[1] but has reciprocity;
is subtle and supremely far reaching;
is superb and supremely refined;
is singular[2] yet bit by bit piles up and accumulates,
is broad yet substantial;
is empty yet full.

The expression *tian rong* 天容 is used in two very different senses in the *Chunqiu fanlu*. The term appears in chapter 16, "Signs and Omens," and chapter 56, "Human Correlates of Heaven's Regularities." In chapter 16.1, we find the following: "He plumbed the principles of things to develop fully what is suitable to the emotions and nature, thereby extending Heaven's prosperity" (極理以盡情性之宜，則天容遂矣). This rendering follows the *Shuowen jiezi*, which glosses the character *rong* with the character *sheng* 盛, meaning "to prosper or flourish." (We also entertain the possibility that in chapter 16, *tian rong* 天容 could be read as *tian rong* 天榮 [Heaven's glory]; see chapter 16, note 2.) In chapter 56, we find: "This is why with the human body, the head, [tilted and] circular, resembles the appearance of Heaven" (是故人之身，首而員，象天容也). We believe that the first sense of the expression to be most germane to the subject matter addressed in this chapter and therefore translated the chapter title as "Heaven's Prosperity."

1. The Lau edition has *ji* 及, but the Su Yu and Lai Yanyuan editions have *fan* 反. We follow Su Yu (*CQFLYZ* 333) and Lai Yanyuan here.
2. The singularity of the Way of Heaven refers to the separate and singular cycles of yin and yang.

The sage observes Heaven and acts. This is why he carefully chooses the appropriate occasion for [displaying] love, hatred, happiness, and anger, wishing to harmonize with Heaven, which will not send forth warming, cooling, chilling, and heating if it is not the appropriate season.

He instructs the people with regulations and commands, but his transformation of customs is cool and subtle, as he wishes to harmonize with Heaven's not[3] inverting the proper sequence of warming, cooling, chilling, and heating that completes the year.

He disdains shallowness and is shamed by extravagance and hypocrisy. He praises honesty and sincerity, wishing to harmonize with Heaven. [Heaven] remains silent and without speech, yet its meritorious virtue accumulates and is brought to perfection.

He does not assent to partisanship and selfishness and praises comprehensive love and universal benefit, wishing to harmonize himself with the way in which Heaven, by giving a minimum of frost and an abundance of dew, brings things to their completion.

He reflects inwardly on what is correct and exhibits outwardly what is appropriate to the season.[4] [45/53/10–15]

Section 45.2

When the ruler is happy or angry, he must not fail to be timely. [Those feelings] are permissible in their time, and in their time they are righteous.[5] When happiness and anger harmonize with things in the same category, their principle is unitary. Thus [the distinction between] what is righteous and what is not righteous [depends on] whether the time is in harmony with the category. Thus happiness and anger each are distinct manifestations of the *qi* of heat and cold. [45/53/15–16]

3. Supplying the negative *bu* 不 after *tian zhi* 天之, as suggested by Liu Shipei (Lai, *CQFLJZJY* 301).
4. Su Yu notes that the text breaks off at this point; something evidently is missing here.
5. Su Yu (*CQFLYZ* 301, note 10) suspects that the text is corrupt here.

Book 11, Part 6

CHAPTER 46

The Heavenly Distinctions Lie in Humans

Section 46.1

Someone raised an objection: In regard to the meeting of yin and yang, during the course of one year they have two encounters. They encounter each other in the southern quarter at the midpoint of summer, and they encounter each other in the northern quarter at the midpoint of winter. Winter is [dominated by] the *qi* of mourning for [the destruction of] things. Why, then, do [yin and yang] meet there?

[Someone responded:] It is like Metal, Wood, Water, and Fire, each of which follow yin and yang to implement that over which they rule. They unify their respective strengths and combine their respective achievements. Their substance is not only that of yin and yang, and yet yin and yang accord with them to arise and help them in that over which they rule. Thus,

Lesser Yang in accordance with Wood arises and assists spring's generating;
Greater Yang in accordance with Fire arises and assists summer's nourishing;
Lesser Yin in accordance with Metal arises and assists autumn's completing;
Greater Yin in accordance with Water arises and assists winter's storing away.

Although yin unites its *qi* with Water and joins winter, their substance is not identical. Therefore Water alone possesses [the *qi* that] mourns [the destruction of] things. Yin does not partake of it. Therefore, yin and yang meet at the midpoint of winter, but it is not they that mourn.

Spring is the loving will;
summer is the joyous will;

autumn is the stern will;

and winter is the sorrowful will.

Therefore to love and yet know sternness, to be joyous and yet know sorrow, are the regulations of the four seasons.

The misfortunes[1] of happiness and anger and the righteousness of sorrow and joy do not reside in human beings alone. They also reside in Heaven.

The yang of spring and summer and the yin of autumn and winter do not reside in Heaven alone. They also reside in human beings.

Without the *qi* of spring, how could human beings love widely and be hospitable toward the multitudes?

Without the *qi* of autumn, how could human beings establish their sternness and perfect their achievements?

Without the *qi* of summer, how could human beings nourish abundantly and rejoice in life?

Without the *qi* of winter, how could human beings pity the dead and commiserate with the mournful?

Likewise,

without the *qi* of happiness, how could Heaven warm and thereby engender and nourish in spring?

Without the *qi* of anger, how could Heaven cool and thereby proceed to kill[2] in autumn?

Without the *qi* of joy, how could Heaven disperse yang and thereby nourish and mature in summer?

Without the *qi* of sorrow, how could Heaven arouse yin and thereby seal up and store away in winter?

Therefore it is said: Heaven surely possesses expressions of happiness, anger, sorrow, and joy, and human beings likewise possess the *qi* of spring, autumn, winter, and summer. This is what is called "joining in accordance with one's kind."

Although commoners are of lowly status, they still can observe the application of bounty and punishment. Thus, the circuits of yin and yang each reach completion in six months, [and] their distance [from each other] is always the same degree, but they lodge themselves at different places.

In its circuit, yin

1. The word *huo* 禍 (misfortune) does not make much sense here and may be an error for some other (unknown) word. Su Yu regards it as intrusive.
2. Following Ling Shu's edition, which reads here *qiu jiu sha* 秋就殺 (Su Yu, *CQFLYZ* 335).

resides in the eastern quarter in spring,
resides in the western quarter in autumn,
has emptiness to its left in summer,
has emptiness to the right in winter,
has emptiness below in summer,
and has emptiness above in winter.[3]

These are the constant places of yin.

In its circuit, yang resides
above in spring,
below in winter.

These are the constant places of yang. Yin completes the yearly cycle with four shifts in location, while yang constantly resides in [positions of] solidity. Is this not a case of embracing yang and rejecting yin, employing accretion and avoiding recision?[4] The will of Heaven constantly places yin in empty places and appropriates yin sparingly to assist [yang]. Therefore punishment is bounty's aide, just as yin is yang's assistant. Yang is the master of the year.

The crawling things of the world follow yang and thereby emerge and withdraw;
the grasses and trees of the world follow yang and thereby thrive and wither;
the Three Kings[5] of the world followed yang and thereby rectified [the first month of the calendar];
the honorable and the base of the world follow yang and thereby set their positions in proper order.[6]

The young reside where yang is immature;
the old reside where yang is elderly;
the honorable reside where yang flourishes;
the base reside where yang declines.

"Hidden" means not being able to match up to yang. Those who are not able to match up to yang are the minister and the son. Those who match up to yang are the ruler and the father. Therefore, the human ruler faces south, taking yang as his position. That yang is honorable and yin is base is [due to] Heaven's regulations. The rites esteem the right. They do not esteem yin. They revere the old and the yang and honor their perfected achievements. [46/53/20–46/54/8]

3. Following Lai Yanyuan's suggestion that the characters for right and left are mistakenly reversed in this line (Su Yu, *CQFLYZ* 335).
4. *De* 德 and *xing* 刑 here also embrace the meanings of "bounty" and "punishment."
5. That is, the founding monarchs of the Xia, Shang, and Zhou dynasties.
6. A similar argument appears in chapter 43.

Book 11, Part 7

CHAPTER 47

The Positions of Yin and Yang

Section 47.1

Yang *qi* first emerges in the northeast and moves toward the south to assume its [dominant] position. It then circles westward and withdraws in the north, where it stores itself away for repose. Yin *qi* first emerges in the southeast[1] and moves toward the north, where it likewise assumes its [dominant] position. It then circles westward and withdraws in the south, where it hides itself away for rest. Thus

yang takes the southern quarter as its position and the northern quarter as its repose;
yin takes the northern quarter as its position and the southern quarter as its retreat.
When yang arrives at its position, there is intense heating;
when yin arrives at its position, there is intense chilling.
When yang arrives at its repose, it withdraws and transforms in the earth;
when yin arrives at its retreat, it shuns accretion below.

1. This passage imagines yang as moving clockwise around the horizon. It emerges from the northeast and, after taking its dominant position in the south, continues to the west until it (implicitly) goes into hiding in the northwest, thus "resting" in the northern quadrant. Yin moves counterclockwise around the horizon circle. It emerges from the southeast, moves northward to its dominant position, and then continues westward, (implicitly) going into seclusion in the southwest and "retreating" in the southern quadrant.

Thus, what emerges and grows above in summer and withdraws and transforms below in winter is yang. What withdraws to guard vacuity belowground in summer and emerges to guard vacuity aboveground[2] in winter is yin.

> Yang emerges from fullness and withdraws to fullness;
> yin emerges from emptiness and withdraws to emptiness.

Heaven employs yang and does not employ yin. It loves accretion and abhors recision in this way. Thus, in the course of the year, yin and yang each emerge one at a time. [47/54/12–17]

2. Emending *wei* 位 to *di* 地, based on the first part of the sentence.

Book 12, Part 1

CHAPTER 48

Yin and Yang End and Begin [the Year]

Section 48.1

Heaven's Way ends and begins anew. Therefore the northern quarter is the place where Heaven begins and ends and the place where yin and yang coincide with and separate from each other. After the winter solstice, yin lowers itself and withdraws in the west while yang lifts itself and emerges in the east. The places where they emerge and withdraw are constantly in opposition, and their [reciprocal] strength and harmonious blending together are constantly in compliance.[1]

When there is more, there is no excess;
when there is less, there is no deficiency.
In spring and summer, yang is more abundant and yin is less abundant.
In fall and winter, yang is less abundant and yin is more abundant.

These quantities are never constant, for there is never a time when yin and yang do not divide up [the whole year] and [keep their respective portions] separate from each other.

As they emerge and withdraw, they correspondingly decrease or increase;
as they increase and decrease, they correspondingly saturate or impede.

What is increasing predominates over what is decreasing, [so] the [rate of] withdrawal doubles. What withdraws is diminished by one, and what emerges is augmented by two. Whichever one is activated by Heaven doubles and redoubles. Its positional advantage is such that it constantly is augmented and tips the balance in its favor. Thus each acts within its own category and responds to

1. For the movements of yin and yang, see chapter 47, note 1.

[its opposite]. Therefore the *qi* [of yin and yang] mix with each other and influence each other with their transformations.

In the middle of spring and autumn, the yin and yang *qi* completely intermingle, in midspring to give birth to [things] and in midautumn to kill [things]. From this we see that

> when Heaven arouses [either yin or yang], its *qi* accumulates;
> when Heaven dampens [either yin or yang], its *qi* dissipates.

Therefore,

> arriving at spring, Lesser Yang emerges in the east and moves into Wood, and together [Lesser Yang and] Wood both engender;
> arriving at summer, Greater Yang emerges in the south and moves into Fire, and together both [Greater Yang and] Fire warm.

Is this not a case of each moving into its kind and arising together with its kind?

> Lesser Yang moves into Wood;
> Greater Yang moves into Fire.

Fire and Wood complement each other as each moves into its [position]. Is this not a case of correcting their proper relationships?

Arriving at the season of autumn, Lesser Yin flourishes but is not permitted to use autumn to accompany Metal. If it accompanied Metal, it would harm the achievements of Fire. Although it is not permitted to accompany Metal, it assuredly uses autumn to emerge in the eastern quarter, lowering its position and adjusting its activities to complete the achievements of the harvest. Is this not a case of expediency?[2]

The movement of yin is [such that it] firmly and constantly resides in vacuity, as it is not permitted to reside in fullness. Arriving at winter, it stops in vacuous emptiness. Then Greater Yang [i.e., the sun] attains the north[3] in accordance with its kind, and, together with Water, stimulates chilling. Thus, the Way of Heaven has its proper relationships, its constant norms, and its expediencies.[4] [48/54/23–48/55/3]

2. "Expediency" (*quan* 權) here implies a flexible responsiveness to the exigencies of the seasons.
3. At the winter solstice, the sun at sunrise reaches its northernmost point on the eastern horizon.
4. The reference to "constant norms of Heaven" (*jing* 經) implies a discussion that does not appear here, indicating that part of this essay may have been lost.

Book 12, Part 2

CHAPTER 49

The Meaning of Yin and Yang

Section 49.1

The constancy of Heaven's Way is for there to be one yin and one yang.

Yang is Heaven's accretion;
yin is Heaven's recision.

If you trace the circuits of yin and yang through to the end of the year, you will thereby observe what Heaven draws near to and relies on. [Yin assists yang] to complete Heaven's achievements, and yet it is still designated "empty," for emptiness is its substance. Therefore, clear [weather] and coolness are to the year what sourness and saltiness are to taste: just enough is all that is needed. The governance of the sage also follows [circumstances] and so is like this.

The Lesser Yin of Heaven is used in activity;
the Greater Yin of Heaven is used in idleness.
The Lesser Yin of human beings is used in sternness;
the Greater Yin of human beings is used in mournfulness.
Mournfulness is likewise idleness.
Idleness is likewise mournfulness.

For this reason, the Way of Heaven relies on three seasons to complete life and one season to mourn death.

Death refers to the withering and decay of the many things;
mourning refers to the grief and sorrow of the yin *qi*.

Heaven also possesses happy and angry *qi* and a joyful and sorrowful heart that mutually complements those of human beings. Thus if a grouping is made according to kind, Heaven and human beings are one.

Spring is the *qi* of happiness and therefore it engenders;
autumn is the *qi* of anger and therefore it kills;
summer is the *qi* of joy and therefore it nourishes;
winter is the *qi* of sorrow and therefore it stores away.

These four are the possessions of Heaven and human beings alike. [Heaven and human beings] possess these principles and are therefore unitary.

Those who use them similarly to Heaven will [engender] great order;
those who use them differently from Heaven [will engender] great disorder.

Therefore when constituting the Way of one who would rule others, nothing is more enlightened than to unify the self with Heaven and use things as Heaven does.

[The ruler] must ensure that his happiness and anger will be displayed only in accordance with righteousness, just as chilling and heating will issue forth only in accordance with the proper season.[1] He must ensure that he uses beneficence more generously than punishment, just as yang exceeds yin. This is why,

in circulating yin *qi*, Heaven appropriates only a small amount of yin to bring autumn to completion while it assigns the remainder to winter;
in circulating yin *qi*, the sage appropriates only a small amount of yin to establish his sternness while he assigns the rest to mournfulness.

Mournfulness is also the winter *qi* of human beings. Thus

the Greater Yin of human beings is not used for punishing but for mourning;
the Greater Yin of Heaven is not used for things but for emptiness.
Emptiness constitutes mourning;
mourning constitutes emptiness.

Their substance is one. Both [exemplify] the heart that mourns death and loss. [49/55/7–18]

1. Note the similar analogy in chapter 79.2: "Happiness and anger have seasons when they ought to issue forth; chilling and heating have seasons when they ought to emerge. Their principle is one."

Book 12, Part 3

CHAPTER 50

Yin and Yang Emerge, Withdraw, Ascend, and Descend

Section 50.1

In the grand design of Heaven's Way, things that are mutually opposed are not permitted to emerge together. Such is the case with yin and yang.

In spring, yang emerges while yin withdraws;
in autumn, yin emerges while yang withdraws;
in summer, yang moves to the right while yin moves to the left;
in winter, yin moves to the right while yang moves to the left.
When yin emerges, yang withdraws;
when yang emerges, yin withdraws.
When yin moves to the right, yang moves to the left;
when yin moves to the left, yang moves to the right.

This is why

in spring both are in the south;
in autumn both are in the north;

yet they do not share [the same] circuit.

In summer they intersect in the front;
in winter they intersect in the rear,

yet their pattern is not the same.

They circulate simultaneously but do not disrupt each other;
they cross [paths], but each maintains its respective duties.

This is called Heaven's intention.

How does [Heaven] discharge its business? Heaven's Way [is such that] with the approach of the beginning of winter, yin and yang each come from their respective quarters and shift to the rear:

Yin comes westward from the eastern quarter,
and yang comes eastward from the western quarter.

Arriving at the middle month of winter, they meet each other in the northern quarter, where they combine to become one. This is called the ["winter] solstice." They then divide and withdraw from each other,

yin heading to the right
and yang heading to the left.
Those that head left follow a compliant path;
those that head right follow a retrograde path.
Retrograde *qi* moves to the left and ascends;
compliant *qi* moves to the right and descends.

Thus

what descends warms,
what ascends chills.

From this it can be seen that in winter,

Heaven moves yin to the right and yang to the left.
Heaven promotes what is to the right and demotes what is to the left.
When the winter months draw to their conclusion, both yin and yang return to the south.
When yang returns to the south, it emerges at *yin* [the third position];
when yin returns to the south, it withdraws at *xu* [the eleventh position].[1]

These are the manifestation points of yin and yang when they first emerge from the earth and withdraw into the earth.

Arriving at the middle month of spring,

yang lies due east,
and yin lies due west.

1. The twelve Earthly Branches (*di zhi* 地支) were used in early China to denote the twelve months and to plot their positions around the horizon circle. The first of the branches, *zi* 子, denoted the first astronomical month (in which the winter solstice occurs), correlated with the direction north. The third branch, *yin* 寅, marked the first month of the civil calendar and the beginning of spring, correlated with the direction east-northeast.

This is called the "spring equinox." At the spring equinox, yin and yang are evenly divided. Therefore,

day and night are of even length;
cold and heat are of equal proportion.
Yin daily decreases and gives way to yang;
yang daily increases and strengthens.

Thus warmth and heat are produced.

At the beginning of the month of the height of summer, [yin and yang] meet each other in the southern quarter where they combine to become one. This is called the ["summer] solstice." They then divide and withdraw from each other.

Yang heads to the right;
yin heads to the left.
Heading left, [yin] comes from below;
heading right, [yang] comes from above;
[what comes from] above heats;
[what comes from] below chills.

From this we see that in summer,

Heaven moves yang to the right
and moves yin to the left;
promotes what is to the right
and demotes what is to the left.

When the summer months draw to their conclusion, both yin and yang return to the north.

When yang returns to the north, it withdraws at *shen* [the ninth position];
when yin returns to the north, it emerges at *chen* [the fifth position].

These are the manifestation points of yin and yang when they first emerge from the earth and withdraw to the earth.

Arriving at the middle month of autumn,

yang lies due west,
and yin lies due east.

This is called the "autumn equinox." At the autumn equinox, yin and yang are evenly divided. Therefore,

day and night are of even length;
cold and heat are of equal proportion.
Yang daily decreases and gives way to yin;
yin daily increases and strengthens.

Thus, arriving at the third month of autumn, frost begins, and arriving at the first month of winter, cold first arrives. [At the time of the] "Light Snow,"[2] all things are mature. [By the time of the] "Great Cold,"[3] things are gathered together and stored away, as the achievements of Heaven and Earth are brought to a conclusion. [50/55/22–50/56/5]

2. "Light Snow" is the twentieth of the twenty-four "fortnightly periods" that comprise the Chinese solar calendar, which commences with "Beginning of Spring" on approximately February 4 or 5 (forty-six days after the winter solstice). The date for the beginning of "Light Snow" is approximately November 23 or 24.

3. "Great Cold," the last of the twenty-four "fortnightly periods," begins on approximately January 21 or 22.

Book 12, Part 4

CHAPTER 51

Heaven's Way Is Not Dualistic

Section 51.1

In Heaven's constant Way, things that are opposed are not permitted to arise simultaneously. Therefore Heaven's Way is said to be singular. What is singular and not dualistic is Heaven's conduct. Yin and yang are mutually opposed. Therefore

> when one emerges, the other withdraws;
> when one is at the right, the other is at the left.
> In spring, both are in the south;
> in autumn, both are in the north.
> In summer, they intersect in the front;
> in winter, they intersect in the rear.
> They move in unison yet do not share [the same] circuit;
> they intermingle in meeting, yet each carries its respective pattern.

Is this not what is prescribed for them?[1]

> It is Heaven's constant way [with regard to yin and yang] that
> one emerges while [the other] withdraws;
> one is in repose while [the other] takes up its position.[2]

Their degree [of separation from each other] is one [i.e., identical], yet their intentions are not identical.

1. These opening lines are virtually identical to those of chapter 50.
2. Emending *fu* 伏 to read *wei* 位, following Zhong, *CQFLJS* 623, note 7.

When yang emerges, it constantly is suspended in the front, taking responsibility for the tasks of the harvest.

When yin emerges, it constantly is suspended in the rear, guarding vacuous emptiness.

When yang rests, its accomplishments have been completed above and stored below.

When yin rests, it is not permitted to be near to righteousness and so moves far [from where righteousness] is located.

Heaven's

using yang and not using yin,

loving accretion [and] not loving recision,

is like this. Thus,

yang emerges and moves to the front;

yin emerges and moves to the rear,

manifesting [Heaven's] mind, which reveres accretion and scorns recision.

Yang emerges and accumulates during the summer, using accretion in the tasks of the harvest.

Yin emerges and accumulates during the winter, relegating recision to vacuous emptiness.

One must analyze it in this way. Heaven is inconstant with regard to things and yet single-minded with regard to the seasons. Whatever is appropriate to a season, [Heaven] does in a unitary fashion.

Therefore, [when Heaven]

opens one, it closes the other,

raises one up, it discards the other,

stopping at the end of a complete [round of] seasons. Having ended, it begins again with one. What is one is unitary. This is why Heaven regards those things that occupy the yin position as all bad and disruptive of goodness; [therefore] yin is not permitted to preside over names. This is Heaven's Way. Therefore, to be constantly unitary and not destructive is Heaven's Way. Whether an act is great or small, difficult or easy, if you oppose Heaven's Way, you will not succeed. This is why

the eyes cannot see two images [simultaneously],

the ears cannot hear two sounds [simultaneously].

One hand cannot do two tasks [simultaneously]. [If you try to] draw a square with one hand while [trying to] draw a circle with the other hand, you will not be able to complete either of them. When people take up small and easy tasks and in the end are unable to complete them, it is [usually] because they likewise do them in a way that contradicts Heaven and cannot be carried out. Thus, when the ancients recorded things in writing, if the mind rested on a single focal point, it was said to be "loyal," but when the mind maintained two focal points, it was said to be "duplicitous."[3] "Duplicitous" means that a person is not centered in the unitary. Not being unitary is the [source] from which duplicity arises. This is why the noble man disdains two and honors one. Who does not have goodness? Yet if their goodness is not unitary, it will not be sufficient for them to establish themselves. What government lacks constant norms? Yet if the constant norms are not unitary, they will be insufficient for [a government] to perfect its achievements. An *Ode* declares:

"The High God is close at hand; do not be double-minded."[4]

These are the words of one who understands Heaven's Way. [51/56/9–23]

3. The author is here playing on the fact that the character for "loyalty," *zhong* 忠, consists of the character *zhong* 中, which means "center," and the character *xin* 心, which means both "heart" and "mind." The character for "duplicity," *huan* 患, closely resembles the character for "loyalty" but doubles the character *zhong* 中. In other contexts, *huan* has a range of meanings, including "calamity" and "to suffer."

4. *Odes* 236, verse 7.

Book 12, Part 5

CHAPTER 52

Heat or Cold, Which Predominates?

Section 52.1

Heaven's Way
  sends forth yang to create warmth and thereby engenders things,
  and sends forth yin to create coolness and thereby completes things.
Therefore
  without heating, nourishment would not be possible,
  and without chilling, maturation would not be possible.

We have emended the title following Su Yu, *CQFLYZ* 347. This chapter consists of two unrelated essays that originally must have circulated independently. The first essay takes up yin-yang cosmology and explains the movements and activities of yin and yang as they pass through the yearly cycle. The second essay attempts to reconcile two contradictory ideas. If anomalies are to be interpreted as Heaven's response to the misdeeds of the ruler and a sign of Heaven's discontent with the ruler's actions, this calls into question the reputation of two of the greatest culture heroes of the Confucian tradition, Tang and Yu, whose legends link them with two major natural calamities, a great drought and a great flood, respectively (for which, see note 3). The author attempts to reconcile that contradiction by introducing the concept of *shi zao zhi bian* 適遭之變, an expression that seems to denote human destiny that is transformed—from auspicious to inauspicious—because of an "untoward alteration of seasonal *qi*." This category of destiny explains why virtuous people may suffer such inauspicious occurrences as floods and droughts. (The subject of "changeable destiny" also appears in chapter 13.3.) Su Yu (*CQFLYZ* 348–49) notes that this idea is also taken up in the *Bohutong* (chapter 16, "Calamities and Extraordinary Events"), in the following passage: "When Yao was visited by the great flood and Tang by the great drought was it also a reproach [from Heaven]? When Yao was visited by the great flood and Tang by the great drought, it was an accident caused by fate" (Tjan Tjoe Som, trans., *Po Hu T'ung: The Comprehensive Discussions in the White Tiger Hall* [Leiden: Brill, 1952], 2:490). The *Wenzi* also contains a short passage dealing with this same subject: "Your humble servant has heard that when evil is practiced, anomalies occur as a response, but when goodness is practiced and anomalies occur, it is a consequence of a sudden encounter with fate. They are not caused by [one who] governs" (quoted in Su Yu, *CQFLYZ* 349).

This is the essence of the year. If you [seek to] regulate[1] your heart but do not scrutinize the [months in which] hot emanations and cold condensations predominate, when using [your heart to carry out policies], you will invariably defy Heaven. People who have defied Heaven, even if industrious, will not be successful. Actually, it is during [the period] from the first month to the tenth month when Heaven completes its achievements. If you calculate during this period the preponderance [of days] occupied by yin and yang, [you will find] whether warm or cold days are more numerous. If you determine the time when something is first engendered to its maturation, [you will find] whether dew or frost is more abundant. The result will be that from the middle of spring until autumn, the *qi* is warm and harmonious. Only when the ninth month of autumn arrives does yin begin to be more abundant than yang. At this time, Heaven emanates cold and sends down frost. The emanation of cold and the sending down of frost is what Heaven confers on living things so that they are inevitably completed. Thus the ninth month is the month in which the achievements of Heaven are nearly completed, and in the tenth month everything is completed. Therefore if you examine Heaven's traces and calculate its substance, [you will find that] the cold days are quite few and, furthermore, that only after Heaven's achievements are completed is yin finally sent forth in great quantity. In the completion of Heaven's achievements, Lesser Yin participates while Greater Yin does not participate.

> Lesser Yin is internal;
> Greater Yin is external.

Therefore

> frost accumulates on things;
> snow accumulates in the void.

The void is simply the earth; it does not extend to things. Once Heaven's achievements have been completed and before things have begun to be generated again, it is suitable for the Greater Yin to emerge. Even though we speak of yin, Greater Yang also helps Greater Yin alter its position, although Greater Yin does not know from where it has received assistance. Therefore when a sagely king occupies the superior position,

> Heaven covers, [and] Earth supports;
> wind commands, and rain spreads.
> Rain, which spreads, corresponds to [the ruler] extending his virtue to all;
> winds, which command, correspond to [the ruler's] upright commands.

An *Ode* declares:

1. Emending *zhi* 知 to *zhi* 治, following Su Yu.

"Do not be clever, do not be knowing;
follow the precepts of the [High] God."[2]

This means that although one is not capable of knowledge or wisdom, nevertheless one can still imitate what Heaven does. [52/56/27–52/57/6]

Section 52.2

Yu's flood and Tang's drought[3] were not due to the constant regularities [of Heaven]. [Both] happened to encounter an untoward alteration of seasonal *qi* in which yin and yang lost their proper balance. Yao looked upon the common people as if they were his sons, and the people looked upon Yao as if he were their father and mother. The *Documents* states: "After twenty-eight years, [Yao] died. The people mourned him for three years as if he had been their parent, and within the Four Seas [i.e., everywhere], the playing of musical instruments ceased for three years."[4] For three years, yang *qi* was suppressed by yin *qi*, so yin *qi* increased substantially. This is why Yu is known for [encountering] a flood.

Jie was the most ruthless and most traitorous man in the world, and Tang was the most virtuous man in the world. When the [people of the whole] world deposed this ruthless and traitorous man and obtained [in his place] someone possessing an abundance of virtue, this amounted to two events of exceptional goodness. Hence, yang *qi* increased twofold. This is why Tang is known for [encountering] a drought.

Both [Yu and Tang] happened to encounter an untoward alteration [of seasonal *qi*]. These disasters were not caused by the transgressions of Yu or Tang. Do not, if you happen to encounter an untoward alteration of *qi*, have doubts about the constancies of everyday life. In this way, what you wish to preserve will not be lost, and the correct way will become increasingly manifest. [52/57/6–11]

2. *Odes* 241, verse 7; translation modified from Arthur Waley, trans., *The Book of Songs: The Ancient Chinese Classic of Poetry*, ed., with additional translations, Joseph R. Allen (New York: Grove Press, 1996), 238. The "High God" here translates *di* 帝 (i.e., *shang di* 上帝), the principal deity of China in high antiquity.
3. According to Chinese tradition, King Yu the Great, founder of the Xia dynasty, encountered a massive flood, and King Tang, founder of the Shang dynasty, encountered a catastrophic drought. How, then, was the author to explain that natural disasters, generally taken as a sign of misrule, occurred during the dynasty-founding reigns of two of the greatest sages in Chinese history? The answer, as we shall see, lay with the actions of their respective predecessors Yao and Jie, the first a great sage and the other a dreadful villain. The abundance of yin produced by the sadness felt by the common people at Yao's death, and the abundance of yang produced by the joy felt by the common people when Jie was deposed and Tang became ruler, gave rise to the subsequent flood and drought in the reigns of Yu and Tang.
4. *Documents*, "Shun dian" (Canon of Shun), 1.13; James Legge, trans., *The Shoo King, or, The Book of Historical Documents*, vol. 3 of *The Chinese Classics*, 2nd rev. ed. (1894; repr., Hong Kong: Hong Kong University Press, 1960), 40–41.

Book 12, Part 6

CHAPTER 53

Laying the Foundation of Righteousness

Section 53.1

All things invariably possess complements. As for these complements:

there must be a superior and there must be a subordinate;
there must be a right, and there must be a left;
there must be a front, and there must be a back;
there must be an outside, and there must be an inside.
[When] there is goodness, there must be evil.
[When] there is compliance, there must be deviation.
[When] there is joy, there must be anger.
[When] there is cold, there must be heat.
[When] there is morning, there must be evening.

These all are complements.

Yin is yang's complement;
the wife is the husband's complement;
the son is the father's complement;
and the minister is the ruler's complement.

Things do not exist without a complement, and each [pair of] complements has its yin and yang [aspects].

Yang unites with yin, and yin unites with yang;
the husband unites with the wife, and the wife unites with the husband;
the ruler unites with the minister, and the minister unites with the ruler.

The righteous [relationships] between ruler and minister, husband and wife, and father and son all derive from the Way of yin and yang:

The ruler is yang; the minister is yin.
The father is yang; the son is yin.
The husband is yang; the wife is yin.

There are no places where the Way of yin circulates alone. At the beginning [of the yearly cycle], yin is not permitted to arise by itself. Likewise, at the end [of the yearly cycle], yin is not permitted to share in [the glories of] yang's achievements. Such is the righteous principle of "joining." Thus,

the minister joins his achievements to the lord;
the son joins his achievements to the father;
the wife joins her achievements to the husband;
yin joins its achievements to yang;
and Earth joins its achievements to Heaven.[1] [53/57/15–21]

Section 53.2

Where there are those who are advanced and promoted, there are those who are restrained and demoted.
Where there are those who are treated dismissively and placed to the right, there are those who are brought forward and placed to the left.
Where there are those to whom one draws near and employs, there are those from whom one keeps away and avoids.
Where there are desires that daily increase, there are desires that daily decrease.

Increase their benefit and decrease their harm.

There are seasons for decreasing what is scarce and increasing what is abundant;
there are seasons for decreasing what is abundant and increasing what is scarce.
Do not allow what is scarce to be completely eradicated.
Do not allow what is abundant to become excessive. [53/57/21–24]

1. This sentence marks the end of the first section (53.1) by functioning as a summation or concluding point to the discussion of the Three Bonds (ruler–minister, father–son, husband–wife) that correlates them with their respective yin-yang counterparts. We treat the seventy characters following this statement as a separate section (53.2). To the extent that they enumerate more examples of the ways in which things belonging to the categories of yin and yang are invariably found as complementary pairs, and so relate to themes described in the opening section, they may appear to be an integral part of section 53.1. But because they do not follow logically from the concluding statement of section 53.1, we have put them in a separate section. These lines, however, may have originally appeared somewhere in section 53.1, perhaps following the list of yin-yang complements that opens the essay in which the parallel grammatical structure *you* x *bi you* y 有 X 必有 Y occurs repeatedly.

Section 53.3

Yin and yang are two [aspects of *qi*]. At the end of the year, each emerges singularly. They emerge singularly, and their proximity or distance [from each other] is identical in degree but not identical in intention.

> Yang emerges and is constantly suspended in the front, taking responsibility for the various undertakings of the yearly cycle.
>
> Yin emerges and constantly is suspended in the rear, guarding vacuous emptiness.[2]

This reveals that

> Heaven draws near to yang while it keeps yin at a distance.
>
> Heaven employs accretion while it does not employ recision.

Thus, the various allotments of humaneness, righteousness, regulations, and limits are ultimately derived from Heaven.

> Heaven is the ruler who shelters and discloses them;
> Earth is the minister who nurtures and supports them.
> Yang is the husband who generates them;
> yin is the wife who assists them.
> Spring is the father who engenders them;
> summer is the son who nourishes them.
> Autumn is the death that enshrouds them;
> winter is the pain that mourns them.

The Three Bonds of the Kingly Way may be sought in Heaven. [53/57/24–28]

Section 53.4

> Heaven sends forth yang to create warming and gives birth to things.
> Earth sends forth yin to create cooling and brings things to maturity.[3]
> Without warming, there is no birth.
> Without cooling, there is no maturation.[4]

---

2. We have emended *kongchu* 空處 to *kongxu* 空虛 based on chapter 51, in which the expression appears in an identical sentence.
3. Two sentences nearly identical to these appear at the beginning of chapter 52. There, however, the activities of both yin and yang are associated with Heaven.
4. Chapter 52 states: "Without heating, nourishment would not be possible, and without chilling, maturation would not be possible."

Nevertheless, if you calculate the quantities of their apportionment, warming and heating constitute one hundred, and cooling and chilling constitute one. Moral education compares to punishments in this same way.[5] Therefore the sage increases his love and decreases his sternness. He extends his bounty and limits his punishments. He relies on this to become a counterpart to Heaven.[6] [53/57/28–30]

Section 53.5

Heaven's great numbers invariably conclude with ten ten-day periods. The ten-day period [conforms to] the numbers of Heaven and Earth. With ten, the enumeration is complete. The ten-day period [governs] the achievements of birth and maturation. With ten [such periods, birth and maturation] are completely accomplished.

[The transformations of] Heaven's *qi* are gradual. It does not suddenly become cold or suddenly become hot.[7] Therefore

when chilling, it does not become frigid;
when heating, it does not become sweltering.

They gradually arise and do not suddenly come to an end.[8] The *Changes* states:

"Frost underfoot, ice will soon follow.
This is to say, it complies [with Heaven's proper sequence]."[9]

The superior must be firm and not violate the proper sequence of things. It is certainly the case that when Heaven acts, it does not complete [its tasks] as soon as it begins them.[10] What human beings do likewise should not all be done when just begun.[11] As a general rule, whenever you initiate an undertaking, gradually implement it and then gradually rescind it, so that the people's hearts will be

5. Note that section 53.4 contrasts *dejiao* 德教 (virtue and education) with *xingfa* 刑法 (punishments and penalties), whereas section 53.3 simply contrasts *de* (bounty) with *xing* (punishment).
6. The ways in which the sage functions as "a counterpart to Heaven" (*pei tian* 配天) also are discussed in chapters 55, 79, and 80A.
7. We have supplied the character *bu* 不, following Lu Wenchao (Su Yu, *CQFLYZ* 352).
8. We have deleted the two characters *you yu* 有餘, following Yu Yue (Su Yu, *CQFLYZ* 352).
9. This citation from the *Changes* (*Yijing*, hexagram *kun*, line 1) differs slightly from extant editions of the text.
10. Liu Shipei suggests excising the character *guo* 果; Zhong Zhaopeng suggests that *guo shi* 果是 is best understood as *guoran shi* 果然是. We followed Zhong's interpretation. See the discussion in Zhong, *CQFLJS* 637, note 21.
11. We have emended the two occurrences of the character *zuo* 作 to *zha* 乍, following Lu Wenchao (Su Yu, *CQFLYZ* 352).

delighted and made secure by it and will not be frightened by it. Thus it is said: "The noble man governs human beings in accordance with their humanity. He understands that they possess the capacity for goodness." This expresses it. The Way of the Sage is identical to Heaven and Earth, stirring all within the Four Seas and transforming their habits and customs. [53/57/30–53/58/5]

Book 12, Part 7

CHAPTER 54

[Title and text are no longer extant.]

Book 13, Part 1

CHAPTER 55

The Correlates of the Four Seasons

Section 55.1

Heaven's Way:

> Spring's warming gives birth,
> summer's heating nourishes,
> autumn's cooling kills,
> winter's chilling stores away.

Warmth, heat, coolness, and cold are different [aspects of] *qi*, yet their achievements are identical: they all are the means by which Heaven completes the year.

The sage correlates himself with Heaven's conduct to create his policies.[1] Therefore,

> with gifts he correlates himself with warming and is the counterpart of spring;[2]
> with rewards he correlates himself with heating and is the counterpart of summer;
> with penalties he correlates himself with cooling and is the counterpart of autumn;
> and with punishments he correlates himself with chilling and is the counterpart of winter.

Gifts, rewards, penalties, and punishments are different affairs, yet their achievements are identical: they all are the means by which the king completes his potency.

---

1. The word *fu* 副 in this context means "correlate." The word also appeared with this meaning in the last sentence of chapter 44.1.
2. The important concept of the ruler as the counterpart of Heaven also appears in chapters 79 and 80.

Gifts, rewards, penalties, [and] punishments and spring, summer, autumn, and winter respond to one another according to kind, like the joining of two halves of a tally. Therefore it is said: "The king is the counterpart to Heaven." This refers to the Way.

Heaven has four seasons;
the king has four policies.

The four policies resemble the four seasons. They are in the same category; they are what Heaven and the ruler have in common.

Gifts are spring;
rewards are summer;
penalties are autumn;
punishments are winter.

With gifts, rewards, penalties, and punishments, you will never be unprepared, just as with spring, summer, autumn, and winter [Heaven] will never be incomplete.

Gifts, rewards, penalties, and punishments must be promulgated in accordance with the appropriate occasion, just as warmth, heat, coolness, and cold must issue forth in accordance with the appropriate season.

Gifts, rewards, penalties, and punishments each have their appropriate occasion, just as spring, summer, autumn and winter each have their appropriate time.

These four policies must not interfere with one another, just as the four seasons must not interfere with one another.

These four policies must not trade places, just as the four seasons must not trade places.

Therefore when there were instances in which gifts, rewards, penalties, and punishments were not implemented on the proper occasion, the *Spring and Autumn* criticized them. [55/58/11–19]

Book 13, Part 2

CHAPTER 56

Human Correlates of Heaven's Regularities

Section 56.1

The virtue of Heaven is to bestow;
the virtue of Earth is to transform;
the virtue of humankind is to be righteous.
Heaven's *qi* is above;
Earth's *qi* is below;
humankind's *qi* is in their midst.
Spring gives birth and summer matures, and so the numerous things flourish;
autumn kills and winter reaps, and so the numerous things are stored away.

Therefore,

nothing is more refined than *qi*;
nothing is more rich than Earth;
nothing is more spiritlike than Heaven.

Of the living things born of the vital essence of Heaven and Earth, none is nobler than human beings. Human beings receive their destiny from Heaven, and therefore they surpass [the lesser creatures] that must fend for themselves.

Other living things suffer troubles and defects and cannot practice humaneness and righteousness. Human beings alone practice humaneness and righteousness.

Other living things suffer troubles and defects and cannot match Heaven and Earth. Human beings alone match Heaven and Earth.

Human beings have 360 joints that match Heaven's numbers.[1] [They have] form, frame, bone, and flesh that match Earth's substantiality.

> Above they have ears and eyes, keen and clear, resembling the sun and moon.
> In their bodies they have orifices and pores, veins and arteries, resembling the rivers and valleys.
> In their hearts they have sorrow and joy, happiness, and anger, which are the same in kind as the spirit *qi* [of Heaven and Earth].

Observe the uniqueness of the human body. How surpassingly lofty a thing it is, and how similar in kind to Heaven!

[Other] things tangentially and meagerly partake of Heaven's yin and yang and thereby survive, but human beings possess [Heaven's] elaborations and patterns in all their brilliance. This is why as a general rule, the forms of other [living] things do not enable them to move about except in a crouched and creeping fashion.[2] Human beings alone stand erect, look straight forward, and assume an upright position. Thus

> those who appropriate a bit of Heaven and Earth assume a non-erect posture;
> those who appropriate much from Heaven and Earth assume an upright posture.

This example makes evident that human beings are distinct from other living things and that they join with Heaven and Earth. This is why with the human body,

> the head, tilted and circular, resembles the appearance of Heaven;
> the hair [. . .][3] resembles the stars and planets;
> the ears and eyes, side and front, resemble the sun and the moon;
> the nose and mouth, inhaling and exhaling, resemble the wind and *qi*;
> the chest and middle, penetrating and knowing, resemble spirit illumination;
> the abdomen and bladder, filling and emptying, resemble the numerous things.

The numerous things are nearest to Earth. Therefore, the portion of the body below the waist corresponds to Earth. As [the body] forms an image of Heaven and Earth, the waist is a sash [dividing the upper and lower parts].

> What lies above the waist[4] is refined, numinous, noble, and majestic, illuminating the features of Heaven's kind.
> What lies below the waist is fertile, full, humble, and lowly, comparable to the richness of the soil.

---

1. The 360 joints corresponded to the number of days in the year, rounded off to six whole sexagenary cycles.
2. Treating *tian di* 天地 as excrescent, following Su Yu, *CQFLYZ* 355.
3. Based on parallelism, two characters must have disappeared from the text here.
4. Here and in the next sentence, we have emended *jing* 頸 (neck) to *yao* 要 (waist), as suggested by Sun Yirang (Zhong, *CQFLJS* 647, note 26).

The feet [side by side] form a square, resembling the Earth's shape. Therefore on ceremonial occasions, when donning a sash or girdle, it must exactly match the waist, to divide [the lower body] from the heart. What is above the sash is entirely yang, and what is below the sash is entirely yin, each with its own function.

Yang is Heaven's *qi*;
yin is Earth's *qi*.

Therefore if the movements of yin and yang cause human beings to have an ailment in the foot and it rises [to become] numbness in the throat, the *qi* of Earth will rise to become clouds and rain, for where there is a resemblance, there is also a response.

The tallies of Heaven and Earth and the correlates of yin and yang always are established in the human body. The [term] "body" resembles [the term] "Heaven." The numerology of the body and that of Heaven are mutually interwoven. Therefore [the body's] destiny and that of Heaven are mutually linked. Heaven completes the human body with the number of days in a full year. Thus the body's 360[5] lesser joints correspond to the number of days in a year, and the twelve larger joints match the number of months.

Inside the body are the five viscera corresponding to the number of the Five Phases;
outside the body are the four limbs corresponding to the number of the four seasons;
the alterations of wakefulness and slumber correspond to day and night;
the alterations of strength and weakness correspond to winter and summer;
and the alterations of sorrow and joy correspond to yin and yang.
Its mind has calculations and deliberations corresponding to degrees and numbers.
Its conduct has conventions and patterns corresponding to Heaven and Earth.

These things, whether obscure or obvious in the body, are innate to human beings. When human beings are compared and matched with Heaven and Earth, they are found to be a fitting match.

In what may be numbered, there is correspondence in number.
In what may not be numbered, there is correspondence in kind.

They all are appropriately identical and correspond to Heaven. This is why [one must]

5. Emending "366" to "360," following Lu Wenchao. See the lengthy discussion justifying this emendation in Zhong, *CQFLJS* 649, note 6.

set out in detail what possesses form to manifest what is formless;
grasp what may be numbered to manifest what may not be numbered.

[When] speaking of the Way in this manner, it is quite fitting that things respond to one another in accordance with their kind. This is just like the human body, which corresponds to Heaven in accordance with its regularities. [56/58/23–56/59/13]

Book 13, Part 3

CHAPTER 57

Things of the Same Kind Activate One Another

Section 57.1

Now if you pour water on level ground, it will avoid the dry area and run to the wet area, but if you expose two similar pieces of firewood to fire, the fire will avoid the wet piece and go to the dry one. All things avoid what is different from them and follow what is similar to them. Therefore,

if *qi* are the same in kind, they will come together;

if tones match, they will respond to each other.

This is clear from the evidence. Now suppose you tune and play a *qin* or a *se*:[1]

Pluck the note *gong*, and other *gong* notes will respond to it;

pluck the note *shang*, and other *shang* notes will respond to it.[2]

Among the five notes, each one that matches will sound spontaneously. This has nothing to do with spirits. Their regularities make them so.

A beautiful thing calls forth things that are beautiful in kind;

an ugly thing calls forth things that are ugly in kind,

for things of the same kind arise in response to each other. For example,

1. The *qin* is a musical instrument, resembling a small version of the later Japanese koto, having a slightly convex sounding board and (usually) five or seven strings, tuned with pegs. The *se* was a zither-like instrument with (usually) twenty-five strings, tuned with movable bridges.
2. The notes of the Chinese pentatonic scale were named *gong*, *shang*, *jue*, *zhi*, and *yu*. The absolute value of the fundamental is a matter of dispute, but if we assume that *gong* is C, then *shang* would be D; *jue*, E; *zhi*, G; and *yu*, A. To demonstrate the principle that like resonates with like, many early Chinese writers used the actual observation that if one string of an instrument is plucked, a similarly tuned string on a nearby instrument will vibrate.

when a horse neighs, horses will respond;
when an ox lows, oxen will respond.

Similarly,

when an emperor or a king is about to arise, auspicious omens first will appear;
when he is about to perish, baleful omens first will appear.

Therefore things of the same kind call forth one another.

Because of the dragon, rain is produced.
By the use of the fan, heat is chased away.
Wherever armies are stationed, briars grow.

Whether beautiful or ugly, all things have their preordained genesis and destiny, but no one knows where they lie.

When the heavens darken and it is about to rain, people's illnesses first will affect them, because their yin has been aroused in response. When the heavens seem about to darken and it is about to rain, people want to sleep. This is because of yin *qi*.

People who are anxious want to lie down, because the yin of anxiety and lying down seek each other;
people who are happy do not want to lie down because the yang of happiness and wakefulness require each other.

Water takes control over the nighttime and stretches out its allotted span; when the east wind arrives, wine ferments more vigorously. Those who are ill worsen at the arrival of night; cocks gather at first light, rousing one another with their crowing. [Different kinds of] *qi* become more and more refined. Therefore,

yang increases yang;
yin increases yin,

for the *qi* of yin and yang can naturally augment or diminish things in accordance with their kind.

Heaven has yin and yang [aspects],
and people have yin and yang [aspects].
When the *qi* of Heaven and Earth arises, the *qi* of people arises in response to it;
when the *qi* of people arises, the *qi* of Heaven and Earth also arises appropriately in response to it.

Their Way is unitary. Those who understand this,

when wishing to bring forth rain, activate yin, causing yin to arise;
when wishing to stop rain, activate yang, causing yang to arise.

Therefore, rain is not caused by the spirits. People suspect that it is the spirits' doing, because its inner principles are subtle and mysterious. It is not only that the *qi* of yin and yang advances or withdraws according to its kind. Even [the reasons for] misfortune, calamities, and blessings are due to the same thing. It is not that these things do not initially arise from within the self, [but even so,] things become active in response to their kind. Therefore, those who are intelligent, sagely, and spiritlike look within and listen to themselves, so their words become intelligent and sagely. The reason why introspection and listening to oneself alone can lead to intelligence and sagacity is because one becomes aware that the original mind lies there. Therefore when the note *gong* is plucked on a *qin* or a *se*, the note *gong* on other [instruments nearby] sounds spontaneously in response. This is a case of things being activated according to kind. Their activity has sound but no form. People do not see a physical form associated with what activates them, so they say that they sound on their own. Furthermore, since they activate each other without [visible] form, it is said that they do so spontaneously. In reality, it is not that they do so spontaneously but that something causes them to be so. There is definitely something concrete that stimulates them, but what stimulates them has no [visible] form. According to a tradition of the *Documents*, when the House of Zhou was about to arise, some big red crows holding seed heads of grain in their bills gathered on the roof of the king's house. King Wu was elated, and all the great officers were elated. The Duke of Zhou said, "Make greater effort. Make greater effort. Heaven reveals this to exhort us."[3] Fearfully we heed this. [57/59/17–57/60/5]

3. *Documents*, "Appendix to the Great Declaration"; James Legge, trans., *The Shoo King, or, The Book of Historical Documents*, vol. 3 of *The Chinese Classics*, 2nd rev. ed. (1894; repr., Hong Kong: Hong Kong University Press, 1960), 298.

Group 6

Five-Phase Principles

THE SEVEN chapters of group 6, "Five-Phase Principles," focus on Five-Phase cosmology and a concern with deriving political norms from the characteristics of that cosmology.

GROUP 6: FIVE-PHASE PRINCIPLES, CHAPTERS 58–64

58. 五行相生 *Wuxing xiang sheng* The Mutual Engendering of the Five Phases[1]
59. 五行相勝 *Wuxing xiang sheng* The Mutual Conquest of the Five Phases
60. 五行順逆 *Wuxing shun ni* Complying with and Deviating from the Five Phases
61. 制水五行 *Zhi shui wuxing* Controlling Water by Means of the Five Phases
62. 制亂五行 *Zhi luan wuxing* Controlling Disorders by Means of the Five Phases
63. 五行變救 *Wuxing bian jiu* Aberrations of the Five Phases and Their Remedies
64. 五行五事 *Wuxing wu shi* The Five Phases and Five Affairs

1. In *CQFL*, the order of chapters 58 and 59 is reversed, with "The Mutual Engendering of the Five Phases" coming after "The Mutual Conquest of the Five Phases." We follow Su Yu (*CQFLYZ* 361), who, in his reconstruction of the *Chunqiu fanlu*, argues that chapter 58 should be "The Mutual Engendering of the Five Phases" and chapter 59, "The Mutual Conquest of the Five Phases." His argument is based in part on literary grounds: the "Mutual Engendering" essay includes an introductory section, but the other does not. We think that the two chapters may once have formed a single essay, with the material arranged in the order proposed by Su Yu.

Description of Individual Chapters

Chapters 58, 59, and 60 are closely related, as they share many of the same Five-Phase correlations and sensibilities and progress logically from one to the next. In addition, all the essays identify the "current dynasty" with the power of the Fire phase, an important point to which we will return. The first two chapters in the group, though not a perfectly matched pair (among other things, the "Mutual Engendering" chapter also includes material on the Mutual Conquest Sequence and is a much more polished production in literary terms), are essentially mirror opposites. The two chapters present a schematic of positive and negative ideals of governance based on the Five Phases. Chapter 58, "The Mutual Engendering of the Five Phases," adheres to the familiar scheme of describing the year in terms of the Mutual Production Sequence, supplying an artificial fifth season of "midsummer" to correlate with Earth. This conception of annual time also implicitly links the Five Phases with the waxing and waning of yin and yang:

Wood = spring = east = Lesser Yang
Fire = summer = south = Greater Yang
Earth = midsummer (sixth month) = center = Mature Yang, Emergent Yin
Metal = autumn = west = Lesser Yin
Water = winter = north = Greater Yin

Chapter 58 correlates each of the Five Phases with the direction, aspect of governance, primary governmental official, virtue, tool, positive exemplar, and secondary official to whom the primary official passes on responsibility in an idealized bureaucracy, as summarized in table 1. The types of activities associated with the "humaneness" of the minister of agriculture exemplify the ways in which these correlative schemes neatly prescribe the conduct of the bureaucracy's highest-ranking officials:

> The minister of agriculture esteems humaneness. He promotes scholars versed in the classical arts and leads them along the path of the Five Emperors and Three Kings. He follows their good points and rectifies their bad points. Grasping the compass, he promotes birth and, with the utmost warmth, saturates those below. He understands the fertility, barrenness, strengths, and weakness of the terrain; establishes affairs; and engenders norms in accordance with what is suitable to the land.[2]

2. *CQFL* 59/61/14–15.

TABLE 1

	Wood	Fire	Earth	Metal	Water
Direction	East	South	Center	West	North
Aspect	Agriculture	Current dynasty	Ruler's administration	Administrator of law	Censor
Primary official	Minister of agriculture	Minister of war	Minister of public works	Minister of mobilization	Minister of justice
Virtue	Humaneness	Wisdom	Trustworthiness	Righteousness	Propriety
Tool	Compass	Balance	Level	Square	Weight
Positive exemplar	Duke of Shao	Duke of Zhou	Grand Duke	Zixu (Wu Zixu)	Confucius
Secondary official	Minister of war	Minister of public works	Minister of mobilization	Minister of justice	Minister of agriculture

Chapter 59 (in our reordering of the first two chapters of this group), "The Mutual Conquest of the Five Phases," also presents each phase in the standard Mutual Production Sequence but concludes the discussion of each phase with a statement of the relevant conquest: Wood (Metal conquers Wood), Fire (Water conquers Fire), Earth (Wood conquers Earth), Metal (Fire conquers Metal), and Water (Earth conquers Water). Each section identifies a particular phase with a primary governmental official, a transgression, a negative exemplar, and (with the exception of the Earth phase) a chastising agent (usually an official) responsible for meting out punishment, as shown in table 2.

TABLE 2

	Wood	Fire	Earth	Metal	Water
Primary official	Minister of agriculture	Minister of war	Minister of public works	Minister of education	Minister of justice
Transgression	Acts treacherously	Acts slanderously	Treats ruler like a spirit	Acts deceptively	Acts disorderly
Negative exemplar	Duke Huan of Qi	Jisun of Lu	King Ling of Chu	Minister De Chen	Ying Tang
Chastising agent	Minister of mobilization	Administrator of the law	The common people	Minister of mobilization	Minister of encampment

The following passage from (the reordered) chapter 59 describing the treachery of the minister of agriculture exemplifies how the radiating influence of the various high-ranking ministers is detailed in every section:

> If the minister of agriculture acts treacherously, he will form factions and partisan cliques. [These in turn will] obstruct the ruler's clarity, force worthy officials into retirement and hiding, extinguish the lineages of nobles and high officers, and teach the people to be wasteful and extravagant. There will be much coming and going of visitors and guests, and people will not exert themselves in agricultural affairs. They will amuse themselves with cockfights, dog racing, and horsemanship. Old and young will lack propriety; the great and small will oppress each other, and thieves and bandits will rise up. Growing arrogant and presumptuous, the people will defy proper principles.[3]

These examples demonstrate how the two chapters function together to provide positive and negative exemplars of how the highest officials of state are to govern themselves, the ethical values they are to embody, and the particular actions that each should ideally follow or avoid if they are to realize those values as they carry out their official responsibilities.

The closely related chapter 60, "Complying with and Deviating from the Five Phases," as its descriptive title suggests, also outlines specific governmental policies commensurate with the Five Phases. In this chapter, it is the ruler, rather than high-ranking ministers of state, who is directed to follow such policies. The descriptions of Wood, Fire, Earth, Metal, and Water again follow a formulaic pattern. Each phase is correlated with a season and its characteristic activity, a set of policies to be implemented by the ruler, and the Heavenly favors that will result if the ruler pursues those policies. The chapter also explains the calamities that Heaven will send down in keeping with the relevant Five-Phase correlations (illnesses befalling the common people, misfortunes afflicting animals, and so on) should the ruler fail to follow the appropriate policies. This chapter follows a long-established tradition of prescribing activities for the months and seasons of the year. In effect, it is an abbreviated version of the familiar "Yue ling" (Monthly Ordinances) of the *Lüshi chunqiu* and the *Liji* (also found in the *Huainanzi* under the title "Shi ze" 時則 [Seasonal Rules]), a text that seems to have been widely circulated in the late Warring States and early Han periods.

3. *CQFL* 58/60/9–11.

Chapters 61 and 62 form a pair as well, as the entire content of both chapters parallels two sections of chapter 3, "Celestial Patterns," in the *Huainanzi*. Chapter 61, "Controlling Water by Means of the Five Phases," closely parallels *Huainanzi* 3.22[4] and presumably is based on that text (or both *Huainanzi* 3.22 and *CQFL* 61 are derived from a common third source, now unknown). Despite its title, the chapter does not explicitly refer to the control of water, but the import of the title becomes clear if it is understood to mean "controlling the negative influence of yin by means of the Five Phases." It begins by identifying the five seventy-two-day periods of the annual cycle, starting with the winter solstice, with the respective phase—Wood, Fire, Earth, Metal, or Water—to be employed in the conduct of governmental affairs and the particular characteristics associated with the *qi*, or vital energy, of that phase. The remainder of the chapter lists specific policies to be followed by the ruler for each of these five seventy-two-day periods. The paired chapters 61 and 62, together with chapter 63, form a distinct subgroup within the Five-Phase group of chapters. All three are devoid of introductions and other literary embellishments and appear to be handbooks in near-tabular form for experts making calendrical predictions or interpreting omens. Many of the seasonal directives that chapter 61 proposes differ from those outlined in chapter 60.[5]

Chapter 62, "Controlling Disorders by Means of the Five Phases," consists of only 142 characters, with neither an introduction nor a conclusion. This brief text is nearly identical to *Huainanzi* 3.23, with only one systematic difference: the *Huainanzi* refers to the phases using the *ganzhi* Heavenly Stem–Earthly Branch sexagenary system, whereas the *Chunqiu fanlu* refers directly to the Five Phases.[6] The chapter lists the twenty anomalies that occur when one of the Five Phases interferes with another phase. Accordingly, the chapter title appears to imply a principle of "forewarned is forearmed"; that is, if one knows that certain configurations of the Five Phases (or, equivalently, the Stems and Branches) are

4. John S. Major, Sarah A. Queen, Andrew Seth Meyer, and Harold D. Roth, trans. and eds., *The "Huainanzi": A Guide to the Theory and Practice of Government in Early Han China* (New York: Columbia University Press, 2010), 128–29. As with the *Chunqiu fanlu*, section divisions within chapters do not appear in the original text of the *Huainanzi* but were added by the translators for the convenience of modern readers and to facilitate the critical analysis of the text.

5. Compare, for example, these two passages: chapter 60: "[When Earth governs], follow the regulations of the palace, heed the distinctions of husband and wife, increase the gratitude of relatives"; chapter 61: "When Earth is in control, nourish the old and elderly, preserve the young and orphaned, demonstrate empathy for the widowed and solitary, give to the filial and brotherly, and bestow grace and favor. Do not raise earthworks."

6. Major et al., *Huainanzi*, 129.

apt to cause disorder or calamity, it might be possible to institute measures to ward off the disaster or mitigate its effects.

The brevity of chapter 62 and its derivative quality suggest that it is an excerpt from the *Huainanzi* or an earlier common source. Like the other chapters in this subgroup, it provides a reference point and an explanation for understanding and interpreting anomalies within a Five-Phase framework. Because chapters 61 and 62 quote material that is consecutive in *Huainanzi* 3, these two *Chunqiu fanlu* chapters might once have been a single text.

Chapter 63, "Aberrations of the Five Phases and Their Remedies," follows a formulaic scheme similar to that of chapters 61 and 62. It runs through each of the five phases—Wood, Fire, Earth, Metal, and Water—defining what an "aberration" in each phase is, what specific governmental policies cause it to occur, what its impact on the common people will be, and what policies can remedy the untoward situation. Again, this chapter is in the spirit of the "Yue ling" and similar annual calendars that link yin-yang and Five-Phase effects to the annual round of the seasons. The chapter is prescriptive and rather moralistic, and its policy prescriptions are so general that they provide little practical guidance for managing government affairs. Nevertheless, the concise and formulaic language of this chapter, like that of the two that precede it, suggests that it may have originated in some kind of early almanac that circulated in governmental circles as a handy reference to help the ruler and his officials track anomalous occurrences and respond to them in cosmologically satisfactory ways.

Chapter 64, "The Five Phases and Five Affairs," also prescribes the ruler's activities based on a Five-Phase cosmological scheme, but on the basis of a Five-Phase scheme different from that in the previous chapters of this group. Whereas chapters 58 through 63 follow the Mutual Production Sequence (Wood/Fire/Earth/Metal/Water), chapter 64 follows the Mutual Conquest Sequence expressed in passive terms (Wood is overcome by Metal, which is overcome by Fire, which is overcome by Water, which is overcome by Earth, which is overcome by Wood). The chapter consists of two essay fragments. Although both are related to the "Great Plan" chapter of the *Documents*, they could not have originally belonged to the same essay. Section 64.1 is a fragment that explains the various disruptions that occur to Wood, Metal, Fire, Water, and Earth when the ruler fails to conduct himself in accordance with the Five Affairs (*wu shi* 五事) of the "Great Plan": when his expression is not solemn, when his speech is not compliant, when his sight is not clear, when his hearing is not acute, and when his mind cannot retain things. The correlations are shown in table 3.

TABLE 3

King's expression is not solemn	**Wood does not bend or straighten**	**Violent winds in summer**	**Wind corresponds to the *qi* of wood**	**Wind corresponds to the note *jue***	**Thus wood responds to the king with violent winds**
King's speech is not compliant	Metal does not follow its refinements	Rumbling thunder in autumn	Rumbling thunder corresponds to the *qi* of metal	Rumbling thunder corresponds to the note *shang*	Thus metal responds to the king with rumbling thunder
King's sight is not clear	Fire does not kindle	Excessive lightning in autumn	Lightning corresponds to the *qi* of fire	Lightning corresponds to the note *zhi*	Thus Fire responds to the king with lightning
King's hearing is not acute	Water does not moisten	Excessive violent rain in summer	Rain corresponds to the *qi* of water	Rain corresponds to the note *yu*	Thus water responds to the king with violent rain
King's mind cannot retain things	Sowing and reaping do not succeed	Excessive thunder in autumn	Thunder corresponds to the *qi* of Earth	Thunder corresponds to the note *gong*	Thus Earth responds to the king with thunder

Section 64.2 contains three explications of the section of the "Great Plan" that defines the ruler's Five Affairs. The first explication concerns the ruler's expression, speech, sight, hearing, and thought. The second focuses on the qualities that those mental processes should ideally manifest: respectfulness, compliance, clarity, astuteness, and retentiveness. The third addresses the solemnity, eminence, wisdom, deliberation, and sagacity that are engendered by the ruler's respectfulness, compliance, clarity, astuteness, and retentiveness. The concluding portion of this explication leaves aside sagacity and its correlate phase, Earth, and associates the ruler's remaining four ideal qualities with the four seasons. It argues that when the ruler realizes these qualities, nature runs smoothly: the *qi* of each respective season functions as it should. Last, this section identifies the anomalies that will result if the ruler implements unseasonable policies.

The list of policies prescribed for the ruler in this chapter once again departs from those recommended in previous chapters. Unlike some of the other chapters in this group, section 64.2 follows the four natural seasons without adding an artificial season of "midsummer." Interestingly, it does not mention the Five Phases as such, though they are implied in the chapter's seasonal correlations.

The content of the chapter, which is in somewhat garbled condition, suggests that it was the work of an exegete of the *Documents*, someone like Liu Xiang, who developed a reputation for his interpretations of the "Great Plan."

Taken as a group, these chapters are certainly linked thematically by their Five-Phase cosmology and their use of the rudiments of this cosmology to describe policies that should be implemented by the ruler and his highest officials. They specify which policies are commensurate with each phase and warn against actions that would disrupt the sequential flow of the Five Phases. The policies identified as being commensurate with the Five Phases are inconsistent across the different chapters, however. In addition, the chapters differ in their understanding of the pertinent sequence of the Five Phases. Thus chapters 58 through 63 take as their starting point the Mutual Production Sequence: Wood, Fire, Earth, Metal, and Water; even chapter 59, which deals with the Mutual Conquest Sequence, arranges its content in Mutual Production order. In contrast, chapter 64 discusses the seasons in the order spring-autumn-summer-winter, corresponding to the passive version of the Mutual Conquest Sequence: Wood, Metal, Fire, Water, and (Earth). These differences suggest that at a minimum, not all these chapters were written by the same person. Are any of them the work of Dong Zhongshu?

Issues of Dating and Attribution

Over the centuries, scholars both East and West have extensively studied the chapters of group 6 and have uniformly expressed doubts that some or all of them are the authentic work of Dong Zhongshu. In fact, they are linked to Dong tenuously, if at all, because there is no indication, in either works confidently attributed to Dong or contemporaneous sources that give reliable information about him, that he ever incorporated Five-Phase concepts into his cosmological theories. In contrast, there is strong evidence that he drew heavily on yin-yang theory to formulate his general cosmological views and on the concept of *ganying* 感應 resonance to develop his interpretations of portents and anomalies. These cosmological views, as seen in the chapters in group 5, "Yin-Yang Principles," were closely tied to the *Spring and Autumn* as interpreted in the *Gongyang Commentary*. Furthermore, the chapters in group 6 contain various kinds of evidence that link them to other intellectual figures, texts, textual traditions, or historical events that postdate Dong's life.

The authenticity of the chapters in group 6 is critical, as it determines the extent to which Dong Zhongshu may be acknowledged as an intellectual link in the development of Five-Phase cosmology between the earlier figure Zou Yan (305–240 B.C.E.) and the later Liu Xiang (77–6 B.C.E.) and Liu Xin (46 B.C.E.–23 C.E.). It now is clear that Lü Buwei (291?–235 B.C.E.), the patron of the *Lüshi chunqiu*, and Liu An (179–122 B.C.E.), the patron of the *Huainanzi* (completed in 139 B.C.E.), demonstrably played a much more important role in the transmission of Five-Phase cosmology between Zou Yan (about whom not much is known) and the Liu father and son.[7] A detailed discussion of this scholarship and these issues may be found in Sarah A. Queen's *From Chronicle to Canon*, so we will summarize here only the most important conclusions.[8]

A Taboo Character

Taboo characters—characters that form part of an emperor's personal name—can be of great value for dating texts. If a text uses a character that later becomes taboo, the text very likely dates to before the time when the character became taboo.[9] Conversely, if a text systematically avoids a taboo character (for example, by always employing a synonym for it), it likely dates from—or at least was copied in—the time after which the taboo took effect. Exactly that kind of internal evidence supports an Eastern Han date for chapter 60. This chapter employs a term for a recommendation category—a category used to designate noteworthy candidates recommended for official posts in the bureaucracy because of a particular outstanding quality—that became current in the Eastern Han only in the

7. See, particularly, chapter 3, "The Celestial Patterns"; chapter 4, "Terrestrial Forms"; and chapter 5, "Seasonal Rules," in Major et al., *Huainanzi*, 109–206.

8. For this discussion, see Sarah A. Queen, *From Chronicle to Canon: The Hermeneutics of the "Spring and Autumn" According to Tung Chung-shu* (Cambridge: Cambridge University Press, 1996), 101–4. See also Gary Arbuckle, "Restoring Dong Zhongshu (BCE 195–115): An Experiment in Historical and Philosophical Reconstruction" (Ph.D. diss., University of British Columbia, 1991), 488–92.

9. Whether such taboos were initiated during the life of a given emperor or following his death is a matter of much debate. B. J. Mansvelt Beck has persuasively argued that taboos were applied only after the death of the emperor, in "The First Emperor's Taboo Character and the Three Day Reign of King Xiaowen: Two Moot Points Raised by the Qin Chronicle Unearthed in Shuihudi in 1975," *T'oung Pao*, 2nd ser., 73, no. 1.3 (1987): 68–85. If that was the case, chapter 60 could not have been written before the end of Guangwu's reign. In any case, evidence from taboo characters can be, as in this case, highly suggestive, but it is rarely probative except in the case of inscriptional or manuscript materials, as the taboo characters may have been altered by a later copyist rather than by the original author. It is also possible, but less common, for taboo characters to be restored by later copyists or editors, rendering them effectively invisible in the historical record.

time of Emperor Guangwu. The term *maocai* 茂才 (cultivated talent) officially replaced the earlier Western Han term *xiucai* 秀才 to avoid the taboo on *xiu*, which was part of Guangwu's personal name. Therefore, chapter 60 probably was written no earlier than, and possibly after, the reign of Emperor Guangwu (r. 25–58 C.E.).

Derivative Materials

In contrast to chapter 60, internal evidence supports an early date for chapters 61 and 62 (though not necessarily an early date for their incorporation into the *Chunqiu fanlu*). As noted earlier, chapter 61, "Controlling Water by Means of the Five Phases," and chapter 62, "Controlling Disorders by Means of the Five Phases," are virtually identical to sections of the *Huainanzi*'s chapter 3, "Celestial Patterns." Lacking introductory or concluding remarks, they appear in the *Chunqiu fanlu* as essay fragments or excerpts. This contrasts with the *Huainanzi* chapter, in which they are well integrated both stylistically and philosophically. These passages appear to have been copied into the *Chunqiu fanlu* either directly from the *Huainanzi* or from some common third source. Thus these two chapters are almost certainly not attributable to Dong Zhongshu. Chapter 63, "Aberrations of the Five Phases and Their Remedies," also appears, on stylistic grounds, to have been copied from some (now unknown) source text. Moreover, because there is no evidence that Dong Zhongshu based his system of omen interpretation on the Five Phases, the content of chapter 63 argues against its being his work. The same is true of chapter 64, "The Five Phases and Five Affairs," which is based on the canonical "Great Plan" chapter of the *Documents* and thus is characteristic of the Han tradition of omen interpretation that developed around that text. It most likely was written by an exegete of the *Documents* working in that tradition. In contrast, Dong Zhongshu derived and developed his ideas on portents and omens based on the *Spring and Autumn* and especially on the *Gongyang Commentary*.

Dong Zhongshu and Five-Phase Theory

The following description of Dong's exegetical activities and cosmological theories, taken from the "Treatise on the Five Phases" in the *Han shu*, makes clear that Dong and some of his successors had quite different views of the theories:

> When the Han arose, it followed on the aftermath of the Qin destruction of learning. In the days of [Emperors] Jing and Wu, Dong Zhongshu mastered the *Gongyang Commentary* to the *Spring and Autumn*, first put forward his yin-yang theories, and was honored by the Confucians. After the days of [Emperors] Xuan and Yuan, Liu Xiang mastered the *Guliang Commentary* to the *Spring and Autumn*, enumerating the inauspicious and auspicious omens [found in them]. His teachings were based on the "Great Plan" [of the *Documents*] and differed from [those of] Dong Zhongshu. Xiang's son Liu Xin mastered the *Zuo Commentary* to the *Spring and Autumn*. His interpretations of the *Spring and Autumn* also were quite extensive. In discussing the commentaries on the Five Phases, he differed as well [from Dong Zhongshu.] For this reason, when citing Dong Zhongshu, I [Ban Gu] have distinguished him from Liu Xiang and Liu Xin.[10]

Dong Zhongshu, Liu Xiang, and Liu Xin, three towering intellectual figures of the Han period, thus followed three different commentarial traditions: the *Gongyang*, *Guliang*, and *Zuo* commentaries, respectively. But differences among their cosmological theories go beyond the commentaries from which they drew their inspiration. Implicit in the *Han shu*'s description of their views is a distinction between yin-yang and Five-Phase cosmology, with Dong firmly identified as favoring the former. Note that the "Treatise on the Five Phases" states that during the reigns of Emperors Jing and Wu, Dong Zhongshu first put forth his "yin-yang theories, and was honored by the Confucians" as a consequence. Had Ban Gu wished to identify Dong with Five-Phase cosmology, he would no doubt have done so in this passage, in which he clearly identifies Liu Xiang and Li Xin with Five-Phase doctrines. Ban Gu states that Liu Xiang's "teachings were based on the 'Great Plan' [of the *Documents*] and differed from [those of] Dong Zhongshu." In addition, the eighty-seven examples of Dong's official responses (*dui* 對) to queries about omens in *Han shu* 27, another place in which we would expect to find evidence of any links between Five-Phase cosmology and Dong's omenology, refer only to yin-yang concepts.[11] (We discuss Dong's yin-yang views at length in our introduction to group 5, "Yin-Yang Principles.")

10. *HS* 27/1317.
11. Gary Arbuckle contends that "the only unquestionably authentic interpretations of the *Chunqiu* by Dong Zhongshu" are "those in the *Han shu*'s 'Wuxing zhi' [Treatise on the Five Phases]," but he goes on to point out that "these . . . interpretations [are] wholly concerned with Yin-Yang . . . interactions" ("Some Remarks on a New Translation of the *Chunqiu fanlu*," *Early China* 17 [1992]: 225). The eighty-seven responses, most of which concern anomalies recorded in the *Spring and Autumn*, include such phenomena as fires, great floods, great droughts, lack of ice, grackles, solar eclipses, stellar aberrations, and falling meteorites.

There is no evidence that Dong wrote the Five-Phase chapters of the *Chunqiu fanlu*. There is little overlap between them and Dong's verifiable views. They were likely written by different authors, some of whom predated or were roughly contemporary with Dong (chapters 61, 62, and possibly 63), and some of whom lived after him (chapters 58, 59, and 60). The author of one chapter may have been a contemporary of Dong Zhongshu, working in the exegetical tradition associated with the *Documents*, possibly Liu Xiang or an exegete closely associated with him (chapter 64).

Even though these chapters are not Dong's work, they are both interesting and valuable. They draw on a long tradition of antecedents stretching back to the third century B.C.E., perhaps to the (now mostly lost) theories of Zou Yan and certainly to such extant works as the "Monthly Ordinances" (Yueling), the earliest version of which is found in the *Lüshi chunqiu*. They help us understand how Five-Phase cosmology developed and how it was applied to political concerns by authors during the Han who sought to derive norms based on it. They also illuminate how Five-Phase theory may eventually have been accepted by and incorporated into the tradition of Gongyang Learning.[12]

The "Current Dynasty" and the Five Phases

The materials comprising the Five-Phase group provide a window into a polemic whose place in the intellectual history of the Han has not been adequately appreciated. The role of Five-Phase theory in Han cosmological debates, its relevance to the politics of the time, and its ramifications in a range of politically charged issues such as calendrical reform and imperial ritual and regalia shed light on this group of chapters and provide additional evidence for assessing their dating and authorship.

One of the most important political tenets of Five-Phase theory was that each dynasty ruled with the power and authority of one or another of the phases. Identifying the ruling phase was thus a matter of the utmost importance, as getting it right meant that the dynasty would be aligned with the force of the

12. We see two possibilities. One is that Five-Phase theory eventually was incorporated into the Gongyang Learning tradition, perhaps two or more generations after Dong Zhongshu's lifetime, and that this accounts for the inclusion of these chapters in the *Chunqiu fanlu*. The second possibility is that Five-Phase theory remained outside the Gongyang Learning tradition but that these Five-Phase chapters were included in the text by its unknown compiler/editor to fill what he saw as an obvious and serious lacuna in the work overall.

cosmos itself, and getting it wrong was to place the dynasty at odds with Heaven's norms.

Chapter 58, "The Mutual Engendering of the Five Phases"; chapter 59, "The Mutual Conquest of the Five Phases"; and chapter 60, "Complying with and Deviating from the Five Phases" all identify the "current dynasty" with the Fire phase of the Five Phases. This is extremely interesting and important to the dating of these chapters. As we shall see, the correlation of Fire with the Han dynasty was probably not hypothesized until well after Dong Zhongshu's death and became accepted only late in the first century B.C.E. The correlation of Fire with the Han achieved prominence with the writings of Liu Xin and was adopted officially in 27 C.E., two years after Emperor Guangwu assumed the throne as the first ruler of the restored Eastern (or Latter) Han.

Efforts to align dynastic politics with Five-Phase cosmology already can be found in late Warring States and Qin works, such as the *Lüshi chunqiu* and parts of the *Guanzi*. Evidence that such political-cosmological views were taken seriously and actively debated at court from the earliest years of the Han period is easy to find—for example, in the practices of the imperial cult. Worship of the Five *di* (*wudi*)—the Bluegreen, Red, Yellow, White, and Black Thearchs—was one of the Han's most important imperial rites. It was instituted by the founding emperor, Gaozu (r. 202–195 B.C.E.), and continued for almost two centuries to the reign of Emperor Ping (r. 1 B.C.E.–5 C.E.). That monarch instituted the Suburban Sacrifice to Heaven, which superseded worship of the Five Thearchs. The issue of imperial worship remained unsettled, however, with change and counterchange until the reign of Wang Mang, when finally it was "firmly determined that worship should be addressed to Heaven, and that the services should take place at sites near the capital. From then (5 C.E.) until the end of the imperial period, Chinese emperors have worshipped Heaven as their first duty."[13]

The influence of Five-Phase cosmology on the Western Han court extended far beyond the great religious center at Yong, where the shrines to the Five Thearchs were located. The question of the proper ruling phase of the Han dynasty provoked heated and prolonged debate at court. Establishing which of the Five Phases corresponded to the reigning dynasty was critical to the legitimizing rhetoric supporting the establishment of a dynasty, believed crucial

13. Michael Loewe, "The Religious and Intellectual Background: Religious Beliefs and Practices," in *The Ch'in and Han Empires, 221 B.C.–A.D. 220*, ed. Denis Twitchett and Michael Loewe, vol. 1 of *The Cambridge History of China* (Cambridge: Cambridge University Press, 1986), 664. For the details of the Suburban Sacrifice, see the introduction to group 7, "Ritual Principles." For a discussion of worship of the "five powers," see Loewe, "Religious and Intellectual Background," 663.

to the dynasty's success. The identification of the ruling phase was typically accompanied by important regulatory reforms initiated by imperial decree—for example, a change in the astronomical system (including the beginning of the calendar year), the type and color of sacrificial animals, and the color of imperial regalia, including court costume, flags and banners. As Michael Loewe explains: "Choice of the patron element [i.e., Phase] constituted a declaration of faith that the dynasty was entitled to its appropriate place in the universal and unbreakable sequence; it also affirmed the view of how the dynasty fitted in that cycle and thereby defined its relationship to its predecessors."[14]

Determining which phase was the correlate of the current dynasty was very complicated. The issue hinged on three separate but related questions. The first was which Five-Phase cycle of change would be used to determine the correlate of the current dynasty. As the *Shiji* and *Han shu* records demonstrate, scholars might avail themselves of two prevalent cycles. One was the Mutual Conquest Sequence associated with Zou Yan and adopted in the *Shiji*, particularly the "Treatise on the Feng and Shan Sacrifices." Typically expressed in passive terms, it yielded the sequence Wood-Metal-Fire-Water-Earth, in which each phase is said to be conquered or overcome by the one that follows: Wood is overcome by Metal (cutting tools), which is overcome by Fire (melting), which is overcome by Water (dousing), which is overcome by Earth (damming), which is overcome by Wood (sprouting).[15] The other is the Mutual Production Sequence, associated with Liu Xin and adopted in the *Han shu*'s "Treatise on the Pitch Pipes and Mathematical Astronomy." It yields the sequence Wood-Fire-Earth-Metal-Water, in which each phase produces its successor: Wood produces Fire (burning), which produces Earth (ashes), which produces Metal (ores), which produces Water (molten metal), which produces Wood (irrigation). The Mutual Conquest Sequence governs processes in which violence brings about change, and the Mutual Production Sequence applies to processes of spontaneous evolution or production.

Which cycle was used to determine the present also weighed on the past because typically the appropriate phase for the current dynasty was determined in relation to the preceding dynasties. For the Han, those referred most immediately to the Zhou and Qin dynasties, but some scholars named schemes that went back farther in time, extending even to the Five Thearchs of legendary

14. Michael Loewe, "The Concept of Sovereignty," in *Ch'in and Han Empires*, 737.

15. The Mutual Conquest Sequence can also be expressed in active terms, Wo-E-Wa-F-M, but this cycle cannot be used to describe a sequence of dynasties because it would imply a logical impossibility: that each dynasty was conquered by its predecessor.

antiquity. Accordingly, which list of historical dynasties would be used and with which correlates was the second important question determining the debate. As we will see, in the Western Han, as exemplified by Sima Qian in the *Shiji*, the historical chronology associated with Five-Phase theory reached back to the Yellow Emperor. In the Eastern Han, however, as exemplified by Liu Xin in the *Han shu*, the historical chronology associated with Five-Phase theory reached back still farther to the time of Paoxi (or Fuxi), the first of the Three Kings.

The third question affected all the debate concerning the ruling phase of the current dynasty in both the Western and Eastern Han: Was the previous dynasty legitimate or illegitimate? This had important ramifications for the debate as the Western Han looked back at the Qin, and again as the Eastern Han looked back at Wang Mang's interregnum from the perspective of Emperor Guangwu's subsequent restoration of the Han. Different intellectuals maintained various views concerning whether these reigns should be considered legitimate or illegitimate and thus whether they should be included in the legitimate progression of the Five Phases. Once determined, the ruling phase for any given dynasty was supposed to stay the same as long as the dynasty maintained the Mandate of Heaven, which might last for decades or even centuries.

The First Emperor of Qin and the Reign of Water

According to the *Shiji*'s "Basic Annals of the Qin," after the Qin ruler assumed his new title as emperor in 221 B.C.E., he declared Water to be the patron power of the dynasty:

> The First Emperor advanced the theory of the cyclical revolutions of the Five Phases. He maintained that inasmuch as the Zhou had held the power of Fire and Qin had supplanted Zhou, to follow it would amount to negating Qin's victory. Since the present time marked the beginning of the cycle of the power of Water, he altered the beginning of the year. . . . Court clothing, pennants, and flags all honored black [this color being the correlate of water]. With regard to numbers, he made six the standard [this number being the correlate of water]. All contract tallies and official hats were six inches, and the chariots were six feet. Six feet made one double-pace, and each equipage consisted of six horses. The [Yellow] River was renamed the Potent Water because it was supposed that this marked

> the beginning of the power of water. With harshness, violence, and extreme severity, everything was determined by law. For by punishing and oppressing, by having no humanity or kindliness, harmony or righteousness, there would come an accord with the numerical succession of the Five Phases [policies obtaining in winter, the seasonal correlate of water].[16]

As Sima Qian makes clear in the *Shiji*'s "Treatise on the Feng and Shan Sacrifices," the Qin identification with the Water ruling phase was contingent on a number of factors. First, the choice of ruling phase was typically associated with an omen that signaled its ascendancy. Second, the ruling phase was established with reference to the preceding dynasties. Third, it was accompanied by a number of reforms. Chief among them were a change in the first month of the calendar and the privileging of a color, number, musical tone, and style of government, all determined by the correlative characteristics of the dynasty's ruling phase:

> When the First Emperor of the Qin had united the world and proclaimed himself emperor, someone advised him, saying, "The Yellow Emperor ruled by the power of Earth, and therefore a yellow dragon and a great earthworm appeared in his time. The Xia dynasty ruled by the power of Wood, and so a bluegreen dragon came to rest in its court and the grasses and trees grew luxuriantly. The Shang dynasty ruled by metal, and silver flowed out of the mountains. The Zhou ruled by fire, and therefore it was given a sign in the form of a red bird. Now the Qin has replaced the Zhou, and the era of the power of water has come. In ancient times when Duke Wen of Qin went out hunting, he captured a black dragon. This is an auspicious omen indicating the power of Water." Consequently, the First Emperor of Qin changed the name of the Yellow River to "Potent Water." He established the tenth month of winter as the beginning of the year; with regard to color, he honored black; with regard to measurements, he established six as the standard; with the tones he honored *dalu*; and with affairs of government, he honored law above all else.[17]

---

16. *SJ* 6/237. This passage is from "The Basic Annals of Qin." Translation modified from Derk Bodde, "The State and Empire of Ch'in," in *Ch'in and Han Empires*, 77.
17. *SJ* 28/1366, "The Treatise on the Feng and Shan Sacrifice," modified from Burton Watson, trans., *Records of the Grand Historian of China*, vol. 2, *The Age of Emperor Wu, 140 to Circa 100 B.C.* (New York: Columbia University Press, 1971), 12. Additional references to the Qin association with the power of the Water are found in *SJ* 26, "The Treatise on the Calendar."

TABLE 4

Yellow Emperor	Xia	Shang	Zhou	Qin
Earth	Wood	Metal	Fire	Water

As this passage indicates, the Qin choice of Water as the ruling phase depended on identifying the ruling phases of previous dynasties. The correlations accepted as valid by the court cosmologists are presented in table 4.[18] From these correlations, it is clear that the sequence followed in determining that Water was the appropriate correlate for the Qin was the "passive" Mutual Conquest Sequence in which Wood is conquered by Metal, Metal is conquered by Fire, Fire is conquered by Water, and Water is conquered by Earth.

The Han Dilemma: Water or Earth?

The *Shiji* suggests that discussions to determine the ruling phase for the Western Han surfaced quite early, under the reign of Emperor Gaozu, but that a full century of discussion and debate would ensue before the issue was finally settled during the reign of Emperor Wu. Apparently, shortly after assuming the throne, Emperor Gaozu expressed support for the power of Water. He is said to have declared, "The altar of the north awaits me to be erected."[19] Since the north was associated with the Water phase, Gaozu's statement was interpreted as an affirmation that the dynasty had rightly obtained the power of Water, inheriting it from the preceding Qin dynasty. This reading was confirmed by Zhang Cang, a high-ranking official who had served the Qin and who may have harbored personal reasons for continuing the Qin agenda.

Ming Xili and Zhang Cang supported the emperor's suggestion that the Han simply conform to the Qin calendar and color of court vestments by citing a number of additional factors: "The empire is just beginning to become settled; the square grid pattern [of the imperial capital] is just being laid out; the high empress and her court ladies do not yet have leisure [to sew and embroider new

18. Note that the *Shiji* does not mention the reigns of the four additional "sage-emperors," who supposedly ruled around the time of the Yellow Emperor and are generally grouped with him as the Five Sovereigns, nor does it mention Kings Yao and Shun; if they had been included in the sequence, the later correlations would have changed.

19. *SJ* 26/1260, "Treatise on the Calendars."

court garments in a different color]; thus it is appropriate to conform to the first month of the year and the color of court vestments established by the Qin."[20]

Given the brevity of Qin rule, Emperor Gaozu of the Han might naturally have assumed that the Water phase had not yet exhausted its power and therefore it was appropriate to simply assume the Qin's ruling phase. In any case, he pursued that policy, augmenting the reign of the Water phase by establishing an altar to the Black Thearch.[21]

Zhang Cang appears to have been a key factor in the continuation of Qin practices, not only during the reign of Emperor Gao, but during the succeeding reign of Emperor Wen as well. During the latter's reign, when Zhang served as chancellor, he opposed proposals by Gongsun Chen and Jia Yi that the Han be identified with the Earth phase.[22] Gongsun Chen, for example, following the logic that Earth conquers Water, just as the Han had conquered the Qin, submitted a letter to the throne:

> Formerly the Qin dynasty ruled by the power of Water. Now that the Han has succeeded the Qin, in accordance with the revolutions of the Five-Phase sequence, Han must [correspond to] the power of Earth. The [confirming] response [from Heaven that this is the case] will be the appearance of a yellow dragon. It is proper, then, to alter the first month of the year, change the color of court vestments, and honor the color yellow.[23]

After the letter was received, the emperor directed Zhang to call a court deliberation to discuss the matter. Zhang, who enjoyed a reputation for being well versed

20. *SJ* 26/1260, "Treatise on the Calendars."
21. *SJ* 28/1378, "Treatise on the Feng and Shan Sacrifices"; Watson, *Records of the Grand Historian of China*, 2:19.
22. "The Biography of Qu Yuan and Master Jia" explains:

> Jia Yi believed that, since by the reign of Emperor Wen the Han had already been in power for over twenty years and the empire was at peace, it was time for the dynasty to alter the month upon which the year began, change the color of the vestments, put its administrative code in order, fix the titles of officials, and encourage the spread of rites and music. He therefore drew up a draft of his proposals on the proper ceremonies and regulations to be followed, maintaining the dynasty should honor the colour yellow and the number five, and should invent new official titles instead of following the practices used by the Qin. But Emperor Wen had just come to the throne and he modestly declined any ability or leisure to put into effect such far-reaching measures. He did, however, direct revisions in the pitch pipes and in the statutes and order the marquises to leave the capital and reside in their own territories, both of which measures originated from suggestions made by Jia Yi. (Burton Watson, trans., *Records of the Grand Historian of China*, vol. 1, *Early Years of the Han Dynasty, 209 to 141 B.C.* [New York: Columbia University Press, 1971], 444)

23. *SJ* 28/1381, "Treatise on the Feng and Shan Sacrifices"; Watson, *Records of the Grand Historian of China*, 2:21.

in astronomy and mathematical harmonics, was in a position to speak authoritatively on the subject and apparently did so. He contended that the Han belonged to the period in which the power of Water was still in the ascendancy. Thus the Yellow River having burst its dikes at a place called Metal Embankment (that is, Water was ascendant over Metal, which generates it according to the Mutual Production Sequence) should be taken as the verification: "Now the year begins in winter in the tenth month, and the colors of court vestments are black on the outside and red on the inside, corresponding perfectly to the power [of Water]. Gongsun Chen's opinion is false, and the matter should be dropped." Despite the apparent finality of Zhang Cang's opinion, the matter was soon reopened because an omen did appear to confirm Gongsun Chen's prediction. As the "Treatise on the Feng and Shan Sacrifices" explains, "Three years later, a yellow dragon appeared in Chengji. Emperor Wen thereupon summoned Gongsun Chen to court, made him an Erudite, and set him to work with the other court scholars to draft a plan to alter the calendar and the color of court vestments." The emperor subsequently issued an edict confirming the appearance of the auspicious creature, declaring his intention to perform the Suburban Sacrifice, and calling on his officials in charge of the rites to deliberate the matter and set forth their recommendations.[24]

Emperor Wen followed through in the summer of the same year, when he personally performed the Suburban Sacrifice to the Five Thearchs north of the Wei River. Having recently come under the influence of a man from Zhao named Xinyuan Ping, the details of the performance were influenced heavily by the interpretations of this new favorite. Emperor Wen seemed to be on the verge of making momentous changes that would have included an imperial declaration of Earth as the new reigning phase. But after the emperor had performed the Suburban Sacrifice, Xinyuan Ping's interpretations were deemed fraudulent. Exhausted and disgruntled by the affair, the emperor is said to have "lost interest in changing the calendar and the color of court vestments and in matters concerning the spirits."[25] Even though the sacrificial officials maintained the requisite ceremonies, the emperor did not again visit the altars or personally offer a sacrifice. Nor did he ever declare a change in the ruling phase of the Han. During the reign of Emperor Jing, discussions to determine the dynasty's ruling phase thus appear to have abated, perhaps because of the emperor's lack of interest in it.

---

24. *SJ* 28/1381, "Treatise on the Feng and Shan Sacrifices"; Watson, *Records of the Grand Historian of China*, 2:21. Zhang Cang's support of the power of Water also is detailed in *SJ* 96, "The Biography of Zhang Cang"; Watson, *Records of the Grand Historian of China*, 1:212.

25. *SJ* 28/1381, "Treatise on the Feng and Shan Sacrifices"; Watson, *Records of the Grand Historian*, 2:23–24.

Emperor Wu

The declaration of a new ruling phase of the Han and the promulgation of a new calendar came with Emperor Wu, who finally instituted the earlier recommendations of Gongsun Chen and Jia Yi and declared Earth as the patron phase of the Han in 104 B.C.E. This momentous change was duly noted in the "Treatise on the Feng and Shan Sacrifices":

> In the summer [of 104 B.C.E.] the calendar of the Han dynasty was changed so that the official year began with the first month. Yellow, the color of Earth, was chosen as the color of the dynasty, and the titles of the officials were recarved on seals so that they all consisted of five characters, five being the number appropriate to the phase Earth. This year was designated as the first year of the era *taichu*, or "Grand Inception."[26]

The *Han shu*'s "Annals of Emperor Wu" also recorded:

> In the summer, the fifth month, [the emperor] corrected the calendar and took the first month as the beginning of the year; [among] the colors, he took yellow [as the ruling color], and [among] the numbers, he used five. He fixed official titles and harmonized the sounds of the musical pipes.[27]

The basic impetus of the Grand Inception reform of 104 B.C.E. was the need to correct the computational system used to calculate the dates and locations of various phenomena that appear in the sky, including solstices and equinoxes, phases of the moon, positions of the planets, and the astrological implications of all of these.[28] Because all such astronomical systems accumulate errors over time, occasionally it is necessary to recalibrate them. Toward the end of Emperor Wu's reign, it was obvious (for example, from disparities in the dates of the equinoxes

26. *SJ* 28/1402; modified from Watson, *Records of the Grand Historian of China*, 2:49.
27. *HS* 6/199; Homer H. Dubs, trans., *History of the Former Han Dynasty*, 3 vols. (Baltimore: Waverly Press, 1938–1955), 2:99.
28. Nathan Sivin, Kiyoshi Yabuuchi, and Shigeru Nakayama, *Granting the Seasons: The Chinese Astronomical Reform of 1280, with a Study of Its Many Dimensions and a Translation of Its Records* (New York: Springer, 2009), 38–42. As they point out, the conventional translation of the Chinese term for this process, *gaili* 改曆, as "calendar reform" is misleading because what was involved was the recalculation of methods used to produce a comprehensive ephemeris and not simply the correction of a sequence of days comprising a civil calendar.

and solstices) that the computational system required correction. The necessary corrections were made, and the promulgation of the Grand Inception calendar provided the occasion for a corresponding rethinking of the Han dynasty's ruling phase. Perhaps reflecting Emperor Wu's confidence that the Han securely possessed the Mandate of Heaven and was not merely a continuation of the Qin dispensation, the ruling phase was finally changed from Water to Earth. The Grand Inception reform involved not only changes in the astronomical system itself but also comprehensive changes in the color and design of vestments and emblems; the recalibration of weights and measures and of the standard pitch of musical notes; as well as changes in numerology, astrology, cosmology, historiography, and other fields that had implications for political, ethical, and moral thought.[29]

During the final decades of the Western Han and into the Eastern Han, the need for further reform of the astronomical system once again became the focus of a wider debate. A new position began to emerge from Five-Phase theory that pertained to the dynasty's ruling phase, along with much else. The new consensus depended largely on the developing views of the famous polymath courtiers Liu Xiang (77–6 B.C.E.) and his son Liu Xin (ca. 50 B.C.E.–23 C.E.).[30] The *Han shu*'s "Treatise on the Suburban Sacrifice" says,

> Liu Xiang the father and his son [Liu Xin] maintained that the [cycle of] thearchs began with [the Earthly Branch] *chen*, therefore Master Paoxi [i.e., Fuxi] was the first to receive the power of Wood. His descendants through the maternal line [were part of] an endless cycle that ended and began anew from Shen Nong and the Yellow Emperor down through the ages to Tang Yu and the Three Dynasties to the Han, who obtained the power of Fire.[31]

This new view of Five-Phase theory had two aspects. The first was the correlation of the phases with ever more distant dynasties stretching all the way back to the legendary Three Kings Fuxi, Shen Nong (the Divine Farmer), and the Yellow Emperor and progressing through the Five Thearchs (Shao Yao, Zhuanxu, Di Ku, Yao, and Shun) and the Three Dynasties (Xia, Shang, and

29. Mark Edward Lewis, *Writing and Authority in Early China* (Albany: State University of New York Press, 1999), 283; Hans Ulrich Vogel, "Aspects of Metrosophy and Metrology During the Han Period," *Extrême Orient, Extrême Occident* 16 (1994): 135–52.
30. For a detailed discussion of this subject, see Aihe Wang, *Cosmology and Political Culture in Early China* (Cambridge: Cambridge University Press, 2000), 129–72.
31. *HS* 25/1270–71.

TABLE 5

	Three Kings			Five Thearchs					Three Dynasties		
Ruler	Paoxi	Shen Nong	Yellow Emperor	Shao Yan	Zhuanxu	Di Ku	Yao	Shun	Xia	Shang	Zhou
Phase	Wood	Fire	Earth	Metal	Water	Wood	Fire	Earth	Metal	Water	Wood

Zhou) to the Han.[32] The second was a shift from the old paradigm of using the (passive) Mutual Conquest Sequence of the Five Phases to calculate the ruling phases of sage-emperors and dynasties to a new one using the Mutual Production Sequence for the same purpose. Thus the sage-emperors and dynasties were associated with phases entirely different from those calculated according to the Mutual Conquest Sequence in the Grand Inception calendar to confirm the legitimacy of the Han conquest over the Qin, but in the view of Liu Xiang and Liu Xin, the Mutual Production Sequence was better suited to the emergent historical narrative of peaceful dynastic change. In this historical narrative crafted by Liu Xin, the Qin dynasty was deemed illegitimate and the Han became associated with the power of Fire. This new historical narrative was laid out in detail in the "Treatise on the Pitch Pipes and Mathematical Astronomy"[33] incorporated into the *Han shu.* The correlations associated with this new narrative are represented in table 5. The treatise explains: "The August Emperor of the Han, Gaozu, promulgated a written document, [saying that] we have chastised the Qin and [directly] succeeded the Zhou. Wood engenders Fire, therefore [Han] corresponds to the power of Fire."[34]

This historical sequence that now identified the Han dynasty with Fire spurred a new round of computational reform. Liu Xin had begun working on computational issues early in the reign of Emperor Cheng (r. 32–6 B.C.E.), and his *san tong* (Triple Concordance) astronomical system was promulgated in 7 B.C.E. Its mathematical features did not amount to a complete reform of the Grand Inception system, as it merely revised some of its key features. But the

32. The *Han shu*'s "Treatise on the Pitch Pipes and Mathematical Astronomy" attributes these correlations (probably spuriously) to Zou Yan (*HS* 21/1011).

33. This treatise is based on the writings of Liu Xin and may incorporate his work verbatim. For Liu Xin and the *san tong* (Triple Concordance) calendar, see Christopher Cullen, *Astronomy and Mathematics in Ancient China: The "Jou Bi Suan Jing,"* Needham Research Institute Studies, no. 1 (Cambridge: Cambridge University Press, 2007), 32–33.

34. *HS* 21/1023.

emperor, approving of Liu Xin's recommendations, took the opportunity presented by the new calendar to adopt comprehensive changes in regalia, weights and measures, music, and so on, all reflecting the new understanding that Fire was the ruling phase of the Han. Thus by the end of the Western Han, both Emperor Wu's adoption of Earth as the dynasty's ruling phase and his Grand Inception astronomical system had been repudiated, replaced by the consensus that Fire was the dynasty's ruling phase as embodied in the Triple Concordance system.

Wang Mang

These developments in Five-Phase discourse, with associated upheavals in numerology, metrology, omenology, and other esoteric fields, laid the crucial intellectual groundwork on which Wang Mang built his case that he was the legitimate successor to Emperor Ping of the Han. As emperor of the Xin dynasty, he argued that he ruled under the reigning power of Earth because, according to the Mutual Production Sequence, Fire engenders Earth. Accordingly, we find the following verification in the *Han shu*'s "Biography of Wang Mang" that the power of Fire was destined to give way to that of Earth:

> The red stone at Wugong appeared in the last year of Emperor Ping of the Han dynasty, when the virtue of Fire had been completely dissipated and the virtue of Earth was due to take [its] place]. August Heaven was solicitous [on account of this circumstance] and so rejected the Han [dynasty] and gave [His Mandate] to the Xin [dynasty], using the red stone as its first Mandate to the Emperor. The Emperor, [Wang] Mang, however humbly refused to accept [this title] and hence occupied [the throne] as regent.[35]

Wang Mang's reception of the Mandate on January 8, in 9 C.E., is described as follows:

> The day of receiving the Mandate was *dingmao* [sexagenary day 4]. *Ding* is Fire, which is the virtue of the Han dynasty; *mao* is what makes the [Han dynasty's] surname, Liu, into this written character [the surname Liu 劉 is written by adding the radical *mao* 卯 to the word *zhao* 釗]. It makes plain that the virtue of Fire,

35. Dubs, *History of the Former Han Dynasty*, 290.

> [which was that of] the Han [dynasty] and of the Liu [clan], is exhausted, and that [the Mandate] has been transmitted to the house of Xin.[36]

Finally, Wang Mang promulgated a new astronomical system, although it was essentially the same as Liu Xin's Triple Concordance system with minor modifications.[37] Nonetheless, this act proclaimed to the world his belief that the new dynasty's Mandate was secure.

Emperor Guangwu

Wang Mang's abortive Xin dynasty collapsed in 23 C.E. After two years of chaos, rebellion, and civil warfare, the Han imperial kinsman Liu Xiu mounted the imperial throne in 25 C.E., proclaiming the restoration of the Han dynasty. (At that time, the imperial capital was moved to Luoyang, giving the Latter Han dynasty its alternative name of Eastern Han.) The *Hou Han shu*'s "Annals of Emperor Guangwu" reports that in 27 C.E., the emperor engaged in a number of solemn religious acts. They depicted his reign as a restoration of the Han: he erected a temple to the founding father of the Han, Emperor Gaozu; he established an altar of Heaven at Luoyang; and he built the suburban altar south of the city. He also proclaimed Fire to be the dynasty's ruling phase, thereby affirming with very powerful symbolism that his dynasty was a restoration of the Han and a continuation of its Mandate, not an entirely new regime. (Emperor Guangwu also took the retrograde step of restoring many of the Western Han's regional kingdoms, with various imperial princes as kings, thereupon bequeathing no end of trouble to his successors.)[38]

Implications for the Dating and Attribution of the Five-Phase Chapters

To recapitulate: the First Emperor of Qin chose Water as the ruling phase of his dynasty, having conquered the Zhou, whose ruling phase was taken to be Fire.

36. Modified from Dubs, *History of the Former Han Dynasty*, 293.
37. Liu Xin became a high official under Wang Mang, serving until he was implicated in a plot to restore the Han (he was a member of the Han imperial Liu clan). He was executed in 23 C.E., not long before the fall of Wang Mang.
38. Hans Bielenstein, "Wang Mang, the Restoration of the Han Dynasty, and Later Han," in *Ch'in and Han Empires*, 256–59.

The Qin's choice of Water remained in force under the Han emperor Gaozu and his immediate successors, signifying that the Han had inherited Qin's Mandate and ruled by its same phase. Emperor Wu instituted Earth as the ruling phase as part of the Grand Inception astronomical system reform of 104 B.C.E., based on the argument that Earth overcomes Water, just as the Han had overcome the Qin. Emperor Cheng accepted Liu Xin's arguments that the Mutual Production Sequence, rather than the Mutual Conquest Sequence, governed the choice of a ruling phase. Accordingly, he proclaimed Fire as the ruling phase of the Han as part of the Triple Concordance astronomical system reform of 7 B.C.E. (This assumes that the Qin dynasty was illegitimate and that the Han succeeded directly to the Mandate of the Zhou, whose ruling phase was Wood.) Wang Mang accepted that logic and so chose Earth (engendered by Fire) as the ruling phase of the Xin dynasty. The Latter Han emperor Guangwu reverted to Fire as a symbol that his dynasty was a restoration of the Han, and Fire remained the ruling phase for the duration of the Latter Han.[39] All these choices involved new arguments about the ruling phase of the Zhou dynasty and its predecessor dynasties and sage-emperors.

Although Wang Mang, like Emperor Wu before him, chose Earth as the patron phase of his dynasty, as Michael Loewe argued many years ago[40] and as our research has affirmed, he did so for very different reasons. Emperor Wu justified his identification with Earth with references to Qin's identification with Water and followed the Mutual Conquest Sequence. In contrast, Wang Mang's identification with Earth was based on the understanding that Han ruled by the power of the Fire phase, a position that was articulated by Liu Xin in the waning years of the Western Han and assumed that the Mutual Production Sequence was the proper way to determine the ruling phase. This theory was opportune for Wang Mang, who wished to present himself as the legitimate successor to the Han. (He encouraged the idea that he had come to the throne not by conquest but because the last emperor of the Han had peacefully ceded the Mandate to him, even though the Mandate, in classical theory, was conferred by Heaven, not passed from one human to another.)

We have seen that chapters 58, 59, and 60 identify the "current dynasty" (*ben chao*) with Fire. Up through the time of Emperor Wu and for several decades thereafter, the Han debate on the ruling phase was confined to either Water or

39. The question of Five-Phase theory and dynastic symbolism continued to be debated throughout the imperial period. See John B. Henderson, *The Development and Decline of Chinese Cosmology* (New York: Columbia University Press, 1984), esp. chaps. 2 and 3.

40. Michael Loewe, "Water, Earth and Fire—The Symbols of the Han Dynasty," *Nachrichten der Gesellschaft für Natur-und Völkerkunde Ostasiens/Hamburg* 125 (1979): 63–68.

Earth. The question of Fire entered the debate only with the theoretical work of Liu Xin near the end of the Western Han. The choice of Fire was accepted by Emperor Guangwu in 27 C.E. and remained in force for the duration of the Latter Han. Thus the essays that identify the "current dynasty" with Fire cannot date to a time earlier than Liu Xin (ca. 50 B.C.E.–23 C.E.) and are most unlikely to be earlier than the reign of Emperor Guangwu. They are, in other words, very likely to date from some time in the Latter Han period. The entire group of Five-Phase chapters in the *Chunqiu fanlu* (chapters 58–64) thus appears to span a time period from the early Han (chapters 60 and 61) to sometime in the Latter Han. As such, they are a valuable record of the development of Five-Phase theory and its gradual incorporation into the Confucian mainstream via the masters of Gongyang Learning. That none of these chapters can plausibly be associated directly with Dong Zhongshu and that some certainly cannot have been written by him, is noteworthy but does not diminish their inherent value.

Finally, it is interesting to observe that the Mutual Production Sequence of the Five Phases lends itself easily to interpretations linked to the production of life as a parent produces offspring. In this line of reasoning, the relationship of the Xin dynasty to the Han, for example, would be that of a son to his father. We might therefore expect the virtue of filial piety to come into play in the development of Five-Phase theory, and this does turn out to be the case: the *Hou Han shu* records a dialogue between a disciple and a teacher that says in part: "The Han wielded the power of Fire; Fire is born from Wood; Wood reaches its apogee in Fire; thus its power is that of filial piety."[41] Are there essays in the *Chunqiu fanlu* that might conform to such a view? The only other chapters that develop Five-Phase theory, chapters 38 and 42, do just this.[42] They promote the ethical value of filial piety in a Five-Phase scheme that privileges Earth and thus appear to represent a moment of integration of Five-Phase theory into Han Confucian ideology.

41. *Hou Han shu* 62/52/2051: 荀韓鍾陳列傳.
42. See the discussion of these chapters in the introduction to group 4, "Ethical Principles."

Book 13, Part 4

CHAPTER 58

The Mutual Engendering of the Five Phases

Section 58.1

The *qi* of Heaven and Earth
when combined becomes one,
when divided becomes yin and yang,
when broken up becomes the four seasons,
and when arrayed becomes the Five Phases.

"Phases" mean "conduct."[1] The conduct [of each of the Five Phases] is not identical. Thus they are designated "the Five Phases." The Five Phases [correspond to] the Five Officials. They engender one another and overcome one another in turn. Thus, in constituting your governance,
if you oppose them, there will be disorder;
if you comply with them, there will be order.

The eastern quarter [corresponds to] Wood. It is the root of agriculture, and [its corresponding office is] the minister of agriculture. The minister of

We usually follow Lau, but in Su Yu and Lai Yanyuan's editions, "The Mutual Engendering of the Five Phases" is chapter 58 and "The Mutual Conquest of the Five Phases" is chapter 59. We believe that this is a better arrangement, as the opening paragraph of "The Mutual Engendering of the Five Phases" functions as an introduction to both essays and thus should ideally precede "The Mutual Conquest of the Five Phases." We have therefore reversed the order of Lau's chapters 58 and 59 to follow Su Yu's edition, although page and line references to the Chinese text still follow Lau's edition.

1. The text defines the term for phase based on a play on words: the character *xing* 行 has the basic meaning "to move" and thus, by extension, "conduct"; but in the binome *wuxing* 五行, it means "Five Phases," the five paradigmatic manifestations of *qi*.

agriculture esteems humaneness. He promotes scholars versed in the classical arts and leads them along the path of the Five Emperors and Three Kings. He

follows their good points
and rectifies their bad points.

Grasping the compass,[2] he promotes birth and, with the utmost warming, saturates those below.

He understands the fertility, barrenness, strengths, and weakness of the terrain; establishes affairs; and engenders norms in accordance with what is suitable to the land. The duke of Shao[3] exemplifies this. He went into the southern[4] fields and oversaw the people as they opened new lands and cultivated the five [i.e., various] kinds of grain. A surplus accumulated; families were able to provide sufficiently for their members; and the granaries and storehouses were filled to capacity. The minister of war verifies [the supply of] grain. The minister of war corresponds to the current dynasty, and the current dynasty corresponds to Fire. Therefore it is said: Wood gives birth to fire.

The southern quarter [corresponds to] Fire, the current dynasty,[5] and the minister of war. The minister of war esteems wisdom. He promotes worthy and sagely scholars and understands the patterns of Heaven above so that

before their tangible signs have become evident
and before their tender shoots have been generated,

they already are apparent to him. Thus he alone observes

the incipient tendencies of survival and destruction,
the essentials of gains and losses,
the origins of order and disorder,

preparing against them well in advance. Grasping the balance beam,[6] he brings things to maturity. With utmost loyalty, generosity, and humanity, he assists his lord. The Duke of Zhou[7] exemplifies this. When King Cheng was young

2. Here "compass" refers to an instrument for drawing circles, not a navigational magnetic compass.
3. He was an official who served King Wu of the Zhou and held the title of "grand protector." In return for his meritorious services, he was given Shao as a fief.
4. Here "southern" might be a mistake for "eastern."
5. Supplying *ye* 也 after *ben chao* 本朝, following Su Yu, *CQFLYZ* 363.
6. The text here reads "square"; Su Yu suggests that the instrument should be the "balance beam." Accordingly, we have corrected "south" to "balance beam," "west" to "square," and "north" to "weight," as in John S. Major, Sarah A. Queen, Andrew Seth Meyer, and Harold D. Roth, trans. and eds., *The "Huainanzi": A Guide to the Theory and Practice of Government in Early Han China* (New York: Columbia University Press, 2010), 3.6. See also Su Yu, *CQFLYZ* 364.
7. He was the younger brother of King Wu of Zhou, whom he helped in annihilating the Shang and establishing the Zhou dynasty. Later he put down a rebellion of Zhou nobles and then withdrew to his own allocated territory when his ward, King Cheng, came of age. He thus is an exemplar of loyalty and the proper use of military force.

and weak and the Duke of Zhou was the prime minister, he punished Guan Shu and Cai Shu to pacify the world. Only then was the world peaceful and secure. Among the ruler's officials is the minister of public works. The minister of public works corresponds to Earth. Therefore it is said: Fire gives birth to Earth.

The central region [corresponds to] Earth, the ruler's administration, and the minister of public works.[8] The minister of public works esteems trustworthiness. He

> humbles his person and disparages himself,
> rises early and retires late,

praising and evaluating remote antiquity to exert the ruler's mind to clarify successes and losses. He remonstrates with subtle words to promote the ruler's goodness and restrain his evil, cutting it off at its source and making good his faults. Grasping the marking cord, he orders the four regions with utmost loyalty, generosity, and trustworthiness to serve his ruler. In accordance with righteous principles, he severs his private affections. The Grand Duke exemplifies this.[9] Responding to Heaven, he complied with the transformations of the seasons, relied on his awesome martiality to control the powerful and violent, and thereby obtained success. The administrator of the law corresponds to the minister of mobilization. The minister of mobilization corresponds to Metal. Therefore it is said: Earth gives birth to Metal.

The western quarter [corresponds to] Metal, the administrator of the law, and the minister of mobilization. The minister of mobilization esteems righteousness. [Thus]

> the ministers [are willing to] die for their ruler;
> the commoners [are willing to] die for their fathers;
> relatives follow the distinctions between eminent and humble;
> and those in positions of authority follow the distinctions between superior and inferior.

Each is willing to die to fulfill their tasks, and no task oversteps the proper bounds. Grasping the [carpenter's] square, he carries out attacks.

> His military actions are not cruel, but he subjugates [the enemies];
> his exactions are not cruel, but he obtains what is due.

8. We follow the emendation of Liu Shipei (Lai, *CQFLJZJY* 337, note 1).
9. The Grand Duke was the former tutor to Kings Wen and Wu, later enfeoffed in Qi.

He [determines what is] righteous and only then acts; he is utterly incorruptible, stern, direct, and resolute. Zixu[10] exemplifies this.

He punished the guilty
and chastised the unrighteous.

Thus, the populace drew near to him; the border regions grew tranquil; and bandits did not rise up. The villages were free of litigations, and relatives lived in peace. The censor[11] corresponds to the minister of justice. The minister of justice corresponds to Water. Therefore it is said: Metal gives birth to Water.

The northern quarter [corresponds to] Water, the censor, and the minister of justice. The minister of justice esteems propriety. Thus

between ruler and minister, there will be proper position;
between young and old, there will be proper hierarchy;
and between the [royal] court and [aristocratic] divans, there will be proper rank.

In the villages and hamlets, age will take precedence. In ascending and descending, there will be polite yielding and prostrations and bows from subordinates to superiors. Movements will be centered and proper. Standing, he bends his body as if playing the chime stones; clasping his hands, it is as if he were holding a drum. Grasping the weight, he collects and stores the myriad things. Utterly pure, incorruptible, and just,

gifts and bribes he will not accept;
requests and pleas he will not heed.

He relies on the law to judge cases and is free from favoritism. Confucius exemplifies this. When he acted as the minister of justice in the state of Lu, his legal decisions always were sincere. He followed the majority opinion, never daring overstep his authority. Thus

those who were sentenced to death did not despise him,
and those who were allowed to live [and yet were punished] did not begrudge him.

The various artisans finished making [the different kinds of] implements at the appropriate time. When the implements were completed, they were given to the minister of agriculture. The minister of agriculture corresponds to the Bureau of Agricultural Lands. The Bureau of Agricultural Lands corresponds to Wood. Therefore it is said: Water gives birth to Wood. [59/61/11–59/62/9]

10. This is Wu Zixu, a nobleman of Chu; see chapter 7.1. For the *Gongyang* version of the Wu Zixu story, see Duke Ding 11.4.13–14.

11. Beginning in the reign of Wang Mang, the official variant designation for the censor (*yushi* 御史) is *zhifa* 執法, as defined in Charles O. Hucker, *A Dictionary of Official Titles in Imperial China* (Stanford, Calif.: Stanford University Press, 1985), 157.

Book 13, Part 5

CHAPTER 59

The Mutual Conquest of the Five Phases

Section 59.1

Wood [corresponds to] the minister of agriculture. If the minister of agriculture acts treacherously, he will form factions and partisan cliques. [These, in turn, will] obstruct the ruler's clarity, force worthy officials into retirement and hiding, extinguish the lineages of nobles and high officers, and teach the people to be wasteful and extravagant. There will be much coming and going of visitors and guests, and people will not exert themselves in agricultural affairs. They will amuse themselves with cockfights, dog racing, and horsemanship. Old and young will lack propriety; the great and small will oppress each other, and thieves and bandits will rise up. Growing arrogant and presumptuous, the people will defy proper principles. [Consequently,] the minister of mobilization will punish [the errant minister of agriculture]. Duke Huan of Qi exemplifies this.[1] In carrying out his duties as hegemon, he employed soldiers and attacked Cai; Cai was defeated. Later he attacked Chu, and the people of Chu submitted. In this way he brought peace to the Central States. [The phase] Wood [corresponds to one of] the ruler's officials. Wood [corresponds to the minister of] agriculture; the minister of] agriculture [is in charge of] the people. If the people do not submit and [instead] rebel, then to order the minister of mobilization to punish their leaders is the correct [course of action]. Thus it is said: Metal conquers Wood.

1. For Duke Huan of Qi, see chapters 4.3, 5.4, 6.4, 6.5, and 7.1.

Fire [corresponds to] the minister of war. If the minister of war acts slanderously, with rebellious words and a quick tongue he will defame others. Within [the court,] he will become isolated from flesh and blood relatives, while outside [the court] he will grow distant from [the ruler's] loyal ministers. Sages and worthies will be expelled or exterminated, while slander and evil will grow stronger day by day. Grand Minister Jisun of Lu exemplifies this.[2] He seized authority, usurped power, and depleted the state's awe-inspiring Virtue. Instead, he relied on hateful means to slander his numerous officials and rob and mislead his ruler. Confucius became the minister of justice in Lu, and relying on the righteous principles [of the *Spring and Autumn*,] he implemented the law. Jisun yielded his power [to Confucius] and destroyed the cities of Fei and Hou; armor and weapons [were stored there in accordance with the appropriate] distinctions [in rank]. Fire corresponds to the current dynasty.[3] When the minister of war slanders and misleads the ruler, the administrator of the law will punish him. The administrator of the law [corresponds to] Water. Thus it is said: Water conquers Fire.

Earth [corresponds to one of] the ruler's officials. Its counterpart is the minister of public works. If the minister of public works treats the ruler as if he were a deity,[4]

> whatever the ruler does, he will support;
> and whatever the ruler says, he will praise.

He will comply with the ruler's precepts, listening and following him to win favor. He will promote whatever the ruler praises to satisfy the ruler's desires. He will lead the ruler into depravity and corrupt him with unrighteous principles.

> How grand will he make palaces and halls;
> how numerous will he make terraces and towers,

with carved ornaments, inlaid with gold, and radiant with the five colors. [But] his taxes and levies will know no limits, robbing the people of their livelihood. He will increase military expeditions and corvée labor, robbing the people of their time. He will engage the people in limitless projects, robbing them of their

2. Duke Ding 11.12.5: "Jisun Si and Zhongsun Heyuan led a force and razed the city of Fei." *Gongyang*:

> Why did they lead troops and raze the cities of Hou and Fei? When Jisun held the power of Lu in his hands, he followed the words of Confucius and for three months did not defy him. Confucius said: "The homes of ministers should not store armor and weapons. The cities where great officers are enfeoffed should not have walls measuring more than 100 *chi* 尺 [i.e., about 75 feet thick in modern measure]." Thereupon, they led troops and razed the city of Hou and the city of Fei.

3. Following Lu Wenchao, who emends *da chao* 大朝 to *ben chao* 本朝, as in subsequent chapters (Su Yu, *CQFLYZ* 368).

4. Treating *wei shen* 為神 as a contraction of *yi zhu wei shen* 以主為神.

strength. [Consequently,] the common people will grow distressed and rebel or flee from the state. King Ling of Chu exemplifies this.[5] He built the watchtower at Qianxi, and after three years when it still was not completed, the people were so exhausted that they revolted and assassinated him. Earth [corresponds to one of] the ruler's officials. [Wood corresponds to the minister of public works.] When the ruler is recklessly extravagant, exceeds the proper limits, and loses [his sense of] propriety, the people will rebel. When the people rebel, the ruler will be lost. Thus it is said: Wood conquers Earth.

Metal [corresponds to] the minister of mobilization. If the minister of mobilization acts deceptively, inside the court he will obtain what properly belongs to the ruler, and outside the court he will behave arrogantly toward the soldiers and officers. Seizing authority and usurping power, he will kill the innocent, invade and attack brutally and recklessly, wage war, and loot indiscriminately. He will fail to carry out orders and will not stop at what is prohibited; he will insult the military leaders and misuse the troops. The troops will grow weary; territory will be lost; and the ruler will be disgraced. [Consequently,] the minister of war will punish [the errant minister of mobilization]. Chu's killing the minister [Ziyu] Dechen exemplifies this. Dechen repeatedly attacked and defeated his enemies; inside [the palace] he obtained what properly belonged to the ruler, [and outside] he behaved arrogantly and proudly and did not show sympathy toward his subordinates, so the soldiers were not willing to be led. Thus when facing the enemy, they were weak and the state of Chu was endangered.[6] [Consequently,] the minister of war punished him. Metal [corresponds to] the minister of mobilization. When the minister of mobilization is weak and unable to lead his soldiers, the minister of war will punish him. Thus it is said: Fire conquers Metal.

Water [corresponds to] the minister of justice. If the minister of justice acts in a disorderly fashion, he will use excessive respect and petty caution, employ crafty words and an insinuating countenance, accept bribes when hearing cases, and become partisan and unjust, tardily carrying out orders but hastily punishing others and executing the guiltless. [Consequently,] the minister of public works will punish him. Ying Tang exemplifies this.[7] He was the minister of justice in the state of Qi. When Grand Duke [Wang] was enfeoffed in the state of Qi, he

5. For King Ling of Chu, see chapter 6.8.
6. Duke Xi, 5.28.6: "Chu executed their great minister Dechen." He Xiu comments: "Ziyu Dechen was a scornful minister who repeatedly instructed his lord to attack the central states. Thus he is censured." For the Chinese text, see *Chunqiu Gongyang Zhuan He Shi jiegu*, chap. 12, p. 8.
7. Ying Tang does not appear in the *Spring and Autumn* or in the *Gongyang Commentary*.

questioned him about the essentials of ordering the state. Ying Tang responded: "Employ humaneness and righteousness. That is all." Grand Duke [Wang] said: "How does one employ humaneness and righteousness?" Ying Tang responded: "Humaneness means to love others. Righteousness means to respect the old." Grand Duke [Wang] asked: "How then does one love others and respect the old?" Ying Tang answered: "In the case of loving others, this means that when you have sons, [you] do not sap their strength. In the case of respecting the old, this means that when the wife is older than the husband, he submits to the wife." Grand Duke [Wang] responded: "I want to use humaneness and righteousness to order the state of Qi, but currently you are using humaneness and righteousness to disorder the state of Qi. I must punish you and bring order to the state of Qi."[8] Water [corresponds to] the administrator of the law [and] the minister of justice. When the administrator of the law is partisan and unjust and manipulates the law to punish others, the minister of public works will punish him. Thus it is said: Earth conquers Water. [58/60/9–58/61/7]

8. *Hanfeizi* ("Waizhu shuo") states:

> Taigong Wang was enfeoffed in Qi. By the eastern sea of Qi there were retired scholars named Kuangyu and Haoshi. These two brothers set forth their principles as follows: "Neither of us would [serve as] ministers to the Son of Heaven or make friends with the Lords of the Land. We would till and work and live on the crops, and dig a well and drink the water. We would not ask anybody for help and would not accept either title from any superior or emolument from any ruler. We attend not to any official post but to our own physical strength." When Taigong Wang arrived at Encampment Hill, he sent men to arrest and punish them with execution. (*Hanfeizi* 34/99/28–30)

Bohutong 11 ("Executions") states:

> Why should sycophants be executed? Because they disturb good conduct and upset the state's government. The *Han shi nei zhuan* says: "When Confucius became minister of justice of Lu, his first act was to execute Shao Zhengmao, of whom he said that his sycophantic ways had always brought confusion to the government of the state." (*Bohutong* 11/29/24–25; Tjan Tjoe Som, trans., *Po Hu T'ung: The Comprehensive Discussions in the White Tiger Hall* [Leiden: Brill, 1952], 2:457)

Book 13, Part 6

CHAPTER 60

Complying with and Deviating from the Five Phases

Section 60.1

Wood [corresponds to] spring. Its nature is to give birth. It is the root of agriculture. [When Wood governs,] make every effort to encourage agricultural affairs, and do not impinge on the common people's seasonal [tasks]. Employ the people not more than three days annually, tax them [only] one-tenth of their output, and promote scholars versed in the classical arts. Relax the numerous prohibitions, pardon light offenses, release the detained and incarcerated, and remove handcuffs and shackles. Open doors and covers, and penetrate barriers and obstructions. Then [Heaven's] favor will extend to the grasses and trees; the plants and trees will flourish beautifully; and the numerous [kinds of] grasses[1] will germinate. [Heaven's] favor also will extend to the scaly creatures: fish will spawn abundantly; sturgeons and whales will not appear; and numerous dragons will descend.

If, however, the people's ruler is untimely in his comings and goings, his sporting dogs and trained horses will run away and gallop off and not return to the palace halls. If he is fond of lewd music, drinks wine and sinks into drunkenness, is unrestrained and indulgent, and does not attend to his governance; and if his public works proliferate, calling forth numerous people to serve him, impinging on the time necessary for the people to attend to their agricultural tasks, [and] making plans and increasing taxes so that he steals the resources of the people,

1. Accepting the emendation of 朱 to 諸; see *CQFL* 60/62/15, note 5.

the people will suffer sores from itching, scratching their bodies until they grow feverish, and their feet and shins will [be racked with] pain. Then [Heaven's] calamities will extend to Wood, so that trees that once flourished will become withered, and the cart wheels hewn by artisans will become badly broken. Noxious waters will engulf the teeming masses [of living things], and the banks of ponds will dry up, [strewn with] stranded fish. [Heaven's] calamities also will visit scaly creatures, so that fish will not spawn, the numerous dragons will hide themselves in the depths, and the great whales will appear.

Fire corresponds to summer, growth and maturation, and the present dynasty. [When Fire governs,] promote the Worthy and Excellent,[2] and advance the Cultivated Talent[3] so that

offices secure their abilities
and posts secure their strengths.
Reward the meritorious
and enfeoff the virtuous.

Distribute goods and resources to supplement those in need. Correct the boundaries of the principalities and send envoys to the four quarters. Then [Heaven's] favors will extend to Fire.[4] Fire will comply with the people's [needs,] and sweet dew will descend. [Heaven's] favors also will extend to the feathered creatures. Flying birds will greatly proliferate; the yellow crane will appear; and the male and female phoenix will soar.

If, however, the people's ruler is deluded by the slanderous and deceitful,

inside his household he will grow estranged from his relatives,
and outside his household he will grow distant from his loyal officials.
The heir apparent will be summarily killed;
the innocent will be punished with execution;
and loyal ministers will be expelled.

If he takes his concubine as a wife, disregards [his own] laws and orders, lets women run the government, and bestows gifts on the unworthy, the people will

2. Following Lau, we have corrected the order of these two terms. The "Worthy and Excellent" (Xianliang 賢良) was a recommendation category for men nominated by local officials to be considered at the capital for selection and appointment to government posts, as defined in Charles O. Hucker, *A Dictionary of Official Titles in Imperial China* (Stanford, Calif.: Stanford University Press, 1985), 242.

3. During the Eastern Han, the term "Cultivated Talent" (*maocai* 茂才) was adopted as an official variant of *xiucai* 秀才 to avoid the taboo on Emperor Guangwu's name. Cultivated talent was a rubric under which talented men were nominated to be considered for official appointments.

4. The Lau text has 恩及於人, but the Su Yu and Lai Yanyuan editions have 恩及於火, which makes better sense in the context of the paragraph. We have followed Su Yu (*CQFLYZ* 363) and Lai Yanyuan here.

suffer ailments of the blood, their bodies will swell, and their sight will become unclear. Then [Heaven's] calamities will extend to Fire and there will be a great drought. Conflagrations will be inevitable. Birds' nests will be destroyed and nestlings snatched. [Heaven's] calamities will extend to winged creatures so that flying birds will not proliferate, "winter responders"[5] will not arrive, owls will gather shrieking together, and the male and female phoenix will fly high and away.

Earth [corresponds to] midsummer, the maturing and ripening of the numerous kinds of [crops], and the ruler's officials. [When Earth governs,]

> follow the regulations of the palace,
> heed the distinctions of husband and wife,
> increase the gratitude of relatives.

Then [Heaven's] favors will extend to Earth.

> The five [types of] grain will mature,
> and the best [types of] millet will flourish.

[Heaven's] favors also will extend to the "naked creatures."[6] The populace will grow intimate and close; cities and suburbs will fill to capacity; worthies and sages will transfer their lodgings; and immortals will descend.

If, however, the people's ruler is fond of lewdness and indolence, his wives and concubines will exceed the proper limits,

> offending his close and distant relatives
> and insulting his father and elder brothers.

If he defrauds and cheats the populace, erects grand open air pavilions, dazzles the eyes with the five colors, carves ornaments and sculpts rafters, the people will suffer "the yellow and black" illnesses of the heart and stomach, and their tongues will burn with pain. Then [Heaven's] calamities will extend to Earth, so the five [types of] grain will not ripen, and there will be much violence and suffering. [Heaven's] calamities also will extend to naked creatures. Naked creatures will not reproduce; the populace will rebel and flee; and worthies and sages will be banished and lost.

Metal [corresponds to] autumn and the inception of the "killing *qi*." [When Metal governs,]

---

5. This refers to migratory birds that normally arrive from the south in spring or early summer to breed in China and then migrate south again when cold weather arrives, hence the term *dongying* 冬應 (winter responders).
6. That is, humans and animals lacking feathers, fur, scales, or shells.

set up flags and drums,
take hold of tassled spears and battle-axes

in order to

execute the violent and injurious,
restrain the oppressive and cruel,

and thereby bring security to and gather together the populace.[7] Thus, when arousing the multitudes and raising armies, you must respond with righteous principles. When embarking on military expeditions, control your forces; when returning from [expeditions], regulate your forces. In periods of leisure, be sure to drill them, taking advantage of the seasonal hunts to do so.

In times of survival, do not forget the possibility of destruction.
In times of peace, do not forget the possibility of danger.
Renovate your cities and suburbs,
repair walls and ramparts,
reexamine the various prohibitions,
refurbish weapons and armor,
admonish the numerous officials,
and execute the unlawful.

Then [Heaven's] favors will extend to metal and stone,[8] and cool winds will arise. [Heaven's] favors also will extend to hairy creatures, so that running animals will greatly proliferate and the *qilin* will arrive.

If, however, the people's ruler is fond of warfare and he attacks and oppresses the Lords of the Land,

coveting the goods of the marketplace
and scorning the lives of the commoners,

the people will suffer coughing throats, lethargic muscles, and congested noses from colds. Then [Heaven's] calamities will extend to Metal so that

casting and smelting will be congealed and weak,
cold tempering will not succeed.

[If you] set up nets on all sides, and [then] set fire to the forests to flush the game, [Heaven's] calamities also will extend to hairy creatures so that running creatures will not proliferate, the white tiger will attack wildly, and *qilins* will stray far away.

---

7. Several early commentators correctly point out that two characters appear to be missing following 安集. We follow one suggested emendation and supply *baixing* 百姓 (Zhong, *CQFLJS* 689, note 2).
8. That is, musical instruments such as bells and chime stones.

Water [corresponds to] winter, storing up, and the height of yin *qi*. It marks the beginning of the sacrifices and offerings at the ancestral temple, the sacrifices that reverence the four seasons, and the proper sequence of the Di and Xia[9] sacrifices before the ancestral spirit tablets, left and right.

[When Water governs,]

the Son of Heaven sacrifices to Heaven;
the Lords of the Land sacrifice to Earth.
Shut doors and gates,
investigate strangers,
apprehend the condemned,
garrison the passes and bridges,
and prohibit travel abroad.

Then [Heaven's] favors will extend to Water. Sweet springs will gush forth. [Heaven's] favors also will extend to armored [i.e., shell-covered] creatures; sea turtles and water lizards will greatly proliferate; and loggerhead turtles will appear.

If, however, the people's ruler neglects the ancestral temples, does not pray and make offerings to the spirits, abandons the sacrifices, does not administer the laws compliantly, and defies Heaven's seasons, the common people will suffer the illnesses of weeping swellings, dropsy,[10] paralysis, rheumatism, and constipation. Then [Heaven's] calamities will extend to Water, so that fog will grow murky and dark and inevitably there will be great floods, the water wreaking havoc on the common people. [Heaven's] calamities also will extend to armored creatures so that loggerhead turtles will go into deep hiding, and sea turtles and water lizards will gasp for air. [60/62/13–60/63/17]

9. The Di sacrifice was an offering to the remotest ancestor from whom the founder of the dynasty traced his descent, and the Xia sacrifice was a collective offering to remote ancestors.
10. Following Ling Shu's edition, which has *chang* 脹 (accumulation of water), instead of *chang* 長 (to extend) (Su Yu, *CQFLYZ* 381).

Book 13, Part 7

CHAPTER 61

Controlling Water by Means of the Five Phases

Section 61.1

Beginning at the winter solstice,

for seventy-two days, Wood is used to conduct affairs. Its *qi* is drying, turbid, and bluegreen.[1]

For seventy-two days, Fire is used to conduct affairs. Its *qi* is drying, heating, and vermilion.

Previous commentators have been troubled by the title of this chapter and have proposed emending it in various ways, but we are persuaded that the title, "Zhi shui wuxing" 治水五行, is correct in its received form and that it means "Controlling Water by Means of the Five Phases." Our reasoning is that water is correlated with yin, and the chapters of group 5, the group immediately preceding this one, explain at length that yin is a subordinate and pernicious force and that its influence is confined to the northern quadrant and the winter months. This chapter now presents a scheme for bringing the influence of water/yin under control: in this scheme, Wood begins to be used to manage affairs, not beginning with *li chun* (beginning of spring), forty-six days after the winter solstice (as in the conventional solar calendar of twenty-four, two-week periods), but instead, right at the winter solstice, for a period of seventy-two days. So Wood is already in charge for the second half of winter (which in Chinese reckoning extends for forty-six days on either side of the winter solstice), thus keeping in check the baleful yin power of water. Thus the chapter title: "Zhi shui wuxing" (Controlling Water by Means of the Five Phases).

1. In this chapter, a year consists of five, seventy-two-day periods dominated by Wood, Fire, Earth, Metal, and Water, respectively. A similar system is mentioned briefly in chapter 44.2. The version found here closely resembles that in *Huainanzi* 3.22. See John S. Major, Sarah A. Queen, Andrew Seth Meyer, and Harold D. Roth, trans. and eds., *The "Huainanzi": A Guide to the Theory and Practice of Government in Early Han China* (New York: Columbia University Press, 2010), 128–29; and D. C. Lau, ed., *Huainanzi zhuzi suoyin* (*A Concordance to the "Huainanzi"*), Chinese University of Hong Kong, Institute of Chinese Studies Ancient Chinese Text Concordance Series (Hong Kong: Commercial Press, 1992), 3/23/20–23. The *Huainanzi* passage does not refer directly to the Five Phases, but to five of the Heavenly Stems of the sexagenary cycle: *jia*, *bing*, *wu*, *geng*, and *ren*. But because these Heavenly Stems are correlated with the Five Phases (*jia* with Wood, *bing* with Fire, *wu* with Earth, *geng* with Metal, and *ren* with Water), the net effect is the same.

For seventy-two days, Earth is used to conduct affairs. Its *qi* is moistening, turbid, and yellow.

For seventy-two days, Metal is used to conduct affairs. Its *qi* is drying, chilling, and white.

For seventy-two days, Water is used to conduct affairs. Its *qi* is clear, chilling, and black.

For the next seventy-two days, Wood again receives control.

When Wood is in control, act gently and graciously, and relax the many prohibitions. At the beginning of spring, pardon light offenses, release the detained and incarcerated, and remove handcuffs and shackles. Open doors and covers, penetrate barriers and obstructions, preserve the young and orphaned, and demonstrate empathy for the widowed and solitary. Do not cut down trees.

When Fire is in control, correct the boundaries of the principalities and inspect the agricultural lands. At the beginning of summer, promote the Worthy and Excellent,[2] enfeoff the virtuous, reward the meritorious, and send envoys to the four quarters. Do not carelessly set fires.

When Earth is in control, nourish the old and elderly, preserve the young and orphaned, demonstrate empathy for the widowed and solitary, give to the Filial and Brotherly,[3] and bestow grace and favor. Do not raise earthworks.

When Metal is in control, strengthen city walls and fortifications, improve walls and enclosures, scrutinize prohibitions, refurbish the armor of the troops, admonish officials, punish the lawless, and preserve the old and elderly. Do not smelt metal or stone [ores].

When Water is in control, shut doors and gates, investigate strangers, apprehend the condemned, garrison passes and bridges, and prohibit travel abroad. Do not destroy dikes or embankments. [61/63/21–28]

2. *Xianliang* 賢良 was a recommendation category for men nominated by local officials to be considered at the capital for selection and appointment to government posts, as defined in Charles O. Hucker, *A Dictionary of Official Titles in Imperial China* (Stanford, Calif.: Stanford University Press, 1985), 242.

3. *Xiaodi* 孝弟 also refers to a category of men whom local officials recommended as potential official appointees, as defined in Hucker, *Dictionary of Official Titles*, 238.

Book 14, Part 1

CHAPTER 62

Controlling Disorders by Means of the Five Phases

Section 62.1

When Fire opposes Wood, hibernating insects will hatch prematurely, and there will be [unseasonably] early thunder.
When Earth opposes Wood, the pregnant will suffer calamities, eggs will be infertile, and birds and insects will suffer great injuries.
When Metal opposes Wood, there will be military operations.
When Water opposes Wood, there will be spring frosts.

When Earth opposes Fire, there will be much thunder.
When Metal opposes Fire, herbaceous plants and trees will die out.
When Water opposes Fire, there will be summer hail.
When Wood opposes Fire, there will be earthquakes.

This chapter records the occurrence of twenty anomalies that arise when one of the Five Phases opposes another. This chapter parallels *Huainanzi* 3.23, as *CQFL* 61 parallels *Huainanzi* 3.22. See John S. Major, Sarah A. Queen, Andrew Seth Meyer, and Harold D. Roth, trans. and eds., *The "Huainanzi": A Guide to the Theory and Practice of Government in Early Han China* (New York: Columbia University Press, 2010), 129; and D. C. Lau, ed., *Huainanzi zhuzi suoyin* (*A Concordance to the "Huainanzi"*), Chinese University of Hong Kong, Institute of Chinese Studies Ancient Chinese Text Concordance Series (Hong Kong: Commercial Press, 1992), 3/23/27–3/24/5.

When Metal opposes Earth,[1] the five grains will suffer calamities.
When Water opposes Earth, there will be cold in summer, rain, and frost.
When Wood opposes Earth, silkworms will not mature.
When Fire opposes Earth, there will be great droughts.

When Water opposes Metal, fish will not grow.
When Wood opposes Metal, herbaceous plants and trees will [die and then] sprout again.
When Fire opposes Metal, herbaceous plants and trees will bloom in autumn.
When Earth opposes Metal, the five grains will not mature.

When Wood opposes Water, creatures will not hibernate in winter.
When Earth opposes Water, hibernating creatures will emerge in winter.
When Fire opposes Water, there will be meteors.
When Metal opposes Water, there will be severe cold in winter. [62/64/5–18]

1. Correcting "Wood" to "Earth."

Book 14, Part 2

CHAPTER 63

Aberrations of the Five Phases and Their Remedies

Section 63.1

When aberrations of the Five Phases occur, one ought to remedy them with virtue and disseminate it throughout the world. Then calamities will be eradicated. If one does not remedy them with virtue, before three years have passed, Heaven will send thunder[1] and rain down stones.

When Wood encounters aberrations, in spring there is decay and in autumn there is flourishing. In autumn, trees are covered with ice, and in spring it rains too much. These aberrations occur

when corvée labor is excessive
and when taxes are burdensome.

The populace becomes impoverished and destitute, leading people to flee or rebel, and the thoroughfares are filled with starving people. To remedy the situation,

decrease corvée labor,
lighten taxes,
and distribute the stored grain

to relieve the distressed and destitute.

When Fire encounters aberrations, in winter it is warm, and in summer it is cold. These aberrations occur

when the king is unenlightened,

1. Reading *lei* 雷 in place of *dang* 當, following Lau's emendation in *CQFL* 64, note 10.

when the good are not promoted,
when the bad are not dismissed,
when fools occupy positions of authority,
and when worthies go into hiding,

so that cold and warmth lose their proper sequence, and the populace is visited by diseases and epidemics. To remedy the situation,

promote the worthy and excellent,
reward the meritorious,
and grant land to the virtuous.

When Earth encounters aberrations, great winds arrive, and the five [kinds of] grain suffer harm. These aberrations occur

when the humane and worthy are not trusted,
when fathers and elder brothers are not respected,
when lusts and desires are not regulated,
and when [the ruler's] dwellings and apartments are excessive.

To remedy the situation,

reduce the number of dwellings and apartments,
abandon carved ornamentation,
promote the filially pious and fraternally respectful,
and show sympathy for the populace.

When Metal encounters aberrations, [the determinative stars for the lunar lodges] Net and Pleiades reverse positions.[2] If this happens three times, there will be war. Armies will increase, and bandits will proliferate. These aberrations occur

when [the ruler] abandons righteousness and covets wealth,
when [he] takes lightly the lives of the people and attaches importance to material gain,

so that the people seek profit, and outlaws and rebels proliferate. To remedy the situation,

promote the honest and pure,
establish the upright and forthright,
set aside the martial, and implement the civil.

When Water encounters aberrations, in winter it grows damp, and there is too much fog. In spring and summer, there is rain and hail. These aberrations

2. The intended meaning of this line is unclear because it is physically impossible for stars to switch positions.

occur when laws and ordinances are lax, and punishments and penalties are not implemented. To remedy the situation,

be painstaking about prisons and jails,
try cases against traitors and rebels,
punish those who have committed crimes,
and carry out investigations every five days. [63/64/22–63/65/4]

Book 14, Part 3

CHAPTER 64

The Five Phases and Five Affairs

Section 64.1

When the king does not [act with] propriety toward his ministers and his expression is not solemn and reverent, wood cannot be bent or straightened. In summer there will be too much violent wind. Wind [corresponds to] the *qi* of Wood and the note *jue*. Thus Wood responds to the king with violent winds.

When the king's speech is not compliant, metal will not follow its [successive] refinements [in smelting]. In autumn there will be too much rumbling thunder. Rumbling thunder corresponds to the *qi* of Metal and the note *shang*. Thus Metal responds to the king with rumbling thunder.

When the king's sight is not clear, fire will not kindle. In autumn there will be too much lightning. Lightning corresponds to the *qi* of Fire and the note *zhi*. Thus Fire responds to the king with lightning.

When the king's hearing is not acute, water will not moisten [the soil].[1] In summer there will be too much violent rain. Rain corresponds to the *qi* of Water and the note *yu*. Therefore, Water responds to the king with violent rains.

When the king's thought cannot retain [things], sowing and reaping will not succeed. In autumn there will be too much thunder. Thunder corresponds to the *qi* of Earth and the note *gong*. Thus Earth responds to the king with thunder. [64/65/8–13]

1. Treating the graph *chun* 春 (spring) as excrescent.

Section 64.2

The five affairs:

The first is called expression;
the second is called speech;
the third is called sight;
the fourth is called hearing;
and the fifth is called thought.[2]

What does this mean? The five affairs are the destiny that human beings receive from Heaven. The king cultivates them [so as] to bring order to the people. Therefore the king, on behalf of the people, [ensures that]

[his] governance does not fail to be enlightened and
[his] level and marking cord do not fail to be true.

The king's expression is said to be respectful. Respectful means that it is reverent.

[The king's] speech is said to be compliant. Compliant means that it can be obeyed.

[The king's] sight is said to be clear. Clear means that it knows the distinction between the sage and the fool; it distinguishes clearly between black and white.

[The king's] hearing is said to be astute. Astute means that it can hear of an affair and discern its significance.

[The king's] thought is said to be capacious. To be capacious means that there is nothing that it does not contain.

Respectfulness makes solemnity;
compliance makes eminence;
clarity makes wisdom;
astuteness makes deliberation;
and retention makes sagacity.[3]

What does this mean?

"Respectfulness makes solemnity." This means that if the king sincerely internalizes the bearing of respectfulness and reverence, there will be no one in the world who will not be awed.

"Compliance makes eminence." This means that the king's speech can be obeyed; being brilliant and correct, it is obeyed and implemented, and the world becomes ordered.

"Clarity makes wisdom." To be wise means to know. [This means] that when the king is enlightened, then

2. These lines are from the "Great Plan" chapter of the *Documents*.
3. These lines are from the "Great Plan" chapter of the *Documents*.

those who are sages will be promoted;
those who are fools will be demoted;
the world will recognize the good and be encouraged by it;
and the world will recognize the evil and be shamed by it.

"Astuteness makes deliberation." Deliberation means to plan affairs. When the king is astute, upon hearing of an affair, he will make plans together with his ministers. Thus in managing affairs, he will be free from erroneous plans.

"Retention makes sagacity." Sagacity means to establish. When the king's mind is broad and expansive, there will be nothing that it does not contain. His sagacity can be put into effect and established, and each one of his undertakings will achieve what is fitting [to the circumstance].

If the king is able to be reverent, he will be solemn. When he is solemn, the spring *qi* will obtain. Thus solemnity governs spring. In spring, the yang *qi* is incipient, and the myriad things are tender and supple. Their influence is weak, and they are easily transformed. During this season, the yin *qi* is fractious. Thus the king is mindful. Being mindful, he does not discuss affairs pertaining to yin. Only then will the myriad things follow their natural course, and only then can wood [be worked to become] bent or straight. In spring,

if the king implements autumn policies, the grasses and trees will wither;
if the king implements winter policies, there will be snow;
and if the king implements summer policies, there will be killing.

[Thus] in spring, if the king diverges from the appropriate policies. . . .[4]

If the king is able to bring order, righteousness will be established. When righteousness is established, the autumn *qi* will obtain. Thus eminence governs autumn. In autumn, the yin[5] *qi* begins to kill. If the king implements minor punishments and penalties and the common people do not violate [the laws and prohibitions], propriety and righteousness will be perfected. During this season, the yang *qi* is fractious. Thus the king assists with the affairs of the overseers of the herdsmen. Only then are the myriad things brought to completion and fruition. In autumn, the grasses and trees will not prosper and flower. Metal follows its [successive processes of] refinement. In autumn,

if the king implements spring policies, there will be [unseasonable] flowering;
if the king implements summer policies, there will be excessive growth;
if the king implements winter policies, there will be fallen [fruit].

4. The text breaks off at this point.
5. We have supplied the character *yin* 陰 based on parallelisms with the ensuing text and the fact that the yin *qi* does the killing in fall and winter.

Thus in autumn, if the king diverges from the appropriate policies, in spring there will be great winds that do not let up, and thunder will not sound forth.

If the king is able to know, he will know [the difference between] good and evil. When he knows [the difference between] good and evil, the summer *qi* will obtain. Thus wisdom governs summer. In summer, the yang *qi* begins to flourish, and the myriad things prosper and mature. If the king does not hide his clarity, the Way will not recede or be obstructed. After the summer solstice, the Great Heat declines, and the myriad things propagate abundantly and become pregnant.[6] During this season, chilling causes injury. Thus the king assists with the tasks of rewarding with gifts. Only then in summer, the grasses and trees will not be injured by frost, and fire will be kindled. In summer,

> if the king implements spring policies, there will be winds;
> if the king implements autumn policies, there will be floods;
> and if the king implements winter policies, there will be fallen [fruit].

Thus in summer, if the king diverges from the appropriate policies, there will be no freezing in winter, the five [kinds of] grain will not be stored away, and the Great Cold will not let up.

If the king is free from erroneous deliberations, the winter *qi* will obtain. Thus deliberations govern winter. In winter, the yin *qi* begins to flourish, and the grasses and trees inevitably will die. If the king is capable of staying informed of affairs and exhibiting caution in his planning and reflecting, he will not invade or chastise other states. If he does not invade or chastise other states or kill [those not deserving execution], then those who die will not despise him, and those who live will not resent him. After the winter solstice, the Great Cold declines, and the myriad things hide themselves under the earth. During this season, heating causes injury. Thus the king assists with the task of urgent judgments. [. . .] with water saturating what lies below the earth.[7] In winter,

> if the king implements spring policies, there will be steam;
> if the king implements summer policies, there will be snow;
> if the king implements autumn policies, there will be drought.

Thus in winter, if the king diverges from the appropriate policies, the grasses and trees will not bear fruit in the summer, there will be frost, and the five [kinds of] grains will fail and wither away. [64/65/13–64/66/12]

6. We have treated the next thirteen characters (beginning with *wang* 王 and ending with *hei* 黑) as an interpolation, following Su Yu, *CQFLYZ* 393.
7. Missing text precedes this fragment.

Group 7

Ritual Principles

GROUP 7, "Ritual Principles," is made up of twelve thematically linked chapters devoted to various aspects of ritual and sacrifice.

GROUP 7: RITUAL PRINCIPLES, CHAPTERS 65–76

65. 郊語 *Jiao yu* Sayings Pertaining to the Suburban Sacrifice
66. 郊義 *Jiao yi* The Principles of the Suburban Sacrifice
67. 郊祭 *Jiao ji* Sacrificial Rites of the Suburban Sacrifice
68. 四祭 *Si ji* The Four [Seasonal] Sacrificial Rites
69. 郊祀 *Jiao si* The Suburban Sacrifice
70. 順命 *Shun ming* Following Orders
71. 郊事對 *Jiao shi dui* An Official Response Regarding the Suburban Sacrifice
72. 執贄 *Zhi zhi* Presenting Gifts to Superiors
73. 山川頌 *Shan chuan song* Hymn to the Mountains and Rivers
74. 求雨 *Qiu yu* Seeking Rain
75. 止雨 *Zhi yu* Stopping Rain
76. 祭義 *Ji yi* The Principles of Sacrificial Rites

Most of these chapters discuss specific rites and sacrifices from the perspective of the *Gongyang Commentary* to the *Spring and Autumn*. Five of the twelve chapters as reconstructed by Su Yu (65, 66, 67, 69, and 71) describe the Suburban Sacrifice, and two chapters (68 and 76) address the seasonal sacrifices performed at the ancestral temple. These two chapters are closely related to those on the Suburban Sacrifice, as they offer a way to reconcile the two possibly incompatible filial obligations of the ruler, to his actual genetic ancestors, and to his Heavenly father in his role as the Son of Heaven. Chapters 74 and 75 detail the rites for dealing with a dearth or surfeit of rain, and the remaining three chapters in this group (70, 72, and 73) address assorted themes dealing with ritual obligations.

In chapters 65, 67, 68, 69, and 70, the reconstructions proposed by D. C. Lau and Su Yu differ. We are generally persuaded by Su Yu's reasoning, which offers a more coherent reading of the various essay fragments. Therefore, both our introductory discussion of these chapters and our translation follow Su Yu rather than Lau. But where we move blocks of text, following Su Yu, we provide the page references in Lau's edition so that readers will have a straightforward way of finding the Chinese text. (Thus all the text in Lau's edition is translated here, but not necessarily where it is placed in that edition.)

The Chapters on Seeking and Stopping Rain

Ancient Chinese procedures for procuring and stopping rain already have been extensively analyzed by a number of scholars, so our introduction to these chapters will be brief.[1]

1. See, especially, Michael Loewe, "The Cult of the Dragon and the Invocation for Rain," in *Chinese Ideas About Nature and Society: Essays in Honour of Derk Bodde*, ed. Charles Le Blanc and Susan Blader (Hong Kong: Hong Kong University Press, 1987), 195–213, revised and reprinted in Michael Loewe, *Divination, Mythology and Monarchy in Han China* (Cambridge: Cambridge University Press, 1994), 142–59. The structure, content, and authenticity of chapters 74 and 75 have been analyzed in detail in Sarah A. Queen, *From Chronicle to Canon: The Hermeneutics of the "Spring and Autumn" According to Tung Chung-shu* (Cambridge: Cambridge University Press, 1996), 106–11, to which we refer the reader for a more extensive discussion of these chapters. See also Gary Arbuckle, "Restoring Dong Zhongshu (BCE 195–115): An Experiment in Historical and Philosophical Reconstruction" (Ph.D. diss., University of British Columbia, 1991), 218–62, 499–537.

   Readers may recall that rain-procuring and rain-stopping procedures also are described in the second section of chapter 5, "The Quintessential and the Ornamental." That passage avers that since yang naturally dominates yin, a drought (caused by an excess of yang) is merely an exaggeration of the normative order and that all that is required is to restore the proper balance. Excessive rain, however, indicates that yin is dominating yang, a reversal of the normative order. In restoring the natural balance, it is necessary to punish the crime of "the inferior defying the superior." Therefore, chapter 5.2 proposes that to stop excessive rainfall, aggressive procedures are needed that involve beating drums and physically assaulting, chastising, and intimidating the altar of Earth. Procedures of that sort do not appear in chapters 74 and 75.

Chapter 57, "Things of the Same Kind Activate One Another," explains the principles of yin and yang that both account for and provide the means for overcoming drought and excessive rainfall:

> Heaven has yin and yang [aspects], and people have yin and yang [aspects]. When the *qi* of Heaven and Earth arises, the *qi* of people arises in response to it; when the *qi* of people arises, the *qi* of Heaven and Earth also arises appropriately in response to it. Their Way is unitary. Those who understand this, when wishing to bring forth rain, activate yin, causing yin to arise; when wishing to stop rain, activate yang, causing yang to arise. Therefore, rain is not caused by the spirits. People suspect that it is the spirits' doing because its inner principles are subtle and mysterious.[2]

Chapter 74, "Seeking Rain," brings together two separate essays of quite different provenance, so we divided the chapter into two sections. The first is a long essay that extensively uses Five-Phase cosmology, and the second simply summarizes a straightforward procedure that uses yin-yang principles to bring rain during any season of the year. In trying to overcome the imbalance of yang over yin, both sections of chapter 74 employ several tried-and-true methods of generating yin energy. Women are encouraged to frequent the market and walk abroad; men are excluded from the market and required to stay indoors. Men and women are encouraged to have sexual intercourse, which was believed to generate yin energy. A shamanka is exposed to the rays of the sun in an open field, in the hope that her concentrated yin spiritual power will counteract the force of the Great Yang. At an extreme, this would amount to an act of human sacrifice. Other shamankas engage in rituals and offer prayers.

The chief instrument for attracting rain is an earthen dragon, an effigy of the quintessential water-loving beast. Section 74.1 amplifies these measures by associating them with an elaborate scheme of Five-Phase correlations. For example, 74.1 divides the year into five seasons (using the now-familiar procedure of designating the seventh month as a separate midsummer season correlated with Earth), rather than the four natural seasons more typical of Dong Zhongshu's writings. The details of the construction and placement of the earthen dragon in each season emphasize Five-Phase correlations. The dragons' specifications vary, and in every case their color, dimensions, direction,

2. *CQFL* 57/59/26–28.

and other details conform exactly to the seasonal correlative characteristics of Wood, Fire, Earth, Metal, and Water.

Chapter 75, "Stopping Rain," compiles materials on that topic from diverse sources, which divide naturally into three sections. Section 75.1 describes relatively simple and brief procedures for generating yang energy and suppressing yin energy, commensurate with but the obverse of the techniques to procure rain outlined in chapter 74.2. In section 75.1, women are sequestered, men conspicuously appear in public, and a pig and other sacrificial goods are ritually offered at the altar of the soil, with prayers that the excessive yin might be made to subside. The brief fragment making up section 75.2 affirms that the main point of the steps outlined in 75.1 is that women should be kept out of sight and men should join together joyfully in generating yang energy. Section 75.2 also specifies that the celebrants wear vermilion vestments (the color of maximum yang) and that the altar of the soil be encircled by a vermilion cord (perhaps to confine and restrict its yin energy).[3] The chapter ends, in 75.3, with an account of the efforts by Dong Zhongshu himself, while serving as administrator of Jiangdu, to put these procedures into practice.[4] His efforts were apparently successful, as Sima Qian makes a point of recording:

> After the present emperor assumed the throne, he appointed Dong Zhongshu to be the administrator to Jiangdu. Relying on the untoward changes such as natural disasters and strange events recorded in the *Spring and Autumn,* he deduced what caused yin and yang to fall into disorder. Therefore when seeking rain, he repressed yang and released yin; when stopping rain, he inverted those techniques. When he implemented those techniques in that single state, he never failed to obtain the desired results.[5]

Because of its heavy reliance on Five-Phase techniques, the long first section of chapter 74 is, in our judgment, not the work of Dong Zhongshu.[6] But section

3. Chapter 5.2 also specifies vermilion vestments and a vermilion cord. One commentator describes the cord as part of the procedure for chastising the altar of the soil for permitting the yin-over-yang inversion of the natural order, but another explains that the cord is to safeguard the altar from people who might otherwise blunder into it in the dark. See chapter 5, note 6.
4. See also similar passages attributed to Dong Zhongshu quoted in commentaries to the *Hou Han shu,* translated in Queen, *From Chronicle to Canon*, 57–59.
5. *SJ* 121/3128.
6. The *Hou Han shu* makes it clear that Dong's rain-controlling efforts were based entirely on yin and yang: "Zhongshu memorialized the king of Jiangdu, saying: 'The formula for seeking rain is that of decreasing the yang and increasing the yin'" (5/3118; Queen, *From Chronicle to Canon*, 111).

74.2 and all of chapter 75 appear to be authentic works by Dong himself. Section 74.1 may represent the efforts of one of Dong's disciples to develop his teacher's rain-seeking techniques and incorporate Five-Phase correlations to keep abreast of the burgeoning popularity of Five-Phase cosmology in the later decades of the Western Han.

The chapters on procuring or stopping rain are best understood as representing Dong's efforts to develop the Rain-Seeking Sacrifice (*yu* 雩) found in the *Spring and Autumn* in a manner compatible with the ideas of yin-yang resonance that informed his cosmological views.[7] Thus procuring and stopping rain is not the work of the spirits, but rather harnesses man's ability to understand and manipulate the Heaven-endowed principles that drive the cosmos itself.[8] Like the other chapters in this group, which deal largely with the Suburban Sacrifice and the Sacrifices of the Four Seasons, the chapters on rain and the additional chapters on ritual obligations were collected at this point in the *Chunqiu fanlu* because they deal with rites and sacrifices recorded in the *Spring and Autumn* and sanctioned by the *Gongyang Commentary.*

Additional Chapters on Ritual Obligations

Chapters 70, 72, and 73 deal with the general subject of ritual obligations. Chapter 70, "Following Orders," clarifies the moral meritocracy implicit in the hierarchical ranking system of the *Spring and Autumn* and its corresponding terminology. This essay maintains that following orders is ultimately a matter of revering Heaven, and through a variety of examples, it demonstrates how the *Spring and Autumn* uses the "subtleties of its terminology" or patterns of notation to identify and assign lesser rank to those who fail in

7. Dong's efforts are explicitly recognized in Wang Chong's *Lunheng*:

> Dong Zhongshu developed the Yu sacrifice of the *Spring and Autumn*. He erected a clay dragon to attract the rain. His intention was to rely on the clouds and the dragon to summon each other. The *Changes* states: "The clouds follow the dragon; the winds follow the tiger." He sought rain by relying on things of the same category. Therefore he erected a clay dragon, yin and yang followed their kind, and clouds and rain spontaneously arrived. (*Lunheng* 22/86/5–10; compare 45/206/3–9, 47/213/24–25, 55/243/23–27, 55/244/18–22, and 63/274/23–25)

8. Likewise, chapter 52.2 says that Yu's flood and Tang's drought were of human origin and not the product of the "constant regularities of Heaven." When Yao died, the people's mourning created so much yin energy that a flood ensued; the tyrant Jie, last ruler of the Xia, created so much baleful yang energy that the reign of his virtuous conqueror Tang was marred at first by a great drought. See the note at the beginning of chapter 52.

that obligation. Section 70.4 links the downfall of rulers and the extinction of states to ritual irregularities.

Chapter 72, "Presenting Gifts to Superiors," describes the appropriate gifts to be offered by various members of the hierarchy to their respective superiors: the Son of Heaven offers black millet wine to Heaven and Earth, the dukes and marquises offer jade ritual regalia to the Son of Heaven when they attend a royal audience, and so on down to the great officers. This chapter is fragmentary and incomplete; fuller parallels can be found in the *Liji*, the *Shuoyuan*, and the *Bohutong*.[9]

Chapter 73, "Hymn to the Mountains and Rivers" (Shan chuan song 山川頌), is a *song*, a praise-hymn or panegyric, apparently composed as part of the liturgy of a sacrifice to the spirits of the mountains and the rivers. It may be related to the sacrifices to Mount Tai, the Yellow River, and the Sea recorded in the *Spring and Autumn* as the "Triple Gazing" (*san wang* 三望),[10] in which the celebrant ritually "gazes from afar" (*wang*) at those conspicuous features of the topography of northern China.[11]

The Chapters on the Four Seasonal Sacrifices

Chapter 68, "The Four [Seasonal] Sacrificial Rites," and chapter 76, "The Principles of Sacrificial Rites," describe in similar terms a program of "first fruits" sacrifices to be performed in the ancestral temple at the beginning of each of the

9. For example, the "Qu li" (Summary of Ritual) chapter of *Liji* (James Legge, trans., *Li Chi: Book of Rites*, ed. Ch'u Chai and Winberg Chai [New Hyde Park, N.Y.: University Books, 1967], 1:119); the "Xiu wen" (Promoting Civility) chapter of the *Shuoyuan*; and the "Rui zhi" (Ritual Presents) of the *Bohutong* (Tjan Tjoe Som, trans., *Po Hu T'ong: The Comprehensive Discussions in the White Tiger Hall*, 2 vols. [Leiden: Brill, 1949, 1952], 2:543–45).

10. The *Gongyang Commentary* at Duke Xi 5.31.3 explains:

> What does "Triple Gazing" mean? It is the Gazing sacrifice. Who then received the sacrifice? It was a sacrifice to Mount Tai, the rivers and the seas. Why were sacrifices to Mount Tai, the rivers, and the seas performed? The mountain waters can enrich things for a hundred *li*. The Son of Heaven, in an orderly fashion, offers sacrifice accordingly. [The clouds] touch its stones and disperse, spread over every inch [of the land] and gather and in the space of one morning bring rain to the whole world. [This happens] only on Mount Tai. The rivers and the seas enrich things for a thousand *li*. Why the term "still"? . . . It was a criticism because the Suburban Sacrifice was not performed yet the Triple Gazing sacrifice was performed.

11. Based on parallels with Liu Xiang's *Shuoyuan*, Gary Arbuckle argues persuasively that Liu Xiang drew on this source, that the "Shan chuan song" was likely written during Dong's lifetime, and that there is no reason to doubt that he could have been the author of this work, in "A Note on the Authenticity of the *Chunqiu Fanlu*," *T'oung Pao* 75 (1989): 226–34.

four seasons.[12] According to section 68.1, the spring sacrifice features scallions; the summer, wheat; the autumn, glutinous panicled millet; and the winter, newly harvested rice. Collectively, these crops are referred to (in chapter 76.1) as "Heaven's gifts." Up to this point, chapters 68 and 76 are quite similar. Then chapter 76 (but not 68) adds punning explanations for the names of the sacrifices and the types of bronze vessels employed in each and launches into a lengthy explanation of the principles of sacrifice, emphasizing the obligation of rulers to offer these fruits of the harvest to their ancestors before they are consumed by living humans. Sacrifice is explained as being the principal means of connecting and communing with the spirits and therefore is a solemn affair of state. Both Confucius and the *Odes* are quoted regarding the necessity of performing the seasonal sacrifices with the utmost gravity. As we will demonstrate later, Dong Zhongshu is using the records of these sacrifices found in the *Spring and Autumn*, and explicated by the *Gongyang Commentary*, to construct and recommend to Emperor Wu a coherent program of imperial sacrifices. Even though Emperor Wu ignored Dong's recommendations, in the longer run Dong's views had a significant impact on how imperial sacrifices would be conducted in the Latter Han period.

The next section in chapter 68 is a brief hymn praising the sacrificial rituals. We moved this section here from chapter 70, following Su Yu's reconstruction. But because Lau's text includes it in chapter 70, we labeled it 70.2 here.

The final part of chapter 68 (which we labeled 68.2) appears to be a stray fragment that associates King Wen with the Suburban Sacrifice but has no direct bearing on the four seasonal sacrifices. However, it is a link to the group's general perspective on sacrifice: despite the importance of the seasonal sacrifices,

12. The *Spring and Autumn* mentions the Zheng 烝 sacrifice at Duke Huan 2.8.1 and 2.8.3, and the Chang 嘗 sacrifice at Duke Huan 2.14.5. Both, according to the *Gongyang*, are mentioned to note a ritual violation. Duke Huan 2.8.1: "The eighth year. Spring. The first month. *Jimao*. There was the Zheng sacrifice." *Gongyang*:

> What is implied by the term Zheng? It was a winter sacrifice. The spring [sacrifice] was called Zi; the summer [sacrifice] was called Yue; the autumn [sacrifice] was called Chang; and the winter [sacrifice] was called Zheng. Regular events were not recorded. Why did [the *Spring and Autumn*] make a record here? In order to criticize. What was there to criticize? [The *Spring and Autumn*] criticized its frequency. [If a sacrifice is presented too] frequently, [the one who offers sacrifice] becomes negligent. [If one becomes] negligent, [one grows] disrespectful. When the Superior Man offers sacrifice, he is respectful and not negligent. If a sacrifice is presented too seldom, then the one who presents the sacrifice becomes idle. If one becomes idle, one becomes forgetful. If an officer is prevented from attending these four [seasonal sacrifices], he must not wear a fur coat in winter, nor a light dress in summer. (Adapted from Göran Malmqvist, "Studies on the *Gongyang* and *Guliang* Commentaries," *Bulletin of the Museum of Far Eastern Antiquities* 43 [1971]: 103)

The "Wang zhi" (Royal Regulations) chapter of the *Liji* states: "The sacrifices in the ancestral temples of the Son of Heaven and the Lords of the Land were that of spring, called Yue; that of summer, called Di; that of autumn, called Chang; and that of winter, called Zheng" (Legge, *Li Chi*, 1:224–25).

the Suburban Sacrifice takes absolute priority in the annual round of the Son of Heaven's sacrificial obligationsL "Having received the Mandate to become king, [the king] must first sacrifice to Heaven, and only then [may he] implement the tasks of a king."[13] The passage's description of the circumstances under which the Suburban Sacrifice is performed is quite different from that in the Suburban Sacrifice chapters themselves. In these chapters, the Suburban Sacrifice is an annual rite to be performed at the very beginning of each civil calendar year, whereas section 68.2 suggests that its primary purpose is to confirm the ruler's authority at the beginning of his reign. But the key point remains that the Suburban Sacrifice, being a sacrifice to Heaven rather than to the royal ancestors, is the most important of the ruler's ritual tasks. Here the *Chunqiu fanlu* ventures onto highly contested ground, a circumstance that prompts an extended examination of the Suburban Sacrifice itself.

The Chapters on the Suburban Sacrifice

The chapters on the Suburban Sacrifice articulate a program of worship based on Confucius's authority, especially as expressed in the *Gongyang Commentary* to the *Spring and Autumn* and complemented by the *Analects* and the *Classic of Odes*.[14] The chapters provide programmatic details concerning this sacrifice, as well as comments on their relationship to the ancestral sacrifices, based on these canonical sources. All the chapters assert that the emperor must faithfully follow the proper sequence of sacrifice. The Suburban Sacrifice is presented as the most important of all sacrificial rituals performed by the emperor because the object of worship is Heaven, the most honored of all the spirits that populate the numinous realm. This priority is literal: the yearly cycle of services performed by the Son of Heaven must begin with an offering to Heaven at the suburban altar at the new year, in the first month, on the first *xin* day, a prescription that faithfully follows the *Gongyang Commentary*.[15] As chapter 67,

13. *CQFL* 68/68/16.
14. These chapters were explored by Gary Arbuckle in "The *jiao* 'Suburban' Sacrifice in the *Chunqiu fanlu*" (paper presented at the annual meeting of the Association for Asian Studies, New Orleans, April 13, 1991).
15. Duke Cheng 8.17.6: "The ninth month. *Xinchou*. We made use of the Suburban Sacrifice 九月辛丑用郊." In explicating these lines, the *Gongyang Commentary* explains: "The Suburban Sacrifice should be made use of in the first month on the first *xin* day." The *Gongyang Commentary* explicitly regards performing the Suburban Sacrifice in the ninth month as a violation of ritual norms.

"Sacrificial Rites of the Suburban Sacrifice" ("The Suburban Sacrifice" in Su Yu's reconstruction), puts it, "Thus every time [the Son of Heaven] arrives at the new year, he must first perform the Suburban Sacrifice to supplicate Heaven. Only then does he dare to sacrifice to Earth."[16]

The Suburban Sacrifice also must precede offerings to the ancestors:

> According to the standards of the *Spring and Autumn*, the king once a year presents sacrificial offerings to Heaven at the suburban altar and four times presents sacrificial offerings at the ancestral temple. The [sacrificial offerings] at the ancestral temple follow the changes in the four seasons; the [sacrificial offerings] at the suburban altar follow the beginning of the new year.... This is to say that one sacrifices to the most honored at the head of the year before all others and [that] each time there is a change in the year, the Suburban offering is presented first. This is the principle of giving priority to the honorable and the Way of revering Heaven.[17]

Finally, the Suburban Sacrifice must precede offerings to the mountains and rivers. This is clear, chapter 69, "The Suburban Sacrifice," argues, from the example of King Xuan of Zhou,[18] conventionally considered the voice in the following stanza from the ode "Yun Han" (The River of Clouds), who, guilty and fearful, laments that his ritual failures have prompted Heaven's disasters:

> Heaven sends down death and chaos;
> repeatedly there is famine and starvation.
> It is not that we have not sacrificed to the spirits;
> it is not that we begrudge the victims;
> We have used up the jade scepters and jade disks;
> how can none [of the spirits] hear us? . . .
> We have unceasingly offered the Yin and Zi sacrifices,
> [hastening between] suburban altar and ancestral temple. . . .[19]

The essay explains that although King Xuan believed that these calamities occurred because he had not properly communicated with Lord Millet or the Lord on High, in fact the king encountered disastrous natural anomalies because

16. In Su Yu's reconstruction, this material has moved from chapter 69 to chapter 67, "The Suburban Sacrifice," where we labeled it chapter 69.1. For the Chinese text, see *CQFL* 69/68/24–69/69/1.
17. *CQFL* 66/67/7–10.
18. King Xuan of Zhou 周宣王 (ca. 841–781 B.C.E.) was the eleventh sovereign of the Zhou dynasty.
19. *Odes* 258, verses 1 (in part) and 2 (in part).

he had failed to follow the proper sequence of sacrifice, having placed the lesser spirits before Heaven:

> Therefore whenever the *Spring and Autumn* raised criticisms concerning the Suburban Sacrifice, it never once held the virtue of the ruler to be insufficient to perform it. However, if sacrifices to the mountains and rivers were performed and the Suburban Sacrifice was not performed, [the *Spring and Autumn* considered this to] violate ritual norms, [the king] having lost the proper sequence of sacrifice. Therefore it necessarily criticized these instances. From this, we see that those who do not sacrifice to Heaven cannot sacrifice to the lesser spirits.[20]

Again at Duke Xi 5.31.3, the *Spring and Autumn* records that the Suburban Sacrifice was not performed but that the Triple Gazing Sacrifice—a sacrifice to Mount Tai, the Yellow River, and the Sea—was performed. The *Gongyang Commentary* maintains that this fact was recorded to criticize the ruler for performing a lesser sacrifice while suspending the Suburban Sacrifice. Reading the *Spring and Autumn* through the lens of the *Gongyang Commentary*, Dong Zhongshu argues once again that there is never a good excuse for performing lesser sacrifices such as the Triple Gazing rite while suspending the Suburban Sacrifice.

In the *Chunqiu fanlu*'s view, then, the yearly cycle of services performed by the Son of Heaven invariably had to begin with an offering to Heaven at the suburban altar at the new year, in the first month, on the first *xin* day. It then would be ritually correct to offer sacrifices to Earth, to the ancestors at the beginning of each season, and to major topographical features later in the year. The Suburban Sacrifice chapters are highly attentive to the need to harmonize the ruler's obligations to Heaven with those due his ancestors. Chapters 68 and 76 describe the four seasonal sacrifices offered to the ancestors and leave no doubt about their importance. But the text relies on the *Spring and Autumn* to justify the priority given to the Suburban Sacrifice over that of the ancestral sacrifices: the Son of Heaven is bound by filial piety to worship his Heavenly father before all other deities, including his deceased parents and more remote ancestors. This is true even when the ancestral sacrifices themselves must be suspended: "It is a righteous principle of the *Spring and Autumn* that when the state conducts the Grand Mourning [of a deceased parent], [the ruler] suspends sacrifices at the ancestral temple but does not suspend the Suburban Sacrifice,

20. *CQFL* 69/69/9–11.

for he does not dare, on account of the funeral of his father or mother, abandon a ritual meant to serve Heaven."[21]

Indeed, the emperor's obligation to offer sacrifices to Heaven comes before all his familial obligations. Not only must the emperor not suspend the Suburban Sacrifice during the mourning period for his deceased parents, but his filial obligations to provide sustenance and succor for his Heavenly father preempts his fatherly responsibilities to his metaphorical sons and grandsons: the common folk who populate his empire. Even at the risk of the people's starving, sacrificial food must be offered on the suburban altar. Moreover, these chapters also argue that the Suburban Sacrifice should be performed in accordance with the Way, which is to say, flawlessly. Even though the ruler could expect to avoid disasters should he err in performing services to the lesser gods, in the case of Heaven the disasters visited on the ruler would correspond to the degree to which he transgressed the ritual norms. All the many examples of ritual violations explicated in the *Gongyang Commentary* reinforce the point that service to Heaven must come before that to the lesser divinities and must be properly performed lest disasters ensue. Chapter 70.4 gives examples of the sorts of injury to, or the unsuitability of, sacrificial animals that can vitiate the power of the sacrifice. For example, the chosen bull might suffer an injury to its mouth or (in a bizarre contingency) have its horns gnawed by ground squirrels. The failure to take precautions, or an outright abandonment of the sacrifice in the face of adverse circumstances, would, the text claims, inevitably lead to disaster.

In Dong Zhongshu's understanding of the *Spring and Autumn*, the Suburban Sacrifice was the prerogative—and the duty—of the Son of Heaven alone. He admits only one modification of that stance. In chapter 71, "An Official Response Regarding the Suburban Sacrifice," Dong defends as legitimate the performance of the Suburban Sacrifice by the Duke of Zhou in his capacity as regent for King Cheng. The Duke of Zhou's virtuous service earned him the authority to perform a rite normally reserved for the Son of Heaven alone, during the period when the king was too young to carry out the sacrifice by himself. But because of the unusual circumstances, the young king and the duke made sure that the duke's performance of the sacrifice was ritually distinguished (by altering the color of the bull employed as a sacrificial victim) from the rite as it normally would be performed by the Son of Heaven. Building on that precedent, subsequent dukes of Lu also

21. *CQFL* 67/67/14–15. In the phrase *tiandi* 天地, we treat *di* 地 as excrescent, following Su Yu (*CQFLYZ* 404), who notes that the *Taipingyulan* 527 citation of this passage does not contain the graph for "Earth."

arrogated to themselves the right to offer the Suburban Sacrifice. Their rationale for doing so is explained in *Liji* 22, "Ji tong" (A Summation of the Sacrificial Rites):

> Anciently, Dan, the Duke of Zhou, meritoriously exerted himself for the sake of the world. After the Duke of Zhou passed away, kings Cheng and Kang, bearing in mind how he meritoriously exerted himself, desired to honor [his home state of] Lu. Consequently they granted to its lords the right of offering the most important sacrifices. . . . The descendants of the Duke of Zhou have continued them, and down to the present day they have not been abandoned, thereby manifesting the virtue of the Duke of Zhou and the importance of his state.[22]

In the Suburban Sacrifice chapters of the *Chunqiu fanlu*, however, Dong upholds the orthodox position of the *Gongyang Commentary*, maintaining that the Suburban Sacrifice was uniquely the prerogative and the responsibility of the Son of Heaven.[23] In taking this position, Dong continues to build his case that Han practice with respect to the Suburban Sacrifice and other imperial sacrifices should reflect the practices of the early Zhou era.

Why do these chapters argue so forcefully for the importance of the Suburban Sacrifice and the need to give it ritual priority over all of the Son of Heaven's other sacrificial obligations, even those to his own ancestors? Why, when, and for whom were these chapters written?

Issues of Dating and Attribution

As Sarah A. Queen's *From Chronicle to Canon* points out, the circumstances under which different chapters and sections of the *Chunqiu fanlu* were

22. *Liji*, "Ji tong" (A Summary of the Sacrificial Rites); Legge, *Li Chi*, 2:253–54.

23. Sarah A. Queen, "The Rhetoric of Dong Zhongshu's Imperial Communications," in *Facing the Monarch: Modes of Advice in the Early Chinese Court*, ed. Garret P. S. Olberding, Harvard East Asian Monographs (Cambridge, Mass.: Harvard University Press, 2013), 166–202. The *Gongyang Commentary* at Duke Xi 5.31.3 states unambiguously:

> The Lu performance of the Suburban Sacrifice violated ritual norms. Why did the Lu performance of the Suburban Sacrifice violate ritual norms? The Son of Heaven sacrifices to Heaven; the regional lords sacrifice to [the God of] the Soil. The Son of Heaven presides over matters in all directions as far as the eye can see, there is no place where he does not penetrate. In the case of the regional lords, the mountains and rivers that do not lie within their territorial allotment do not receive [their] sacrifice.

Thus while Dong Zhongshu accepted the performance of the Suburban Sacrifice by the Duke of Zhou *in his capacity as regent for King Cheng*, he did not accept that the performance of that sacrifice then descended by hereditary right to the subsequent dukes of Lu.

composed and the audiences for which they were composed were not necessarily the same. Of those portions of the text reliably attributable to Dong Zhongshu, some are perhaps best understood as meant to teach students; others appear to derive from various court debates and official communications; and still others seem to offer advice to the emperor and address his concerns. Many parts of the text appear to be the work of others, including chapters that may have been written by Dong's students or other followers. What circumstances, then, may have prompted the Suburban Sacrifice chapters to be written? Fortunately, internal and external evidence enable us to affirm the attribution of these chapters to Dong Zhongshu and date them to the reign of Emperor Wu. We begin with chapter 71 because it contains the strongest and most unambiguous evidence for confirming authorship and dating. As the title and the content of the chapter suggest, it is an official response (*dui* 對) to Emperor Wu. The opening lines identify the author of the document as Chamberlain for Law Enforcement Zhang Tang. He formally reports to the emperor the content of an interview around 123 B.C.E.[24] with Dong Zhongshu, now living at home in retirement. Dong answers Emperor Wu's questions through that emissary, who reports his answers using the conventions of imperial exchange.[25]

Ban Gu's "Biography of Dong Zhongshu" provides the background to this document. The biography notes that after a brief tenure as administrator to King Yu of Jiaoxi (Liu Duan, an elder brother of Emperor Wu), whose conduct Dong found reprehensible,[26] Dong retired to his home in fear for his life. Ban Gu notes that even in retirement, Dong stayed in contact with the imperial court: "When Zhongshu was retired, if the central court held an important deliberation, [the emperor would] send emissaries, including even the Chamberlain for Law Enforcement Zhang Tang himself, to travel to his home and question him. His responses all possessed clear standards."[27] As it happened, the

24. Zhang Tang was active in this post from 126 to 121 B.C.E., but Dong Zhongshu did not retire before 123 B.C.E. So the document must date no earlier than 123 B.C.E. and no later than 121 B.C.E. See Queen, *From Chronicle to Canon*, 31–36.

25. For example, in the opening line, Zhang Tang employs the phrase "risking death for daring to report [to your Majesty]." As Enno Giele noted, the phrase "risking death" was actually an abbreviation of "risk committing a crime that merits capital punishment, a Qin convention employed by officials when submitting letters to the throne that continued in use under the Han" (*Imperial Decision-Making and Communication in Early China: A Study of Cai Yong's "Duduan"* [Wiesbaden: Harrassowitz, 2006], 92). See also Queen, "Rhetoric of Dong Zhongshu's Imperial Communications."

26. *SJ* 59/2097; Burton Watson, trans., *Records of the Grand Historian of China*, vol. 1, *Early Years of the Han Dynasty, 209 to 141 B.C.* (New York: Columbia University Press, 1971), 393; Ban Gu's much abbreviated criticisms of Liu Duan at *HS* 56/2525.

27. *SJ* 59/2097; Watson, *Records of the Grand Historian of China*, 1:393; Ban Gu's much abbreviated criticisms of Liu Duan at *HS* 56/2525.

year 123 B.C.E., when Zhang Tang interviewed Dong Zhongshu, was a momentous one for the Suburban Sacrifice. Emperor Wu resumed performing this rite after a hiatus of more than a decade. As the emperor made plans to resume the Suburban Sacrifice, it would have made sense to seek Dong's advice on the many rites he knew intimately and had written about extensively.

Commensurate with his other writings on the Suburban Sacrifice, in Zhang Tang's report Dong emphasized the Suburban Sacrifice to Heaven as the emperor's most important rite of veneration. Although performed only a few times by the Han emperors who preceded Emperor Wu, and only intermittently by Emperor Wu himself, the Suburban Sacrifice had been established as reserved for the emperor alone. That this came to be very likely involved debate and a certain jostling for power. In the early decades of the Han period, much of the empire was divided into semiautonomous kingdoms ruled by imperial kinsmen of the Liu clan (such as King Yu of Jiaoxi, whom Dong Zhongshu served for a short time as administrator), who could easily have claimed that they had the right to perform the Suburban Sacrifice on their own behalf, by analogy to the performance of that sacrifice by the dukes of Lu. The relationship between the imperial throne and the regional kings was one of the most important, and most difficult, political problems of the early Han period. Dong's position thus aligned him firmly with the imperial centralists and in opposition to the neofeudal claims of the regional kings.[28]

Accordingly, we can be quite confident that the official exchange preserved in chapter 71 dates from the end of Dong's career around 123 B.C.E. The other essays on the Suburban Sacrifice most likely were written earlier, during the years when Emperor Wu had suspended his performance of the Suburban Sacrifice. The content of the chapters suggest this, for they are marked by one overriding theme: the desire to reform the views of an emperor who not only was failing to attend properly to this sacrifice but also was distracted by many lesser gods of the pantheon. The content of these chapters suggests that the crucially important (to Dong) Suburban Sacrifice should have been regularly performed by the emperor. It also implies that in contemporary practice, it followed no set ritual schedule and that the justifications for and the details of the sacrifice were the subject of much debate. Clearly, Dong was just one of many would-be religious advisers to the emperor and was struggling to make his voice heard in the

28. For a brief account of this political struggle, see John S. Major, Sarah A. Queen, Andrew Seth Meyer, and Harold D. Roth, trans. and eds., *The "Huainanzi": A Guide to the Theory and Practice of Government in Early Han China* (New York: Columbia University Press, 2010), 2–6.

cacophony. Such circumstances appear to color the arguments set forth in these chapters in several ways.

Why else, for example, would the author of chapter 65 ask bluntly: "What, then, of those who abandon the rite of the Suburban Sacrifice?" And why else would he answer:

> The rite of the Suburban Sacrifice was what the sages most deeply valued.[29] If you abandon what the sages deeply valued, the causes of good and bad fortune, and of benefit and harm, will remain shrouded in darkness, so that you are unable to perceive them when in its midst. Even though you have already suffered extreme harm from them, how will you understand them?

As we have seen, the author argues forcefully that the ancients did not dare suspend the Suburban Sacrifice, even in times of mourning, a sign of how deeply the ancients feared and revered Heaven. How, then, would the ruler dare abandon the Suburban Sacrifice, "[the rite that] the sages most deeply valued"? Dong does not accept the legitimacy of circumstantial excuses for suspending the sacrifice. He notes that some contemporaries have argued that "'when the myriad commoners are so impoverished, suffering from starvation and cold, how can it suffice to perform the Suburban Sacrifice?'" Dong's response is emphatic: "How mistaken are such claims!" Regardless of external circumstances, the ruler should no more abandon the Suburban Sacrifice to Heaven than a filial son should neglect to feed his parents. In the event that the ruler should claim—or did claim—that he could not perform the Suburban Sacrifice because he was morally unworthy, in chapter 69.2, King Xuan of Zhou's response to a drought that ruined the harvest is used to demonstrate that for the *Spring and Autumn*, the issue is never whether the virtue of the ruler is sufficient to sacrifice but whether the ruler is willing to place Heaven before all other spirits. In fact, nearly every one of the Suburban Sacrifice chapters addresses this potential violation of ritual norms, arguing that the Suburban Sacrifice to Heaven must come before those to the lesser gods.

Citing the practices of the sage kings of antiquity, chapter 67.2 (now part of chapter 65, in Su Yu's reconstruction) maintains that none among the kings of the former ages failed to perform the Suburban Sacrifice and attach great importance to it. The Qin alone neglected and abandoned it. The Zhou dynasty stood

29. Following Su Yu and Lau, who supply *sheng* 聖 before *ren* 人 (Lai, *CQFLJZJY* 66, note 8).

at one end of the spectrum, embodying the ideal of the Suburban Sacrifice in all its perfection, while the Qin stood at the other end, failing to offer the sacrifice at all. With this example, the author argues that although the emperor may offer sacrifice to all the spirits of the realm, if he fails to serve Heaven, service to these lesser spirits will not make his realm prosperous.

The tone of these chapters strongly suggests that they were written when the Suburban Sacrifice had been neglected by the Han emperors for some time and when Emperor Wu showed no inclination to reinstitute the rite on a regular basis. Perhaps some scholars and officials at court argued that there was simply too much poverty among the common folk to support such an expensive ritual. Possibly Emperor Wu himself contended that his reputation as a virtuous sovereign had not yet been confirmed by Heaven. Whatever the case, Dong Zhongshu is quite insistent here about the need to offer the Suburban Sacrifice to Heaven to lead off the annual cycle of sacrifices. What could this be a response to, other than an emperor who was sacrificing to many other spirits and who had abandoned the Suburban Sacrifice? As it happens, Emperor Wu appears to have done just that.

Imperial Cults and the Suburban Sacrifice in the Western Han

The history of imperially sponsored religion in the Western Han period is confused and somewhat chaotic.[30] Under Emperor Wu especially, but under other emperors as well, worship of various deities was instituted, continued, neglected, or abolished, apparently depending on the whims and attention spans of the emperors themselves and on which advisers were in favor at the time. The Suburban Sacrifice was performed on a number of occasions, but with no uniformity; indeed, every aspect of the sacrifice was in dispute. Contested issues included in what month of the year the sacrifice should be performed, how frequently it should be performed, who should perform it (the emperor personally or ritual

30. Sources for the events and issues discussed in this subsection are *SJ* 28, "Treatise on the Feng and Shan Sacrifices"; *HS* 25/5, "The Suburban Sacrifice," which is heavily based on the *Shiji*; and the *Han shu* annals of the various Western Han emperors. Relevant studies include Michael Puett, *To Become a God: Cosmology, Sacrifice, and Self-Divinization in Early China* (Cambridge, Mass.: Harvard University Press, 2002), 287–315; and Michael Loewe, "K'uang Heng and the Reform of Religious Practices—31 BC," in *Crisis and Conflict in Han China, 104 BC to AD 9* (London: Allen & Unwin, 1974), 154–92.

stewards acting on his behalf), where the sacrifice should be performed, which deity or deities should receive the offerings, what sacrificial victim should be offered, what ritual or liturgical procedures should be followed, and how the sacrifice should be understood in relation to services for the emperor's deceased parents and more remote ancestors, as well as for other spirits. Dong Zhongshu was apparently only one of many advisers offering opinions about these matters, and his voice—as usual in the context of Emperor Wu's court—was by no means the decisive one.

In the "Treatise on the Feng and Shan Sacrifices" (*Shiji* 28), Sima Qian quotes the *Zhouli* as saying that the purpose of the Suburban Sacrifice was to welcome the lengthening of the days: "At the winter solstice a sacrifice shall be made to Heaven in the southern suburbs in order to greet the arrival of lengthening days. At the summer solstice a sacrifice shall be made to the Earth God. At both ceremonies music and dances shall be performed. Thus one may pay respect to the spirits."[31] This accords with the view expressed in the *Liji*: "At the [Great] Border [i.e., Suburban] Sacrifice, [the Son of Heaven] welcomed the arrival of the longest day."[32] Sima Qian also states that during the Qin dynasty, "the Suburban Sacrifice was performed once every three years. Since the Qin dynasty had designated the tenth month as the beginning of its [civil] year, it was always in the tenth month that the emperor fasted and journeyed to the suburbs to visit the deity."[33]

The founding Han emperor, Gaozu, continued Qin ritual practices with little change. There is no record of his having performed the Suburban Sacrifice or of his having caused it to be performed, but he did institute worship of the Five Thearchs, considered as personifications of the five directions. Emperor Wen performed what was explicitly called the Suburban Sacrifice in the suburb of Yong in 165 B.C.E. and again at a new shrine at Weiyang in 164 B.C.E. After discussion with his ritual specialists, he performed the rite in the fourth month of each of those two years; the object of worship was the Five Thearchs.

Of Emperor Jing it is said that "during the sixteen years of his reign the officials in charge of sacrifices continued to perform their various duties at the appropriate seasons but no new forms of worship were introduced."[34] He carried out the Suburban Sacrifice at Yong in 144 B.C.E., again directed at the Five Thearchs.

31. Burton Watson, trans., *Records of the Grand Historian of China*, vol. 2, *The Age of Emperor Wu, 140 to Circa 100 B.C.* (New York: Columbia University Press, 1971), 6.
32. *Liji*, "Jiaote sheng" (The Single Victim at the Suburban Sacrifice) 9.2.2; Legge, *Li Chi*, 1:427.
33. Watson, *Records of the Grand Historian of China*, 2:18.
34. Watson, *Records of the Grand Historian of China*, 2:24.

Emperor Wu is first recorded as having performed the Suburban Sacrifice in 134 B.C.E. The *Shiji* states that in that year, the emperor "journeyed to Yong for the first time to perform the Suburban Sacrifice at the Five Altars." It also claims that "from that time on he invariably performed the Suburban Sacrifice once every three years."[35] The reference to the Five Altars indicates that the sacrifices were again devoted to the Five Thearchs. The statement that the emperor then performed the Suburban Sacrifice every three years is not, however, confirmed by what follows in either the *Shiji* or the *Han shu*. The "Basic Annals of Emperor Wu" notes that Emperor Wu performed the Suburban Sacrifice in 123 B.C.E. Thereafter, he is recorded as having performed the sacrifice six additional times: in 122, 114, 113, 110, 108, and 92 B.C.E.[36]

The history of Emperor Wu's religious practices during the decade-long hiatus between the first recorded performance of the Suburban Sacrifice in 134 B.C.E. and the second in 123 B.C.E., as described in the "Treatise on the Feng and Shan Sacrifices," is essentially an account of the emperor's coming under the influence of a motley succession of men who persuaded him to worship various gods that they proposed in turn. This began with a man named Li Shaojun, who persuaded Emperor Wu to worship the god of the hearth while following Li's theories on how to achieve immortality through a dietary regimen. When Li Shaojun died, the emperor almost immediately fell under the influence of a magician named Miu Ji, who persuaded the emperor to institute sacrifices to the star divinity Great Unity (Tai yi), maintaining that this deity was "the most honored of all the spirits of Heaven." He described the Five Thearchs, formerly the objects of the Suburban Sacrifice, as Grand Unity's "helpers." Emperor Wu carried out the recommendation and ordered the master of invocations to establish a place of worship southeast of Chang'an. The emperor performed the rites to Tai yi there in 113 B.C.E. The rituals included sacrifices to the sun and the moon, and the worship of Tai yi continued sporadically during the reigns of Emperor Wu and several of his successors. Emperor Wu inaugurated a variety of other imperially sponsored altars and cults, depending on which self-styled ritual authority currently had the emperor's ear. A notable example was the establishment in 114 B.C.E. of an altar to the Earth Queen (Hou tu) at Fenyin, Hedong Commandery, at the direct command of the emperor (and presumably at the suggestion of one of his *fangshi* advisers). Emperor Wu apparently took

35. Watson, *Records of the Grand Historian of China*, 2:24; note that the date given there is incorrect.
36. *HS* 6/162, 6/174, 6/175, 6/183, 6/185, 6/193, 6/195; Homer H. Dubs, trans., *The History of the Former Han Dynasty* (Baltimore: Waverly Press, 1941), 2:57, 60, 74, 76, 89, 93, 113.

this cult seriously, as he performed rites to the Earth Queen again in 107, 105, 104, 103, and 100 B.C.E.[37] (His successors Emperors Xuan and Yuan revived the cult, worshipping at the altar of the Earth Queen in 61, 55, 41, 39, and 37 B.C.E.)

The performance of the Suburban Sacrifice by Emperor Wu in 123 B.C.E. took place late in the year, during the tenth month, and was devoted to the Five Thearchs. Some ambiguity surrounds the performance of the ritual in the following year (again in the tenth month). The *Shiji* describes it as having been devoted to the High Thearch, a divinity that could be equated to Heaven, and remarks specifically that the rite was paired with another sacrifice devoted to Earth. The *Han shu* records, however, that the object of worship was once again the Five Thearchs.[38] The Suburban Sacrifices of 114, 113, 110, 108, and 92 B.C.E. all were late-year rituals devoted to the Five Thearchs. The only variants reported in the sources suggest that the sacrifice of 113 B.C.E. was paired or coordinated with (or possibly replaced by) a rite devoted to Grand Unity, held in 110 B.C.E. Emperor Wu also journeyed to Mount Tai to celebrate the Feng and Shan Sacrifices, rites explicitly devoted to Heaven and designed to affirm that the reigning dynasty was securely in possession of the Mandate of Heaven.

In all of this there is no attention to Dong Zhongshu's position: that the Suburban Sacrifice should be the first imperial sacrifice of the civil calendar year, that it should be devoted to the worship of Heaven, and that it should take precedence over all other imperial sacrificial rites. It appears that the position so forcefully argued in the Suburban Sacrifice chapters of the *Chunqiu fanlu* found no favor with the emperor himself.

After the Suburban Sacrifice of 92 B.C.E., near the end of Emperor Wu's long reign, the Suburban Sacrifice was neglected for many years. There was a long hiatus through the reign of Emperor Zhao and into that of Emperor Xuan. The latter finally resumed the rite in 56 B.C.E. as a first-month ritual (as Dong Zhongshu had recommended all along): "In the second year, in the spring, the first month, [the Emperor] traveled and favored Yong [with a visit where he] sacrificed at the altars to the Five [Thearchs]." Emperor Yuan performed the sacrifice in 46 B.C.E., again in the first month, but no longer at Yong (where the Suburban Altar had been since Emperor Wu's time), and devoted to Grand Unity rather than to the Five Thearchs: "In the fourth year, in the spring, the first month, [the Emperor] traveled and favored Ganquan [with a visit, where he

37. For the various cults instituted by Emperor Wu mentioned in this paragraph, see Watson, *Records of the Grand Historian of China*, 2:25–27.

38. Watson, *Records of the Grand Historian of China*, 2:30; Dubs, *History of the Former Han Dynasty*, 2:60.

performed] the Suburban Sacrifice at the altar of Grand Unity." Six years later, in 40 B.C.E., Emperor Yuan again performed the sacrifice, this time in the third month of the year, back at Yong, and once again devoted to the Five Thearchs. He repeated the performance two years later: "In the [reign-period] *jianzhao* (Establishing Brightness, 38–33 B.C.E.), the first year, in the spring, the third month, [the Emperor] favored Yong [with a visit, where he sacrificed] at the altars to the Five [Thearchs]."[39]

Generally, during the first century and a half of the Western Han, the Suburban Sacrifice seems consistently to have been worship of the Five Thearchs, usually performed at the Suburban Altar at Yong, but with some disagreement over the appropriate season. Although Dong Zhongshu's arguments for a Heaven-centered sacrificial system fell on deaf ears during the reign of Emperor Wu, it appears that ultimately they may have been influential in the later debates over religious reform under Emperors Cheng, Ai, and, finally, Ping. In 31 B.C.E., the imperial counselors Kuang Heng and Zheng Tan presented to Emperor Cheng a severe critique of Emperor Wu's religious innovations. They apparently were persuasive, for in that year Emperor Cheng instituted a Suburban Sacrifice to Heaven at an altar south of Chang'an. He went on to abolish a number of sacrifices initiated by Emperor Wu. Subsequently, however, the famous official Liu Xiang argued, in opposition to Kuang Heng and Zheng Tan, that the emperor should restore the sacrificial system established under Emperor Wu. The emperor then reversed course and followed Liu Xiang's advice. Dissension, confusion, and further changes in direction continued through the reign of Emperor Ai. At last, however, Emperor Ping, in response to Wang Mang's memorials, decisively implemented the reforms suggested by Kuang Heng in 31 B.C.E., and chief among those reforms was the establishment of sacrifices to Heaven and to Earth.[40] Change and counterchange followed until the reign of Wang Mang, when finally it was "firmly determined that worship should be addressed to Heaven, and that the services should take place at sites near the capital. From then (5 C.E.) until the end of the imperial period, Chinese emperors have worshiped Heaven as their first duty."[41] It took a century or so, but Dong Zhongshu's position on these matters was finally, at least to some extent, vindicated.

---

39. Dubs, *History of the Former Han Dynasty*, 2:248, 313, 324, 329.
40. For all these events, see Loewe, "K'uang Heng and the Reform of Religious Practices—31 BC."
41. Michael Loewe, "The Religious and Intellectual Background," in *The Ch'in and Han Empires, 221 B.C.–A.D. 220*, ed. Denis Twitchett and Michael Loewe, vol. 1 of *The Cambridge History of China* (Cambridge: Cambridge University Press, 1986), 664.

Book 14, Part 4

CHAPTER 65

Sayings Pertaining to the Suburban Sacrifice

Section 65.1

Sayings of the common people:

Vinegar dissipates smoke,
and owl feathers dispel dust blindness.
A lodestone attracts iron,
and a concave metal [mirror] attracts fire.[1]
When silkworms secrete fragmented silk in the side room,
the [*shang*] string snaps in the center hall.[2]
When grains mature in the fields,
millet grows scarce in the granaries.
When weeds spring up in Yan,
oranges die in Jing.

Chapter 65, "Sayings Pertaining to the Suburban Sacrifice" 郊語, is the first of several chapters devoted to the Suburban Sacrifice. Others include chapter 66, "The Principles of the Suburban Sacrifice" 郊義; chapter 67, "Sacrificial Rites of the Suburban Sacrifice" 郊祭; chapter 69, "The Suburban Sacrifice" 郊祀; and chapter 71, "An Official Response Regarding Matters of the Suburban Sacrifice." There is much debate among the commentators regarding the original form of these essays. Some have argued that these five chapters were originally a single essay. Furthermore, these chapters are rather difficult to follow owing to omissions, interpolations, and disordering of the original text. But the current arrangement also is highly contested.

1. A similar saying is found in *Huainanzi* 3.2. See John S. Major, Sarah A. Queen, Andrew Seth Meyer, and Harold D. Roth, trans. and eds., *The "Huainanzi": A Guide to the Theory and Practice of Government in Early Han China* (New York: Columbia University Press, 2010), 116.
2. Following Lau's emendation, based on the similar statements in *Huainanzi* 3.2 and 6.2. See D. C. Lau, ed., *Huainanzi zhuzi suoyin* (*A Concordance to the "Huainanzi"*), Chinese University of Hong Kong, Institute of Chinese Studies Ancient Chinese Text Concordance Series (Hong Kong: Commercial Press, 1992), 3/19/11, 6/50/14–15; and Major et al., *Huainanzi*, 116, 216.

These ten things all are uncanny and can be marveled at. They are not something people understand. Since they are not something people understand, they are taken as given once they appear. Some are auspicious and some [are] inauspicious; some indicate bad fortune and some indicate good fortune. [Nonetheless,] there is nothing uncanny about the causes of benefit and harm. How is it that people do not understand them in this way? Such things are truly awesome.

Confucius said: "A noble man is awestruck by three things:

He is awestruck by the Mandate of Heaven;
he is awestruck by the Great Man;
and he is awestruck by the words of the sages."[3]

Even though these things do not harm the people, someone like Confucius was awestruck by them! From this example it is evident that

Heaven cannot but be fearfully revered,
just as the ruler above cannot but be respectfully served.
If you do not respectfully serve the ruler,
the ruler's misfortunes will rise and be utterly evident;
If you do not fearfully revere Heaven,
Heaven's calamities will rise and be utterly baffling.

Baffling means that one cannot perceive their causes, as if they were spontaneous. Thus it is said: "Grave and severe as Heaven['s calamities]."[4] This means that one cannot necessarily verify them:

They are silent and soundless;
they are hidden and formless.

Looking at things from this perspective, the difference between Heaven's calamities and the ruler's punishments is that one is abstruse while the other is obvious. Nonetheless, in arriving and affecting the people, they probably do not differ.[5] [Thus] Confucius [treated them] as identical and said that both are awesome.

The heart of the spirit illumination of Heaven and Earth
and the reality of successes and failures of human endeavors

certainly are things that no [ordinary] person can perceive. Only the sage can perceive them. The sage can see what others cannot see. Thus the words of the sage are awesome as well.

3. *Analects* 16.8. The same lines are quoted in chapter 70.4.

4. This appears to be a quotation from some now unidentifiable source, as it does not appear in the received canon.

5. Treating *bu* 不 before *ran* 然 as excrescent, following Lai, *CQFLJZJY* 367, note 25.

What, then, of those who abandon the rite of the Suburban Sacrifice? The rite of the Suburban Sacrifice was what the sages most deeply valued.[6] If you abandon what the sages deeply valued, the causes of good and bad fortune, and of benefit and harm, will remain shrouded in darkness, so that you are unable to perceive them when in its midst. Even though you have already suffered extreme harm from them, how will you understand them? Thus it is said: When questioning the sage, ask what he does, but do not ask why he does what he does. If you ask him why he does what he does, you will never understand it, so it is better not to ask at all. [But]

> if you ask him what he does and you do it,
> and if you ask him what he does not do and you refuse to do it,

this amounts to being substantially at one with the sage. What could be wrong with that?

An *Ode* says:

> "Do not err, do not forget.
> Follow the ancient statutes."[7]

"The ancient statutes" are the ancient writings of the former sages. "To follow" means that in each case they are followed[8] and obeyed. This means that with regard to the ancient writings of the former sages, even if you are unable to investigate them deeply or know them minutely, you still have not lost sight of their good and glorious achievements. The Suburban [Sacrifice] exemplifying the righteous principle of serving Heaven [is what] the sages spoke about [again and again].[9] [65/66/16–65/67/1]

Section 67.2

Therefore, the sage-kings of antiquity[10] considered [the Suburban Sacrifice] the most important [topic in the received] writings. None among the kings of the former ages failed to follow [this practice of] attaching importance to it. With the most refined millet, they made their offerings to serve Heaven

6. Following *CQFL* 66, note 8, citing Su Yu in supplying *sheng* 聖 before *ren* 人.
7. *Odes* 249, verse 2.
8. Emending *xiu* 修 to *xun* 恂, following Su Yu (Lai, *CQFLJZJY* 367, note 37) and supported by Lai Yanyuan.
9. In the Lau edition, chapter 65 ends here. We follow Su Yu, who, in turn, follows Qian Tang and Lu Wenchao, in moving chapter 67.2 and 67.3 (*CQFL* 67/67/20–67/68/7, beginning with 故古之聖王, 文章之最重者也 and ending with 疾于法令) to the end of chapter 65 (Su Yu, *CQFLYZ* 397–401).
10. Su Yu treats the five characters *gu gu zhe sheng wang* 故古之聖王 as excrescent (Lai, *CQFLJZJY* 369, note 40).

above. Coming to the time of the Qin, the Qin alone neglected and abandoned it. How could they fail to follow the ancient statutes that were of such great significance!

Heaven is the great lord of the spirits. [Thus] if service to Heaven is not provided, then even if [you sacrifice to] the numerous [lesser] spirits, it will be of no benefit to you. Why do I say that this is so? Those who did not sacrifice to the spirit of Heaven but sacrificed to the spirit of the land were criticized in the *Spring and Autumn*.[11] Confucius said: "If you commit a crime against Heaven, you will have no one to whom you can pray."[12] This was his standard. Thus we have not seen the state of Qin attract Heaven's blessings as the state of Zhou did. An *Ode* says:

> "This King Wen, watchful and reverent,
> brightly served the High God
> and so secured many blessings."[13]

"Many blessings" does not refer to his person but to his meritorious service [to Heaven]. It refers to what Heaven blesses. A tradition states: "Among the sons of the Zhou state, there were many worthies. They flourished all the way down to the time of Pin, who conceived four sons. These four in turn produced eight sons. They all were noble men, brave and eminent."[14] This was how Heaven brought prosperity to the state of Zhou. This was not something the state of Zhou could accomplish on its own. Now Qin, like Zhou, also attained the [rank of] Son of Heaven, and yet the way in which Qin served Heaven differed from [that of] Zhou. Zhou considered the Suburban Sacrifice to come before [the services to] all the other spirits. When they first entered the new year, they performed the sacrifice on the first *xin* day of the first month. They first made offerings to Heaven, and only after this was done did they dare sacrifice to Earth. This is the principle of placing the honorable first. Performing the Suburban Sacrifice annually before all other [sacrificial services] is a far cry from not performing it at all in the course of a year.

With regard to the blessings of the world, it is not as if there were anything [about them] that one might consider uncanny. Rather, during this

11. Following Lu Wenchao and Yu Yue, we believe that this sentence is incomplete. Following Yu Yue, we emended it to read: 不祭天神而祭地神者,春秋譏之. This makes sense, as the *Chunqiu* notes several occasions in which the various dukes of Lu do not perform the Suburban Sacrifice but do perform the Three Vistas sacrifice to the spirits of the land, such as Mount Tai (Duke Xi 5.31.3–4; Duke Xuan 7.3.1–7.3.3; Duke Cheng 8.10.2; Su Yu, *CQFLYZ* 398).
12. *Analects* 3.13.
13. *Odes* 236, verse 3.
14. This quotation is from an unknown source; it does not appear in the received canon.

long period when [the Suburban Sacrifice] was not observed, it is not that it was completely obvious that it ought to have been observed and was not, but that the officials in charge of ritual affairs were in doubt about the matter and none of them were able to make it clear that [the sacrifice] ought to have been observed. As for whether or not it should have been carried out, they could have turned inward to look into their hearts to make a decision. Yao said to Shun, "The succession ordained by Heaven has fallen on your person." This means that if you look into your own person, you will know Heaven. Now among those who have sons, who does not desire that their sons practice the [appropriate] rites? The sage rectifies names. Names do not arise from nowhere. Those who become the Son of Heaven are Heaven's sons and must rely on their person to investigate Heaven. How could Heaven alone not want his sons to carry out the rites proper to a son? Now, if you are the Son of Heaven and you do not sacrifice to Heaven, why should Heaven have to approve of that? [67/67/20–67/68/4]

Section 67.3[15]

I have heard it said that when the world has achieved harmony and tranquillity, then disasters and calamities will no longer arise. At present, disasters and calamities arise to indicate that the world has not yet achieved harmony and tranquillity. The reason that harmony and tranquillity have not yet been achieved is that the Son of Heaven's education and transformation [of the people] have not been carried out. An *Ode* says:

"To [one who] displays upright and virtuous conduct,
all in the Four Quarters render obedient homage."[16]

Jue [覺] means "to display." The king is one who displays his virtuous conduct to the world. Then no one in the Four Quarters will fail to respond [like an] echo to his transforming influence. This is superior to all else. Thus it is said,

"It is more pleasing than favors and rewards,
more awe inspiring than punishments and penalties,
and swifter than laws and commands." [67/68/4–7]

15. Su Yu places this passage from chapter 67 here at the end of chapter 65, but it clearly does not belong with the text that precedes it. It seems to be a stray fragment of text, which in style and content most closely resembles Dong Zhongshu's memorial to Emperor Wu.

16. *Odes* 256, verse 2.

Book 15, Part 1

CHAPTER 66

The Principles of the Suburban Sacrifice

Section 66.1

The principles of the Suburban [Sacrifice]: According to the standards of the *Spring and Autumn*, the king

> once a year presents sacrificial offerings to Heaven at the suburban altar
> and four times presents sacrificial offerings at the ancestral temple.
> The [sacrificial offerings] at the ancestral temple follow the changes in the four seasons;
> the [sacrificial offerings] at the suburban altar follow the beginning of the new year.

The sage had reasons for initiating such practices. In making sacrifices, you cannot fail to be bound by familial obligations.

Heaven is the lord of the numerous spirits and is what the king reveres above all other spirits. Because the ruler is most reverent toward Heaven, when there is a change in the year he initiates the Suburban Sacrifice. The Suburban offering must be presented in the first month on the first *xin* day.[1] This is to say that one sacrifices to the most honored at the head of the year before all others and [that] each time there is a change in the year, the Suburban offering is presented first. This is

> the principle of giving priority to the honorable
> and the Way of revering Heaven. [66/67/7–10]

---

1. For a description of the sacrifice, see *Liji*, "Jiaote sheng," part 2, para. 1–4; James Legge, trans., *Li Chi: Book of Rites*, ed. Ch'u Chai and Winberg Chai (New Hyde Park, N.Y.: University Books, 1967), 1:426–29.

Book 15, Part 2

CHAPTER 67

Sacrificial Rites of the Suburban Sacrifice

Section 67.1

It is a righteous principle of the *Spring and Autumn* that when the state conducts the Grand Mourning [of a deceased parent], [the ruler] suspends sacrifices at the ancestral temple but does not suspend the Suburban Sacrifice, for he does not dare, on account of the funeral of his father or mother, abandon a ritual meant to serve Heaven.[1] Mourning a father or mother is utterly sorrowful and painful. If the ruler dare not abandon the Suburban Sacrifice, who else would have sufficient cause to abandon it? Thus, with regard to the rites, there is also the saying: "In times of mourning, do not sacrifice; only in the sacrifice to Heaven is one able to violate this [general principle] of mourning and observe this service."

The ancients feared and revered Heaven and therefore deeply emphasized the Suburban Sacrifice to Heaven. At present, however, numerous officials and learned scholars do not look deeply into this sacrifice. They say: "When the myriad commoners are so impoverished, suffering from starvation and cold, how can it suffice to perform the Suburban Sacrifice?" How mistaken are such claims!

The Son of Heaven, serves Heaven as his father and mother;
[he] tends to the myriad commoners as his sons and grandsons.

1. Treating *di* 地 (Earth) as excrescent, following Su Yu (*CQFLYZ* 404), who notes that the *Taiping yulan* 527 recension of this passage does not contain the word for Earth.

[To claim that when] the people have not yet eaten their full, it is useless to sacrifice to Heaven is like [claiming that when] sons and grandsons have not yet secured their own food, it is useless to feed their fathers and mothers. There are no claims more pernicious than this. They depart very far from [the standards of] propriety. If we place the honorable first and the base last, who is more honorable than the Son of Heaven? The Son of Heaven is designated as "Heaven's son." How can one who receives the designation of "Son of Heaven" fail to perform the rites appropriate to the Son of Heaven? The Son of Heaven must not fail to sacrifice to Heaven. This is no different from the son who must not fail to provide food for his father. [67/67/14–20][2]

Section 69.1

To be someone's son and not serve his father: no one in the world could approve of that. Now how does that differ from a Son of Heaven failing to serve Heaven? Thus

> every time he arrives at the new year, he first must perform the Suburban Sacrifice to supplicate Heaven. Only then does he dare to [sacrifice to] Earth. This is to perform the rituals of a son.
>
> Every time he raises troops, he must first perform the Suburban Sacrifice to inform Heaven. Only then does he dare to mount a punitive expedition. This is to enact the Way of the Son.

When King Wen received the Mandate of Heaven and became king over the world, he first performed the Suburban Sacrifice and only then carried out his [kingly] tasks and raised troops to attack Chong. An *Ode* declares:

> "Luxuriant are the oak clumps.
> We make firewood of them; we heap them up.
> Stately is our ruler and king;
> to the left and right, they hasten to him.
> Stately is our ruler and king;
> to the left and right [of him] they hold up [their] insignia.
> They hold the insignia high
> as befits the fine officers."[3]

2. We have followed Su Yu (*CQFLYZ* 405–6) in placing sections 67.2 and 67.3 (*CQFL* 67/67/20–67/68/7) at the end of chapter 65, so have omitted those sections here. We also have followed Su Yu in transferring section 69.1 (*CQFL* 69/68/24–69/69/1) to this location in chapter 67.

3. *Odes* 238, verses 2 and, immediately after, 3.

These words describe the Suburban Sacrifice. The next stanza declares:

"Floating along are those boats on the Jing [River],
many men are rowing them;
the king of Zhou marches,
and the six armies[4] go along with him."

These words describe the attack. Farther on, it says:

"King Wen received the appointment,
he had these martial achievements;
when he had made the attack on Chong,
he built a city in Feng."[5]

From these words it is evident that after receiving the Mandate, King Wen performed the Suburban Sacrifice. He performed the Suburban Sacrifice and only then attacked Chong. When he attacked Chong, how could the people find calamity in this? [69/68/24–69/69/1]

4. "Six armies" is a conventional term for the armed forces available to the Zhou king (drawn in part from the armed forces of the landholdings of the Lords of the Land).

5. *Odes* 244, verse 2. Note that this stanza is not part of *Ode* 238, as the text seems to imply.

Book 15, Part 3

CHAPTER 68

The Four [Seasonal] Sacrificial Rites

Section 68.1

The ancients annually performed four sacrifices. These four sacrifices followed the four seasons' cycle of birth and fruition. Offerings were made to their remote ancestors and their fathers and mothers. Accordingly,

> the spring [sacrifice] was called Zi;
> the summer [sacrifice] was called Yue;
> the autumn [sacrifice] was called Chang;
> and the winter [sacrifice] was called Zheng.[1]

That is as if to say [with these designations], do not stray from the appropriate season when making offerings and sacrifices to your remote ancestors. For if a season passes without [the appropriate] sacrifice, that is to lose the Way proper to anyone's son.

> The Zi sacrifice occurs in the first month with a food offering of scallions;
> the Yue sacrifice occurs in the fourth month with a food offering of wheat;
> the Chang sacrifice occurs in the seventh month with a taste offering of glutinous panicled millet;
> the Zheng sacrifice occurs in the tenth month with an offering of newly harvested rice.

1. 曰祠.夏曰礿.秋曰嘗.冬曰烝. See the introduction to group 7, "Ritual Principles," note 12.

Such is Heaven's norm and Earth's righteousness. The filial son and the dutiful[2] wife base themselves on the seasons of Heaven and avail themselves of the benefits of Earth. [68/68/11–14]

Section 70.2[3]

"Oh the earth's vegetables, gourds, and fruits! [4]
Oh the plants' rice, wheat, and millet!
The greens sprout forth, and the grains mature,
We think constantly of an auspicious day
to offer in worship these sacrificial items:
Having fasted and bathed,
Pure, clean, and utterly reverent,
we offer sacrifice to our remote ancestors and parents."

If filial sons and dutiful wives do not allow the seasonal [sacrifices] to exceed [what is appropriate],

managing the sacrifices with love and reverence,
performing the sacrifices with admiration and yielding,

perhaps they will avoid the punishments [visited on the unfilial]. [70/69/25–27]

Section 68.2

Having received the Mandate to become king, [the king] must first sacrifice to Heaven and only then [may he] implement the tasks of a king. King Wen's attack on Chong is a case in point. The *Ode* declares:

"Stately is our ruler and king;
to the left and right [of him] they hold up [their] insignia.
They hold the insignia high
as befits the fine officers."[5]

---

2. The term here is *xiao* 孝, usually translated as "filial," but in English, that word has strong connotations of "behavior appropriate to a son" and seems awkward when applied to a wife. Hence, we translate *xiao* here as "dutiful."
3. We follow the arrangement of the text by Su Yu (*CQFLYZ* 407–8), who moves chapter 70.2 (*CQFL* 70/69/25–27, beginning with 地之菜茹瓜果 and ending with 亦殆免於罪矣) to this location in chapter 68.
4. Su Yu (*CQFLYZ* 407) contends that the character *di* 地 (earth) is erroneous, but we see no reason to support this claim, based on the parallelism and rhyming scheme.
5. *Odes* 238, verses 2–3. These stanzas also are quoted in chapter 69.1, which now is part of chapter 67, following Su Yu's arrangement of the text.

This [describes] King Wen's Suburban Sacrifice. The next stanza reads:

> "Floating along are those boats on the Jing [River],
> many men are rowing them;
> the king of Zhou marches,
> and the six armies go along with him."

This [describes] King Wen's punitive expedition against Chong. The first stanza describes the holding of the insignia [at the Suburban Sacrifice]; the next stanza describes the punitive expedition against Chong. From this perspective, it is evident that King Wen first performed the Suburban Sacrifice and only afterward carried out his punitive expedition [against Chong]. King Wen received the Mandate and performed the Suburban Sacrifice. Having performed the Suburban Sacrifice, he then attacked Chong. The commoners of the state of Chong were troubled by a violent and rebellious lord. Yet they were not able to receive the virtuous beneficence of the sagely ruler until King Wen had performed the Suburban Sacrifice. How could [a king] who has not yet ordered [the world] through virtuous beneficence not be permitted to perform the Suburban Sacrifice?[6] [68/68/16–20]

6. The argument here is that the dynastic founder should perform the Suburban Sacrifice at the earliest opportunity and not wait until the entire realm has been pacified by his virtuous beneficence. The obligation for the king to serve Heaven as a filial son precedes all other obligations.

Book 15, Part 4

CHAPTER 69

The Suburban Sacrifice

Section 69.2[1]

During the time of King Xuan of Zhou, Heaven sent down a drought, and the harvest was ruined.[2] [Consequently,] the king worried about this. An *Ode* declares:

"Bright is the River of Clouds [i.e., the Milky Way],
shining it encircles the sky;
the king says:
Alas, what guilt rests upon us now?
Heaven sends down death and chaos;
repeatedly there is famine and starvation.
It is not that we have not sacrificed to the spirits;
it is not that we begrudge the victims;
We have used up the jade scepters and jade disks;
how can none [of the spirits] hear us?
The drought is long and very severe,
with heat and thunder and sultry weather.
We have unceasingly offered the Yin and Zi sacrifices,
[hastening between] suburban altar and ancestral temple.
To [the powers] above and below, we have offered up and buried [sacrificial gifts];

1. Following Su Yu, we have moved section 69.1 (*CQFL* 69/68/24–69/69/1) to the end of chapter 67.
2. The *Spring and Autumn* at Duke Xuan 7.7.9 records the occurrence of a great drought.

> there are no spirits to which we have not given reverence;
> but Lord Millet does not avail us,
> and the High God does not come near;
> They spread destruction and slaughter above and below;
> why do they smite us?"[3]

King Xuan thought that these calamities occurred because he was not able to communicate with Lord Millet or the High God. When these calamities occurred, he grew ever more anxious and attempted to serve Heaven further. If Heaven had not given [the Mandate] to this family, how could this family have been established as the Son of Heaven? It was established as the Son of Heaven because Heaven gave [the Mandate] to it. "Heaven gives [the Mandate] to this family" means that Heaven commands this family. If Heaven had already given [the Mandate] to this family and commanded it, how could it not be able to communicate with Heaven! Therefore whenever the *Spring and Autumn* raised criticisms concerning the Suburban Sacrifice, it never once held the virtue of the ruler to be insufficient to perform it. However, if sacrifices to the mountains and rivers were performed and the Suburban Sacrifice was not performed, [the *Spring and Autumn* considered this to] violate ritual norms, [the king] having lost the proper sequence of sacrifice. Therefore it necessarily criticized these instances. From this, we see that those who do not sacrifice to Heaven cannot sacrifice to the lesser spirits.

The Suburban Sacrifice accords with the divination that precedes it. If [the divination] is inauspicious, [the king] will not dare perform the Suburban Sacrifice. The sacrifices to the numerous [lesser] spirits are not preceded by divination; only the Suburban Sacrifice is preceded by divination. The Suburban Sacrifice is the most important sacrifice. The *Spring and Autumn* criticizes the performance of [ordinary] sacrifices during mourning [for a parent], but it does not criticize the performance of the Suburban Sacrifice during mourning. If performing the Suburban Sacrifice does no harm to mourning, and moreover, mourning itself is not harmed by it, how much less [can it harm] other things? The Suburban Invocation states:

> "How august is Heaven above.
> Heaven radiates and approaches earth below.
> Heaven gathers together the numerous beings of the earth.
> Heaven sends down fragrant winds and rain,

3. *Odes* 258, verses 1–2.

and the multitudes of living things obtain what is proper to each.
Whether present or past, Heaven confers it on the one man [that is, the ruler,]
who is reverently thankful for august Heaven's blessings."

[The Son of Heaven] does not speak one his own behalf but for the growth and development of the multitude of living things. If the people approach Heaven in a heartfelt way, they will not be criticized [by Heaven]. If Heaven makes no reproach and your words are reverent and compliant, it is fitting that it should bring happiness.[4] [69/69/3–15]

4. Treating as excrescent the last eleven graphs *you jiao si jiu ju, jiu ju zhe yang shu ye* 右郊祀九句，九句者陽數也 which mean "[concerning] the preceding [literally, "to the right"] nine sentences about the Suburban Sacrifice, the nine sentences constitute a yang number." We suspect that this is a fragment from a commentary that has crept into the text by mistake.

Book 15, Part 5

CHAPTER 70

Following Orders

Section 70.1

The father is the son's Heaven;
Heaven is the father's Heaven.

It has never been the case that something comes into existence without Heaven. Heaven is the ancestor of the myriad things. The myriad things cannot come into existence without Heaven.

With yin alone, they will not come into existence;
with yang alone, they will not come into existence.

Only after yin and yang combine with Heaven and Earth do the myriad things come into existence. Therefore it is said:

The father's son can be honored;
the mother's son can be humbled.
What is honored appropriates a lofty designation;
what is humbled appropriates a lowly designation.

Therefore those whose virtue accompanies Heaven and Earth [are those whom] August Heaven sets to the right and treats as sons by bestowing on them the title Son of Heaven. Those next in line obtain the five levels of rank (duke, marquis, earl, viscount, and baron) and thereby are honored. They all take their respective states and city [names] as their designations. Those who do not possess the virtue of Heaven and Earth [are designated with reference only to] a province,[1]

---

1. The word *zhou* 州 (province) here appears to refer to a perhaps fanciful scheme attributed to the mythical founder of the Xia dynasty, Yu the Great, who divided China into nine provinces. Here the term has the general sense of a geographic area larger than a "state" (*guo* 國).

a state, a man, or a family name.[2] In the most extreme cases, they are not associated with either their state or [their] city. They are cut off from any associations with those [of the same] bones and flesh [i.e., blood relatives]. Having departed from human norms, they are simply called gatekeepers and thieves. Those lacking a surname, personal name, style, or family name are lower than the most lowly.

Deeply[3] honor those who possess Utmost Virtue.
Promote them to a lofty position that cannot be made loftier.
Deeply[4] humble those who are utterly base.
Demote them to a lowly position that cannot be made lowlier.

The *Spring and Autumn* sets the various ranks in order and arranges the lofty and the base.[5]

How intricate! Its details can be obtained and observed. Even if a person is unenlightened and a fool, no one will fail to be enlightened [by the *Spring and Autumn*'s designations].[6] [70/69/19–25]

Section 70.3

The duke's son Jingfu was guilty of a grave crime, and so it was not appropriate to associate him with his state.[7] Considering that he was closely related [to the ruler], [the *Spring and Autumn*] concealed [his identity] and referred to him in terms of his mother's state as Zhongsun of Qi in order to expunge his close relationship as the duke's son. Therefore those who commit the grave crime

2. Emending *min* 民 to *ming* 名, following Ling Shu (Su Yu, *CQFLYZ* 411). *Gongyang Commentary* at Duke Zhuang 3.10.6:

   [In the designation of a barbarian nation,] the name of a department (*jing* 境) is inferior to the name of the state (*guo* 國); the name of the state is inferior to the family name (*shi* 氏); the family name is inferior to the term *ren* 人 [man]; the term *ren* is inferior to the personal name (*ming* 名); the personal name is inferior to the style (*zi* 子); and the style is inferior to the title of viscount. (Adapted from Göran Malmqvist, "Studies on the *Gongyang* and *Guliang* Commentaries," *Bulletin of the Museum of Far Eastern Antiquities* 43 [1971]: 130)

3. Emending *qi* 其 to *shen* 甚, following *CQFL* 69, note 10.
4. Emending *qi* 其 to *shen* 甚, following *CQFL* 69, note 11.
5. Emending *beizun* 卑尊 to *zunbei* 尊卑, following *CQFL* 69, note 12.
6. Following Su Yu's arrangement of the text, we have moved section 70.2 (*CQFL* 70/69/25–27) to chapter 68 and thus omitted it here.
7. Duke Min 4.1.6: "In Winter, Zhongsun of Qi came." *Gongyang*: "Who was this Zhongsun of Qi? He was the duke's son Jingfu. If so, why is he not referred to as the duke's son Jingfu? In order to associate him with Qi. Why so? In order to estrange him. Why estrange him? [The *Spring and Autumn*] conceals for the sake of the noble, for the sake of those who are closely related [to the ruler], and for the sake of the worthy."

of disregarding Heaven's commands are always cut off from their Heaven-endowed relationships.

With respect to Heaven, humans receive their fate in accordance with the Way.
With respect to [other] humans, they receive their orders in the form of [the ruler's] verbal instructions.
Those who do not follow the Way are cut off by Heaven.
Those who do not follow [the ruler's] verbal instructions are rejected by others.

When the minister receives important commands from the ruler, he is given verbal instructions and then journeys abroad. Only when the altars of the grain and soil or the state are endangered is it permissible for him to abandon his instructions and act on his own discretion to restore [the ruler's] security. When the duke's son Jie, the marquis of Ji, and the duke of Song[8] made a covenant, it exemplified this principle.[9]

The Son of Heaven receives orders from Heaven;
the Lords of the Land receive orders from the Son of Heaven;
sons receive orders from fathers;
ministers receive orders from the ruler;
and wives receive orders from husbands.

What all those who receive orders show respect for, in every case, is Heaven. Although it also is permissible to say that they receive their orders from Heaven. . . .[10]

When the Son of Heaven was incapable of carrying out Heaven's orders, [the *Spring and Autumn*] discarded [his proper rank] and designated him with the lower rank of duke. The descendants of the kings exemplify this principle.

When a duke or marquis was incapable of carrying out an order from the Son of Heaven, [the *Spring and Autumn* referred to him by] his personal name,

8. Supplying the following eight characters based on Su Yu's restoration of the text: 公子結及齊侯宋公 (Lai, *CQFLJZJY* 385, note 20).

9. *Gongyang Commentary* at Duke Zhuang 3.19.3:

> Why does [the *Spring and Autumn*] record this instance? [The duke's son Jie] acted on his own discretion, and therefore [the *Spring and Autumn*] records it. A great officer does not act on his own discretion. Why, then, does [the *Spring and Autumn*] use the term *sui* 遂? According to the ritual of a mission of friendly inquiries, a great officer receives orders but no specific verbal instructions. If, on a journey abroad, he finds himself in a position to act in the interest of his own state, it is permissible for him to do so on his own accord. (Adapted from Malmqvist, "Studies on the *Gongyang* and *Guliang* Commentaries," 135)

10. Following Lu Wenchao, we take the next four characters 不天亦可 to be an intrusion into the text. There must have been additional text here, now missing, to complete the previous dependent clause (Su Yu, *CQFLYZ* 412).

disassociated him [from his rank], and did not allow him to return to his position. Shuo, marquis of Wey, exemplifies this principle.[11]

When a son did not carry out his father's order, [the *Spring and Autumn* records that] a punitive expedition was mounted to punish him. Peng Gui, the heir apparent of Wey, exemplifies this principle.[12]

When a minister did not carry out his ruler's order, even if he achieved goodness, [the *Spring and Autumn* used] the term "rebellion" to describe the affair. Zhao Ying of Jin entering Jin Yang and "rebelling" exemplifies this principle.[13]

When a concubine did not carry out her lord's order, [the *Spring and Autumn* records] that she was given as a dowry in marriage and was the first to be sent to her mistress's future home.[14]

When the wife did not respectfully receive her husband's orders, [the *Spring and Autumn*] disassociates her from her husband. Avoiding the expression "and"

---

11. Duke Huan 2.16.5: "In the eleventh month, Shuo, marquis of Wey, left [his state] and fled to Qi." *Gongyang*:

    Why is Shuo, marquis of Wey, referred to by his personal name? In order to disassociate him. Why disassociate him? He was guilty of an offense against the Son of Heaven. Under what circumstances was he guilty of an offense against the Son of Heaven? Being charged with the protection of Wey, Shuo [the marquis of Wey] was not even capable of employing a small body of men in his own state. [The marquis of Wey] had violated that part of Qi that was situated at the northern side of Mount Dai. [He] claimed illness, stayed [where he was], and did not submit to punishment. (Adapted from Malmqvist, "Studies on the *Gongyang* and *Guliang* Commentaries," 111)

12. Peng Gui, the heir apparent of Wey, was Duke Zhuang of Wey. His personal name was Peng Gui. Peng Gui acted immorally, so Duke Ling rejected him and established his brother Peng Che as the heir apparent. Peng Gui fled to a place called Qi. Consequently, Guo Xia of Wey and Dan Mangu of Wey led troops on a punitive expedition. Duke Ai 12.3.1: "Guo Xia of Qi and Dan Mangu of Wey led troops to surround Qi." *Gongyang*: "Why is it that Guo Xia of Qi and Dan Mangu of Wey led troops to surround Qi? It was a hegemonic attack."

13. Duke Ding 11.13.7: "Zhao Ying of Jin returned home to Jin." *Gongyang*:

    This was a rebellion. Why then does the text use the term "return home"? He relied on his territory to rectify the state. Under what circumstances did he rely on his territory to rectify the state? Zhao Ying of Jin appropriated the troops of Jin Yang to expel Xun Yin and Shiji Xie. Why the reference to Xun Yin and Shiji Xie? They were evil men who were close to the ruler. This was a case of expelling evil men who were close to the ruler. Why, then, is it described as a rebellion? [Zhao Ying] did not have his ruler's orders [to do so].

14. In ancient times when a regional lord married a woman from another state to be his consort, the norm was that to accompany the prospective bride, both states sent a woman who was called an "escort" (*ying* 媵). When Duke Xi of Lu married, Qi sent a woman as an escort. Because they arrived first in Lu, before Lu had agreed, Duke Xi was coerced into establishing the woman from Qi as his bride. Duke Xi 5.8.3: "We conducted the Di ceremony in the Grand Temple and performed the Yong and the Zhi sacrifices to install the lady consort." *Gongyang*:

    What does [the term] *yong* indicate? The term *yong* indicates that it was not suitable to perform the Yong sacrifice. The term *zhi* indicates that it was not suitable to perform the Zhi sacrifice. To perform the Di ceremony and the Yong and Zhi sacrifices to install the lady consort violated ritual protocol. Why did [the *Spring and Autumn*] not refer to the lady consort as Lady Jiang? In order to censure her. Why did [the *Spring and Autumn*] censure her? [The *Spring and Autumn*] criticized the duke for taking a concubine as a primary wife. Under what circumstances did he take a concubine as a primary wife? In fact, he was coerced, because the woman escort from Qi arrived first.

[to describe a husband and wife together] exemplifies this principle.[15] [Thus] I say, those who do not respectfully follow Heaven are guilty of crimes like these. [70/69/27–70/70/8]

Section 70.4

Confucius said: "[A noble man is awestruck by three things:]

He is awestruck by the Mandate of Heaven;
he is awestruck by the Great Man;
and he is awestruck by the words of a sage."[16]

When sacrificing to the spirits of the grain and soil, the ancestors, the mountains and rivers, or the ghosts and spirits, if you do not do so in accordance with the Way, you [still] will avoid disaster and harm. But regarding [circumstances under which] sacrifices to Heaven are not presented, [it may be that] the divination was not auspicious, [or something] caused the bull's mouth to suffer injury,[17] or ground squirrels gnawed at the bull's horns.[18] Sometimes [the record] states that "[ground squirrels] gnawed at the bull"; sometimes "[ground squirrels] gnawed [at the bull], and it died"; sometimes "[ground squirrels] gnawed at [the bull], and it lived"; sometimes "[ground squirrels] did not gnaw at [the bull], and it died of its own accord"; sometimes "there was a second divination, and the bull died"; and sometimes "there was a divination, and [ground squirrels] gnawed at the bull's horns."

Transgressions may be deep or shallow, significant or trivial;
disasters may be insignificant or significant, severe or light.

You must examine this. With regard to [any particular] aberration [that occurs during] the Suburban Sacrifice, deduce the cause of the disaster from

---

15. Duke Huan 2.18: "Our lord [and] the lady consort of the Jiang clan subsequently entered Qi." *Gongyang*: "Why does [the *Spring and Autumn*] not state '*and* the lady consort' with reference to our lord? The lady consort was estranged. What does 'the lady consort was estranged' indicate? It is an expression used in the inner [palace]. In fact, the lady consort was estranged from our lord."

16. This passage from *Analects* 16.8 also is quoted in chapter 65.1. As quoted here, the introductory line, "A noble man is awestruck by three things," is missing; we supply it in square brackets.

17. Duke Xuan 7.3.1: "Spring. The royal first month. The mouth of the bull intended for the Suburban Sacrifice was injured." Duke Xuan 7.3.2: "We did a different divination [to choose] a bull, and the bull died. Accordingly, we did not conduct the Suburban Sacrifice."

18. Duke Cheng 8.7.1: "Spring. The royal first month. Ground squirrels ate the horns of the bull intended for the Suburban Sacrifice." Duke Cheng 8.7.2: "We did a different divination [to choose] a bull, and ground squirrels again ate its horns. Accordingly, we released the bull and did not conduct the Suburban Sacrifice."

the aberration, and in response, do not act [in that manner again].[19] This is a "response," not an overt action. We see that the alterations of the numerous affairs seem unknowable, and so we attribute them to natural causes. But cannot such things be thoroughly explained? Looking at what is awesome from this perspective, is it not Heaven, the one alone who possesses the power to execute and kill?

[The *Spring and Autumn* records] more than thirty instances of ministers killing their lords and sons killing their fathers. [The *Spring and Autumn*] denigrated those in lowly positions [by omitting their name and referring to them as "men."][20] Looking at what is awesome from this perspective, it is surely the Mandate of Heaven.[21]

[The *Spring and Autumn*] records more than fifty instances of states perishing. All of them failed to be in awe. How much more so is this true of being awestruck by the Great Man, who alone possesses the power to take life. When a lord is about to suffer extinction, what days are left to him?

Duke Xuan of Lu disobeyed the sage's words, altering the ancient [practices] and changing the constant norms, so he was immediately visited by calamity.[22] How can one fail to heed the words of the sage! These three things that can be feared have different manifestations but identical ends. Thus the sage identified them and said that collectively they could be feared. [70/70/10–18]

19. Reading *you* 猶 as homophonous with 由. We treat the characters *zhi* 之 and *er* 而 as excrescent, following Liu Shipei (see also *CQFL* 70, note 3).

20. Lu Wenchao suspects these six characters are corrupt (Su Yu, *CQFLYZ* 413).

21. Treating the three characters *da ren hu* 大人乎 as intrusions, following Ling Shu, as cited in Su Yu, *CQFLYZ* 413.

22. Duke Xuan 7.15.8: "There was the first tax by *mu*." *Gongyang*:

What is meant by the term "first"? It means "for the first time." What is meant by the expression "tax by *mu*"? It means to [measure by] pacing the *mu* and tax [its agricultural production] accordingly. Why was this entry made? In order to criticize. Why criticize? [The *Spring and Autumn*] criticizes the duke for being the first to [measure by] pacing the *mu* and tax [its agricultural production] accordingly. What was there to criticize in this? The ancients based their tribute on [the agricultural production of] one part in ten. Why did the ancients base their tribute on [the agricultural production of] one part in ten? This was the correct average throughout the empire. When tribute was more than one part in ten, it was called "Greater Jie" and "Lesser Jie." When tribute was less than one part in ten, it was called "Greater Mo" and "Lesser Mo." Tribute of one part in ten was the correct average in the realm. When it was implemented, songs of praise were composed.

See also *Mencius* 5A.8a and 5A.8b.

Book 15, Part 6

CHAPTER 71

An Official Response Regarding the Suburban Sacrifice

Section 71.1

"The chamberlain for law enforcement, your servant [Zhang] Tang, deserves death for daring to report [to Your Majesty]: Your servant [Zhang] Tang has received an imperial decree to question the former administrator of Jiaoxi, [Dong] Zhongshu, regarding the Suburban Sacrifice."

"Your servant Dong Zhongshu responded stating: '[Your servant] has heard that among the rituals of the Son of Heaven in ancient times, none was more important than the Suburban [Sacrifice]. The Suburban [Sacrifice] was always offered in the first month on the first *xin* day. In order to precede the sacrifices to the numerous spirits, it was placed at the very beginning [of the sacrificial schedule]. In accordance with the rites, during the three-year mourning period, although one did not sacrifice to the ancestors, one did not dare abandon the Suburban [Sacrifice]. The suburban [altar] was more important than the ancestral temple, [just as] Heaven is more venerable than humankind. "The Regulations of the King" state:

> "Of the bulls used to sacrifice to Heaven and Earth, their horns should be [no larger than] a cocoon or a chestnut;

This exchange dates to around 123 B.C.E., when Dong Zhongshu retired from his official duties. See Sarah A. Queen, *From Chronicle to Canon: The Hermeneutics of the "Spring and Autumn" According to Tung Chung-shu* (Cambridge: Cambridge University Press, 1996), 36.

"of the bulls used in the ancestral temple, their horns should be [no larger than] what one can grasp in one's hands;

"of those used for feasting guests, their horns should be [no larger than] a foot long."[1]

This means that the greater the virtue, the smaller was the sacrifice.

'The *Spring and Autumn* states: "In the Lu sacrifice, the Duke of Zhou used a white bull."[2] The color white symbolized reverence and purity. It further states: "The victim for the sacrifice to the [High] God underwent cleansing for three months."[3] The victim was valued for its plumpness and purity and not sought for its size. As a general rule, the way to raise sacrificial victims is to exert oneself in finding a victim that is plump and unblemished. A foal or calf that already can eat grass or grain is not as good as one that still drinks its mother's milk.' "[4]

"Your servant [Tang] respectfully asked Zhongshu: 'In the Lu sacrifice, the Duke of Zhou used a white bull. Was this not [in accordance with] the rites?' Your servant Zhongshu responded: 'It was [in accordance with] the rites.' "

"Your servant Tang asked: 'The Zhou Son of Heaven used a red bull to offer in sacrifice, whereas the numerous dukes used multicolored bulls to offer in sacrifice. The Duke of Zhou was a duke. How then was he able to use a pure-colored bull to offer in sacrifice?' Your servant Zhongshu responded, stating: 'King Wu had died and King Cheng had been established [as Son of Heaven], but he was still a child. The Duke of Zhou inherited the undertaking of Kings Wen and Wu and brought to completion the merit of these two sagely kings. His virtue extended to all that lay between Heaven and Earth, and his generosity filled all within the Four Seas. Thus King Cheng recognized his virtue and ability and revered and respected him. An *Ode* declares:

"No virtuous deed is without recompense."[5]

Thus when King Cheng ordered the sacrificial offering, the Duke of Zhou used a white bull. With respect to his superior, he was not allowed to use the same color sacrificial victim as that used by the Son of Heaven. With respect to his

1. Restoring these lines following Lu Wenchao, who notes that in the *Gu wen yuan*, all three lines contain the character *jiao* 角 following the character *niu* 牛 (*CQFL* 71, note 8). This passage is quoted from *Liji*, "Wang zhi" (Royal Regulations), part 3, para. 10; James Legge, trans., *Li Chi: Book of Rites*, ed. Ch'u Chai and Winberg Chai (New Hyde Park, N.Y.: University Books, 1967), 1:227.
2. *Gongyang Commentary* to Duke Wen 6.13.5.
3. *Gongyang Commentary* to Duke Xuan 7.3.1.
4. The text here reads "Cannot yet eat grass or grain," which makes no sense, as it renders the whole statement self-contradictory. We think this originally must have said "already can" and emended it accordingly.
5. *Odes* 256, verse 6.

subordinates, [the color of the sacrificial victim] differed from that of the Lords of the Land. Your servant Zhongshu, in his stupidity, is of the opinion that this was an act of propriety to recompense the Duke of Zhou's virtue.' "

"Your servant Tang asked Zhongshu: 'The Son of Heaven made sacrificial offerings to Heaven, and the Lords of the Land made sacrificial offerings to the altar of the soil. Under what circumstances was it permissible for Lu to carry out the Suburban Sacrifice?' Your servant Zhongshu responded by stating: 'The Duke of Zhou assisted King Cheng; King Cheng consequently achieved the status of a sage. There is no achievement more meritorious than this. The Duke of Zhou was a sage, in possession of [the authority] to sacrifice to the Way of Heaven. Therefore King Cheng ordered Lu to perform the Suburban Sacrifice.' "

"Your servant Tang respectfully asked Zhongshu: 'In the Lu sacrifice, the Duke of Zhou used a white victim. When it performed the Suburban Sacrifice [to Heaven], what color victim did Lu use?' [Your servant] Zhongshu responded by stating: 'When Lu offered the Suburban Sacrifice, they used a pure-red bull. The Zhou dynasty revered the color red. Since Lu received orders from the Son of Heaven to perform the Suburban Sacrifice, they used a red bull.' "

"Your servant Tang asked Zhongshu: 'When performing the sacrifices at the ancestral temple, some substitute a domesticated duck for a wild duck. A domesticated duck is not a wild duck. Is it or is it not permissible to use a domesticated duck?' [Your subject] Zhongshu responded: 'A domesticated duck is not a wild duck; a wild duck is not a domesticated duck. Your servant has heard that when Confucius entered the ancestral temple of the Son of Heaven, he made inquiries concerning each thing he encountered. This was the epitome of vigilance. His Majesty personally performs the Suburban Sacrifice. [Before performing the sacrifice, His Majesty] fasts and purifies himself, cleansing body and mind. In offering sacrifices at the ancestral temple, he is extremely reverent. Why, then, substitute a domesticated duck for a wild duck? Neither the name nor the reality of the thing would match. Using a domesticated duck to sacrifice at the ancestral temple would be quite a mismatch! In his stupidity, your servant Zhongshu considers that such a substitution is not permissible.

'Your servant is but a decrepit hound or broken-down horse, having been granted permission [to rest his] weary bones and to live out his days in this humble lane. Still, His Majesty has graciously sent one of the nine ministers to question your servant on an important matter of the court. Your servant is stupid and vulgar. [His abilities] do not suffice to receive this enlightened instruction [from His Majesty] and submit a significant response. Your servant Zhongshu risks death to inform [Your Majesty].' " [71/70/22–71/71/10]

Book 16, Part 1

CHAPTER 72

Presenting Gifts to Superiors

Section 72.1

General rules for presenting gifts to superiors:

The Son of Heaven uses black millet wine;
a duke or a marquis uses jade;
a minister uses a lamb;
a great officer uses a wild goose.

The wild goose has [qualities] that are the same in kind as elders. Elders occupy a position above the people.

Invariably they arrange themselves in hierarchical order;
invariably they reverently form themselves into an orderly row.

Thus a great officer uses the wild goose as his gift.

The lamb has [qualities] that are the same in kind as Heaven.[1]

The Way of Heaven is to rely on yang and not to rely on yin.
The Way of a king is to rely on beneficence and not to rely on punishments;

Su Yu points out that this chapter does not discuss gifts presented by officers (*shi* 士) and commoners (*shuren* 庶人), as seen in similar discussions in the "Qu Li" (Summary of the Rites) chapter of *Liji* (James Legge, trans., *Li Chi: Book of Rites*, ed. Ch'u Chai and Winberg Chai [New Hyde Park, N.Y.: University Books, 1967], 1:119; the "Xiu wen" (Promoting Civility) chapter of the *Shuoyuan*; and the "Rui zhi" (Ritual Presents) chapter of the *Bohutong* (Tjan Tjoe Som, trans., *Po Hu T'ong: The Comprehensive Discussions in the White Tiger Hall* [Leiden: Brill, 1952], 2:543–45). Thus Su Yu (*CQFLYZ*, 419) suspects that portions of this essay have been lost.

1. Lu Wenchao suggests that the next twenty-seven graphs are an intrusion. We believe, however, that these sentences fit well with the context and retained them in our translation (*CQFL* 71, note 5).

this is how he complies with Heaven. The lamb has horns but does not use them. It is fully equipped [with horns] yet does not use them, being the same in kind as one who loves humaneness.

When you seize it, it does not bleat;
when you kill it, it does not cry out,

being the same in kind as one who will die for righteousness. When feeding from its mother, the lamb always kneels to receive, being the same in kind as one who understands propriety. Thus the name for sheep, *yang* 羊, resembles *xiang* 祥, meaning auspicious.[2] Thus a minister uses the lamb as his gift.

Jade has qualities that resemble a noble man. "The Master said: 'There is nothing I can do with a man who is not constantly saying, "What am I to do? What am I to do?" ' "[3] Thus, those who hide their illness will not secure a good doctor, and those who avoid seeking instruction will be shunned by the sage. Considering that such people distance themselves from success while they draw near to disaster, [the doctor and sage] have nothing to do with them.

Jade is utterly clear and does not conceal its imperfections. Should a blemish exist on the inside, it will always be visible from the outside. Thus [similarly] a noble man does not hide his shortcomings.

When he does not know something, he seeks an answer.
When he cannot do something, he learns how

and so appropriates [the qualities] of jade. The noble man is comparable to jade. Jade is lustrous and undefiled: these [are the qualities of] the humane and utterly incorruptible. [Jade can be made] pointed, but it is not injurious: these [are the qualities of] the righteous who do not harm others.

[Jade is] hard but indestructible,[4]
warm to the touch but not clammy.[5]
At first glance it appears commonplace;
inspected closely, it [reveals itself as] precious stone.[6]

2. The right-hand component of the character *xiang*, meaning "auspicious," consists of the phonetic *yang* meaning "sheep."

3. *Analects* 15.16; D. C. Lau, trans., *The Analects* (Harmondsworth: Penguin, 1979), 134.

4. Following Su Yu, we emended the character *jian*—no. 24251 in Morohashi Tetsuji, *Dai Kan-Wa jiten*, 13 vols. (Tokyo: Taishūkan, 1955–1960) (like 堅 but with the "stone" radical 石 in place of the "earth" radical), meaning "hard, stiff, rigid"—to *mo* 磨, based on an unnamed earlier edition of the *Chunqiu fanlu* (Lai, *CQFLJZJY* 395, note 14).

5. Reading the character *guo* 過 as a mistake for *wen* 溫, following Su Yu (Lai, *CQFLJZJY* 395, note 15).

6. Treating the three characters *zhuang ru she* 狀如石 as intrusions into the text from what possibly was an early commentary, following Su Yu (Lai, *CQFLJZJY* 395, note 17).

It can be carved but cannot be bent.[7] It is pure and white as unadorned [silk] but cannot be stained. Things in the category of "jade" are replete with virtue.[8] Thus a duke or a marquis uses jade as his gift.

Black millet wine has [qualities] that are the same in kind as the sage, who is pure, humane, pellucid, and unadulterated and who possesses the highest kind of knowledge.

> What [the sage] contains within himself is inexhaustible in its virtue and accord;
> What [the sage] exhibits in his actions is inexhaustible in its magnanimity and fructification.

Its refined aroma, pleasant and fragrant, penetrates up to Heaven.[9]

Black millet is obtained from the most fragrant of all the grasses.[10] It is ground into flour and mixed until it is uniform; and when it attains its particular fragrance, the aroma wafts up to Heaven. Its being pellucid and unadulterated, without anything to pick out, is as one with [the qualities of] the sage. Thus the Son of Heaven uses black millet wine as his gift, on each and every occasion using it to serve [Heaven] above.

Observe the significance of these various gifts, and you will understand their various usages. [72/71/16–28]

---

7. Treating the character *cong* 從 as excrescent, following Su Yu (Lai, *CQFLJZJY* 395, note 18).
8. Supplying the character *de* 德 between *bei* 備 and *zhe* 者, following Lu Wenchao (Lai, *CQFLJZJY* 395, note 20).
9. Treating the character *ji* 積 beginning this line as excrescent, following Su Yu (Lai, *CQFLJZJY* 395, note 23).
10. Emending *xiang* 香 to *cao* 草 and *xin* 心 to *xiang* 香, following Su Yu (Lai, *CQFLJZJY* 395, note 24).

Book 16, Part 2

CHAPTER 73

Hymn to the Mountains and Rivers

Mountains:

How jagged and precipitous, sheer and steep,
soaring and colossal, towering and craggy,
long enduring, they do not collapse or crumble,

Just like the humane man or resolute scholar-gentleman.

Confucius said: "Mountains![1] Spirits and earth divinities [must have] erected them."[2]

Treasures to store and amass,
implements to use and enrich.

[Whether] crooked or straight, [their trees are equally] suitable.

The large [trees] can be crafted into palaces, dwellings, terraces, and pavilions;
the small [trees] can be made into boats, carts, pontoons, and rafts.[3]
None of the large ones are not just right;
none of the small ones are unacceptable.
Take up the ax and fell [their trees];
take up the sickle and reap [their grasses].

There,

living people support themselves,
wild animals take refuge,
and the dead are interred.

---

1. Treating *chuan* 川 as excrescent, following Lu Wenchao (Lai, *CQFLJZJY* 397, note 3).
2. This saying, attributed to Confucius, does not appear in the received canon. Some editions of the *Chunqiu fanlu* read *zhi* 只 in place of *qi* 祇: "Only a spirit [could have] erected them."
3. Following Su Yu's emendations (Lai, *CQFLJZJY* 397, note 7).

Numerous are the achievements [of mountains], yet they say nothing; this is why the Noble Man compared himself to them.

Moreover, as earth piles up to become a mountain,

it causes no injury;
as it attains its height,
it does no harm;
as it grows in size,
it causes no loss.
Small at the apex
and massive at the base,
it long remains stable

for future generations, without the slightest movement, majestically standing alone.

Such is the virtue of the mountain.

An *Ode* says:

"How lofty is the Southern Mountain,
with rocks so steep and precipitous!
Majestic and awesome are you, Grand Master Yin.
The people all revere you!"[4]

This expresses it.

Water:

How it gushes forth and rushes forth from sources and springs;

day and night it is never depleted,
resembling those who are strong.
It overflows every barrier and moves on,
resembling those who are just.
It flows downward through tiny fissures,
not neglecting the smallest gaps,
resembling those who are discerning.
It flows through gully and ravine without going astray;
even rushing forth for ten thousand *li*, it always reaches its destination,
resembling those who are knowledgeable.

4. *Odes* 191, verse 1.

Though obstructions hinder it,
it remains fresh and calm,
resembling those who understand their destiny.
Unclean, one enters it,
to emerge refreshed and clean;
it resembles those who excel at transforming others.
Flowing toward a gorge a thousand fathoms[5] deep,
it enters it without hesitation,
resembling those who are courageous.

All things are destroyed by fire;
water alone conquers it.
It resembles those who are martial.
Getting it, one lives,
losing it, one dies.
It resembles those who possess virtue.

While standing by a river, Confucius said, "What has passed away resembles this flowing water. Day and night it does not cease."[6] This expresses it. [73/72/3–8]

5. Literally, "a thousand *ren* 刃 deep." A *ren* is eight Chinese feet (*chi* 尺). In modern measurements, the length of a Han foot was about nine inches, so the distance described here is about six thousand feet, more than a mile. The general sense of the phrase is "very deep."

6. *Analects* 9.17.

Book 16, Part 3

CHAPTER 74

Seeking Rain

Section 74.1

To seek rain during a spring drought, instruct the [officials of] prefectures and towns, on a Water day,[1] to order the people to pray at the altars [of the soil and grain] and the members of households to sacrifice to the door [god]. Do not fell prominent trees. Do not clear mountain forests. Expose shamankas[2] [to the sun] and assemble emaciated persons.

On the eighth day [of these proceedings], construct an earthen altar outside the eastern gate of the city, with openings on all four sides and [measuring] eight feet square.[3] Set out on it eight pieces of azure[4] silk. Its presiding spirit is Gong Gong.[5] Sacrifice to Gong Gong with eight live fish and dark wine.[6]

Prepare clear wine and cured meats. Select those among the shamankas who are pure and unblemished and eloquent in uttering auspicious phrases to act as the invocators. They pray and fast for three days. Donning azure clothing,

---

For an analysis of this chapter, see Michael Loewe, "The Cult of the Dragon and the Invocation for Rain," in *Chinese Ideas About Nature and Society: Studies in Honour of Derk Bodde*, ed. Charles Le Blanc and Susan Blader (Hong Kong: Hong Kong University Press, 1987), 206–10.

1. That is, on a day designated as *ren* 壬 or *gui* 癸, the ninth and tenth days of the ten-day "week" denoted by the ten Heavenly Stems (*tian gan* 天干).
2. *Wu* 巫, generally understood in Han contexts to refer to female shamans.
3. In modern measurements, the length of a Han "foot" (*chi* 尺) was about nine inches, so this altar would be about six feet square. The same conversion applies to other dimensions given in this chapter.
4. Cang 蒼 is the color of kingfisher feathers: brilliant azure blue.
5. Gong Gong was a mythical figure associated with the north. See John S. Major, Sarah A. Queen, Andrew Seth Meyer, and Harold D. Roth, trans. and eds., *The "Huainanzi": A Guide to the Theory and Practice of Government in Early Han China* (New York: Columbia University Press, 2010), 3.1, 115.
6. Eight is a yin number, and square is a yin shape, so all these measures are designed to attract water.

they first bow twice [and] then kneel in a row. Having knelt in a row, they bow twice again, then rise and pray, saying: "August Heaven generates the five [kinds of] grain to nourish the people. Now the five [kinds of] grain are stricken by drought. We fear that they will not ripen. We respectfully bring forward this clear wine and cured meat." They then bow twice again and request rain. When blessed with timely rains, they present a sacrificial animal.

On a *jia* or *yi* day,[7] fashion one large azure dragon, eighty feet long, to position at the center. Fashion seven smaller dragons, each forty feet long, to be placed to the east. All dragons face east, separated from one another by a distance of eight feet. Eight young boys fast for three days, don bluegreen clothing, and dance [around] the dragons. The bailiffs in charge of fields,[8] also having fasted for three days and donned bluegreen clothing, [are the ones who] erect [the dragons].

Excavate a tunnel through the altar [of the soil][9] to connect it with the water course beyond the city gate. Take five frogs and set them randomly at the center of the altar. [Make] a pool eight feet square and one foot[10] deep; fill it with water; and put the frogs into it. Prepare clear wine and cured meat. Fast and pray for three days, and don azure clothing. The worshipping, kneeling, and lining up in a row is the same as the beginning.

Take a three-year-old cock and a three-year-old boar, and cook them on a spirit altar with four openings. Instruct the people to close the southern gates of the towns and villages, set out water beyond the gates, and open the northern gates of the towns and villages.[11] Prepare one older boar and set it out beyond the northern gates. Place an additional boar at the center of the marketplace. With the sound of drumming and chanting, begin burning the tails of the boars.

Collect the bones of the dead and bury them; open up mountain streams; gather firewood and burn it; open up the obstructions and blockages in roads, bridges, and thoroughfares not traveled owing to impediments and barriers.[12] When favored with rain, repay it with one pig and a sufficiency of wine, salt, and millet. Make a mat of rushes, but do not trim [the rushes in making] it.

---

7. First and second days of the ten-day cycle.
8. *Tian se fu* 田嗇夫.
9. Emending *zhu li she* 諸噁里社 to *zuo she* 鑿社, following *CQFL* 72, note 15.
10. Emending "two" to "one" to match the other seasons.
11. This is to exclude yang *qi* and to allow yin *qi* to enter.
12. Following Su Yu's reordering of the six graphs *bu xing zhe jue du zhi* 不行者決瀆之 (Lai, *CQFLJZJY* 401, note 28).

To seek rain during a summer drought, instruct the [officials of] prefectures and towns, on a Water day, [to order the people to pray at the altars of the soil and grain, and] the members of households to sacrifice to the stove [god]. Do not initiate tasks involving earth, augment the water [supply], or dig wells. Expose cooking pans on the altar and mortars and pestles in the alleys.

On the seventh day [of these proceedings], construct an earthen altar outside the southern gate of the city, with openings on all four sides and [measuring] seven feet square. Set out on it seven pieces of red silk. The presiding spirit is Chi You.[13] Sacrifice to Chi You with seven red cocks and dark wine.

Prepare clear wine and cured meat. Pray and fast for three days, and don red clothing. Bowing, kneeling, forming ranks, and praying is similar to the instructions for spring.

On a *bing* or *ding* day,[14] fashion one large red dragon that is seventy feet long, to position at the center. Again, fashion six smaller dragons, each thirty-five feet long, to be placed to the south. All dragons face south, separated from one another by a distance of seven feet. Seven full-grown men fast for three days, don red clothing, and dance [around] the dragons. The bailiffs in charge of public works,[15] also having fasted for three days and donned red clothing, [are the ones who] erect [the dragons].

Excavate a tunnel through the altar of the soil to connect it with a water course beyond the city gate. Take five frogs, and set them randomly at the center of the altar. [Make] a pool seven feet square and one foot deep. The wine, meat, fasting, and praying, the donning of red clothing, and the bowing and kneeling in a row is the same as in the beginning.

Take a three-year-old cock and a three-year-old boar, and cook them on a spirit altar with four openings. Open up the yin and close off the yang, as in spring.

To seek rain during a late summer [drought],[16] pray to the spirits of the mountains and tumuli to assist [the rituals]. Instruct all the prefectures and towns to

13. A mythical deity of high antiquity, associated with red, the south, and other Five-Phase Fire correlates. He is said to have battled the Yellow Emperor for supremacy among the ancient sage-rulers but was defeated by him.
14. Third and fourth days of the ten-day cycle.
15. *Si kong se fu* 司空嗇夫.
16. This artificial "fifth season" of high summer was added to the calendar to conform to Five-Phase theory; see chapter 42, note 4. The same arrangement is found in chapter 5, "Seasonal Rules," in Major et al., *Huainanzi*, 5.6, 189–90.

relocate their markets outside the southern gate of the towns for ten days. For five days, prohibit young men from going into the markets. Members of households sacrifice to the central ridgepole [god]. Do not initiate any tasks involving earth. Assemble the shamankas beside the markets, and make a canopy for them.

Construct an earthen altar in the center of the city, with openings on all four sides [and measuring five feet square]. Set out on it five pieces of yellow silk. The presiding spirit is Lord Millet.[17] Sacrifice to Lord Millet with five servings of fried pickled meat with millet and dark wine.

Prepare clear wine and cured meat.[18] Pray and fast for three days, and don yellow clothing, all similar to the spring sacrifice.

On a *wu* or *ji* day,[19] fashion one large yellow dragon that is fifty feet long, to position at the center. Again, fashion four smaller dragons, each twenty-five feet long, to be placed to the south. All dragons face south, separated from one another by a distance of five feet. Five men in their prime fast for three days, don yellow clothing, and dance [around] the dragons. Five elders, also having fasted for three days and donned yellow clothing, [are the ones who] erect [the dragons]. Also excavate a tunnel through the altar of the soil to connect it with a water course beyond the city gate. Take five frogs, and set them randomly at the center of the altar. [Make] a pool five feet square and one foot deep. All the remaining instructions are the same as before.[20]

[To seek rain during an] autumn [drought], expose shamankas and emaciated persons [to the sun] for nine days. Do not initiate any activities involving fire or cook in metal vessels. Members of households sacrifice to the gate [god].

Construct an earthen altar outside the western gate of the city, with openings on all four sides and [measuring] nine feet square. Set out on it nine pieces of

17. A mythical deity of high antiquity, associated with the center, yellow, and the phase Earth. Lord Millet was considered the founding ancestor of the Zhou royal clan.
18. Treating the three characters *ling ming wei* 令名爲 as excrescent, following Lu Wenchao (Lai, *CQFLJZJY* 404, note 7).
19. Fifth and sixth days of the ten-day cycle.
20. Treating as excrescent the two lines from *The Divine Farmer Seeks Rain* at 74/73/23–24 (Lai, *CQFLJZJY* 73, note 13):

> If on the nineteenth day it has not rained on a *wu* or *ji* day, order the construction of a yellow dragon and also the construction of a large dragon. The celebrants dance around them and set them up in accordance with the season. It also is said: In the east, young children dance around them; in the south, men in their prime [dance around them]; in the west, diseased men [dance around them]; and in the north, commoners dance around them.

white silk. The presiding spirit is Shao Hao.[21] Sacrifice to Shao Hao with paulownia wood, nine fish, and dark wine.

Prepare clear wine and cured meat. Don white clothing. The rest is similar to the spring sacrifice.

On a *geng* or *xin* day,[22] fashion one large white dragon that is ninety feet long, to position at the center. Again, fashion eight smaller dragons, each forty-five feet long, to be placed to the west. All dragons face west, separated from one another by a distance of nine feet. Nine widowers fast for three days, don white clothing, and dance [around] the dragons. Commanders, also having fasted for three days and donned white clothing, [are the ones who] erect [the dragons].

The pool for the frogs is nine feet square and one foot deep. All the remaining instructions are the same as before.

[To seek rain during a] winter [drought], dance the dragon [dance] for six days. Pray to renowned mountains to assist [the rites]. Members of households sacrifice to the well [god]. Do not impede [the flow of] water.

Construct an earthen altar outside the northern gate of the city, with openings on all four sides and [measuring] six feet square. Set out on it six pieces of black silk. The presiding spirit is Xuan Ming.[23] Sacrifice to Xuan Ming with six young black dogs and dark wine.

Prepare clear wine and cured meat. Pray and fast for three days and don black clothing. The rest is similar to the spring sacrifice. The rites for the invocation are similar to spring.

On a *ren* or *gui* day,[24] fashion one large black dragon that is sixty feet long, to position at the center. Again, fashion five smaller dragons, each thirty feet long, to be placed to the north. All dragons face north, separated from one another by a distance of six feet. Six elders fast for three days, don black clothing, and dance [around] the dragons. Bailiffs, also having fasted for three days and donned black clothing, [are the ones who] erect [the dragons].

The frogs and pool all are the same as [the instructions for] spring. [74/72/19–74/7]

21. A mythical deity of high antiquity, associated with the west, white, and the phase Metal.
22. Seventh and eighth days of the ten-day cycle.
23. A mythical deity of high antiquity, associated with the north, black, and the phase Water.
24. Ninth and tenth days of the ten-day cycle.

Section 74.2

During [each of] the four seasons, in every case on a Water day, construct a dragon. You must take pure clay to construct it. Bind and cover the dragon. When the dragon is completed, discard [the cords and cover]. During the four seasons, in every case on a *gengzi* day,[25] order the wives and husbands among the officials and commoners to have sexual intercourse. In general, when seeking rain, the main point is that men should be withdrawn and secluded and women should be harmonious and joyous.[26] [74/74/9–10]

25. Thirty-seventh day of the sexagenary cycle.
26. Treating as excrescent the line from *The Book of the Divine Farmer* at 74/74/12 (*CQFL* 74, note 2): "It is also said: Open up [the shrines of] the spirits of mountains and the spirits of chasms. Pile up firewood. At night, beat drums; make a great racket until [the throats of the celebrants] are parched; keep this up until dawn."

Book 16, Part 4

CHAPTER 75

Stopping Rain

Section 75.1

When rain is excessive, order the [officials of] prefectures and counties to select an Earth day[1] to seal up irrigation canals, block off channels, and cover wells. Prohibit women from going into the market. Order all the prefectures, districts, and hamlets to sweep out the altars of the god of the soil. Send down orders to the prefectures and counties that if there are three or more assistants, chief clerks, and bailiffs, one of them [from each category] should serve as an invoker. If there are three or more functionaries under the county bailiff, one of them should serve as an invoker. If there are three or more elders in the hamlets and counties, one of them should serve as an invoker. In every case, the invokers should fast for three days, each wearing clothing appropriate to the season. Prepare a young pig, grain, salt, and wine sufficient for the altar of the god of the soil. Beat the drums for three days. The invokers first bow twice and then kneel down, arranging themselves in a row. They again bow twice before rising. The invokers [then] say: "Alas! Heaven gives birth to the five [kinds of] grain in order to nourish humanity. Now the rain is excessive. The five [kinds of] grain are not in harmony [with Heaven]. We respectfully present this fattened sacrificial animal and pure wine to implore the god of the soil to favor us by stopping the rain, thereby eradicating the people's hardships. Do not let the yin destroy the yang. When the yin destroys the yang, this does not accord with Heaven.

1. That is, a day designated *wu* 戊 or *ji* 己, the fifth and sixth days in the ten-day cycle.

It is the constant intent of Heaven to benefit human beings. We human beings wish to stop the rain, so we dare announce [our distress] to the god of the soil." Beat the drums but do not chant. Arriving at the end [of the ceremony], the rain will stop. [75/74/16–22]

Section 75.2

In general, when stopping rain, the main point is that women should hide themselves away in seclusion and men should unite together in joy. Open up the yang, and block up the yin. Obstruct water and liberate fire. Take a vermilion cord, and encircle the [altar of the] god of the soil ten times. Wear vermilion clothing and a vermilion cap. After three days, [the rain will] stop. [75/74/22–23]

Section 75.3

In the twenty-first year,[2] in the eighth month, on a day designated *gengshen*, the month having begun on the day designated *bingwu*,[3] the administrator of Jiangdu, [Dong] Zhongshu, notified the clerk of the capital and the commandant of the capital: "The yin rain has persisted for some time, and [I] fear that it will damage the five [kinds of] grain. Let us hasten to stop the rain. The rite for stopping the rain dispels the yin and arouses the yang. Notify the seventeen prefectures, eighty separate districts, and all officials of the capital [with an annual salary of] one thousand bushels[4] and below as follows: Those men who hold office should instruct their wives to return to their homes. Prohibit women from entering the market, and do not allow those who are in the market to go to the wells. Cover the wells so they do not leak water. Beat the drums, and offer a sacrificial animal at the altar of the god of the soil. Pray to the god of the soil saying: 'The rain already has been excessive. The five

2. The twenty-first year of King Yi, the ruler of the kingdom of Jiangdu, corresponds to 133 B.C.E. Dong Zhongshu served as the administrator of Jiangdu from ca. 134 to 130 B.C.E. For a chronology of his life, see Sarah A. Queen, *From Chronicle to Canon: The Hermeneutics of the "Spring and Autumn" According to Tung Chung-shu* (Cambridge: Cambridge University Press, 1996), chap. 1. Michael Loewe dates this precisely to November 10, 134 B.C.E., in "The Cult of the Dragon and the Invocation for Rain," in *Chinese Ideas About Nature and Society: Studies in Honour of Derk Bodde*, ed. Charles Le Blanc and Susan Blader (Hong Kong: Hong Kong University Press, 1987), 211.

3. *Gengshen* 庚申 is the fifty-seventh day and *bingwu* 丙午 is the forty-third day of the sexagenary cycle.

4. During the Han dynasty, the annual salary of officials was calculated in bushels of grain.

[kinds of] grain are not harmonious. We respectfully present this fattened sacrificial animal to implore the god of the soil to favor us by stopping the rain, thereby eradicating the people's hardships. Do not let the yin destroy the yang. When the yin destroys the yang, it does not comply with Heaven. It is the constant intent of Heaven to bring benefit to its people. We implore you to stop the rain, so we dare make these pronouncements.' Then they drummed and presented the sacrificial animal at the altar of the soil. All this was done [beginning] on a *xinhai* day.[5] When the written orders arrived, [the officials] immediately arose; the district magistrates of the prefectures and towns, the heads of departments, the bailiffs of the city and town altars, and the village chiefs and village attendants all went out and assembled at the altar of the soil. At the time of the evening meal, [the ceremonies] stopped. After three days, [the rituals] were brought to a close. Before the three days were up, the sky cleared and [the rain] stopped. [75/74/25–31]

5. The forty-eighth day of the sexagenary cycle.

Book 16, Part 5

CHAPTER 76

The Principles of Sacrificial Rites

Section 76.1

The essential nature of the five grains and other foodstuffs is that they are things that Heaven bestows on the people. The foodstuffs maturing during the four seasons that are offered at the ancestral temples are the gifts that the people receive from Heaven, and [they therefore] offer them at the ancestral temples. This is an expression of utmost reverence, and to devote them for use as sacrificial offerings is most suitable. The sacrificial offerings of the ancestral temple are the highest expression of the plenitude of things.

In spring, one presents the fruits of the Dou vessel;
in summer, one presents the fruits of the Suan vessel;
in autumn, one presents the fruits of the Gui vessel;
in winter, one presents the fruits of the Dui vessel.[1]

"Fruits of the Dou vessel" mean scallions, which are the first crop to emerge in the spring.[2]

"Fruits of the Suan vessel" means cooked wheat, which is the first [grain] received in the summer.[3]

"Fruits of the Gui vessel" means glutinous panicled millet, which is the first [grain] to mature in the autumn.

1. *Dou* 豆, *suan* 筭, *gui* 机, and *dui* 敦 all are specific types of bronze vessels used in performing the ancestral rites.
2. Emending *chun zhi shi suo sheng ye* 春之始所生 to *chun zhi suo shi sheng* 春之所始生 to restore parallelism with the three following lines.
3. Emending *xia zhi suo shou chu* 夏之所受初也 to *xia zhi suo chu shou* 夏之所初受也 to restore parallelism with the preceding line and the two following lines.

"Fruits of the Dui vessel" means paddy rice, which is the last [grain] to mature in the winter.

Being the first to emerge in the spring, [the sacrifice of scallions] is called "Ci"[4] to commend [its ability] "to take control";

being the first received in the summer,[5] [the sacrifice of wheat] is called "Yue" to honor [its ability] "to ferment";[6]

being the first to mature [*cheng*] in the autumn, [the sacrifice of glutinous panicled millet] is called "Chang" [to taste], which means "sweet" (*gan*);[7]

being the last to ripen [*shu*] in the winter, [the sacrifice of newly harvested rice] is called "Zheng" [steam], which means "numerous" (*zhong*).[8]

To present and offer what is received from Heaven during the four seasons constitutes the four sacrifices.[9] They venerate Heaven's gifts and honor the ancestral temple. Upon receiving his lord's gifts, Confucius always offered a sacrifice; how much more so when Confucius received Heaven's gifts! Within the span of a single year, Heaven's gifts arrive four times. When they arrive, one makes offerings. This is why there are four sacrifices a year at the ancestral temple.

There is not a single noble man who does not [wish to] eat freshly harvested foodstuffs. But when the gifts of Heaven arrive, [the noble man] invariably first presents them at the ancestral temple, and only then does he dare partake of them. Such is the heart that venerates Heaven and is respectful of the ancestral temple. To venerate Heaven is to beautify righteousness; to show respect for the ancestral temple is to make much of the rites. Now the sage was extremely cautious of such matters, so

he did not begrudge[10] that the sacrificial victims were numerous but desired [only] that they be unblemished.

He did not begrudge that the sacrifices were incessant, but desired [only] to be reverent and respectful.

---

4. Ci 祠. In this and the following three sentences, the meaning depends on the partial graphic and phonetic similarity of the paired terms: Ci 祠 (the name of a sacrifice) and *si* 司 (to take control), and so on.
5. Emending *xia yue* 夏約 to *chu shou* 初受 to restore parallelism, following Lai, *CQFLJZJY* 412, note 15.
6. After reviewing a variety of suggested emendations, we have emended *gui suo chu yue ye* 貴所初礿也 to *gui suo yue ye* 貴所汋也 to yield: 初受故礿, 貴所汋也. Following the *Gongyang Commentary* at Duke Huan 2.8.5, in which this sacrifice is mentioned, He Xiu explains: "When the wheat first ripens, it can be fermented; thus [the sacrifice] is called Yue [meaning to bubble up or ferment]" (麥始熟可汋,故曰汋. 春秋繁露校辭) (Zhong, *CQFLJS* 816, note 18).
7. *Cheng* 成, *chang* 嘗, *gan* 甘.
8. *Shu* 熟, *zheng* 烝, *zhong* 衆.
9. Emending *shang ji* 上祭 to *si ji* 四祭, following Su Yu (Lai, *CQFLJZJY* 412, note 20).
10. Supplying *tan* 歎 between *bu* 不 and *duo* 多, following Su Yu (Lai, *CQFLJZJY* 412, note 23).

When the noble man carries out sacrifice, he does so personally [and] expresses his innermost sincere intentions, manifesting to the fullest the Way of respect and purity to receive with the highest honors [the ancestral spirits]. Thus the ancestral spirits arrive to accept [his offerings]. One who makes offerings in this way can be said to be able to sacrifice. Sacrifice means perspicacity.[11] It refers to being good at reaching the ghosts and spirits. Once good [at reaching the ghosts and spirits], one can reach what cannot be heard or seen. Therefore, it is called "perspicacity." I use the term ["perspicacity"] to refer to what [causes the ghosts and spirits] to accept [the offerings]. Therefore making offerings is not an empty practice. How could it not require perspicacity?

"To sacrifice" also means "to commune." When one offers sacrifices, one then can see what cannot be seen.

> One who sees what cannot be seen can then understand Heaven's commands [concerning] ghosts and spirits.
>
> One who understands Heaven's commands [concerning] ghosts and spirits can then understand the meaning of the sacrifices.
>
> One who understands the meaning of the sacrifices can then understand [the need for] attaching importance to sacrificial matters.

Confucius said: "If I do not take part in a sacrifice, [it is as if I did not sacrifice]. Sacrifice to the spirits as if the spirits were present."[12] One attaches importance to the sacrifices as if one were serving one's living [parents]. Therefore with regard to the ghosts and spirits, the Sage [Confucius]

> feared them and dared not cheat them;
> trusted them but did not count on them alone;
> served them and did not merely rely on them.
> He relied on their generosity to repay those who possessed virtue;
> he relied on their lack of selfishness to bring happiness to the people.

This sentiment can be seen in the *Ode* that states:

> "Oh you noble men!
> Do not reckon your peace and rest will persist.
> Quietly fulfill the duties of your offices.
> Show fondness for the correct and upright.

11. This and the following paragraph rely for their force of meaning on a visual pun among three written characters: *ji* 祭 (sacrifice), *cha* 察 (perspicacity), and *ji* 際 (to commune). The commonality of the written form of these words implied to the *Chunqiu fanlu* author that they also overlapped substantially in meaning.

12. *Analects* 3.12. As quoted here, the passage is somewhat different from the received version.

And the spirits will hear you.
And give you great blessings."[13]

Those who are correct and upright receive blessings. Those who are not correct and not upright do not receive blessings. This is [Heaven's] standard. With this poem, it became a standard for the whole world. What does "not to accord with the standard" mean? The language of the poem is straightforward and repeatedly uses expressions of regret in the hopes that people will examine its intent. But those who still do not examine it: How lost they are! Confucius said: "The weighty documents! The memorable sayings! Aha! One must not let them go unexamined. Surely one will find worthy principles in them."[14] This expresses it. [76/75/3–21]

13. *Odes* 207, verse 4.
14. This quotation, attributed to Confucius, is not in the received canon.

Group 8

Heavenly Principles

WE HAVE named group 8, consisting of five thematically linked chapters, "Heavenly Principles" because all are devoted to clarifying how various political and moral values derived from Heaven are instrumental to the health of the physical body and the body politic. In this respect, this last group exhibits clear affinities with the cosmological chapters found earlier in the *Chunqiu fanlu*, as most contain repetitions and revisit themes that appear in earlier chapters.

GROUP 8: HEAVENLY PRINCIPLES, CHAPTERS 77–82

77. 循天之道 *Xun tian zhi dao* Conform to Heaven's Way
78. 天地之行 *Tian di zhi xing* The Conduct of Heaven and Earth
79. 威德所生 *Wei de suo sheng* The Origins of Severity and Beneficence
80. 如天之為 *Ru tian zhi wei* In Imitation of Heaven's Activities
81. 天地陰陽 *Tian di yin yang* Heaven, Earth, Yin, and Yang
82. 天道施 *Tian dao shi* The Way of Heaven Bestows

Despite their thematic links, these chapters are the worst preserved in the entire collection. They are a ragbag of essay fragments that appear to have been sorted into different chapters according to the similarity of their topics. Their fragmentary condition has inspired many attempts over the centuries by editors and commentators to restore them to some semblance of order. Among them, Su Yu has provided the most coherent arrangements. Consequently, in addition to our translation of the standard D. C. Lau text, we have translated Su Yu's arrangements for those chapters (78, 80, 81, and 82) that depart from that text, and our discussions of them follow Su Yu rather than Lau. The Su Yu versions of these chapters are numbered 78A, 80A, 81A, and 82A.

Description of Individual Chapters

In Su Yu's reconstruction, chapter 77, "Conform to Heaven's Way," is a collection of six essays and essay fragments, all of which address themes germane to nourishing life.[1] These materials apparently are linked to the supposed works of Confucius's famous disciple Gongsun Nizi. We discuss those links in our remarks on dating and attribution. Section 77.1 derives principles for nourishing the body from the annual path of Heaven, with its "two conjunctions" and "two midpoints," the equinoxes and solstices mentioned in several of the chapters in group 5, "Yin-Yang Principles." Section 77.1 echoes these chapters, describing the conjunctions and midpoints and their respective functions and critical roles in the annual cycle of Heaven: "[The myriad things] are completed by a conjunction; their birth also must arise from a conjunction. They begin at a midpoint; their ending also must be at a midpoint. The midpoints are that by which Heaven and Earth begin and end things. The conjunctions are that by which Heaven and Earth engender and complete things."[2] These two aspects of Heaven's yearly cycle are then linked to the ethical values "harmony" and "centrality." The force of the argument here, that ethical principles are derivative of nature's cycles, comes from a clever play on words for the astronomical terms for "midpoint" (*zhong*) and "conjunction" (*he*), which are homophonous with the political/moral value "centrality" (also *zhong*) and "harmony" (also *he*). The essay concludes: "Therefore, the virtue of those who are able to rely on centrality and harmony to govern the world will greatly flourish; the life span of those who are able to rely on centrality and harmony to nourish their bodies will be greatly prolonged."[3]

Section 77.2 develops standards of healthy living and sexual practices for men and women derived from the yearly circuit of yin and yang described in 77.1.

1. For the details of the various number of essays (five or six) in this chapter in the various editions of the *Chunqiu fanlu*, see chapter 77, first note.
2. *CQFL* 77/75/30–76/1.
3. *CQFL* 77/75/25–76/3.

By imitating these natural cycles, people can make themselves healthy and long-lived. They also can ensure that their sexual unions will synchronize with those times that are optimal for procreation without being excessive (and thus impairing longevity).

Section 77.3 addresses "midpoints" and "conjunctions" once again, but in this essay the conjunctions of Heaven and Earth are said to "represent the balance points of Heaven and the equilibrium of yin and yang." These cosmic moments, in turn, provide the template for human beings wishing to restore the harmony and centrality of their own persons so as to promote longevity. The specific techniques to do so take as their point of departure Mencius's claim to have developed techniques to nourish his "floodlike *qi*." Section 77.3 expands on this theme with a long citation from Gongsun Nizi's work *Nourishing Qi*, which enumerates the various decentering and disharmonious conditions that are injurious to one's bodily *qi*. When such conditions arise, the noble man takes concerted steps to revert to the norms of centrality and harmony within his person: "when angry [he] reverts to centrality by satisfying his *qi* with harmony; when happy [he] reverts to centrality by collecting his *qi* with uprightness; when worried [he] reverts to centrality by calming his *qi* with determination; when startled [he] reverts to centrality by solidifying his *qi* with refinement." The key to restoring these desired states, the essay continues, is the mind within (*nei xin*), because the bodily *qi* invariably follows the mind. With the mind properly balanced, *qi* will flow through the four extremities of the body, promoting health and long life. Thus nourishing and regulating the *qi* with a centered mind is the key. The noble man understands these truths and therefore deeply cherishes his bodily *qi*. Even when enjoying "the pleasures of the bedchamber," he matches Heaven's timeliness, regulating his sexual activities with the rhythms of the cosmos so as not to harm or dissipate his bodily *qi*:

> [W]hen he has just entered puberty, he seeks pleasure in the bed chamber once every ten days; when he is in his middle years, he doubles the interval of the adolescent; when he has just begun to decline, he doubles the interval of the middle-aged man; when he has arrived at his middle years of decline, he doubles the interval of the man just entering his declining years; and when he is well into his years of decline, he takes a month for each of the adolescent's days, thereby identifying his self-regulation with that of Heaven and Earth above.[4]

4. *CQFL* 77/77/8–10.

Therefore, people must cherish their Heavenly *qi* as they naturally cherish clothing and food. But unlike these rudiments of life that can be replenished when exhausted, when one's bodily *qi* is used up, it cannot be replenished and death is inevitable. Therefore, the essay concludes, nothing is more essential than the *qi* for nourishing life.

With the essay fragment preserved in section 77.4, the reader encounters the argument well after it has begun. From what survives of the original essay, it appears that it described how the noble man directs the people to consume certain foods beneficial to the body and to avoid those that are harmful. Diet is thus correlated with the rhythms of Heaven, which is said to ripen certain grains at certain times of the year to nourish the various species of living things.[5] Section 77.6 returns to the themes of centrality and harmony and their benefit for achieving longevity, but here longevity is discussed in relation to the allotted life span that people receive at birth:

> Attaining the eminence of Heaven and Earth extends and lengthens one's life span; failing to attain the eminence of Heaven and Earth harms and shortens one's life span. The basic substance of a long or short [life span] is something that human beings receive from Heaven. . . . But whether they live out their life span or die prematurely rests with their own actions. For those who through their own actions follow the Way of longevity, their life span is comparatively long; for those who through their own actions do not follow the Way of longevity, their life span is comparatively less long.[6]

Longevity, then, is partly a matter of fate, but it is also partly under the control of individuals, who can enhance or diminish their fated life spans.

Chapter 78A, "The Conduct of Heaven and Earth," consists of two essays, both of which articulate general standards of conduct for the ruler and his ministers. Section 78A.1 correlates the roles of the ruler and his ministers with Heaven and Earth, and section 78A.2 makes an analogy between the ruler and his ministers with different parts of the human body. Section 78A.1, as mentioned in the introduction to group 2, "Monarchical Principles," appears to be either a more complete recension or a later reworking of the essay preserved in chapter 18, "Departing from and Conforming to the Fundamental." There are

5. *CQFL* 77/77/18–21.
6. *CQFL* 77/77/23–25.

some telling differences between these two essays that suggest the second possibility is more likely. Using cosmological notions such as *qi*, yin and yang, and quintessence, section 78A.1 details the ways in which Heaven and Earth provide standards of conduct for the ruler and his ministers, whereas such concepts do not appear in chapter 18. Moreover, it identifies the ruler with the Way of Yang, whereas chapter 18 emphasizes the ruler's non-active attributes. Section 78A.1 emphasizes the importance of the minister's loyalty to his ruler, as in chapter 18, but with an even greater emphasis on ethical values typically identified with Confucius. For example, it maintains that the minister is instrumental in assisting the ruler "in becoming a noble man" and identifies as righteous the minister's willingness to attribute his accomplishments to his ruler.

The discussion in section 78A.1 of how the ruler secures worthy and capable men to staff his bureaucracy is far more elaborate than that in chapter 18, depicting a ruler who enjoys a more symbiotic relationship with his ministers. The ruler leads his ministers by implementing a series of bureaucratic techniques that emphasize impartiality, constancy, and transparency and that allow the ruler to promote men based on reliable criteria. The result is that capable men are employed, the worthy are attracted to his court, those who truly possess merit are promoted, and those who do not are demoted. For their part, the ministers who emulate Earth dedicate themselves to their ruler, deriving honor from their accomplishments, healing the ruler when ill, sacrificing their lives if necessary, and serving without thoughts of usurpation. In short, they apply themselves to the utmost to promote the ruler's excellence. This symbiotic vision of the ruler-minister relation has none of the negative attitude toward ministers found in chapter 18, in which the ruler is advised to hide from his ministers and take on the mysterious and recondite qualities of a spirit.

Section 78A.2, as in chapter 22, "Comprehending the State as the Body," views the body politic as analogous to the human body. In this instance, the ruler of a unified state is likened to the mind of a unified body: the mind ideally works in concert with the components of the body, just as the ruler ideally works in concert with the components of his bureaucracy. In such conditions, the ruler attracts auspicious omens, just as the adept summons potent symbols of immortality.

The two essays of chapter 79, "The Origins of Severity and Beneficence," revisit one of the ruler's most important functions: the proper dispensation of rewards and punishment, a theme discussed earlier in chapter 55, "The Correlates of the Four Seasons." They recommend that the ruler dispense rewards and punishments in accordance with models of conduct derived from Heaven.

Section 79.1, like many previous chapters, argues that the principles of governance lie in Heaven. In this case, harmony, beneficence, impartiality, and severity are identified in quite standard fashion with Heaven and its respective seasons of spring, summer, autumn, and winter. Thus the ruler—interestingly referred to here as "the Perfected"—embodies "Heavenly Virtue" by emulating these cosmic patterns.

Section 79.2 begins by reminding the ruler that his awesome power and responsibility over life and death mirror that of the Way of Heaven: "One who would rule others occupies the position of Utmost Potency and grasps the positional advantage of life and death, thereby altering and transforming the people. The people follow their master [just] as the grasses and trees respond to the four seasons." It instructs the ruler to synchronize his happiness, anger, severity, and beneficence with the cold, heat, winter, and summer of Heaven. When he does so, he becomes a "counterpart to Heaven."

Chapter 80A, "In Imitation of Heaven's Activities," has been restored by Su Yu from the two chapter fragments that we identify as sections 80A.1 and 80A.2. The essay begins with themes that by now are thoroughly familiar to the reader of the *Chunqiu fanlu*. It repeats that Heaven and humanity share a characteristic organic unity defined in terms of *qi* and explains that in human beings, this *qi* is manifest as love, hate, happiness, and anger. These four human emotions are correlated with Heaven's heat, cold, warmth, and coolness expressed in the four seasons. These correlations between the emotions and the seasons appeared earlier in chapter 43.2, "Yang Is Lofty, Yin Is Lowly"; chapter 44, "The Kingly Way Penetrates Three"; and chapter 45, "Heaven's Prosperity," in which the ruler's emotional states also were the focus of discussion. Similarly, chapter 80A argues that the ruler's four emotions should not be restrained from issuing forth when he has a desire to express himself, just as Heaven's four climates should not be obstructed when their respective seasons arrive. But then, rather than suggesting, as in earlier chapters, that the ruler should simply regulate his emotions and his policies in accordance with the seasons, the essay modifies these earlier claims to make room for those exceptional circumstances when the ruler is compelled to depart from these seasonal correlations:

> [But] when urgent situations arise, one should not wait for the normal season [to take action]. Such is Heaven's will. The sage receives Heaven's will and governs accordingly. For this reason, in spring he cultivates humaneness and seeks out goodness; in autumn he cultivates righteousness and seeks out evil. . . . This is how he complies with Heaven and Earth and embodies yin and yang.

> Nevertheless, when he has just begun to seek goodness, if he sees evil he does not dismiss it; . . . if he sees a grave malefaction he immediately eradicates it. He thereby imitates . . . Heaven and Earth.[7]

In this way, the essay modifies the claims about the seasonal rules made in the earlier yin-yang chapters, affording the ruler a degree of flexibility not present in earlier versions of that long-standing theory and allowing him to follow seasonal imperatives overall but also to respond to compelling circumstances when necessary.

Chapter 81A, "Heaven, Earth, Yin, and Yang," also has been restored as a continuous essay, thanks to Su Yu. This essay revisits several themes touched on earlier in the *Chunqiu fanlu*—for example in chapter 43, "Yang Is Lofty, Yin Is Lowly"; chapter 52, "Heat or Cold, Which Predominates?"; and chapter 53.5, "Laying the Foundation of Righteousness." As in those earlier chapters, chapter 81A emphasizes the number ten, which is seen as the complete expression of Heaven's numbers. In turn, Heaven's numbers symbolically account for all the essential components of the cosmos: "Heaven, earth, yin, yang, wood, fire, earth, metal, and water constitute nine things. Together with human beings, they total ten, completing Heaven's numerical categories." This Heavenly numerology is key to understanding, in turn, the nobility of humankind, a theme broached in chapter 41, "Heaven, the Maker of Humankind," and chapter 56, "Human Correlates of Heaven's Regularities," and in Dong's memorials to Emperor Wu. Chapter 81A asks, "Why are human beings noble?"[8] and replies, "[It is because] what originates with Heaven extends to human beings [and thus] is brought to completion."[9] The chapter concludes that the ruler must be absolutely vigilant because he is in a position to "stir and shake" the world.

Chapter 82A, "The Way of Heaven Bestows," begins with a claim made earlier in chapter 56.1: "The virtue of Heaven is to bestow; the virtue of Earth is to transform; [and] the virtue of humankind is to be righteous." In section 82A.1, however, the righteousness of humankind is not grounded in the numerical correspondence between Heaven and humankind, as it is in chapter 56; rather, it derives from the rituals that the sage creates. As is also the case in the *Xunzi*, this essay argues that the sage understands the source of depravity and disorder and consequently creates rituals to bring tranquillity to the people. In this

7. *CQFL* 80/83/1–5.
8. Following Yu Yue and Su Yu, treating the character sheng 聖 as excrescent (*CQFLYZ*, 463–464).
9. *CQFL* 81/84/11–14.

way, they can live lives defined by the cardinal Confucian virtue, righteousness: "Now ritual is what embodies the emotions and prevents disorder. Human emotions cannot control desires, so we cause them to be regulated by the rites [so that] the eyes gaze on correct colors; the ears listen to correct sounds; the mouth savors correct flavors; and the person carries out the correct Way."[10] This does not mean, however, that people are encouraged to become ascetics.

After all, emotions are internal and integral to human nature, but the influences that stimulate the emotions to manifest themselves clearly are external. Although such external influences may become so habitual as to appear to be part of human nature, and therefore part of the very self that defines humankind, to assume that they are part of the self is a mistake. The essay concludes: "[It is] like a discarded cicada skin [lying] amid turbidity and filth: how could it muster the means to affect you? To follow along with the myriad things but not lose the [essence of] the self—this is the mind of the sage."[11]

Section 82A.2 revisits the important Confucian theory of the rectification of names, a subject treated extensively in chapter 35, "Deeply Examine Names and Designations." In a manner similar to that in chapter 35, this essay interprets the *Spring and Autumn* to be an expression of this critical approach to naming:

> The terminology [of the *Spring and Autumn*] does not conceal the true nature of things. It illuminates the true nature of things but does not neglect proper terminology. If people's minds follow it and do not struggle against it, it will penetrate and connect the ancient and contemporary without the least disorder. Such are the righteous principles of [its use of] names.[12]

The names and designations of the *Spring and Autumn* follow the Human Way, which uses varied expressions of propriety and righteousness that, in turn, deviate from or comply with the Way of Heaven. Thus the careful reader who observes the distinctions expressed in the *Spring and Autumn* will ultimately come to understand its underlying moral message and learn to "find joy in the rites." Given the fragmentary quality of this material, this section may very well once have been part of chapter 35 and certainly should be read today alongside that chapter. Or this may be all that remains of an independent essay that found justification for the rectification of names in the terminology of the *Spring and*

10. *CQFL* 82/85/27–28.
11. *CQFL* 82/86/2–3.
12. *CQFL* 82/86/5–6.

Autumn. Whatever the case, this essay once again illuminates the ways in which Gongyang exegetes linked Confucian theories to the subtle language of the *Spring and Autumn*.

Issues of Dating and Attribution

We suggested earlier that most of the chapters of group 8 revisit themes addressed in those of group 5, "Yin-Yang Principles." Some, in fact, repeat verbatim lines that appear in these earlier essays, showing the close links and affinities to these writings. The following list clarifies these affinities:

GROUP 8: "HEAVENLY PRINCIPLES"	EARLIER CHAPTERS OF *CHUNQIU FANLU*
Chapters 77.1 and 77.3	Chapter 48
Chapter 78A.1	Chapter 18
Chapter 78A.2	Chapter 22
Chapter 79	Chapter 55
Chapter 80A	Chapters 43, 44, and 45
Chapter 81A	Chapters 41, 43, 52, and 53.5
Chapter 82A.1	Chapter 56.1
Chapter 82A.2	Chapter 35

A closer look at these repetitions and affinities uncovers clues to understanding the general structure of the text as well as the dating and attribution of these chapters.

By now, the reader must recognize the poor condition of the *Chunqiu fanlu*, having already encountered numerous instances in which we have pointed out the fragmented nature and questionable arrangement of materials in many of the chapters. This last group of chapters is in the worst condition, which may account for their placement at the end of the text; they seem like leftovers. The content of these chapters, with their thematic links to the earlier group 2, "Monarchical Principles"; group 5, "Yin-Yang Principles"; and group 6, "Five-Phase Principles," would indicate that they properly belong with them. So in this respect, the archaeology of the *Chunqiu fanlu* illuminates important underlying and pervasive features of the text. It once again suggests the existence of an unknown compiler intent on preserving all he could find that was relevant to and associated with Gongyang Learning in the Han, no matter how garbled or fragmented the materials.

Chapter 78A, "The Conduct of Heaven and Earth," repeats many lines that appear in chapter 18, "Departing from and Conforming to the Fundamental," although here we find a much fuller account of the themes found in chapter 18.

Chapter 79, "The Origins of Severity and Beneficence," draws on Heaven to establish guidelines for how the ruler should reward and punish the populace, as does chapter 55, "The Correlates of the Four Seasons."

Chapter 80A, "In Imitation of Heaven's Activities," develops arguments that the ruler's emotional states should be restrained and regulated in accordance with their seasonal correlations, as does chapter 43.2, "Yang Is Lofty, Yin Is Lowly"; chapter 44, "The Kingly Way Penetrates Three"; and chapter 45, "Heaven's Prosperity." Here, once again, we find resonances with earlier arguments that are developed and modified in new ways.

Chapter 81A, "Heaven, Earth, Yin, and Yang," revisits several themes touched on earlier in the *Chunqiu fanlu*, for example, in chapter 43, "Yang Is Lofty, Yin Is Lowly"; chapter 52, "Heat or Cold, Which Predominates"; and chapter 53.5, "Laying the Foundation of Righteousness."

In chapter 82A, "The Way of Heaven Bestows," section 82.1 repeats the opening claim of chapter 56.1, "Human Correlates of Heaven's Regularities," but seeks the ontological origins of humankind's righteousness not in correlations with Heaven but as the product of rituals created by the sages of the past. Once again, we find a new development of a theme addressed earlier in the text.

These links to earlier chapters in the *Chunqiu fanlu* have several possible explanations. They may indicate that over the centuries, these chapters migrated from their original locations earlier in the text to the end of the collection. Or perhaps the anonymous compiler purposefully placed these chapters at the end of the text precisely because they were later productions, essays that consciously addressed earlier themes but developed them in new ways. Or they may be here as added materials, the last gleanings of Gongyang materials available to the compiler. Whatever the case, they are generally in keeping with the larger contours of the *Chunqiu fanlu* and the spirit of Gongyang Learning that permeates other parts of the text. They are equally valuable for understanding the ways in which Gongyang Learning developed during the Han dynasty and the approaches taken by exegetes of this tradition to address the institutional issues of that period.

The Arts of Nourishing Life: Chapters 78A.2 and 77.2

What about the two chapters in this group that do not have links to earlier chapters? How can they be contextualized? The essays and essay fragments in chapter 77, "Conform to Heaven's Way," and in chapter 78A.2, "The Conduct of Heaven and Earth," contain themes and express concerns not seen in earlier chapters of the *Chunqiu fanlu*: they recommend a panoply of bodily techniques and sexual practices to promote health, longevity, and immortality. Rather than simply dismiss these essays as spurious because there is no historical evidence linking Dong Zhongshu to a "nourishing-life" (*yang sheng*) tradition, we prefer to ask: How did essays on nourishing life, longevity, and immortality find their way into a collection attributed to a Confucian scholar working in the tradition of Gongyang Learning during the middle years of the Western Han? The answer may lie in a tradition of hagiography with roots in the Western Han. To identify these roots, we must digress briefly to *Traditions of Divine Transcendents* (*Shen xian zhuan* 神仙傳), the hagiographical collection attributed to Ge Hong (283–343). There, in a classic conversion story, we find a narrative describing Li Shaojun that links Dong Zhongshu to one of the most famous nourishing-life practitioners of the Han period. At the outset of the story, Dong is adamantly opposed to the practices proposed, in this case a certain medicinal regimen. The more opposed he is, however, the more dramatic the conversion is:

> In the beginning, Li Shaojun had been a close friend of Court Gentleman for Consultation Dong Zhongshu. Seeing that Dong was bedridden with a chronic illness, his body withered and his breath shallow, Li produced two doses of medicine for him along with instructions.... But Dong Zhongshu was stubborn and upright in his ways. He had studied the Five Classics extensively but had never attained an understanding of arts of the Dao. He often scoffed at people of the world for ingesting drugs and practicing the Dao. He presented memorials to Emperor Wu arguing that human life was limited by an allotted life span and that aging was a naturally given process, so that [human life] was not something that arts of the Dao could possibly lengthen. He maintained that even if there were apparent exceptions to this rule, they were due to natural endowment, not to these arts. So, when he obtained [Li's] medicine, he did not take it, nor did he ask for the method for making it.[13]

13. Robert Ford Campany, *To Live as Long as Heaven and Earth: A Translation and Study of Ge Hong's Traditions of Divine Transcendents* (Berkeley: University of California Press, 2002), 224.

Only when Dong's illness takes a turn for the worse does he begin to warm to the practices of the nourishing-life tradition:

> Several months after Li Shaojun had departed, Dong Zhongshu's illness worsened. When he heard Emperor Wu speak on several occasions about his dream and how regretful he was about the loss of Li, he remembered the medicine Li had given him. He tried taking less than half a dose: his body grew light and strong, and his illness was suddenly healed. Then he took a full dose, his breath and strength were as they had been when he was young. Only now did he believe that there was a way of long life and deathlessness. He quit his official post and traveled in search of a master of the Dao whom he could ask about the method [for making the drug he had taken]. He never succeeded in grasping all of it; he only managed to prevent his hair from going white and to stay very healthy. Only when he was more than eighty years old did he finally die. Before that, he told his son, Daosheng, "When I was still young, I obtained Li Shaojun's esoteric medicine. At first I didn't believe in it; after I used it, I regained strength, but then I was never able to grasp [the method for making] it. I will carry this regret with me to the Yellow Springs. You must go and search among people for a master of esoteric arts, someone who can explain the meaning of this method. If you persist in taking this medicine, you will certainly transcend the world."[14]

Robert Campany explains: "Dong Zhongshu's portrayed conversion is a powerful apologetic device: the sometime skeptic who, badly ill, takes the proffered medicine and by its results becomes convinced—too late to save himself—of the efficacy of the arts of transcendence."[15]

In addition to this conversion story, Ge Hong supplies a further link between Dong Zhongshu and Li Shaojun, portraying Dong as the author of the "Family Records of Li Shaojun" (李少君家錄). Dong also appears in the hagiography of Wang Xing, in which he is described as fasting and meditating on the gods in a Daoist meditation chamber at the behest of Wang Xing while accompanying Emperor Wu on a pilgrimage to Mount Song.[16]

Even though no historical sources confirm that Dong actually took up the longevity arts, these references, as well as the ascription to Dong Zhongshu of a book describing Li Shaojun's esoteric methods, demonstrates that by the

14. Campany, *To Live as Long as Heaven and Earth*, 225.
15. Campany, *To Live as Long as Heaven and Earth*, 226.
16. Campany, *To Live as Long as Heaven and Earth*, 226–27, 341.

late third to early fourth century, Dong had become associated with the quest for immortality. In addition, a reading of Ge Hong's works shows that he was undiscriminating in his acceptance of tales of life-nourishing techniques. Living in a world in which Dong Zhongshu was said to have promoted the arts of nourishing life as well as the Confucian tradition of Gongyang Learning, our anonymous compiler had ample reason to include chapters 77 and 78 in a comprehensive collection of the works of Dong Zhongshu and his disciples.

Book 16, Part 6

CHAPTER 77

Conform to Heaven's Way

Section 77.1

Conforming to Heaven's Way to nourish the body is called the Way. Heaven has two conjunctions[1] and thereby completes two midpoints.[2] It yearly establishes its midpoints, employing them ceaselessly. Thus,

The title of the chapter derives from the opening lines of the first section. The composition of the chapter varies across the extant editions of the *Chunqiu fanlu*. Ling Shu's *Chunqiu fanlu* of 1816, Su Yu's *Chunqiu fanlu yizheng* of 1910, and Lai Yanyuan's *Chunqiu fanlu jinzhu jinyi* of 1984 all contain six sections. The *Sibu congkan* and *Chunqiu fanlu zhuzi suoyin* (Lau) editions contain five sections, and the *Sibu beiyao* preserves four sections. We have included all the sections in our translation. The various editions share the following materials:

SECTIONS	1	2	3	4	5	6
CQFL (D. C. Lau)	X	X	X		X	X
CQFL[LS] (Ling Shu)	X	X	X	X	X	X
CQFLJZJY (Lai Yanyuan)	X	X	X	X	X	X
CQFLYZ (Su Yu)	X	X	X	X	X	X
CQFL SBCK (*Sibu congkan*)	X	X	X		X	X
CQFL SBBY (*Sibu beiyao*)	X	X	X			X

The six sections in the *CQFLYZ* are made up of fragments of six originally separate essays. The Chinese text of the fourth section of *CQFLJZJY* 77 and *CCFLYZ* 77 may be found at *CQFL* 78/78/10–23.

1. *Liang he* 兩和 refers to the spring and autumn equinoxes.
2. *Liang zhong* 兩中 refers to the summer and winter solstices. Some of the force of the argument in section 77.1 comes from a play on words: between the astronomical/calendrical term "midpoint" (*zhong*) and the political/moral value "centrality" (also *zhong*), and between the astronomical/calendrical term "conjunction" (*he*) and the political/moral value "harmony" (also *he*).

the midpoint of the northern region [i.e., the winter solstice][3] employs blended yin, and the myriad things begin to move below [the ground].

The midpoint of the southern region [i.e., the summer solstice][4] employs blended yang, and the [process of] nourishment begins to perfect [things] above [the ground].

When [the myriad things] stir below [the ground], without the conjunction of the eastern region, they would not be able to come into existence. This refers to the middle month of spring [i.e., the spring equinox].[5]

When [the myriad things] flourish above, without the conjunction of the western region, they would not be able to mature. This refers to the middle month of autumn [i.e., the autumn equinox].[6]

It follows that the good and evil of Heaven and Earth reside at the two places of conjunction [in the eastern and western regions] and where the midpoints come from and return to as they complete their tasks. Thus

the conjunction of the eastern region brings things into existence;

the conjunction of the western region brings things to maturity.

That the conjunction of the eastern region produces birth is due to what arises in the northern region;

that the conjunction of the western region brings things to maturity is due to what is nourished in the southern region.

With regard to their giving rise to things, if they do not arrive at the place of the conjunction, things will not be able to produce and grow.

With regard to their nourishing things, if they do not arrive at the place of the conjunction, things will not be able to mature and ripen.

[The myriad things] are completed by a conjunction; their birth also must arise from a conjunction.

---

3. *Beifang zhi zhong* 北方之中 refers to the eleventh month, in which the yin and yang meet in the northern quadrant and give rise to the winter solstice. Chapter 50.1, states: "Yin comes westward from the eastern quarter, and yang comes eastward from the western quarter. Arriving at the middle month of winter, they meet each other in the northern quarter, where they combine to become one. This is called the ['winter] solstice.'"

4. *Nanfang zhi zhong* 南方之中 refers to the fifth month, in which yin and yang unite in the southern quadrant and give rise to the summer solstice. Chapter 50.1 explains: "Yin daily decreases and gives way to yang; yang daily increases and strengthens. Thus warmth and heat are produced. At the beginning of the month of the height of summer, [yin and yang] meet each other in the southern quarter where they combine to become one. This is called the ['summer] solstice.'"

5. Chapter 50.1 states: "Arriving at the middle month of spring, yang lies due east, and yin lies due west. This is called the 'spring equinox.' At the spring equinox, yin and yang are evenly divided. Therefore, day and night are of even length; cold and heat are of equal proportion."

6. Chapter 50.1 states: "Arriving at the middle month of autumn, yang lies due west, and yin lies due east. This is called the 'autumn equinox.' At the autumn equinox, yin and yang are evenly divided. Therefore, day and night are of even length; cold and heat are of equal proportion."

They begin at a midpoint; their ending also must be at a midpoint.
The midpoints are that by which Heaven and Earth begin and end things.
The conjunctions are that by which Heaven and Earth engender and complete things.

Now,

there is no virtue greater than harmony.
There is no way more correct than centrality.

With centrality, the perfection of Heaven and Earth penetrates the underlying principles [of all living things]. It is what the sage preserves and protects. An ode declares:

"Neither hard nor soft. Gently he spreads his instructions abroad."[7]

Does this not refer to centrality and harmony? Therefore,

the virtue of those who are able to rely on centrality and harmony to govern the world will greatly flourish;
the life span of those who are able to rely on centrality and harmony to nourish their bodies will be greatly prolonged. [77/75/25–77/76/3]

Section 77.2

The standards for men and women emulate yin and yang.

Yang *qi* arises in the northern region and flourishes when reaching the southern region.
When its flourishing reaches its end point, it unites with yin.
Yin *qi* arises during the middle month of summer [i.e., at the summer solstice] and flourishes when reaching the middle month of winter [i.e., at the winter solstice].
When its flourishing has reached its end point, it unites with yang.

If they did not reach their end points, they would not [be able to] unite. Thus in ten months,[8] each flourishes once, and at the end of the year they join together again. The long-standing regularities of Heaven and Earth are constant in this way. Thus, first imitate them within your person. Nourish the body and thereby make it whole.

7. *Odes* 304, verse 4.
8. One commentator suggests emending ten months to six months. But 43.1, says that yang dominates for ten months of the year and yin dominates for the other two.

If a man is impotent, do not allow him to form a household;
if [her] yin *qi* is not at its height, do not allow [a woman] to engage in sex.

When the body's essence is bright, it will not readily decline, and [the body will] remain strong and stable. Longevity is dependent on a lack of excessiveness. This is the Way of Heaven and Earth.

Heaven's *qi* first causes maleness to flourish and only then produces semen. Therefore the semen is strong.
Earth's *qi* first causes femaleness to flourish and only then produces transformation.
Thus its transformations are good.

Therefore, with regard to the union of yin and yang,

in winter they unite in the north, and the myriad things begin to stir below;
in summer they unite in the south, and the myriad things begin to stir above.

The great stirrings above and below both take place after the [winter and summer] solstices.

When cold, it freezes water and cracks earth.
When hot, it burns sand and melts stone.

The quintessential *qi* achieves such things as this. Therefore, with the transformations of Heaven and Earth,

spring *qi* engenders, and all living things emerge;
summer *qi* nourishes, and all living things grow;
autumn *qi* kills, and all living things die;
and winter *qi* reaps, and all living things hide themselves.

This is why only the *qi* of Heaven and Earth is quintessential. Its comings and goings are formless, and yet all living things respond to them. This is the perfection of its true nature. The noble man imitates the Heaven and Earth that he reveres.

The yin and yang of Heaven and Earth correspond to the female and male;
the female and male of human beings correspond to the yin and yang.
Yin and yang can also be called male and female.
Male and female can also be called yin and yang. [77/76/3–13]

Section 77.3

It is the constant course of Heaven and Earth that

when [the sun] arrives at the midpoint of the eastern region [i.e., at the spring equinox], what has been born is greatly nourished.

when [the sun] arrives at the midpoint of the western region [i.e., at the autumn equinox], what has been nourished is greatly completed.

In one year there are four risings. The [accomplishment of their] respective tasks depends on the midpoints.[9] What is done at the midpoints necessarily proceeds to the conjunctions. Therefore it is said: "The conjunctions are essential." The conjunctions represent the balance points of Heaven and the equilibrium of the yin and yang. Their *qi* is the most excellent; it is what brings the myriad things into existence. Those who sincerely appropriate [the qualities of] the conjunctions will greatly obtain the blessings of Heaven and Earth. The Way of Heaven and Earth is such that

even though it is sometimes disharmonious, it invariably returns to harmony so that what it achieves is efficacious;

even though it is sometimes decentered, it invariably returns to centrality so that what it achieves is free from error.

Thus,

the path of yang begins at the midpoint of the northern region [i.e., the winter solstice] and ends at the midpoint of the southern region [i.e., the summer solstice];

the path of yin begins at the midpoint of the southern region [i.e., the summer solstice] and ends at the midpoint of the northern region [i.e., the winter solstice].

The paths of yin and yang are not identical with regard to when they flourish, but both stop at the midpoint, and the place from which they arise is also necessarily the midpoint. The midpoint is the Great Ultimate of Heaven and Earth, the place where the sun and moon arrive and reverse their direction, and the limits of long and short do not surpass it.

The regulations of Heaven and Earth unite the harmonious and disharmonious, the centered and the decentered in accordance with the seasons employing them and reaching the ultimate of success. Thus what is never untimely is the Way of Heaven and Earth.

Compliance is Heaven's Way;[10]
intervals are Heaven's regulations;

---

9. Spring presides over birth; summer presides over nourishment; autumn presides over maturation; and winter presides over storage. The task of generating occurs at the midpoint of the east (i.e., the spring equinox); the task of nourishing occurs at the midpoint of the south (i.e., the summer solstice); the task of ripening occurs at the midpoint of the west (i.e., the autumn equinox); and the task of storing occurs at the midpoint of the north (i.e., the winter solstice). Note that in section 77.1, the term "midpoint" (*zhong*) refers to the solstices, whereas the word "conjunction" (*he*) refers to the equinoxes. In this passage, though, somewhat confusingly, both solstices and equinoxes are called "midpoints."

10. We have emended *xun tian zhi dao* 循天之道 to *xun zhe, tian zhi dao ye* 循者,天之道也 to accord with the parallelism of the following five lines.

yang is Heaven's generosity;
yin is Heaven's stinginess;
centrality is Heaven's application;
harmony is Heaven's achievements.

For perfecting the Way of Heaven and Earth, there is nothing more beautiful than harmony.[11] This is why every living thing invariably cherishes its *qi* and tries to nourish it. It is as Mencius said: "I am good at nourishing my floodlike *qi*."[12] He meant that when conduct invariably accords with the rites,[13] the mind is naturally pleased, and one constantly relies on yang to achieve and promote one's intentions. Gongsun [Nizi]'s *Nourishing Qi*[14] states:

When the viscera are too full, the *qi* will not circulate;
when they are too empty, the *qi* will not be sufficient;
when heat prevails, the *qi* will . . . [missing character];
when cold prevails, the *qi* will . . . [missing character];
when the viscera are too fatigued, the *qi* will not enter;
when they are too relaxed, the *qi* will stagnate;
when angry, the *qi* will become heightened;
when happy, the *qi* will become scattered;
when anxious, the *qi* will become reckless;
when frightened, the *qi* will become dissipated.

As a general rule, these ten conditions are injurious to the *qi*, and all come into existence when a person is not centered and harmonious. Therefore the noble man,

when angry, reverts to centrality by satisfying his *qi* with harmony;
when happy, reverts to centrality by collecting his *qi* with uprightness;
when worried, reverts to centrality by calming his *qi* with determination;
when startled, reverts to centrality by solidifying his *qi* with refinement.

One cannot help but revert back to centrality and harmony in this manner. Therefore when the Way of the Noble Man is achieved, *qi* flourishes and moves upward.

As a general rule, *qi* follows the mind. The mind is the master of the *qi*. How, then, can the mind act without the *qi* following it? This is why those in the

11. Following Su Yu, we have inserted the character *mo* 末 before *mei* 美 (Lai, *CQFLJZJY* 421, note 44).
12. *Mencius* IIA, 2.
13. Emending *zhong* 終 (to end) to *zhong* 中 (to hit the mark), following Su Yu (Lai, *CQFLJZJY* 421, note 46).
14. This work, attributed (probably spuriously) to the second-generation Confucian disciple Gongsun Nizi, is no longer extant.

world who possess the Way all say that the inner mind is the foundation. Therefore the reason why humane people enjoy longevity is because externally they are free of envy and internally they are pure and unsullied. Their minds are balanced and harmonious, and they do not lose centrality and uprightness. They appropriate the beauty of Heaven and Earth to nourish their bodies. Therefore [their days] are numerous, and [their bodies] are well regulated.

The reason why a crane lives long is because it has no flaccid *qi* [in its body]. Thus it can eat ice. The reason why a monkey lives long is because it is fond of stretching its limbs. Thus *qi* circulates to its four extremities.

> Heaven's *qi* constantly descends and spreads to Earth below. Thus those who cultivate the Way likewise draw *qi* into their feet.
>
> Heaven's *qi* constantly circulates and does not stagnate. Thus those who cultivate the Way likewise do not stifle their *qi*.

If you do not regulate the *qi*, then even though full of *qi*, you invariably will feel empty.[15] Therefore the noble man nourishes and harmonizes it, moderates and regulates it.[16]

> He avoids accumulating excess;
> he encourages a plenitude of harmony.
> A high tower is excessively yang;
> a broad house is excessively yin.

Both depart from the harmony of Heaven and Earth. Therefore the sage does not build such structures. He simply keeps to the mean and nothing more.

> The average man is eight feet tall;[17] four feet is the midpoint.
> *Gong* is the central note;
> sweetness is the central flavor;
> and four feet is the central measure.

Therefore the rites of the Three Kings

> esteemed sweetness with respect to flavor
> and esteemed harmony with respect to sounds.

They located themselves [in this way] and therefore constantly saturated themselves with the Way of Heaven and Earth. Their Ways were the same in kind, but

15. Following Lu Wenchao, emending *bu* 不 to *bi* 必 (Lai, *CQFLJZJY* 421, note 59).
16. Following Su Yu, emending *fa* 法 to *zhi* 治 (Lai, *CQFLJZJY* 421, note 60).
17. That is, eight *chi* 尺. A Han "foot" was about nine inches long, so this equates to about six feet tall in modern measure (which seems tall for an "average person" of the Han). The *Liezi*, chapter 2, "The Yellow Emperor," writes of a "seven-foot (*qi chi* 七尺 [i.e., five-foot, three-inch]) skeleton," which seems more reasonable (A. C. Graham, trans., *The Book of Lieh-tzu: A Classic of Tao* [New York: Columbia University Press, 1990], 53).

each was distinguished by his own *qi*. Those who model themselves on Heaven also model themselves on these human distinctions.

It is the Way of Heaven that

when fall and winter approach, yin arrives;

when spring and summer approach, yin departs.

This is why, at the frost's descent, the men of old welcomed women [for marriage], and when the ice melted, sexual relations [became] taboo. In this way they moved close to yin and away from yang. When the *qi* of Heaven and Earth is not flourishing and abundant, the yin and yang do not intermingle. This is why the noble man deeply cherishes his *qi* and, when seeking pleasure in the bedchamber, embodies Heaven. *Qi* is not harmed when it accords with [Heaven's] flourishing and penetrating, yet it is harmed when it is untimely, [because] Heaven rejects it. Not to accord with the movements of yin and yang is called untimeliness. To wantonly follow your desires and not observe the norms of Heaven is called "what Heaven rejects." The noble man regulates his body and does not dare defy Heaven. Therefore

when he has just entered puberty, he seeks pleasure in the bedchamber once every ten days;

when he is in his middle years, he doubles the interval of the adolescent;

when he has just begun to decline, he doubles the interval of the middle-aged man;

when he has arrived at his middle years of decline, he doubles the interval of the man just entering his declining years;

and when he is well into his years of decline, he takes a month for each of the adolescent's days,

thereby identifying his self-regulation with that of Heaven and Earth above.[18] This is the general overview. Yet the essential point is that you should not have intercourse when the [yin] *qi* has not yet reached the limit of its flourishing. "Sparing in spring and abstinent in summer"[19] refers to not departing from the norms of Heaven and Earth.

All people know to cherish their clothing and food, but they do not cherish Heaven's *qi*. The Heavenly *qi* in human beings is more important than clothing and food. If clothing and food are exhausted, one is still able to replenish them.

18. In other words, the mature man has sex every twenty days; the man in early decline, every forty days; the man in the middle years of decline, every eighty days; and the elderly man, every ten months.

19. In other words, in spring one should decrease the number of sexual encounters, and in summer one should refrain from sexual relations altogether.

If the *qi* is exhausted, one has arrived at the end. Therefore, the most important aspect of nourishing life is cherishing the *qi*. The *qi* follows the spirit and is perfected; the spirit emerges from intentions. The direction of the mind is its intentions. When the will labors excessively, the spirit becomes agitated. When the spirit is agitated, the *qi* dissipates. When the *qi* dissipates, it is difficult to endure for long. Therefore the noble man restrains his likes and restricts his dislikes in order to balance his intentions.

He balances his intentions in order to still his spirit.
He stills his spirit in order to nourish his *qi*.

When his *qi* is abundant and regulated, he has achieved the most important aspect of nourishing life. The ancient masters of the Way had an expression that said:

"If you wish to avoid decline,
resolutely guard your unitary potency."

This states that when the spirit does not leave the body, then the *qi* is abundant and the interior is full, so one can withstand hunger and cold. Harmony and joy augment life from without, but they are not as good as [something that] enhances life from within. And what if one is harmed from without? Anger and anxiety harm the life force, while pleasure and happiness nourish the life force. The noble man is cautious about trivial matters and so avoids significant setbacks. His conduct is centered and correct; his voice is clear and full; his *qi* and intentions are harmonious and balanced; and his dwellings and abodes are peaceful and happy. One can say that he nourishes life. As a general rule, for those who nourish life, nothing is more essential than *qi*.[20] [77/76/13–77/77/18]

Section 77.4[21]

The movements of Heaven and Earth are excellent. For this reason,

in spring, wear coarse cloth;
in summer, keep to the cool shade;
in autumn, avoid the deadly winds;
and in winter, avoid the heavy rains,

20. Following Lu Wenchao, we treat the five characters *gu tian xia zhi jun* 故天下之君 as excrescent (*CQFL* 77, note 6).

21. As pointed out in note 1 of this chapter, Su Yu's *CQFLYZ* and Lai Yanyuan's *CQFLJZJY* depart from Lau at this point, including here the passage that in *CQFL* begins chapter 78 [78/78/10–23]. We follow Lu Wenchao and Su Yu in including the passage as section 77.4, but we also follow Lau in including it as the first section of (Lau's version of) chapter 78.

and so follow [Heaven's] harmony.

With clothing, one's desire is to ameliorate cold;
with food, one's desire is to ameliorate hunger;
with the body, one's desire is to ameliorate toil but be free from prolonged idleness.

As a general rule, creatures that live within Heaven and Earth
spring up during their [i.e., Heaven and Earth's] period of ascendancy and so are born,
and become exhausted during their period of conquest and so die.

The alterations of the four seasons are like this. Therefore winter's *qi* of Water [moves] eastward, increasing until spring, when Wood is born, springing up during its period of ascendancy. What is born in spring [moves] westward [until it] arrives at Metal and dies, being exhausted by conquest.

What is born by Wood arrives at Metal and dies.
What is born by Metal arrives at Fire and dies.
What is born in spring does not last beyond autumn.
What is born in autumn does not last beyond summer.

These are Heaven's regularities.

Among the various aromas and flavors of food and drink, each arrives at a particular season. Each has a time when it is ascendant and a time when it is not ascendant; these patterns should be investigated. The *qi* of the four seasons is not alike, and each kind of *qi* has a particular suitability. Where the suitability [of each] resides is where things succeed one another in their excellence. Observe the successions of excellence and successively nourish them. Variously eat those things that are excellent in their own season. In every case, this will be what is suitable. Therefore the water chestnut attains its excellence in winter, and mustard greens ripen in summer. From this we can observe what is suitable to winter and summer. Winter is the *qi* of Water. The water chestnut has a sweet taste. What avails itself of the *qi* of Water and thereby flourishes corresponds to sweetness conquering cold. The word *ji* (water chestnut) corresponds to the word *ji*, which means "great flood."[22] Summer is the *qi* of Fire. Mustard greens have a bitter taste. What takes advantage of the *qi* of Fire and thereby ripens corresponds to bitterness conquering heat.

22. *Ji* 薺 (water chestnut). Here *ji* 濟 is defined as a "great flood," associating it with the phase Water, which is dominant in winter. More often, however, the word means "to assist" or "to ford a stream."

Heaven does not say anything but expresses its will by means of living things. Those things that do not live or die at the same time as the majority of other things [of the same sort] must be deeply investigated, for such things are the means by which Heaven informs people. Therefore, with the ripening of the water chestnut, [Heaven] informs people of sweetness. With the ripening of mustard greens, [Heaven] informs people of bitterness. The noble man investigates the ripening of things and announces that [it is necessary to be] circumspect. This is why [when] arriving at the season when water chestnuts are inedible, he completely avoids sweet things until the season when mustard greens ripen. Just as Heaven alone successively brings things to maturity, the noble man alone successively [eats] them. Such are the things appropriate to winter and summer. In spring and autumn, various foodstuffs are in harmony, but in winter and summer, he successively submits to what is suitable and so obtains exactly the excellence of Heaven and Earth and the harmony of the four seasons. In general, the main principle in selecting flavors is that there is an excellence appropriate to each season and [that one must] avoid departing far from Heaven. [78/78/10–23]

Section 77.5

Thus during the season when the myriad things are mostly engendered, all the various living things spring to life,[23] yet these things alone die. [Regarding] what is edible, announce: "Its flavor is beneficial to human beings." [Regarding] what is not edible, announce: "Eliminate their pollution and eradicate their harm; you need not wait for autumn." During the season when things are mostly withering away, [almost] all the various things die. In this way, only [a few] things still live. Of those things that are edible, eat as much of them as you can. Heaven does this to benefit human beings. Heaven alone successively gives birth to them. Of those things that are not edible, increase feeding cattle with them. Heaven pities those who live in the Zhouhua [marshes], so it creates "camp wheat" and, at midyear, brings it to maturity. The noble man investigates the differences among things to seek out Heaven's will, which is discernible to a great extent. [77/77/18–21]

23. Based on Su Yu's *CQFLYZ* and Lai Yanyuan's *CQFLJZJY*, we have supplied the thirteen characters that begin this section: *shi gu dang bai wu da sheng zhi shi chun wu jie sheng* 是故當白物大生之時群物皆生 (Su Yu, *CQFLYZ* 455).

Section 77.6

Thus the male and female embody the flourishing [of Heaven and Earth].

The stinking and fragrant partake of their supremacy;
dwellings and habitations follow their harmony;
toil and leisure dwell in their centrality;
cooling and heating do not depart from their suitability;
hunger and fullness do not exceed their balance;
likes and dislikes are regulated and ordered;
movement and quiescence comply with their nature;
happiness and anger stop at the mean [i.e., are not immoderate];
worry and anxiety revert to uprightness.

Thus when centrality and harmony constantly reside in one's person, it is said that one has greatly attained the eminence of Heaven and Earth.

Attaining the eminence of Heaven and Earth extends and lengthens one's life span;
Failing to attain the eminence of Heaven and Earth harms and shortens one's life span.

The basic substance of a long or short [life span] is something that human beings receive from Heaven. This is why

one's life span can be short or long,
nourishing [vitality] can succeed or fail.

Arriving at the end [of one's life span], it is universally the case that one compares it [with that of others]. Being that way, no one can depart [from that situation]. Therefore to speak of *shou* [meaning "life span"] is to *chou* [meaning "make a comparison"].[24] Although people are numerous, all of them individually compare their allotted life spans [with those of others]. But whether they live out their life span or die prematurely rests with their own actions.

For those who through their own actions follow the Way of longevity, their life span is comparatively long.
For those who through their own actions do not follow the Way of longevity, their life span is comparatively less long.

The nature of a long or less long life lies in the comparison of one's actions throughout life. Whether you arrive [at the end of your life] now or later, ultimately you cannot win. This is why it is said that *shou* [longevity] means *chou*

24. *Shou* 壽; *chou* 讎.

[comparison]. Thus what human beings can do by themselves still can augment or hinder [a person's basic endowment of] longevity or brevity.

If their actions are lax but their life span is long, fate increases it.

If their actions are by themselves upright but their life span is short, fate lessens it.

On account of what Heaven's fate increases or decreases, to doubt the successes and failures of men's action is to be greatly confused. This is why

in a case when Heaven lengthens it but humans harm it, its length is shortened;

in a case when Heaven shortens it but men nourish it, its shortness is lengthened.

What shortens or lengthens [the life span] fated by Heaven is, in every case, human beings. Are not human beings the heirs of Heaven? [Heaven] sends forth its basic substance, but people do not carry it out. This is most regrettable! [77/77/21–77/78/4]

Book 17, Part 1

CHAPTER 78

The Conduct of Heaven and Earth

Section 78.1

The movements of Heaven and Earth are excellent. For this reason,

in spring, wear coarse cloth;
in summer, keep to the cool shade;
in autumn, avoid the deadly winds;
and in winter, avoid the heavy rains,

and so follow [Heaven's] harmony.

With clothing, one's desire is to ameliorate cold;
with food, one's desire is to ameliorate hunger;
with the body, one's desire is to ameliorate toil but be free from prolonged idleness.

As a general rule, creatures that live within Heaven and Earth

spring up during their [i.e., Heaven and Earth's] period of ascendancy and so are born,
and become exhausted during their period of conquest and so die.

The alterations of the four seasons are like this. Therefore winter's *qi* of Water [moves] eastward, increasing until spring, when Wood is born, springing up during its period of ascendancy. What is born in spring [moves] westward [until it] arrives at Metal and dies, being exhausted by conquest.

What is born by Wood arrives at Metal and dies.
What is born by Metal arrives at Fire and dies.

This is Lau's version of chapter 78 (*CQFL* 78/78/18–78/80/2). For Su Yu's version (Lau 78/80/6–78/81/4), see chapter 78A.

What is born in spring does not last beyond autumn.
What is born in autumn does not last beyond summer.

These are Heaven's regularities.

Among the various aromas and flavors of food and drink, each arrives at a particular season. Each has a time when it is ascendant and a time when it is not ascendant; these patterns should be investigated. The *qi* of the four seasons is not alike, and each kind of *qi* has a particular suitability. Where the suitability [of each] resides is where things succeed one another in their excellence. Observe the successions of excellence and successively nourish them. Variously eat those things that are excellent in their own season. In every case, this will be what is suitable. Therefore the water chestnut attains its excellence in winter, and mustard greens ripen in summer. From this we can observe what is suitable to winter and summer. Winter is the *qi* of Water. The water chestnut has a sweet taste. What avails itself of the *qi* of Water and thereby flourishes corresponds to sweetness conquering cold. The word *ji* (water chestnut) corresponds to the word *ji*, which means "great flood."[1] Summer is the *qi* of Fire. Mustard greens have a bitter taste. What takes advantage of the *qi* of Fire and thereby ripens corresponds to bitterness conquering heat.

Heaven does not say anything but expresses its will by means of living things. Those things that do not live or die at the same time as the majority of other things [of the same sort] must be deeply investigated, for such things are the means by which Heaven informs people. Therefore, with the ripening of the water chestnut, [Heaven] informs people of sweetness. With the ripening of mustard greens, [Heaven] informs people of bitterness. The noble man investigates the ripening of things and announces that [it is necessary to be] circumspect. This is why [when] arriving at the season when water chestnuts are inedible, he completely avoids sweet things, until the season when mustard greens ripen. Just as Heaven alone successively brings things to maturity, the noble man alone successively [eats] them. Such are the things appropriate to winter and summer. In spring and autumn, various foodstuffs are in harmony, but in winter and summer, he successively submits to what is suitable and so obtains exactly the excellence of Heaven and Earth and the harmony of the four seasons. In general, the main principle in selecting flavors is that there is an excellence appropriate to each season and [that one must] avoid departing far from Heaven. [78/78/10–23]

1. *Ji* 薺 (water chestnut). Here *ji* 濟 is defined as a "great flood," associating it with the phase Water, which is dominant in winter. More often, however, the word means "to assist" or "to ford a stream."

Section 78.2[2]

Thus, during the season when the myriad things are mostly engendered, all the various living things spring to life. . . . [78/78/23]

Section 78.3

The norms of the people's ministers are derived from and modeled on Earth. Therefore from morning to evening, they come and go. . . .[3] When facing death, [they] do not covet life; that is what makes them [able to] relieve others in distress.

They promote his radiance and splendor, and extol and praise [the ruler's] goodness; that is what makes them enhance [his] brilliance.

They follow his orders and make known [the ruler's] grace, and assist him in becoming a noble man; that is what makes them enhance his transforming influence.

They complete [their] achievements and finish tasks, and ascribe all beneficence to [the ruler] on high; that is what makes them achieve righteousness.

For this reason,

Earth makes clear its principles and acts as the mother of the myriad things.
The minister makes clear his duties and acts as the councillor of a unified state.
It is imperative that the mother not be untrustworthy.
It is imperative that the councillor not be disloyal.
If the mother were untrustworthy, grasses and trees would suffer injury at their roots.
If the councillor were disloyal, treacherous ministers would endanger the ruler.
When the roots suffer injury, trees and grasses lose their branches and leaves.
When the ruler is endangered, the ruler loses his state.

Therefore,

Earth's task is to dutifully show its form;
the minister's task is to manifest his true nature. [78/78/23–27]

---

2. This sentence begins chapter 77.5 in Su Yu's version of chapter 77. Here it is an isolated fragment.
3. Inserting the sentence *wei ren chen zhe, qi fa qu xiang yu di* 爲人臣者,其法取象於地, copied from 78A/80/17, based on Su Yu's version of chapter 78. The following passage is separated into two passages in Lau's version, one part here and the rest at the end of section 78.5. For a different arrangement, proposed by Su Yu, see chapter 78A.1.

Section 78.4

The ruler of a unified state is like the mind of a unified body.

He is hidden deep within the palace, just as the mind is hidden within the chest.

He is the most honored without an equal, just as the mind's spirit has no counterpart.

The ruler

drafts men for official posts and elevates officers, promoting the pure and brilliant while demoting the impure and stupid, just as the body honors the eyes and slights the feet.

employs the multitudinous ministers without favoritism, just as the four limbs perform their respective tasks;

within relies on the four supports,[4] just as the mind relies on the liver, lungs, spleen, and kidneys;

without relies on officialdom,[5] just as the mind relies on the body and apertures;

draws near sages and promotes worthies, just as spirit illumination jells in the mind;

moves upward and downward finding mutual recognition and compliance, just as the limbs and body mutually act and direct each other;

extends his grace and spreads his favor, just as the primal energy flows to the hair of the skin and the vessels of the muscles.

All the hundred surnames obtain their place, just as when harmonized and tranquil, the blood and *qi* cause the body to be free from pain.

Non-action brings Great Peace, just as spirit *qi* naturally penetrates to the source.

With non-action, the ruler summons the yellow dragon and the phoenix,[6] just as spirit illumination summons the Jade Maiden and the *zhiying* fungus.[7]

The ruler is brilliant while the minister conceals his achievements, just as with the mind's spirit, the body finds perfection.

The minister is worthy while the ruler conceals his grace, just as the mind obtains the stillness of the body and so is calmed.

4. *Sifu* 四輔 was a collective reference to the ruler's four highest assistants, as defined in Charles O. Hucker, *A Dictionary of Official Titles in Imperial China* (Stanford, Calif.: Stanford University Press, 1985), 446.
5. *Baiguan* 百官 (literally, "one hundred officials") refers to all officials, military and civilian, serving in the governmental hierarchy, as defined in Hucker, *Dictionary of Official Titles*, 388.
6. The yellow dragon and the phoenix were considered auspicious signs from Heaven.
7. These are symbols of immortality. In early China, people who sought to lengthen their lives believed that the emanations from the star named Jade Maiden and the fungus known as *zhiying* 芝英 promoted immortality.

When the ruler is chaotic, his inferiors suffer harm, just as when the ears and eyes are beclouded, the hands and feet suffer injury.

When the minister is disloyal, the ruler is destroyed, just as when the body moves recklessly, the mind is lost.

For this reason, the propriety between the ruler and minister resembles the mind's relation to the body.

The mind must be firm, [just as] the ruler must be sagely.
The body must comply, [just as] the minister must be loyal.
The mind is perfected by the efforts of the body.
The ruler is secured by the achievements of the ministers. [78/79/1–10]

Section 78.5

For this reason, Heaven

elevates its position yet sends down its manifestations;
conceals its form yet reveals its light;[8]
orders the arrayed stars and draws near the Utmost Essence;
relies on yin and yang and sends down frost and dew.
It elevates its position; that is what makes it honorable.
It sends down its manifestations; that is what makes it humane.
It conceals its form; that is what makes it spiritlike.
It reveals its light; that is what makes it brilliant.[9]
It orders the arrayed stars; that is what gives it continuity.
It draws near the Utmost Essence; that is what makes it endure.
It relies on the yin and yang; that is what makes it complete [each] year.
It makes fall frost and dew; that is what makes it engender or slay.

The norms of the people's ruler are derived from and modeled on Heaven. Therefore,

he values rank and [treats the] states as vassals; that is what makes him humane.

He dwells in seclusion, not revealing his form; that is what makes him spiritlike.

He appoints the worthy and employs the capable, observing and listening to the four quarters of his realm; that is what makes him brilliant.

He confers office according to capability, distinguishing the worthy from the stupid; that is what gives him continuity.

8. These two parallel lines are identical to the opening lines of chapter 18.
9. These four parallel lines also are found in chapter 18.

He induces worthy men to draw near, employing them as his legs and arms; that is what makes him endure.

He investigates the true nature of his ministers' achievements, ranking and ordering them from worst to best; that is what makes him achieve [the full span of] his reign.

He promotes those who possess merit and demotes those who lack merit; that is what enables him to reward and punish.

For this reason,

Heaven cleaves to the Way and [thus] is the master of all things.

The ruler maintains [Heaven's] constant regularities and [thus] is the master of a unified state.

It is imperative that Heaven be resolute.

It is imperative that the ruler be firm.

If Heaven were not resolute, the arrayed stars would be disordered in their movements.

If the ruler were not firm, evil ministers would be disorderly in their offices.

When stars become disordered, they create havoc for Heaven.

When ministers become disordered, they create havoc for the ruler.

Therefore,

Heaven's task is to stabilize its *qi*;

the ruler's task is to stabilize his government.

[He must be] resolute and firm; only then will the Way of yang regulate his Mandate.

Earth

humbles its position and sends up its *qi*;

shows its forms and manifests its true nature;

receives the dead and offers up the living;

completes its tasks and confers its merit [on Heaven].

It

humbles its position; this is what makes it serve Heaven;

sends up its *qi*; this is what makes it nourish yang;

shows its forms; this is what makes it loyal;

manifests its true nature; that is what makes it trustworthy;

receives the dead; that is what makes it store away the end [of life];

offers up the living; that is what makes it enhance Heaven's brilliance;

completes its tasks; that is what makes it enhance Heaven's transformations;
confers its merit [on Heaven]; that is what makes it achieve righteousness.

The norms of the people's ministers are derived from and modeled on Earth. Therefore, from morning to evening, they come and go.

They take up various tasks and respond to various inquiries; that is what makes them serve the honorable [ruler].

They provide food and drink and attend to him in sickness and illness; that is what makes them nourish [the ruler].

They dedicate themselves and sacrifice their lives and serve without usurping [the ruler's prerogatives]; that is what makes them loyal.

They expose their ignorance and manifest their true nature and do not gloss over their mistakes; that is what makes them trustworthy.

They suffer setbacks and die for righteousness [78/79/12–26]

Section 78.6

Successively there are four seasons. Regarding what human beings govern, how can they maintain a pattern of appropriate action for a long period of time while they [also] must wait for the [alterations of the] four seasons? This is called "obstruction." It is not the Mean.

Human beings have happiness, anger, sorrow, and joy,
just as Heaven has spring, summer, fall, and winter.

When happiness, anger, sorrow, and joy arrive at their time, they desire to issue forth,

just as when spring, summer, fall, and winter arrive at their time, they desire to issue forth.

In every case, it is due to the inherent character of Heaven's *qi*. That [the regularities appropriate to humans] ought to move uniformly, free from obstruction or repression, is identical [in principle]. Heaven completes the year with one revolution of these four [seasons], but when the master of the people completes the days [of a year] and does not know whether [or not] he has exceeded these four numbers, then their patterns certainly cannot support one another. Moreover, Heaven's desiring to benefit human beings is not limited to desiring to bring benefit to the grain [crops]. If removing what is rotting [in the fields] does not wait for the right time, what about rotten human beings? [78/79/28–78/80/2]

Book 17, Part 1A

CHAPTER 78A

The Conduct of Heaven and Earth

Section 78A.1

The conduct of Heaven and Earth is beautiful. For this reason, Heaven

elevates its position yet sends down its manifestations;
conceals its form yet reveals its light;[1]
orders the arrayed stars and draws near the Utmost Essence;
relies on yin and yang and sends down frost and dew.
It elevates its position; that is what makes it honorable.
It sends down its manifestations; that is what makes it humane.
It conceals its form; that is what makes it spiritlike.
It reveals its light; that is what makes it brilliant.[2]
It orders the arrayed stars; that is what gives it continuity.
It draws near the Utmost Essence; that is what makes it endure.
It relies on yin and yang; that is what makes it complete [each] year.
It makes fall frost and dew; that is what makes it engender or slay.

The norms of the people's ruler are derived from and modeled on Heaven. Therefore,

he values rank and [treats the] states as vassals; that is what makes him humane.
He dwells in seclusion, not revealing his form; that is what makes him spiritlike.

This is Su Yu's reconstruction of chapter 78, included in Lau's text as book 17, part 1A (*CQFL* 78/80/6–78/81/4).

1. These two parallel lines are identical to the opening lines of chapter 18.
2. These four parallel lines also are found in chapter 18.

He appoints the worthy and employs the capable, observing and listening to the four quarters of his realm; that is what makes him brilliant.

He confers office according to capability, distinguishing the worthy and the stupid; that is what gives him continuity.

He induces worthy men to draw near, employing them as his legs and arms; that is what makes him endure.

He investigates the true nature of his ministers' achievements, ranking and ordering them from worst to best; that is what makes him achieve [the full span of] his reign.

He promotes those who possess merit and demotes those who lack merit; that is what enables him to reward and punish.

For this reason,

Heaven cleaves to the Way and [thus] is the master of all things.

The ruler maintains [Heaven's] constant norms and [thus] is the master of a unified state.

It is imperative that Heaven be resolute.

It is imperative that the ruler be firm.

If Heaven were not resolute, the arrayed stars would be disordered in their movements.

If the ruler were not firm, evil ministers would be disorderly in their offices.

When stars become disordered, they create havoc for Heaven.

When ministers become disordered, they create havoc for the ruler.

Therefore,

Heaven's task is to stabilize its *qi*;

the ruler's task is to stabilize his government.

[He must be] resolute and firm; only then will the Way of yang regulate his Mandate.

Earth

humbles its position and sends up its *qi*;

shows its forms and manifests it true nature;

receives the dead and offers up the living;

completes its tasks and confers its merit [on Heaven].

It

humbles its position; that is what makes it serve Heaven;

sends up its *qi*; that is what makes it nourish yang;

shows its forms; that is what makes it loyal;
manifests its true nature; that is what makes it trustworthy;
receives the dead; that is what makes it store away the end [of life];
offers up the living; that is what makes it enhance Heaven's brilliance;
completes its tasks; that is what makes it enhance Heaven's transformations;
confers its merit [on Heaven]; that is what makes it achieves righteousness.

The norms of the people's ministers are derived from and modeled on Earth. Therefore, from morning to evening, they come and go.

They take up various tasks and respond to various inquiries; that is what makes them serve the honorable [ruler];

They provide food and drink, and attend to him in sickness and illness; that is what makes them nourish [the ruler].

They dedicate themselves and sacrifice their lives, and serve without usurping [the ruler's prerogatives]; that is what makes them loyal.

They expose their ignorance and manifest their true nature, and do not gloss over their mistakes; that is what makes them trustworthy.

They suffer setbacks and, when facing death, do not covet life; that is what makes them [able to] relieve others in distress.

They promote his radiance and splendor, and extol and praise [the ruler's] goodness; that is what makes them enhance [his] brilliance.

They follow his orders and make known [the ruler's] grace, and assist him in becoming a noble man; that is what makes them enhance his transforming influence.

They complete achievements and finish tasks, and ascribe all beneficence to [the ruler] on high; that is what makes them achieve righteousness.

For this reason,

Earth makes clear its principles and acts as the mother of the myriad things.

The minister makes clear his duties and acts as the councillor of a unified state.

It is imperative that the mother not be untrustworthy.

It is imperative that the councillor not be disloyal.

If the mother were untrustworthy, grasses and trees would suffer injury at their roots.

If the councillor were disloyal, treacherous ministers would endanger the ruler.

When the roots suffer injury, trees and grasses lose their branches and leaves.

When the ruler is endangered, the ruler loses his state.

Therefore,

Earth's task is to dutifully show its form;
the minister's task is to manifest his true nature. [78/80/6–23]

Section 78A.2

The ruler of a unified state is like the mind of a single body.

He is hidden deep within the palace, just as the mind is hidden within the chest.

He is the most honored without an equal, just as the mind's spirit has no counterpart.

The ruler

Drafts men for official posts and elevates officers, promoting the pure and brilliant while demoting the impure and the stupid, just as the body honors the eyes and slights the feet;

employs the multitudinous ministers without favoritism, just as the four limbs perform their tasks;

within relies on the four supports,[3] just as the mind relies on the liver, lungs, spleen, and kidneys;

without relies on officialdom,[4] just as the mind relies on the body and apertures;

draws near sages and promotes worthies, just as spirit illumination jells in the mind;

moves upward and downward, finding mutual recognition and compliance, just as the limbs and body mutually act and direct each other;

extends his grace and spreads his favor, just as the primal energy flows to the hair of the skin and the vessels of the muscles.

All the people [literally, the "hundred surnames"] obtain their place, just as the blood and *qi*, when harmonized and tranquil, cause the body to be free from pain.

Non-action brings Great Peace, just as spirit *qi* naturally penetrates to the source.

With non-action, the ruler summons the yellow dragon and the phoenix,[5] just as spirit illumination summons the Jade Maiden and the *zhiying* fungus.[6]

The ruler is brilliant while the minister conceals his achievements, just as with the mind's spirit, the body finds perfection.

3. *Sifu* 四輔 was a collective reference to the ruler's four highest assistants, as defined in Charles O. Hucker, *A Dictionary of Official Titles in Imperial China* (Stanford, Calif.: Stanford University Press, 1985), 446.
4. *Baiguan* 百官 (literally, "one hundred officials") refers to all officials, military and civilian, serving in the governmental hierarchy, as defined in Hucker, *Dictionary of Official Titles*, 388.
5. The yellow dragon and the phoenix were considered auspicious signs from Heaven.
6. These are symbols of immortality. In early China, people who sought to lengthen their lives believed that the emanations from the star named Jade Maiden and the fungus known as *zhiying* 芝英 promoted immortality.

The minister is worthy while the ruler conceals his grace, just as the mind obtains the stillness of the body and so is calmed.

When the ruler is chaotic, his inferiors suffer harm, just as when the ears and eyes are beclouded, the hands and feet suffer injury.

When the minister is disloyal, the ruler is destroyed, just as when the body moves recklessly, the mind is lost.

For this reason, the propriety between the ruler and minister resembles the mind's relation to the body.

The mind must be firm, [just as] the ruler must be sagely.

The body must comply, [just as] the minister must be loyal.

The mind is perfected by the efforts of the body, [just as] the ruler is secured by the achievements of the ministers. [78/80/25–78/81/4]

Book 17, Part 2

CHAPTER 79

The Origins of Severity and Beneficence

Section 79.1

Heaven possesses
harmony and beneficence,
impartiality and severity,
intentions that correspond to [what is] received,
principles that create governance.
You must not fail to examine this.
Spring is Heaven's harmony;
summer is Heaven's beneficence;
autumn is Heaven's impartiality;
and winter is Heaven's severity.
Heaven's sequence is
invariably to be first harmonious and only afterward to be beneficent;
invariably to be first impartial and only afterward to be severe.
From this it can be seen that
if not [first] harmonious, Heaven cannot [then] display the beneficence of favors and rewards;
if not [first] impartial, Heaven cannot then display the severity of penalties and punishments.
One can also see that
beneficence is born from harmony;
severity is born from impartiality.

Without harmony, there can be no beneficence;
without impartiality, there can be no severity.

This is the Way of Heaven. The Perfected view things from this perspective.

Though having what pleases me and makes me happy, I must first harmonize my mind in order to seek what is appropriate. Only then can I bestow gifts and rewards to establish beneficence.

Though having what distresses me and makes me angry, I must first calm my mind to seek what is just. Only then can I implement penalties and punishments to establish severity.

The ability to constantly act in this manner is called Heavenly Virtue. Those who implement Heavenly Virtue are called sages. [79/81/8–13]

Section 79.2[1]

One who would rule others
occupies the position of Utmost Potency
and grasps the positional advantage of life and death,

thereby altering and transforming the people. The people follow their master [just] as the grasses and trees respond to the four seasons.

Happiness and anger correspond to chilling and heating.
Severity and beneficence correspond to winter and summer.
Winter and summer match up to severity and beneficence.
Chilling and heating are the counterparts of happiness and anger.
Happiness and anger have seasons when they ought to issue forth;
chilling and heating have seasons when they ought to emerge.

1. This marks the beginning of a separate essay, as the argument shifts dramatically at this point. Before this, the essay focused on the four qualities of harmony, beneficence, impartiality, and severity. The author maintains that the severity of punishments and the beneficence of rewards must be applied only after the ruler has tempered his joy or anger by achieving a harmonious and impartial mind. Thus rewards and punishments properly emanate from these affective states and not from the emotive states of joy or anger. In section 79.2, the argument shifts in two distinct ways. First, the four qualities of harmony, beneficence, impartiality, and severity are replaced by a discussion of happiness, anger, beneficence, and severity. Second, the author correlates the proper expression of these qualities with the proper seasonality of heating and chilling, summer and winter. The two sections appear to be at odds with each other because this second part does not try to temper the expression of emotions by recourse to psychological training but instead allows for the full expression of the emotions as long as that expression follows the model provided by the course of nature with its constant changes in the seasons and weather.

Their principle is one.

Not being happy when one ought to be happy resembles [the weather's] not being hot when it ought to be hot.

Not being angry when one ought to be angry resembles [the weather's] not being cold when it ought to be cold.

Not being beneficent when one ought to be kind resembles [the season's] not being summer when it ought to be summer.

Not being severe when one ought to be severe resembles [the season's] not being winter when it ought to be winter.

Happiness, anger, severity, and beneficence must issue forth at the appropriate occasion, just as chilling and heating, winter and summer, must issue forth at the proper time.[2] When the display of happiness and anger and the application of severity and beneficence in every case hits the mark, such responses partake of the way in which chilling and heating, winter, and summer do not stray from their proper time. Thus it is said: "The sage is a counterpart to Heaven." [79/81/14–21]

2. This sentence is followed by forty-two characters (79/81/18–19) that do not belong to this essay. Since the passage is wholly incongruous with the subject matter before and after, we have excluded it from the preceding translation. The passage reads:

> Therefore, one must be cautious with respect to the germination of good and evil. How can you verify what is so? In embracing goodness, [the *Spring and Autumn*] does not disregard the slightest instance of goodness; in rejecting evil, it does not neglect the greatest instance of evil. It avoids but does not conceal; it condemns but does not despise. [Two characters missing.] [It relies on] correct principles to praise and blame.

Book 17, Part 3

CHAPTER 80

In Imitation of Heaven's Activities

Section 80.1

Yin and yang *qi* are present above[1] in Heaven and also in human beings.

In human beings, they constitute love, hate, happiness, and anger.
In Heaven, they constitute warming, cooling, chilling, and heating.
Emerging and retiring,
ascending and descending,
leftward and rightward,
forward and backward,

they circulate uniformly and ceaselessly. There has never been anything that has hindered, restrained, obstructed, or repressed them. In human beings likewise, it is fitting that they circulate without restraint, like the four seasons that follow one another in good order. Now the cessation and movement of happiness, anger, sorrow, and joy constitute the nature and destiny that Heaven confers on human beings. When their time arrives, they desire to issue forth. Their responses also are Heaven's responses. It is no different from the way in which warmth, coolness, cold, and heat want to issue forth when their season arrives. If you restrain your beneficence in anticipation of spring and summer, or restrain your punishments in expectation of autumn and winter, you might gain a reputation for complying with the four seasons; but in reality, you will defy the constant norms of Heaven and Earth. As with human beings, so also with Heaven: Why, then,

1. Lu Wenchao suggests that the character *shang* 上 is an interpolation. Su Yu (*CQFLYZ* 463) notes, however, that the character is found in Huang Zhen's citation of this passage in his *Daily Notes*.

detain and restrain Heaven's *qi*, causing it to become obstructed and repressed so that it is unable to circulate properly? Thus, according to the cycles of Heaven, millet rots by the *yin* month,[2] whereas wheat sprouts in autumn, thereby informing the people to eliminate what is rotting and to replenish what is deficient. In this way, [Heaven] completes its achievements and replenishes what is deficient to provide for humankind. In Heaven's engendering of things, there are grand norms,[3] but in its circulation, there also are misfortunes and accomplishments. Under exceptional circumstances [involving] killing and corporal punishment, when urgent situations arise, do not wait for the normal season [to take action]. Such is Heaven's will. The sage receives Heaven's will and governs accordingly. For this reason,

> in spring he cultivates humaneness and seeks goodness;
> in autumn he cultivates righteousness and seeks evil;
> in winter he cultivates punishments and extends his purity;
> and in summer he cultivates beneficence and extends his magnanimity.

This is how he complies with Heaven and Earth and embodies yin and yang. Nevertheless,

> when he has just begun to seek goodness, if he sees evil he does not dismiss it;
> when he has just begun to seek malefaction, if he sees goodness he immediately implements it;
> when he has just begun to extend his purity, if he sees a great goodness, he immediately advances it;
> when he has just begun to extend his magnanimity, if he sees a grave malefaction he immediately eradicates it.

He thereby imitates the way that Heaven and Earth, just at the time of giving life, also bring death and that, just at the time of bringing death, also give life. Thus,

> his will and intentions follow Heaven and Earth,
> and his tarrying and hurrying follow yin and yang.

Human affairs that are appropriate to be carried out will encounter no delay. Moreover, showing reciprocity to others and complying with Heaven, so that the Way of Heaven and the Way of humankind are mutually realized, is called "grasping the mean." Heaven does not,

> on account of spring, give life to human beings
> or, on account of autumn, bring death to human beings.

2. That is, the first month of the civil calendar, early spring.
3. Su Yu (*CQFLYZ* 464) notes that the next six characters, *er suo zhou xing zhe you* 而所周行者又, contain errors and lacunae, so our translation here is tentative.

To those who ought to live, [Heaven] says live;
to those who ought to die, [Heaven] says die.

It is not that the righteousness of killing things must await the four seasons. [80/81/25–80/82/5]

Section 80.2

[Even when] spirit illumination arises in a chaotic age, it is widespread. Both [well-governed and chaotic ages] rely on the transformations of Heaven and Earth to bring success or failure to things, and both depend on the assistance of yin and yang to take responsibility for what they do. Thus doing what is evil causes one's strength to diminish and one's achievements to suffer injury; one's reputation will thus decline.

The space between Heaven and Earth contains yin and yang *qi* that constantly immerses human beings, [just] as water constantly immerses fish. The way in which they differ is that [water] can be seen, whereas [*qi*] cannot be seen, as it is colorless and clear. Nevertheless, human beings' dwelling in the space between Heaven and Earth is like fish not[4] leaving the water; they are the same. Its seamlessness is like that of *qi*, but [*qi*] is more fluid than water. Water is to *qi* what mud is to water. Hence, the space between Heaven and Earth appears empty but is full. Human beings are constantly immersed in this colorless clarity. [When they] avail themselves of this chaos-quelling *qi*, it flows forth, penetrates, and intermingles with them. Thus when the *qi* of human beings blends harmoniously, the transformations of Heaven and Earth are beautiful; when it intermingles hatefully, its fragrance is destroyed. This is something that is easy to understand. If you infer from the categories of things and rely on what is easy to understand to see what is difficult to understand, the true situation may be apprehended: Orderly or disorderly *qi* and noxious or salutary customs intermingle with the transformations of Heaven and Earth. Born of the transformations of Heaven and Earth and returning to intermingle with the transformations of Heaven and Earth, they join together with the cycles of Heaven and Earth. When the *Spring and Autumn* makes known the way of worldly affairs, it also writes of what can and cannot be [understood]

4. Supplying the negative *bu* 不 here for logical sense.

exhaustively with regard to Heaven, for such are the responsibilities of the true king. An *Ode* declares:

> "Heaven is hard to trust;
> it is not easy to be a king."[5]

This expresses it. The ruler must know Heaven. "Knowing Heaven" is what the poem calls "difficult." Heaven's intentions are difficult to see, and its Way is difficult to get straight. Thus, the ruler clarifies the emerging and retiring of yin and yang and the places where it is full or empty and thereby observes the Will of Heaven; he distinguishes the root and branches, compliance and deviance, contraction and expansion, [and] broadening and narrowing of the Five Phases and thereby observes the Way of Heaven. The Will of Heaven is humane; its Way is righteous.

> One who acts as the people's ruler
> gives or takes, lets live or executes, in each case in accordance with its [respective] righteous principle; [thus he is] like the four seasons.
> He classifies the officials and establishes the functionaries, ensuring accordance with their abilities; [thus he is] like the Five Phases.
> He loves humaneness and loathes vileness, relying on virtue and avoiding punishments; [thus he is] like yin and yang.

Of such a ruler it is said, "He is a counterpart to Heaven."[6] It is the Way of Heaven to nourish living things, and it is the way of the ruler to nourish human beings.

> The greatness of the ruler lies in his forming a triad with Heaven and Earth;
> the distinction between what he likes and loathes lies in the principles of yin and yang;
> the expression of his approval and disapproval lies in the comparison of chilling and heating;
> the tasks of the officials lie in the righteous principles of the Five Phases.

With such things, the ruler nourishes all that lies within the space between Heaven and Earth and stirs all that lies within the Four Seas. [80/82/5–19]

5. *Odes* 236, verse 1.
6. The important notion of the ruler as the "counterpart of Heaven" (*pei tian* 配天) also is developed in chapters 55 and 79.

Book 17, Part 3A

CHAPTER 80A

In Imitation of Heaven's Activities

Section 80A.1

Yin and yang *qi* are present above[1] in Heaven and also in human beings.

In human beings, they constitute love, hate, happiness, and anger.
In Heaven, they constitute warming, cooling, chilling, and heating.
Emerging and retiring,
ascending and descending,
leftward and rightward,
forward and backward,

they circulate uniformly and ceaselessly. There has never been anything that has hindered, restrained, obstructed, or repressed them. In human beings likewise, it is fitting that they circulate without restraint, like the four seasons that follow one another in good order. Now the cessation and movement of happiness, anger, sorrow, and joy constitute the nature and destiny that Heaven confers on human beings. When their time arrives, they desire to issue forth. Their responses also are Heaven's responses. It is no different from the way in which warmth, coolness, cold, and heat want to issue forth when their season arrives. If you restrain your beneficence in anticipation of spring and summer, or restrain your punishments in expectation of autumn and winter, you might gain a reputation for complying with the four seasons, but in reality you will defy the constant norms

This is a translation of Su Yu's reconstruction of chapter 80, included in Lau's text as book 17, part 3A (*CQFL* 80/82/23–80/83/11).

1. Lu Wenchao suggests that the character *shang* 上 is an interpolation. Su Yu (*CQFLYZ* 463) notes, however, that the character is found in Huang Zhen's citation of this passage in his *Daily Notes*.

of Heaven and Earth. As with human beings, so also with Heaven: Why, then, detain and restrain Heaven's *qi*, causing it to become obstructed and repressed so that it is unable to circulate properly? Thus, according to the cycles of Heaven, millet rots by the *yin* month,[2] whereas wheat sprouts in autumn, thereby informing the people to eliminate what is rotting and to replenish what is deficient. In this way, [Heaven] completes its achievements and replenishes what is deficient to provide for humankind. In Heaven's engendering of things, there are grand norms,[3] but in its circulation there also are misfortunes and accomplishments. Under exceptional circumstances [involving] killing and corporal punishment, when urgent situations arise, do not wait for the normal season [to take action]. Such is Heaven's will. The sage receives Heaven's will and governs accordingly. For this reason,

> in spring he cultivates humaneness and seeks out goodness;
> in autumn he cultivates righteousness and seeks out evil;
> in winter he cultivates punishments and extends his purity;
> and in summer he cultivates beneficence and extends his magnanimity.

This is how he complies with Heaven and Earth and embodies yin and yang. Nevertheless,

> when he has just begun to seek goodness, if he sees evil he does not dismiss it;
> when he has just begun to seek malefaction, if he sees goodness he immediately implements it;
> when he has just begun to extend his purity, if he sees a great goodness he immediately advances it;
> when he has just begun to extend his magnanimity, if he sees a grave malefaction he immediately eradicates it.

He thereby imitates the way that Heaven and Earth, just at the time of giving life, also bring death and that, just at the time of bringing death, also give life. Thus,

> his will and intentions follow Heaven and Earth,
> and his tarrying and hurrying follow yin and yang.

Human affairs that are appropriate to be carried out will encounter no delay. Moreover, showing reciprocity to others and complying with Heaven, so that the Way of Heaven and the Way of humankind are mutually realized, is called "grasping the mean." Heaven does not,

2. That is, the first month of the civil calendar, early spring.
3. Su Yu (*CQFLYZ* 464) notes that the next six characters, *er suo zhou xing zhe you* 而所周行者又, contain errors and lacunae, so our translation here is tentative.

> on account of spring, give life to human beings;
> or, on account of autumn, bring death to human beings.
> To those who ought to live, [Heaven] says live;
> to those who ought to die, [Heaven] says die.

It is not that the righteousness of killing things must await the four seasons. So how can those things that are governed by human beings maintain the principles of appropriate action for a long period of time while they must [also] wait for the [alterations of the] four seasons? This is called "obstruction." It is not the mean. [80A/82/23–80A/83/8]

Section 80A.2

> Human beings have happiness, anger, sorrow, and joy,
> just as Heaven has spring, summer, fall, and winter.
> When happiness, anger, sorrow, and joy arrive at their time, they desire to issue forth,
> just as when spring, summer, fall, and winter arrive at their time, they desire to issue forth.

In every case, it is due to the spontaneous action of Heaven's *qi*.[4] That they ought to move uniformly, free from obstruction or repression, is [due to] their being as one. Heaven completes the year with one revolution of these four [seasons], but when the people's master completes his days and does not know when he is overstepping these four regularities, then their patterns cannot maintain [their proper order]. Moreover, Heaven's desiring to benefit human beings is not limited to desiring to bring benefit to the [harvest of] grain. If removing what is rotting [in the fields] does not wait for a particular time, what about [the removal of] rotten human beings? [80A/83/8–11]

4. Supplying *zi* 自 before *ran* 然, following Su Yu, *CQFLYZ* 465.

Book 17, Part 4

CHAPTER 81

Heaven, Earth, Yin, and Yang

Section 81.1

Heaven, earth, yin, yang, wood, fire, earth, metal, and water constitute nine things. Together with human beings, they total ten, completing Heaven's numerical categories. Therefore,

> when counting, you arrive at ten and stop.
>
> When writing, you take the tenth stroke as the last one.

Both examples derive from [Heaven's numerical categories]. Why are human beings noble?[1] [It is because] what originates with Heaven extends to human beings [and thus] is completed. What lie outside this completion are called "things." Although things may take on the incipient qualities of nobility, they do not fall within the compass of [the word] "noble." From this, it can be seen that human beings are, by a great margin, superior to other things, the noblest in the world. Below, human beings nurture the myriad things; above, they form a triad with Heaven and Earth. Thus, their orderly or disorderly status and the motion, rest, compliance, or deviance of their *qi* can injure or benefit the transformations of yin and yang, and stir and shake everything within the Four Seas. Things, being difficult to comprehend, are like spirits; you cannot say it is not so. Now,

> if you fall onto the ground, you will die or suffer injury, and you will be unable to move.

1. Following Yu Yue and Su Yu, we treat the character *sheng* 聖 as excrescent (*CQFLYZ* 465–66).

If you fall into mud, you will be able to move in some direction, but only for a short distance.

If you fall into water, you will be able to move in some direction for a longer distance.

From this, one can see that the more fluid a thing is, the more readily it alters, moves, stirs, and shakes. Now the fluidity of the transformations of *qi* is not so limited as that of water. The people's ruler, with his numerous activities, moves it ceaselessly. Thus, his orderly or disorderly *qi* constantly intermingles with the transformations of Heaven and Earth, producing disorder [in response to the ruler's disorder].

When the age is ordered and the people are harmonious, when the will is tranquil and the *qi* is upright, the transformations of Heaven and Earth will be quintessential, and the beauty of the myriad things will arise.

When the age is disordered and the people vie with one another, when the will is biased and *qi* grows malign, the transformations of Heaven and Earth will be harmful, and catastrophes will arise.

This is why the virtue of a well-ordered age enriches the plants and trees; its beneficence flows to [all within] the Four Seas; and its achievements are surpassing. [81/83/15–23]

Section 81.2

Names are the means by which one distinguishes things.

For [relationships that are] close, there are significant names;
for [relationships that are distant], there are less significant names;
for [people who are] noble, there are refined names;
for [people who are] base, there are plain names;
for [ages that are] near, there are detailed names;
for [ages that are] distant, there are general names.

The terminology [of the *Spring and Autumn*] does not conceal the true nature of things. It illuminates the true nature of things but does not neglect proper terminology. If people's minds follow it and do not struggle against it, it will penetrate and connect the ancient and contemporary without the least disorder. Such are the righteous principles of [its use of] names.

Men and women are like the Way. People's inborn differences are discussed [by means of] propriety and righteousness. The origin of names and designations arise from human affairs. What does not comply with the Way of Heaven is designated as unrighteous.

Observe the distinctions between Heaven and humankind;
scrutinize the differences between the Way and fate;
and you will understand the delightfulness of propriety.

Observing goodness, one cannot but like it;
observing evil, one cannot but dislike it.

But likes and dislikes come and go and cannot be preserved and guarded [permanently]; therefore we have the Human Way. The Human Way is what human beings follow. It is the source from which people obtain joy, but it is not chaotic; it is [reliably] repetitious without being tiresome. [Each of] the myriad things comes into existence bearing a name. The sage names them in accordance with their appearance. However, [names] can be modified, in every case in accordance with righteous principles. Thus, one rectifies names so that the names are righteous. The term "thing" is a general name for something, an all-inclusive name for something. But things also have their particular names, which are specific names and not names for things in general. Thus it is said:

"What the myriad things move but has no form is intention;
what takes form but does not change is virtue;
what is joyous without being chaotic and [reliably] repetitious without being tiresome is the Way." [81/83/25–81/84/3]

Section 81.3

[Everything] within the Four Seas blends with the *qi* of yin and yang and intermingles with Heaven and Earth. Thus there is the popular expression that states: "One who may be called a king forms a triad with Heaven and Earth." If he forms a triad with Heaven and Earth, then he has undergone a transformation. How could such a transformation be due solely to the quintessence of Heaven and Earth? The king also participates in and blends together with it.

When he is orderly, salutary *qi* blends with the transformations of Heaven and Earth.
When he is disorderly, noxious *qi* blends with the transformations of Heaven and Earth.

The norms of Heaven are such that

when he identifies with Heaven, there is mutual benefit;
when he differs from Heaven, there is mutual harm.

This cannot be doubted. [81/84/3–7]

Book 17, Part 4A

CHAPTER 81A

Heaven, Earth, Yin, and Yang

Section 81A.1

Heaven, earth, yin, yang, wood, fire, earth, metal, and water constitute nine things. Together with human beings, they total ten, completing Heaven's numerical categories. Therefore,

> when counting, you arrive at ten and stop.
>
> When writing, you take the tenth stroke as the last one.

Both examples derive from [Heaven's numerical categories]. Why are human beings noble?[1] [It is because] what originates with Heaven extends to human beings [and thus] is brought to completion. What lie outside this completion are called "things." Although things may take on the incipient qualities of nobility, they do not fall within the compass of [the word] "noble." From this, it can be seen that human beings are, by a great margin, superior to other things, the noblest in the world. Below, human beings nurture the myriad things; above, they form a triad with Heaven and Earth. Thus, their orderly or disorderly status and the motion, rest, compliance, or deviance of their *qi* can injure or benefit the transformations of yin and yang, and stir and shake everything within the Four Seas. Things, being difficult to comprehend, are like spirits; you cannot say it is not so. Now,

> if you fall onto the ground, you will die or suffer injury, and you will be unable to move.

This is Su Yu's reconstruction of chapter 81, included in Lau's text as book 17, part 4A (*CQFL* 81/84/10–81/85/7).

1. Following Yu Yue and Su Yu, we treat the character *sheng* 聖 as excrescent (*CQFLYZ* 465–66).

If you fall into mud, you will be able to move in some direction, but only for a short distance.

If you fall into water, you will be able to move in some direction for a longer distance.

From this, one can see that the more fluid a thing is, the more readily it alters, moves, stirs, and shakes. Now the fluidity of the transformations of *qi* is not so limited as that of water. The people's ruler, with his numerous activities, moves it ceaselessly. Thus, his orderly or disorderly *qi* constantly intermingles with the transformations of Heaven and Earth, producing disorder [in response to the ruler's disorder].

When the age is ordered and the people are harmonious, when the will is tranquil and the *qi* is upright, the transformations of Heaven and Earth will be quintessential, and the beauty of the myriad things will arise.

When the age is disordered and the people vie with one another, when the will is biased and *qi* grows malign, the transformations of Heaven and Earth will be harmful, and catastrophes will arise.

This is why the virtue of a well-ordered age enriches the plants and trees; its beneficence flows to [all within] the Four Seas; and its achievements surpass spiritlike understanding. [81A/84/10–18]

Section 81A.2

The influences of a chaotic age are equally widespread. Both [well-governed and chaotic ages] rely on the transformations of Heaven and Earth to bring success or failure to things, and both depend on the assistance of yin and yang to take responsibility for what they do. Thus doing what is evil causes one's strength to diminish and one's achievements to suffer injury; one's reputation will thus decline.

The space between Heaven and Earth contains yin and yang *qi* that constantly immerses human beings, [just] as water constantly immerses fish. The way in which they differ is that [water] can be seen, whereas [*qi*] cannot be seen, as it is colorless and clear. Nevertheless, human beings' dwelling in the space between Heaven and Earth is like fish not[2] leaving the water; they are the same. Its seamlessness is like that of *qi*, but [*qi*] is more fluid than water. Water is to *qi* what mud is to water. Hence, the space between Heaven and Earth appears

2. Supplying the negative *bu* 不 here for logical sense.

empty but is full. Human beings are constantly immersed in this colorless clarity. [When they] avail themselves of this chaos-quelling *qi*, it flows forth, penetrates, and intermingles with them. Thus when the *qi* of human beings blends harmoniously, the transformations of Heaven and Earth are beautiful; when it intermingles hatefully, its fragrance is destroyed. This is something that is easy to understand. If you infer from the categories of things, and rely on what is easy to understand to see what is difficult to understand, the true situation may be apprehended: Orderly or disorderly *qi* and noxious or salutary customs intermingle with the transformations of Heaven and Earth. Born of the transformations of Heaven and Earth and returning to intermingle with the transformations of Heaven and Earth, they join together with the cycles of Heaven and Earth. When the *Spring and Autumn* makes known the way of worldly affairs, it also writes of what can and cannot be [understood] exhaustively with regard to Heaven, for such are the responsibilities of the ruler. An *Ode* declares:

> "Heaven is hard to trust;
> it is not easy to be a king."[3]

This expresses it. The ruler must know Heaven. "Knowing Heaven" is what the poem calls "difficult." Heaven's intentions are difficult to see, and its Way is difficult to get straight. Thus, the ruler clarifies the emerging and retiring of yin and yang and the places where it is full or empty and thereby observes the Will of Heaven; he distinguishes the root and branches, compliance and deviance, contraction and expansion, [and] broadening and narrowing of the Five Phases and thereby observes the Way of Heaven. The Will of Heaven is humane; its Way is righteous.

One who acts as the people's ruler

> gives or takes, lets live or executes, in each case in accordance with its [respective] righteous principle; [thus he is] like the four seasons.
>
> He classifies the officials and establishes the functionaries, ensuring accordance with their abilities; [thus he is] like the Five Phases.
>
> He loves humaneness and loathes vileness, relying on virtue and avoiding punishments; [thus he is] like yin and yang.

Of such a ruler it is said, "He is able to be the counterpart of Heaven."[4] It is the Way of Heaven to nourish living things, and it is the way of the ruler to nourish human beings.

---

3. *Odes* 236, verse 1.
4. The important notion of the ruler as the "counterpart of Heaven" (*pei tian* 配天) also is developed in chapters 55 and 79.

The greatness of the ruler lies in his forming a triad with Heaven and Earth;
the distinction between what he likes and loathes lies in the principles of yin and yang;
the expression of his approval and disapproval lies in the comparison of chilling and heating;
the tasks of the officials lie in the righteous principles of the Five Phases.

With such things, the ruler nourishes all that lies within the space between Heaven and Earth and stirs all that lies within the Four Seas. [81A/84/18–81A/85/5]

Section 81A.3

[Everything within the Four Seas] blends with the *qi* of yin and yang and intermingles with Heaven and Earth. Thus the popular expression states: "One who may be called a king forms a triad with Heaven and Earth." If he forms a triad with Heaven and Earth, then he has undergone a transformation. How could such a transformation be due solely to the quintessence of Heaven and Earth? The king also participates in and blends together with it.

When he is orderly, salutary *qi* blends with the transformations of Heaven and Earth.
When he is disorderly, noxious *qi* blends with the transformations of Heaven and Earth.

The norms of Heaven are such that

when he identifies with Heaven, there is mutual benefit;
when he differs from Heaven, there is mutual harm.

This cannot be doubted. [81A/85/5–7]

Book 17, Part 5

CHAPTER 82

The Way of Heaven Bestows

Section 82.1

The Way of Heaven is to bestow;
the Way of Earth is to transform;
the Way of humankind is to be righteous.
The sage observes the twigs and understands the root; this is the perfection of quintessence.
The sage takes one [thing] and responds with ten thousand; this is the orderliness of classification.
[There are] those who agitate the roots but do not know how to calm the branches.
[There are] those who take on affairs at the outset but are unable to predict their outcome.
Profit is the root of depravity.
Wantonness is the beginning of disorder.

If you accept the beginnings of disorder and stir the root of depravity, although you want to bring tranquillity to the people, you will not be able to do so. Therefore, the noble man

does not speak if it is not in accordance with the rites;
does not move if it is not in accordance with the rites.
Those who are fond of sex but do not follow the rites become unrestrained;
those who eat and drink but do not follow the rites become contentious.

Lack of restraint and contentiousness gives rise to disorder.

Now ritual is what embodies the emotions and prevents disorder. Human emotions cannot control desires, so we cause them to be regulated by the rites [so that]

> the eyes gaze on correct colors,
> the ears listen to correct sounds,
> the mouth savors correct flavors,
> and the person carries out the correct Way.

This is not meant to deprive one of emotions; rather, it is the means by which the emotions are calmed. Alterations [of feelings] are termed "emotions." Although the various alterations of human emotions must await stimulation by various external things [to be expressed], they also are an aspect of nature. Therefore they are said to be internal. The alterations that cause altered [emotional states] are designated as external. Therefore, although they are due to the emotions, they nonetheless are not explained as being part of nature. Thus it is said: The activation of nature by externals is like the impermanence of the spirit. Accumulated habits and gradual weaknesses are the subtle influences of [external] things. They unwittingly become part of the self. One forgets that they are only habits, as they become like part of one's nature. It is imperative that this be examined.

> Only with pure knowledge and upright thoughts will your plans succeed.
> Only with moderate desires and compliant actions will your relationships obtain.
> Take remonstrance, struggle, dignity, and calm as your dwelling.
> Take Propriety, Righteousness, the Way, and Virtue as your model.[1]

Therefore, perfect sincerity leaves things behind and is not altered by them. Personal liberality that is not contentious cannot be vulgarized or influenced by them. Various strong [pressures] cannot enter [the self]. [It is] like a discarded cicada skin [lying] amid turbidity and filth: how could it muster the means to affect you? To follow along with the myriad things but not lose the [essence of] the self—this is the mind of the sage. [82/85/11–20]

1. Emending the line from *yi li yi wei dao ze wen de* 以禮義為道則文德 to *yi li yi dao de wei ze* 以禮義道德為則, following Lai, *CQFLJZJY* 444, note 18.

Book 17, Part 5A

CHAPTER 82A

The Way of Heaven Bestows

Section 82A.1

The Way of Heaven is to bestow;
the Way of Earth is to transform;
the Way of humankind is to be righteous.
The sage observes the twigs and understands the root; this is the perfection of quintessence.
The sage takes one [thing] and responds with ten thousand; this is the orderliness of classification.
[There are] those who agitate the roots but do not know how to calm the branches.
[There are] those who take on affairs at the outset but are unable to predict their outcome.
Profit is the root of depravity.
Wantonness is the beginning of disorder.

If you accept the beginning of disorder and stir the root of depravity, although you want to bring tranquillity to the people, you will not be able to do so. Therefore the noble man

does not speak if it is not in accordance with the rites;
does not move if it is not in accordance with the rites.
Those who are fond of sex but do not follow the rites become unrestrained;
those who eat and drink but do not follow the rites become contentious.

This is Su Yu's reconstruction of chapter 82, included in Lau's text as book 17, part 5A (*CQFL* 82/85/24–82/86/12).

Lack of restraint and contentiousness gives rise to disorder.

Now ritual is what embodies the emotions and prevents disorder. Human emotions cannot control desires, so we cause them to be regulated by the rites [so that]

> the eyes gaze on correct colors,
> the ears listen to correct sounds,
> the mouth savors correct flavors,
> and the person carries out the correct Way.

This is not meant to deprive one of emotions; rather, it is the means by which the emotions are calmed. Alterations [of feelings] are termed "emotions." Although the various alterations of human emotions must await stimulation by various external things [to be expressed], they also are an aspect of nature. Therefore they are said to be internal. The alterations that cause altered [emotional states] are designated as external. Therefore, although they are due to the emotions, they nonetheless are not explained as being part of nature. Thus it is said: The activation of nature by externals is like the impermanence of the spirit. Accumulated habits and gradual weaknesses are the subtle influences of [external] things. They unwittingly become part of the self. One forgets that they are only habits, as they become like part of one's nature. It is imperative that this be examined.

> Only with pure knowledge and upright thoughts will your plans succeed.
> Only with moderate desires and compliant actions will your relationships obtain.
> Take remonstrance, struggle, dignity, and calm as your dwelling.
> Take Propriety, Righteousness, the Way, and Virtue as your model.[1]

Therefore, perfect sincerity leaves things behind and is not altered by them. Personal liberality that is not contentious cannot be vulgarized or influenced by them. Various strong [pressures] cannot enter [the self]. [It is] like a discarded cicada skin [lying] amid turbidity and filth: how could it muster the means to affect you? To follow along with the myriad things but not lose the [essence of] the self—this is the mind of the sage. [82A/85/24–82A/86/3]

1. Emending the line from *yi li yi wei dao ze wen de* 以禮義為道則文德 to *yi li yi dao de wei ze* 以禮義道德為則, following Lai, *CQFLJZJY* 444, note 18.

Section 82A.2

Names are the means by which one distinguishes things.

For [relationships that are] close, there are significant names;
for [relationships that are distant], there are less significant names;
for [people who are] noble, there are refined names;
for [people who are] base, there are plain names;
for [ages that are] near, there are detailed names;
for [ages that are] distant, there are general names.

The terminology [of the *Spring and Autumn*] does not conceal the true nature of things. It illuminates the true nature of things but does not neglect proper terminology. If people's minds follow it and do not struggle against it, it will penetrate and connect the ancient and contemporary without the least disorder. Such are the righteous principles of [its use of] names.

Men and women are like the Way. People's inborn differences are discussed [by means of] propriety and righteousness. The origin of names and designations arise from human affairs. What does not comply with the Way of Heaven is designated as unrighteous.

Observe the distinctions between Heaven and humankind;
scrutinize the differences between the Way and fate;

and you will understand the delightfulness of propriety.

Observing the good, one cannot but like it;
observing the bad, one cannot but dislike it.

But likes and dislikes come and go and cannot be preserved and guarded [permanently]; therefore we have the Human Way. The Human Way is what human beings follow. It is the source from which people obtain joy, but it is not chaotic; it is [reliably] repetitious without being tiresome. [Each of] the myriad things comes into existence bearing a name. The sage names them in accordance with their appearance. However, [names] can be modified, in every case in accordance with righteous principles. Thus, one rectifies names so that the names are righteous. The term "thing" is a general name for something, an all-inclusive name for something. But things also have their particular names, which are specific names and not names for things in general. Thus it is said:

"What the myriad things move but has no form is intention;
what takes form but does not change is virtue;
what is joyous without being chaotic and [reliably] repetitious without being tiresome is the Way." [82A/86/5–12]

APPENDIX A

Biographies of the Confucian Scholars

DONG ZHONGSHU was a native of Guangchuan. When he was a youth, he mastered the *Spring and Autumn*. During the reign of Emperor Jing, he was made an Erudite.[1] [From behind] a lowered curtain, he lectured to and recited for his disciples, who in turn transmitted [his teachings] from those with greatest seniority to those with least seniority, so that some of his disciples never even saw his face. His concentration was such that for three years he did not even glance at his garden. His movements were composed and self-effacing. If something was not in keeping with propriety, he would not do it. Students and scholars all revered him as a teacher.

After the present emperor assumed the throne, he appointed Dong Zhongshu to be the administrator to Jiangdu. By consulting ominous changes such as natural disasters and strange events recorded in the *Spring and Autumn*, Zhongshu deduced the causes of disorderly interactions between yin and yang. Therefore when inducing rain, he repressed yang and released yin; when stopping rain, he reversed these techniques. When he carried out these techniques in this single state, he never failed to obtain the desired results. In the midst of his tenure as administrator to Jiangdu, he was dismissed from his post and appointed as a grand master to the palace.

SJ 121.3127–28. For another translation, see Burton Watson, trans., *Records of the Grand Historian*, rev. ed. (New York: Columbia University Press, 1993), 2:368–70. Michael Loewe provides a detailed summary of this biography in *Dong Zhongshu, a "Confucian" Heritage, and the "Chunqiu fanlu,"* Brill China Studies, no. 20 (Leiden: Brill, 2011), 45–47.

1. That is, an expert on one of the classical texts, appointed to an official sinecure and supported by the state.

Residing at home, Zhongshu composed the *Record of Disasters and Anomalies*. At this time, there was an ominous fire in the temple of Emperor Gao in Liaodong. Zhufu Yan, being jealous of Zhongshu, stole his composition [on portents] and sent it to the Son of Heaven with a memorial.[2] The Son of Heaven summoned an audience with various scholars and showed them the composition, which was roundly criticized and satirized. Zhongshu's disciple Lü Bushu, who was unaware that it was his teacher's composition, pronounced it "utterly foolish." Subsequently, Zhongshu was remanded to the legal officials, who sentenced him to death, but an imperial instruction pardoned him. After this incident, Zhongshu did not dare speak again of disasters and anomalies.

Zhongshu personally was incorruptible and frank. At that time, the four tribes that lived beyond the limits of the empire were being pressured to submit to the emperor. Gongsun Hong's mastery of the *Spring and Autumn* did not compare with that of Zhongshu, yet Hong put himself forward on every possible occasion and so rose up the ladder of officialdom to achieve high ministerial rank. Zhongshu considered Hong to be an obsequious toady, and Hong, for his part, despised [Dong Zhongshu]. [Now it happened that] the king of Jiaoxi, an elder brother of the emperor, was particularly unrestrained, having mistreated his two-thousand-bushel officials numerous times.[3] Hong consequently spoke to the emperor and said: "Only Dong Zhongshu is up to the task of being appointed administrator to the king of Jiaoxi."[4] Having heard that Zhongshu was a great Confucian, the king of Jiaozi treated him well, [but] Zhongshu feared that if he remained long [in this post], he would be [falsely] accused of some crime. So he retired on the grounds of illness.

When Zhongshu retired from his post and returned home to live, for the rest of his life he did not pay attention to [enhancing] his family's livelihood but instead occupied his time cultivating his scholarship and writing books. Thus from the time the Han arose and across a span of five [imperial] generations, only Dong Zhongshu gained a reputation for elucidating the *Spring and Autumn* and transmitting the interpretations of Master Gongyang.

2. Dong's essay on portents must have contained material that could be construed as critical of the emperor or one of his imperial ancestors.
3. Official salaries were computed in terms of bushels of grain.
4. The king of Jiaoxi was a "hawk" with respect to frontier policy, which added to the danger of being in his administration.

APPENDIX B

The Biography of Dong Zhongshu

Early Years[1]

DONG ZHONGSHU was a native of Guangchuan. When he was a youth, he mastered the *Spring and Autumn*. During the reign of Emperor Jing, he was made an Erudite.[2] [From behind] a lowered curtain, he lectured to and recited for his disciples, who in turn transmitted [his teachings] from those with greatest seniority to those with least seniority, so that some of his disciples never even saw his face. His concentration was such that for three years, he did not even glance at his garden. His movements were composed and self-effacing. If something was not in keeping with propriety, he would not do it. Students and scholars all revered him as a teacher.

After Emperor Wu assumed the throne, he [called for] the recommendation of scholars who were "worthy, excellent, and learned,"[3] numbering several hundred. Dong Zhongshu was among those recommended as "worthy and excellent" who responded to the imperial inquiry.

Ban Gu, *Han shu* (*History of the [Former] Han Dynasty*), chap. 56. For a detailed paraphrase of the three imperial instructions and Dong Zhongshu's responses contained in this biography, see Michael Loewe, *Dong Zhongshu, a "Confucian" Heritage, and the "Chunqiu fanlu,"* Brill China Studies, no. 20 (Leiden: Brill, 2011), 87–97.

1. The Chinese original does not contain subheads; we have added them for the convenience of readers.
2. That is, an expert on one of the classical texts, appointed to an official sinecure.
3. *Xianliang wenxue* 賢良文學 was "a recommendation category for men nominated by local officials to be considered at the capital for selection and appointment to government posts" (Charles O. Hucker, *A Dictionary of Official Titles in Imperial China* [Stanford, Calif.: Stanford University Press, 1985], 242).

The First Imperial Instruction

The imperial instruction[4] stated:

We have secured and inherited [this position of] utmost reverence and refined virtue and [wish] to transmit its legacy without flaw so that it operates everywhere. Yet the responsibility is great and the undertaking weighty. Thus day and night, [We] take no time to rest, thinking constantly of the governance of the myriad affairs, ever fearful that [We] have fallen short. Therefore [We] have searched widely and deeply for the "eminent and brave"[5] from the Four Quarters [of the empire] and [ordered] the Lords of the Land and the dukes of the commanderies and kingdoms to recommend scholars who are worthy and excellent, who cultivate their integrity, and who are widely versed [in the classical literature], because [We] desire to hear the essentials of the great Way and the ultimate truths of its highest principles. Now you, gentlemen, have been honored to stand at the head of those recommended. We deeply admire this [achievement]. You, gentlemen, refine your thoughts and stretch your minds, for We have condescended to listen to and question you. [*HS* 56/2495]

Verily [We] have heard that the Way of the Five Thearchs and the Three Kings was to reform institutions and compose music so that the world would obtain harmony. The numerous kings [that followed] did the same. Of the music of Master Shun, none flourished more than the *shao*, and under the Zhou, none flourished more than the *shuo*. After the demise of the sage-kings, though the music of the bells, drums, flutes, and strings had not yet declined, the great Way became flawed, reaching its nadir with the conduct of Jie and Djou, when the Kingly Way was laid to ruin. Now in the past five hundred years, there have been numerous rulers bent on preserving civility, and scholars who have followed this path have desired to emulate the models of the Former

4. For the general meaning of the term *ce*, see Enno Giele, *Imperial Decision-Making and Communication in Early China: A Study of Cai Yong's "Duduan"* (Wiesbaden: Harrassowitz, 2006), 268–84.

5. *Huainanzi* 20.23 explains: "Those whose knowledge surpassed ten thousand men were called 'talented'; those whose knowledge surpassed a thousand men were called 'eminent'; those whose knowledge surpassed a hundred men were called 'brave'; those whose knowledge surpassed ten men were called 'prominent'" (John S. Major, Sarah A. Queen, Andrew Seth Meyer, and Harold D. Roth, trans. and eds., *The "Huainanzi": A Guide to the Theory and Practice of Government in Early Han China* [New York: Columbia University Press, 2010], 833).

Kings to sustain and protect their age. Yet none have been able to return [to those models]. [Instead,] they were neglected day by day and fell into disuse, until the time of the Later Kings when they finally ceased altogether. How could it be that all [those rulers] were wrong and erroneous and strayed from the tradition of rule [set forth by the Five Thearchs and the Three Kings]? Surely the Mandate ordained by Heaven is irrevocable. But does it mean that the Way of the Three Kings must end in utter decline and ultimately cease to exist altogether? Alas! Will all that we have taken pains to accomplish, rising before dawn and retiring after dusk, doing the utmost to emulate the rulers of remote antiquity, be of no avail? Where are the auspicious signs that the Mandate received by the [rulers of the] Three Dynasties now rests at the present time [with Us]? What caused disasters and anomalies to arise? The disposition of allotted life span and nature is such that [a person's allotted life span] is sometimes short and sometimes long; [a person's nature] is sometimes humane and sometimes degenerate. These designations are often heard of, but their principles are not well understood. Our wish is that customs be propagated and commands enacted, punishments lightened, and treachery rectified, so that the common people will be harmonious and joyful and governmental affairs will be fitting and clear. What [policies] must be cultivated and what [policies] must be refined so that sweet dew descends, the numerous grains flourish, [Our] virtue permeates all who live within the Four Seas, and Our bounty enriches the grasses and plants, the Three Luminaries shine forth in all their splendor, and cold and heat arrive in even measure? [How can We] receive the assistance of Heaven and enjoy the numinous efficacy of the ghosts and spirits? How will Our virtue and bounty spread forth and extend beyond the empire so that it reaches to all living things?

You, gentlemen, understand the undertakings of the Former Sages and are well versed in the alternations of customary change and the proper sequence of their cycles. For many long days you have been discussing and deliberating these lofty and proper principles. Communicate your insights to Us. Explain every detail as a separate item. Do not crowd your points together. Select each item in accordance with a clear method. Carefully consider your replies. If you know of any instance of impropriety, dishonesty, disloyalty, laxity, or negligence in the administration, write a letter, do not leak the information, and submit it to Us personally. Do not dread the repercussions. You, gentleman, speak your minds. Do not conceal anything. We will personally examine [your responses]. [2498]

Dong Zhongshu's Reply to the First Instruction

Your Highness[6] has spoken in virtuous tones and sent down this enlightened announcement inquiring into Heaven's Mandate and into the disposition and nature. These all are beyond the reach of your ignorant servant.

Your servant respectfully notes that the *Spring and Autumn* scrutinizes affairs that occurred in an earlier age to draw conclusions about the mutual interaction between Heaven and humankind. Truly, it is something to hold in awe. When a state is about to suffer a defeat because [the ruler] has strayed from the proper path, Heaven first sends forth disastrous and harmful [signs] to reprimand and warn him. If the [ruler] does not know to look into himself [in response], then Heaven again sends forth strange and bizarre [signs] to frighten and startle him. If he still does not know [that he should] change, only then will he suffer ruin and defeat. From this, we observe that Heaven's heart is humane and loving toward the people's ruler and that Heaven desires to keep him from chaos. During those ages when there is no great loss of proper principles, Heaven still desires to support and secure him. His task is simply to exert himself. He must make efforts to learn and inquire, and then what he hears and sees will be pervasive, and his knowledge will become increasingly enlightened. He must exert himself to practice the proper principles, and then his virtue will increase daily, and he will be in possession of great achievements. These efforts will enable him to quickly achieve results.

The *Odes* state: "From dawn to dusk unceasing."[7]

The *Documents* state: "Make the effort. Make the effort."[8]

Both refer to exerting oneself.[9] [2498–99]

The Way is the most suitable path to good government. Humaneness, righteousness, ritual, and music all are its instruments. Thus, although the sage-kings have already expired, their sons and grandsons have enjoyed security and peace for several hundred years. This is all due to the merit of the morally instructive transformational [quality] of ritual and music. During the time when the

6. Neither ministers or subjects dared address the throne directly. Instead, they addressed "*bixia*" 陛下, which literally means "below the steps of the throne," a phrase that we approximate as "Your Highness."
7. *Odes* 261, verse 1.
8. *Documents*, "Yu da mo" (Counsels of Yu the Great) 11; James Legge, trans., *The Shoo King, or, The Book of Historical Documents*, vol. 3 of *The Chinese Classics*, 2nd rev. ed. (1894; repr., Hong Kong: Hong Kong University Press, 1960), 59.
9. This passage, beginning with "your servant respectfully notes" and continuing through "exerting oneself" is quoted in chapter 30.2.

king has yet to compose [his own dynasty's] music, he still uses the music of the former kings that is suitable to the age to deepen and extend transformation through moral instruction to the common people. If the proper implementation of transformation through moral instruction is not carried out, the music of the *ya* and *song* will not be perfected. Thus when the king's achievements are brought to a conclusion, music is composed to celebrate his virtue. Music is the means to change the habits of the common people and transform their customs. It changes people readily, and it transforms people visibly. Therefore, when its sounds issue forth from harmony and they are rooted in [a person's] disposition, they link up to the sinews and muscles and are stored away in the bones and marrow. Even though the Kingly Way has become flawed, the sounds of the flutes and strings have not yet been lost. A long time passed since Master Shun governed, yet some of the music that he bequeathed still survived, so that when Confucius traveled to Qi, he heard the *shao* [of Master Shun].

Now among the many who have ruled others, there have been none who did not desire security and survival and none who did not loathe danger and death. Yet those whose governments became disordered and whose states became endangered are quite numerous, because the men whom they employed were not the right men and the path that they followed was not the right Way. Accordingly, their governments daily declined, [finally reaching] the point of destruction. Now the Way of Zhou declined under [the rulers] Yu and Li, not because the Way was lost, but because these rulers failed to follow it. But in the time of King Xuan, being mindful of the Virtue of the Former Kings, reviving the defunct and making good the defective, he set forth the noble achievements of [Kings] Wen and Wu, so that the Way of the Zhou Kings was restored to all its glory. The poets consequently praised him with their compositions while Heaven blessed him by providing him with worthy assistants. Later generations sang his praises, and down to the present day they have yet to cease. Such was the outcome of practicing goodness "from dawn to dusk unceasing." Confucius said: "People can broaden the Way. It is not the Way that broadens people."[10] Thus, order or disorder and decline or prosperity rest in your person. It is not the case that the Mandate ordained by Heaven is irrevocable. [2499–2500]

Your servant has heard that when one is about to become king by means of the great appointment of Heaven, he will invariably possess things that cannot be brought about by human effort, yet he finds himself in possession of them. There are the auspicious signs that he has received the Mandate. The people of the

10. *Analects* 15.28.

world will turn to him with one heart as if they are returning home to their father and mother. Thus Heaven's auspicious signs always arrive in response to sincerity. The *Documents* says: "A white fish entered the king's boat. Fire spread back into the king's chamber, taking [the shape of] a bird." These were surely signs that the Mandate had been received. [Therefore] the Duke of Zhou exclaimed: "I have been repaid! I have been repaid!"[11] Confucius said: "Virtue never stands alone. It is bound to have neighbors."[12] These all are the result of accruing goodness and amassing virtue.

Yet coming down to the later ages, [in contrast] there was indulgence, indolence, decline, and decay, qualities incapable of [serving as the basis for] ruling and ordering the numerous forms of life. The Lords of the Land grew rebellious and oppressed and tyrannized the innocent multitudes, wresting their land from them. They abandoned moral instruction and instead relied on punishments. If punishments and penalties are not appropriate, they will engender a noxious *qi*. If a noxious *qi* accumulates below, resentments and hatreds will proliferate above. If above and below are not harmonious, yin and yang will fall out of step, and inexplicable evils will be engendered. This is what causes disasters and anomalies to arise. [2500]

Your servant has heard that [a person's] life span is Heaven's command; nature is the inherent quality humans possess at birth; and disposition is [a function of] human desire. Some people die prematurely, while others are long-lived; some are humane, while others are degenerate. When the potter molds them and brings them to completion, it is not always possible to refine and improve them because of [the factors] that arise in a well-ordered or chaotic age. Consequently, they are not uniform. Confucius said: "The virtue of the noble man is like the wind; the virtue of the petty man is like grass. Let the wind blow over the grass, and it is sure to bend."[13] When Yao and Shun practiced their virtuous ways, the people were humane and lived out their natural life spans; when Jie and Djou practiced their violent ways, the people were degenerate and died prematurely. Therefore, for the ruler to transform the ruled and for the ruled to submit to the ruler resembles the clay on a potter's wheel: only a potter can shape it. It resembles metal in a mold: only a metalsmith can cast it. This is precisely what Confucius meant when he said: "Having brought peace to them, they turned to him; having set them tasks, they worked harmoniously."[14] This expresses it. [2501]

11. Loewe cites Yan Shigu in identifying these two quotations from the *Documents* as coming from the *jinwen* (New Text) version of the "Tai shi," in *Dong Zhongshu*, 89n.23.
12. *Analects* 4.25.
13. *Analects* 12.19.
14. *Analects* 19.25.

Your servant has respectfully examined the text of the *Spring and Autumn* in search of the starting point of the Kingly Way and has found it in the term *zheng* (the first). [In the first entry for each reign in the *Spring and Autumn*,] the term *zheng* (the first) follows the term *wang* (king), and the term *wang* (king), follows the term *chun* (spring).[15] The spring [season] is established by Heaven; the first [month] is established by the king. The intention of the *Spring and Autumn* is to say that the ruler receives what Heaven establishes and he uses it to rectify his activities. This is what I mean when I say that "the first" is the starting point of the Kingly Way. This being the case, whenever the ruler desires to do something, it is fitting that he derive his starting point from Heaven.

The most important aspect of Heaven's Way is yin and yang. Yang corresponds to beneficence; yin corresponds to punishment. Punishment presides over death; beneficence presides over life. Thus yang always takes up its position at the height of summer, taking engendering, nurturing, nourishing, and maturing as its tasks; yin always takes up its position at the height of winter, accumulating in empty, vacuous, and useless places. From this perspective, we see that Heaven relies on beneficence and does not rely on punishment. Heaven causes yang to emerge, circulate, and operate above the ground to preside over the achievements of the year. Heaven causes yin to retire and prostrate itself below the ground, seasonally emerging to assist yang. If yang does not obtain yin's assistance, it cannot complete the year on its own. Ultimately, however, it is yang that is noted for completing the year. Such is Heaven's intent.

The king receives Heaven's intent and thereby implements his affairs. Accordingly, he relies on moral instruction and does not rely on coercive punishment. Coercive punishment cannot be relied on to order the age, just as yin cannot be relied on to complete the year. To govern by relying on coercive punishment does not conform to Heaven. Thus none among the Former Kings dared do so. Is not the present dismissal of officials who promote the moral instruction of the Former Kings, and the sole reliance on officials who uphold the rule of law to bring order to the people, a case of relying on coercive punishments? Confucius said: "To impose the death penalty on those you have not educated is called tyranny."[16] When tyrannical government is applied to the lower reaches of society, it is exceedingly difficult to fulfill the desire to spread moral instruction throughout the world within the Four Seas! [2501–2]

15. In other words, the first entry for each ruler reads *chun wang zheng yue* 春王正月 (Spring. The royal first month).
16. *Analects* 20.2.

Your servant has respectfully examined the reason why the *Spring and Autumn* refers to "the first [year of each lord's reign]" as "the originating [year]."[17] The first is that from which all things begin. The Origin is what the Great Appendix [of the *Changes*] calls "great." To refer to the first as the originating [year] is to recognize the importance of the beginning and to desire to rectify the root [of all things.] The *Spring and Autumn* explores deeply the root [of things], and so it retraces back to begin from the noble. Therefore, one who would rule others rectifies his mind to rectify the court; [he] rectifies the court to rectify the hundred officials; he rectifies the numerous officials to rectify the myriad people; and [he] rectifies the myriad people to rectify the Four Quarters of the world. If the Four Quarters of the world are rectified, then no one, near or far, will dare fail to be one with his rectitude, and there will be no noxious *qi* to defile those around him. For this reason, yin and yang will be harmonious; and wind and rain will arrive in their appropriate seasons; all living things will be in harmony and the multitudes will prosper; the five [kinds of] grain will reach fruition; and the subsidiary crops will flourish. All within Heaven and Earth will be showered by these blessings, and all within the Four Seas will hear of the ruler's flourishing virtue and flock to him to become his subjects. Of all possible blessings and every conceivable auspicious omen that may be summoned, none will fail to arrive, and the Kingly Way will be fulfilled.

Confucius said: "The Phoenix does not appear; the River does not offer up its Chart. I am done for."[18] Confucius was grieved that even though he had the ability to summon these auspicious omens, since he occupied a lowly station in the world, he had no opportunity to [exercise that ability]. Now Your Highness holds the exalted position of Son of Heaven and enjoys the riches of the Four Seas. He occupies the highest station that it is possible to attain and is endowed with the greatest ability. His actions are noble and his generosity abundant; his wisdom is manifest and his intentions are excellent. He loves his people and favors his scholars. He is assuredly a righteous ruler. Why, then, have Heaven and Earth not responded and auspicious signs not yet appeared? It is because transformation through moral instruction has not been established, and consequently the people are not yet rectified. The people continue to seek profit, [just] as water naturally tends to flow downward. If you do not rely on transformation through moral instruction to dam up this tendency, you will not be able to stop it. Hence, when moral instruction has been established, wicked and corrupt

17. The first entry for each successive ruler begins with "*yuan nian*" 元年 (the first year).
18. *Analects* 9.9.

practices cease because the dikes have been perfected. When moral transformation has been neglected, villainy and wickedness appear. Punishments and penalties cannot overcome them because the dikes have deteriorated. The kings of antiquity understood this principle. Accordingly, when they faced south to rule the world, they all considered transformation through moral instruction [to be] their most important achievement. They set up institutions for study in the country and created schools for transformation in the villages. They saturated the people with humaneness, refined them with upright conduct, and restrained them with ritual. Hence, the reason the prohibitions were not disobeyed, even though the punishments were light, was because transformation through moral instruction was practiced so that mores and customs became good.

When the sage-kings succeeded to the disorder of former ages, they swept away all traces of it and restored moral instruction to its original position of honor. Instruction thus established and customs defined, their descendants followed their example for five hundred or six hundred years without fail. But in their final days, the Zhou went completely counter to the Way and lost the empire. The Qin succeeded the Zhou but, far from improving things, made them even worse. They proscribed the classical literature, so that their texts became unavailable; they rejected propriety and righteousness and sought to discredit them with the aim of completely eradicating the Way of the Former Kings and establishing their own irresponsible and licentious rule. Consequently, after a period of only fourteen years, their dynasty collapsed. From antiquity to the present day, there has never been any government that, in seeking to remedy disorder with more disorder, has oppressed the people more cruelly than the Qin. Even today, traces survive of their poisonous legacy, causing [correct] customs to be treated with contempt and the people to be obstinate and obstructive; such is the seriousness of its corruption.

Confucius said: "A piece of rotten wood cannot be carved, nor can a wall of dried dung be troweled."[19] Now Han has succeeded to the legacy of the Qin, which resembles rotten wood or dried dung. Although you desire to improve and repair it, how can it be done? Although laws are enacted, crime proliferates. Although orders are disseminated, deception increases. The situation resembles one who tries to stop water from boiling by adding hot water, or one who attempts to extinguish a fire by putting wood on it. This simply makes matters worse and avails nothing. I would liken [this situation] to a *qin* or a *se* that has gone out of tune. In serious cases, it must be unstrung and restrung before

19. *Analects* 5.9.

it can be played again. Similarly, when governmental policies are enacted but they prove ineffective, in serious cases it is necessary to change and reform them before they can be set in good order. When one must restring [an instrument] and fails to do so, then even a gifted artist cannot make the tuning correct. When one must reform [the government] but fails to do so, then even a great and worthy ruler cannot govern well. Therefore, since the Han obtained the empire, it has constantly desired to govern well, but up to the present day it has failed to accomplish this because it did not reform when it was appropriate to do so. The ancients had a saying: "Looking down into a pond and coveting the fish does not compare to withdrawing and weaving a net." Now looking down at the government and desiring to govern for more than seventy years does not compare with withdrawing and instituting reform. Having instituted reform, it will be possible to govern well. If the state is well governed, disasters will diminish day by day, and blessings will increase. The *Odes* declare: "He treats his people correctly; he treats his officials correctly; and so he receives his reward from Heaven."[20] Those who govern by treating the people correctly will surely be rewarded by Heaven. It is the Five Virtues of Humaneness, Righteousness, Propriety, Wisdom, and Trustworthiness that the king should cultivate. When the king cultivates them, he will receive the assistance of Heaven and enjoy the numinous efficacy of the ghosts and spirits. His virtue and bounty will spread forth and extend beyond the empire so that it reaches all living things. [2502–5]

The Second Imperial Instruction

The Son of Heaven examined Dong Zhongshu's reply but did not agree with it and so again issued an imperial instruction, which stated:

Verily [We] have heard that when Yu Shun ruled, he strolled leisurely along his palace corridors with his hands clasped idly together, doing nothing at all, yet the world enjoyed an era of Great Peace. [In contrast,] King Wen of Zhou had no time for a repast until well past noon, yet the world also was well governed. Now was not the Way of the Thearchs and Kings bound by the same connecting thread? Why, then, could one ruler sit idle while the other toiled? [2506]

20. *Odes* 249, verse 1.

Verily, the Frugal One (Shun) made no great display of flags and banners. But when it came to the Zhou dynasty, large city gates were erected and the rulers rode forth in sumptuous carriages. Their shields were decorated with vermilion, and their battle-axes wrought of jade. Eight teams of dancers performed in their courtyards, and the music of the *Odes* rang forth. Yet surely the tenets of the Kingly Way [underlying these different practices] were not different?

Some say that good jade should not be carved. Yet others say that without external ornamentation, there is no way to give expression to the inherent quality. These two principles are contradictory. The Yin [dynasty] upheld the Five Mutilating Punishments to reprove wrongdoing. They injured the body to punish crime. But Cheng and Kang of the Zhou did not avail themselves of these punishments; yet for more than forty years, the empire was free of crime and the prisons stood empty. The Qin dynasty [once again] employed the Five Mutilating Punishments so that the dead proliferated and the mutilated were common passersby. How wasteful! How pitiful!

Alas! We retire after dusk and rise before dawn, pondering the examples of the former thearchs and kings and thinking constantly of how to uphold [their position of] utmost reverence and how to honor and manifest their vast achievements, all of which lie in encouraging the root [of agriculture] and employing worthy men. Accordingly, [We] personally till the fields to emphasize the primacy of agriculture, encourage the Filial and Fraternal, and exalt the Virtuous. Our emissaries are dispatched in great numbers, inquiring into the conditions of those who toil and comforting the orphaned and the childless. [We] have exhausted [Our] mind and depleted [Our] spirit but cannot even begin to say that [We] have obtained any merit or reward for all We have done. Currently, yin and yang are out of step, and noxious *qi* fills and obstructs the atmosphere so that the numerous forms of life rarely reach maturity and the common people have yet to find relief. The honest and corrupt are mixed together and the worthy and degenerate are confused, having not yet obtained their true identities.

Thus who among the scholars that [We] have so carefully selected will speak the truth? Currently, among the one hundred or so gentlemen who await this imperial announcement, some have said that the challenges of the present age have yet to be relieved. You have explicated the different policies of remote antiquity, but when applying them to the present circumstances, you have [claimed that they are] difficult to implement. Is it the case that you have been so fettered by the constraints of literary form that you have been unable to avail yourself of your talents? Or is it that you have recommended conflicting methods [to be adopted] or presented me with differing advice? Each of you should consider your response carefully and write it down in clearly defined sections. Do not conceal your opinions from the responsible officials. Illuminate both your specific points and a broader overview. Cut and polish your investigations in order to fulfill Our wish. [2506–7]

Dong Zhongshu's Reply to the Second Instruction

Your servant has heard that when Yao received the Mandate of Heaven, he considered the empire to be a worrisome responsibility and did not consider assuming the throne to be a joyful occasion. Accordingly, he punished and expelled his rebellious servants and labored to search out worthy and sagely men. This is how he secured [the assistance of] Shun, Yu, Ji, Xie, and Gao You. These sagely men augmented his virtue, and their sagely abilities assisted him in his various tasks. Moral instruction was widely disseminated, and the empire enjoyed harmony and tranquillity as the multitudes found security in humaneness and rejoiced in righteousness. Each found his rightful place, complied with ritual, and readily conformed to the centrality of the Way. Yet Confucius said: "Even if a sage appeared, it would take a generation for humaneness to prevail."[21] This is what is meant. [2508]

When Yao had been on the throne for seventy years, he abdicated in favor of Shun. When he passed away, the empire did not return its allegiance to Yao's son Danzhu but instead to Shun. Only when he realized that he could not decline did Shun assume the throne. He appointed Yu as his chancellor and relied on Yao's assistants to transmit the governmental institutions that Yao had established. This is why Shun could clasp his hands together idly and do nothing at all, and yet the empire was well governed. Thus Confucius said: 'The *shao* is not only the ultimate in beauty but in goodness as well."[22] This is what he meant.

Coming to Djou of the Yin [dynasty], in contrast, in defiance of Heaven, he violated living beings, executed by strangulation the worthy and wise, and oppressed and tyrannized the common people. Bo Yi and Tai Gong, though worthy men of the age, hid themselves in reclusion and refused to serve. All those who held office fled for their lives, taking refuge in far-away places beyond the rivers and seas. The empire fell into chaos, and the people did not live in peace.

21. *Analects* 13.12.
22. *Analects* 3.25.

The people of the empire therefore abandoned the Yin and gave their allegiance to the Zhou. King Wen conformed to Heaven and brought order to the myriad things. For his teachers, he employed worthy men. This is why the likes of Hong Yao, Tai Dian, and San Yisheng gravitated to his court. His love was bestowed on the multitudes, and the empire submitted to him. Thus Tai Gong emerged from retirement to become one of the Three Ministers. At this time, although Djou still occupied the throne, the noble and mean had become muddled and confused, and the common people had become scattered and destitute. Consequently, King Wen was grieved and pained and desired to bring peace to their lot. This is why he had no time for a repast until well past noon.

When Confucius was writing the *Spring and Autumn*, he entered the terms *zheng* (the first) and *wang* (king) at the beginning of the first entry and related them to the myriad affairs of governance, thus revealing [his] writings [to be those] of an uncrowned king. Viewed from this perspective, there is indeed only one thread binding together the thearchs and kings, yet the difference between toiling away or remaining idle is due to the different ages that rulers encounter. And so Confucius also said: "The *wu* [music] is the ultimate in beauty, but not quite in goodness."[23] This is what he meant. [2509]

Your servant has heard that sumptuary regulations and the ornamental black and yellow insignia were the means to distinguish the lofty from the base and to differentiate the noble from the mean in order to encourage the virtuous. Thus in the *Spring and Autumn*, the first things to be regulated by those who received Heaven's Mandate were the change in the first month of the year and the alteration of the color of court dress to respond to Heaven. Nonetheless, the regulations concerning palaces and dwellings and flags and banners were [kept] as they were because they were based on particular models. Thus Confucius said: "Extravagance leads to insubordination; frugality leads to stubbornness."[24] Frugality is not the mean when it comes to the regulations of a sage.

Your servant has heard that good jade is never carved because its inherent disposition, being moist and beautiful, does not permit being cut and polished. This is no different from the boy of Daxiang village, who did not [need to] study because he was intuitively wise.[25] However, if ordinary jade is not carved, it will not complete the outward form of its inherent qualities. [Likewise,] if the gentleman does not study, he will not complete his virtue. [2510]

23. *Analects* 3.25.
24. *Analects* 7.36.
25. The boy from Daxiang village is mentioned in *Analects* 9.2.

Your servant has heard that when the sage-kings ruled the empire, they refined the people's habits by educating them when they were young. [Then] they employed their talents by appointing them to official posts when they matured. Ranks and emoluments were meant to nourish their virtue, while punishments and penalties were meant to repress their depravities. Thus the common people came to understand ritual and righteousness and were ashamed to disobey their ruler. King Wen conducted himself with immense righteousness, thereby pacifying the treacherous and rebellious. The Duke of Zhou created rites and music to give outward expression to King Wen's righteousness. Coming down to the time of [Kings] Cheng and Kang, the prisons were empty for more than forty years. This all was due to the incremental influence of moral instruction and the dissemination of humaneness and righteousness. It was not at all the consequence of mutilating the bodies [of miscreants].

Coming down to the [First Emperor of the] Qin, however, it was not to be so. Taking as his guide the methods of Shen Buhai and Shang Yang and implementing the theories of Han Feizi, he loathed the Way of the Thearchs and Kings and instead took greed and avarice to be customary. He lacked both the outward form and the inner virtue with which to instruct and teach his subjects below. He inflicted punishments by the letter of the law but did not examine the inner realities [of the supposed crimes], so that those who did good did not necessarily avoid punishment, and those who committed transgressions were not necessarily punished. Consequently, his numerous officials made a display of empty words, without any regard for their relationship to reality. Outwardly they conformed to the propriety of serving their lord while inwardly they harbored hearts set on defying their ruler. They committed all kinds of deceits and shamelessly pursued profit. The ruler of Qin also was fond of employing cruel and vindictive officials who imposed taxes and levies without limit and who exhausted the resources and strength of the common people. Consequently, the people became scattered and lost, as they could not fulfill their livelihoods tilling and weaving. Bands of thieves arose in droves. Thus the numbers of people who were punished proliferated while [the corpses of] those who were executed could be seen everywhere. Yet wrongdoing did not cease to exist. The change in customs caused things to be so. Thus Confucius said: "If you lead the people with laws and you regulate them with punishments, they will evade [the laws and punishments,] but they will have no sense of shame."[26] This is what is meant. [2511]

26. *Analects* 2.1.

Currently Your Highness has united the whole world. All who live within the [Four] Seas have submitted to Your Highness. Your Highness has observed broadly and listened widely, reaching the limits of what your subjects know and exhausting the beauty of what the empire provides. Your supreme Virtue brilliantly operates beyond the borders of the empire: from Yelang to Kangju; territories separated by ten thousand *li* delight in your Virtue and revert to your righteousness. Surely this is the coming of Great Peace. But Your achievements have yet to benefit the common people because Your kingly heart has yet to cleave to them. Zengzi said: "He reveres what he has heard, so his loftiness becomes brighter; he implements what he has learned, so his radiance becomes greater. Making bright his loftiness and making great his radiances do not rest with anything other than applying his mind to it."[27] Your servant implores Your Highness to follow and use what [Your Highness] has heard, establish it sincerely in [Your Highness's] heart, and extend and implement it [throughout the empire]. If done, how would Your Highness differ from the Three Kings?

Your Highness has personally tilled the fields to emphasize the primacy of agriculture, rising before dawn and retiring after dusk, constantly pondering remote antiquity and striving to search out worthy men. In this way, Your Highness has also applied his mind as Yao and Shun did. But Your Highness cannot yet say that he has obtained any rewards for his efforts, because previously scholars have not been encouraged. Now desiring to seek out worthy men when one has not previously encouraged scholars is like seeking out the brilliant shape of jade without carving it. Therefore, among the important ways to nurture scholars, none is greater than a grand academy. A grand academy is an institution to which scholars will attach themselves. It is the root and source of transformation through moral instruction. Currently, despite the numerous [recommended] scholars from the commanderies and kingdoms, among those who responded, none has provided a [satisfactory] answer to your communication. This surely indicates that the Kingly Way is heading toward extinction. Your servant implores Your Highness to establish a grand academy and appoint enlightened teachers in order to nurture the empire's scholars. Frequently test and question them in order to make the most of their talents. Then [the services of] the eminent and brave surely will be secured.

At the present time, the governors of the commanderies and prefects of the provinces are the teachers and leaders of the common people. They are the ones who have been commanded to propagate transformation [among the common

27. *Da Dai liji* 5.

people]. Thus if the teachers and leaders are not worthy, then the ruler's virtue will not be proclaimed, and his benevolent and saturating [moral influence] will not flow forth. Now the subofficial functionaries[28] are lacking in education and instruction in the lower echelons of government. Some fail to accept and employ the laws of their ruler and superiors. [Instead,] they tyrannize the common people and proffer deals with the treacherous so that the poor and destitute, and the orphaned and infirm, suffer injustice and hardship and consequently lose their livelihoods. Surely such actions hardly express Your Highness's intent! This is why yin and yang are out of step and noxious *qi* fills and chokes the heavens, so that the numerous forms of life rarely reach maturity and the common people have yet to find relief. In all cases, it is the lack of enlightenment among the chiefs and subofficial functionaries that brought this about. [2511–12]

The chiefs and subofficial functionaries come mainly from the ranks of the gentlemen of the interior[29] and the inner gentlemen,[30] who in turn are selected through recommendations from the sons and younger brothers of two-thousand-bushel [high-ranking] officials. Just because they are wealthy does not necessarily mean that they are worthy. Moreover, in antiquity officials who were deemed meritorious were ranked in accordance with the extent to which they fulfilled the responsibilities of their assigned posts and not in accordance with the length of time they served. Thus those officials whose capabilities were limited remained in minor posts even if they served for a long time, whereas those whose capabilities were worthy, even if they had not served for long, were not precluded from possibly being promoted to a high post. This is why officials employed all their strength and fully developed their knowledge, exerting themselves to the utmost to master their tasks and thereby accrue merit. Nowadays the circumstances are not the same. Officials earn various honors because of their seniority. The longer their tenure in office is, the higher their post will be. This is why the honest and the corrupt are mixed together and the worthy and degenerate are confused, and their true abilities are not yet ascertained. Your servant, in his ignorance, is of the opinion that Your Highness should direct the Lords

28. "Throughout history the most common generic term used for Sub-official Functionary [*li* 吏, was] a category of state employees who performed the clerical and more menial tasks in all governmental agencies at all levels and had not ranked civil service status, though at times they could be promoted into official status for meritorious service" (Hucker, *Dictionary of Official Titles*, 301).
29. Official salaries were computed in terms of bushels of grain. The "gentleman of the interior" was "the lowest of 3 rank categories (= 300 bushels) into which most expectant appointees serving as court attendants were divided" (Hucker, *Dictionary of Official Titles*, 301).
30. "In Han, the highest status accorded expectant officials serving as courtiers, rank = 600 bushels" (Hucker, *Dictionary of Official Titles*, 191).

of the Land, the governors of commanderies, and the two-thousand-bushel officials each to select the most worthy men among their functionaries and annually supply two men to serve as guards of the lodgings and observe the abilities of the great ministers. Those who recommend worthy men should be rewarded; those who recommend unworthy men should be punished. In this manner, the imperial marquises and two-thousand-bushel officials will devote their minds to seeking out worthies, and it will be possible to secure the scholars of the empire and employ them in office. If everywhere in the empire, worthy men are identified, prosperity [comparable to that] of the Three Kings will be readily achieved, and a reputation [comparable to that] of Yao and Shun will be attained. Do not consider the longevity of an official's tenure to be meritorious, but, rather, give priority to substantiating and testing an official's worthiness and ability. Assess his capabilities and appoint him to office; appraise his virtue and determine his rank. Then the honest and the corrupt will follow distinct paths, and the worthy and foolish will occupy different posts.

Your Highness has been most generous in overlooking your servant's crimes. [Your Highness] has sent down an imperial command not to be fettered or constrained by the demands of literary form, enabling [your servant] to cut and polish [his] investigations of these matters. Your servant's daring not to fully develop [his response] is due to his ignorance. [2512–13]

The Third Imperial Instruction

Subsequently, the Son of Heaven again issued an imperial instruction, which stated:

Verily, [We] have heard "Those who excel at speaking of Heaven invariably find verification in humankind; those who excel at speaking of the past invariably find proof in the present." Thus We have condescended to question you concerning the responsiveness between Heaven and humankind. We have shown admiration for Yao and Shun and expressed remorse for Jie and Djou with regard to the gradually diminishing and extinguishing [Way] and the gradually brightening and shining Way, with the purest of intentions to enact reform.

Now, you gentlemen understand how yin and yang create and transform, and you are well versed in the Way of the Former Kings, yet your literary compositions have yet to reach the ultimate. Could it be that you are confused concerning which endeavors are most appropriate to the present age? Or does the fact that the threads of your arguments do not connect [and] the central skein [of your formulations] does not compass the subject indicate that you feel We will not understand? That We will listen as if dazed? Now, [some claim] that the teachings of the Three Kings differed in their origins and that each had its failings. [Yet] others say that to endure without changing is the Way. How strange these opinions are! Now, you gentlemen have already expounded on the highest principles of the Great Way and the starting point of order and chaos. You have elaborated on these issues in great detail. Who will return to these issues once more? Does not the *Odes* declare: "Alas! You, noblemen! Do not anticipate that your repose will endure forever. . . . The spirits are listening to you and will bring you radiant happiness!"[31] We will personally examine [your responses]. You gentlemen, do your utmost to clarify the issues raised. [2513–14]

Dong Zhongshu's Reply to the Third Instruction

Your servant has heard that the *Analects* states: "It is perhaps the sage alone who, having started something, will always see it through to the end."[32] Currently Your Highness has sent down favor and bestowed kindness by retaining and heeding his servant who has inherited the learning [of the sages]. Once again, [Your Highness] has promulgated an enlightened edict [inviting scholars] to parse His ideas, so as to fully investigate the virtue of the sages. This is not something Your ignorant servant, with his limited capabilities, is equipped to do. Previously in the response submitted to the throne, the thread [of the arguments] did not connect, the central skein [of the formulations] did not compass the subject, the language was not clear, and the principles [were] not distinguished. This all is due to the faults of Your servant, who is vile and lowly. [2514–15]

The imperial instruction states: "Those who excel at speaking of Heaven invariably find verification in humankind; those who excel at speaking of the past invariably find proof in the present."

Your servant has heard that Heaven is the ancestor of all things. Thus it covers and envelopes [all things] so that there is nothing separate from it.

31. *Odes* 207, verse 5.
32. *Analects* 19.12.

> It establishes the sun and moon, wind and rain, to harmonize things.
>
> It regulates yin and yang, cold and heat, to complete things.

Thus the sages emulated Heaven in establishing the Way. With universal love and free from selfish desires, they spread their bounty and displayed their humaneness to benefit [the people]. They established righteous principles and set out behavioral norms to instruct [the people].

> Spring is the means by which Heaven generates things; humaneness is the means by which the ruler loves things.
>
> Summer is the means by which Heaven develops things; beneficence is the means by which the ruler nurtures things.
>
> Frost is the means by which Heaven kills; punishments are the means by which the ruler penalizes.

Speaking from this perspective, the verifications of Heaven in the human world are principles that endure from antiquity to the present.

When Confucius composed the *Spring and Autumn*, he planned it with regard to the Way of Heaven above and substantiated it with regard to the sentiments of humankind below. He compared [its accounts] with ancient practices and tested them against the present. Therefore,

> [conduct] that the *Spring and Autumn* condemned engendered anomalies.
>
> [Conduct] that the *Spring and Autumn* despised gave rise to disasters.

Confucius recorded the faults of the states and related them to various anomalous and disastrous transformations to demonstrate that no matter how good or how evil, the actions of human beings pervade and penetrate Heaven and Earth, and past and future respond to one another. Such is the paramount principle of Heaven.

The ancient [rulers] cultivated officials who took charge of instruction and training, striving to transform the people with virtue and goodness. After the people had been greatly transformed, there was not a single criminal case throughout the empire. The present age, however, has abandoned and failed to cultivate [such officials.] Consequently, it lacks the means to transform the common people. Thus the common people have ceased to practice righteousness and instead risk death for the sake of wealth and profit. They defy the laws, and their crimes proliferate so that criminal cases in a single year number in the millions. Thus we can see why the practices of the ancients must be followed and why the *Spring and Autumn* criticized those who departed from them.

Heaven's command is called the "Mandate." Without a sage, the Mandate cannot be implemented. The unadorned substance [of a living creature] is called the "nature." Without transformation through moral instruction, the nature cannot be perfected. Human desire is called the "disposition." Without limiting regulations, the disposition cannot be moderated. For this reason, with regard to what lies above, the king is careful to recognize the intentions of Heaven in order to comply with Heaven's Mandate. With regard to what lies below, the king strives to enlighten his people by means of transformation through moral instruction in order to complete their nature. He rectifies the suitability of the various laws and measures and establishes the hierarchy of superior and inferior in order to guard against [unrestrained] desires. If the ruler cultivates these three, the great root will be promoted.

Human beings receive their destiny from Heaven.[33] Consequently, they differ immeasurably from other forms of life. Inside their households, they have the kinship relations of father and son, and of elder and younger brother. Outside their households, they have the propriety of ruler and minister, and of superior and inferior. When they gather together in social intercourse with others, they have the various social distinctions of seniority and youth. How splendid are the cultural forms with which they communicate with one another! How peaceful the sense of compassion with which they relate to one another! These are the reasons why human beings are so noble. They raise the five [kinds of] grain to feed themselves, silk and hemp to clothe themselves, and the six beasts of burden to nourish themselves. They yoke the ox and harness the horse, trap the leopard and cage the tiger. This is how they obtain the numinous quality of Heaven and why they are nobler than other things. Therefore Confucius said: "Of all the forms of life that exist within Heaven and Earth, humans are the noblest."[34]

If [someone] is aware of the [true] nature of Heaven, he will understand that he is nobler than all other things.

> Only after a person realizes that he is nobler than all other things will he understand humaneness and righteousness.
>
> Only after a person understands humaneness and righteousness will he value ritual and etiquette.
>
> Only after he values ritual and etiquette will he find contentment in abiding in the good.
>
> Only after he finds contentment in abiding in the good will he find joy in conforming to the patterns [of Heaven].
>
> Only after he finds joy in conforming to the patterns [of Heaven] will he be deemed a noble man.

33. Compare with *CQFL* 44.1.
34. *Xiao jing* (*Classic of Filial Piety*) 9.

Therefore Confucius said: "One has no way of becoming a noble man unless he understands the Mandate."[35] This is what he meant. [2515–16]

The imperial instruction states: "[We] have shown admiration for Yao and Shun and expressed remorse for Jie and Djou with regard to the gradually diminishing and extinguishing [Way] and the gradually brightening and shining Way, with the purest of intentions to enact reform."

Your servant has heard that one achieves abundance by amassing things little by little; one attains significance by accumulating what is insignificant. Therefore the sage relies on what is hidden to become manifest; he relies on the insignificant to become significant. Thus Yao appeared among the ranks of the Lords of the Land, and Shun emerged from deep within the mountains. Neither achieved fame in the course of a day. On the contrary, they achieved it only gradually. Words that come from the heart cannot be repressed; acts that emanate from the core of one's person cannot be concealed. Speech and conduct are the most vital aspects of governance. They are the means by which the noble man moves Heaven and Earth. Therefore, those who concentrate on small things will become great, and those who are cautious about subtle things will become manifest. The *Odes* declare: "King Wen was circumspect and reverent."[36] Consequently, Yao trembled as he daily pursued the Way, and Shun proceeded fearfully as he daily extended his filial piety. Their small acts of goodness accumulated, and their reputations became prominent; their virtue became ever more manifest, and their persons revered. Such is the manner in which the Way gradually became illustrious and prosperous.

One accumulates goodness just as days lengthen so gradually that no one perceives it. Unless you are able to see clearly the disposition and nature of human beings, and unless you look deeply into mores and customs, how will you be able to perceive [such gradual phenomena]? This is how Yao and Shun gained their commanding reputations, and how Jie and Djou were able to cause so much bitterness and dread. Now, goodness begets goodness and wrongdoing begets wrongdoing, just as the shadow corresponds to the form and the echo to the sound. When Jie and Djou were violent and cruel, bandits and thieves arose in droves while the worthy and knowledgeable hid themselves away. Wrongdoing daily became more prominent while the state daily grew more chaotic. Although [Jie and Djou] considered themselves as secure as the sun in the sky, they finally came to a disreputable end. Those who are violent and devoid of humanity

35. *Analects* 20.3.
36. *Odes* 236, verse 3.

cannot be eradicated in a single day. This, too, is brought about gradually. Accordingly, although Jie and Djou lost the Way, [each] clung to power for more than a decade. Such is the manner in which the Way gradually became obscure and lost. [2517]

The imperial instruction states: "Now, [some claim] that the teachings of the Three Kings differed in their origins and each had its failings. [Yet] others say that to endure without changing is the Way. How can these differences be explained?"

Your servant has heard that what brings joy and yet does not cause disorder, what is repeatedly applied yet is not oppressive, is called "the Way." The Way has endured for ten thousand generations without flaw. If flaws should arise, this means that the Way has been lost. The Way of the Former Kings necessarily possessed aspects that were biased and undeveloped because the governments [they inherited] were, in certain respects, unenlightened and ineffective. They implemented corrective measures in order to repair such flaws and nothing more. "The teachings of the Three Kings differed in their origins" does not mean that their Ways were opposed to one another but that in restraining what was excessive and propping up what was declining, the changing circumstances they encountered differed from one another. Thus Confucius said: "Was it not Shun who ruled by taking no action?"[37] He simply altered the first month of the year and changed the color of court dress to comply with the Mandate of Heaven. In the remaining matters of governance, he completely followed the Way of Yao. Why would he have changed anything else? Thus a king might outwardly change regulations, but he does not inwardly alter the substance of the Way. Accordingly, the Xia esteemed loyalty, the Yin esteemed respectfulness, and the Zhou esteemed refinement, because it was suitable to employ [those qualities] to restrain [the flaws] that each had inherited. Confucius said: "The Yin observed the rituals of the Xia. What they diminished and what they augmented can be known. The Zhou observed the ritual of the Yin. What they diminished and what they augmented can [also] be known."[38] What the ruler who will succeed the Zhou [will diminish and what he will augment] will be known a hundred generations from now. This means that what the next one hundred kings do

37. *Analects* 15.5.
38. *Analects* 2.23.

will consist of these three and nothing more. The Xia followed [the rituals of] Shun. In this case alone, Confucius did not speak of diminishing or augmenting because their Way was as one and what they esteemed was identical. The great source of the Way emanates from Heaven. Heaven does not change; the Way also does not change. Thus when Yu succeeded Shun and Shun succeeded Yao, these three sages received and safeguarded the same Way. There were no policies [needed] to repair flaws, and so there is no discussion of what they diminished and what they augmented. Looking at the issue from this perspective, for a ruler who succeeds a well-governed age, the Way remains the same. For a ruler who succeeds a chaotic age, the Way changes. Now the Han [dynasty], having succeeded a profoundly chaotic government, should diminish the refined policies of the Zhou and employ the loyalty of the Xia. [2518–19]

Your Highness, being in possession of enlightened virtue and the outstanding Way, is saddened by the dissipating customs of our age and remorseful that the Kingly Way does not shine forth. Thus Your Highness has recommended scholars who are worthy and excellent, straightforward and upright[39] to discuss and deliberate and to be tested and questioned, desiring to restore the excellent virtues of Humaneness and Righteousness, to clarify the laws and institutions of the thearchs and kings, and to establish the Way of Great Peace. Your servant, being stupid and degenerate, merely transmits what he has heard and recites what he has studied, speaking the words of his teachers, and in doing so, he is scarcely able to avoid error. To discuss the successes and failures of governmental policies and investigate what the empire is at stake to lose or gain are the duty of the bulwarks and assistants of the grand ministers, and the responsibility of the Three Dukes and Nine Ministers. They are not issues Your servant Zhongshu is capable of addressing. Nonetheless, Your servant humbly submits the following perverse [opinion].

Now, the empire of antiquity is no different from the empire of today, and the empire of today is no different from the empire of antiquity. Both are empires, but in antiquity the empire was immeasurably well ordered. Superior and inferior were harmonious and cooperative. Practices and customs were exquisite and

39. *Xianliang fangzheng* 賢良方正 was a recommendation category "for men nominated by local officials to be considered at the capital for selection and appointment for government posts" (Hucker, *Dictionary of Official Titles*, 242). Note that the recommendation category referred to here differs from that mentioned by Ban Gu in introducing the first imperial edict, providing additional evidence that Ban Gu preserved official documents from more than one imperial communication between Dong Zhongshu and Emperor Wu. For a detailed discussion of additional evidence, see Sarah A. Queen, *From Chronicle to Canon: The Hermeneutics of the "Spring and Autumn" According to Tung Chung-shu* (Cambridge: Cambridge University Press, 1996), app. 2.

prosperous. Without being commanded, [the people] acted; without being prohibited, they desisted. The clerks were free from wrongdoing, the people were free from banditry, and the prisons stood empty. Virtue watered the grasses and plants, and favors showered the Four Seas. Phoenixes came to form flocks, and *qilins* came to roam about. Measuring the past against the present, how far removed is the present from the past! How is it that we have arrived at such a state of insult and injury? Is there anything in our intentions that has erred from the Way of Antiquity? Is there anything that has defied Heaven's principles? If we try to trace it back to antiquity and refer it back to Heaven, then surely we will know!

Now, Heaven apportions its gifts. [Creatures] that are given upper teeth are not [also] permitted to have horns; those to which wings are attached are given [only] two feet. Likewise, those who have been endowed with great things may not appropriate small things as well. In antiquity, those who were given salaries did not eat by means of their own physical labor, nor did they participate in the branch occupations. This is also a case of being endowed with great things, not appropriating small things, and thereby identifying with Heaven's will. Now, if Heaven could hardly provide sufficiently for those who, having received great things, also sought to appropriate small things, how much less can humans do so! [That those in high positions appropriate more than their fair share] is why the people wail bitterly about their insufficiencies.

How can the people tolerate those who are favored with positions of eminence, having warm houses and enjoying substantial salaries, availing themselves of the resources of their wealth and position to compete for profit with them? They increase the numbers of their servants, multiply the numbers of their livestock, enlarge the sizes of their land and estates, augment the fruits of their professions, and amass supplies of grain. They exert their utmost on these endeavors and nothing else, oppressing the common people so that as the days and months pass by, the common people are gradually reduced to utter destitution. If the wealthy are extravagant and wasteful, the poor will become destitute and aggrieved. If the poor become destitute and aggrieved and the emperor does not relieve them, then the people will find no joy in living. If the people find no joy in living, they will do nothing to avoid death. How is it possible, then, that they will avoid committing crimes? This is why depravity cannot be overcome even if punishments are increased. Therefore, the households that receive an official salary should live off their official salaries and nothing more. They should not compete for resources with the common people. Only then will benefits be distributed equally, and the people will be able to provide sufficiently for their households. Such policies esteem the principles of Heaven and also the Way of Remote Antiquity. They are what the Son of Heaven should emulate in devising his institutions and what officials ought to follow and implement.

Thus when the prime minster of Lu, Master Gongyi,[40] returned home and saw his wife weaving silk, he grew angry and banished her. When he went home to dine and [saw his servants] pickling vegetables, he grew vexed and uprooted the vegetables, exclaiming: "I already live off an official salary. How could I deprive the farmers and weavers of their profit?"[41] All the worthy and noble men of antiquity who took up various official positions were like this. Thus all their subordinates admired their conduct and followed their teachings, while the common people were transformed by their incorruptibility and were no longer scornful. But coming to the decline of the Zhou dynasty, in contrast, the chief ministers were lax in practicing righteousness, yet frantic to pursue profit. Though utterly lacking retiring and deferential habits, they occupied themselves with lawsuits to vie for land. Accordingly, the poets despised and satirized them, saying: "How lofty is the Southern Mountain! How massive its boulders! How awesome are you, Master Yin! The people all look to you."[42] If You[43] are fond of righteousness, the people will turn to humaneness, and customs will become good. If You are fond of profit, the people will grow fond of depravity, and customs will become corrupt. From this perspective, it is clear that the Son of Heaven and his chief ministers are those whom the common people watch and emulate, and those whom the inhabitants of distant regions on all sides look to for guidance. Surely it is not possible for one to whom people both near and far look for their example to occupy the position of the worthy man, yet conduct himself as the common man! If the August Emperor seeks wealth and profit, ever fearful that He will not have enough, His intentions will be those of a common man. If the August Emperor seeks humaneness and righteousness, ever fearful that He will not be able to transform the people, His intentions will be those of a noble man. The *Changes* states: "Carrying his burdens on his back, he avails himself of a carriage and thereby invites robbers to attack him."[44] To avail oneself of a carriage reflects the station of the noble man; to carry a burden's on one's

40. Gongyi Xiu 公儀休 was prime minister under Duke Mu of Lu (r. 407–376 B.C.E.), who enjoyed a reputation for frugality and incorruptibility.
41. For other Han versions of this popular narrative, see *Huainanzi* 12.32 [12/113/22–26] and *SJ* 119/3101–2. For English translations, see Major et al., *Huainanzi* 463–64; and Burton Watson, trans., *Records of the Grand Historian*, rev. ed. (New York: Columbia University Press, 1993), 2:375–76.
42. *Odes* 191, verse 1.
43. Note here the use of the pronoun *er* 爾, a more formal second person pronoun than *ru* 汝.
44. *Changes* 40 ("Jie"), line 3.

back reflects the station of the small man. This means that one who occupies the station of the noble man yet follows the pursuit of the common man will inevitably be overtaken by disaster. If one wishes to occupy the position of a noble man and engage in conduct appropriate to that station, then one can never forsake the example of Gongyi Xiu when he was a minister in Lu. [2520–21]

The *Spring and Autumn* magnifies unified rule.[45] This is the eternal warp thread binding together Heaven and Earth and the penetrating righteousness pervading the past and the present. Today teachers differ in their instructions, men differ in their theories, and the numerous lineages of learning differ in their prescriptions, so that principles and their interpretations diverge from each other. Thus the throne has no means with which to unify rule. Moreover, laws and institutions have changed repeatedly so that His subjects do not know what to sustain. Your servant, in his ignorance, considers that what does not lie within the Six Disciplines and the Arts of Confucius should be proscribed and should not be allowed to be pursued. Only after bad and perverse doctrines are stopped will Your rule be unified, the laws be clarified, and the people know what to follow. [2522]

Administrator of Jiangdu

When [Dong Zhongshu's] responses were concluded, the Son of Heaven appointed him to be the administrator to Jiangdu to serve King Yi [personal name Liu Fei]. King Yi was the elder brother of the emperor. He was unrefined and haughty and was fond of bravado. Zhongshu employed propriety and righteousness to correct and rectify [the king]. [Consequently,] the king respected [Dong] and took him seriously.

After some time had passed, the king inquired about Zhongshu:[46] "The king of Yue, together with the great officers [Shi] Yong, [Wen] Zhong, and [Fan] Li, made a plan to attack [the state of] Wu. Confucius said: 'There were three humane men [during] the Yin [dynasty].'[47] I, the Orphaned One [i.e., the king] submit that

45. The concept that in writing the *Spring and Autumn*, Confucius tried to underscore the importance of unified rule is discussed explicitly and implicitly throughout the *Gongyang Commentary*. It is no accident that the commentary opens with this claim in its first entry under Duke Yin.

46. This exchange with the king of Jiangdu is preserved, with minor editorial variations, as chapter 32 of the *Chunqiu fanlu*.

47. *Analects* 18.1.

there also were three humane men in Yue. As Duke Huan [of Qi] handed off his questions to Guan Zhong, so do I, the Orphaned One, hand off mine to you." Zhongshu responded, saying:

> Your servant is stupid, and [his knowledge] is not sufficient to submit a significant response. [2523] [Your servant] has heard that in earlier times, the lord of Lu asked Liuxia Hui: "I wish to attack Qi. What do you think?" Liuxia Hui responded: "That is not permissible." Having returned home with a worried expression, he said: "I have heard that when [the ruler] is going to attack another state, he does not question those who are humane. Why were these questions directed at me?" Liuxia Hui was ashamed even when he was merely asked about the subject. How much more [would he have been ashamed] if he had plotted [along with King Goujian] to treacherously attack Wu. Looking at the question from this perspective, [the kingdom of] Yue fundamentally lacked even one humane man. A humane man is one who
>
> > corrects his Way but does not calculate what benefits that will bring him;
> > adheres to principles without hurrying after success.
>
> The righteousness of the *Spring and Autumn* honors trustworthiness and censures deceit. To deceive others in order to achieve victory, even if successful, is not something a noble man would do. This is why even a five-foot-tall boy[48] who lodges within the gate of [i.e., follows the teachings of] Confucius is ashamed to mention the Five Hegemons, because they placed treachery and force before humaneness and righteousness. They engaged in treachery and nothing else. Therefore they are not worthy of being mentioned within the gate of the great Noble Man [Confucius]. Compared with other Lords of the Land, the Five Hegemons were worthy; compared with the Three Kings, they were but coarse stone to polished jade.

The king responded: "Excellent." [2524]

Zhongshu brought order to the state [of Jiangdu] by using ominous changes such as the natural disasters and strange events recorded in the *Spring and Autumn* to deduce the causes of disorderly conduct among the yin and yang. Therefore,

48. The length of a Han "foot" was about nine inches in modern measure, so a "five-foot-tall boy" would have stood about three feet, eleven inches—a very young boy.

when inducing rain, he repressed yang and released yin; when stopping rain, he reversed those techniques. When he implemented those techniques in this single state, he never failed to obtain the desired results.

Danger at Court

In the midst of his tenure as administrator to Jiangdu, [Dong Zhongshu] was dismissed from his post and appointed as a grand master to the palace.[49] Before this, there were ominous fires in the temple to Emperor Gao in Liaodong and in the side hall of his funerary temple in Zhangling. Zhongshu, residing at home, deduced and analyzed their significance. He had not yet submitted his draft [report] to the throne when Zhufu Yan paid a visit to Zhongshu. When he caught sight of the draft, being jealous of Zhongshu, he stole the composition and sent it to the throne [with a covering] memorial. The emperor summoned an audience with the various Confucian scholars. Zhongshu's disciple Lü Bushu, who was unaware that it was his teacher's composition, pronounced it "utterly foolish." Subsequently, Zhongshu was remanded to the legal officials, who sentenced him to death; however, an imperial instruction pardoned him. After this incident, Zhongshu did not dare speak again of disasters and anomalies.

Zhongshu personally was incorruptible and frank. At that time, the four tribes that lived beyond the limits of the empire were being pressured to submit to the emperor. Gongsun Hong's mastery of the *Spring and Autumn* did not compare with that of Zhongshu, yet Hong put himself forward on every possible occasion and so rose up the ladder of officialdom to achieve high ministerial rank. Zhongshu considered Hong to be an obsequious toady, and Hong, for his part, despised [Dong Zhongshu].

Administrator of Jiaoxi

[Now it happened that] the king of Jiaoxi, an elder brother of the emperor, was particularly unrestrained, numerous times having mistreated his

49. This was one of three policy consultants to the emperor, as defined in Hucker, *Dictionary of Official Titles*, 194.

two-thousand-bushel officials. Hong consequently spoke to the emperor and said: "Only Dong Zhongshu is up to the task of being appointed administrator to the king of Jiaoxi."[50] The king of Jiaozi, having heard that Zhongshu was a great Confucian, treated him well, [but] Zhongshu feared that he if remained long [in this post,] he would be [falsely] accused of some crime. So he retired on the grounds of illness.

Retirement

As the administrator of two states, in both instances he served an arrogant king yet remained upright in his person in order to lead his subordinates. He repeatedly submitted letters to the throne in remonstration and resistance. Teaching and commanding those within the states [he served], wherever he resided was well governed. When he retired from his post and returned home to live, to the end of his days he did not pay attention to [enhancing] his family's livelihood, but instead occupied his time cultivating his scholarship and writing books.

When Zhongshu was retired, if the central court held an important deliberation, [the emperor would] send emissaries, including even the chamberlain for law enforcement, Zhang Tang himself, to travel to his home and question him. All his responses had clear standards. From the time that Emperor Wu was first established on the throne and when the marquis of Weiqi and the marquis of Wuan [each] served as supreme commander and exalted the Confucians,[51] Dong Zhongshu's responses to imperial instructions promoted and clarified [the teachings of] Confucius. The repression and proscription of the One Hundred Lineages and the establishment of official organs of education [that enabled] provinces and commanderies to recommend "flourishing talent" and "filial and incorrupt" [young men] all emanated from Zhongshu. When he was old, he lived out his years and died a natural death at home. [After his death,] his family was moved to Maoling. Owing to their erudition, his sons and grandsons achieved high office.

50. The king of Jiaoxi was a "hawk" with respect to frontier policy, which added to the danger of being in his administration.

51. Dou Ying, marquis of Weiqi, served as supreme commander under Emperor Jing and held various offices early in the reign of Emperor Wu. Tian Fen, marquis of Wuan, held that office briefly early in the reign of Emperor Wu. Both were noted proponents of classical learning. See *SJ* 107, "Biographies of the Marquises of Weiqi and Wuan"; Watson, *Records of the Grand Historian*, 2:89–106.

All of Zhongshu's compositions elucidated the meaning of the classical arts. Memorials submitted to the throne and items of instruction totaled 120 *pian*. His expositions of the successful and unsuccessful affairs [recorded in] the *Spring and Autumn*, such writings as *Heard and Promoted*, *Jade Cup*, *Luxuriant Gems*, *Pure Brightness*, and *Bamboo Grove* came to an additional several tens of *pian*, amounting to more than a hundred thousand characters. All were transmitted to later generations. Selections from compositions relating to matters of the court at the time comprised additional *pian*.

The encomium states: Liu Xiang declared: "Dong Zhongshu had the ability to assist a true king. Even Yi [Yin] and Lü [Wang] [would have] lacked the means to augment [his talents], while the likes of Guan [Zhong] and Yan [Ying] certainly did not compare with him." Liu Xiang's son Liu Xin remarked, "Yi Yin and Lü Wang were partners of the sage-kings. If the kings had not emulated them, they would not have prospered. Thus when Yan Yuan died, Confucius said: 'Alas! Heaven is destroying me.' "[52] If one man alone was able to bring Confucius to this, then Cai Wo, Zi You, and Zi Lu did not compare with him. Zhongshu encountered the aftermath of Qin's destruction of learning, [the effects of which were] inherited by the Han. The Six Classics had been torn asunder. [Yet] with lowered curtain, he expressed his ardor, diligently pursuing his grand undertaking, enabling future scholars to enjoy [the classical learning] he had gathered into one and unified. He was a leader among the various Confucians, yet if you examine those teachers and friends who were influenced by his instruction, they still did not compare with Zi You and Zi Xia. To say "Yan [Ying] certainly did not compare with him" or "Even Yi [Yin] and Lü [Wang] [would have] lacked the means to augment [his talents]" is excessive. Yet coming down to Liu Xiang, who compared and discussed the ideal of the noble man on numerous occasions with Dong's grandson Gong, Liu Xiang's words are what they are.[53]

52. *Analects* 11.8.

53. In other words, Liu Xin thinks that his father exaggerated Dong's importance but is unwilling to say so in writing.

Selected Bibliography

Michael Loewe's biographical study *Dong Zhongshu, a "Confucian" Heritage, and the "Chunqiu fanlu"* (Leiden: Brill, 2011) contains an extensive and up-to-date bibliography of relevant works, which it would seem pointless to duplicate here. Accordingly, this bibliography lists only our reference editions for classical Chinese texts, translations of the *Chunqiu fanlu* into modern Chinese, and important secondary studies (including partial translations of the *Chunqiu fanlu* into Western languages).

Arbuckle, Gary. "The *jiao* 'Suburban' Sacrifice in the *Chunqiu fanlu*." Paper presented at the annual meeting of the Association for Asian Studies, New Orleans, April 13, 1991.

——. "A Note on the Authenticity of the *Chunqiu Fanlu*." *T'oung Pao* 75 (1989): 226–34.

——. "Restoring Dong Zhongshu (BCE 195–115): An Experiment in Historical and Philosophical Reconstruction." Ph.D. diss., University of British Columbia, 1991.

——. "Some Remarks on a New Translation of the *Chunqiu fanlu*." *Early China* 17 (1992): 215–33.

——. "The Works of Dong Zhongshu and the Text Traditionally and Incorrectly Titled *Luxuriant Dew of the Annals (Chunqiu fanlu)*." Formerly available at http://www.sagesource.net/dong/works_part_A.html. Last updated 2004 and last accessed July 29, 2008. [This URL is now defunct, and we do not know where, if at all, this paper is now available]

Bujard, Marianne. "La vie de Dong Zhongshu: Enigmes et hypothèses." *Journal Asiatique* 280 (1992): 145–217.

Chan, Wing-Tsit, trans. and comp. *A Source Book in Chinese Philosophy*. Princeton, N.J.: Princeton University Press, 1965.

Cheng, Anne. "Ch'un ch'iu 春秋, Kung yang 公羊, Ku liang 穀梁, and Tso chuan 左傳." In *Early Chinese Texts: A Bibliographical Guide*, edited by Michael Loewe, 67–76. Early China Special

Monograph Series, no. 2. Berkeley: Society for the Study of Early China and the Institute of East Asian Studies, University of California, 1993.

——. *Étude sur le Confucianisme Han: L'élaboration d'une tradition exégétique sur les Classiques*. Paris: Collège de France, Institut des hautes études chinoises, 1985. [Includes translation of chapter 12]

Cullen, Christopher. *Astronomy and Mathematics in Ancient China: The "Zhou bi suan jing."* Needham Research Institute Studies, no. 1. Cambridge: Cambridge University Press, 2007.

Dubs, Homer H., trans. *The History of the Former Han Dynasty*. 3 vols. Baltimore: Waverly Press, 1938–1955.

Elman, Benjamin. *Classicism, Politics, and Kinship: The Ch'ang-chou School of New Text Confucianism in Late Imperial China*. Berkeley: University of California Press, 1990. [Includes translation of chapter 12]

Eno, Robert. *The Confucian Creation of Heaven: Philosophy and the Defense of Ritual Mastery*. Albany: State University of New York Press, 1990.

Feng Youlan 馮友蘭. *Zhongguo zhexue shi* 中國哲學史. Shanghai: Commercial Press, 1934.

Franke, Otto. *Studien zur Geschichte des konfuzianischen Dogmas und der chinesischen Staatsreligion*. Hamburg: Friederichsen, 1920. [Includes translation of chapter 12]

Fung Yu-lan [Feng Youlan]. *A History of Chinese Philosophy*. Vol. 1, *The Period of the Philosophers (From the Beginnings to Circa 100 B.C.)*. Translated by Derk Bodde. Princeton, N.J.: Princeton University Press, 1952.

——. *A History of Chinese Philosophy*. Vol. 2, *The Period of Classical Learning (From the Second Century B.C. to the Twentieth Century A.D.)*. Translated by Derk Bodde. Princeton, N.J.: Princeton University Press, 1953.

Gassmann, Robert. *Üppiger Tau des Frühling-und-Herbst-Klassikers: Übersetzung und Annotation der Kapitel eins bis sechs*. Schweitzer Asiatische Studien Monographien, no. 8. Bern: Peter Lang, 1988. [Includes translations of chapters 1–6]

Gentz, Joachim. "Confucius Confronting Contingency in the *Lunyu* and the *Gongyang zhuan*." *Journal of Chinese Philosophy* 39, no. 1 (2012): 60–70.

——. *Das "Gongyang zhuan": Auslegung und Kanonisierung der "Frühlings- und Herbstannalen (Chunqiu)."* Wiesbaden: Harrassowitz, 2001. [Includes translations of chapters 12 and 17 and passages from chapters 1–9]

——. "Language of Heaven, Exegetical Skepticism, and the Reinsertion of Religious Concepts in the Gongyang Tradition." In *Early Chinese Religion: Part One: Shang Through Han (1250 BC–220 AD)*, edited by John Lagerwey and Marc Kalinowski, 813–38. Leiden: Brill, 2008.

——. "Long Live the King! The Ideology of Power Between Ritual and Morality in the *Gongyang zhuan* 公羊傳." In *Ideology of Power and Power of Ideology in Early China*, edited by Yuri Pines, Paul Rakita Goldin, and Martin Kern, 69–117. Leiden: Brill, 2015.

——. "Mohist Traces in the Early *Chunqiu fanlu* Chapters." *Oriens Extremus* 48 (2009): 55–70.

——. "The Past as a Messianic Vision: Historical Thought and Strategies of Sacralization in the Early Gongyang Tradition." In *Historical Truth, Historical Criticism, and Ideology: Chinese Historiography and Historical Culture from a New Comparative Perspective*, edited by Helwig Schmidt-Glintzer, Achim Mittag, and Jörn Rüsen, 227–54. Leiden: Brill, 2005.

——. "Ritual Meaning of Textual Form: Evidence from Early Commentaries of the Historiographic and Ritual Traditions." In *Text and Ritual in Early China*, edited by Martin Kern, 124–48. Seattle: University of Washington Press, 2005.

Giele, Enno. *Imperial Decision-Making and Communication in Early China: A Study of Cai Yong's "Duduan."* Wiesbaden: Harrassowitz, 2006.

Graham, A. C. *Disputers of the Tao: Philosophical Argument in Ancient China*. LaSalle, Ind.: Open Court, 1989.

Han shu buzhu 漢書補注. Beijing: Zhonghua shuju, 1983.

Henderson, John B. *The Development and Decline of Chinese Cosmology*. New York: Columbia University Press, 1984.

Hucker, Charles O. *A Dictionary of Official Titles in Imperial China*. Stanford, Calif.: Stanford University Press, 1985.

Knoblock, John. *Xunzi: A Translation and Study of the Complete Works*. 3 vols. Stanford, Calif.: Stanford University Press, 1988, 1990, 1994.

Knoblock, John, and Jeffrey Riegel, trans. *The Annals of Lü Buwei: A Complete Translation and Study*. Stanford, Calif.: Stanford University Press, 2000.

Lai Yanyuan 賴炎元. *Chunqiu fanlu jinzhu jinyi* 春秋繁露今注今譯. Taibei: Commercial Press, 1984.

Lau, D. C., trans. *The Analects*. Harmondsworth: Penguin, 1979.

——, ed. *Bohutong zhuzi suoyin* 白虎通逐字索引 (*A Concordance to the "Bohutong"*). Chinese University of Hong Kong, Institute of Chinese Studies Ancient Chinese Text Concordance Series. Hong Kong: Commercial Press, 1995.

——, trans. *The Book of Mencius*. Harmondsworth: Penguin, 1970.

——, ed. *Chunqiu fanlu zhuzi suoyin* 春秋繁露逐字索引 (*A Concordance to the "Chunqiu fanlu"*). Chinese University of Hong Kong, Institute of Chinese Studies Ancient Chinese Text Concordance Series. Hong Kong: Commercial Press, 1992.

——, ed. *Gongyang zhuan zhuzi suoyin* 公羊傳逐字索引 (*A Concordance to the "Gongyang Commentary"*). Chinese University of Hong Kong, Institute of Chinese Studies Ancient Chinese Text Concordance Series. Hong Kong: Commercial Press, 1995.

——, ed. *Guanzi zhuzi suoyin* 管子逐字索引 (*A Concordance to the "Guanzi"*). Chinese University of Hong Kong, Institute of Chinese Studies Ancient Chinese Text Concordance Series. Hong Kong: Commercial Press, 2001.

——, ed. *Huainanzi zhuzi suoyin* 淮南子逐字索引 (*A Concordance to the "Huainanzi"*). Chinese University of Hong Kong, Institute of Chinese Studies Ancient Chinese Text Concordance Series. Hong Kong: Commercial Press, 1992.

——, ed. *Lunheng zhuzi suoyin* 論衡逐字索引 (*A Concordance to the "Lunheng"*). Chinese University of Hong Kong, Institute of Chinese Studies Ancient Chinese Text Concordance Series. Hong Kong: Commercial Press, 2008.

——, ed. *Lunyu zhuzi suoyin* 論語逐字索引 (*A Concordance to the "Analects"*). Chinese University of Hong Kong, Institute of Chinese Studies Ancient Chinese Text Concordance Series. Hong Kong: Commercial Press, 1995.

——, ed. *Mengzi zhuzi suoyin* 孟子逐字索引 (*A Concordance to the "Mencius"*). Chinese University of Hong Kong, Institute of Chinese Studies Ancient Chinese Text Concordance Series. Hong Kong: Commercial Press, 1995.

——, ed. *Xin shu zhuzi suoyin* 新書逐字索引 (*A Concordance to the "Xin shu"*). Chinese University of Hong Kong, Institute of Chinese Studies Ancient Chinese Text Concordance Series. Hong Kong: Commercial Press, 1994.

——, ed. *Yan tie lun zhuzi suoyin* 鹽鐵論逐字索引(*A Concordance to the "Debates on Salt and Iron"*). Chinese University of Hong Kong, Institute of Chinese Studies Ancient Chinese Text Concordance Series. Hong Kong: Commercial Press, 1994.

Legge, James, trans. *The Chinese Classics*. 2nd rev. ed. 5 vols. in 4. 1894. Reprint. Hong Kong: Hong Kong University Press, 1960.

——, trans. *Li Chi: Book of Rites*. Edited by Ch'u Chai and Winberg Chai. 2 vols. New Hyde Park, N.Y.: University Books, 1967.

Lewis, Mark Edward. *Writing and Authority in Early China*. Albany: State University of New York Press, 1999.

Liang Cai. "Who Said 'Confucius Composed the *Chunqiu*'? The Genealogy of the *Chunqiu* Canon in the Pre-Han and Han Periods." *History of China* 5, no. 3 (2010): 363–85.

Loewe, Michael. *A Biographical Dictionary of the Qin, Former Han, and Xin Periods (221 BC–AD 24)*. Leiden: Brill, 2000.

——. "The Concept of Sovereignty." In *The Ch'in and Han Empires, 221 B.C.–A.D. 220*, edited by Denis Twitchett and Michael Loewe, 726–46. Vol. 1 of *The Cambridge History of China*. Cambridge: Cambridge University Press, 1986.

——. *Crisis and Conflict in Han China, 104 BC to AD 9*. London: Allen & Unwin, 1974.

——. "The Cult of the Dragon and the Invocation for Rain." In *Chinese Ideas About Nature and Society: Studies in Honour of Derk Bodde*, edited by Charles Le Blanc and Susan Blader, 195–213. Hong Kong: Hong Kong University Press, 1987.

——. "The Cult of the Dragon and the Invocation for Rain." Rev. version. In *Divination, Mythology and Monarchy in Han China*, 142–59. Cambridge: Cambridge University Press, 1994.

——. *Divination, Mythology, and Monarchy in Han China*. Cambridge: Cambridge University Press, 1994.

——. *Dong Zhongshu, a "Confucian" Heritage, and the "Chunqiu fanlu."* Brill China Studies, no. 20. Leiden: Brill, 2011.

——. "The Former Han Dynasty." In *The Ch'in and Han Empires, 221 B.C.–A.D. 220*, edited by Denis Twitchett and Michael Loewe, 103–222. Vol. 1 of *The Cambridge History of China*. Cambridge: Cambridge University Press, 1986.

——. "K'uang Heng and the Reform of Religious Practices—31 B.C." In *Crisis and Conflict in Han China, 104 BC to AD 9*, 154–92. London: Allen & Unwin, 1974.

——. "The Religious and Intellectual Background." In *The Ch'in and Han Empires, 221 B.C.–A.D. 220*, edited by Denis Twitchett and Michael Loewe, 649–725. Vol. 1 of *The Cambridge History of China*. Cambridge: Cambridge University Press, 1986.

——. "Water, Earth and Fire—The Symbols of the Han Dynasty." *Nachrichten der Gesellschaft für Natur-und Völkerkunde Ostasiens/Hamburg* 125 (1979): 63–68.

Mair, Victor H., trans. *The Art of War*. New York: Columbia University Press, 2007.

——, trans. *Wandering on the Way: Early Tales and Parables of Chuang Tzu*. Honolulu: University of Hawai'i Press, 1998.

Major, John S. "The Five Phases, Magic Squares, and Schematic Cosmography." In *Explorations in Early Chinese Cosmology*, edited by Henry Rosemont Jr., 133–66. JAAR Thematic Studies, vol. 50, no. 2. Chico, Calif.: Scholars Press, 1984.

——. *Heaven and Earth in Early Han Thought: Chapters Three, Four, and Five of the "Huainanzi."* Albany: State University of New York Press, 1992.

——. "New Light on the Dark Warrior." *Journal of Chinese Religions* 13–14 (1985/1986): 63–86.

Major, John S., Sarah A. Queen, Andrew Seth Meyer, and Harold D. Roth, trans. and eds., with additional contributions by Michael Puett and Judson Murray. *The "Huainanzi": A Guide to the Theory and Practice of Government in Early Han China*. New York: Columbia University Press, 2010.

Malmqvist, Göran. "Studies on the *Gongyang* and *Guliang* Commentaries." *Bulletin of the Museum of Far Eastern Antiquities* 43 (1971): 67–222; 47 (1975): 19–69; 49 (1977): 33–215.

Needham, Joseph. *Science and Civilisation in China*. Vol. 3, *Mathematics and the Sciences of the Heavens and the Earth*. Cambridge: Cambridge University Press, 1959.

Nylan, Michael. "The Chin wen / Ku wen Controversy in Han Times." *T'oung Pao* 80 (1994): 83–145.

——. *The Five "Confucian" Classics*. New Haven, Conn.: Yale University Press, 2001.

Puett, Michael. *To Become a God: Cosmology, Sacrifice, and Self-Divinization in Early China*. Cambridge, Mass.: Harvard University Press, 2002.

Queen, Sarah A. "Beyond Liu Xiang's Gaze: Debating Womanly Virtue in Early China." *Asia Major* (forthcoming).

——. *From Chronicle to Canon: The Hermeneutics of the "Spring and Autumn" According to Tung Chung-shu*. Cambridge: Cambridge University Press, 1996.

——. "The Rhetoric of Dong Zhongshu's Imperial Communications." In *Facing the Monarch: Modes of Advice in the Early Chinese Court*, edited by Garret P. S. Olberding, 166–202. Harvard East Asian Monographs. Cambridge, Mass.: Harvard University Press, 2013.

Queen, Sarah A., and Michael Puett, eds. *The "Huainanzi" and Textual Production in Early China*. Leiden: Brill, 2014.

Rickett, W. Allyn, trans. *Guanzi: Political, Economic, and Philosophical Essays from Early China*. 2 vols. Princeton, N.J.: Princeton University Press, 1985, 1998.

Riegel, Jeffrey. "The Four 'Tzu Ssu' Chapters of the *Li Chi*: An Analysis and Translation of the *Fang Chi, Chung Yung, Piao Chi*, and *Tzu I*." Ph.D. diss., Stanford University, 1978.

Saiki Tetsurō 齋木哲郎. "*Shunjū hanro* no gishosetsu ni tsuite" 春秋繁露の僞書說について (On Theories That the *Chunqiu fanlu* Is a Forgery). *Kyūko* 汲古 17 (1990): 17–22.

Seufert, Wilhelm. "Urkunden zur staatlichen Neuordnung unter der Han-Dynastie." *Mitteilungen des Seminars für Orientalische Sprachen* 23–25 (1922): 1–55. [Includes translation of the Three Imperial Instructions]

Shiji 史記. Beijing: Zhonghua shuju, 1959.

Sivin, Nathan, Kiyoshi Yabuuchi, and Shigeru Nakayama. *Granting the Seasons: The Chinese Astronomical Reform of 1280, with a Study of Its Many Dimensions and a Translation of Its Records*. New York: Springer, 2009.

Su Yu 蘇輿. *Chunqiu fanlu yizheng* 春秋繁露義證. Beijing: Zhonghua shuju, 1992.

Tjan, Tjoe Som, trans. *Po Hu T'ung: The Comprehensive Discussions in the White Tiger Hall*. 2 vols. Leiden: Brill, 1949, 1952.

Twitchett, Denis, and Michael Loewe, eds. *The Ch'in and Han Empires, 221 B.C.–A.D. 220*. Vol. 1 of *The Cambridge History of China*. Cambridge: Cambridge University Press, 1986.

Van Auken, Newell Ann. "Who Is a *rén* 人? The Use of *rén* in *Spring and Autumn* Records and Its Interpretation in the *Zuǒ, Gōngyáng*, and *Gǔliáng* Commentaries." *Journal of the American Oriental Society* 131, no. 4 (2011): 555–90.

Van Ess, Hans. "The Old Text / New Text Controversy: Has the 20th Century Got It Wrong?" *T'oung Pao* 80 (1994): 146–70.

Van Zoeren, Steven. *Poetry and Personality: Reading, Exegesis, and Hermeneutics in Traditional China.* Stanford, Calif.: Stanford University Press, 1991.

Vogel, Hans Ulrich. "Aspects of Metrosophy and Metrology During the Han Period." *Extrême Orient, Extrême Occident* 16 (1994): 135–52.

Waley, Arthur, trans. *The Book of Songs: The Ancient Chinese Classic of Poetry*. Edited, with additional translations, by Joseph R. Allen. New York: Grove Press, 1996.

Wang, Aihe. *Cosmology and Political Culture in Early China.* Cambridge: Cambridge University Press, 2000.

Watson, Burton, trans. *Records of the Grand Historian*. Rev. ed. 2 vols. New York: Columbia University Press, 1993.

Woo Kang. *Les trois théories politiques du Tch'ouen Ts'ieou interpretées par Tong Tchong-chou d'après les principes de l'école de Kong-yang.* Paris: Leroux, 1932. [Includes translation of chapter 12]

Yan Li 阎丽. *Dongzi Chunqiu fanlu yizhu* 董子春秋繁露译注. Heilongjiang: People's Publishing, 2003.

Yu Kam-por. "Confucian Views on War as Seen in the *Gongyang Commentary* on the *Spring and Autumn* Annals." *Dao* 9, no. 1 (2010): 97–111.

Zhang Shiliang 張世亮, Zhong Zhaopeng 钟肇鹏, and Zhou Guidian 周桂钿. *Chunqiu fanlu* 春秋繁露. Beijing: Zhonghua shuju, 2012.

Zhong Zhaopeng 鍾肇鵬. *Chunqiu fanlu jiaoshi* 春秋繁露校釋. Jinan: Shandong youyi chubanshe, 1994.

Zhu Yongjia 朱永嘉 and Wang Zhichang 王知常. *Xinyi Chunqiu fanlu* 新譯春秋繁露. 2 vols. Taibei: San Min Book, 1996.

Index

TRANSLATIONS FROM THE ASIAN CLASSICS

Major Plays of Chikamatsu, tr. Donald Keene 1961

Four Major Plays of Chikamatsu, tr. Donald Keene. Paperback ed. only. 1961; rev. ed. 1997

Records of the Grand Historian of China, translated from the Shih chi of Ssu-ma Ch'ien, tr. Burton Watson, 2 vols. 1961

Instructions for Practical Living and Other Neo-Confucian Writings by Wang Yang-ming, tr. Wing-tsit Chan 1963

Hsün Tzu: Basic Writings, tr. Burton Watson, paperback ed. only. 1963; rev. ed. 1996

Chuang Tzu: Basic Writings, tr. Burton Watson, paperback ed. only. 1964; rev. ed. 1996

The Mahābhārata, tr. Chakravarthi V. Narasimhan. Also in paperback ed. 1965; rev. ed. 1997

The Manyōshū, Nippon Gakujutsu Shinkōkai edition 1965

Su Tung-p'o: Selections from a Sung Dynasty Poet, tr. Burton Watson. Also in paperback ed. 1965

Bhartrihari: Poems, tr. Barbara Stoler Miller. Also in paperback ed. 1967

Basic Writings of Mo Tzu, Hsün Tzu, and Han Fei Tzu, tr. Burton Watson. Also in separate paperback eds. 1967

The Awakening of Faith, Attributed to Aśvaghosha, tr. Yoshito S. Hakeda. Also in paperback ed. 1967

Reflections on Things at Hand: The Neo-Confucian Anthology, comp. Chu Hsi and Lü Tsu-ch'ien, tr. Wing-tsit Chan 1967

The Platform Sutra of the Sixth Patriarch, tr. Philip B. Yampolsky. Also in paperback ed. 1967

Essays in Idleness: The Tsurezuregusa of Kenkō, tr. Donald Keene. Also in paperback ed. 1967

The Pillow Book of Sei Shōnagon, tr. Ivan Morris, 2 vols. 1967

Two Plays of Ancient India: The Little Clay Cart and the Minister's Seal, tr. J. A. B. van Buitenen 1968

The Complete Works of Chuang Tzu, tr. Burton Watson 1968

The Romance of the Western Chamber (Hsi Hsiang chi), tr. S. I. Hsiung. Also in paperback ed. 1968

The Manyōshū, Nippon Gakujutsu Shinkōkai edition. Paperback ed. only. 1969

Records of the Historian: Chapters from the Shih chi of Ssu-ma Ch'ien, tr. Burton Watson. Paperback ed. only. 1969

Cold Mountain: 100 Poems by the T'ang Poet Hanshan, tr. Burton Watson. Also in paperback ed. 1970

Twenty Plays of the Nō Theatre, ed. Donald Keene. Also in paperback ed. 1970

Chūshingura: The Treasury of Loyal Retainers, tr. Donald Keene. Also in paperback ed. 1971; rev. ed. 1997

The Zen Master Hakuin: Selected Writings, tr. Philip B. Yampolsky 1971

Chinese Rhyme-Prose: Poems in the Fu Form from the Han and Six Dynasties Periods, tr. Burton Watson. Also in paperback ed. 1971

Kūkai: Major Works, tr. Yoshito S. Hakeda. Also in paperback ed. 1972

The Old Man Who Does as He Pleases: Selections from the Poetry and Prose of Lu Yu, tr. Burton Watson 1973

The Lion's Roar of Queen Śrīmālā, tr. Alex and Hideko Wayman 1974

Courtier and Commoner in Ancient China: Selections from the History of the Former Han by Pan Ku, tr. Burton Watson. Also in paperback ed. 1974

Japanese Literature in Chinese, vol. 1: *Poetry and Prose in Chinese by Japanese Writers of the Early Period*, tr. Burton Watson 1975

Japanese Literature in Chinese, vol. 2: *Poetry and Prose in Chinese by Japanese Writers of the Later Period*, tr. Burton Watson 1976

Love Song of the Dark Lord: Jayadeva's Gītagovinda, tr. Barbara Stoler Miller. Also in paperback ed. Cloth ed. includes critical text of the Sanskrit. 1977; rev. ed. 1997

Ryōkan: Zen Monk-Poet of Japan, tr. Burton Watson 1977

Calming the Mind and Discerning the Real: From the Lam rim chen mo of Tsoṇ-kha-pa, tr. Alex Wayman 1978

The Hermit and the Love-Thief: Sanskrit Poems of Bhartrihari and Bilhaṇa, tr. Barbara Stoler Miller 1978

The Lute: Kao Ming's P'i-p'a chi, tr. Jean Mulligan. Also in paperback ed. 1980

A Chronicle of Gods and Sovereigns: Jinnō Shōtōki of Kitabatake Chikafusa, tr. H. Paul Varley 1980

Among the Flowers: The Hua-chien chi, tr. Lois Fusek 1982

Grass Hill: Poems and Prose by the Japanese Monk Gensei, tr. Burton Watson 1983

Doctors, Diviners, and Magicians of Ancient China: Biographies of Fang-shih, tr. Kenneth J. DeWoskin. Also in paperback ed. 1983

Theater of Memory: The Plays of Kālidāsa, ed. Barbara Stoler Miller. Also in paperback ed. 1984

The Columbia Book of Chinese Poetry: From Early Times to the Thirteenth Century, ed. and tr. Burton Watson. Also in paperback ed. 1984

Poems of Love and War: From the Eight Anthologies and the Ten Long Poems of Classical Tamil, tr. A. K. Ramanujan. Also in paperback ed. 1985

The Bhagavad Gita: Krishna's Counsel in Time of War, tr. Barbara Stoler Miller 1986

The Columbia Book of Later Chinese Poetry, ed. and tr. Jonathan Chaves. Also in paperback ed. 1986

The Tso Chuan: Selections from China's Oldest Narrative History, tr. Burton Watson 1989

Waiting for the Wind: Thirty-six Poets of Japan's Late Medieval Age, tr. Steven Carter 1989
Selected Writings of Nichiren, ed. Philip B. Yampolsky 1990
Saigyō, Poems of a Mountain Home, tr. Burton Watson 1990
The Book of Lieh Tzu: A Classic of the Tao, tr. A. C. Graham. Morningside ed. 1990
The Tale of an Anklet: An Epic of South India—The Cilappatik ram of Iḷaṅkō Aṭikaḷ, tr. R. Parthasarathy 1993
Waiting for the Dawn: A Plan for the Prince, tr. with introduction by Wm. Theodore de Bary 1993
Yoshitsune and the Thousand Cherry Trees: A Masterpiece of the Eighteenth-Century Japanese Puppet Theater, tr., annotated, and with introduction by Stanleigh H. Jones, Jr. 1993
The Lotus Sutra, tr. Burton Watson. Also in paperback ed. 1993
The Classic of Changes: A New Translation of the I Ching as Interpreted by Wang Bi, tr. Richard John Lynn 1994
Beyond Spring: Tz'u Poems of the Sung Dynasty, tr. Julie Landau 1994
The Columbia Anthology of Traditional Chinese Literature, ed. Victor H. Mair 1994
Scenes for Mandarins: The Elite Theater of the Ming, tr. Cyril Birch 1995
Letters of Nichiren, ed. Philip B. Yampolsky; tr. Burton Watson et al. 1996
Unforgotten Dreams: Poems by the Zen Monk Shōtetsu, tr. Steven D. Carter 1997
The Vimalakirti Sutra, tr. Burton Watson 1997
Japanese and Chinese Poems to Sing: The Wakan rōei shū, tr. J. Thomas Rimer and Jonathan Chaves 1997
Breeze Through Bamboo: Kanshi of Ema Saikō, tr. Hiroaki Sato 1998
A Tower for the Summer Heat, by Li Yu, tr. Patrick Hanan 1998
Traditional Japanese Theater: An Anthology of Plays, by Karen Brazell 1998
The Original Analects: Sayings of Confucius and His Successors (0479–0249), by E. Bruce Brooks and A. Taeko Brooks 1998
The Classic of the Way and Virtue: A New Translation of the Tao-te ching of Laozi as Interpreted by Wang Bi, tr. Richard John Lynn 1999
The Four Hundred Songs of War and Wisdom: An Anthology of Poems from Classical Tamil, The Puṟanāṉūṟu, ed. and tr. George L. Hart and Hank Heifetz 1999
Original Tao: Inward Training (Nei-yeh) *and the Foundations of Taoist Mysticism*, by Harold D. Roth 1999
Po Chü-i: Selected Poems, tr. Burton Watson 2000
Lao Tzu's Tao Te Ching: *A Translation of the Startling New Documents Found at Guodian*, by Robert G. Henricks 2000
The Shorter Columbia Anthology of Traditional Chinese Literature, ed. Victor H. Mair 2000
Mistress and Maid (Jiaohongji), by Meng Chengshun, tr. Cyril Birch 2001
Chikamatsu: Five Late Plays, tr. and ed. C. Andrew Gerstle 2001
The Essential Lotus: Selections from the Lotus Sutra, tr. Burton Watson 2002
Early Modern Japanese Literature: An Anthology, 1600–1900, ed. Haruo Shirane 2002; abridged 2008
The Columbia Anthology of Traditional Korean Poetry, ed. Peter H. Lee 2002
The Sound of the Kiss, or The Story That Must Never Be Told: Pingali Suranna's Kalapurnodayamu, tr. Vecheru Narayana Rao and David Shulman 2003
The Selected Poems of Du Fu, tr. Burton Watson 2003
Far Beyond the Field: Haiku by Japanese Women, tr. Makoto Ueda 2003
Just Living: Poems and Prose by the Japanese Monk Tonna, ed. and tr. Steven D. Carter 2003
Han Feizi: Basic Writings, tr. Burton Watson 2003
Mozi: Basic Writings, tr. Burton Watson 2003
Xunzi: Basic Writings, tr. Burton Watson 2003
Zhuangzi: Basic Writings, tr. Burton Watson 2003
The Awakening of Faith, Attributed to Aśvaghosha, tr. Yoshito S. Hakeda, introduction by Ryuichi Abe 2005
The Tales of the Heike, tr. Burton Watson, ed. Haruo Shirane 2006
Tales of Moonlight and Rain, by Ueda Akinari, tr. with introduction by Anthony H. Chambers 2007
Traditional Japanese Literature: An Anthology, Beginnings to 1600, ed. Haruo Shirane 2007
The Philosophy of Qi, by Kaibara Ekken, tr. Mary Evelyn Tucker 2007
The Analects of Confucius, tr. Burton Watson 2007
The Art of War: Sun Zi's Military Methods, tr. Victor Mair 2007
One Hundred Poets, One Poem Each: A Translation of the Ogura Hyakunin Isshu, tr. Peter McMillan 2008
Zeami: Performance Notes, tr. Tom Hare 2008
Zongmi on Chan, tr. Jeffrey Lyle Broughton 2009
Scripture of the Lotus Blossom of the Fine Dharma, rev. ed., tr. Leon Hurvitz, preface and introduction by Stephen R. Teiser 2009
Mencius, tr. Irene Bloom, ed. with an introduction by Philip J. Ivanhoe 2009
Clouds Thick, Whereabouts Unknown: Poems by Zen Monks of China, Charles Egan 2010
The Mozi: A Complete Translation, tr. Ian Johnston 2010
The Huainanzi: A Guide to the Theory and Practice of Government in Early Han China, by Liu An, tr. and ed. John S. Major, Sarah A. Queen, Andrew Seth Meyer, and Harold D. Roth, with Michael Puett and Judson Murray 2010
The Demon at Agi Bridge and Other Japanese Tales, tr. Burton Watson, ed. with introduction by Haruo Shirane 2011

Haiku Before Haiku: From the Renga Masters to Bashō, tr. with introduction by Steven D. Carter 2011

The Columbia Anthology of Chinese Folk and Popular Literature, ed. Victor H. Mair and Mark Bender 2011

Tamil Love Poetry: The Five Hundred Short Poems of the Aiṅkuṟunūṟu, tr. and ed. Martha Ann Selby 2011

The Teachings of Master Wuzhu: Zen and Religion of No-Religion, by Wendi L. Adamek 2011

The Essential Huainanzi, by Liu An, tr. and ed. John S. Major, Sarah A. Queen, Andrew Seth Meyer, and Harold D. Roth 2012

The Dao of the Military: Liu An's Art of War, tr. Andrew Seth Meyer 2012

Unearthing the Changes: Recently Discovered Manuscripts of the Yi Jing (I Ching) *and Related Texts*, Edward L. Shaughnessy 2013

Record of Miraculous Events in Japan: The Nihon ryōiki, tr. Burton Watson 2013

The Complete Works of Zhuangzi, tr. Burton Watson 2013

Lust, Commerce, and Corruption: An Account of What I Have Seen and Heard, *by an Edo Samurai*, tr. and ed. Mark Teeuwen and Kate Wildman Nakai with Miyazaki Fumiko, Anne Walthall, and John Breen 2014

Exemplary Women of Early China: The Lienü zhuan *of Liu Xiang*, tr. Anne Behnke Kinney 2014

The Columbia Anthology of Yuan Drama, ed. C. T. Hsia, Wai-yee Li, and George Kao 2014

The Resurrected Skeleton: From Zhuangzi to Lu Xun, by Wilt L. Idema 2014

The Sarashina Diary: *A Woman's Life in Eleventh-Century Japan*, by Sugawara no Takasue no Musume, tr. with introduction by Sonja Arntzen and Itō Moriyuki 2014

The Kojiki: *An Account of Ancient Matters*, by Ō no Yasumaro, tr. Gustav Heldt 2014

The Orphan of Zhao *and Other Yuan Plays: The Earliest Known Versions*, translated and introduced by Stephen H. West and Wilt L. Idema 2014

GPSR Authorized Representative: Easy Access System Europe, Mustamäe tee 50, 10621 Tallinn, Estonia, gpsr.requests@easproject.com

www.ingramcontent.com/pod-product-compliance
Lightning Source LLC
Chambersburg PA
CBHW020937310726
48980CB00007B/810/J
* 9 7 8 0 2 3 1 1 6 9 3 2 5 *